Scotland Highlands & Islands

Alan Murphy

Every self-respecting Scot comes over all proprietorial when introducing the glories of their country to a friend or loved one for the first time. So much so, you'd think they'd designed the whole place themselves. As if the jaw-dropping scenery of Wester Ross, or the Trossachs, was some kind of DIY makeover: 'oh, yes, we got rid of all that woodchip and planted the hillsides in Caledonian pine forest. The native woodland look is in this year.'

The Scots have every right to be proud, for when the rain stops falling and the mist clears, there is, quite simply, no more beautiful place on Earth. If there is a heaven, it must surely look like the Highlands and islands, but let's hope the petrol's cheaper.

Scotland is one of the least densely-populated countries in Europe. Not much smaller than its southern neighbour, England, it has only a tenth of its population – and most of those are crammed into the narrow central belt, leaving two-thirds of the country virtually empty. This is Europe's last great wilderness; one of the few places in this increasingly cluttered continent where you can really get away from it all.

About the only thing the Highlands doesn't have going for it is a dependable climate. Let's face it; if you want to lie on a beach all day soaking up rays, then you really ought to try somewhere else. Ironically, though, this makes the Scottish Highlands and islands the perfect destination for a romantic break. Think about it: if the weather's rubbish then you'll have more time to stay in bed. It could give a whole new meaning to the term Highland fling.

This page An Teallach, Western Ross.
Previous page Neist Point lighthouse, Isle of Skye.

3

Stromness ⑪ ○ Kirkwall
Orkney Islands

Dunnett Pentland
Head Firth
Durness ⑦ ○ John o'Groats
Thurso○
Ben Hope
(3042ft) ○ Wick

Ben Klibreck
(3154ft)

⑩ St Kilda
57° 50'
8° 30'

Stornoway ⑧
Lewis

Outer
Hebrides   *Harris*   *The Minch*

Stac Pollaidh
(2012ft)   Ullapool○   Tain○
An Teallach
(3485ft)   *Sgurr Mor*   Cromarty○   *Moray Firth*   Elgin○
(3643ft)
Lochmaddy○   Uig○   Torridon   Huntly○
North Uist   *Sgorr Ruadh*   Inverness○   *Tap o'Noth*
Benbecula   Portree○ ⑥   *(3151ft)*   *(1848ft)*
Applecross○   *Loch*
Skye   Kyle of   *Ness*   Aviemore○
South Uist   Lochalsh○   *Cairn Gorm*
Fort Augustus○   *(4086ft)*   *An Sgarsoch*   Lochnagar
Rùm   Mallaig○   *(3479ft)* ▲ *(3791ft)*
⑨ *Barra*   *Eigg*   ④   *Grampian*   *Mayar*
Inner   *Ben Nevis*   *Mountains*   Pitlochry○ ▲ *(3046ft)*
Hebrides   *(4411ft)*   Fort
Coll   *Ardnamurchan*   William
Meall a'Bhuiridh
Tiree   Tobermory○   *(3636ft)*   Crieff○   Dundee
Staffa   ⑤   St Andrews○
Atlantic   *Iona* ①   Oban○   Crianlarich○   Perth○
Ocean   *Mull*   Callander○
Aberfoyle○   Stirling○   Dunfermline○
Colonsay   Lochgilphead○   *Loch*
Jura   *Lomond*   *Firth of Forth*
② ③   Greenock○   **EDINBURGH** □
Islay   Tarbert○ *Bute*   Glasgow○
Port Ellen○   *Arran*   Peebles○
Brodick○   *Southern*   Selkirk○
Ayr○   *Uplands*   Hawick○
Shetland
Islands   Campbeltown○
Orkney
Islands   Dumfries○
Newton
Stewart○   Kirkcudbright○
Stranraer○   *Solway*
Firth   ENGLAND

Highlights

See colour maps in centre of book

1 Hire a bike and explore the divine little island of Iona. ▶▶ page 100.

7 Sit on the beach at Sandwood Bay and watch the sun set. ▶▶ page 282.

2 Savour the delights of an Islay malt on a tour of one of the island's distilleries. ▶▶ page 123.

8 Discover the eerie mystery of 5000-year-old Calanais. ▶▶ page 348.

3 Take a ferry to Jura, and trek to the summit of her legendary Paps. ▶▶ page 122.

9 Fly to Barra and land on the world's only beach runway. ▶▶ page 368.

4 Climb aboard the West Highland Railway for one of the world's great train rides. ▶▶ page 228.

10 Voyage across perilous seas to the mysterious haunted islands of St Kilda. ▶▶ page 376.

5 Glen Coe has it all: amazing scenery, a tragic past and a great ridge walk. ▶▶ page 230.

11 Be blown away at Europe's best preserved Stone Age village at Skara Brae. ▶▶ page 389.

6 Enjoy super-fresh seafood at the glorious Applecross Inn. ▶▶ page 262.

12 Explore the dramatic coastal landscape of Hermaness National Nature Reserve. ▶▶ page 424.

---

12 Unst

Shetland Islands

Yell

Mainland

Lerwick ○

○ Peterhead

○ Aberdeen

North Sea

N

40 km
40 miles

Top One of Islay's famous distilleries.
Middle The Isle of Iona.
Bottom The distinctive Paps of Jura.

Opposite page top The standing stones of Calanais.

Opposite page bottom Skara Brae.

The West Highland Railway passes through some of Scotland's most delicious scenery.

Top Welcome to Barra-dise.

Top right Plate of seafood at the Applecross Inn.

Bottom Abandoned village on St Kilda.

Opposite page top Sandwood Bay.

Opposite page bottom Hermaness National Nature Reserve.

Despite being one of Scotland's most accessible places, Glen Coe retains a tangible sense of tragic beauty.

Contents

ORKNEY & SHETLAND

Atlantic Ocean

OUTER HEBRIDES

North Sea

NORTH & NORTHWEST

SKYE & SMALL ISLES

CENTRAL HIGHLANDS

ARGYLL & INNER HEBRIDES

Contents

Footprint features

Essentials

Where to go

Scotland is a small country but there's a lot to see. There are many, many places of great natural beauty and the country's long, turbulent history has left a rich heritage of medieval castles, cathedrals, palaces, abbeys, neolithic stone circles, Bronze Age brochs and even a 5000-year-old village.

The Scottish mainland is surrounded by hundreds of islands, each one with its own distinct history and culture. Crossing to some of these islands doesn't just feel like entering a different country, but stepping into another time zone. Where else would you see sheep in a phone box (Harris), cattle wandering the beach (Berneray and Tiree), deer easily out-numbering the human population (Jura) and park swings padlocked to ensure strict observance of the Sabbath (Lewis).

Lying off the west coast are the Hebrides, home of the Gaelic culture, where the road signs include English spellings almost as an afterthought and local people speak Gaelic as their native tongue. Off the northern tip of the mainland is Orkney, an archipelago of 70 islands, which has spawned some of Scotland's greatest writers; not surprising, perhaps, given that Orkney has such a fascinating and eventful history. The islands were ruled by the Vikings for 650 years, until the 15th century and, despite their remote location, played a dramatic role at the end of the First World War when the German fleet was scuttled in Scapa Flow. But if you think Orkney seems remote, you ain't seen nothing yet. The Shetland Islands are so far north they can only be included on maps as an inset and the nearest mainland town is Bergen, in Norway. Little wonder that there are some inhabitants who feel a greater affinity to Norway than mainland Scotland. Unbelievable as it may seem, Shetland is made to look like the hub of civilization by St Kilda, the most remote community in Europe until the evacuation of its entire population in 1930. The white-knuckle boat trip across perilous Atlantic seas must surely rank as one of the great adventures.

Yet don't think that remote always equates to waving goodbye to modern comforts. On Harris and Jura you'll find stunning, five- star accommodation boasting amenities almost as fabulous as the scenery beyond your window. Likewise, Highland kitchens increasingly recognize Scotland's rich natural larder, offering diners a taste of local cheeses, shellfish, game, preserves and malt whisky.

The Highlands and Islands' green and dramatic scenery offers a sense of immersion in nature – a true escape from the stress of urban life. There are mountains to climb, lochs to fish and wildlife to watch; or you can just sit back and take in all the stunning scenery. There are countless opportunities to leave civilization a long way behind. You can explore Scotland's long-distance footpaths, such as the West Highland Way, which snake through some of the country's finest scenery. The more adventurous can try their hand (or feet) at 'Munro bagging', which is the name given to the popular pursuit of climbing Scotland's 284 mountains higher than 3000 ft. This offers the chance to explore wild areas of unparalleled beauty such as Glen Coe, Torridon, Kintail or the Cairngorms. If even that is too tame for you, then don't worry, Scotland is fast becoming the outdoor capital of the Northern Hemisphere with some of the best climbing, diving, sea kayaking, surfing and mountain biking in the world, in addition to pursuits like canyoning and fun yakking.

Scotland's wide, open spaces are also home to a rich and diverse wildlife. On land, you can see pine martens, red squirrels, reindeer and even wildcats, while golden eagles, ospreys and rare sea eagles rule the skies. In the lochs and seas of the Northwest Highlands live otters, dolphins, porpoises, whales and, according to some, even the occasional prehistoric monster.

One week

Thirty minutes north of Glasgow is Loch Lomond and the Trossachs National Park, gateway to the mountain and lochside scenery of the Western Highlands. From Loch Lomond, drive north through atmospheric Glen Coe to Fort William and Lochaber, the self-proclaimed outdoor capital of the UK, which lies in the shadow of Ben Nevis, Britain's highest peak.

From Fort William, there's the option to hop aboard the West Highland Railway for a journey through spectacular scenery to the fishing port of Mallaig, where you can board a ferry for Skye to spend several days touring its glens, mountains and clan sites.

Travelling directly north from Fort William, stop in Fort Augustus for the engineering wonder of the Caledonian Canal, before hiking or driving up the west side of the dark, 'Nessie'-inhabited waters of Loch Ness. Be sure to stop at the impressive Urquhart Castle by the lochside and consider a detour further west to hike the beautiful, remote and wildlife-rich country of Glen Affric.

Pressing north into Inverness, tuck into delicious Highland fare, hop aboard a dolphin cruise in the Moray Firth and visit the Culloden battlefield site. There's also the option to drive one hour northwest to spend a day or two enjoying the rugged mountain scenery and seafood around the fishing port of Ullapool.

From Inverness, drive south down the A9, briefly stopping at the Tomatin malt whisky distillery. Twenty miles south at Carrbridge, let the kids run off steam in the natural play-park of Landmark and travel up the funicular railway at Cairngorm to dine in Britain's highest restaurant.

From Aviemore, pass through the big tree country of highland Perthshire with the chance to fish or visit the likes of Scone Palace, before returning to Glasgow via the rich forest canopy and lochs of the Trossachs.

Two weeks

Consider a Caledonian MacBrayne Rover ticket to island hop and venture off the beaten track. South of Glasgow, sail across to the Isle of Arran to hike the dramatic mountains, spot seals and visit ancient castles. From Lochranza, sail for Claonaig where it's a short hop across the Kintyre Peninsula to the pristine beaches, wildlife, clan history and whisky distilleries of the Isle of Islay. Return to Kennacraig and drive north for Oban through the walking country of Argyll, stopping to explore the Neolithic remains around Kilmartin.

Directly off Oban lies the tiny rugged Isle of Kerrera and the Isle of Mull beyond. Spend a few days on Mull, wonderful for its birds of prey, atmospheric Duart Castle and for access to Staffa and the holy island of Iona.

In picturesque Tobermory, tuck into fresh seafood before departing Mull for the wilds of the Ardnamurchan Peninsula, where you may spot minke whales from the lighthouse. Head northwest, past the silver sands of Morar for Mallaig and sail to Skye for a taste of castles, mountain scenery and fine Highland hospitality.

From Skye, cross back onto the mainland at Kyle of Lochalsh and head east for Fort Augustus and a peek at Loch Ness. But first stop to admire Eilean Donan Castle, where the mountains rise majestically off the sea loch.

From Fort Augustus head south, past the Commando Memorial at Spean Bridge, then east along Loch Laggan before popping into the distillery at Dalwhinnie. Joining the A9, head south with a final stop at impressive Blair Atholl Castle before returning to Glasgow.

Packing for Scotland

You'll be able to find everything you could possibly need for your trip in Scottish cities, so if you wish you can pack light and buy supplies as you go along. Given the variable climate, whatever the time of year it's advisable to include warm and waterproof clothing in your suitcase. Also bring light clothes in the summer, preferably long-sleeved to protect you from the midges, see page 51. If you're planning on doing some hillwalking you should come properly prepared, as the weather can change rapidly in the mountains (see page 22 for details). It's worth treating your boots with a waterproofing agent as some of the trails cross boggy ground.

If you are backpacking, a sleeping bag is useful in hostels, and a sleeping sheet with a pillow cover is needed if staying in Scottish Youth Hostel Association (SYHA) hostels (or you can hire one there). A padlock can also be handy for locking your bag if it has to be stored in a hostel for any length of time. Other useful items include an alarm clock (for those early ferry departures), an adaptor plug for electrical appliances, an elastic clothes line and, if you're hillwalking or camping, a map, Swiss Army knife, torch (flashlight) and compass are essential. If planning to undertake watersports, it's a good idea to bring a waterproof pouch for your wallet/purse and other small essential items.

Three to four weeks

Discover the rich history and wildlife of Orkney and Shetland or the Outer Hebrides. Both areas are easily accessible by plane and ferry.

From Glasgow, take in Loch Lomond, reaching the west coast port of Oban via the scenic waters of Loch Fyne and Inverary Castle. After sampling seafood by the quay-side, board the ferry for Barra and the Outer Hebrides. En route, enjoy the classic West Highland scenery of Mull and Ardnamurchan.

On Barra, visit formidable Kisimul Castle and watch planes land on the UK's only beach runway. The white, deserted beaches of neighbouring Vatersay deserve your attention, before you sail north for Eriskay where Bonnie Prince Charlie landed to launch his campaign for the Scottish crown. Via causeways, explore the Gaelic speaking Isles of South and North Uist, with their windswept beaches, wonderful food and soul-nurturing slower pace of life.

Moving on from North Uist, excellent food, stunning coastal scenery, authentic tweed and superb surfing can be found on Harris and Lewis, from where you can sail from Stornoway for Ullapool on the mainland.

Alternatively, sail from Lochmaddy to Uig on the Isle of Skye to enjoy several days of great food, castles and mountain scenery.

Bid farewell to Skye and spend a week winding north through the picturesque coastal villages of the remote northwest with its starkly beautiful, almost primeval landscapes, including the mountains of Torridon and Assynt, and enchanting Sandwood Bay. There are limitless opportunities for wildlife spotting and hillwalking and there is fabulous game and seafood on offer. From Durness, press eastwards to the seabird-peppered cliffs at Dunnet Head, the most northerly point on the mainland. Close by, consider a short boat trip to explore the many Neolithic wonders on Orkney.

Inverness is your next stop, via a dolphin cruise off Cromarty. Explore the west side of atmospheric Loch Ness, visiting the ruin of Urqhhart Castle and searching for Nessie.

Hikers are rewarded with a detour into Glen Affric whilst beyond Fort Augustus you'll spy Ben Nevis, Britain's highest peak looming behind Fort William. Further south, pass through dramatic Glen Coe with its fabulous mountain terrain for the experienced hillwalker and climber.

At the head of Loch Lomond, pop in to the Drover's Inn at Inverarnan, once frequented by clan folk hero, Rob Roy MacGregor. In Arrochar take a boat cruise of the bonnie banks before heading back to Glasgow.

When to go

The high season is from May to September, and this is when Scotland receives the vast majority of its visitors. Though the weather tends to be better during the summer months, prices for accommodation are higher, and hotels and guesthouses in the most popular places need to be booked in advance. It's also a good idea to make reservations on ferries to the islands during this period, especially to Skye and Mull. A major advantage to visiting in the summer months are the long hours of daylight, especially in the far north, where the sun doesn't set till around 2300 or later in June and July.

From October to Easter, many sights are closed, and travelling around the Highlands and Islands can be difficult, as public transport services are limited. Many of the smaller tourist offices are also closed during the low season. Although some hotels and guesthouses close too, the majority are now open all year round, as are most restaurants. Taking everything into consideration, May and September are probably the best months for a visit to the Scottish Highlands and Islands.

The Scottish climate is notoriously unpredictable, especially on the west coast, where a bright, sunny morning can turn into a downpour in the time it takes to butter your toast. Predicting the weather is not an exact science and tables of statistics are most likely a waste of time. There's an old saying in Scotland that if you don't like the weather, then wait 20 minutes, and this just about sums it up. The west coast receives far more rain than the rest of the country and the east coast gets more sunshine. The west coast is also milder in the winter due to the relatively warm waters of the Gulf Stream. Winters in the north can be very harsh, especially in the mountains and glens, making hiking conditions treacherous. Winter storms also make it difficult to travel around the islands as ferry services are often cancelled.

Generally, May to September are the warmest months, with an average summer high of around 18-19°C and, though they are often the driest months, you can expect rain at any time of the year. Remember the old hikers' adage that there's no such thing as bad weather, only inadequate clothing.

Go green

▶▶ If you picnic or BBQ on a beach, be sure to carry away all of your litter. Don't bury it.

▶▶ A landscape that may look 'empty' to you may be common grazing land maintained by the local crofter, so think twice before parking your 4WD on it.

▶▶ On remote islands like Vatersay, the beaches are stunning and deserted but don't ignore the small signs requesting you don't walk on the (fragile) dune systems.

▶▶ Scotland has plenty of wildlife operators, try and book with those accredited to schemes like the Whale and Dolphin Conservation Society.

Responsible tourism

The Highlands and Islands of Scotland are beautiful, dramatic and wild, but also a living, working landscape and a fragile and vulnerable place.

There are many simple steps you can take to ensure your footprint on Scotland's landscape is minimal. For a start, consider cycling or walking through the countryside – or at least using the ever-improving public bus network. Admittedly, it's slower than a car but with no need for fuel you'll notice a healthy impact on your body and your wallet.

Equally, seek out tour operators who pride themselves on their green credentials. Whether sea kayaking or wildlife watching, Wilderness Scotland (www.wildernessscotland. com) and Islay Birding (www.islaybirding.co.uk) are just two of many 'green' tourism businesses on these shores.

Moreover, try to use restaurants and cafés that source their fresh produce from the local area. Why pay for exotic fish that has been shipped in from the other side of the world when many island communities offer superb seafood caught on their doorstep. By purchasing even basic foodstuffs from a village shop, you're also helping sustain a vital business in a remote community.

Finally, to sleep easy with a green conscience, minimize energy wastage by asking yourself if it's really necessary to switch on every light and electrical appliance in your hotel room or use every bath towel.

For further information on how to be a 'green' tourist, contact Tourism Concern, www. tourismconcern.org.uk, or the Tourism and Environment Forum, www.green tourism.org.uk.

Sports and activities

Blessed with wild, rugged mountains, windswept lochs, idyllic islands and miles of remote coastline, Scotland is paradise for the visitor who comes to unwind or in search of adventure amidst breathtaking scenery. Indeed, enlightened access legislation, www.outdooraccess-scotland.com, now provides almost limitless opportunities for the responsible tourist to roam freely through the countryside, cycle through miles of forest, paddle down tumbling rivers or scramble up mountains to bag Munros (mountains over 3000 ft). Furthermore, come rain, hail or shine, tour operators now offer a variety of thrilling, adrenaline-packed activities from canyoning, fun yakking and whitewater rafting, to telemark skiing, skydiving and surfing, demonstrating that Scotland's growing reputation as an adventure sports mecca is no idle boast.

Birdwatching

ⓘ **Royal Society for the Protection of Birds**, 25 Ravelston Terrace, Edinburgh, EH4 3TP, T01767-680551, www.rspb.org.uk. **Scottish Ornithologists Club**, Waterstone House, Aberlady, East Lothian, EH32 0PY, T01875-871330, www.the-soc.org.uk. **Scottish Wildlife Trust**, Cramond House, 3 Kirk Cramond, Edinburgh EH4 6HZ, T0131-3127765, www.swt. org.uk, which owns and runs over 100 nature reserves.

Scotland is great for birdwatching. Over 450 species have been recorded, including vast colonies of seabirds, birds of prey and many rare species. Among the best places in Scotland to see birds are Handa Island off the coast of Sutherland, and the Treshnish Islands, off Mull, where you'll see colonies of shags, razorbills, guillemots and puffins. Another excellent place for birdwatching is Loch Garten by Boat of Garten, where you can see ospreys. Many of the Hebridean islands, such as Islay, Mull and Tiree, are home to a rich variety of seabirds and you can also see golden eagles here. Orkney and Shetland are famous for their rich variety of birdlife and are home to large colonies of seabirds and migratory birds. There are puffins, kittiwakes, fulmars, shags, razorbills, guillemots and even auks. A more unusual and rare resident of Shetland is the snowy owl.

Canoeing, kayaking and rafting

ⓘ **Canoe Hebrides**, T01851-820726, www.canoehebrides.com; **Canoe Scotland**, T0131-317 7314, www.canoescotland.com; **Hebridean Pursuits**, T01631-710317, www. hebrideanpursuits.com; **Monster Activities**, T07710-540398, www.monsteractivities. com; **Nae Limits**, Ballinluig, near Pitlochry, T08450-178177, www.naelimits.co.uk; **National Kayak School**, T01631-565310, www.nationalkayak school.com; **Sea Kayak Shetland**, T01595-840272, www.seakayakshetland.co.uk; **Rockhopper Sea Kayaking**, T0773-983 7344, www.rockhoppersscotland.co.uk; **Skyak Adventures**, Isle of Skye, T01471-820002, www.skyakadventures.com; **Splash**, Aberfeldy, T01887-829706, www.rafting.co.uk.

Scotland's rivers, lochs and deeply indented coastline offer great opportunities for canoeing, surf kayaking, sea kayaking and careering down rivers in inflatable two-man fun yaks and whitewater rafts. Perthshire, served by the Tummel, Garry and Tay rivers is arguably Scotland's kayaking hub and the place to find adventure operators such as Nae Limits and Splash. However, whilst legions of river kayakers head for the slalom gates of Grandtully, it's the azure waters of the Inner and Outer Hebrides, that have helped establish Scotland as one of Europe's top sea kayaking destinations.

Canyoning

ⓘ **Nae Limits**, Oban, T08450-178177, www.naelimits.co.uk; **Vertical Descents**, 8 miles south of Fort William, T01855-821593, www.verticaldescents.com.

This involves heading downriver in a gorge and dropping several hundred feet by swimming, jumping into plunge pools, sliding down log flumes and abseiling. In Perthshire and Lochaber you can go cliff-jumping from heights of up to 60 ft into rock pools, combined with head-first descents of waterfalls. If that's too tame try the Tyrolean Traverse, crossing a gorge at 300 ft.

Mountain safety

Visitors to Scotland should be aware of the need for caution and safety preparations when walking or climbing in the mountains. The nature of Scottish weather is such that a fine sunny day can turn into driving rain or snow in a matter of minutes. Remember that a blizzard can be raging on the summit when the car park at the foot of the mountain is bathed in sunshine. It is essential to get an up-to-date weather forecast before setting off on any walk or climb. Whatever the time of year, or conditions when you set off, you should always carry or wear essential items of clothing. A basic list for summer conditions would be: boots with a good tread and ankle support, and a thick pair of socks; waterproof jacket and trousers, even on a sunny day; hat and gloves are important if the weather turns bad;

warm trousers should be worn or carried, tracksuit bottoms are okay if you also have waterproof trousers; a spare woolly jumper or fleece jacket will provide an extra layer; a map and compass are essential to carry and to know how to use. Other essentials are food and drink, a simple first-aid kit, a whistle and a torch. A small 25-30 litre rucksack should be adequate for carrying the above items. Also remember to leave details of your route and expected time of return with someone, and remember to inform them on your return.

In the winter extra warm clothing is needed, as well as an ice axe and crampons, and the ability to use them. The skills required for moving over ice or snow should be practised with an experienced and qualified mountain guide or instructor.

Climbing

ⓘ **Glenmore Lodge**, Aviemore, T01479-861256, www.glenmorelodge.org.uk; **Mountaineering Council of Scotland**, The Old Granary, West Mill St, Perth, T01738-493942, www.mcofs.org.uk; **Wilderness Scotland**, T0131-625 6635, www.wildernessscotland.com. Other useful websites: **www.naelimits.co.uk**, **www.scotclimb.org.uk**.

With hundreds of summer and winter climbing routes, rock climbers and winter mountaineers alike are spoilt for choice. From Glencoe and Lochaber to the Cuillin ridge on Skye, the Cairngorms and majestic hills of Torridon and Assynt, there's no lack of opportunity to test one's nerve. Scotland is a great place to try rock climbing and its arduous winter cousin, ice climbing. The Cairngorms and Cuillins offer the most challenging climbing, as do Glencoe and Torridon. Most mountaineering clubs have regular weekend meets in the hills as well as social gatherings closer to home.

Cycling

ⓘ **Cyclists' Touring Club (CTC)**, Parklands, Railton Rd, Guilford, Surrey, T0131-448 0930 (Scotland), www.ctc.org.uk, is the largest cycling organization in the UK. **Forestry Commission Scotland**, www.forestry.gov.uk/scotland, details of sites with mountain-biking trails. **Scottish Cyclists' Union (SCU)**, The Velodrome, Meadowbank Stadium, London Rd, Edinburgh EH7 6AD, T0131-652 0187, http://newbritishcycling.org.uk/scotland, produces an annual handbook and calendar of events for road racing, time trialling and mountain biking. **SUSTRANS**, T0845-113 0065, www.sustrans.org.uk, is the UK's leading sustainable transport charity. **VisitScotland tourist office**, www.visit scotland.

com, for maps and details of cycle routes in their area. It also publishes Cycling in Scotland (free), listing bike repair shops and operators. See also **www.spokes.org.uk**.

The bicycle was invented in Scotland, so it seems appropriate that travelling by bike is one of the best ways to explore the country. Thanks to SUSTRANS and other hard- working voluntary organizations, Scotland boasts a growing number of traffic-free cycle routes.

Cycling, particularly cross-country and downhill mountain biking, has really taken off in Scotland over the past decade, with over a dozen purpose-built trail centres now established in forests around the country, including by Fort William and Golspie.

If road racing or touring is your thing, Scotland's miles of rural roads are a delight to explore, with routes using disused railway tracks and upgraded canal towpaths, including the dedicated tracks on the Isle of Arran. The wild and remote Highlands are very popular with cycle tourers. Routes such as Torridon and Applecross provide challenging climbs and exhilarating descents. However, some routes are shared with walkers and horse-riders so caution and consideration should be exercised at all times.

You can cut down on the amount of pedalling you have to do by transporting your bike by train. Bikes can be taken free on all FirstScotRail services including the sleeper rail services on a first come, first served basis (call ScotRail bookings, T08457-550033, www.firstscotrail.com). However, check with Virgin Rail and GNER for their conditions of carriage. Regardless, space is always limited on trains so it's a good idea to book as far in advance as possible. With a few exceptions, such as the Dearman coach between Ullapool and Durness, buses are unable to carry bikes unless they are dismantled and boxed. Ferries transport bikes for a small fee and airlines will often accept them as part of your baggage allowance. Check with the ferry company or airline about any restrictions.

Diving

ⓘ **The Puffin Dive Centre**, see page 75, T01631-566088, www.puffin.org.uk, is the UK's most comprehensive diving facility (based in Oban) and runs intensive PADI courses.

Scotland may not have the Great Barrier Reef but it does have some of the finest dive locations in the world, featuring shipwrecks, reefs, sheer underwater cliffs, soft corals and abundant sea life. The west coast offers the best diving, as the water is warmed by the effects of the Gulf Stream and is not as cold as you might expect, even without a dry suit. Among the best sites are the west coast of Harris, the Summer Isles and the remote island of St Kilda. There are lots of wrecks in the Sound of Mull, and the chance to find a Spanish Galleon off Tobermory. Scapa Flow in Orkney is world-renowned as the burial site of the German First World War fleet.

Fishing

ⓘ **Scottish Federation of Sea Anglers**, T01573-470612, www.fishsea.co.uk, provides comprehensive information on the main species to fish for and advice on where to fish. See also **www.visitscotland.com/fish**; **www.fishscotland.co.uk**, for a complete listing and key information about locations in Scotland; **www.fishhebrides.co.uk**; and **www.fishtweed.co.uk**.

Scotland's rivers, streams, lochs and estuaries are among the cleanest waters in Europe and are filled with salmon, trout (sea, brown and rainbow) and pike. Not surprisingly, fishing (coarse, game and sea) is hugely popular in Scotland.

There is no close season for coarse fishing or sea angling. For wild brown trout the close season is early October to mid-March. The close season for salmon and sea trout varies from area to area and between net and rod fishing. It is generally from late August to early February for net fishing, and from early November to early February for rod fishing. No licence is required to fish in Scotland, but most of the land and rivers are privately owned so you must obtain a permit from the owners or their agents. These are often readily available at the local fishing tackle shop and usually cost from around £15, though some rivers can be far more expensive.

Golf

ⓘ **VisitScotland**, www.visitscotland.com. VisitScotland's *Golfing in Scotland* brochure provides a comprehensive break-down of prices and courses across the country, plus lists of accommodation providers. To arrange golfing holidays, visit **www.scotland-golf-tours.co.uk**.

Scotland has over 400 golf courses, with more being built all the time, and therefore has more courses per head of population than any other country in the world. Any decent-sized town in Scotland will have a golf course nearby and most, if not all, are available for play. There are many public courses, which tend to be both cheap and extremely busy, and often have excellent layouts. The majority of private clubs allow visitors, although many have restrictions as to what days these visitors can play. Weekends are usually reserved for club competitions for the members, so it is best to try to play on a weekday. All private clubs have a dress code and it is inadvisable to turn up in a T-shirt and jeans. These minor caveats aside, you are likely to receive a warm, courteous welcome.

Many clubs offer a daily or weekly ticket with the cost depending on the course and area. For example, a Perthshire Highlands Ticket (T01887-829010) costs £35 for three days and allows access to up to 11 nine-hole layouts on courses including Blair Atholl and Killin. The Carnoustie Country Dream Ticket (T0800-975 5955, T0141-305 5050) provides access to four of the world's classic links courses for £230 (Apr-Oct, £120 in winter).

Hillwalking

ⓘ **Forestry Commission Scotland**, www. forestry.gov.uk. **Scottish Rights of Way Society**, www.scotways.com. **Woodland Trust**, www.woodlandtrust.org.uk.

Scotland is a walker's paradise. Throughout the country there are numerous marked trails, ranging from short walks to long- distance treks from one side of the country to the other. Whatever your taste or level of fitness and experience, you'll find plenty of opportunities to get off the beaten track and explore the countryside.

The best time for hiking in the mountains depends solely on the weather and your experience. Mountain weather conditions change so fast that one moment it can be a clear, crisp day in November and the next a blizzard. So, though April to October is arguably the 'safest' period for the less experienced, always carry clothing that will keep you warm should conditions deteriorate. Winter walking in the Highlands requires technical equipment such as ice axes and crampons, and a lot of experience. June to August are the busiest times, though only the most popular routes, such as Ben Nevis, get really crowded. Another problem during these months are midges, see page 51. May to mid-June is probably the most pleasant time overall, as the weather can often be fine and the midges have yet to appear. September is also a good time, though it can be a lot colder.

Five great short walks

Scotland is a walker's paradise. Whether you are looking for family strolls on the beach, a challenging 3000-ft mountain hike or an adventure on one of Scotland's numerous long-distance trails, you are spoilt for choice. Wherever you choose to roam ensure you dress appropriately, for the weather conditions on Scotland's hills and mountains are notoriously fickle.

Sandwood Bay (Blairmore)

Scotland's coastline is peppered with beaches but Sandwood Bay, 10 miles south of Cape Wrath is arguable one of the best (see page 283). This vast stretch of golden, deserted sand is accessed over peatland from Blairmore via a 4-mile track. At Sandwood, look south for the magnificent Am Buachaille sea stack that rises over 30 yds out of the waves. The whole area sits within a protected 11,490-acre estate of crofting land managed by the John Muir Trust. Enjoy your picnic but don't overstay your welcome. It's rumoured that ghosts of shipwrecked mariners roam the deserted dunes.

Reinigeadal to Tarbert (Isle of Harris)

Of the six walks, this 7-mile hike across the rugged eastern hills of Harris to Tarbert is the most challenging and exposed. The sea views are spectacular, but spare a thought for the hardy kids who, for generations, could only reach school via this tortuous track above the sea. Cloaked in silence, the trail winds through deer-inhabited wilds managed by the North Harris Community Land Trust. The ruins of long abandoned crofts poke through the heather as you walk west over Beinn a' Chaolais. On skirting high above the remote sea loch of Trollamarig, look for the abandoned hamlet of Molingeanais.

Sanna Bay (Ardnamurchan)

The wildlife and rugged scenery of the Ardnamurchan Peninsula, barely scratched by the human hand, remains one of Scotland's best-kept secrets. On a fine day, pack a picnic and head for the remote village of Sanna – the westernmost point on the British mainland. Here, a beautiful expanse of fine golden sand caressed by turquoise waters will convince you that this is the Caribbean, until you dip your toe in the chilly water. As you walk the 2 miles south to the hamlet, gaze seaward for a breath-taking panorama of the Small Isles and the distant peaks of Skye. Keep a look out for seals, dolphins and basking sharks.

Glenmore Forest (Cairngorm)

Glenmore Forest Park (est 1948) offers an invigorating 4½-mile hike from above the shores of Loch Morlich to the tranquil waters of An Lochan Uaine (the Green Lochan) and beyond to the rustic, simple shelter of Ryvoan Bothy. This walk is ideal for a family outing on a well-marked path. Aside from views of the Cairngorms, it's a rare opportunity to hike through remnants of ancient Caledonian pinewood and juniper that long ago covered the landscape. Look out for red squirrels, pine marten and red deer.

Conic Hill (Loch Lomond)

It's a short, sharp 45-minute climb from the car park at Balmaha on the southeastern shores of Loch Lomond. However, on reaching the rounded summit of Conic Hill (1115 ft) you are rewarded with magnificent views across the forested islands of the southern part of Loch Lomond – at over 22 miles long, it's the largest stretch of fresh water in the UK and the hub of the Loch Lomond and Trossachs National Park. Further westward enjoy the jagged peaks of the Arrochar Alps, whilst to the northeast lies the magnificent heather- and forest-strewn hills once roamed by the 17th-century clansman and folk hero, Rob Roy MacGregor. See page 160.

Scotland has a long tradition of enabling access to mountain and moorland. This free access, of course, relies on walkers behaving responsibly and recognizing that the countryside is a place of work as well as recreation. It's the Land Reform (Scotland) Act 2003 that underpins one's right to roam in Scotland but with the proviso that it's undertaken responsibly and in accordance with the Outdoor Access Code (see page 41). In particular, it's the walker's responsibility to ensure he or she doesn't damage fences, crops or worry livestock. By adhering to these common-sense rules, all who come to enjoy Scotland's countryside will be helping to maintain access that is the envy of every other country in the UK. However, most land in Scotland remains privately owned and at certain times of the year, such as the main shooting seasons, walkers may be asked to respect certain restrictions on access. The main deer stalking season runs from mid-August to mid-October and the grouse shooting season is between 12 August (referred to as the 'Glorious Twelfth') and 10 December. There may also be restricted access during the lambing season from March to May.

Kitesurfing

① **Kite Sports Scotland (KSS)**, St Andrews (also Dunbar and Gullane in East Lothian), T07875-773346, www.kss.uk.com, recommended for advice; **Wild Diamond**, T01879-220399, www.wilddiamondsurf.co.uk, offers lessons and hire.

Kitesurfing, which involves whizzing over the sea with a tiny board strapped to your feet and body harnessed to a powerful kite, is growing in popularity in Scotland with Tiree a popular location for 'grabbing air'. However, windsurfing and particularly wave-sailing amidst the powerful surf of Tiree and Machrihanish remains extremely popular, with the former hosting the annual Tiree Wave Classic every October.

Mountain biking

① **Scottish Cyclists' Union (SCU)**, The Velodrome, Meadowbank Stadium, London Rd, Edinburgh, T0131-652 0187, www.scuonline.org, produces an annual handbook and calendar of events for road racing, time trialling and mountain biking, its excellent website is packed with information; **www.forestry.gov.uk**, has details of Forestry Commission Scotland sites with mountain biking trails; **www.visitscotland.com/adventure**, provides a good description of the key mountain bike centres and trails across Scotland. It's also worth picking up a copy of the Scottish Mountain Biking Trails Guide.

The sport of cycling, and particularly cross-country and downhill mountain biking, has really taken off over the past decade. Indeed, today Scotland is regarded, by no less than the International Mountain Biking Association, as one of the world's top mountain-biking destinations. This country boasts no less than a dozen dedicated mountain bike trail centres, including the Wolf Trax mountain bike trail centre by Laggan, and Learnie Forest in the Black Isle, www.himba.org.uk. These are hot mountain bike destinations but arguably the most famous is to be found at Fort William where the 'Witch's Trail' and nerve-wracking 1½-mile 'black' run downhill track annually attracts the world's best riders for a stage of the UCI MTB World Cup, www.ridefortwilliam.co.uk. The Fort William downhill track (May to September) is accessed by the gondola system (1000-1700). An adult multi-trip ticket costs £18 per day, single trip ticket £10. A youth (12-17) multi-trip ticket costs £13.50 and a single ticket, £7.25, and all participants under 16 years-of-age must have their parent or guardian sign a special participation form before purchasing a ticket. Bike hire is available from the Nevis Range centre or at Off Beat Bikes in Fort William, T01397-704008, www. offbeatbikes.co.uk.

Paragliding

ⓘ **Flying Fever Paragliding**, Isle of Arran, T01770-303899, www.flyingfever.net, daily May-October, offers a tandem flight as part of a Funday for £100.

If you fancy getting high during your visit, you can try your hand at the exciting sport of paragliding. Flying Fever on the Isle of Arran offers tandem and solo paragliding lessons, courses from beginner to advanced and hire.

Pony trekking and horse riding

ⓘ **British Horse Society Scotland** (**BHS**), Woodburn Farm, Crieff, T01764-656334, www. bhs.org.uk, the BHS website provides a full listing of all BHS-approved riding schools in Scotland and details of forthcoming major events. **Trekking and Riding Society of Scotland** (**TRRS**), Bruaich-Na-H'Abhainne, Margowan, Killin, Perthshire, KF21 8TN, T01567-820909, www.ridinginscotland.com.

Pony trekking is a long-established activity in Scotland and miles of beautiful coastline, lochsides, and moorland are accessible on horseback. There are numerous equestrian centres around the country catering to all levels of riders. VisitsScotland produces a *Riding Scotland* brochure listing riding centres around the country, all of them approved by the Trekking and Riding Society of Scotland (TRSS) or the British Horse Society (BHS). Centres offer pony trekking (leisurely strolls at walking pace for novices), hacks (short rides at a fast pace for experienced riders) and trail riding (long- distance rides at no more than a canter). For general information contact the TRSS.

Skiing

ⓘ **Snowsport Scotland**, T0131-445 4151, www.snowsportscotland.org, for information on all aspects of Scottish skiing and snowsports; also useful is **www.ski-scotland.com**.

Conditions in Scotland are not as reliable as the Alps, but with short, steep descents off- piste, dozens of beginner/intermediate groomed pistes and breathtaking mountain scenery, snowboarders, skiers and telemark skiers are handsomely rewarded when the snow falls and the sun shines. The core season is from January to April, but it is possible to ski from as early as November to as late as May. Ski packages and lessons are available, though it's easy to arrange everything yourself. There's plentiful accommodation in and around the ski centres.

Ski centres There are five ski centres in Scotland and the largest are Glenshee, which has the most extensive network of lifts and selection of runs, and Cairngorm, which has over 30 runs spread over an extensive area. Glencoe is the oldest of the ski resorts, and with runs like the 'flypaper', offers tremendous skiing for experts. Nevis Range Aonach Mor near Fort William, has the highest ski runs and the only gondola in Scotland. The Lecht is ideal for beginner and intermediate skiers or boarders and also has a 'tubing' piste.

Costs Ski equipment and clothing can be hired at all resorts, but lessons should be booked in advance. Prices vary from centre to centre, but on average expect to pay around £15-20 per day for hire of skis, poles and boots or snowboard and boots. Adult lift passes cost around £22-30 per day (junior/senior around £15-20) with seven-day packages around

£150. Reduced price half-day tickets are offered at most centres. Group ski lessons are around £25-30 for half-day. Packages including ski hire, and tuition and lift pass vary in cost according to location.

Information Details for each of the five resorts, including phone numbers and websites, are given in the appropriate place in the main text. For further general information contact VisitScotland for its Ski Scotland brochure and accommodation list, or visit their website, www.visitscotland.com/adventure, which is updated daily. Or you can contact Snowsport Scotland (see above). During the ski season, resort websites publish up-to-date snow and weather conditions, and outline which pistes are open. To hire, buy or seek advice when ski touring and ski mountaineering in Scotland, it's recommended that you contact Mountain Spirit in Aviemore, T01479-811788, www.mountainspirit.co.uk.

Surfing

ⓘ **Coast 2 Coast Surf School**, Belhaven Bay, East Lothian, T07971-990361, www. c2csurfschool.com, 'surf safaris' throughout Scotland; **Scottish Surfing Federation**, www.scottishsurfingfederation.com. Useful websites are, **www.sas.org.uk** and **www. hebrideansurf.co.uk**.

Scotland has some of the best surfing beaches in Europe, a fact recognised by its hosting of a World Pro Surf Tour (qualifying) competition in 2006. But despite the clean coral and beach breaks, powerful waves and pristine (island) beaches, this is no sun-drenched Hawaii. Surfing in Scotland is decidedly chillier with temperatures in the spring and autumn as low as 4-5°C! However, you could be pleasantly surprised at the temperature between July and October, but remember a good wetsuit is essential.

The best beaches on the West Coast are to be found at the northern tip of the Isle of Lewis, on North and South Uist, the north coast of Scotland (including Thurso), Machrihanish at the southwestern tip of the Mull of Kintyre and all along the coast east of Edinburgh. On the north coast the top spot is Thurso, home to the world-class Thurso East break (strictly for experts). In recent years, a host of reputable surf schools have sprung up, also try the surf shops, which sell equipment and provide information on the best breaks.

From the famous Thurso East break and surf competitions in northeast Scotland, to the massive waves on the Isle of Lewis and Tiree, to instruction and hire on a string of beaches, Scottish surfing is really taking off.

Wildlife watching

ⓘ **Hebridean Whale and Dolphin Trust**, www.whaledolphintrust.co.uk; **Sea Watch Foundation**, www.seawatchfoundation.org.uk. Also try www.outdooraccess-scotland. com for further details on wildlife watching.

Almost anywhere around the western and northern coasts of Scotland there is a chance to see bottlenose dolphins, white-beaked dolphins, Risso's dolphins, common dolphins, white-sided dolphins, pilot whales, minke whales, porpoises, seals and, occasionally orcas (killer whales). The best places to see bottlenose dolphins are at Cromarty and Chanonry Point, both on the Moray Firth. Other good places to catch glimpses of bottlenose and other dolphins, as well as porpoises and minke whales, are the westerly tip of Ardnamurchan, Mull, Neist Point on Skye, Gairloch and Rubha Reidh Lighthouse, Stoer Head, Handa Island, Cape Wrath, Strathy Point, Dunnet Head, Duncansby Head, Lybster, Brora and Golspie, Tarbat Ness and off the Isle of Mull (T01688-302916, www.sealifesurveys.com). The North

Kessock Dolphin and Seal Centre, near Inverness, has more information on where to see dolphins and seals locally. Generally speaking, the best time to see the various species of marine mammals (cetaceans) is late summer, from late July to early September.

Seals can be seen in abundance, particularly on the rocks around the wonderfully serene Lochranza Bay in the north of Arran. From Harris to Plockton and Oban, there are plenty of seal-spotting boat trips on offer from spring to autumn. To be guaranteed to spot seals visit the Scottish Sea Life Sanctuary, T01631-720 386, www.sealsanctuary.co.uk, north of Oban. Otters are more elusive. They tend to live on undisturbed remote stretches of the seashore or quiet areas of a river. If you are determined to spot the creatures, contact Skye Environmental Centre, home to the International Otter Survival Fund, T01471-822487, www.otter.org, who can provide more information.

Getting there

Air

Generally speaking, the cheapest and quickest way to travel to Scotland from outside the UK is by air. There are good links to Edinburgh and Glasgow, with direct flights from many European cities, and direct flights from North America to Glasgow. There are also flights from a few European cities to Aberdeen and Inverness. There are no direct flights from North America to Edinburgh; these are usually routed via London or Dublin. There are also daily flights from Ireland and regular flights to most Scottish airports from other parts of the UK. There are no direct flights to Scotland from Australia, New Zealand, South Africa or Japan; you will have to get a connection from London.

From the UK and Ireland
There are direct flights to Scotland's four main airports – Glasgow, Edinburgh, Aberdeen and Inverness – almost hourly from London Heathrow, Gatwick, Stansted and Luton airports. There are also daily flights from provincial UK airports and from Dublin. To fly on to the smaller airports, you'll need to change planes, see page 33, for domestic flights. The cheapest flights leave from London Luton or Stansted, plus a few provincial airports, with **Ryanair** and **easyJet**. If you book online, fares can be as little as £5 one-way during promotions (excluding taxes), but usually you can expect to fly for under £70 return if you can be flexible with dates and times. These tickets are often subject to rigid restrictions, but the savings can make the extra effort worthwhile. Cheaper tickets usually have to be bought at least a week in advance and apply to only a few midweek flights. They are also non-refundable, or only partly refundable, and non-transferable. A standard flexible and refundable fare from London to Glasgow or Edinburgh will cost at least £150-200 return. The flight from London to Glasgow and Edinburgh is roughly one hour.

There are flight to Inverness from London and from many regional UK airports, as well as flights from Glasgow to Islay, Tiree, Barra, Benbecula, Stornoway, Kirkwall (Orkney) and Sumburgh (Shetland), from Edinburgh to Wick, Stornoway, Kirkwall and Sumburgh and from Inverness to Benbecula, Stornoway, Kirkwall and Sumburgh with Flybe franchise partner, Loganair (www.flybe.com or www.loganair.co.uk). For full details of all flights to Highlands and Islands airports from the rest of the UK, visit the **Highlands and Islands Airports Ltd** website, www.hial.co.uk.

From the rest of Europe

There are direct flights to **Glasgow International** from many European capitals, including Copenhagen, Amsterdam, Paris (Beauvais), Dublin, Frankfurt, Stockholm, Brussels, Milan, Oslo and Barcelona. There are flights to **Edinburgh** from Paris (CDG), Zurich, Amsterdam, Brussels, Copenhagen and Frankfurt; direct flights to **Aberdeen** from Amsterdam, Copenhagen and Stavanger; and to **Inverness** from Amsterdam and Zurich.

From North America

Because of the much larger number of flights to London, it is generally cheaper to fly there first and get an onward flight, see above for the best deals. For low season Apex fares, expect to pay around US$500-700 from New York and other East Coast cities, and around US$700-900 from the West Coast. Prices rise to around US$700-1000 from New York, and up to US$1000 from the West Coast in the summer months. Low season Apex fares from Toronto and Montreal cost around CAN$700-900, and from Vancouver around CAN$800-900, rising during the summer. East Coast USA to Glasgow takes around six to seven hours direct. To London it takes seven hours. From the West Coast it takes an additional four hours.

To Glasgow International **Continental Airlines** and **KLM** fly from New York, **Aer Lingus** and **KLM** fly from Chicago and **Air Canada** from Toronto.

Airlines flying to Scotland

Aer Arann, www.aerarann.com.
Aer Lingus, www.aerlingus.com.
Air Canada, www.aircanada.com.
Air France, www.airfrance.co.uk.
American Airlines, www.aa.com.
BMI, www.flybmi.com.
British Airways, www.britishairways.com.
Continental, www.continental.com.

Eastern Airways, www.easternairways.com.
easyJet, www.easyjet.com.
Flybe, www.flybe.com.
Icelandair, www.icelandair.com.
KLM, www.klm.com.
Lufthansa, www.lufthansa.com.
Ryanair, www.ryanair.com.
ScotAirways, www.scotairways.com.

Airport information

Glasgow International ⓘ *T0844-481 5555*, is 8 miles west of the city, at junction 28 on the M8. It handles domestic and international flights. Terminal facilities include car hire, bank ATMs, currency exchange, left luggage, tourist information (T0141-848 4440), and shops, restaurants and bars. For all public transport information T0871-200 2233. **Edinburgh airport** ⓘ *T0844-4812 8989 for general enquiries*, has all facilities, including a tourist information desk, currency exchange, ATMs, restaurants and bars (first floor), shops (ground floor and first floor) and car hire desks in the terminal in the main UK arrivals area. For details of facilities and amenties at all Highlands and Islands airports, visit www.hial.co.uk.

Rail

There are fast and frequent rail services from London and other main towns and cities in England to Glasgow, Edinburgh, Aberdeen and Inverness. Journey time from London is about 4½ hours to Edinburgh, five hours to Glasgow, seven hours to Aberdeen and eight hours to Inverness. Two companies operate direct services from London to Scotland:

National Express trains leave from King's Cross and run up the east coast to Edinburgh, Aberdeen and Inverness, and **Virgin** trains leave from Euston and run up the west coast to Glasgow. **ScotRail** operate the *Caledonian Sleeper* service if you wish to travel overnight from London Euston to Aberdeen, Edinburgh, Glasgow, Inverness and Fort William. This runs nightly from Sunday to Friday. Fare start from £59 per person. For more information, see www.scotrail.co.uk or the excellent www.seat61.com.

    Eurostar ① *T08705-186186 (+44-123-361 7575), www.eurostar.com*, operates high-speed trains through the Channel Tunnel to London St Pancras International from Paris (2½ hours), Brussels (two hours) and Lille (1½ hours). You then have to change trains, and stations, for the onward journey north to Scotland. If you're driving from continental Europe you could take *Le Shuttle*, which runs 24 hours a day, 365 days a year, and takes you and your car from Calais to Folkestone in 35 to 45 minutes. Standard return fares on *Le Shuttle* range from £98 per carload. Depending on how far in advance you book, or when you travel, cheaper fares are available, call T08705-353535 for bookings.

Enquiries and booking

National Rail Enquiries ① *T08457-484950, www.nationalrail.co.uk*, are quick and courteous with information on rail services and fares but not always accurate, so double check. They can't book tickets but will provide you with the relevant telephone number. The website, www.qjump.co.uk, is a bit hit-and-miss but generally fast and efficient, and shows you all the various options on any selected journey, while www.thetrainline.co.uk, also has its idiosyncrasies but shows prices clearly. For advance card bookings, contact **National Express**, T08457-484950, www.nationalexpresseastcoast.com; **ScotRail**, T08457-550033, www.scotrail.co.uk; and **Virgin**, T08457-222333, www.virgintrains.co.uk.

Fares

To describe the system of rail ticket pricing as complicated is a huge understatement and impossible to explain here. There are many and various discounted fares, but restrictions are often prohibitive, which explains the long queues and delays at ticket counters in railway stations. The cheapest ticket is an Advance ticket or Value Advance (Virgin), which must be booked in advance (obviously), though this is not available on all journeys. A GNER London–Edinburgh Advance Single costs between £14-100. Advance Singles with ScotRail on this route start from £39.50 for direct trains. All discount tickets should be booked as quickly as possible as they are often sold out weeks, or even months, in advance. A Caledonian Sleeper 'Bargain Berth' single ticket from London to Edinburgh or Glasgow costs from £19; to book visit www.travelpass.buytickets.scotrail.co.uk.

Railcards

There are a variety of railcards which give discounts on fares for certain groups. Cards are valid for one year and most are available from main stations. You need two passport photos and proof of age or status.

Young Person's Railcard For those aged 16-25 or full-time students aged 26+ in the UK. Costs £26 for one year and gives 33% discount on most train tickets and some other services (www.16-25railcard.co.uk).

Senior Citizen's Railcard For those aged over 60. Same price and discounts as above (www.senior-railcard.co.uk).

Disabled Person's Railcard Costs £18 and gives 33% discount to a disabled person and one other. Pick up an application form from stations and send it to Disabled Person's

On the buses

With Citylink, www.citylink.co.uk, running services to all the key cities, ferry links and the West Highland Flyer, www.road-to-the-isles.org.uk, carrying your bike for the handy link between Oban and Mallaig (via Fort William), it's only when wanting to venture off the beaten track that you may bemoan the fact that fewer buses ply the remote rural roads.

Consequently, a great cheap way to quickly experience the more famous sites around Scotland is on one of the backpacker bus tours. These leave from Edinburgh daily, except Sunday, and stop off at independent hostels in Perth, Pitlochry, Inverness, Loch Ness, the Isle of Skye, Fort William, Glen Coe, Oban and Glasgow. There's tremendous rivalry between the various operators so you benefit from keen prices for what are excellent value tours of the Highlands and Islands.

Tours vary from a one-day tour of Loch Lomond and Glencoe (£33) to a two-day tour of Loch Ness (£55) and three days around Skye (£59), to a five-day jaunt around the Highlands and Skye (from £105). However, prices with these 'backpacker' operators don't tend to include accommodation (from £15 per night) in, for the most-part, clean and comfortable hostels. See page 57 for a list of tour operators.

Railcard Office, PO Box 163, Newcastle-upon-Tyne, NE12 8WX. It may take up to 21 days to process, so apply in advance (www.disabledpersons-railcard.co.uk).
Family Railcard Costs £26 and gives 33% discount on most tickets for up to four adults travelling together, and 60% discount for up to four children.

Road

Bus/coach

Road links to Scotland are excellent, and a number of companies offer express coach services day and night. This is the cheapest form of travel to Scotland. The main operator between England and Scotland is **National Express** ① *T08717-818178, www.national express.com*. There are direct buses from most British cities to Edinburgh, Glasgow, Aberdeen and Inverness. Tickets can be bought at bus stations or from a huge number of agents throughout the country. Fares from London to Glasgow and Edinburgh with **National Express** start at around £25 return for a Funfare return (online discount fare). Fares to Aberdeen and Inverness are a little higher. The London to Glasgow/Edinburgh journey takes around eight hours, while it takes around 11 to 12 hours for the trip to Aberdeen and Inverness. From Manchester to Glasgow takes around 6½ hours.

Car

There are two main routes to Scotland from the south. In the east the A1 runs to Edinburgh and in the west the M6 and A74(M) runs to Glasgow. The journey north from London to either city takes around eight to 10 hours. The A74(M) route to Glasgow is dual carriageway all the way. A slower and more scenic route is to head off the A1 and take the A68 through the Borders to Edinburgh. There's an Autoshuttle Express service to transport your car overnight between England and Scotland and vice versa while you travel by rail or air. For further information and reservations, T08705-502309. See also page 35.

Sea

P&O Irish Sea ⓘ *T0871-664 2020, www.poferries.com*, has several crossings daily from Larne to Cairnryan (one hour), and from Larne to Troon (two hours). Fares are from £79 each way for for car and driver. **Stena Line** ⓘ *T0870-570 7070, www.stenaline.co.uk*, runs numerous ferries (three hours) and high-speed catamarans (1½ hours) from Belfast to Stranraer, fares from £79 single for car and driver.

Getting around

It is easy to visit the main towns and tourist sights by bus or train, but getting off the beaten track without your own transport requires careful planning and an intimate knowledge of rural bus timetables. Public transport can also be expensive, though there's a whole raft of discount passes and tickets which can save you a lot of money. Hiring a car can work out as a more economical, and certainly more flexible, option, especially for more than two people travelling together. It will also enable you to get off the beaten track and see more of the country. Even if you're driving, however, getting around the remote Highlands and Islands can be a time-consuming business as much of the region is accessed only by a sparse network of tortuous, twisting single-track roads. Be sure to refuel regularly, allow plenty of time for getting around and book ferries in advance during the busy summer season.

Air

As well as the main airports of Glasgow, Edinburgh, Aberdeen and Inverness, there are also numerous small airports, many of them on islands (one of them, on Barra, uses the beach as an airstrip). Internal flights are relatively expensive, however, and not really necessary in such a small country, unless you are short of time. For example a return flight from Edinburgh or Glasgow to Shetland can cost over £200. There are discounted tickets available, which must be booked at least 14 days in advance, and special offers on some services. There is no departure tax on flights from Highlands and Islands airports.

The majority of flights are operated by **Flybe/Loganair** ⓘ *T0871-700 2000, www.fly be.com, www.loganair.co.uk*. For inter-island flights in Orkney, you should book direct through **Loganair**, T01856-873457. For information on flight schedules, call the airports listed on page 30, or **British Airways**. The British Airports Authority (BAA) publishes a free *Scheduled Flight Guide*.

Rail

The rail network in Scotland is limited and train travel is comparatively expensive, but trains are a fast and effective way to get around and also provide some beautifully scenic journeys. The West Highland line to Fort William and Mallaig and the journey from Inverness to Kyle of Lochalsh are amongst the most beautiful rail journeys in the world and well worth doing. Services between Glasgow, Edinburgh, Stirling, Perth, Dundee and Aberdeen are fast and frequent, and there are frequent trains to and from Inverness.

ScotRail operates most train services within Scotland. You can buy train tickets at the stations, from major travel agents, or over the phone with a credit or debit card. For information and advance credit or debit card bookings visit www.scotrail.co.uk. Details of services are given throughout the guide. For busy long-distance routes it's best to reserve a seat. Seat reservations to Edinburgh, Glasgow, Aberdeen or Inverness are included in the price of the ticket when you book in advance. If the ticket office is closed, there's usually a machine on the platform. If this isn't working, you can buy a ticket on the train. Cyclists should note that though train companies have a more relaxed attitude to taking bikes on trains, reservations at a small fee for bikes are still required on some services. Cycles are carried free of charge on ScotRail services, although reservations are required on longer distance routes.

Eurorail passes are not recognized in Britain, but **ScotRail** offers a couple of worthwhile travel passes. The most flexible is the **Freedom of Scotland Travelpass**, which gives unlimited rail travel within Scotland. It is also valid on all **CalMac** ferries on the west coast, many **Citylink** bus services in the Highlands, some regional buses and offers discounts on some city centre bus tours. It also gives 20% discount on **Northlink Ferries** between Scrabster–Stromness, Aberdeen–Lerwick and Aberdeen–Kirkwall–Lerwick. It costs £114 for four days' travel out of eight consecutive days, £153 for eight out of 15. The **Highland Rover** and Central Scotland Rover Tickets are more limited. The Highland Rover allows unlimited rail travel in the Highlands region, plus the West Highland line from Glasgow, and travel between Aberdeen and Aviemore. It also allows free travel on **Citylink** buses between Oban, Fort William and Inverness. Ferry travel between Oban–Mull and Mallaig–Skye is also included on this ticket. It costs £74 for any four out of eight consecutive days. The Central Scotland Rover allows unlimited travel in the central belt of Scotland from the East Coast, Edinburgh, Stirling and Fife to Glasgow, and also covers unlimited travel on the Glasgow Underground network. It costs £33 for any three out of seven consecutive days.

Road

Bus and coach

Travelling around Scotland by bus takes longer than the train but is much cheaper. There are numerous local bus companies, but the main operator is **Scottish Citylink** ① *T08705-505050, www.citylink.co.uk*. Bus services between towns and cities are good, but far less frequent in more remote rural areas. To identify bus times and the myriad of operators in the Highlands it's worthwhile visiting www.rapsons.co.uk, and downloading the relevant timetable. Note that long-distance express buses are called coaches. There are a number of discount and flexible tickets available and details of these are given on the **Citylink** website, which is fast and easy to use.

Available to overseas passport holders, the **Brit Xplorer Pass** offers unlimited travel on all **National Express** buses. Passes cost from £79 for seven days, £139 for 14 days and £219 for its month-long Rolling Stone pass. They can be bought from major airports and bus terminals. **Scottish Citylink** runs a daily bus service between Scotland's six cities and strategic ports including Oban, Uig (Skye) and Ullapool. It offers a diverse range of discount and saver cards including an Explorer Pass that offers unlimited travel on its routes for a specified number of days. Passes start from £35 for three days.

Many parts of the Highlands and Islands can only be reached by Royal Mail **postbuses**. Admittedly, in recent years many routes have disappeared to be replaced by Dial-a-Bus services, such as in Gairloch. These operate on demand and don't follow a fixed timetable, see www.highland.gov.uk or www.royalmail.com/postbus. However, in places you can still find the friendly, red postbus. These are minibuses that follow postal delivery routes and carry up to 14 fare-paying passengers. They set off early in the morning from the main post office and follow a circuitous route as they deliver and collect mail in the most far-flung places. They are often very slow on the outward morning routes but quicker on the return routes in the afternoons. It can be a slow method of getting around, but you get to see some of the country's most spectacular scenery, and it is useful for walkers and those trying to reach remote hostels or B&Bs. There's a restricted service on Saturdays and none on Sundays.

Car and campervan

Travelling with your own private transport is the ideal way to explore the country, particularly the Highlands. This allows you to cover a lot of ground in a short space of time and to reach remote places. The main disadvantages are rising fuel costs (around £1.30 per litre for diesel), traffic congestion and parking, but the latter two are only a problem in the main cities and on the motorways in the Central Belt. Roads in the Highlands and Islands are a lot less busy than those in England, and driving is relatively stress-free, especially on the B-roads and minor roads. In more remote parts of the country, on the islands in particular, many roads are single track, with passing places indicated by a diamond-shaped signpost. These should also be used to allow traffic behind you to overtake. Remember that you may want to take your time to enjoy the stupendous views all around you, but the driver behind may be a local doctor in a hurry. Don't park in passing places. A major driving hazard on single track roads are the huge number of sheep wandering around, blissfully unaware of your presence. When confronted by a flock of sheep, slow down and gently edge your way past. Be particularly careful at night, as many of them sleep by the side of the road (counting cars perhaps). Also keep a sharp lookout for deer, particularly at night.

To drive in Scotland you must have a current **driving licence**. Foreign nationals also need an international **driving permit**, available from state and national motoring organizations for a small fee. Those importing their own vehicle should also have their vehicle registration or ownership document. Make sure you're adequately **insured**. In all of the UK you drive on the left. **Speed limits** are 30 miles per hour (mph) in built-up areas, 70 mph on motorways and dual carriageways, and 60 mph on most other roads.

It's advisable to join one of the main UK motoring organizations during your visit for their 24-hour breakdown assistance. The two main ones in Britain are the **Automobile Association (AA)** ① *T0800-085 2721, www.theaa.com*, and the **Royal Automobile Club (RAC)** ① *T08705-722722, www.rac.co.uk*. One year's membership of the AA starts at £30 and £28 for the RAC. They also provide many other services, including a reciprocal agreement for free assistance with many overseas motoring organizations. Check to see if your organization is included. Both companies can also extend their cover to include Europe. Their emergency numbers are: **AA**, T0800-887766; **RAC**, T0800-828282. You can call these numbers even if you're not a member, but you'll have to a pay a large fee. In remote areas you may have to wait a long time for assistance. Also note that in the Highlands and Islands you may be stranded for ages waiting for spare parts to arrive.

Car hire need not be expensive in Scotland if you shop around for the best deals. **AVIS** (see below) offers weekend rates from around £45 and £126 for the week, though whichever operator you choose be wary of high charges for additional mileage. Even without deals you should be able to hire a small car for a week from £150. Local hire companies often offer better deals than the larger multi-nationals, though **easyCar** can offer the best rates, at around £10 per day, if you book in advance and don't push up the charges with high mileage. They are based at Aberdeen, Glasgow, Edinburgh and Inverness airport. Many companies such as **Europcar** offer the flexibility of picking up in Glasgow and leaving in Edinburgh, and vice versa. Most companies prefer payment with a credit card, otherwise you'll have to leave a large deposit (£100 or more). You'll need a full driver's licence (one or two years) and be aged over 21 (23 in some cases).

Alternatively, why not hire your own transport and accommodation at the same time by renting a campervan. Campervans can be rented from a number of companies and it's best to arrange this before arriving as everything gets booked up in the high season (June-August). Inverness based **Highland Camper Vans** is a good bet with its new two-berth 'Adventure Van' starting at around £385 per week and £75 per day, or £525 per week for its four-person touring van.

Car/campervan hire companies

Arnold Clark, T0844-576 5425, www.arnoldclarkrental.com.
Avis, T0870-608 6338, www.avis.co.uk
Budget, T0844-581 9998 and T0844-581 2231, www.budget.co.uk. From outside UK T+44 1344-484100.
Europcar, T08457-585375, www.europ car.co.uk. In the US dial T877-940 6900.
easyCar.com, T08710-500444, www.easy car.com.
Hertz, T08705-996699, www.hertz.co.uk, in the US T800-654 3001.

Highland Camper Vans, T01667-493976, www.highlandcampervans.com. Family-run, this friendly and efficient Inverness based operator is also the longest running camper van hire business in the Highlands.
National Car Rental, T0131-333 1922 (Edinburgh Airport), in the US T800-CAR-RENT, www.nationalcar.com.
Thrifty, T0131-337 1319 (Edinburgh), T0141-248 3868 (Glasgow), in the US T800-367 2277, www.thrifty.com.

Hitching
As in the rest of the UK, hitching is never entirely safe, and is certainly not advised for anyone travelling alone, particularly women travellers. Those prepared to take the risk should not find it too difficult to get a lift in the Highlands and Islands, where people are far more willing to stop for you. Bear in mind, though, that you will probably have to wait a while even to see a vehicle in some parts.

Sea

There are around 60 or so inhabited islands off the coast of Scotland, and nearly 50 of them can be reached by a scheduled ferry service. Most ferries carry vehicles and can be booked in advance. If you're travelling to the islands by car, it's a good idea to book ferries in advance whatever the time of year, particularly to the more popular islands.

The majority of ferry services on the west coast are operated by **Caledonian MacBrayne** ⓘ *Ferry Terminal, Gourock, T01475-650100, T0800-066 5000, www.calmac.co.uk*, or **CalMac** as they're more commonly known. They sail from Oban, Mallaig and Ullapool to over 20 islands in the Inner and Outer Hebrides. They also run services on the Firth of Clyde. Fares are expensive, especially with a car, but if you're planning on using ferries a lot, you can save a lot of money with an **Island Hopscotch ticket**, which offers reduced fares on 26 set routes. The ticket is valid for one month and you need to follow your set itinerary, though this can be changed en route without too much fuss. For more details and some sample fares, see under the relevant destination. A more flexible option is the **Island Rover**, which offers unlimited travel on **CalMac** ferries for a set period, though you still need to make reservations. An eight-day pass costs £48.50 per passenger and £232 for a car, and a 15-

day pass costs £70 per passenger and £348 for a car. **CalMac** schedules are complicated, but details of sailings are given under each relevant destination in this guide. **Western Ferries** ⓘ *T0136-970 4452, www.western-ferries.co.uk*, runs services between Gourock and Dunoon, and Islay and Jura.

Northlink Ferries ⓘ *T0845-6000 449, www.northlinkferries.co.uk*, run car ferries to Orkney and Shetland. Ferries to Orkney depart from Aberdeen or from Scrabster, near Thurso. There are also car and passenger ferries to Orkney with **Pentland Ferries** ⓘ *www. pentlandferries.co.uk*, and a passenger-only ferry (summer only) with **John o'Groats Ferries** ⓘ *www.jogferry.co.uk*. See pages 386 and 393 for full details of these. Ferries to Shetland sail from Aberdeen.

The Orkney Islands are linked by services run by **Orkney Ferries** ⓘ *www.orkney ferries. co.uk*, while Shetland's heavily subsidized inter-island ferries are run by **Shetland Islands Council** ⓘ *www.shetland.gov.uk*. There are also numerous small operators offering day-trips to various islands. Details of these are given in the relevant chapters.

Maps

You'll find a good selection of maps of Scotland in many bookshops and at the main tourist offices. Road atlases can be bought at most service stations. The best of these are the large-format ones produced by the **AA**, **Collins** and **Ordnance Survey**, which cover all of Britain at a scale of around 3 miles to one inch and include plans of the major towns and cities. The **Michelin** and **Bartholomew** fold-out maps are also excellent, as are the official regional tourist maps published by **Estate Publications**, which are ideal for driving and are available from most tourist offices.

The best detailed maps for walking are the Ordnance Survey (OS) maps, which are unsurpassed for accuracy and clarity. These are available at different scales. The Landranger series at 1:50,000 (1¼ inches to a mile) covers the whole of Britain and is good for most walkers. The new Explorer and Outdoor Leisure series are 1:25,000 and offer better value for walkers and cyclists. An excellent source of maps is **Stanfords** ⓘ *12-14 Longacre, London, T0207-836 1321, www.stanfords.co.uk*. There are branches of Stanfords in Bristol and Manchester too.

Sleeping

Staying in the Highlands and Islands of Scotland can mean anything from being pampered to within an inch of your life in a baronial mansion to roughing it in a tiny island bothy with no electricity. If you have the money, then the sky is very much the limit in terms of sheer splendour and excess. We have listed many of the top class establishments in this book, with a bias towards those that offer that little bit extra in terms of character. Those spending less may have to forego the four-posters and Egyptian cotton sheets but there are still many good-value small hotels and guesthouses with that essential wow factor – especially when it comes to the views. At the bottom end of the scale, there are also some excellent hostels in some pretty special locations.

We have tried to give as broad a selection as possible to cater for all tastes and budgets but if you can't find what you're after, or if someone else has beaten you to the draw, then the tourist information centres (TICs) will help find accommodation for you. They can recommend a place within your particular budget and give you the number to phone up and book yourself, or will book a room for you. Some offices charge a small fee (usually £1) for booking a room, while others ask you to pay a deposit of 10% which is deducted from your first night's bill. Details of town and city TICs are given throughout the guide. There are also several websites that you can browse and book accommodation. Try www.visitscotland.com, www.scottishaccommodationindex.com, www.aboutscotland.com, www.scotland200.com, and www.assc.co.uk.

Accommodation in Scotland will be your greatest expense, particularly if you are travelling on your own. Single rooms are in short supply and many places are reluctant to let a double room to one person, even when they're not busy. Single rooms are usually more than the cost per person for a double room and in some cases cost the same as two people sharing a double room.

Hotels, guesthouses and B&Bs

Area tourist boards publish accommodation lists that include campsites, hostels, self-catering accommodation and VisitScotland-approved hotels, guesthouses and bed and breakfasts (B&Bs). Places participating in the VisitScotland system will have a plaque displayed outside which shows their grading, determined by a number of stars ranging from one to five. These reflect the level of facilities, as well as the quality of hospitality and service. However, do not assume that a B&B, guesthouse or hotel is no good because it is not listed by the tourist board. They simply don't want to pay to be included in the system, and some of them may offer better value. If you'd like to stay in a Scottish castle as a paying guest of the owner, contact **Scotts Castle Holidays** ⓘ *T01208-821341, www.scottscastles.com*.

Hotels

At the top end of the scale there are some fabulously luxurious hotels, often in spectacular locations. Many of them are converted baronial mansions or castles, and offer a chance to enjoy a taste of aristocratic grandeur and style. At the lower end of the scale, there is often little to choose between cheaper hotels and guesthouses or B&Bs. The latter often offer higher standards of comfort and a more personal service, but many smaller hotels are really just guesthouses, and are often family-run and every bit as friendly. Note that some hotels, especially in town centres or in fishing ports, may also be rather noisy, as the bar

Sleeping price codes

L	£160 and over	D	£50-69
A	£130-159	E	£30-49
B	£90-129	F	£29 and under
C	£70-89		

Accommodation prices in this book are based on the cost for two people sharing a double room with en suite bathroom during the high season. Cheaper rooms with shared bathrooms are available in many hotels, guesthouses and B&Bs. Many places, particularly larger hotels, offer substantial discounts during the low season and at weekends. All places listed are recommended as providing good quality and value within their respective price category. Note that outside the major cities, the vast majority of youth hostels and backpackers cost less than £20 per night.

can often be the social hub. Rooms in most mid-range to expensive hotels almost always have bathrooms en suite. Many upmarket hotels offer excellent room-only deals in the low season. An efficient last-minute hotel booking service is www.laterooms.com, which specializes in weekend breaks. Also note that many hotels offer cheaper rates for online booking through agencies such as www.lastminute.com.

Guesthouses

Guesthouses are often large, converted family homes with up to five or six rooms. They tend to be slightly more expensive than B&Bs, charging between £30 and £50 per person per night, and though they are often less personal, usually provide better facilities, such as en suite bathroom, colour TV in each room and private parking. In many instances they are more like small budget hotels. Many guesthouses offer evening meals, though this may have to be requested in advance.

Bed and breakfasts (B&Bs)

B&Bs provide the cheapest private accommodation. At the bottom end of the scale you can get a bedroom in a private house, a shared bathroom and a huge cooked breakfast for around £20-25 per person per night. Small B&Bs may only have one or two rooms to let, so it's important to book in advance during the summer season and on the islands where accommodation options are more limited. More upmarket B&Bs have en suite bathrooms and TVs in each room and usually charge from £25-35 per person per night. In general, B&Bs are more hospitable, informal, friendlier and offer better value than hotels. Many B&B owners are also a great source of local knowledge and can even provide OS maps for local walks. B&Bs in the Outer Hebrides and other remote locations also offer dinner, bed and breakfast, which is useful as eating options are limited, especially on a Sunday.

Some places, especially in ferry ports, charge room-only rates, which are slightly cheaper and allow you to get up in time to catch an early morning ferry. However, this means that you miss out on a huge cooked breakfast. If you're travelling on a tight budget, you can eat as much as you can at breakfast time and save on lunch as you won't need to eat again until evening. This is particularly useful if you're heading into the hills, as you won't have to carry so much food. Many B&B owners will even make up a packed lunch for you at a small extra cost.

For those travelling on a tight budget, there is a large network of hostels offering cheap accommodation. These are also popular centres for backpackers and provide a great opportunity for meeting fellow travellers. Hostels have kitchen facilities for self-catering, and some include a continental breakfast in the price or provide cheap breakfasts and evening meals. Advance booking is recommended at all times, particularly from May to September and on public holidays, and a credit card is often useful.

Scottish Youth Hostel Association (SYHA)

The **Scottish Youth Hostel Association** (**SYHA**) ① *7 Glebe Cres, Stirling, T01786-891400, www.syha.org.uk*, is separate from the YHA in England and Wales. It has a network of over 60 hostels, which are often better and cheaper than those in other countries. They offer bunk-bed accommodation in single-sex dormitories or smaller rooms, kitchen and laundry facilities. The average cost is £10-20 per person per night. Though some rural hostels are still strict on discipline and impose a 2300 curfew, those in larger towns and cities tend to be more relaxed and doors are closed as late as 0200. Some larger hostels provide breakfasts for around £2.50 and three-course evening meals for £4-5. For all EU residents, adult membership costs £10, and can be obtained at the SYHA National Office, or at the first SYHA hostel you stay at. SYHA membership gives automatic membership of Hostelling International (HI). The SYHA produces a handbook (free with membership) giving details of all their youth hostels, including transport links. This can be useful as some hostels are difficult to get to without your own transport. You should always phone ahead, as many hostels are closed during the day and phone numbers are listed in this guide. Many hostels are closed during the winter, details are given in the SYHA Handbook. Youth hostel members are entitled to various discounts, including 20% off Edinburgh bus tours, 20% off Scottish Citylink tickets and 33% off the Orkney Bus (Inverness–Kirkwall).

Independent hostels

Details of most independent hostels (or 'bunkhouses') can be found in the annual Independent Hostel Guide, www.independenthostelguide.com. The Independent Backpackers Hostels of Scotland is an association of nearly 100 independent hostels/ bunkhouses throughout Scotland. This association has a programme of inspection and lists members in their free '*Blue Guide*'. Independent hostels tend to be more laid-back, with fewer rules and no curfew, and no membership is required. They all have dormitories, hot showers and self-catering kitchens. Some include continental breakfast, or provide cheap breakfasts. All these hostels are listed on their excellent website, www.hostel-scotland.co.uk.

Campsites

There are hundreds of campsites around Scotland. They are mostly geared to caravans, and vary greatly in quality and level of facilities. The most expensive sites, which charge up to £15 to pitch a tent, are usually well-equipped. Sites are usually only open from April to October. If you plan to do a lot of camping, you should check out www.scottish camping. com, which is the most comprehensive service with over 500 sites, many with pictures and reviews from punters. North Americans planning on camping should invest in an international camping carnet, which is available from home motoring organizations, or

Wild camping

The Land Reform (Scotland) Act 2003, which together with the Scottish Access Code came into effect in February 2005, ensures Scotland offers walkers, canoeists, cyclists and campers some of the most liberal land access laws in Europe. Technically it means you have the 'right to roam' almost anywhere, although the emphasis is on 'responsible access' (see www.outdooraccess-scotland.com).

from **Family Campers and RVers (FCRV)** ⓘ *4804 Transit Rd, Building 2, Depew, NY 14043, T1-800-245 9755, www.fcrv.org*. It gives you discounts at member sites.

Self-catering

One of the most cost-effective ways to holiday in the Highlands and Islands is to hire a cottage with a group of friends. There are lots of different types of accommodation to choose from, to suit all budgets, ranging from luxury lodges, castles and lighthouses to basic bothies with no electricity.

The minimum stay is usually one week in the summer peak season, though many offer shorter stays of two, three or four nights, especially outside the peak season. Expect to pay at least £200-400 per week for a two-bedroom cottage in the winter, rising to £400-1000 in the high season, or more if it's a particularly nice place. A good source of self-catering accommodation is the VisitScotland's guide, which lists over 1200 properties and is available to buy from any tourist office, but there are also dozens of excellent websites to browse. Amongst the best websites are the following: www.cottages-and- castles.co.uk; www.scottish-country-cottages.co.uk; www.cottages4you.co.uk; www.rural retreats. co.uk, www.assc.co.uk. If you want to tickle a trout or feed a pet lamb, www.farm stay. co.uk, offer over a thousand good value rural places to stay around the UK, all clearly listed on a clickable map.

The **National Trust for Scotland** ⓘ *28 Charlotte Sq, Edinburgh, T0844-493 2100, www. nts.org.uk*, owns many historic properties which are available for self-catering holidays, sleeping between two and 15 people. Prices start at around £300 per week in high season rising to £1000 for the top of the range lodges.

Eating and drinking

While Scotland's national drink is loved the world over, Scottish cooking hasn't exactly had good press over the years. This is perhaps not too surprising, as the national dish, haggis, consists of a stomach stuffed with diced innards and served with mashed tatties (potatoes) and *neeps* (turnips). Not a great start. And things got even worse when the Scots discovered the notorious deep-fried Mars bar.

However, Scottish cuisine has undergone a dramatic transformation in the last decade and Scotland now boasts some of the most talented chefs, creating some of the best food in Britain. The heart of Scottish cooking is local produce, which includes the finest fish, shellfish, game, lamb, beef and vegetables, and a vast selection of traditionally made cheeses. What makes Scottish cooking so special is ready access to these foods. What could be better than enjoying an aperitif whilst watching your dinner being delivered by a local fisherman, knowing that an hour later you'll be enjoying the most delicious seafood?

Eating price codes

Modern Scottish cuisine is now a feature of many of the top restaurants in the country. This generally means the use of local ingredients with foreign-influenced culinary styles, in particular French. International cuisine is also now a major feature on menus all over the country, influenced by the rise of Indian and Chinese restaurants in recent decades. In fact, so prevalent are exotic Asian and Oriental flavours that curry has now replaced fish and chips (fish supper) as the nation's favourite food.

Food

Fish, meat and game form the base of many of the country's finest dishes. Scottish beef, particularly Aberdeen Angus, is the most famous in the world. This will, or should, usually be hung for at least four weeks and sliced thick. Game is also a regular feature of Scottish menus, though it can be expensive, especially venison (deer), but delicious and low in cholesterol. Pheasant and hare are also tasty, but grouse is, quite frankly, overrated.

Fish and seafood are fresh and plentiful, and if you're travelling around the northwest coast you must not miss the chance to savour local mussels, prawns, oysters, scallops, langoustines, lobster or crab. Salmon is, of course, the most famous of Scottish fish, but you're more likely to be served the fish-farmed variety than 'wild' salmon, which has a more delicate flavour. Trout is also farmed extensively, but the standard of both remains high. Kippers are also a favourite delicacy, the best of which come from Loch Fyne or the Achiltibuie smokery, see page 271. Proper fish and chips in Scotland are made with haddock; cod is for Sassenachs (the English) and cats.

Haggis has made something of a comeback, and small portions are often served as starters in fashionable restaurants. Haggis is traditionally eaten on Burns Night (25 January) in celebration of the great poet's birthday, when it is piped to the table and then slashed open with a sword at the end of a recital of Robert Burns' *Address to the Haggis*. Other national favourites feature names to relish: **cock-a-leekie** is a soup made from chicken, leeks and prunes; **cullen skink** is a delicious concoction of smoked haddock and potatoes; while at the other end of the scale of appeal is **hugga-muggie**, a Shetland dish using fish's stomach. There's also the delightfully named **crappit heids** (haddock heads stuffed with lobster) and **partan bree** (a soup made form giant crab's claws, cooked with rice). Rather more mundane is the ubiquitous **Scotch broth**, made with mutton stock, vegetables, barley, lentils and split peas, and **stovies**, which is a hearty mash of potato, onion and minced beef.

Waist-expanding puddings or desserts are a very important part of Scottish cooking and often smothered in butterscotch sauce or syrup. There is a huge variety, including cranachan, a mouth-watering mix of toasted oatmeal steeped in whisky, cream and fresh raspberries, and **Atholl Brose**, a similar confection of oatmeal, whisky and cream.

Eaten before pudding, in the French style, or afterwards, are Scotland's many home-produced cheeses, which have made a successful comeback in the face of mass-produced varieties. Many of the finest cheeses are produced on the islands, especially Arran, Mull, Islay and Orkney. **Caboc** is a creamy soft cheese rolled in oatmeal and is made in the Highlands.

Anyone staying at a hotel, guesthouse or B&B will experience the hearty **Scottish breakfast**, which includes bacon, egg, sausage, 'tattie scone' and black pudding (a type of sausage made with blood), all washed down with copious quantities of tea. Coffee is readily available everywhere, with most places now offering a selection of cappuccinos and café lattes. You may also be served kippers (smoked herring) or porridge, an erstwhile Scottish staple. Made with oatmeal and with the consistency of Italian polenta, it is traditionally eaten with salt, though heretics are offered sugar instead. Oatcakes (oatmeal biscuits) may also be on offer, as well as potato scones, baps (bread rolls) or bannocks (a sort of large oatcake). After such a huge cooked breakfast you probably won't feel like eating again until dinner.

Drink

Beer

Beer is the alcoholic drink of choice in Scotland. The most popular type of beer is lager, which is generally brewed in the UK, even when it bears the name of an overseas brand, and is almost always weaker in both strength and character than the lagers in mainland Europe. However, examples of the older and usually darker type of beers, known as ales, are still widely available, and connoisseurs should try some of these as they are far more rewarding. Indeed, the best of them rival Scotland's whiskies as gourmet treats.

Traditionally, Scottish ales were graded by the shilling, an old unit of currency written as /-, according to strength. This system is still widely used by the older established breweries, though many of the newer independents and 'micros' have departed from it. 70/- beers at around 3.5% ABV (alcohol by volume), known as 'heavy', and 80/- beers (4.5% sometimes known as 'export'), are the most popular, while 60/-, 'light' (3-3.5%) is harder to find. Very strong 90/- beers (6.5% + ABV), known as 'wee heavies', are also brewed, mainly for bottling.

The market is dominated by the giant international brewers: Scottish Courage with its McEwans and Youngers brands; Interbrew with Calders and Carslberg; and Tetley with Tennents lagers. Tennents was the first British brewery to produce a continental-style lager commercially back in the 19th century, and, despite a competitive marketplace, remains a favourite for many Scots.

Much better are the ales from smaller independent breweries. Edinburgh's Caledonian is a world-class brewer producing many excellent beers, including a popular 80/- and a renowned golden hoppy ale, Deuchars IPA. Belhaven, an old, established family brewery in Dunbar, has some superb traditional beers including a malty 80/-, once marketed as the Burgundy of Scotland. Broughton, a microbrewery in the Borders, produces the fruity Greenmantle and an oatmeal stout. Another micro, Harviestoun of Clackmannanshire (once an important brewing country) offers a wide and adventurous range of specialities, including Ptarmigan 80/- and a naturally brewed cask lager, Schiehallion. The Heather Ale Company, near Glasgow, has the spicy and unusual Fraoch (pronounced 'Frooch'), which is flavoured with real heather as well as hops.

Turn water into whisky

Malt whisky is made by first soaking dry barley in tanks of local water for two to three days. Then the barley is spread out on a concrete floor or placed in cylindrical drums and allowed to germinate for between eight and 12 days, after which it is dried in a kiln, heated by a peat fire. Next, the dried malt is ground and mixed with hot water in a huge circular vat called a 'mash tun'. A sugary liquid called 'wort' is then drawn from the porridge-like result and piped into huge containers where living yeast is stirred into the mix in order to convert the sugar in the wort into alcohol. After about 48 hours the 'wash' is transferred to copper pot stills and heated till the alcohol vaporizes and is then condensed by a cooling plant into distilled alcohol which is passed through a second still. Once distilled, the liquid is poured into oak casks and left to age for a minimum of three years, though a good malt will stay casked for at least eight years.

Draught beer in pubs and bars is served in pints, or half pints, and you'll pay between £2.50 and £3.50 for a pint (unless you discover a 'Happy Hour' offering good deals on drinks, usually for much more than one hour! Happy hours usually apply in late afternoon or early evening). In many pubs the basic ales are chilled under gas pressure like lagers, but the best ales, such as those from the independents, are 'real ales', still fermenting in the cask and served cool but not chilled (around 12°C) under natural pressure from a handpump, electric pump or air pressure fount. All Scottish beers are traditionally served with a full, creamy head.

Whisky

No visit to the Scottish Highlands would be complete without availing oneself of a 'wee dram'. There is no greater pleasure on an inclement evening than enjoying a malt whisky in front of a roaring log fire whilst watching the rain outside pelt down relentlessly. The roots of Scotland's national drink (*uisge beatha*, or 'water of life' in Gaelic) go back to the late 15th century, but it wasn't until the invention of a patent still in the early 19th century that distilling began to develop from small family-run operations to the large manufacturing business it has become today. Now more than 700 million bottles a year are exported, mainly to the United States, France, Japan and Spain.

There are two types of whisky: single malt, made only from malted barley; and grain, which is made from malted barley together with unmalted barley, maize or other cereals, and is faster and cheaper to produce. Most of the popular brands are blends of both types of whisky – usually 60-70% grain to 30-40% malt. These blended whiskies account for over 90% of all sales worldwide, and most of the production of single malts is used to add flavour to a blended whisky. Amongst the best-known brands of blended whisky are Johnnie Walker, Bells, Teachers and Famous Grouse. There's not much between them in terms of flavour and they are usually drunk with a mixer, such as water or soda.

Single malts are a different matter altogether. Each is distinctive and should be drunk neat to appreciate fully its subtle flavours, though some believe that the addition of water helps free the flavours. Single malts vary enormously. Their distinctive flavours and aromas are derived from the peat used for drying, the water used for mashing, the type of oak cask used and the location of the distillery. Single malts fall into four groups: Highland, Lowland, Campbeltown and Islay. There are over 40 distilleries to choose from, most

Which whisky?

Opinions vary as to what are the best single malts and as to when you should drink them. As a rough guide, we would recommend a Speyside malt such as Glenmorangie or Glenlivet before dinner and one of the Islay malts – Ardbeg, Bowmore, Bunnahabhain (pronounced 'bun-a-haven'), Lagavulin, or the very wonderful Laphroaig (pronounced 'la-froig') – after dinner.

If the Islays are not to your taste, then you could try instead the versatile Highland Park from Orkney or perhaps Tamdhu or Aberlour from Speyside. Those eternal favourites, Glenfiddich and The Macallan, can be enjoyed at any time.

offering guided tours. The majority are located around Speyside, in the northeast. The region's many distilleries include that perennial favourite, Glenfiddich, which is sold in 185 countries. Recommended alternatives are the produce of the beautiful and peaceful Isle of Islay, whose malts are lovingly described in terms of their peaty quality and the produce of the island known as 'Scotland in Miniature', Arran, whose 10-year-old malt, distilled in Lochranza, has won recent international acclaim. Scots tend to favour the 10-year-old Glenmorangie, while the most popular in the USA is The Macallan.

Eating out

There are places to suit every taste and budget. In the large towns and cities you'll find a vast selection of eating places, including Indian, Chinese, Italian and French restaurants, as well as Thai, Japanese, Mexican, Spanish and, of course Scottish, but beyond the main cities, choice is much more limited. More and more restaurants are moving away from national culinary boundaries and offering a wide range of international dishes and flavours, so you'll often find Latin American, Oriental and Pacific Rim dishes all on the same menu. This is particularly the case in the many continental-style bistros, brasseries and café-bars, which now offer a more informal alternative to traditional restaurants. Vegetarians are increasingly well catered for, especially in the large cities, where exclusively vegetarian/ vegan restaurants and cafés are often the cheapest places to eat. Outside the cities, vegetarian restaurants are thin on the ground, though better-quality eating places will normally offer a reasonable vegetarian selection.

For a cheap meal, your best bet is a pub, hotel bar or café, where you can have a one-course meal for around £5-7 or less, though don't expect gourmet food. The best value is often at lunchtime, when many restaurants offer three-course set lunches or business lunches for less than £10. You'll need a pretty huge appetite to feel like eating a three-course lunch after your gigantic cooked breakfast, however. Also good value are the pre-theatre dinners offered by many restaurants in the larger towns and cities (you don't need to have a theatre ticket to take advantage). These are usually available from around 1730-1800 until 1900-1930, so you could get away with just a sandwich for lunch. At the other end of the price scale are many excellent restaurants where you can enjoy the finest of Scottish cuisine, often with a continental influence, and these are often found in hotels. You can expect to pay from around £30 a head up to £40 or £50 (excluding drinks) in the very top establishments.

The biggest problem with eating out in Scotland, as in the rest of the UK, is the ludicrously limited serving hours in some pubs and hotels, particularly in remoter locations. These places only serve food during restricted hours, seemingly ignorant of the eating habits of foreign visitors, or those who would prefer a bit more flexibility during their holiday. In small places especially, it can be difficult finding food outside these enforced times. Places that serve food all day till 2100 or later are restaurants, fast-food outlets and the many chic bistros and café-bars, which can be found not only in the main cities but increasingly in smaller towns. The latter often offer very good value and above-average quality fare.

Entertainment

Bars and clubs

As in the rest of Britain, pubs are the main focus of social life and entertainment for most Scots. These vary greatly, from traditional old inns full of character to chic and trendy bars where you can order foccacia bread with sundried tomatoes washed down with a bottle of continental lager. Many pubs in large towns are owned by the large breweries and only serve their own particular beers, while in more remote parts the local hotel bar is often the only watering hole for miles around. Visitors should also note that the Scottish parliament passed a law in 2006 banning smoking in pubs and bars, which means that those wishing to light up will have to step outside. Pubs are generally open Monday to Saturday from 1100 till 2300, and Sunday from 1100-1200 till 2230, though some close for a couple of hours between 1400 and 1600, which can be annoying on a wet afternoon. In towns and cities many pubs are open till 2400 or later on Friday and Saturday nights.

Cinema

Scotland, like the rest of the UK, has succumbed to the rise of home entertainment and many of the finest cinemas have long gone, replaced by bingo halls and out-of-town leisure and entertainment complexes showing a vast array of Hollywood blockbusters and little else. That's not to say that independent cinema is dead. Inverness, Perth and Oban all have independent cinemas showing arthouse films.

Dance

One of the most vibrant expressions of Celtic culture is the ceilidh (pronounced 'kay-lee') an evening of Scottish music and dance, the music provided by a ceilidh band, which normally consists of a fiddler, an accordionist, a drummer and a singer or 'caller' (who announces and sometimes explains the dances). Here you can spend the evening sampling the delights of Gay Gordons or Dashing White Sergeants, Scottish country dances which, along with eightsome reels, figure prominently in the ceilidh dance-band repertoire. Beware the well-meaning local lad or lassie bearing gifts of whisky, however – an excellent evening enjoying the music can often lead to a spectacular hangover the following morning. The local TIC, or newspaper, will have details of what's on where.

Music

Folk music clubs still thrive in Scotland although, sadly, seem to be restricted to an 'early-in-the-week' slot of a Monday or Tuesday evening in bars, as landlords attempt to bring in customers on what are generally quieter nights for business. Even the Scots, with their fearsome (and well-earned) reputation for partying, can't do it every night of the week. Look out for boards outside pubs which proclaim 'Live Music Tonight' or 'Folk Music

Session – All Welcome', when the atmosphere of the local pub is transformed into something resembling a scene from a Hollywood film featuring Julia Roberts in an Aran jumper.

Theatre

The main focal points of Scottish theatre are, not surprisingly, the cities of Edinburgh and Glasgow. The latter in particular stages some of the UK's most exciting and innovative drama in its Citizens' and Tramway Theatres. Outside the big two, Perth, Pitlochry and Inverness all have thriving summer programmes.

Festivals and events

There is a huge range of organized events held throughout Scotland every year, ranging in size and spectacle from the Edinburgh Festival, the largest arts festival in the world, to more obscure traditional events featuring ancient customs dating back many centuries. For all events in Scotland, by far and away the best website to visit is www.eventscotland. org. The most popular tourist events are the **Highland Games** (or **Gatherings**), a series of competitions involving lots of kilts, bagpipes and caber-tossing, which are held across the Highlands and Islands, the northeast and Argyll from June to September. The best known is the **Braemar Gathering**, see box, page 159, which is attended by various members of the royal family. Those at Oban and Dunoon are large events, but smaller gatherings are often more enjoyable and 'authentic'. Details of Highland Gatherings can be obtained through the Event Scotland website, see above.

Folk festivals take place all over the country, from Arran to Shetland, and are great fun. Musicians from all over Scotland gather to play the tunes, sing the songs and maybe, just maybe, drink the odd beer or two. Among the best of the folk festivals is the **Shetland Folk Festival**, usually held over a long weekend in April or early May. Also recommended are those held in Inverness, Islay, Arran, Skye and Kirriemuir. All are usually held during the summer months, but check in advance for dates. Details of all these festivals, and many others, are available from the VisitScotland regional office. Details of local festivals are given in the listings sections of individual town and cities; also visit www.whatsonwhen.com.

Festivals

Jan New Year's Day A variety of ancient local celebrations take place, including the Kirkwall Ba' Game, a mixture of football and mud wrestling.

Up Helly-Aa Re-enactment of the ancient Viking fire festival held on Shetland on the last Tue in Jan, see page 416.

Burns Night Burns suppers held on 25 Jan all over the country to celebrate the poet's birthday. Lots of haggis, whisky and poetry.

May Spirit of Speyside Whisky Festival Held on Speyside in May.

Sep Braemar Highland Gathering, www. braemargathering.org. Attended by the royal family, the 1st Sat in Sep.

Oct National Mod Competitive Gaelic music festival held at various locations.

Tour of Mull Rally The highlight of the Scottish rally season, run over the island's public roads (no wonder they're in such appalling condition) in Oct.

31 Dec Hogmanay Old year's night, and the most important national celebration. Possible derivations of the word include Holag Monath, Anglo Saxon for 'holy month', and Hoog min dag, which is Dutch for 'great love day'. Edinburgh's huge street party is the largest in the northern hemisphere.

Bank holidays

1 Jan New Year's Day
2 Jan Also a holiday in Scotland.
Mar-Apr Good Friday and Easter Monday
1 May May Day
May Victoria Day (the last Mon in May).
25 Dec Christmas Day
26 Dec Boxing Day

There are also local public holidays in spring and autumn. Dates vary from place to place. Banks are closed during these holidays, and sights and shops may be affected. Contact the relevant Area Tourist Board for more details.

Shopping

Scottish textiles, especially the **tartan** variety, are popular and worth buying. You can get hold of everything from a travelling rug to your own kilt outfit. Shops up and down the country, and especially in Inverness, can tell which clan your family belongs to and make you a kilt in that particular tartan. For the full outfit, including kilt, sporran, jacket, shoes and *skeann dhu* dagger, expect to pay in the region of £600, or more if you want elaborate accessories. **Harris Tweed** is also a good buy and you can watch your cloth being woven on the Hebridean islands of Harris and Lewis.

Knitwear is also good value and sold throughout Scotland. Shetland is a good place to find high-quality wool products. Note that Aran jumpers are not from the island of Arran, but from Aran (with one 'r') in Ireland. **Jewellery** is another popular souvenir and there are many excellent craft shops throughout the Highlands and Islands making beautiful jewellery with Celtic designs. **Glassware** is also popular, particularly Edinburgh crystal and Caithness glass, as well as pottery. You can order Scottish crafts at www.papastour.com.

Food is another good souvenir and not just the ubiquitous shortbread sold in tartan tins. If you haven't far to travel home, smoked salmon, or any other smoked product, is good value. Two of the best islands for food products are Mull and Arran, where you can buy their delicious local mustards and preserves, smoked fish and game, and cheeses. And, of course, there's **whisky**. Most distilleries will refund the cost of their guided tour in the form of a discount voucher on a bottle of their brand whisky.

Shop hours in Scotland are generally Monday to Saturday 0900-1730 or 1800. In larger towns and cities, many shops also open on Sundays and late at night, usually on a Thursday and Friday. Large supermarkets and retail complexes found outside large towns are open till 2000 or later Monday to Saturday and till 1600 on Sunday. There are some 24-hour superstores in and around major cities. In the Highlands and Islands, few shops are open on Sunday, most notably in the Outer Hebrides. Also note that in many rural areas there is an early-closing day when shops close at 1300. This varies from region to region, but the most common day is Wednesday.

Essentials A-Z

Accident and emergency

For police, fire brigade, ambulance and, in certain areas, mountain rescue or coastguard, T999 or T112.

Children

Visiting the Scottish Highlands with kids is no different from other parts of the UK, though you may find that the locals are just that little bit more tolerant and helpful. If you're near a beach, toddlers will be in rock pool heaven, rooting around to their little heart's content as you sit nearby, shivering in the rain. Even teenagers should have no reason to moan as there are all manner of thrill-a-minute adventure sports to try.

If you're travelling with babies and/ or toddlers you may find eating out a frustrating experience in some establishments, though the days of families being banished to some grubby room at the back, well out of the way of other diners, are, thankfully, a thing of the past in most places. The attitude to breastfeeding, while some way behind the likes of Scandinavia, is more relaxed than the US and becoming ever more civilized and progressive. In major towns and cities, Italian restaurants are generally more child- friendly. The child may not be quite be king, but they are allowed to be seen and heard.

If you are flying, inform the airline in advance that you're travelling with a baby or toddler, and check out the facilities when booking as these vary with each aircraft. British Airways operates a Skyflyers programme specifically to help passengers travelling with young children. Facilities include special seats for under 2s, allowing foldable pushchairs to be taken on-board or stored in the hold and the provision of skycots for long-haul flights. With 24-hrs' advance notice, children's meals can also be provided on-board. However, take snacks and toys for in-flight entertainment, and remember that swallowing food or drinks during take-off and landing will help prevent ear problems.

A recommended website is www.baby goes2.com, while www.mumsnet.com/ bigissues/travel.html, is useful for parents with older kids.

Customs and duty free

Visitors from EU countries do not have to make a declaration to customs on entry into the UK. The limits for duty-paid goods from within the EU are 3200 cigarettes and 200 cigars, 10 litres of spirits, 20 litres of fortified wine, 90 litres of wine and 110 litres of beer. There is no longer any duty-free shopping. Visitors from non-EU countries are allowed to import 200 cigarettes, or 250 g of tobacco, 2 litres of wine, and 2 litres of fortified wine or 1 litre of spirits. There are various import restrictions, most of which should not affect the average tourist. There are tight quarantine restrictions which apply to animals brought from overseas (except for Ireland). For more information on British import regulations, contact **HM Customs and Excise**, Dorset House, Stamford St, London SE1 9PJ, T0845-010 9000, www.hmce.gov.uk.

Many goods in Britain are subject to a Value Added Tax (VAT) of 17.5%, with the major exception of books and food. Visitors from non-EU countries can save money through the Retail Export Scheme, which allows a refund of VAT on goods to be taken out of the country. Note that not all shops are participants in the scheme and that VAT cannot be reclaimed on hotel bills or other services.

Disabled travellers

For travellers with disabilities, visiting Scotland independently can be a difficult business. While most theatres, cinemas, libraries and modern tourist attractions are accessible to wheelchairs, tours of many historic buildings and finding accommodation remains problematic. Many large, new hotels do have disabled suites, but far too many B&Bs, guesthouses and smaller hotels remain ill-equipped to accept bookings from people with disabilities. However, through the work of organizations like **Disability Scotland** the Government is being pressed to further improve the Disability Discrimination Act and access to public amenities and transport. As a result, many buses and FirstScotRail's train services now accommodate wheelchair-users whilst city taxis should carry wheelchair ramps.

Wheelchair users, and blind or partially sighted people are automatically given 30-50% discount on train fares, and those with other disabilities are eligible for the Disabled Person's Railcard, which costs £18 per year and gives a third off most tickets. If you will need assistance at a railway station, call FirstScotRail before travelling on T0800-912 2901. There are no discounts on buses.

If you are disabled you should contact the travel officer of your national support organization. They can provide literature or put you in touch with travel agents specializing in tours for the disabled. **VisitScotland** produces a guide, *Accessible Scotland*, for disabled travellers, and many local tourist offices can provide accessibility details for their area. Alternatively call its national booking hotline on T0845-225 5121. A useful website is www.atlholidays. com, which specializes in organizing holidays for disabled travellers, recommends hotels with good facilities and can also arrange rental cars and taxis.

Useful organizations include:
Capability Scotland, ASCS, 11 Ellersly Rd, Edinburgh EH12 6HY, T0131-313 5510, or Textphone 0131-346 2529, www.capability-scotland.org.uk,
The Holiday Care Service, T0845-124 9974, www.holidaycare.org.uk, www.tourismfor all.org.uk. Both websites are excellent sources of information about travel and for identifying accessible accommodation in the UK.
The Royal Association for Disability and Rehabilitation (RADAR), Unit 12, City Forum, 250 City Rd, London EC1V 8AF, T020-7250 3222, www.radar.org.uk. A good source of advice and information. It produces an annual *National Key Scheme Guide* for gaining access to over 6000 toilet facilities across the UK (£10.70 including P&P).

Electricity

The current in Britain is 240V AC. Plugs have 3 square pins and adapters are widely available.

Embassies and consulates

The **Foreign Office** website, www.fco. gov.uk, has a directory of all British embassies overseas.

Gay and lesbian travellers

Don't assume that because men are wearing skirts in the Highlands that people take a relaxed attitude to homosexuality. The same prejudices apply as elsewhere in rural parts of the UK. Though Scotland is generally tolerant of homosexuality, overt displays of affection are not advised. Gay couples may also come up against subtle forms of discrimination, such as B&Bs spontaneously 'losing' bookings for a double room and being left with the option of taking 2 singles. The *Scotsgay* magazine, www.scotsgay.co.uk, is a good source of information, as is the **Stonewall Scotland** organization, www.stonewall scotland.org.uk. *The List Magazine*, www.list. co.uk, published fortnightly and available at newsagents in Scottish cities, includes listings

Once bitten, twice shy

The major problem facing visitors to the Highlands and Islands of Scotland during the summer months is *Culicoides impunctatus* – or the midge, as it's more commonly known. These tiny flying creatures are savage and merciless in the extreme and hunt in huge packs (it is estimated that midges cost the Scottish tourist industry nearly £300 million a year in lost revenue). No sooner have you left your B&B for a pleasant evening stroll, than a cloud of these bloodthirsty little devils will descend, getting into your eyes, ears, nose and mouth – and a few places you forgot you even had. The only way to avoid them is to take refuge indoors, or to hide in the nearest loch.

Midges are at their worst in the evening and in damp, shaded or overcast conditions, and between late May and September, but they don't like direct sunlight, heavy rain, smoke and wind. Make sure you're well covered up and wear light-coloured clothing (they're attracted to dark colours). Most effective is a midge net, if you don't mind everyone pointing and laughing at you. Insect repellents have some effect, particularly those with DEET, but those who don't fancy putting chemicals on their skin can try Mozzy Off, www.mozzy off.com, which comprises 100% plant oils, while the Thurso-made Essential Spirit, www. essentialspirit.co.uk, is also made from natural ingredients. A more radical approach is the Midgeater, a trap which emits carbon dioxide to lure the little blighters within range and then sucks them in at high speed. Those who see prevention as the best form of cure can log on to www.midgefore cast.co.uk, a new online midge forecast service that gives five-day predictions of midge movements.

If you do get bitten, spare a thought for the gravedigger from Rùm. According to legend, as punishment for not burying a body properly he was stripped naked, tied to a post and left outside with only the midges for company. The poor chap eventually died of the countless bites.

of venues and events that may appeal to the gay, lesbian and bisexual community.

Health

No vaccinations are required for entry into Britain. Citizens of EU countries are entitled to free medical treatment at National Health Service (NHS) hospitals on production of a European Health Insurance Card (EHIC). For details, see the Department of Health website, www.dh.gov.uk/travellers. Also, Australia, New Zealand and several other non-EU European countries have reciprocal healthcare arrangements with Britain. Citizens of other countries will have to pay for all medical services, except accident and emergency care given at Accident and Emergency (A&E) Units at most (but not all) National Health Service hospitals. Health insurance is therefore strongly advised for citizens of non-EU countries.

Pharmacists can dispense only a limited range of drugs without a doctor's prescription. Most are open during normal shop hours, though some are open late, especially in larger towns. Local newspapers will carry lists of which are open late. Doctors' surgeries are usually open from around 0830-0900 till 1730-1800, though times vary. Outside surgery hours you can go to the casualty department of the local hospital for any complaint requiring urgent attention. For the address of the nearest hospital or doctors' surgery, www.nhs24. com. See also individual town and city directories throughout the book for details local medical services.

You should encounter no major problems or irritations during your visit to Scotland. The only exceptions are the risk of hyperthermia if you're walking in the mountains in difficult conditions, and the dreaded midge, see box, above.

Insurance

It's a good idea to take out some form of travel insurance, wherever you're travelling from. This should cover you for theft or loss of possessions and money, the cost of all medical and dental treatment, cancellation of flights, delays in travel arrangements, accidents, missed departures, lost baggage, lost passport, and personal liability and legal expenses. There are a variety of policies to choose from, so it's best to shop around to get the best price. Your travel agent can also advise you on the best deals available. **STA Travel**, www.statravel.com, with branches nationwide, and other reputable student travel organizations often offer good-value travel policies. Another company worth calling for a quote is **Columbus Direct**, T0870-033 9988, www.columbusdirect. com. Older travellers should note that some companies won't cover people over 65 years old, or may charge high premiums. The best policies for older travellers are offered by **Age Concern**, T0800-009966, www.age concern.org.uk. Some other recommended travel insurance companies in North America include **Travel Guard**, T1-800 826 4919, www.travelguard.com; **Access America**, T1-800-284 8300, www. accessamerica.com; **Travel Insurance Services**, T1-800-937 1387, www.travel insure.com; and **Travel Assistance International**, T1-800-821 2828, www.travelassistance.com.

Points to note: you should always read the small print carefully. Some policies exclude 'dangerous activities' such as scuba-diving, skiing, horse riding or even trekking. Not all policies cover ambulance, helicopter rescue or emergency flights home. Find out if your policy pays medical expenses direct to the hospital or doctor, or if you have to pay and then claim the money back later. If the latter applies, make sure you keep all records. Whatever your policy, if you are unfortunate enough to have something stolen, make sure you get a copy of the police report, as you will need this to substantiate your claim.

Internet

Even in the Highlands of Scotland, internet access is extensive. Every major town now has at least 1 internet café, with more springing up daily. Email works out much, much cheaper than phoning home and is also useful for booking hotels and tours, and for checking out information on the web. Many hotels now have Wi-Fi access and many hostels also offer internet access to their guests. Websites and email addresses are listed where appropriate in this guide. VisitScotland and area tourist boards have their own websites and these are given on page 60. Internet cafés are also listed under each relevant section. In the absence of any listed under a particular town try the public library or ask at the TIC.

Language

Though the vast majority of Scots speak English, to the untutored ear the Scottish dialect can be hard to understand, as many words and expressions are derived not from English but from Lowland Scots, or lallans, which is now recognized as a separate language as opposed to simply a regional dialect. In the Highlands and Islands, however, the accent is very clear and easy to understand.

Scotland's oldest surviving language is Scottish Gaelic (*Gaidhlig*, pronounced 'Gallic'), spoken by only about 2% of the population. Notably, a 2001 Census found Glasgow has the highest concentration of Gaelic speakers. Generally however, the Highlands, Outer Hebrides and Argyll have the greatest numbers of Gaelic-speaking inhabitants. Indeed, on many islands including Harris and Lewis road signs are written in both Gaelic and English. In recent years greater efforts have been made to revive the language, including the creation by the BBC of wholly Gaelic TV and radio programming, www.bbc.co.uk/ scotland/ alba. A good phrasebook for getting to grips with the basics of the ancient Celtic language is *Scots Gaelic, an introduction to the basics* by George McLennan (Argyll Publishing). *Macbain's Etymological Dictionary of the Gaelic language* contains a wealth of words and information. For information on Gaelic language schools including on the Isle of Islay visit www. gaelic-scotland.co.uk. For more on the history of Gaelic, see page 459, and for a glossary of Gaelic words, see page 470.

Laundry

Most towns have coin-operated launderettes. The average cost for a wash and tumble dry is about £3-4. A service wash, where someone will do your washing for you, costs around £5-6. In more remote areas, you'll have to rely on hostel and campsite facilities. An increasing number of SYHA hostels have excellent 'drying rooms' and washing facilities.

Media

Newspapers and magazines
The main British daily and Sun newspapers are widely available in Scotland and some of them publish special Scottish editions, among them the *Scottish Daily Mail*, *Scottish Daily Express* and Rupert Murdoch's notorious scandal sheet, *The Sun*.

The Scottish press produces 2 main 'quality' newspapers, *The Scotsman*, published in Edinburgh, and *The Herald*, published in Glasgow, which is the oldest daily newspaper in the English-speaking world, dating from 1783. The biggest-selling

daily is the *Daily Record*, a tabloid paper. The *Press and Journal*, published in Aberdeen, also enjoys one of the highest circulations in the country. The weekend equivalents of the dailies are *Scotland on Sunday* from the Scotsman stable, the *Sunday Herald* and the *Sunday Mail*, published by the Daily Record, while the rather couthy *The Sunday Post*, is popular with the older generation. Provincial newspapers are widely read in Scotland. The main Highlands varieties are the weekly *Oban Times* and the radical, crusading *West Highland Free Press* published on Skye.

TV and radio
There are 5 main television channels in Scotland; the publicly funded BBC 1 and 2, and the independent commercial stations, ITV, Channel 4, Channel 5. The main commercial TV network in Scotland is STV, providing national coverage.

The BBC network also broadcasts several radio channels, most of which are based in London. These include: *Radio 1* aimed at a young audience; *Radio 2* targeting a more mature audience; *Radio 3* which plays mostly classical music; *Radio 4* which is talk-based and features arts, drama and current affairs; and *Radio 5 Live* which is a mix of sport and news. *Radio Scotland* (92-95FM, 810MW) provides a Scottish-based diet of news, sport, current affairs, travel and music. It also provides an ever-expanding Gaelic network in the northwest, and local programmes in Orkney and Shetland. There are also a number of local commercial radio stations, stretching from Shetland in the north to the Borders.

Money → *US$1 = £0.64, 1 Euro = £0.83 (Jan 2011).*

The British currency is the pound sterling (£), divided into 100 pence (p). Coins come in denominations of 1p, 2p, 5p, 10p, 20p, 50p, £1 and £2. Bank of England banknotes are legal tender in Scotland, in addition to those issued by the Bank of Scotland, Royal Bank of Scotland and Clydesdale Bank.

These Scottish banknotes (bills) come in denominations of £5, £10, £20, £50 and £100 and regardless of what you are told by shopkeepers in England the notes are legal tender in the rest of Britain.

Banks
The larger towns and villages have a branch of at least one of the big 4 high street banks – **Bank of Scotland**, **Royal Bank of Scotland**, **Clydesdale** and **TSB Scotland**. Bank opening hours are Mon-Fri from 0930 to between 1600 and 1700. Some larger branches may also be open later on Thu and on Sat mornings. In small and remote places, and on some islands, there may be only a mobile bank which runs to a set timetable. This timetable will be available from the local post office.

Banks are usually the best places to change money and cheques. You can withdraw cash from selected banks and ATMs (or cashpoints as they are called in Britain) with your cash and credit card. Though using a debit or credit card is by far the easiest way of keeping in funds, you must check with your bank what the total charges will be; this can be as high as 4-5% in some cases. In more remote parts, and especially on the islands, ATMs are few and far between and it is important to keep a ready supply of cash on you at all times and many guesthouses in the remoter reaches of Scotland will still request payment in cash. Outside the ferry ports on most of the smaller islands, you won't find an ATM. Your bank will give you a list of locations where you can use your card. **Bank of Scotland** and **Royal Bank** take **Lloyds** and **Barclays** cash cards; **Clydesdale** takes **HSBC** and **National Westminster** cards. **Bank of Scotland**, **Clydesdale** and most building society cashpoints are part of the Link network and accept all affiliated cards. See also Credit cards below. In addition to ATMs, bureaux de change can be used outside banking hours. These can be found in most city centres and also at the main airports and train stations. Note that some charge high commissions for changing cheques. Those at international airports, however, often charge less than banks and will change pound sterling cheques for free. Avoid changing money or cheques in hotels, as the rates are usually very poor.

Credit cards
Most hotels, shops and restaurants accept the major credit cards such as MasterCard and Visa and, less frequently, Amex, though some places may charge for using them. They may be less useful in more remote rural areas and smaller establishments such as B&Bs, which will often only accept cash or cheques.

Visa card holders can use the **Bank of Scotland**, **Clydesdale Bank**, **Royal Bank of Scotland** and **TSB** ATMs; Access/MasterCard holders the Royal Bank and Clydesdale; Amex card holders the Bank of Scotland.

Traveller's cheques
The safest way to carry money is in traveller's cheques. These are available for a small commission from all major banks. **American Express (Amex)**, **Visa** and **Thomas Cook** cheques are widely accepted and are the most commonly issued by banks. You'll normally have to pay commission again when you cash each cheque. This will usually be 1%, or a flat rate. No commission is payable on Amex cheques cashed at Amex offices, www.americanexpress.co/feefree. Make sure you keep a record of the cheque numbers and the cheques you've cashed separate from the cheques themselves, so that you can get a full refund of all uncashed cheques should you lose them. It's best to bring sterling cheques to avoid changing currencies twice. Also note that in Britain traveller's cheques are rarely accepted outside banks or foreign exchange bureaux, so you'll need to cash them in advance and keep a good supply of ready cash.

Money transfers

If you need money urgently, the quickest way to have it sent to you is to have it wired to the nearest bank via **Western Union**, T0800-833 833, www.westernunion.co.uk, or **Money-gram**, T0800-8971 8971. Charges are on a sliding scale; ie it will cost proportionately less to wire out more money. Money can also be wired by **Thomas Cook**, www.thomasexchangeglobal.co.uk, or transferred via a bank draft, but this can take up to a week.

Cost of travelling

The Highlands and Islands of Scotland can be an expensive place to visit, and prices are higher in more remote parts, but there is plenty of budget accommodation available and backpackers will be able to keep their costs down. Petrol is a major expense and won't just cost an arm and a leg but also the limbs of all remaining family members. Expect to pay up to 15p per litre more than in central and southern parts of Scotland and don't pass a fuel station in the Highlands and Islands if short of fuel. Accommodation and restaurant prices also tend to be higher in more popular destinations and during the busy summer months.

The minimum daily budget required, if you're staying in hostels, very cheap B&Bs or camping, cycling or hitching (not recommended), and cooking your own meals, will be around £25-30 per person per day. If you start using public transport and eating out occasionally that will rise to around £35-40. Those staying in slightly more upmarket B&Bs or guesthouses, eating out every evening at pubs or modest restaurants and visiting tourist attractions, such as castles or museums, can expect to pay around £50-60 per day. If you also want to hire a car and use ferries to visit the islands, and eat well, then costs will rise considerably and you'll be looking at least £75-80 per person per day. Single travellers will have to pay more than ½ the cost of a double room in most places, and should budget on spending around 60-70% of what a couple would spend.

Opening hours

Businesses are usually open Mon-Sat 0900-1700. In towns and cities, as well as villages in holiday areas, many shops open on a Sun but they will open later and close earlier (for further details, see page 48). For TIC opening hours, see page 58. Those visiting the Outer Hebrides need to be aware of the strict observance of the Sabbath on those islands.

Post

Most post offices are open Mon-Fri 0900 to 1730 and Sat 0900-1230 or 1300. Smaller sub-post offices are closed for an hour at lunch (1300-1400) and many of them operate out of a shop. Post offices keep the same ½-day closing times as shops.

Stamps can be bought at post offices, but also from vending machines outside, and also at many newsagents. A 1st-class letter weighing up to 100 g to anywhere in the UK costs 36p and should arrive the following day, while 2nd-class letters weighing up to 100 g cost 27p and take between 2-4 days. For more information about Royal Mail postal services, call T08457-740740, or visit www.royalmail.com.

Safety

Incidences of serious crime in Highlands and Islands tend to be the exception rather than the rule and are so rare that they always make front page news. In fact, if someone failed to say 'good morning' – heaven forfend – it would provoke such an outrage that locals would be talking about little else for weeks to come. Orkney, for example, has the lowest crime rate in the UK (though there was one reported drive-by shouting back in the 1980s). In most island communities, even sizeable ones such as

Tobermory on Mull, people don't even lock their doors at night, and will even leave their car keys still in the lock. The major safety issue when visiting the Highlands and more remote parts relates to the unpredictable weather conditions. Everyone should be aware of the need for caution and proper preparation when walking or climbing in the mountains. For more information on mountain safety, see www.mountaineering-scotland.org.uk/safety.

Student travellers

Discount passes

There are various official youth/student ID cards available. The most useful is the **International Student ID Card (ISIC)**. For £9 the ISIC card gains you access to the world of student travel with a series of discounts, including most forms of local transport, cheap or free admission to museums, theatres and other attractions, cheap meals in some restaurants and discounted fares on certain ferry, rail and even Scotland tour operators. You'll also receive the ISIC handbook, which ensures you get the most out of services available. ISIC cards are available at student travel centres. US and Canadian citizens are also entitled to emergency medical coverage, and there's a 24-hr hotline to call in the event of medical, legal or financial emergencies.

If you're aged under 26 but not a student, you can apply for an **International Youth Travel Card (IYTC)**, which for £9 gives you much the same discounts. If you're 25 or younger you can qualify for a **Go-25 Card**, which gives you the same benefits as an ISIC card. These discount cards are issued by student travel agencies and hostelling organizations, see page 40.

Studying in Scotland

If you want to study in Scotland you must first prove you can support and accommodate yourself without working and without recourse to public support. Your studies should take up at least 15 hrs a week for a minimum of 6 months. Once you are studying, you are allowed to do 20 hrs of casual work per week in the term time and you can work full-time during the holidays. In North America full-time students can obtain temporary work or study permits through the **Council of International Education Exchange (CIEE)**, 300 Fore St, Portland, ME 01401, T1-800-40-STUDY, www.ciee.org. For more details, contact your nearest British embassy, consulate or high commission, or the **Foreign and Common- wealth Office** in London, T020-7270 1500, www.fco.gov.uk. See also www.ukvisas.gov.uk.

Telephone → *Country code +44.*

Useful numbers: operator T100; international operator T155; directory enquiries T192; overseas directory enquiries T153.

Most public payphones are operated by **British Telecom (BT)** and can be found in towns and cities, though less so in rural areas. Numbers of public phone booths have declined in recent years due to the advent of the mobile phone, so don't rely on being able to find a payphone wherever you go. BT payphones take either coins (20p, 50p and £1) or phonecards, which are available at newsagents and post offices displaying the BT logo. These cards come in denominations of £2, £3, £5 and £10. Some payphones also accept credit cards.

For most countries (including Europe, USA and Canada) calls are cheapest Mon-Fri between 1800 and 0800 and all day Sat-Sun. For Australia and New Zealand it's cheapest to call from 1430-1930 and from 2400-0700 every day. Area codes are not needed if calling from within the same area. Any number prefixed by 0800 or 0500 is free to the caller; 08457 numbers are charged at local rates and 08705 numbers at the national rate. To call Scotland from overseas, dial 011 from USA and Canada, 0011 from Australia and 00 from New Zealand, followed by 44, then the area code, minus the first zero, then the number. To call overseas from Scotland dial 00 followed by the country code. Country codes include: Australia 61; Ireland 353; New Zealand 64; South Africa 27; USA and Canada 1.

Time

Greenwich Mean Time (GMT) is used from late Oct to late Mar, after which time the clocks go forward an hour to British Summer Time (BST). GMT is 5 hrs ahead of US Eastern Standard Time and 10 hrs behind Australian Eastern Standard Time.

Tipping

Believe it or not, people in Scotland do leave tips. In a restaurant you should leave a tip of 10-15% if you are satisfied with the service. If the bill already includes a service charge, you needn't add a further tip. Tipping is not normal in pubs or bars. Taxi drivers will expect a tip for longer journeys, usually of around 10%; and most hairdressers will also expect a tip. As in most other countries, porters, bellboys and waiters in more up-market hotels rely on tips to supplement their meagre wages.

Tour operators

There are many companies offering general interest or special interest tours of Scotland. Travel agents will have details, or you can check the small advertisements in the travel sections of newspapers, or contact VisitBritain or VisitScotland for a list of operators.

In the UK
About Argyll Walking Holidays, Letters Lodge South, Strathlachlan, Argyll, T01369-860272, www.aboutargyll.co.uk. As its name suggests, this operator specializes in offering guided and self-guided walking trips of Argyll and the islands.
Cape Adventure, Ardmore, Rhiconich, by Lairg, Sutherland IV27 4RB, T01971-521006,

www.capeventure.co.uk. Whether you want to spend a weekend sea kayaking and climbing, or a week trekking the wilds of northwest Scotland, this acclaimed operator offers bags of adventure for families and individuals.
c-n-do Scotland, 32 Stirling Enterprise Park, Stirling, T01786-445703, www.cndoscotland. co.uk. A highly reputable walking holiday specialist with diverse itineraries across the Highlands and Islands, including a 4-day walk in Perthshire to a 14-day wilderness experience in the far northwest of Scotland.
Escape 2 Scotland, 27/10 Maxwell St, Edinburgh EH10 5HT, T/F0131-447 2570, www.escape2scotland.co.uk. Organizes tailor-made trips for groups and individuals.
Gael Connexions, T01855-841219, T0776-992 2463 (mob), www.gaelconnexions. co.uk. Fort William-based company organizing genealogy tours for foreigners wishing to trace their ancestors. Their guide and researcher will point you in the right direction or plan your entire journey. Free consultation offered.
Haggis Adventures, 11 Blackfriars St, Edinburgh EH1 1NB, T0131-557 9393, www. haggisadventures.com. Award-winning operator specializing in offering a variety of day and week-long tours for independent travellers including backpackers. Tours include the 7-day Island Explorer for £279.
Heart of Scotland Tours, T01828-627799, www.heartofscotlandtours.co.uk. Runs 1-day coach tours, priced from £37 and departing from Edinburgh city centre. Loch Ness and highland castles are among the guided itineraries.
HF Holidays, 720 Centennial Court, Elstree, Hertfordshire WD6 3SY, T0208-732 1220, www.hfholidays.co.uk. Holiday operator organizing a variety of self-guided and supported trekking packages including of the Rob Roy Way and West Highland Way.
Macbackpackers, Edinburgh, T0131-558 9900, www.macbackpackers.com. Well-established tour operator for independent budget travellers with 2-5 day minibus tours

ranging from £50-125 of the Highlands and Islands that depart from Edinburgh and use a network of hostel accommodation.

National Trust for Scotland (NTS), 28 Charlotte Sq, Edinburgh EH2 4ET, T0844-4932100, www.nts.org.uk. With over 300 historic properties and landscapes under its care, Scotland's largest conservation charity also offers the chance to stay in historic cottages and country houses or participate in archaeological digs and conservation weekends.

North-West Frontiers, Viewfield, Strathpeffer IV14 9DS, T/F01997-421474, www.nwfrontiers.com. Offers a good range of guided and self-guided hiking and walking tours across north of Scotland and islands including a trip focused on Assynt's world reknown geology. See also www.highland-tours.co.uk.

Valasay, 25 Valasay, Great Bernera, Isle of Lewis HS2 9NB, T01851-612288, www.hebridean-holidays.co.uk. Offers walking and sightseeing packages that reveal the wildlife, archaeology and history of Lewis and Harris in the Outer Hebrides.

Rabbie's Trail Burners, 207 High St, Edinburgh, T0131-226 3133, www.rabbies.com. From Glasgow and Edinburgh runs insightful 1- and multi- day, minibus based tours of the Highlands and Islands for independent travellers.

Scottish Cycling Holidays, 87 Perth St, Blairgowrie, T01250-876100, www.scotcycle.co.uk. Perthshire based operator that for over 30 years has offered guided and self-guided 2-day to 8-day pedal powered trips throughout Scotland. Prices from £130 with options for accommodation and luggage transportation.

Timberbush Tours, 555 Castlehill, Edinburgh, T0131-226 6066, www.timberbush-tours.co.uk. Award winning, family-run run operator offering a variety of 1-3 day guided coach tours around the country.

Walkabout Scotland, 2F2, 70 Strathearn Rd, Edinburgh EH9 2AF, T0845-686 1344, www.walkaboutscotland.com. Day, weekend and week-long walking tours

around Scotland including day jaunts up Ben Lomond or Ben Lawers.

Wild in Scotland, 9 South St Andrew St, Edinburgh, T0131-478 6500, www.wild-in-scotland.com. Run various coach tours from 3 days (£89) to 6 days (£129).

Wilderness Scotland, T0131-625 6635, www.wildernessscotland.com. Specialist Edinburgh-based adventure tour operator offering excellent walking, climbing, kayaking, hiking and photographic trips into Scotland's wild places, plus tailor-made and self-guided trips.

In North America

Abercrombie & Kent, T1-800-554 7016, www.abercrombiekent.com. General sightseeing tours and, it claims, even the chance to sup tea with a clan chief on Mull.

Golf International Inc, T1-800-833 1389, www.golfinternational.com. American-based operator offering golfing tours of Scotland.

Jerry Quinlan's Celtic Golf, T1-800-535 6148, www.celticgolf.com. Organizes golfing packages from the USA.

Prestige Tours, T1-800-890 7375, www.prestigetours.com. Offers general sightseeing tours ranging from 1 to 6 days.

Saga, 222 Berkeley St, Boston, MA 02116, USA. General sightseeing tours.

Tauck, T1-800-788 7885, www.tauck.com. Sightseeing itineraries that include Loch Lomond and highland Perthshire.

Travel and Company, T1-800-888 2247, www.travelandcompany.com. Boston-based operator offering a 9-day Links and Leisure tour.

Tourist information

Tourist Information Centres

Tourist offices – called tourist information centres (TICs) – can be found in most Scottish towns. Their addresses, phone numbers and opening hours are listed in the relevant sections of this book. Opening hours vary depending on the time of year, and many of the smaller offices are closed during the winter months. All tourist offices provide information on accommodation, public transport, local attractions and restaurants, as well as selling books, local guides, maps and souvenirs. Many also have free street plans and leaflets describing local walks. They can also book accommodation for you, for a small fee.

Museums, galleries and historic houses

Most of Scotland's tourist attractions, apart from the large museums and art galleries in the main cities, are open only from Easter-Oct. Full details of opening hours and admission charges are given in the relevant sections of this guide.

Over 100 of the country's most prestigious sights, and 75,000 ha of beautiful countryside, are cared for by the **National Trust for Scotland** (NTS), 26-31 Charlotte Sq, Edinburgh EH2 4ET, T0844-493 2100, www.nts.org.uk. National Trust properties are indicated in this guide as 'NTS', and entry charges and opening hours are given for each property.

Historic Scotland (HS), Longmore House, Salisbury Pl, Edinburgh EH9 1SH, T0131-668 8600, www.historic-scotland.gov.uk, manages more than 330 of Scotland's most important castles, monuments and other historic sites. Historic Scotland properties are indicated as 'HS', and admission charges and opening hours are also given in this guide. Historic Scotland offers an Explorer Pass which allows free entry to 70 of its properties including Edinburgh and Stirling castles. A 3-day pass (can be used over 5 consecutive days) costs £25, concessions £20, family £50, 7-day pass (valid for 14 days) £34, £27, £68. It can save a lot of money, especially in Orkney, where most of the monuments are managed by Historic Scotland.

Many other historic buildings are owned by local authorities, and admission is cheap, · or in many cases free. Most fee-paying attractions give a discount or concession for senior citizens, the unemployed, full-time students and children under 16 (those under 5 are admitted free everywhere). Proof of age or status must be shown. Many of Scotland's stately homes are still owned and occupied by the landed gentry, and admission is usually between £4 and £8.

Finding out more

The best way of finding out more information for your trip to Scotland is to contact Visit Scotland (aka the Scottish Tourist Board), www.visitbritain.com. Alternatively, you can contact VisitBritain, the organization that is responsible for tourism throughout the British Isles. Both organizations can provide a wealth of free literature and information such as maps, city guides and accommodation brochures. If particularly interested in ensuring your visit coincides with a major festival or sporting event, it's also worthwhile having a look at EventScotland's website, www.eventscotland.org. Travellers with special needs should also contact Visit- Scotland or their nearest VisitBritain office. If you want more detailed information on a particular area, contact the specific tourist boards, see below.

VisitScotland regional offices

Aberdeen & Grampian, www.aberdeen-grampian.com.
Argyll, Loch Lomond, Stirling & The Trossachs, www.lochlomond-trossachs.org.
Ayrshire & Arran, www.ayrshire- arran.com.
The Highlands of Scotland, www.visit highlands.com.
Orkney, www.visitorkney.com.
Perthshire, www.perthshire.co.uk.
Shetland, www.visitshetland.com.
VisitScotland, Ocean Point One, 94 Ocean Drive, Edinburgh EH6 6JH, T0845-225 5121, www.visitscotland.com (the phone number is the national booking line for accommodation or to order a brochure). VisitScotland also operates offices around 6 key regional areas.
Outer Hebrides, www.visithebrides.com.

Useful websites

VisitScotland and the various area tourist board sites have information on accommodation, transport and tourist sights as well as outdoor activities such as walking, mountain biking, fishing, etc.

Travel and leisure

www.aboutscotland.co.uk Online resource for information on accommodation.

www.bbc.co.uk/scotland Ideal for grasping key information about news, views, events taking place across Scotland and the weather.

www.britannia.com A huge UK travel site. Click on 'Scotland guide' for a massive selection of subjects plus links to various sites including newspapers.

www.scotland-info.co.uk Good for local information on hotels, shops and restaurants.

www.scotlandbybike If you've ever dreamed of touring the Highlands and Islands on a classy motorbike this operator ensures you can enjoy guided tours, ride pillion or simply take off by yourself.

www.travelscotland.co.uk A good online source for information about Scotland.

www.uktrail.com Very useful for pinpointing budget style hostels around Scotland.

www.undiscoveredscotland.com Another good online source of information for details about villages and towns across the country including their history and with recommendations for accommodation.

Outdoors

http://cycling.visitscotland.com/ mountain_biking; mountain-bike-scotland.com; www.forestry.gov.uk/ scotland To identify Scotland's world-class downhill and cross-country mountain bike routes.

www.golfscotland.co.uk For those who don't share Mark Twain's view that golf is a good walk spoiled, this site has everything you need to know about golf in Scotland.

www.goodbeachguide.co.uk Reveals the 43 of 108 Scottish beaches that in 2008 passed stringent 'MCS Recommended' water quality standards.

www.magicseaweed.com The latest surf conditions around Scotland and the world.

www.mwis.org.uk The weather in Scotland's mountains can change in mins so before you head into the hills log on for the latest forecast.

www.ski.visitscotland.com Information on ski conditions at all centres, updated daily throughout the winter.

www.sustrans.org.uk Official site of the charity that co-ordinates the National Cycle Network. The clickable map lets you zoom in on sections of the route and reveals a network stretching from the Scottish Borders to the Shetland Islands. Happy pedalling!

www.walkingworld.com Perhaps the best directory of British walks though you have to pay to download their detailed maps.

www.walkscotland.com This is a fairly comprehensive site with suggested walks, contacts and practical information for hikers and climbers.

History, politics and culture

www.ceolas.org Celtic music site with lots of information and sounds.

www.electricscotland.com Massive directory with lots of information on clans, travel, etc. In-depth history pages.

www.scotchwhisky.net Everything you ever wanted to know about the 'water of life'.

www.scotland.gov.uk Updates on government affairs in Scotland.

www.scottish.parliament.uk Easy to use guide to the Scottish Parliament.

www.smws.co.uk Worldwide whisky association with its roots in Scotland, offering members the chance to sample rare whiskies.

www.the-mod.co.uk The official website of the Royal National Mod, Scotland's premier Gaelic festival held annually in Oct.

Visas and immigration

Visa regulations are subject to change, so it is essential to check with your local British embassy, high commission or consulate before leaving home. Citizens of all European countries – except Albania, Bosnia Herzegovina, Kosovo, Macedonia, Moldova, Turkey, Serbia and all former Soviet republics (other than the Baltic states) – require only a passport to enter Britain and can generally stay for up to 3 months. Citizens of Australia, Canada, New Zealand, South Africa or the USA can stay for up to 6 months, providing they have a return ticket and sufficient funds to cover their stay. Citizens of most other countries require a visa from the commission or consular office in the country of application.

The **Foreign and Commonwealth Office (FCO)**, T0207-270 1500, www.fco.gov.uk, has an excellent website, which provides details of British immigration and visa requirements. Also the Home Office UK Border Agency is responsible for UK immigration matters and its website is a good place to start for anyone hoping visit, work, study or emigrate to the UK. Call the immigration enquiry bureau on T0870-6067 766 or visit www.bia.homeoffice.gov.uk.

For visa extensions also contact the **Home Office UK Border Agency** via the above number or its website. The agency can also be reached at Lunar House, Wellesley Rd, Croydon, London CR9. Citizens of Australia, Canada, New Zealand, South Africa or the USA wishing to stay longer than 6 months will need an Entry Clearance Certificate from the British High Commission in their country. For more details, contact your nearest British embassy, consulate or high commission, or the Foreign and Commonwealth Office in London.

Weights and measures

Imperial and metric systems are both in use. Distances on roads are measured in miles and yards, drinks poured in pints and gills, but generally, the metric system is used elsewhere.

Women travellers

Travelling in Scotland is neither easier nor more difficult for women than travelling in other parts of the UK. Generally speaking, Scots are friendly and courteous and even lone women travellers should experience nothing unpleasant, however, common sense dictates that single women would do well to avoid hitching on their own in the middle of nowhere. In the main cities and larger towns, the usual precautions need to be taken and you should avoid walking in quiet, unlit streets and parks at night.

Working in Scotland

In today's economic climate and with ever more stringent immigration rules it's not easy picking up work in Scotland. Most citizens of European Union (EU) countries can live and work in Britain freely without a visa, but non-EU residents need a permit to work legally. This can be difficult to obtain without the backing of an established company or employer in the UK. Rules and regulations for working in the UK are constantly being updated by the government so if you are unsure of your visa status, it's worthwhile visiting the website www.ukvisas.gov.uk, for the latest information. Since 2007 new rules have been introduced for students who wish to study in the UK for less than 6 months. For full information look at the Student (INF5) form on the website, www.ukvisas.gov.uk. Also, visitors from Commonwealth countries who are aged between 17 and 30 may apply to be part of the Working holidaymaker Scheme (guidance form INF15) which as part of a (maximum of 2 year) holiday allows participants to work for a maximum of 12 months in the UK. You must have a visa before travelling to the UK as a

Working holidaymaker. These certificates are only available from British embassies and consulates abroad, and you must have proof of a valid return or onward ticket, as well as means of support during your stay. Commonwealth citizens with a parent or grandparent born in the UK can apply for a Certificate of Entitlement to the Right of Abode, allowing them to work in Britain.

An option for citizens of some non-Commonwealth countries is to visit on an au pair placement to learn English by living with an English-speaking family for a maximum of 2 years. Au pairs must be aged between 17 and 27, and come from one of the following countries: Andorra, Bosnia-Herzegovina, Croatia, The Faroe Islands, Greenland, Macedonia, Monaco, San Marino and Turkey. Swiss citizens and members of the European Economic Areas (EEA) can also apply. This can be a good way to learn English, but check out the precise conditions of your placement before taking it up. See guidance form INF16 at www.ukvisas.gov.uk. For information about work permits for the likes of the Seasonal Agricultural Workers Scheme contact the Customer Contact Centre at the UK Border Agency on T0114-207 4074.

Volunteering

See www.volunteerscotland.org.uk.
The British Trust for Conservation Volunteers, Sedum House, Mallard Way, Doncaster DN4 8DB, T01302-388883, www.btcv.org. Get fit in the 'green gym', planting hedges, creating wildlife gardens or improving footpaths.
Earthwatch, 57 Woodstock Rd, Oxford OX2 6HJ, T01865-318838. Team up with scientists studying our furry friends.
Jubilee Sailing Trust, Hazel Rd, South-ampton, T023-804 9108, www.jst. org.uk. Work on deck on an adventure holiday.
National Trust for Scotland, Wemyss House, 28 Charlotte Sq, Edinburgh EH2 4ET, T0844-493 2100, www.nts.org.uk. Among a number of Scotland based charities that offer volunteering opportunities. You could find yourself helping restore buildings on St Kilda or taking part in an archaeological dig on Loch Lomondside.

Contents

Footprint features

At a glance

⊖ **Getting around** There are regular ferry sailings to the islands. Off the main roads it's easier to use a car or bicycle than a bus.

✪ **Time required** There are regular ferry sailings to the islands. Off the main roads it's easier to use a car or bicycle than a bus.

☀ **Weather** Sunshine and rainfall in equal measure. Even in winter there are fine sunny days.

✘ **When not to go** Oct-Mar on Islay, Jura and the more remote areas of Argyll, you may find tourist attractions are closed.

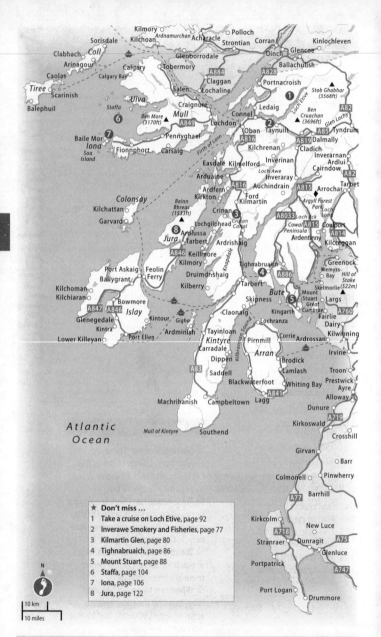

★ Don't miss ...
1 Take a cruise on Loch Etive, page 92
2 Inverawe Smokery and Fisheries, page 77
3 Kilmartin Glen, page 80
4 Tighnabruaich, page 86
5 Mount Stuart, page 88
6 Staffa, page 104
7 Iona, page 106
8 Jura, page 122

10 km
10 miles

Stretching north from the Mull of Kintyre almost to Glencoe and east to the shores of Loch Lomond, the region of Argyll marks the transition from Lowland to Highland. Argyll may be Highlands-lite to some – less starkly dramatic and more lush – but it has its own special beauty. It's a region of great variety, with all the ingredients of the classic Scottish holiday: peaceful wooded glens, heather-clad mountains full of deer, lovely wee fishing ports, romantic castles and beautiful lochs. Despite its proximity to the massive Glasgow conurbation, Argyll is sparsely populated. The main tourist centre and second largest town, Oban, has only 8000 inhabitants. Oban is also the main ferry port for Argyll's Hebridean islands.

The Inner Hebrides comprise the great swathe of islands lying off the western coast of Argyll, each with its own distinct appeal. The most accessible and most popular is Mull, a short ferry ride from Oban. The variety of scenery on offer is astounding and its capital, Tobermory, is the most attractive port in western Scotland. A stone's throw from Mull is tiny Iona, one of the most important religious sites in Europe, with some divine beaches. Boat trips can be made to the dramatic island of Staffa, looming out of the sea like a great cathedral and the inspiration for Mendelssohn's *Hebrides Overture*. Further west, windswept Coll and Tiree offer miles of unspoilt beaches and great windsurfing and, to the south, Colonsay is a stress-free zone that makes Mull seem hectic. Those who enjoy a good malt whisky should head for Islay, famed for its distilleries, while neighbouring Jura is a wild and beautiful place, perfect for some off-the-beaten-track hiking. If you're after some peace and quiet on Jura then you're in good company, for this is where George Orwell came to write Nineteen Eighty-Four. Back on the mainland, the area of Kilmartin is rich in Neolithic and early Christian remains.

Getting there

There are plenty of buses and trains from Glasgow and Fort William to Oban. For details of bus connections, contact **Scottish Citylink** ① *T08705-505050*, or the **Oban Tourist Information Centre (TIC)** ① *T01631-563122*. Bus, train and ferry times can be found in Argyll and Bute Council's free Area Transport Guides to Lorn, Mull and Islay and Jura, available at Oban tourist office. There are flights from Glasgow to Port Ellen (Islay) and to Tiree. For full details of flight times and prices call **Flybe** ① *T0871-700 2000, www.flybe.com*, the local TICs, or **Port Ellen airport** ① *T01496-302022*, and **Tiree airport** ① *T01879-220456*.

CalMac car and passenger ferries sail to Mull, Islay, Coll, Tiree, Colonsay and Gigha, and passenger-only ferries sail to Iona (and to the Small Isles, see page 328). The departure point for ferries to Mull, Coll, Tiree and Colonsay is Oban. Ferry times change according to the day of the week and time of year. Services listed in the Transport sections for each separate island are for the summer period (March-October). For full details see the *CalMac Explore Guide* or call **CalMac** ① *T0800-066 5000, www.calmac.co.uk*. The departure point for ferries to Islay (and on to Jura), and some ferries to Colonsay, is Kennacraig. ▸▸ *For further details, see the Transport sections: Mull, page 112; Coll, Tiree and Colonsay page 117; Islay and Jura, page 126.*

Getting around

Most ferries to the islands and remote peninsulas are run by CalMac, see above for contact details. If you're planning on taking more than a couple of ferries, especially with a car, it may be more economical to buy an **Island Hopscotch ticket**. They can be used on a variety of route combinations and are valid for a month from the date of your first journey. They require advance planning but are better value than buying single tickets. Another excellent option is the **Island Rover ticket**, which is valid for all routes over an 8- or 15-day period. During the peak summer months it's essential to book ferry tickets in advance.

Public transport is steadily improving across much of Argyll, though don't expect the same frequency of bus services as in the main towns. The main bus operators are **Scottish Citylink** ① *T08705-505050*, **Bowmans Coaches** ① *T01631-566809*, and **Westcoast Motors** ① *www.westcoastmotors.co.uk*. The Oban to Glasgow rail line passes through the northern part of the region. Times of local buses and trains can be checked at local tourist offices. ▸▸ *For further details, see the Transport sections, pages 75, 93, 99 and 112.*

Tourist information

There are TICs in Oban, Craignure, Tobermory (Mull) and Bowmore (Islay). Oban TIC has information on all the islands covered in this chapter. Most of this chapter is covered by the **Argyll the Isles, Loch Lomond, Stirling & Trossachs Tourist Board** ① *www.visitscottishheartlands.com*. The main offices, which are open all year round, are in Oban, Inveraray, Dunoon, Rothesay and Campbeltown. There are seasonal offices in Lochgilphead, Tarbert, Ardgarten and Helensburgh. The island of Arran is covered by **Ayrshire & Arran Tourist Board** ① *T0845-225 5121, www.ayrshire-arran.com*.

Oban and around

Oban is a busy little place. Argyll's tourist hub, this Victorian seaside town is also the largest west coast port north of Glasgow and the main departure point for ferries to the Inner and Outer Hebrides. Not surprisingly, it gets very crowded in summer, with passing traffic and people using it as a base for exploring the region. A working port, Oban's main streets narrowly avoid the excesses of tourist kitsch and offer visitors a wide range of hotels, guesthouses, B&Bs, restaurants and shops. Note that many restaurants stop serving by 2200. There are also several tourist attractions of note if stuck here in bad weather. The town itself lies in the beautiful setting of a wide, crescent-shaped bay backed by steep hills, with the tiny, idyllic island of Kerrera, just offshore, providing a natural shelter. Oban is at the centre of the northerly part of Argyll, known as Lorn, which comprises several relatively peaceful islands including Lismore, Kerrera, Seil and Luing. ▸▸ For listings, see pages 72-76.

Ins and outs

Getting there and around Oban and the 'gateway to the isles' is reasonably well served by buses and trains from Glasgow, Fort William and Inverness, and there are a number of west coast local bus services to and from Lochgilphead and Kilmartin. There are regular local buses around town and around Lorn, including to Ellenabeich and North Cuan on Seil, Isle of Luing, North Connel, Dalavich, Bonawe and Ganavan Sands. These are mostly operated by **West Coast Motors** ① *T01586-552319*. **CalMac ferry terminal** ① *T0800-066 5000*, is on the Railway Pier, to the south of the town centre, and the train station is next to the bus terminal. ▸▸ *For further details, see Transport, page 75.*

Tourist information Oban **TIC** ① *Argyll Sq, T01631-563122, Mar-Oct Mon-Sat 0900-1830, Sun 0900-1700; Nov-Feb Mon-Sat 1000-1700, Sun 1100-1500*, has coin-operated internet access (£1 for 20 minutes). There's also a foreign exchange bureau and a huge choice of maps to buy or pick up among the scores of leaflets. It's very busy but the staff are extremely helpful.

Oban → *For listings, see pages 72-76. Colour map 3, B5. Phone code 01631. Population 8000.*

The town's great landmark is **McCaig's Tower**, an incongruous structure that resembles Rome's Coliseum and which dominates the skyline. The tower was built by local banker John Stuart McCaig in the late 19th century, as a means of providing work for unemployed stonemasons. Unfortunately, McCaig died before the project was complete, and to this day no one is quite sure of his intentions. There's not much to see, apart from the exterior walls, but the views of the town and bay are quite magnificent and well worth the climb. There are various routes on foot, but the most direct is to go up Argyll Street and on the left beside the church climb the set of steps known as **Jacob's Ladder**, which lead to Ardconnel Terrace. Turn left and the tower soon comes into view and is well signposted.

Another good walk is to the ruins of seventh-century **Dunollie Castle**, north of town on the Corran Esplanade towards Ganavan, from where there are also wonderful views. The castle was built on the site of an ancient stronghold of the King of Scots, and was then taken over in the 13th century by the MacDougalls, Lords of Lorn. Continue round the corner to **Ganavan Sands**, a long, safe sandy beach about 1½ miles north of the town, for a romantic west coast sunset.

If the weather's bad take a tour round the excellent **Oban Distillery** ① *Stafford St, opposite North Pier, T01631-572004; Jan closed; Feb Mon-Fri 1230-1600; Mar-Easter Mon-Sat 1000-1700; Easter-Jun 0930-1700; Jul-Sep Mon-Fri 0930-1930, Sat and Sun 0930-1700; Oct Mon-Sat 0930-1700; Nov Mon-Fri 1000-1700; Dec Mon-Fri 1230-1600, £7.* The distillery dates

Oban

Sleeping 🛏️
Alexandra **1** *A2*
Barriemore **2** *A1*
Caledonian **3** *C2*
Dungallan House **4** *C1*
Glenburnie House **5** *A1*
Jeremy Inglis
 Hostel **6** *C3*
Manor House **7** *C1*
Oban Backpackers **8** *A3*
Oban Caravan &
 Camping Park **9** *C1*
SYHA Youth Hostel **10** *A1*
Thornloe Guest
 House **11** *B3*

Eating 🍴
Coast **1** *B2*
Ee'usk **2** *B2*
John Ogden's **3** *C2*
MacGillivray's Seafood
 Bar **4** *C2*
Nories **5** *B2*
Studio Steakhouse **6** *B3*
Waterfront **7** *C2*

Bars & clubs 🍸
O'Donnells **8** *A3*
Skipinnish Ceilidh
 House **9** *B3*

back to 1794. The **War and Peace Museum** ⓘ *T01631-570007, May-Sep Mon-Sat 1000-1800, Sun 1000-1600; Mar, Apr, Oct and Nov 1000-1600, free,* has expanded and is worth a look. Staffed by enthusiastic volunteers, it tells the story of Oban's role in the Second World War through a display of old photos and memorabilia. Don't leave town without a visit to **Sweeties**, a glorious, old-fashioned sweet shop with over 350 varieties to choose from, most of them handmade in Scotland.

Dunstaffnage Castle ⓘ *T01631-562465, Apr-Sep daily 0930-1730, Oct daily 0930-1630, Nov-Mar Sat-Wed 0930-1630, castle grounds open all year, £4, concessions £3.20, children £2.40,* 3 miles north of Oban, off the A85, is an impressive 13th-century fort that was a stronghold of the MacDougalls until captured by Robert the Bruce in 1309. Much of its towering curtain wall is still intact. The ruins of the little chapel nearby are worth a look. Long before this castle served as a temporary prison for Flora MacDonald, it's believed the site was used to keep the original Stone of Destiny.

Around Oban → *For listings, see pages 72-76.*

Isle of Kerrera → *Colour map 3, B-C5. Phone code 01631.*
Boasting one of the best short (6-mile) coastal walks in the UK, the tranquil isle of Kerrera lying half a mile offshore and a five-minute **ferry ride** ⓘ *Mon-Sat 0840-1800, Sun 1030-1800, £5.00 return, children £2.50, bikes 50p,* from Oban, provides the perfect antidote to the bustle of the town. Walkers or cyclists to this isle that supports just 35 inhabitants may spot wild goats, otters, sea eagles or even porpoise offshore. Five minutes' walk south of the welcoming Kerrera bunkhouse and tea room visitors are rewarded with the imposing ruins of Gylen Castle and views across to Mull, the Slate Islands, Lismore and Jura. Built by the MacDougall's in 1587, **Gylen Castle** sits proudly on a clifftop looking down the Firth of Lorn. A mile northwest of the ferry jetty is **Slatrach Bay**, a sandy beach providing a terrific place for a family picnic. There are no shops so arrive with provisions. However, at the **Oban Marina** located at the northeastern end of Kerrera, you'll find the excellent **Waypoint Bar and Grill** ⓘ *T01631-570223,* which in addition to great seafood runs a complimentary ferry boat service for guests dining at the restaurant (boat leaves Oban's North Pier at 1210 and every hour between 1700-2200).

Connel to Oban Sealife Centre → *Colour map 3, B5. Phone code 01631.*
Five miles north of Oban an impressive steel cantilever bridge carries the A828 across the mouth of Loch Etive at Connel. It's worth stopping here to see the **Falls of Lora**, a wild tide-race created by the narrow mouth of the sea loch and the reef that spans most of it, thus restricting the flow of water. The result is the impressive rapids, which are best seen from the shore in the village or from halfway across the bridge.

Ten miles north up this road on the shore of Loch Creran and past the turn-off to 16th-century Barcaldine Castle, a most atmospheric B&B option awaits (see Sleeping, page 72). **Oban Sealife Centre** ⓘ *T01631-720386, Apr-Oct daily 1000-1700 (ring for winter opening hours), £12.95, concessions £12.00, children £10.00,* is enormous fun. This environ- mentally friendly facility rescues seals and other aquatic creatures, which are then released back into the wild at the end of the season. Aside from over 30 displays, there's a touch pool, an underwater observatory and a terrific forest adventure trail. Parents can rest their tired feet in the coffee shop. Bus No 405 runs regularly from Oban to the Sealife Centre.

Appin → Colour map 3, B5. Phone code 01631.

The road runs around Loch Creran and enters the district of Appin, made famous in Robert Louis Stevenson's *Kidnapped*, which was based on the 'Appin Murder' of 'The Red Fox – Campbell of Glenure' – in 1752 for which the prominent Jacobite, James Stewart was tried by a 'kangaroo court' of Campbells and subsequently hung in Ballachulish with his body left to rot for three years. A road turns southwest off the main Fort William road to **Port Appin**, on the western tip of the peninsula, the departure point for the passenger ferry to Lismore. To the north of Port Appin is the irresistibly photogenic **Castle Stalker**. Standing on its own tiny island with a background of islands and hills, it's probably second only to the famous Eilean Donan in its portrayal of Scotland's romantic image. It was built upon the remnants of a previous MacDougall stronghold built in the 15th century by the Stewarts of Appin before falling into Campbell hands after the ill-fated 1745 rebellion. The current owners open it to the public for a limited period in July and August. Check opening times at the tourist office in Oban. **Castle Stalker View Café** overlooks the castle from the north and is a great place to eat and photograph the ancient site (see Eating, page 74).

Isle of Lismore → Colour map 3, B5. Phone code 01631.

The island of Lismore lies only a few miles off the mainland, in Loch Linnhe, yet feels a world away. It makes an ideal day trip and offers great opportunities for walking and cycling, as well as wonderful views across to the mountains of Morvern and Mull, the Paps of Jura to the south and Ben Nevis to the north. It's a fertile little island (the name *leis mór* is Gaelic for the big garden) that once supported a population of 1400, though the present population is only 176. Lismore has a long and interesting history as outlined by the award winning, wood clad Gaelic Heritage Centre, 'Ionad Naomh Moluag' that opened in 2007 complete with café and gift shop. Lismore was the ecclesiastical capital of Argyll for several centuries and the **Cathedral of St Moluag** was founded here in the 12th century, just north of Clachan. All that remains is the choir, which is now used as the parish church. The cathedral occupies the site of a church founded by the Irish saint, who established a religious community on the island about the same time as St Columba was busy at work in Iona. Legend has it that the two saints were racing to the island, in an attempt to be the first to land and found a monastery. Such was Moluag's religious zeal that he cut off his finger and threw it on to the shore, thus claiming possession. Not far from the church, is the 2000-year-old **Broch of Tirefour**, one of the best-preserved prehistoric monuments in Argyll, with surviving circular walls up to 16-ft high. Other sights include **Castle Coeffin**, a 13th-century fortress built by the MacDougalls of Lorn on the site of an earlier Viking settlement. In the southwest of the island lies the 13th-century Achadun Castle, built for the Bishops of Argyll. It's a short walk from here to **Bernera Island**, which can be reached at low tide (but don't get stranded).

South Lorn and the Slate Islands → Colour map 3, C4-5. Phone code 01852.

Eight miles south of Oban the B884 turns west off the A816 and wriggles its way round glassy lochs and knobbly, green hills studded with copper-coloured cattle to the tiny Slate Islands, so called because in the mid-19th century, the island's slate quarries exported millions of roofing slates every year. The quarrying industry has long since gone, leaving the area dotted with pretty little villages of whitewashed cottages.

The most northerly of the Slate Islands is **Seil** (or Clachan Seil), which is reached from the mainland across the seriously humpbacked Clachan Bridge. Better known as the 'Bridge over the Atlantic', it was built in 1792, with its high arch allowing ships to pass beneath. Beside the bridge is an old inn, **Tigh an Truish**, or 'House of the Trousers', where islanders once swapped their kilt for trousers in order to conform to the post-1745 ban on the wearing of Highland dress. There's also a petrol pump and souvenir shop here. Two miles south, at **Balvicar** (where there's a bank in the grocery store) the road turns right and climbs up and over to the harbour and attractive village of **Ellenabeich**, which is also, rather confusingly, known by the same name as the nearby island of Easdale. Ellenabeich is home to the Isle of Seil microbrewery (reputedly Scotland's smallest) since 2004. Before sinking a pint of their Corryveckan Ale, try the 130-yd, 12-hole Isle putting green. Apparently, if you beat the course par of 24, a bottle of Oban whisky is yours. The village is also the base for the excellent **Seafari Adventures** (see Activities and tours, page 75), and here too you'll find the **Scottish Slate Islands Heritage Trust Centre** ① *T01852-300449, Apr-Oct daily 1030-1300, 1400-1700, £1.50, children 25p*, with its insight into the area's history.

Endearingly tiny **Easdale** is separated from Seil by a 500-yd-wide channel which has to be dredged to keep it open. The island, only 800 yds by 700 yds, was the centre of the slate industry and, between 1842 and 1861 produced over 130 million roof slates. Now inhabited by just 71 residents, the island once supported over 450 people before the quarries were flooded in the great storm of 1881 and the industry collapsed. A few minutes' walk from the ferry pier you'll find the delightful folk museum run by island volunteers. If the museum is closed, wander past the whitewashed former slate workers' cottages to seek out island information over a pint at the cosy **Puffer Bar**. The island's lively social life also revolves around the community hall with one of the highlights of the year being the keenly contested world stone-skimming championships. See Festivals and events, page 74. For more information on the island, visit www.easdale.org.

Another road runs south from Balvicar to **North Cuan**, from where the car ferry sails across the treacherous Cuan Sound to the long, thin island of **Luing** (pronounced 'Ling'). The island once had a population of around 600, which was drastically reduced during the Clearances to make way for cattle. Luing is still well known for its beef, and is the home of a successful new breed named after it. The island is small, 6 miles by 2 miles, and mostly flat, making it ideal for exploring by bike. Bikes can be hired just 50 yds from the ferry slipway at the **Sunnybrae Caravan Park** ① *T01852-314274*, from where static caravans can be hired from £100 per week. A mile or so further south is the village of **Cullipool**. The only other village is Toberonochy, 3 miles from Cullipool. Wildlife abounds with sightings of otters, seals, eagles and buzzards, whilst visitors can also enjoy a breathtaking panorama of the outlying isles of Mull, Shuna and Scarba.

South of the turn-off to the Slate Islands is **Arduaine Gardens** ① *T0844-493 2216, Apr-Sep daily 0930-1630, £5.50, concessions £4.40*, a beautiful place and an absolute must for all gardening enthusiasts. Gifted to the National Trust for Scotland in 1992, this 20-acre oasis boasts spectacular rhododendrons in early summer, Himalayan lilies, blue Tibetan poppies, a woodland garden, sweeping lawns and inspirational views across to Jura and the Slate Islands.

This is serious boating country, and just south of Arduaine, on the northern coast of the Craignish Peninsula, is surreal **Craobh Haven**, a yachting marina built in the style of a reproduction 18th-century fishing village. South of Craobh Haven is another yachting marina at **Ardfern**, where the **Galley of Lorne Hotel and pub** is invariably packed with yachties. You can arrange boat trips from Ardfern around Loch Craignish and to the offshore islands, see Activities and tours, page 74.

For Sleeping and Eating price codes and other relevant information, see Essentials pages 38-45.

⊜ Sleeping

Oban *p67, map p68*

As the main ferry port for the islands, Oban gets busy in the summer with traffic. It's often an idea to get the tourist office to find you a bed; it'll cost more, but saves time and effort.

L-B Manor House Hotel, Gallanach Rd, T01631-562087, www.manorhouseoban. com. Open year-round. 11 rooms. A beautiful stone house in a secluded location overlooking the bay on the road south towards the Kerrera ferry. Style and comfort assured and with a reputation for fine food.

A-B Caledonian Hotel, Station Sq, T0844-8559135, www.obancaledonian.com. Impressive former grand station built around 1882, overlooking the ferry pier. For a touch of luxury try one of the Captain's rooms with views across Oban bay. Coffee connoisseurs will enjoy the menu in the brasserie (♔♔).

C Dungallan House Hotel, Gallanach Rd, T01631-563799, www.dungallanhotel-oban. co.uk. Built in 1870 by the Duke of Argyll, this tastefully refurbished residence is another great Oban establishment that offers fine dining on locally sourced produce, over 100 malts and excellent views on the road south to the Kerrera ferry.

C Alexandra Hotel, Corran Esplanade, T01631-562381. Large hotel with well-equipped rooms and good facilities, including pool and steam room.

C-D Glenburnie House, Corran Esplanade, T01631-562089, www.glenburnie.co.uk. Open Apr-Oct. A guesthouse renowned for tasteful rooms and excellent breakfasts, including fresh fruit salad and salmon with scrambled eggs.

C-D Barriemore Hotel, Corran Esplanade, T01631-566356, www.barriemore-hotel. co.uk. Open Feb-Dec. A delightful, friendly guesthouse with great views of Oban bay at the quieter end of the Esplanade. Very good value.

C Thornloe Guest House, Albert Rd, T01631-562879, www.thornloeoban.co.uk. Quiet and centrally located guesthouse offering 7 good-sized en suite rooms and limited off-street parking. Enjoy the sea views with a bottle of wine in the conservatory. One of the rooms has a 4-poster bed.

F Jeremy Inglis Hostel, 21 Airds Cres, opposite the tourist office, T01631-565065. Handy for the train station and ferry, these small, quirky rooms include continental breakfast.

F Oban Backpackers, Breadalbane St, T01631-562107, www.obanbackpackers. com. Open year-round and very popular. Book ahead.

F SYHA Youth Hostel, Corran Esplanade, just beyond St Columba's Cathedral, T01631-562025. Open all year. With its 17 rooms and 6 dorms, this superbly equipped, friendly hostel is ideal for individuals and families who are looking for a safe, clean and hospitable budget option in Oban. Recommended.

Camping

Oban Caravan & Camping Park, Gallanach Rd, 2 miles south of town beyond the Kerrera ferry, T01631-562425. Open Apr to mid-Oct. Beautiful setting looking out to Kerrera but beware late-night revellers.

Roseview Caravan and Camping, on the Glenshellach Rd, 1½ miles south of the ferry terminal, T/F01631-562755. Open Mar-Nov. Very good campsite with facilities for kids.

Around Oban *p69*

L Airds Hotel, Port Appin, T01631-730236, F01631-730535, www.airds-hotel.com. One of Scotland's finest family-run hotels. The owners, Saun and Jenny McKivragan, ensure a personal touch pervades this classy establishment, which boasts exquisite views, fine dining and 11 delightful rooms. Recommended.

L-A Willowburn Hotel, Seil, T01852-300276, www.willowburn.co.uk. Open Mar-Nov. 7 rooms with the rate including a delicious 4-course dinner. Just past the 'Bridge over the Atlantic' on Seil island, this house enjoys a delightful, peaceful setting with views over Sound of Seil. The owners bake their own bread, smoke their own salmon, duck and cheeses, and serve local produce including vegetables from the garden. An absolute gem. Recommended.

A Loch Melfort Hotel, Arduaine, T01852-200233, www.lochmelfort.co.uk. Open all year. 23 rooms available. Terrific seafood and game as you enjoy the views over Asknish Bay.

B-A Barcaldine Castle, Benderloch, 9 miles north of Oban and the A828, T01631-720598. Open year-round. This is a rare opportunity to reside in a 16th-century castle and home of the Campbells of Barcaldine (2 rooms available). You'll even step over the dungeon en route to breakfast.

B Pierhouse Hotel, Port Appin, T01631-730302, www.pierhousehotel.co.uk. Open all year. Looking out to the tiny pier and over Loch Linnhe, this stylish little hotel has a reputation for tasty, moderately priced local seafood. The 12 en suite rooms are tidy and comfortable. Also has a bar and pool room.

F Kerrera Bunkhouse, Isle of Kerrera, T01631-570223, www.kerrerabunkhouse. co.uk. Open year-round. 6 rooms. Friendly accommodation complete with tea garden open May-Sep Wed-Sun 1030-1630.

Camping

Camping and Caravanning Club, Oban, Barcaldiine By Connel,Argyll, 12 miles north of Oban, T01631-720348. Open Apr-Oct. Clean and friendly.

Sunnybrae Caravan Park, South Cuan, Isle of Luing, T01852-314274. To enjoy fabulous sunsets towards Jura and an away-from-it-all escape, there's 1 of 6 static caravans for hire (£100-250 per week).

🍴 Eating

Oban *p67, map p68*

🍴🍴🍴 **The Waterfront**, 1 Railway Pier, T01631-563110. Daily 1000-1415, 1730-2130. Good seafood restaurant that owns 2 fishing boats, which land its daily catch. Pricey but the Waterfront Platter of langoustines, sea bass, scallops and garlic mussels is enticing.

🍴🍴🍴-🍴🍴 **Coast**, 104 George St, T01631-569900. Mon-Sat 1200-1400, 1730-2130, Sun 1730-2130. An imaginative menu in a stylish setting. Mouth-watering vegetarian, meat and seafood dishes served with a smile.

🍴🍴🍴-🍴🍴 **The Studio Steakhouse**, Craigard Rd, T01631-562030. Tue-Sun 1800-2100. A cosy restaurant away from the busy waterfront that serves a fine Stornoway black pudding starter and prime steaks in addition to its daily catch.

🍴🍴 **Ee'usk**, North Pier, T01631-565666. Daily 1200-1500, 1800-2100. Busy, glass-fronted trendy fish restaurant, which isn't cheap but prides itself on the quality of its seafood. Service with flair. Huge seafood platter £59. Also good place for a rewarding lunch.

🍴 **John Ogden's**, by the ferry terminal. Daily 0900-1800. After 17 years, Ogden's bustling green shed remains Oban's best takeaway seafood haunt. For an inexpensive quality snack try a pot of squat lobster tails (£2.75), a fresh crab sandwich or the mouth-watering scallops in garlic (£6.75).

🍴 **MacGillivray's Seafood Bar**, just 20 m from **John Ogden's**. Offering the likes of pan fried scallops (£6) and squat lobster.

🍴 **Nories**, George St. After 43 years, it remains Oban's finest and friendliest chippy. Ask for it wrapped in newspaper.

Around Oban *p69*

🍴🍴🍴 **Airds Hotel**, Port Appin, T01631-730236, F01631-730535. Upmarket, award-winning fine dining that draws on the best of local seafood and Scottish meats. Recommended.

🍴🍴🍴-🍴🍴 **Waypoint Bar and Grill**, Isle of Kerrera, T01631-565333. From a hearty seafood platter to a humble BLT sandwich, hop aboard 'The Dirk' at the North Pier in Oban to dine in style with lovely views across the bay. Ferry for guests only runs from 1210 daily.

† The Oyster Inn, Connel Bridge, T01631-710666, www.oysterinn.co.uk. Modern, child-friendly restaurant with wide-ranging menu, real ales and sea views.

††-† Castle Stalker View, Appin, T01631-730444. Feb-Oct daily 0930-1730, Nov-Dec Thu-Sun 1000-1600, Closed Jan. On the hillside overlooking the castle and directly off the Oban to Ballachulish main road, this is an excellent café. Tuck into the likes of Inverawe smoked salmon, freshly baked cakes and coffee. Panoramas down the sea lochs to Oban and unrivalled views over the castle. There are also information boards outlining the history of the castle and the infamous Appin murder. Outside, there's a path down to a viewpoint. Highly recommended.

††-† Oyster Brewery and Restaurant, Ellenabeich Pier, Seil, T01852-300121. This harbourside hostelry is where to sample smooth real ales and a delicious seafood salad whilst bantering with the friendly locals.

ⓝ Bars and clubs

Oban *p67, map p68*
Oban is no party town, but for an unrivalled taste of high energy and informal live ceilidh music head for **Skipinnish Ceilidh House** on George St, T01631-569599.
O'Donnells, Breadalbane St. Popular Irish bar.

Around Oban *p69*
You'll always find a pint and warm welcome at the **Galley of Lorne Hotel** in Ardfern; the **Puffer Bar** in Easdale; and the **Oyster Brewery Bar and Restaurant**, in Ellenabeich.

ⓔ Entertainment

Oban *p67, map p68*
The Highland Theatre, at the north end of George St, T01631-562444. This is, confusingly, the local cinema. It shows most of the popular current releases.

ⓕ Festivals and events

To check for major events in the area, visit www.eventsscotland.org.

Oban *p67, map p68*
Apr-May Highlands & Islands Music & Dance Festival for Children, held at the end of Apr/beginning of May.
Aug Argyllshire Gathering (Oban Games), held during the 4th week of Aug in Mossfield Park, www.obangames.com.
Sep World stone-skimming championships, held on Easdale in late Sep, www.stone skimming.com. Drinking and merriment.

ⓐ Activities and tours

Oban *p67, map p68*
Boat trips
Boat trips can be made from Oban to Mull, Iona, Staffa and The Treshnish Islands with a variety of companies, including:
Argyll Charters, Corran Esplanade, T01631-563387; **Bowman's Tours**, Queens Park Pl, T01631-566809, in association with **Gordon Grant Tours** (Mull and In from Oban from £32); **Turus Mara**, Penmore Mill, Dervaig, Mull, T0800 0858786/01688-400242, www.turusmara.com.
Skipinnish Sea Tours, T07799-275388, T07714-764932, www.skipinnish-sea-tours.co.uk. For information and bookings contact the **Skipinnish Ceilidh House**, George St, T0161-569599. Open 1000-1800. Tickets can also be bought onboard. 1-hr trips around Kerrara cost £15, children £10. Tours run daily Apr-Oct and leave from the steps of Oban seafront.

Diving
Puffin Dive Centre, Gallanach Port, Gallanach Rd, T01631-566088, or booking office on George St, T01631-571190. This dive centre offers a 1½- to 2-hr beginner 'try-a-dive' (£87) and training for all standards including wreck diving.

Fishing
Oban Sea Fishing, Dunstaffnage Marina, T07793-120958, www.obanseafishing.com. Offshore fishing for all standards.

Swimming
Atlantis Leisure, Dalriach Rd, T01631-566800, www.atlantisleisure.co.uk. Sports and leisure centre with pool.

Around Oban *p69*
Boat trips
Craignish Cruises, T07747-023083, Ardfern Yacht Centre, T01852-500247, www.craignishcruises.co.uk. Runs private charters and fishing trips to the Sound of Jura, Corryvreckan and Garvellachs.
Seafari Adventures, Ellenabeich, Seil (also book at Oban TIC), T01852-300003, www.seafari.co.uk. Their 300 hp RIBS take you on a thrilling ride across the Corryvreckan whirlpool, with opportunities to spot seals, porpoises and lots of seabirds, £35, children £27. They also run a new Easdale to Iona day trip (departs 1030 and returns 1630) that's £70, under 16s £55. Travel to Iona to see the Abbey, ample time ashore, includes non landing trip to Staffa. Recommended.

Horse riding
Ardfern Riding Centre, Craobh Haven, T01852-500632. Offers a variety of trails and pub rides, from £23 for 1 hr.
Lettershuna Riding, Appin, T01631-730227. www.lettershunaridingcentre.com Pony trekking.

Watersports
Linnhe Marine Watersports Centre, Lettershuna, just beyond Port Appin and

20 miles north of Oban, T07721-503981. Hire motor boats and sailing dinghies (from £35 for the 1st hr, £20 2nd hr and £10 thereafter),

⊙ Transport

Oban *p67, map p68*
Bus There are regular daily buses to **Inverness**, 4 hrs, via **Fort William** (1 hr 15 mins), **Benderloch** and **Appin** with Scottish Citylink, T08705-505050. Regular daily service to **Glasgow**, 3 hrs, with Scottish Citylink Coaches; Tue and Sat, 3 hrs with McGill's Bus, T01475-711122.

The West Highland Flyer minibus, T07780-724248, Easter-end Oct, links the **Oban** (Mull) and **Mallaig** (Skye) ferries. It will take you just 2½ hrs to do this route and the minibus will also carry your bike. Departs Oban 0945 and arrives in Mallaig at 1215. Travels via Fort William and the Glen Nevis Youth Hostel on request.

Regular daily buses to **Dalmally**, via Cruachan Power Station, **Lochawe** and Taynuilt Hotel, with Awe Service Station, T01866-822612; Scottish Citylink, T08705-505050; and West Coast Motors, T01586-552319.

To **Ardrishaig**, via **Kilmartin** and **Lochgilphead**, Mon-Sat, **Scottish Citylink** and West Coast Motors, T01586-552319. To **Ellenabeich** and **North Cuan**, Mon-Sat, West Coast Motors.
Car hire Flit Van & Car Hire, Glencruitten Rd, T/F01631-566553. From £40 per day.
Cycle hire There are numerous cycling routes and walks in Argyll. Ask at the TIC for the leaflet, *Cycle the Forests of North Argyll*, or visit www.forestry.gov.uk/mtbscotland. Evo Bikes, 29 Lochside St, T01631-566996, rents bikes; Liberty Cycles, Unit 9, Mill Lane, T01631-564000. Rents adult, kids and trailer bikes from £15 per day.
Ferry Oban is the main ferry port for many of the Hebridean islands, for details of the CalMac ferry terminal, see page 67.

The departure point for ferries to **Kerrera** is 1½ miles along the Gallanach Rd. They leave at regular intervals Mon-Fri 0845-1800, Sun 1030-1800.

A passenger ferry leaves to **Lismore island** Mon-Sat 4 times daily, twice on Sun, 50 mins, £5.80 return per passenger, £47.50 per car. A tiny passenger ferry sails from **Ellenabeich** on Seil to **Easdale**, making the 3-min trip at regular intervals Mon-Sat between 0745 and 2100, partly to schedule, partly on request. Ring the bell in the shelter on the pier (T01631-562125). A daily car ferry to **Luing** (South Cuan), T01631-562125, sails from South Cuan on Seil (5 mins), Mon-Sat every 15 mins from 0730 to 1820 (later in summer) and on Sun every 20 mins from 1100-1810. Return fare is £1.50 per passenger and £6.05 per car.

Train There are 3 trains daily to **Glasgow**, via **Crianlarich**, where the Oban train connects with the Mallaig/Fort William to Glasgow train.

Around Oban *p69*
Cycle hire **Isle of Luing Bike Hire**, Isle of Luing, T01852-314274. Hires bikes for £17 per day.

❶ Directory

Oban *p67, map p68*
Banks Several major banks have branches with ATMs in the centre of Oban and you can change foreign currency at the TIC. Note that some B&Bs and pubs on the islands will only take cash. **Internet** Oban SYHA; Oban Library, 77 Albany St, T01631-571444, free access.

Mid-Argyll, Kintyre, Cowal and Bute

Further south from Oban the long finger of Mid-Argyll extends past the offshore 'whisky isles' of Islay and Jura, pointing southwards into the remote Kintyre Peninsula where rolling hills protect the Isle of Arran from the wrath of the Atlantic Ocean. Packed with history, winding roads take visitors on a journey past attractive sea lochs and huge forests, revealing at Kilmartin Glen one of Europe's most important prehistoric sites. Mull of Kintyre is the lonely tip, a stone's throw from Northern Ireland. On the other side of Loch Fyne is the walking haven and giant claw of Cowal Peninsula, looking as if it's about to crush in its grasp the aptly named Isle of Bute, home to one of Scotland's most fantastical stately homes. ▸▸ *For listings, see pages 89-93.*

Tourist information

Cowal's main **TIC** ① *Alexandra Parade, Dunoon, T08707-200629, open all year*; Helensburgh **TIC** ① *clock tower on the waterfront, T01436-672642, open Apr-Oct*; Bute **TIC** ① *Promenade, Rothesay, T01700-502151, open all year*; Inveraray **TIC** ① *Front St, T01499-302063*; Lochgoilphead **TIC** ① *Lochnell St, T01546-602344, open Apr-Oct*; Tarbert **TIC** ① *Harbour St, T01880-820429*; and Campbeltown **TIC** ① *Old Quay, T01586-552056.*

Loch Awe and Loch Etive → *For listings, see pages 89-93. Colour map 3, C5/B5-6.*

Loch Awe is the longest freshwater loch in Scotland and, further north, is the beautiful Loch Etive. Between the two Lochs runs the River Awe, which squeezes through the dark and ominous Pass of Brander. It is so steep and narrow that, according to legend, it was once held against the army by an old woman brandishing a scythe. There's enough to see here to justify a couple of days' exploration, particularly the little visited west shore of Loch Awe, and there are plenty of other places to visit around Inveraray to the south.

At the northeastern tip of Loch Awe, between the villages of of **Dalmally** and **Lochawe**, is the romantic ruin of **Kilchurn Castle**, on a promontory jutting out into the loch. It can be visited by boat from **Ardanaiseig Hotel** ① *T01866-833333*, on the east side of the loch. Also worth a look around here is the lovely, and rather bizarre, **St Conan's Church** ① *free, donation requested*, just off the A85 by Lochawe village. Built in the late 19th century but not used until 1930, the church's serene atmosphere is striking. Inside is an effigy of Robert the Bruce, with one of his bones buried underneath. The exterior, especially the south side overlooking the loch, is a riot of eccentric detail. You can buy fishing permits from the **Tight Line Bar** in the village.

Four miles west of Lochawe, and almost a mile inside Ben Cruachan (3695 ft) is the underground attraction of the **Cruachan Power Station or 'Hollow Mountain'** ① *Apr-Oct 0930-1645, Nov-Mar 1000-1700*. From the visitor centre on the shores of Loch Awe, a bus trip takes you into the heart of the mountain through tunnels until you reach the giant steel doors and generating room. Whilst exploring this Bond- like subterranean warren, it's impossible to forget the millions of tons of rock above your head. Pray Loch Awe doesn't spring a leak!

Further west, and 12 miles east of Oban, is the tiny village of **Taynuilt**, near the shore of Loch Etive. Just before the village, at Bridge of Awe, is a sign for **Inverawe Smokery and Fisheries** ① *T01866-822808, www.smokedsalmon.co.uk, Mar-Dec daily 0830-1700*, where you can take fishing lessons (£30), learn about traditional smoking techniques, or wander

Piscine cuisine

At **Inverawe Fisheries and Smokery**, see page 77, they buy smaller farmed salmon because they believe the lower fat content makes them tastier than larger ones. Traditional methods prevail here. The fish are dry salted, washed, smoked over oak logs for anything from 16 to 24 hours, depending on conditions, and then hand-sliced. The result is a rich and freshly oaky taste. From a 100 g smoked salmon pack (£7.50) to a 750 g pre-sliced side of salmon (£29.95), as well as gravadlax, smoked trout, eel and halibut, there's a diverse range to choose from.

Knipoch Smokehouse, South Lorn near Oban, T01852-316251, www.knipoch smokehouse.co.uk, on the other hand, believes that large salmon, 6-7 kg, produce the best quality. Its approach involves a dry salt cure strengthened with sugar, whisky, juniper and rowan berries, plus a lengthy two- to three-day smoke. The fish comes out so black it has to be washed and trimmed to look presentable, and the taste is rather unusual: strong, sweet, sharp and almondy. A whole side costs £45, but it can be cut to any size: sliced £17.60 per 500 g, unsliced £15.95. Also offer 500 g of smoked scallops for £22.

---

along a series of nature trails. If the weather's fine, you can buy some of their delicious smoked products and have a picnic, see box, above. If you fancy some smoked salmon delivered to your home, make sure you sign up for their mailing list.

One mile north of the village on the shores of Loch Etive is **Bonawe Iron Furnace** ① T01866-822432, Apr-Sep daily 0930-1730, £4.50, concessions £3.60, children £2.70. Founded in 1753 by a group of Cumbrian ironmasters, Bonawe used the abundant woodlands of Argyll to make charcoal to fire its massive furnace. At its height, it produced 600-700 tons of pig-iron a year and provided cannonballs for Admiral Nelson at the Battle of Trafalgar. Iron production ceased at Bonawe in 1876 and it has now been restored as an industrial heritage site, with displays explaining the whole production process.

Beyond Bonawe is the tranquil pier from which **Loch Etive Cruises** depart. Inaccessible except by boat, the cruise of one of Scotland's great hidden treasures is definitely worth it. ▸▸ For further details, see Activities and tours, page 92.

Running south from the village is the very lovely and very quiet Glen Lonan. Three miles along the Glen Lonan road is **Barguillean's Angus Garden** ① T01866-822335, daily 0900-1800, £2, one of Argyll's youngest and smallest gardens, but also one of the most peaceful and evocative, set around the shores of little Loch Angus. It was created in 1957, in memory of Angus MacDonald, a journalist and writer killed in Cyprus in 1956.

Walks around Loch Awe and Loch Etive

A single-track road runs southwest of Kilchrenan along the shores of Loch Awe to the tiny villages of **Dalavich** and **Ford**, through the very beautiful Inverinan Forest, a Forestry Commission property which has a series of undemanding marked trails running through the hills overlooking the loch. The first walk starts out from the little hamlet of **Inverinan**. Red waymarkers lead you from the car park into the woods surrounding the gorge of the River Inan. Part of the route follows the old drove road along which cattle were driven from the Highlands down to the markets in south and central Scotland. The walk is 3 miles long and should take around 1½ hours. Further along the road, half a mile north of Dalavich, is a car park at **Barnaline Lodge**, the starting point for a 9-mile bike route, a way-marked walk through the Caledonian Forest Reserve, and a couple of other woodland walks. The longest of the walks is the 5-mile route that leads along the **River Avich**, then along the shores of **Loch Avich** before returning to the lodge. Two and a half miles south of Dalavich is a car park, which marks the starting point for a blue waymarked walk along the shores of **Loch Awe**. The route passes through **Mackenzie's Grove**, a sheltered gorge containing some of the largest conifers on the west coast. The route then runs along the shores of the loch, from where you can see the remains of a *crannog*, one of over 40 of these Iron Age settlements on Loch Awe. The route then heads back to the car park; about 3 miles in total. These routes are all outlined, with accompanying maps, in the Forestry Commission Scotland leaflet, *A Guide to Forest Walks and Trails in North Argyll*, available at tourist offices. Alternatively visit www.forestry.gov.uk/recreation.

Inveraray and around → *For listings, see pages 89-93. Colour map 3, C6.*

Inveraray → *Phone code 01499.*

Inveraray is the classic 18th-century planned town (don't call it a village), with its straight, wide streets and dignified Georgian houses, and enjoys the most stunning of settings, on the shores of Loch Fyne. It was rebuilt by the third Duke of Argyll, head of the Campbell clan, at the same time as he restored the nearby family home, which now attracts hordes of summer visitors. As well as its natural beauty and elegance, and fine castle, Inveraray has several other attractions that make an overnight stay in the town worthwhile. The sweet-toothed shouldn't walk past the door of **Sweet Memories** on Main Street East (open all year) where shelves are packed with jars of Scottish old world confectionery, including humbugs, aniseed balls and cough candy.

One of Argyll's most famous castles, **Inveraray Castle** ⓘ *T01499-302203, Apr-Oct, Mon-Sun 1000-1745, (last admission 1700), £9, concessions £7.50, children £6.10, under 5s free*, has been the clan seat of the Campbells for centuries and is still the family home of the Duke of Argyll. The present neo-Gothic structure dates from 1745, and its main feature is the magnificent armoury hall, whose displays of weaponry were supplied to the Campbells by the British government to quell the Jacobite rebellion. The elaborately furnished rooms are also on display, as is the fascinating and troubled family history in the Clan room. For £1 from the TIC, the booklet *Five Walks on Inverary Estate* is a worth- while investment.

Inveraray Jail ⓘ *T01499-302381, Apr-Oct 0930-1800, Nov-Mar 1000-1700, £8.25, concessions £6.95, children £5.50*, the Georgian prison and courthouse in the centre of the town has been brilliantly restored as an interesting museum that gives a vivid insight into life behind bars from medieval times up until the 19th century. You can sit in on an 1820 courtroom trial, then visit the cells below and learn all about some of the delightful prison pursuits, such as branding with a hot iron, ear nailing and public whipping. The whole experience is further enhanced by the guides, who are dressed as warders and prisoners. Makes you want to stay on the right side of the law, although, thankfully, conditions have improved – as you will see for yourself.

Another worthwhile diversion, especially if you've got kids in tow, is the **Inveraray Maritime Museum** ⓘ *T01499-302213, daily 1000-1800, £5, concessions £3, children £2.50*, housed in the *SV Arctic Penguin*, one of the world's last iron sailing ships, which is moored at the lochside pier. Below deck are displays on Clyde shipbuilding, the Highland Clearances and footage from the maritime TV classic *Para Handy* as well as the chance to blow the foghorn and relax with an on-board cuppa. Berthed behind the ship is *Vital Spark*, an old Clyde 'puffer' recently purchased by the museum and due to open as an exhibition space in 2009. Your ticket to the Maritime Museum also entitles you to a 20% discount off the ticket price at the jail.

A few miles southwest of town, on the A83 to Lochgilphead, is **Argyll Adventure** ① T01499-302611, www.argylladventure.com, Apr-Oct daily 1000-1700, from £6 per activity. Here, by the banks of Loch Fyne, both children and the young at heart can indulge in laser clay-pigeon shooting, Laser Quest, bungee trampolining, climbing and horse riding (from £25). Call ahead to book pony treks/riding.

Three miles beyond Argyll Adventure is **Auchindrain Township** ① T01499-500235, www.auchindrain-museum.org.uk, Apr-Oct daily 1000-1700 (last admission 1600), £5.50, concessions £4.50, children £3, a restored and authentic West Highland farming village with parts dating to the 1700s. Features include two perfectly restored thatched cottages and barns, furnished and equipped with dairy and household items to give a real insight into what rural life must have been like in centuries past. There's also an informative visitor centre and coffee shop. Recommended.

Four miles further down the A83 is **Crarae Gardens** ① T01546-886614, visitor centre April-Oct daily 1000-1700, gardens open all year daily 0930-sunset, £6, concessions £5, one of Scotland's very best public gardens, dramatically set in a deep wooded glen on the shores of Loch Fyne. Initiated by Lady Campbell in 1912, there are marked woodland walks winding their way through a spectacular array of rhododendrons, azaleas and numerous other exotic plants towards the tumbling waterfalls of the 'Himalayan Gorge'. Any time of year is rewarding to visit including autumn when foliage is resplendent in rich tints.

Kilmartin and around → Colour map 3, C5. Phone code 01546.

Much of this region was once part of the ancient Kingdom of Dalriada, established by the Irish Celts (known as the *Scotti*, hence Scotland) who settled here in the fifth century. North of Lochgilphead, on the A816 to Oban, is **Kilmartin Glen**, an area of Neolithic and Bronze Age chambered and round cairns, stone circles, rock carvings, Iron Age forts and duns, Early Christian sculptured stones and medieval castles. Indeed, there are more than 350 ancient monuments within just a few miles radius of **Kilmartin House** Museum ① T01546-510278, Mar-Oct 1000-1730, Nov-Dec 1100-1600, £4.60, concessions £3.90, children £1.70. Housed in the old manse next to the parish church in the tiny village of **Kilmartin**, the 15-minute audio-visual display and imaginative exhibits provide an invaluable insight into the surrounding landscape. The **Glebe Cairn Café** is well worth a visit (see Eating, page 91). Next door in the church graveyard are the Kilmartin crosses, dating from as far back as the ninth and 10th centuries. Also within the graveyard is one of the largest collections of medieval grave slabs in the West Highlands.

Two miles north of Kilmartin, sitting high above the A816, is **Carnasserie Castle** ① free, it's a little way from the car park, an imposing 16th-century tower house built by John Carswell, Bishop of the Isles, who translated *The Book of the Common Order* in 1567, the first book to be printed in Gaelic.

Most notable of all is the **linear cemetery**, a line of burial cairns that stretch southward from Kilmartin village for over 2 miles. The largest and oldest of the group is the Neolithic cairn, Nether Largie South, which is over 5000 years old and big enough to enter. The other cairns, Nether Largie North, Mid Nether Largie and Ri Cruin, are Bronze Age, and the huge stone coffins show carvings on the grave slabs. Nearby are the Temple Wood Stone Circles, where burials took place from Neolithic times to the Bronze Age.

On the other side of the A816, and visible from the road, is a group of monuments which can all be reached from Dunchraigaig Cairn. This is a huge Bronze Age cairn with some of the covering stones removed to reveal three stone coffins. From here a path is signed to **Ballymeanoch Standing Stones**, the tallest of which is 12-ft high. Two of the stones are decorated with cup marks, prehistoric rock carvings that can be found at numerous locations throughout the Kilmartin area. There's also a henge monument in the same field. These were generally round or oval platforms with an internal ditch, and it's thought they were used for ceremonial purposes. The best example of rock carvings is at Achnabreck, near Cairnbaan village, the largest collection anywhere in Britain. The purpose and significance of these cup- and ring-marked rocks is still a matter of debate.

A few miles south of Kilmartin village is the Iron Age hill fort of **Dunadd**, which stands atop a rocky outcrop and dominates the surrounding flat expanse of **Moine Mhór** (Great Moss), one of the few remaining peat bogs in the country and now a nature reserve. **Dunadd Fort** became the capital of the ancient kingdom of Dalriada around AD 500 and is one of the most important Celtic sites in Scotland. The views from the top are wonderful and worth the visit alone, but you can also see carved out of the exposed rock, a basin and footprint, thought to have been used in the inauguration ceremonies of the ancient kings of Dalriada.

Crinan Canal → *Colour map 3, C5.*
Kilmartin Glen is bordered to the south by the Crinan Canal, a 9-mile stretch of waterway linking Loch Fyne at Ardrishaig with the Sound of Jura. It was designed and built by Sir John Rennie in 1801, with the assistance of the ubiquitous Thomas Telford, to allow shipping to avoid the long and often hazardous journey round the Mull of Kintyre and to help stimulate trade in the islands. These days you're more likely to see pleasure yachts and cruisers sailing on the canal than the cargo vessels, which once transported coal and other goods to the islands and returned with livestock. You don't need to come in a boat to appreciate the canal. You can walk or cycle along the towpath that runs the entire length of the canal, from Ardrishaig to Crinan, and watch boats of all shapes and sizes negotiating a total of 15 locks. The best place to view the canal traffic is at **Crinan**, a pretty little fishing port on Loch Crinan at the western end of the canal.

Knapdale
Running south from the Crinan Canal down to Kintyre is Knapdale, a forested, hilly area that gets its name from its Gaelic description, *cnap* (hill) and *dall* (field). It's an area worth exploring, for there are many walking and cycling trails and superb views from the west coast across to the Paps of Jura. Immediately south of the canal is Knapdale Forest, which stretches from coast to coast over hills dotted with tiny lochs. Forestry Commission Scotland has marked out several trails. Three fairly easy circular routes start from the B8025 which runs south from **Bellanoch**, just east of Crinan.

One trail sets out from the car park at the unmanned Barnluasgan Interpretation Centre and runs up to a point beyond **Loch Barnluasgan**, with great views over the forest and the many lochs. It's a mile in total. A second trail, also a mile long, starts from a car park a little further along the B8025 and heads through the forest to the deserted town- ship of **Arichonan**. The third trail starts out from the car park between the starting points for the first and second trails. It runs right around **Loch Coille-Bharr** and is 3 miles long. A more strenuous walk starts from a car park about 100 yds into the forest, off the B841, about half a mile west of Cairnbaan, and climbs up to the peak of **Dunardy** (702 ft).

At the Barnluasgan Interpretation Centre a little side road turns south down the eastern shore of beautiful Loch Sween, past the village of Achnamara, to the 12th-century **Castle Sween**. First impressions of the castle, situated on the shores of the lovely loch with the forested hills all around, are tainted by the sprawling caravan park and self-catering chalets on a nearby 15,000-acre estate. Unfortunately, the caravans were not there when Robert the Bruce attacked the castle, otherwise he might have done us all a favour by razing them. Three miles south is the ruined 13th-century **Kilmory Knap Chapel**. A new glass roof protects the carved stones inside. Here, visitors will find an 8-ft-high, 15th-century **MacMillan's Cross**, which shows the Crucifixion on one side and a hunting scene on the other. There are also several unmarked graves, believed to be those of 13th-century Knights Templar who fled from France.

Lochgilphead → Colour map 3, C5.

The main town in the area of Mid-Argyll, and administrative centre for the entire Argyll and Bute region, is Lochgilphead, a sleepy little place at the head of Loch Gilp, an arm of Loch Fyne. Lochgilphead started life as a planned town, but the industries came and went, leaving it with the customary grid plan of wide streets but little else. Today it serves as a useful base for exploring the area, with accommodation options, a bank and a supermarket. There's a nice easy walk from the car park at Kilmory Castle Gardens, about a mile east of town, up to Kilmory Loch. It takes about an hour there and back and is well marked. The gardens also make a pleasant stroll and there are other marked walks, including up to **Dun Mór** (360 ft).

Kintyre → For listings, see pages 89-93. Colour map 5, A-B2. Phone code 01880.

The long peninsula of Kintyre is probably best known as the inspiration for Paul McCartney's phenomenally successful 1970s dirge, *Mull of Kintyre*, but don't let that put you off. Historic Kintyre may be isolated but it's also packed with great scenery, wildlife and beaches, which attract the experienced surfer and windsurfer alike. Hardy walkers also have the opportunity to explore the 89-mile **Kintyre Way coastal route** ① www.kintyreway.com, stretching from Tarbert harbour to Dunaverty in the south. The peninsula would be an island, were it not for the mile-long isthmus between West and East Loch Tarbert, a fact not lost on King Magnus Barefoot of Norway. In the 11th century he signed a treaty with the Scottish king, Malcolm Canmore, giving him all the land he could sail round, and promptly had his men drag his longboat across the narrow isthmus, thus adding Kintyre to his kingdom.

Ins and outs

Getting there There is at least one flight daily (35 minutes) from Glasgow to Campbeltown (Machrihanish) airport. For times and reservations, contact **Flybe** ① www.flybe.com T0871-700 2000. There are several daily **Citylink buses** ① T0844-266 3333, from Glasgow to Campbeltown (4½ hours) via Inveraray, Lochgilphead, Kennacraig and Tarbert.

Getting around Public transport on Kintyre has improved, though still requires patience. On the west coast there's a regular (daily) bus service running between Campbeltown, Tarbert, Lochgilphead and Glasgow that also stops at the Kennacraig ferry terminal (for crossings to Islay). From Tarbert to Claonaig (for ferries to Lochranza on Arran) and Skipness there are buses Monday to Saturday. A bus also covers the quiet east route between Campbeltown and Carradale. Details are available from **Argyll & Bute Council** ① T01546-602127, or Tarbert TIC ① Main St, T08707-200023, open Apr-Oct. ▶▶ For further details, see Transport, page 93.

Tarbert → *Colour map 5, A3.*

The fishing village of Tarbert sits at the head of East Loch Tarbert, in a sheltered bay backed by forested hills, and is one the most attractive ports on the west coast. Tarbert (the name derives from the Gaelic *An Tairbeart*, meaning 'isthmus') has a long tradition of fishing, and in the 18th and 19th centuries was a major herring port. Today, prawns and other shellfish are the main catch and though there is still a sizeable fleet, fishing has declined in importance to the local economy. Tourism is now a major source of income, with yachties in particular swelling local coffers when the **Scottish Series**, the second largest yacht race in the UK sails into the picturesque natural harbour.

Overlooking the harbour is the dramatically sited ruin of **Robert the Bruce's 14th-century castle**. There's not much left to see, other than the five-storey 15th-century keep. It's unsafe to investigate the ruins too closely, but the view alone is worth the walk. There are steps leading up to the castle, next to the **Loch Fyne Gallery** on Harbour Street. Behind the castle there are several marked trails leading up into the hills, with great views over Loch Fyne and the islands. Less strenuous is the short walk at the end of Garvel Road, on the north side of the harbour, which leads to the beach. At the end of East Pier road, beyond the Cowal Ferry, is yet another good walk, to the **Shell Beaches**. One mile south, you can also explore the lovely gardens at **Stonefield Castle Hotel**, see Sleeping, page 90.

Gigha → *Colour map 5, A2, www.isle-of-gigha.co.uk.*

The small island of Gigha (pronounced *Gee-a* with a hard 'g') translates from Norse as 'God's Island'. A grand claim, perhaps, but there's no question that this most accessible of islands is also one of the loveliest (and pretty much midge-free). It's only a 20-minute ferry ride away, and is only 7 miles by 1 mile, so it can be visited easily in a day, which is just about enough time to appreciate why the Vikings loved it so much. Like so many of the Hebridean islands, Gigha has had a long list of owners, including various branches of the MacNeils and, more recently, in 1944, Sir James Horlick, he of bedtime drink fame. Now, though, the islanders are the proud owners of their own little piece of paradise, thanks to a successful buy-out in 2001.

It was Horlick who created the islanders self-proclaimed 'Jewel in the Crown'; the wonderful **Achamore Gardens** ⓘ *1 mile south of the ferry terminal, T01583-505254, daily 0900-dusk, £2.* Thanks to Gigha's mild climate, the 50-acre woodland garden has an amazing variety of tropical plants, including rhododendrons, azaleas and camellias. The sight of albino peacocks and palm trees may have you doubting this is a Scottish island at all. There are two marked walks, starting from the walled garden. Managed by the Isle of Gigha Heritage Trust, a three-year, £600,000 garden restoration project has ensured Gigha's 'jewel' continues to shine for years to come.

The island's other delights include some good walks, white sandy beaches and fantastic views across to Jura on one side and Kintyre on the other. One of the best walks is to take the path left after the nine-hole golf course, signed Ardaily, past Mill Loch to the **Mill** on the west shore. The views from here are just magnificent. Another good idea is to walk, or cycle to the peninsula of **Eilean Garbh** at the north of the island. About half a mile beyond Kinererach Farm a path leads left to the peninsula where two crescent-shaped beaches are separated by a thin spit of land. And if the weather's good enough for a picnic, make sure you try some of the island's famously distinctive cheese.

Campbeltown and around → *Colour map 5, B2.*

At the southern end of the Kintyre Peninsula is **Campbeltown**, once home to 34 whisky distilleries and a large fishing fleet. Still the largest town in Kintyre, the two remaining distilleries hint at the town's decline in fortune, though the **Campbeltown Heritage Centre** ① *T07733-485387, Apr-Sep Mon-Sat 1130-1630, £2*, richly documents its history. Another worthwhile local attraction is the **Scottish Owl Centre** ① *Witchburn Rd, T01586-554397, Apr, May, Jun and Sep Wed-Sat, Jul-Aug Mon-Sat 1330-1630, with flying display at 1430, £6, children £4*. Six miles west lies **Machrihanish** and until recently a secretive military airbase beyond which miles of golden sands and gigantic Atlantic breakers beckon beachcombers and experienced wave-sailors alike. Nearby is a dramatic 18-hole championship golf course. The beach can be approached either by walking north from the village, or south from the car park on the main A83 to Tayinloan and Tarbert, where it leaves the coast.

If the weather's good, it's worth taking a walk up to **Beinn Ghulean**, which overlooks the town and loch. Follow the signs for the A83 to Machrihanish until you reach Witchburn Road. After passing the creamery on your left, turn left into Tomaig Road and continue until you come to a wooden gate. Cross over the stile and follow the track through the fields, crossing two more stiles, before you reach the Forest Enterprise sign which marks the start of the walk. It's about 4 miles there and back from of Tomaig Road.

One of the most popular day trips is to the uninhabited **Davaar Island**, connected to the peninsula by a tidal breakwater. Here you can see the cave painting of the Crucifixion, completed in secret by a local artist in 1877. The island can be visited at low tide from Kildalloig Point, a couple of miles east of town. Check tide times at the tourist office before setting out.

It's only a short drive south from Campbeltown to the tip of the peninsula, the Mull of Kintyre. There's nothing much to see in this bleak, storm-battered place, apart from the coast of Ireland, a mere 12 miles away and clearly visible on a good day. The road out to the lighthouse, built in 1788 and remodelled by Robert Stevenson, grandfather of Robert Louis, is both twisty and spectacular. Above the lighthouse is a small poignant cairn in memory to military personnel killed when their helicopter crashed in bad weather almost a decade ago on the remote hillside. It's possible to walk from here up to Machrihanish (about 10 miles), past the ruined township of **Balmavicar** and the **Largiebaan Bird Reserve**. The views are great and there's a chance of seeing golden eagles.

The southernmost village on Kintyre is **Southend**, a bleak, windswept place with a wide sandy beach. At the east end of the beach, jutting out on a rocky promontory, are the scant remains of **Dunaverty Castle**, once a MacDonald stronghold, where 300 Royalists were brutally massacred in 1647 by the Covenanting army of the Earl of Argyll, despite having already surrendered. To the west of Southend, below the cliffs, is the ruined 13th-century **Keil Chapel**, which is said to mark the spot where St Columba first set foot on Scottish soil, before heading north to Iona. Close by is a pair of footprints carved into the rock, known as Columba's footprints.

The slow and winding single track B842 meanders up the east coast from Campbeltown to Skipness and **Claonaig**, departure point for the ferry to Arran, see page 94. The scenery en route is gentle and pleasant, with nice views of Arran, and there are some worthwhile places to stop.

Ten miles up the coast are the idyllic ruins of **Saddell Abbey**, a Cistercian establishment founded by Somerled in 1160. The abbey fell into ruin in the early 16th century and much of the stone was used in the building of 18th-century Saddell Castle for the Bishop of

Argyll. Though little remains, there are some impressive medieval grave slabs, depicting knights, monks, ships, animals and other images.

A few miles further north is the village of **Carradale**, the only place of any size on the east coast, nestling in the sandy sweep of beautiful Carradale Bay. There are several pleasant marked walks through the woods between the B842 and the shore. The shortest of these walks (with green waymarkers) starts from the Network Centre (see below) and is a mile long. There's a 3-mile walk with red waymarkers which starts at the **Port Na Storm** car park and follows the forest road to the left. After 150 yds the route turns left again at the road junction. A mile further on, you turn right off the road and follow the track up to the summit of **Cnoc-nan Gabhor**, from where there are great views of Kintyre and across to Arran. A third walk (6 miles; blue waymarkers) also starts from the Port Na Storm car park. This time the route heads right at the junction 150 yds beyond the car park and then runs north along the shore, with a chance of seeing dolphins and basking shark. The path then swings west towards the road, then turns south with views of Carradale Glen.

Twelve miles north of Carradale the B842 ends at **Claonaig**, which is actually nothing more than a slipway for the ferry to Arran (see page 94). From here the B8001 heads west to meet the A83 near the Kennacraig ferry pier. A dead-end road runs north for a few miles to the tiny village of **Skipness**, where you can visit the substantial ruins of the 13th-century Skipness Castle and nearby chapel.

Cowal Peninsula and the Clyde Coast → *For listings, see pages 89-93. Colour map 5, A3-4.*

The Cowal Peninsula reaches out into the Firth of Clyde, framed by Loch Fyne and Loch Long. This is the most visited part of Argyll due to its proximity to Glasgow, but, despite the summer hordes, many of whom come for the Cowal Highland Gathering in late August, much of it is undisturbed. Most people head straight for the rather drab main ferry port and traditional Clyde seaside resort of Dunoon. More adventurous souls enjoy the forests and mountains of Argyll Forest Park in the north or the peace of the southwest coastline.

Argyll Forest Park
The northern part of the peninsula is largely covered by the sprawling Argyll Forest Park which extends from Loch Lomond south to Holy Loch. This area contains the most stunning scenery in Cowal, and includes the **Arrochar Alps**, a range of rugged peaks north of Glen Croe which offer some of the best climbing in Argyll. The most famous of these is anvil-like Ben Arthur (2891 ft), better known as **The Cobbler**. Less imposing are the hills south of Glen Croe, between Loch Goil and Loch Long, in an area known as Argyll's Bowling Green (not because it's flat, but an English corruption of the Gaelic *Baile na Greine*, meaning 'Sunny Hamlet'). There are many footpaths and cycle tracks threading their way through the park. Details of five are outlined in the excellent *Argyll Forest Park Guide* (£3), available from the Forestry Commission office in Ardgarten.

Arrochar to Dunoon
The gateway to Cowal, Arrochar sits at the head of Loch Long on the main A83, only a few miles west of Tarbet and the shores of Loch Lomond. It's a small, uninspiring place but the setting is dramatic, with The Cobbler towering overhead. A few miles beyond Arrochar, on the shores of Loch Long, is **Ardgarten**, where there's an excellent **Forestry Commission visitor centre** ① *T01301-702403, Apr-Oct daily 1000-1700.* This provides useful information on hillwalking and wildlife and is an excellent start-point for climbing The Cobbler (seven

hours return trip). From Ardgarten, the A83 climbs steeply up Glen Croe to reach one of Scotland's classic viewpoints at the top of the pass, the **Rest and be Thankful** (built under Major Caulfeild after the '45). The hordes of like-minded tourists, eager for that memorable photograph, cannot detract from the majestic views of the surrounding craggy peaks.

Here the road forks. The A83 continues towards **Inveraray**, see page 79, and the single-track B828 heads southwest to meet the B839, which runs down to the village of **Lochgoilhead**, in a beautiful setting on Loch Goil. There are several hotels and B&Bs as well as an unsightly village of self-catering holiday chalets next door. At the end of the road, several miles down the west side of Loch Goil, are the ruins of 15th-century **Carrick Castle**.

The A83 meanwhile runs down through **Glen Kinglas** to reach the village of **Cairndow**, at the head of Loch Fyne. Here, gastronomes must decide whether to drive south down the A815 and east side of Loch Fyne for Inver Cottage, by Castle Lachlan, or continue towards Inveraray and **Clachan**, to dine in the ever popular **Loch Fyne Oyster Bar**, see page 91. At the southern end of Loch Eck, at Benmore, is the **Younger Botanic Garden** ① *T01369-706261, Apr-Sep daily 1000-1800, Mar and Oct 1000-1700, £5, concessions £4, children £1*, a lovely woodland garden and offshoot of the Royal Botanic Garden in Edinburgh. Its 120 acres are laid out with over 300 species of rhododendrons and feature an avenue of giant redwoods.

Dunoon → *Colour map 5, A4.*

The largest town in Cowal, with around 8000 inhabitants, is Dunoon, one-time favourite holiday destination for Glaswegians, who came in their hordes on board the many paddle steamers that sailed "doon the watter" from Glasgow. Dunoon still attracts many visitors, but the town's economy has suffered following the closure of the Holy Loch US nuclear submarine in the 1990s. Nevertheless, Dunoon still comes to life during the **Cowal Highland Gathering**, see page 92. There's not much to detain you here, although the **Castle House Museum** ① *Easter-Oct Mon-Sat 1030-1630, Sun 1400-1630, £2, concessions £1.50, children free*, on Castle Hill overlooking the town offers an insight into clan history and the role of the Clyde in wartime, and allows you to bone up on Cowal's often grisly past. There are CalMac ferries every hour (0620-2020) from Gourock to Dunoon, with train connections from Glasgow Central (25 minutes, £3.20 one way per person, £8.80 per car). There is also a ferry service from McInroy's Point, 2 miles from Gourock, with **Western Ferries** ① *www.western-ferries.co.uk*. It leaves every 15-20 minutes during peak times and runs daily from 0730-2400, £3.50 per passenger, £9.90 per car.

The southwest

One of the most beautiful parts of Argyll is the southwest of Cowal, particularly the route down to the little village of **Tighnabruaich**. The A8003 runs down the west side of Loch Riddon and there are few lovelier sights than the view from this road across the **Kyles of Bute**, the narrow straits that separate Cowal from the island of Bute. Tighnabruaich gets busy in the summer with visitors who come here to enjoy the best sailing on the west coast. A few miles southwest of Kames is **Portavadie**, on the west coast of Cowal. A CalMac car and passenger ferry sails from here to Tarbert, on the Kintyre Peninsula, saving a lot of time if you're heading for the islands of Islay, Jura or Colonsay.

Helensburgh → *Colour map 5, A4.*

Overlooking the Clyde is the town of Helensburgh, its wide, grid-plan streets lined with elegant Georgian houses. The town is most famously known for its connection with the great Glasgow architect, **Charles Rennie Mackintosh**. In the upper part of the town is **Hill House** ① *Upper Colquhoun St, T01436-673900, Apr-Oct daily 1330-1730, £9, concessions £6.50, tea room open 1330-1630, trains from Glasgow Queen Street station to Helensburgh Central,* one of the best examples of Mackintosh's work. The house was designed for Glasgow publisher Walter Blackie in 1902-1904, and is managed by the National Trust for Scotland. In accordance with Blackie's wish to have a house with an individual feel, it is a masterpiece of balanced perfection and artistry with great attention to detail. The use of light and dark, and the symbolism of the floral patterns – hallmarks of his personal art nouveau style – are in evidence. After exploring the house, visit the cosy tea room in the converted kitchen.

Isle of Bute → *For listings, see pages 89-93. Colour map 5, A3.*

Barely a stone's throw off the south coast of Cowal is the island of Bute, another favourite holiday destination for people from Glasgow and Ayrshire, who come here in droves during the busy summer months. But though the island is small (15 miles long by 5 miles wide), it's deceptively easy to escape the hordes, who tend to congregate around the east coast resort of Rothesay, leaving the delights of the sparsely populated west coast free for those who enjoy a bit of peace and quiet.

Ins and outs

Getting there The bus service provided by West Coast Motors is good, though limited on Sunday. There are buses to Rothesay from Tighnabruaich in southwest Cowal at least once a day from April to October, the journey takes one hour. For times, contact **West Coast Motors** ① *T0870-850 6687.* A car/passenger ferry makes the five-minute crossing from Colintraive to Rhubodach, at the northern end of Bute, daily every 30 minutes or hour from Easter until the end of August (Monday-Saturday 0530-2055 and Sunday 0830-2055). It costs £1.40 one way per person and £8.80 per car. Bute is easily accessible from Glasgow. Take a train from Glasgow Central to the ferry terminal at Wemyss Bay, and from there it's a 35-minute crossing to Rothesay. The ferries leave every 45 minutes from 0715 until 1945 (later on Friday, Saturday and Sunday), £4.45 one way per passenger, £17.60 per car. For times and fares, call T08705-650000.

Getting around The best way to see Bute is still by bike, with roads fairly quiet and in good condition beyond Rothesay. The No 93 bus makes at least five trips daily between Guildford Square in Rothesay and Mount Stuart.

Bute

To Colintraive
Rhubodach

Kyles of Bute

Torran
Turach
(745ft)

Windy Hill
(913ft)

St
Colmac

Kildavanan

Kames Bay
Port Bannatyne

A844

Ettrick
Bay

Rothesay Bay

To Wemyss Bay

To Arran

B878

Rothesay

Canada Hill
(532ft)

Straad

B881

Ascog

St
Ninian's
Point

Loch
Fad

Quien Hill
(476ft)

Kerrycroy

Inchmarnock

Loch Quien

Mount Stuart

A844

Scalpsie
Bay

Kingarth

Stravanan
Bay

Kilchattan
Bay

B881

Dunagoil Bay

St Blane's
Chapel

Törr Mòr
(486ft)

Garroch
Head

Glencallum
Bay

Bruchag Point

N

2 km
2 miles

Rothesay

The sole town on Bute is Rothesay, with its handsome period mansions lining the broad sweep of bay, its elegant promenade lined with palm trees and the distinctive 1920s **Winter Gardens**, now refurbished with a cinema, restaurant and the TIC. **Rothesay Castle** ① *T01700-502691, Mon-Sat 0930-1900, closed Thu and Fri afternoon in winter, £4.50, concessions £3.60, children £2.70*. One thing men must do before leaving Rothesay is visit the palatial **Victorian public toilets** ① *Easter-Sep daily 0800-2100, Oct-Mar daily 0900-1700*. This architectural gem enables gents to 'spend a penny' in style.

Mount Stuart

① *T01700-503877, www.mountstuart.com. House and grounds open May-Sep daily 1200-1700, grounds 1000-1800. House and grounds £8, concessions £6.50, children £4; grounds only £4, concessions £3.50, children £2.50.*

One of Bute's main attractions is Mount Stuart, a unique Victorian Gothic house set in 300 acres of lush woodland gardens, 3 miles south of Rothesay. This magnificent architectural fantasy reflects the Third Marquess of Bute's passion for astrology, astronomy, mysticism and religion, and the sheer scale and grandeur of the place almost beggars belief. This is truly one of the great country houses of Scotland and displays breathtaking craftsmanship in marble and stained glass, as well as a fine collection of family portraits and Italian antiques. Much of the existing house dates from 1877, and was built following a terrible fire which destroyed the original, built in 1719 by the Second Earl of Bute. Equally impressive are the landscaped gardens and woodlands, established by the Third Earl of Bute (1713-1792), who advised on the foundation of Kew Gardens in London, and the stunning visitor centre complete with audio-visuals and restaurant. The present owner is Johnny Dumfries (only the Daily Mail calls him the Seventh Marquess of Bute), former racing driver who won Le Mans in 1988 and who, famously, gave up his house for the wedding of Stella McCartney, daughter of Paul, in 2003. It's worth spending a whole day here in order to take in the splendour of the house and to explore the beautiful gardens. And if the weather's fine, why not bring a picnic and enjoy the wonderful sea views.

Other sights around the island

Just before Mount Stuart is the tidy little village of **Kerrycroy**, designed by the wife of the Second Marquess of Bute and featuring an interesting mix of building styles. South of Mount Stuart and the village of Kingarth is **Kilchattan Bay**, an attractive bay of pink sands and the start of a fine walk down to Glencallum Bay, in the southeastern corner of the island.

Southwest of Kilchattan Bay is **St Blane's Chapel**, a 12th-century ruin in a beautifully peaceful spot near the southern tip of the island. The medieval church stands on the site of an earlier monastery, established in the sixth century by St Blane, nephew of St Catan, after whom Kilchattan is named. The ruin can be reached by road from Rothesay, or as part of the walk from Kilchattan Bay. Four miles north of St Blane's, on the west coast, is **Scalpsie Bay**, the nicest beach on the island and a good place for seal spotting. A little further north is **St Ninian's Point**, looking across to the island of **Inchmarnock**. At the end of the beach are the ruins of a sixth-century chapel, dedicated to St Ninian.

The Highland–Lowland dividing line passes through the middle of Bute at Loch Fad, which separates the hilly and uninhabited northern half of the island and the rolling farmland of the south. The highest point on the island is **Windy Hill** (913 ft) in the north, from where there are great views across the island. A less strenuous walk is up **Canada Hill**, a few miles southwest of Rothesay, above Loch Fad. Walk along Craigmore promenade and turn off at the old pier to **Ardencraig Gardens**. Then continue uphill along the golf course to the top of the hill for great views of the Firth of Clyde.

Kilchattan Bay to Glencallum Bay walk

A longer walk is the circular route from Kilchattan Bay south to Glencallum Bay and back, via St Blane's chapel. The bay was once a final staging point for boats bound for overseas. The walk is 5 miles in total. Allow about four hours. There are buses to and from Rothesay. The route is waymarked, but if you want to take a map, it's OS Landranger sheet 63 or Explorer 362. The Rothesay Discovery Centre (TIC) carries a full stock of maps.

Follow the signpost for 'Kelspoke Path' beside Kiln Villas and take the track, which climbs steadily before turning sharply back on itself. Go through a gate and shortly before the next gate turn right. Follow the rough track, which swings right, then left over open ground to the ruins of Kelspoke Castle.

Continue along the grassy path, past a reservoir on your right, then cross the stile and go down and across a small burn. Turn left and follow the burn, before heading right to join the shore path and follow this past the lighthouse on your left and around the headland to **Glencallum Bay**. Continue round the shoreline and at the far end of the bay follow the waymarks as the path climbs to cross the headland. The path then levels out and from here there are great views across to the mountains of Arran.

The path then reaches the col above **Loch na Leighe**. Drop down to the loch and follow the waymarks south over open ground. Before reaching a farm called The Plan, go right over two footbridges, then left below a low ridge. Keep to the right of the buildings, following the waymarks across open ground to the stile that crosses to the ruins of St Blane's Chapel (see above). Leave the chapel by the gap in the boundary wall and go through a gate, turning left on a clear track which climbs steadily to a stile. Cross the stile and turn right, following the edge of the field down to a gate. Walk uphill on the left side of the field to Suidhe Hill. At the top of the field, cross the fence and keep going, turning right at the corner of the fence. Go through a gate at the next corner and look for a waymark about 100 yds downhill. Follow the path steeply downhill, passing through a kissing gate and staying close to the wall. You then reach a drying green at the foot of the hill; turn left and follow a path around the buildings and back onto the road at **Kilchattan**.

⊙ Mid-Argyll, Kintyre, Cowal and Bute listings

For Sleeping and Eating price codes and other relevant information, see Essentials pages 38-45.

⊜ Sleeping

Loch Awe and Loch Etive *p77*

L Ardanaiseig Hotel, 3 miles east of Kilchrenan village (12 miles from Taynuilt) on an unclassified road, T01866-833333, www.ardanaiseig-hotel.com. Open Feb-Dec. A luxurious highland retreat that boasts one of the best hotel restaurants in Scotland (♈♈♈). You'll pay at least £50 per head for

dinner but with delicious food, a delightful ambience (including drinks by the fire in the library bar) and even private boat trips to atmospheric Kilchurn Castle, it's 1st class.
C-D Blarcreen Farm, Ardchattan Estate, T01631-750272, www.blarcreenfarm.com. Open Mar-Dec. A mile past Ardchattan Priory on the road from Oban to Bonawe. Elegant, Victorian farmhouse standing on its own surrounded by lovely countryside. Individually styled rooms, homely ambience and 3-course candelit dinner from £28.50 per person.

Self-catering

Inistrynich, Lochaweside, Dalmally, T01838-200256, www.loch-awe.com/inistrynich. This delightful cottage (sleeps 4-8) is nestled by the loch. Fishing, golf and walking nearby.

Inveraray and around *p79*

L Crinan Hotel, T01546-830261, www.crinanhotel.com. Nestled on the shores of Loch Crinan and by the famous Crinan Canal, guests are assured of fine dining and luxury in this acclaimed retreat. Fantastic views, pampering on a majestic scale and a sensational restaurant make a stay here well worthwhile.

A-D George Hotel, Main St, T01499-302111, www.thegeorgehotel.co.uk. Enjoy genuine hospitality and tasty local produce (see Eating, below) in this atmospheric, late 18th-century hotel with cosy bar, real ales and a resident ghost. The Merchants Room with double jacuzzi is booked up to 12 months in advance.

B-C Fernpoint Hotel, T01499-302111. Located just off the quayside, this grand hotel offers comfort (including whirlpool baths), and good value lunch (1300-1630) and evening (1800-2045) dining.

E Kilmartin Hotel, opposite the church in Kilmartin village, T01546-510250. Offers 4 en suite rooms. Handy, comfortable stop whilst exploring historic Kilmartin Glen.

F Inverary Youth Hostel, Dalmally Rd, T01499-302454. Open Apr-end Oct. The perfect budget base from which to explore the nearby castle and town.

Self-catering

The Paymaster's House, T01499-302003, www.paymastershouse.co.uk. A delightful 1780s dated option, oozing character and history in the heart of Inverary. From £90-165 per night.

Kintyre *p82*

There are at least 4 self-catering options run by the Heritage Trust on the island. Visit www.isle-of-gigha.co.uk, for further details.

L-A Stonefield Castle Hotel, 2 miles north of Tarbert, on the A82 to Lochgilphead, T01422-323200. This impressive 18th-century former castle home of the Campbells provides guests with comfort, eye-catching views of Loch Fyne and acres of garden to walk off the delicious 4-course dinner.

C Kilberry Inn, west of Tarbert on the B8024, T01880-770223, www.kilberryinn. com. 3 rooms. Open Easter-Oct and at weekends in the winter. Offers superb Scottish meat and seafood dishes (ᵀᵀᵀ-ᵀ),and cosy comforts including a roaring log fire. Has a glowing reputation for serving fabulous food, especially seafood and locally sourced beef and lamb that has won the restaurant plaudits by national newspaper food critics. Recommended.

C-E Post Office House, 5 mins from the ferry, Gigha, T01475-650100. B&B and self-catering option. Owners also run the Isle of Gigha post office and general store, and rent out bikes (£10 per day).

D Gigha Hotel, Isle of Gigha, T01583-505254, www.isle-of-gigha.co.uk. Comfortable, friendly hotel with double/family rooms and some looking out over the sea. Good value food including dinner (ᵀᵀ). Non-residents can enjoy breakfast for £9.35.

E Rhu House, Tarbert, T/F01880-820231, Comfortable B&B looking out over west Loch Tarbert. Handy for Islay ferry.

Camping

Portban Holiday Park, Kilberry, Tarbert, T01880-770224. Majestic views towards Jura from the comfort of your tent.

Cowal Peninsula and the Clyde Coast *p85*

L-B An Lauchin, Tighnabruaich, T01700-811 239. This elegant hotel with its own moorings boasts exquisite dining (ᵀᵀᵀ), beautiful decor and many a fine dram in the snug bar.

C Kames Hotel, Kames, T01700-811489. Offers 10 en suite rooms, terrific views down the Kyles and great food.

Self-catering

Cove Park, Rosneath Peninsula, Loch Long, T01436-850123, www.covepark.org. Very unusual and extremely restful place to stay, on the shore of Loch Long, 20 mins by car from Helensburgh. Accommodation in one of 2 'pods' or 3 'cubes'. The former are designed to blend in seamlessly with the surrounding landscape, with balconies overlooking the loch, and can sleep up to 4 in 2 en suite bed- rooms; £100 per pod per night (minimum 2 nights). The 'cubes' are designed for singles or couples and cost £40 per night each. If you're looking for something a bit different, or just to get away from it all, this is the place to come. It is also a centre for the creative arts and runs an annual programme of artists' residences. Recommended.

Camping

Glendaruel Caravan/Campsite, T01369-820267. Terrific secluded location, well maintained and close to amenities.

Isle of Bute *p87, map p87*

L-A Balmory Hall, 3 miles south of Rothesay, at Ascog, T/F01700-500669, www.balmoryhall.com. This Italianate mansion, set in 10 acres of grounds and once home to the 3rd Marquess of Bute, is now a superior guesthouse run by Tony and Beryl. A stay here is a memorable experience, the setting is idyllic and the suites are elegant and sumptuous (sample the Bute Suite for some serious indulgence). The 7-course breakfast is an event in itself. There are also self-catering apartments for weekend breaks (£235 per person).

E-D Cannon House Hotel, Battery Pl, Rothesay, T01700-502819. A comfortable Georgian townhouse. Close to the ferry.

D Kingarth Hotel, in Kingarth, in the south of the island, T01700-831662, www.kingarthhotel.co.uk. Quiet, cosy 1782 inn offering genuine hospitality, terrific seafood or steak platters (♥♥-♥) and the chance to

banter with the locals. A wonderful place to enjoy the food and ambience.

Self-catering

Ardencraig House, Ardencraig Rd, Rothesay. T01700-505077. Luxury 4-apartment option in converted Victorian-era mansion with views of Clyde (£195-495 per week).

❶ Eating

Inveraray and around *p79*
♥♥♥-♥♥ **Loch Fyne Oyster Bar**, at Cairndow on the A83 near Clachan, T01499-600482. Open daily from 0900. Book ahead at this famous seafood restaurant known to attract heavyweight (in both senses of the word) politicians and gastronomes alike. All the seafood is from sustainable stock. There's also an excellent delicatessen to further tempt your taste-buds, though doubt you'll have room after gorging on a seafood platter.
♥♥-♥ **The George Hotel**, Main St, T01499-302111. Real ales on tap, hearty bar meals and reasonably priced dinners using locally sourced meats and seafood. If staying, try the home-made jams.
♥♥-♥ **Kilmartin House (Glebe Cairn) Café**, Kilmartin Hotel, see Sleeping, above. Daily 1000-1700 and Thu-Sat evenings for dinner. Superb cooking, much better than you should expect, and a lesson to many other visitor attractions in how to do things well. Wholesome and healthy soups, snacks, home-made bread and excellent coffee. Book ahead if planning on dinner.

Cowal Peninsula and the Clyde Coast *p85*
♥♥♥-♥♥ **An Lauchin**, T01700-811239. Game terrine, venison with red onion marmalade, cranachan. Provide Scottish cuisine at its best.
♥♥♥-♥♥ **Inver Cottage**, Strathlachlan on B8000, past Strachur, T01369-860537. Mouth-watering starters, succulent game and hand-dived scallops, to-die-for desserts and homely ambience. A gem so book ahead. Recommended.

Isle of Bute *p87, map p87*

♥ West End Café, 1-3 Gallowgate, Rothesay, T01700-503596. Open Tue-Sun. It is a must while you are on Bute to sample the fish and chips at this award-winning chippy. Phone ahead to avoid the massive queues in summer.

⊛ Festivals and events

Kintyre *p82*
Aug Mull of Kintyre Music Festival. If you're around Campbeltown in mid-Aug don't miss 3 days of the best in traditional Celtic music.
Sep Gigha Music Festival, held early in the month.

Cowal Peninsula and the Clyde Coast *p85*
Aug Cowal Highland Gathering, held on the last weekend of the month. The world's largest and culminate in a spectacular march of massed pipes and drums through the streets.
Oct Cowalfest. An action-packed week-long walking and arts festival in early Oct.

Isle of Bute *p87, map p87*
May Isle of Bute Jazz Festival, held during the May Bank Holiday weekend.
Jul Isle of Bute Dunoon Sheepdog Trials and Inverary Highland Games.

⦿ Activities and tours

Loch Awe and Loch Etive *p77*
Boat trips
Loch Etive Cruises, T01866-822430. Cruises depart at 1000 and 1200 (2-hr cruise; £10) and 1400 (3-hr cruise; £15), Easter-Oct Sun-Fri (Sat, charters only). No booking necessary but arrive in plenty of time. The departure point is 1 mile from Taynuilt up the road to the Bonawe Heritage Site.

Fishing
Lochawe Boats, Arbrecknish by Dalavich, off the B840, T01866-833256. All year. £20 per

day for rowing boat or canoe. £40 per day for outboard boat. Loch Awe fishing permits from £10 per day.

Inverary and around *p79*
Adventure and horse riding
Argyll Riding, Dalchenna Farm, 2 miles south of Inveraray on A83, T01499-302611, www.horserides.co.uk. BHS-approved riding school offering trekking (Easter-Oct). Also bungee trampolines, climbing walls and clay-pigeon shooting (daily from 1000).
Argyll Trail Riding, Brenfield Farm, Ardrishaig, T01546-603274, www.brenfield. co.uk. Riding trails or beach gallops from a ½-day to a full week, including 'Day Pub Trails' and the week-long Rob Roy Trail. Also clay-pigeon shooting.
Highland Horse Riding, Tarbert, Argyll, T01880-820333. Located just off the A83 past the southern end of Tarbert. Rides and hacks from 1 hr to a day. Instructional rides from age 8.

Boat trips
Craignish Cruises, Ardfern by Lochgilphead, T0845-3979824, T07747-023038. Aboard the 33 ft long *Sea Leopard*, you'll explore the sealife rich waters of the Firth of Lorn and out to the islands and Corryvreckan. Tours from 2 hr (£20) to 4 hrs (£35). Skipper also offers boat as a water taxi to help cyclists and walkers reach remote locations. Price dependent on route.
Sanda Island, T01586-551987. Summer sailings (£25) from Campbeltown run daily. Spend 3 hrs on the privately owned historic island of Sanda (2 miles off Mull of Kintyre) with its cosy wee pub and ancient sites. Reached aboard the *Seren Las*. There are 6 self-catering cottages (from £360 per week) and a pub serving good food – The Byron Darnton – named after the largest ship to be wrecked on off the island in 1946.

⊖ Transport

Inverary and around *p79*

Bus There are **buses** from **Lochgilphead** to **Cairnbaan**, **Crinan**, **Achnamara** and **Tayvallich**, several times daily Mon-Fri, T01546-870330. There is at least 1 daily bus to **Oban** via **Kilmartin** (Mon-Sat) and several daily buses to **Inveraray**. There's a regular service to **Ardrishaig** and from Argyll to **Glasgow**.

Cycle hire Crinan Cycles, 34 Argyll St, Lochgilphead, T01546-603511. Mon-Sat 0930-1730. Bikes for rent from £8, also parts and repairs and will advise on routes and provide maps.

Kintyre *p82*

Air There is at least 1 flight daily (35 mins), all year round to **Glasgow**.

Bus There are 5 buses a day daily from Campbeltown to **Machrihanish Saddell**, 25 mins; **Carradale**, 45 mins; and to **Southend**, 25 mins. Ask at TIC for an *Area Transport Guide*.

Ferry There is a car and passenger ferry from **Portavadie** on the Cowal Peninsula to **Tarbert**, daily every hr Apr-Oct, 25 mins, £3.30 per passenger, £14.95 per car, less frequent departures in winter.

There are 9 daily ferries to **Lochranza** (Arran) and **Claonaig** on the west coast of Kintyre (and east of Kennacraig), 30 mins, £4.75 per passenger, £21.20 per car. Ferries leave from **Kennacraig**, 5 miles south of Tarbert, to to **Colonsay** (see page 115) and **Islay** (see page 118).

A small car and passenger ferry leaves from **Tayinloan** to the ferry pier at Ardminish on **Gigha**, Mon-Sat 0800-1800, Sun 1100- 1700, 20 mins, £5.70 return per passenger, £21.10 per car.

Cowal Peninsula and the Clyde Coast *p85*

Bus West Coast Motors, T01586-552319, run 3 (No 386) buses Mon-Sat from the **Dunoon** ferry terminal to **Inveraray** via **Benmore Gardens**, **Strachur** and **Cairndow**. The 1st bus leaves at 0850. Alternatively, there are at least 5 buses daily (No 484) Mon-Sat from Dunoon ferry terminal to Lochgoilhead.

To reach the CalMac ferry at Portavadie for the CalMac ferry to Tarbert in mid Argyll, at least 1 bus (No 478) runs Mon-Sat from Dunoon to **Portavadie** ferry terminal via **Tighnabruaich** and **Kames**. The buses leaves Dunoon at 0711 and 1325.

To reach **Bute** from *Cowal* there's 1 bus (No 479) Wed and Fri, 2 on Sat and 3 on Sun from **Dunoon** to the CalMac ferry at **Colintraive**, where on reaching **Rhubodach** (Bute) the bus continues into **Rothesay**, 1 hr 40 mins.

Isle of Bute *p87, map p87*

Bus and ferry To cross from **Rothesay** to **Dunoon** on the Cowal Peninsula using the bus and ferry, there's at least 1 service (No 477) Mon-Sat. This bus travels to the ferry terminal at Rhubodach and on crossing, stops in Kames and Tighnabruaich before Dunoon, 1 hr 40 mins.

Isle of Arran

→ *Colour map A3/B3. Phone code 01770.*

In the wedge of sea between Ayrshire and Kintyre lies the oval-shaped, compact Isle of Arran. A land of beauty and contrast, the rugged, mountainous north is akin in hue and character to the northwest Highlands, whilst the fertile, forested south is lowland country. Unspoiled and alive with ancient history, myths and geological treasures, 25-mile-long Arran deserves its sobriquet, 'Scotland in Miniature'. Moreover, despite its popularity and accessibility from the Central Belt, outside Brodick you're as likely to spot a deer as a fellow tourist. ▸▸ *For listings, see pages 98-99.*

Ins and outs

Getting there The main ferry route to Arran is from the distinctly unappealing Ayrshire town of Ardrossan to the island's main town, Brodick. CalMac car and passenger ferry makes the 55-minute journey Monday to Sunday. The journey costs £5.95 one-way per passenger, £43.50 one-way per car (cheaper in winter). The other ferry route is from Claonaig to Lochranza in the north of the island. The non-bookable car and passenger ferry makes the 30-minute trip seven to nine times daily during the summer (April to October), and there's one daily service in winter to Tarbert. The journey costs £5.40 per passenger and £23.85 per car (cheaper in winter). For ferry times, call T0800-665000 or look at www.calmac.co.uk. There's a regular train connections from Glasgow Central. By car, from the south the main route to Arran is from the M74 motorway, on to the A71 via Kilmarnock, to Irvine and Ardrossan. ▸▸ *For further details, see Transport, page 99.*

Getting around A reliable bus network makes using public transport feasible, although many visitors explore by bike. It is possible to cycle a full circuit of the island in one day. Once on the island, there are regular daily buses from Brodick to Blackwaterfoot via 'The String'; to Lamlash and Whiting Bay and on to Blackwaterfoot; to Corrie, Sannox, Lochranza, Catacol, Pirnmill, Machrie and Blackwaterfoot. Kildonan, Whiting Bay and back to Brodick.

Tourist information The Brodick **TIC** ⓘ *T01770-303774, www.ayrshire-arran.com, Easter-Oct Mon-Fri 0900-1700, Sat 0900-1930), Sun 1000-1700, winter hours vary but are currently Mon-Sat 1000-1700,* is beside the pier and bus terminal.

Brodick

Whether coming to play golf (there are seven courses), walk, climb or sample the ales, whisky and cheese produced by proud Arranachs, the largest town and port of Brodick is where most visitors step ashore. Lying in a 'broad bay', (hence its Norse name *breidr vik*), Brodick offers up guesthouses, eateries and shops but little of the scenic charm that awaits along the outlying winding roads.

Two miles north of town and overlooking Brodick Bay is the impressive **Brodick Castle** ⓘ *T01770-302202, castle and restaurant, Easter-Oct daily 1100-1600 (castle closes 1500 in Oct), walled garden 1000-1630, country park open all year, daily 0930-sunset; castle, garden and country park £11, concessions £8.* The ancient seat of the Dukes of Hamilton, it is now a flagship NTS property. Parts of the castle date from the 13th century and extensions were added in the 16th, 17th and 19th centuries. With paintings, antiques and (apparently) ghosts aplenty, it's worth exploring the sumptuously furnished rooms and the walled garden. The surrounding country park has 11 miles of marked trails and an adventure playground.

Halfway between the village and the castle is the excellent **Arran Heritage Museum** ① *T01770-302636, www.arranmuseum.co.uk, Apr-Oct daily 1030-1630, £3, concessions £2, children £1.50, family (children under 16) £7.* Within a former croft and smiddy, visitors can discover a wealth of information about the island's archaeology, geology and social history before popping next door to **Café Rosaburn** (April to October).

Just over a mile north you'll find **Arran Aromatics**, where nature has been harvested to produce handmade soaps and oils. Continuing to Cladach by the castle, there's the chance to undertake a 45-minute sampling tour of real ales including a tasty Arran Blonde at the **Arran Brewery** ① *T01770-302353, Easter-Oct Mon-Sat 1000-1700, Sun 1230-1700, Nov-Mar Mon-Sat 1000-1500, £2.50 guided tour (by arrangement), self-guided tour £2, children free.*

South Arran

The south of Arran is a fertile landscape of rolling hills and pretty little seaside villages, where you'll find the bulk of the island's population and tourists. A few miles south of

Arran

Brodick is **Lamlash**, a quiet and attractive village boasting a wide, sheltered bay but also an unappealing mud beach.

Lying just offshore is humpbacked **Holy Island** ① *www.holyisland.org*. Owned by Buddhists since 1992 they have established a meditative retreat and since 2003 a Peace Centre (see Sleeping, page 98) on slopes grazed by feral goats and countless rabbits. A ferry runs to Holy Island between April and September, with a limited service in winter (£11 return). For further information on getting to Holy Island, call T01770-600998. For day visitors, there's just enough time to ascend **Mullach Mór** (1030 ft).

Renowned for its golf, the little fishing village of **Blackwaterfoot** is set round a bay with a tiny harbour. Two miles (45 minutes' walk) north along the coast are the **King's Caves**, where, according to legend, Robert the Bruce watched the spider that inspired him. The cathedral-like main cave has an unlocked iron gate to keep out sheep.

Four miles north of Blackwaterfoot, off the main coast road, is **Machrie Moor**, site of the most impressive of Arran's Bronze Age **stone circles**. Park by the Historic Scotland sign and then walk for 1½ miles up the farm track to reach an area boasting six stone circles. Many are barely visible above the ground, but the tallest is over 18 ft high. A few miles further on, just south of the turn-off to Machrie village, is another Historic Scotland sign for **Moss Farm Road Stone Circle**, which lies about half a mile walk along the farm track.

North Arran

The northern half of Arran, with its wild, heather-strewn hillsides, brooding glens and dramatic mountains, contrasts sharply with the south. Sparsely populated, this remote region is paradise for the dedicated hillwalker. Six miles north of Brodick is the quaint village of **Corrie**. In addition to its craftshop, hotel and friendly pub, Corrie is also an alternative start-point to Brodick for the ascent of Goatfell. The main coastal road continues north from Corrie to **Sannox**, with its sandy beach and fine hotel before winding northwest into the heather-strewn glen and dropping into the former herring village of Lochranza.

Nestling under dramatic mountains and reached by road or the ferry from Claonaig, Arran's most northerly village of **Lochranza** is dominated by the ruins of 13th-century **Lochranza Castle** and the seal rich, U-shaped bay in which it stands. If the herds of deer grazing on the golf course contribute to Lochranza's air of serenity, the Highland atmosphere is accentuated by the presence of **Isle of Arran Distillery** ① *T01770-830264, www.arranwhisky.com, Mar-Oct daily 1000-1800, Sun 1100-1800, call for winter opening hours, informative 1 hr guided tours cost £4.50, concessions £3.50*. Opened in 1995, it's the island's first legal whisky distillery for over 170 years.

Walks on Arran → *OS map No 69 covers these walks.*

Arran is paradise for the outdoor enthusiast, offering a variety of forest, hilltop and coastal walks. There's even a 60-mile circuitous island route called the **Arran Coast Way** ① *www. coastalway.co.uk*. The north part of the island boasts ten peaks of over 2000 ft and several challenging ridge walks while the gentler south features less strenuous forest walks. Note all mountain routes should only be undertaken in good weather, whilst some – **A'Chir**, **Witches Step**, **Suidhe Fherghas** and **Cioch Na Oighe** – involve scrambling and can be very dangerous for the inexperienced and unprepared. In all cases, good OS maps (and ropes) are available from the TIC office in Brodick. Local advice must be sought before venturing onto the hills during the deer-stalking season (August to October).

The **Glenashdale Falls and Giants' Graves walk** is one of the most popular in south. It's a steady, easy climb through woodland with the considerable incentive of a beautiful waterfall at the end of it. Both walks can be done together and should take around two to three hours in total, though you should allow some time to enjoy the falls. If you want to take a picnic, pop into the village shop which has a wide range of deli-type foods and local cheeses. The trail starts by the bridge over **Glenashdale Burn**. There's a map board here showing the route. Walk up the track alongside the burn until you see the sign for the path leading to the left up to the **Giants' Graves**. It's about 40 to 45 minutes up to the graves and back to this point, but it's a stiff climb up a steep staircase of 265 steps. At the top continue left along a path through the trees, which then curves right until you reach a clearing and the graves, which are chambered tombs, believed to be around 5000 years old. Depending on the light, this can be a very eerie, but almost magical place. Return back down the steps, and head left along the main path as it climbs steadily above the burn, past smaller falls, until you reach the main falls. The setting is stunning and the falls are spectacular as they plummet 140 ft into the pools below. You can rest and have a picnic at the top of the falls, or follow the paths down to the pools below which you can swim. The path back down to **Whiting Bay** passes the scant remains of an Iron Age fort, then turns back uphill to reach a broad track. Turn right, cross a small burn by stepping stones, then follow the track downhill all the way to the main road, a short way along from the car park.

Arran's most popular peak, **Goatfell**, is also its highest, at 2866 ft. There's a path leading up from Corrie, but most people begin the walk from the car park at Cladach sawmill, near Brodick Castle. The path is well marked and, apart from the final section, relatively easy. It runs initially through the **Brodick Country Park**, then follows the Cnocan burn as it rises steadily through woodland before crossing the Mill burn. Beyond the burn is a deer fence above which the landscape changes to heather moorland and the path begins to climb the flanks of the mountain. The final 650 ft up to the top is steep and rocky though the path is clear even when undertaking a gentle scramble on loose scree. Hopefully, your climb will be rewarded with spectacular views down the Firth of Clyde, over Arran's ridges and westwards towards Islay and Jura. In total the walk should take about five hours. Despite the hordes of walkers, treat this ascent with the same caution and respect as on any Scottish mountain. Certainly, the adjacent ridges should only be attempted by experienced hill-goers. In all instances, you should be dressed and equipped appropriately and be prepared for any sudden change in the weather.

Many of the walks start from Glen Rosa Farm. One of these takes in the three Beinns; **Beinn Nuis**, **Beinn Tarsuinn** (2681 ft) and **Beinn A'Chliabhain**. Start at Glen Rosa Farm and go up the Wood Road to the High Deer Gate, then to Torr Breac and the 'Y' junction at the top of the Garbhalt and on to the path which runs round the Three Beinns. This is a full day's walk.

Another excellent walk is from Glen Rosa to the head of the Glen; then take the path up into the Coire Buidhe and on to the ridge between **Cir Mhor** (2617 ft) and **A'Chir** (known as the Ceems Ridge). Then follow the path around the west side of A'Chir. This is not easy to find, but takes you around the back of A'Chir to Bowman's Pass and the north end of Beinn Tarsuinn. From here take the path to Beinn A'Chliabhan and down to the foot of Garbhalt Ridge and back down to Glen Rosa.

Cir Mhor can also be climbed from Glen Rosa. Before going over into Glen Sannox take the steep path straight up. On the way back down, head into Coire Buidhe and back down the glen. You can also continue from the top of Cir Mhor and take the path around the west side of A'Chir to the north end of the Bowman's Pass up on to Beinn Tarsuinn and along the ridge to Beinn Nuis, then down the path to the Garbhalt Bridge.

Finally, in **Lochranza** there's an easy two-hour coastal walk from the youth hostel along the north shore of Lochranza Bay (Newton Shore) to the viewpoint at Kirn Point affording lovely views down the Kilbrannan Sound. A mile northwards, past the geological phenomenon known as Hutton's unconformity is the rustic cottage of 'Fairy Dell' above which a track briefly climbs and leads back to North Newton and past the creative croft at The Whins where artist Reg assembles and sells his delightfully quirky 'stone-men'.

There are also several walks in and around **Glen Sannox**. It's a pleasant walk just to make your way up the head of the Glen and return the same way. You can walk up the Glen to beyond the old mine then make your way up towards the Devil's Punchbowl until you reach the main path and follow that down into the Coire. Take the main path back down into Glen Sannox instead of trying to climb out of the Devil's Punchbowl. You can also walk from Glen Sannox to Glen Rosa, which takes around four hours.

◉ Isle of Arran listings

For Sleeping and Eating price codes and other relevant information, see Essentials pages 38-45.

◉ Sleeping

Brodick *p94*
L Kilmichael Country House Hotel, T01770-302219, www.kilmichael.com. Take the road towards the castle, turn left at the golf course and follow the signs. Enjoy refined elegance in the island's oldest house. Their restaurant is the best on the island. Booking is essential for non-residents. No children under 12.
L-A Auchrannie Country House Hotel, just beyond the turning to **Kilmichael**, T01770-302234, www.auchrannie.co.uk. Superb child-friendly facilities, and also has a 36-bedroom spa resort. Their Eighteen 69 (♥♥♥) is highly rated and **Brambles Bistro** serves bar meals. Self-catering available. Very popular.
D Belvedere Guest House, T01770-302397. Friendly guesthouse combining B&B with complimentary reiki or aromatherapy.

Camping
Glen Rosa, 2 miles from town on the road to Blackwaterfoot, T01770-302380, www.glenrosa.com. Open Apr-Oct. Fairly basic but beautifully situated campsite.

South Arran *p95*
C-F Holy Isle Peace Centre, T01770-601100, www.holyisland.org. Comfortable rooms and 3 vegetarian meals a day form part of relaxing experience on this Buddhist-run isle.
D Eden Lodge Hotel, Whiting Bay, T01770-700357, www.edenlodgehotel.co.uk. Friendly, with home-cooking and a beer garden.

North Arran *p96*
E Castlekirk, Lochranza, T01770-830202, www.castlekirk.co.uk. Pleasant B&B in a converted church with views of the castle.
F Lochranza SYHA, Lochranza, T08701-553255, T01770-830631. Open Feb-Oct. Friendly hostel with views over the bay.

Self-catering
Butt Lodge, T01770-302303, www.buttlodge.com. Secluded, luxury house with hinoki hot-tub. £1200-1700 per week.

Camping
Campsite next to the golf course near the **Arran Distillery**, Lochranza, T01770-820273, www.lochranzagolf.com. Open Apr-Oct.

◉ Eating

Brodick *p94*
♥♥♥-♥♥ **Creelers Seafood Restaurant**, at Home Farm, near the castle, T01770-302797,

www.creelers.co.uk. Excellent seafood, game and vegetarian dishes.
♯-♯ Café Rosaburn, by Heritage Museum, T01770-302636. Delicious, freshly made salads and home-cooking in a converted croft.

North Arran *p96*
♯ Catacol Bay Hotel, Catacol, T01770-830231, www.catacol.co.uk. Hearty meals 1200-2200, Sun buffet popular with the islanders.
♯ Isle of Arran Distillery, T01770-830264. Apr-Oct Mon-Sat 1000-1800, Sun 1100-1800, call for winter or evening opening hours. Locally sourced produce.

☉ Activities and tours

Brodick *p94*
Arran Adventure, T01770-302244, www.arranadventure.com. Hire a bike here from £6. Also offer sea kayaking, climbing, abseiling, archery and gorge walking.
Flying Fever, Strathwhillan Farm, Cottage 2, Strathwilan Rd, T01770-303899, T07717-712727 (mob), www.flyingfever.net. May-Oct. Quad-bike at Balmichael and paraglide. Offers a tandem flight as part of a Funday for £100.

North Arran *p96*
North Sannox Pony Trekking Centre, T01770-810222. Mon-Sat. £18 for a 1-hr trek.

☉ Transport

Brodick *p94*
Bus Bus to **Lochranza** connects with the **Claonaig ferry** or to **Brodick** for the ferry to **Ardossan**.
Car hire Arran Transport, at Brodick pier, T01770-302121. Car hire from £25.
Ferry The main ferry route is to **Ardrossan** from **Brodick**. CalMac ferry, 55-mins.
  The other route is to **Claonaig** from **Lochranza** in the north of the island. A non-bookable car/passenger ferry, 30 mins, for times, T0800-665000, www.calmac.co.uk.

☉ Directory

Brodick *p94*
Banks Brodick has banks with ATMs, but these are the only ones on the island.
Post Post office, opposite the pharmacy.

Mull and Iona

→ *Colour map 3, B3-4, C3-4.*

Whether bathed in sunshine or shrouded in mist, each of Scotland's isles possess a magical quality. The Isle of Mull, a 50-minute sail from Oban and the third largest of the Hebridean islands, is no different. Teeming with wildlife and a gateway to the tiny and spiritual isle of Iona, Mull (derived from the Norse meaning 'high, bold headland') supports 2800 inhabitants and remains one of Scotland's most popular Hebridean isles. Indeed, Mull, just 26 miles east to west and 24 miles north to south, has enough going for it to appeal to most tastes: spectacular mountain scenery, 300 miles of wild coastline, castles, a narrow-gauge railway, fine cuisine and, in Tobermory, one of Scotland's prettiest coastal villages that also served as the main setting for the cult children's TV series, Balamory. ▶▶ *For listings, see pages 109-113.*

Ins and outs

Getting there and around Mull is served by regular car/passenger ferry services, mostly from Oban but also from Kilchoan on the Ardnamurchan Peninsula and Lochaline on the Morvern Peninsula. Once on the island you can get to most places by bus. Services given in the Transport section are for April to October. Winter services are less frequent. There are regular five-minute sailings from Iona. ▶▶ *For further details, see Transport page 112.*

Tourist information The Craignure TIC ① *T01680-812377, open all year daily*, is opposite the pier in the same building as the CalMac office. Tobermory TIC ① *at the far end of Main St, T01688-302182, Apr-Sep*, is also in the same building as the CalMac office.

Mull → *For listings, see pages 109-113 Colour map 3, B3-4,C3-4.*

Ins and outs

For bus times, contact the operators listed under Transport, or ideally pick up the comprehensive *Mull Area Transport Guide* at the tourist offices in Oban, Tobermory or Craignure. This also includes ferry times.

Craignure to Tobermory

The arrival point for visitors is the village of Craignure. One and a half miles south of here is **Torosay Castle and Gardens** ① *T01680-812421, Apr to mid-Oct daily 1030-1700, £7, concession £6, children £4*, more of a baronial family home than a full-blown castle. The best way to arrive is by the **Mull and West Highland Railway** ① *T01680-812494, Easter to Oct 1100-1700, £5, children £3.50 return*, affectionately known as the Balamory Express.

A couple of miles east of Torosay is **Duart Castle** ① *T01680-812309, Apr Sun-Thu 100-1600, May to mid-Oct daily 1030-1730, £5.50, concessions £4.80, children £2.65*. The 13th-century ancestral seat of the Clan Maclean stands imperiously at the end of a promontory, commanding impressive views over Loch Linnhe and the Sound of Mull. Every five years (the next is in 2012) the castle and Mull hosts the Clan Maclean Gathering. The castle's main feature is the tower house, built in the late 14th century when it became the main residence of the Macleans of Duart. Today it's a fascinating place to visit, with many relics and artefacts on display.

Midway between Craignure and Tobermory, on the main A849, is the pretty village of **Salen**, where a fantastic culinary experience awaits at **Mediterranea** (see Eating, page 110). Salen, situated at the narrowest point on the island, has several sites of interest on its doorstep. Two miles south is Mull's tiny and only airfield, adjacent to which is the excellent **Glenforsa Hotel** (see Sleeping, page 109) where majestic views down the Sound of Mull can also be enjoyed. One mile north of Salen, overlooking the bay, is the ruin of **Aros Castle**, built in the 14th century and one of the strongholds of the Lords of the Isles. Tradition holds that the treasure of the Spanish galleon sunk in Tobermory Bay in 1588, was recovered by the Macleans and lies buried beneath Aros Castle.

Four miles southwest of Salen, near Gruline and Loch Ba, is the **MacQuarrie Mausoleum**, which houses the remains of Major-General Lachlan MacQuarrie (1761-1824). He took over as Governer-General of New South Wales from the unpopular William Bligh, formerly of the *Bounty*, and became known as the 'Father of Australia'. The mausoleum is maintained by the NTS, on behalf of the National Trust of Australia.

Tobermory

There is surely no prettier port in the west of Scotland than Tobermory, Mull's main village and setting for most of the popular children's TV series *Balamory*. Followers of the now-defunct series should ask for the Balamory leaflet at the TIC office, which highlights the key filming locations. Tobermory got its name from a small settlement once situated northwest of the current village where there's a spring known in Gaelic as Tobar (well) Mhoire (Mary). The brightly painted houses that line Tobermory's harbour front date from the late 18th

Mull

century when the British Fisheries Society built Tobermory as a planned herring port. During the Second World War, as a naval training base Tobermory was euphemistically called HMS Western Isles. Nowadays, only a few fishing boats, but dozens of yachts, bob at anchor in the protected waters of the natural harbour. Lying at the bottom of the harbour is a galleon of the Spanish Armada, which sank in mysterious circumstances, along with its treasure of gold doubloons, see box opposite. Remnants of a Spanish galleon can be

Tobermory

Isle of Mull Landrover Wildlife Expeditions

An Tobar Arts Centre

Back Brae

Ruarigan Terr

Jubilee Terr

Victoria St

Church Brae

Dervaig Rd

Albert St

Argyll Terr

Post Office Brae

Mull Museum

Hebridean Whale & Dolphin Trust

Island Bakery & Deli

CalMac Ferry Terminal

Breadalbane St

West St

Tobermory Chocolate Company

Prison Brae

Harbour

Tobermory River

Tobermory Distillery

To Aros Park ▼

Mull Pottery

To Standing Stones

N

To Salen & Craignure

To Isle of Mull Cheese & Dervaig

Sleeping	Eating	Schmooze 4
Lonan B&B 1	Café Fish 1	
Tobermory SYHA 2	MacGochan's 2	
Western Isles 3	Mishnish Hotel 3	

seen on Main Street in the wonderful **Mull Museum** ① *T01688-301100, Easter-Oct Mon-Fri 1000-1600, £2*, housed in an old bakery. Raining or not, it's worth visiting to gleen an insight of the island's history.

The harbour front (Main Street) is where you'll find most of what you want: the tourist office, tours, hotels, guesthouses, restaurants, pubs and the award-winning baker. Mercifully, though, it's free from the tartan tat that blights so many other tourist hot-spots. At the foot of the main road down to the harbour is the tiny **Tobermory Distillery** ① *T01688-302645, www.burnstewartdistillers.com, Mon-Fri 1000-1700, £3, concessions £1, children free*, which offers a guided tour rounded off with a sampling of the island's single malt. At the top of Back Brae, on Argyll Terrace, is **An Tobar** ① *T01688-302211, www.antobar.co.uk, Mon-Sat 1000-1600, Sun 1400-1700, free*, an excellent arts centre housed in the old school and featuring a varied programme of exhibitions, music and workshops. Or you can just have a coffee and cake by the fire and admire the view.

West coast Mull

Mull's west coast is where you'll find some of the island's most stunning scenery. The B8073 winds its way anti-clockwise from Tobermory in a series of twists and turns as it follows the contours of the coastline. The road climbs west from Tobermory then makes a dramatic descent, with hairpin bends, to Dervaig.

Dervaig is a lovely village of whitewashed cottages, beautifully situated at the head of Loch Cuin. Here sits **Kilmore Church**, with its unusual pencil-shaped spire. Until its closure in 2006, Dervaig was also the home of the smallest professional theatre in Britain. A fundraising campaign is helping to establish a new theatre south of Tobermory for the famous **Mull Touring Theatre Company** ① *T01688-302673*. One mile beyond Dervaig take the turn-off to Torloisk to reach Glen Bellart and the highly informative **Old Byre Heritage Centre** ① *T01688-400229, Easter-Oct Wed-Sun 1030-1830, £4, concessions £3, children £2*. In addition to a new geology exhibition there are dozens of exhibits and several films (including one for toddlers) that highlight the history of Mull through the ages and its varied wildlife. Ask about the location of the nearby Neolithic standing stones. The tea rooms delicious home-baking is an additional treat, see Eating, page 110.

Five miles west of Dervaig is **Calgary Bay**, Mull's most beautiful beach ringed by steep wooded slopes with views across to Coll and Tiree. Calgary in Alberta, Canada, was named after the former township. Many emigrants were forcibly shipped to Canada from here during the Clearances. There are some wonderful paths through Calgary Wood, just past **Calgary Farmhouse Hotel**, including a half-hour circular walk.

Isle of Ulva

If you have the time and need to escape the hectic bustle of Mull, then take a day out on idyllic Ulva (meaning 'wolf island' in Norse), just off the west coast. You won't see any wolves around, but you're almost guaranteed to spot deer, golden eagles, buzzards and seals offshore. There are several woodland and coastal trails across the island, including one to the southwest where there are basalt columns similar to those on Staffa. Alternatively, you can follow the trail to the top of the hill for views across to the Cuillins on Skye (on a clear day), or else cross the causeway to Ulva's even smaller neighbour **Gometra**. For more information on the island walks and on its history, visit the **Boathouse Heritage Centre** ① *A restored thatched croft house close to the ferry slip, T01688-500241, Easter-Oct Mon-Fri 0900-1700 and Sun Jun-Aug only, £5, children £2, entry is included in the ferry fare (see Transport, page 112)*. There's also a tea room where you can try the local oysters with

Guinness. Note that there are no camping facilities on Ulva, but ask the ferryman for advice on possible places to wild camp.

Staffa

The tiny uninhabited island of Staffa, 5 miles off the west coast of Mull, is one of the most spectacular sights not just in Scotland but anywhere in the world. It consists of immense hexagonal, basalt pillars, which loom up out of the sea like a giant pipe organ. Staffa was formed 60 million years ago by the slow cooling of Tertiary basalt lavas. These have been carved by the pounding sea into huge cathedral-like caverns such as the mightily impressive **Fingal's Cave**. The sound of the sea crashing against the black crystalline columns made such an impression on Felix Mendelssohn in 1829 that he immortalized the island in his *Hebrides Overture*. The composer was obviously aware of its original name in Gaelic, which means 'The Melodious Cave'. You can land on the island – if the weather is good enough – and walk into the cave via the causeway; an experience not be missed. But even if the seas are too rough, it's worth making the 90-minute boat trip just to witness the columns and cave.

South Mull

From Ulva Ferry the B8073 heads east along the north shore of **Loch na Keal** then enters a wide flat valley, where the road forks east to Salen and west along the south shore of Loch na Keal. This part of Mull is dominated by **Ben More** (3170 ft), the island's highest mountain. All around is a spectacular region of high jutting mountains and deep glens, extending west to the **Ardmeanach Peninsula**. The peninsula may look impenetrable, but with the proper walking gear can be explored on foot. On the north coast, about a mile from the road, is the massive entrance to **MacKinnon's Cave**, which runs for about 100 yds back under the cliffs. Make sure to visit only at low tide. The area around the headland, now owned by the National Trust for Scotland, is known as **The Wilderness**. Near the headland is **MacCulloch's Tree**, a fossilized tree 40 ft high and thought to be 50 million years old, which was discovered in 1819. The tree is only accessible by a 7-mile footpath which begins at Burg Farm. You should have a map of the area and also time your arrival with low tide.

Mull's southernmost peninsula stretches west for 20 miles from the head of Loch Scridain as far as Iona. Most visitors use it merely as a route to Iona but there are a couple of interesting little detours along the way. A twisting side road leads south from Pennyghael over the hills and down to **Carsaig Bay**, from where you can head east or west along the shore for some dramatic coastal scenery. Two roads lead south from Bunessan. One leads to **Scoor**, near where is a great beach at Kilveockan. The other road splits near the coast: the left branch leads to **Uisken Bay**; the right-hand branch leads to **Ardlanish Bay**, each with a good beach.

The road ends at **Fionnphort**, the departure point for the small passenger-only ferry to Iona, just a mile across the Sound of Iona. The village is little more than a car park, a row of houses, a pub and a shop, but there are several inexpensive B&Bs for those arriving too late to make the crossing. Even if you're not staying, it's worth stopping off in the village to visit the **Columba Centre** ⓘ *Apr-Sep daily 1100-1700, free*, where interpretive displays tell the story of St Columba.

A road runs south from Fionnphort to **Knockvologan**, opposite **Erraid Island**, which is accessible at low tide. The island has literary connections, for it was here that Robert Louis Stevenson is believed to have written *Kidnapped*. **Balfour Bay** on the south of the island is named after the novel's hero who was shipwrecked here.

Things to do on Mull when it's wet

It rains a lot on Mull, but luckily there's a fairly large number of indoor options to keep you nice and dry until the weather changes. If you've just arrived off the ferry from Oban and it's chucking it down, then head straight for **Torosay Castle** (page 100), just to the south of Craignure. And if the weather changes whilst exploring the interior, don't miss the gardens. Just beyond the castle is **Wings Over Mull**, a bird of prey conservation centre, which offers indoor hawk-handling and a chance to learn about the island's incredible bird life. Nearby is Mull's greatest fortification, **Duart Castle** (page 100), which is also worth a peek.

If all that history gets too much then you could do worse than hole up in the bar of the **Craignure Inn** (page 109) and relax in front of the roaring log fire.

In the north of the island, the most appealing option by far is the **Old Byre Heritage Centre** (page 110), not far from the picturesque village of Dervaig. When in Tobermory do as the locals do, and get yourself down to the **The Mish** bar, see Eating and Entertainment page 110, though you shouldn't really need the excuse of inclement weather. Meanwhile, over in Fionnphort, the departure point for the pilgrimage to Iona, you can seek a wee dram in the cosy **Keel Row Bar**.

Walks on Mull → *OS Landranger maps 47, 48 and 49 cover the entire island.*

Mull presents numerous walking opportunities, ranging from gentle forest trails to wild and dramatic coastal routes, or even a spot of Munro-bagging for the more intrepid. With the exception of the Cuillins on Skye, Mull's highest peak, **Ben More** (3170 ft) is the only Munro not on the mainland.

The trail starts at a lay-by on the B8035, at Dishig, and is fairly clear, though it can be tricky near the top. Return the same way, or more experienced climbers could continue down the narrow ridge to the eastern summit, **A'Chioch**, then descend the eastern face to the road that skirts **Loch Ba**. The views from the top are magnificent, across the other Hebridean islands and even as far as Ireland. If it's a cloudy day, it's worth postponing the ascent until there's clear weather. Allow around six hours for the round trip.

There are a couple of excellent coastal walks which start out from Carsaig Bay. A good path heads west along the shore to **Carsaig Arches** at Malcom's Point. The path runs below the cliffs out to the headland and then around it, and after about a mile reaches **Nun's Cave**, a wide and shallow cave where the nuns of Iona took refuge after being expelled during the Reformation. The path continues for another mile or so, but becomes a bit exposed in places and traverses a steep slope above a sheer drop into the sea. The famous arches are columnar basalts worn into fantastic shapes. One is a free-standing rock stack and another is a huge cave with two entrances. You'll need to allow about four hours in total plus some time at the arches.

Heading east from Carsaig Bay is a spectacular 4½-mile walk to **Lochbuie**, past **Adnunan stack**. It starts out through woodland, then follows the shore below the steep cliffs, with waterfalls plunging straight into the sea. It's easy at first but then gets very muddy in places and there's quite a bit of wading through boggy marsh, so make sure you've got good walking boots. Allow about five to six hours in total.

A shorter walk takes you to the Bronze Age Lochbuie Stone Circle at the foot of **Ben Buie**. Leave your car at the stone bridge before you reach the village. Look for the green sign on the gate to your left and follow the white marker stones across the field. The stone circle is hidden behind a wall of rhododendrons, so follow the marker stones across the plank bridge until you see it. It takes about 30 minutes.

There are several marked trails through Forestry Commission land on Mull. The first walk is to **Aros Park**, on the south side of Tobermory Bay. Start out from the car park near the distillery in Tobermory and follow the shoreline for about a mile to Lochan a'Ghurrabain, which is good for trout fishing. From here there is also a marked path around the loch (1 mile). A longer walk is to **Ardmore Bay**, 3 miles north of Tobermory. The trail/cycle path starts at the car park by the road that runs northwest from Tobermory. From here, it runs out almost to Ardmore point and back again, passing a couple of ruined villages on the way. There's a good chance of seeing seals and sea birds in Ardmore Bay. The trail is 4 miles in total.

Four miles north of Craignure is the car park and picnic site at **Garmony Point**, where a 2-mile trail leads to the ferry terminal at **Fishnish**, hugging the shore all the way. Another trail (4 miles) runs out to Fishnish Point and back through the forest to the car park.

Iona → *For listings, see pages 109-113. Colour map 3, C3. Phone code 01681. Population 130.*

Iona is a small island – barely 3 miles long and a little over a mile wide – but its importance to Christianity is out of all proportion to its size. Iona's place in religious history was guaranteed when St Columba arrived in the land of the Gaels with his 12 disciples and founded a monastery there in AD 563. The Irish monk then set about converting a large part of pagan Scotland (for the head-hunting Picts to the north and east followed the teachings of Druids) and much of northern England. Iona went on to become the most sacred religious site in Europe and has been a place of pilgrimage for several centuries. Today that pilgrimage has turned into more of an invasion, with day-trippers making the five-minute ferry trip from Mull to visit the abbey. Few, however, venture beyond the main village, **Baile Mór**, and it's easy to find a quiet spot, particularly on the west coast with its sparkling silver beaches washed by turquoise sea. It's worth spending a day or two here to soak up the island's unique spiritual peace so well conveyed in the words of Dr Johnson: "that man is little to be envied whose … piety would not grow warmer among the ruins of Iona".

Background

Iona is known as the 'Cradle of Christianity in Scotland', and was once a centre of the arts. The monks produced elaborate carvings, manuscripts, ornate gravestones and Celtic crosses. Their greatest work was the beautiful *Book of Kells*, which dates from AD 800, and which is now on display in Dublin's Trinity College. This proved to be the high point of the church's history. Shortly after came the first of the Viking raids, in AD 806, when many monks were slaughtered at Martyrs' Bay, followed by another in AD 986 which destroyed the work of many years. The relentless pressure from the established church ended with the suppression of the Celtic Church by King David in 1144.

In 1203 Iona became part of the mainstream church with the establishment of a nunnery for the Order of the Black Nuns, as well as a Benedictine Abbey by Reginald of the MacDonalds of the Isles. Iona became overshadowed by the royal city of Dunfermline, and its final demise came with the Reformation when buildings were demolished and all but three of the 360 carved crosses destroyed.

The abbey lay in ruins until, in 1899, the island's owner, the eighth Duke of Argyll, donated the buildings to the Church of Scotland on condition that the abbey church was restored for worship. Then, in 1938, the Reverend George Macleod founded the Iona

Community as an evangelical Church of Scotland 'brotherhood', with the abbey buildings as its headquarters, and by 1965 had succeeded in rebuilding the remainder of the monastic buildings. Now the abbey complex has been completely restored and the island of Iona, apart from the abbey buildings, is owned by the National Trust for Scotland.

The abbey

ⓘ *Apr-Sep daily 0930-1730; Oct-Mar 0930-1630. £5.50, concessions £4.50, children £3.30.*

The present abbey dates from around 1200, though it has been rebuilt over the centuries and was completely restored in the 20th century. The oldest part is the restored **St Oran's Chapel**, to the south of the abbey on the right, which is plain and unadorned save for its splendid 11th-century Norman doorway. You get a good view of the whole complex from

Iona

Eilean Chalbha

Dun I (300ft)

Bishop's Walk Farm

MacDougal's Cross

Iona Abbey

St Oran's Chapel

Eilean nam Ban

▲ Dun Bhuirg

Iona Heritage Centre

Cnoc Mor ▲

Maclean's Cross

Nunnery

Baile Mór

To Fionnphort, Mull

Bay at the Back of the Ocean

Sound of Iona

St Columba's Bay

N

Sleeping 🛏
Argyll **1**   Iona Hostel **2**

500 metres
500 yards

The story of St Columba

St Columba (Colum Cille in Gaelic), a prince of Ireland and grandson of the Irish King, Niall of the Nine Hostages, came to Scotland not as a missionary, but as an act of self-imposed penance for his actions. He stubbornly refused to hand over his copy of the Gospels, illegally copied from St Finian's original, which led to a bitter dispute with the king. This ended in a pitched battle in which Columba's supporters prevailed, but he was so overcome with remorse at the bloodshed he had caused that he fled Ireland, finally settling on Iona as it was the first place he found from where he couldn't see his homeland. Columba, however, was not retiring into obscurity.

His missionary zeal drove him to begin building the abbey. He banished women and cows from the island, declaring that "where there is a cow there is a woman, and where there is a woman there is mischief". Workers at the abbey had to leave their womenfolk on nearby Eilean nam Ban (Women's Island). Not content with that, he also banished frogs and snakes from Iona, though there are plenty on Mull. He is even said to have pacified the Loch Ness Monster during a visit to Inverness. He went on to found the Celtic Church, or the Church of the Culdees, with centres throughout Scotland, which differed in many ways from the Church of Rome.

the top of the small grassy knoll opposite the abbey entrance. It is said that Columba was prevented from completing the building of the original chapel until a living person had been buried in the foundations. His friend Oran volunteered and was duly buried. Columba later asked for the face to be uncovered so that he could bid a final farewell to his friend, but Oran was found to be alive and claimed he had seen Heaven and Hell, describing them in such blasphemous terms that Columba ordered he be covered up immediately!

Surrounding the chapel is the **Reilig Odhrain**, the sacred burial ground, which is said to contain the graves of 48 Scottish kings, including Macbeth's victim, Duncan, as well as four Irish and eight Norwegian kings. The stones you see today are not the graves of kings but of various important people from around the West Highlands and Islands, including that of John Smith, leader of the British Labour Party from 1992 until his death in 1994.

Beside the Road of the Dead, which leads from the abbey church to St Oran's Chapel, stands the eighth-century **St Martin's Cross**. This is the finest of Iona's Celtic high crosses and is remarkably complete, with the Pictish serpent-and-boss decoration on one side and holy figures on the other. Standing in front of the abbey entrance is a replica of **St John's Cross**, the other great eighth-century monument. The restored original is in the Infirmary Museum, at the rear of the abbey, along with a fine collection of medieval gravestones.

No part of St Columba's original buildings survives, but to the left of the main entrance is **St Columba's Shrine**, the small, steep-roofed chamber which almost certainly marks the site of the saint's tomb. This is **Torr an Aba**, where Columba's cell is said to have been. The abbey itself has been carefully restored to its original beautiful simplicity and inside, in a side chapel, are marble effigies of the eighth Duke of Argyll and his third wife, Duchess Ina.

Baile Mór

The passenger ferry from Fionnphort on Mull lands at Baile Mór, Iona's main village, which is little more than a row of cottages facing the sea. There are over a dozen places to stay but, as demand far exceeds supply during the busy summer season, it's best to book in advance at one of the tourist offices on Mull or in Oban. There's also a post office, a very good craft shop and general store in the village. Just outside the village, on the way to the abbey, are the ruins of the **Augustinian nunnery**. Just to the north, housed in the parish church manse, built by Thomas Telford, is the **Iona Heritage Centre** ① *T01681-700576 Apr-Oct Mon-Sat 1030-1630, £2.20*, which features displays on the island's social history. Nearby stands the intricately carved 15th-century **Maclean's Cross**.

Around the island
On the west coast are some lovely beaches of white sand and colourful pebbles. The best of the lot is the **Bay at the Back of the Ocean**, beside the golf course, and only a 1½-mile walk from the ferry. This was one of John Smith's favourite places and it's easy to see why. At the southern tip of the island is another sandy beach at **St Columba's Bay**, believed to be the spot where the saint first landed. Another good walk is to the top of **Dun I**, the only real hill, which rises to a height of 300 ft. To get there, continue on the road north from the abbey, past MacDougal's Cross, then go through a gate to the right of Bishop's Walk Farm and follow the fence up to where you join a footpath up to the top. It's only about half an hour up and down and there are great views from the top of the entire island and the coastline of Mull.

◉ Mull and Iona listings

For Sleeping and Eating price codes and other relevant information, see Essentials pages 38-45.

● Sleeping

Craignure to Tobermory *p100*
C-D Glenforsa Hotel, 2 miles south of Salen, T01680-300377. Open Easter-Oct. Delightful hotel run by friendly hotelier and aviator above whose reception hangs a propeller off a WWI aircraft. 27 tasteful, wood furnished rooms, beautiful views down the Sound of Mull and a lovely restaurant serving wild salmon, Mull oysters (🍴), and real ales.
E-F Arle Lodge, Aros, T01680-300299, www.arlelodge.co.uk. Friendly, independent hostel that offers continental breakfast as part of the deal.
D-E Craignure Inn, Craignure, T01680-812305, www.craignure-inn.co.uk. This 18th-century inn, complete with an interior of rough hewn stone walls, wooden floor and open fire has an atmospheric cosy bar serving real ales and food that includes Hebridean lamb(🍴-🍴). Shortlisted for Pubof the Year in 2008. Has 3 rooms available.

F Glenaros Lodge, Salen, T01680-300301, www.glenaroslodge.net. 18 bed hostel close to public transport between Craignure and Tobermory.

Camping
Balmeanach Park, Fishnish, T/F01680-300342. Well-equipped, child-friendly caravan and campsite.

Tobermory *p101, map p102*
B-C Western Isles Hotel, T01688-302012. Open all year. Owners Esplin Chapman and Richard Nealon are proud this grand, sand- stone hotel with commanding views over Tobermory harbour is no longer part of a chain. Step inside and it's clear the pair are on a mission to transform this 23 room, Victorian era hotel back to its former glory. The Master Seaview rooms are worth the additional pounds for the breathtaking view but whatever room you choose, expect great food and a warm welcome.
F Lonan B&B, off Western Rd, T01688-302082. Open Easter-Oct. Welcoming, small B&B with lovely garden, terrific breakfasts and only 5 mins' walk from Main St.

F Tobermory SYHA, Main St, T01668-302481. Terrific harbour-front location. Always busy so book ahead.

West coast Mull p103
D Druimard Country House Hotel, Dervaig, T01688-400491, www.druimard.co.uk. Open end Mar-Oct. 6 tastefully furnished rooms with views to Glen Bellart. Good breakfast and can arrange wildlife and island tours.
F Dervaig Bunkhouse, 6 miles from Tobermory, in tiny Dervaig, T01688-400249. A terrific budget option.

South Mull p104
C-D Pennyghael Hotel, in Pennyghael, overlooking the loch, T01681-704288, www.pennyghaelhotel.com. Serving locally farmed meats and seafood in the restaurant and a 4-course set dinner (♥♥♥-♥♥). 2 self- catering cottages in the grounds from £375 per week.

Iona p106, map p107
B-D Argyll Hotel, T01681-700334, www.argyllhoteliona.co.uk. Open Apr-Oct. This remains the better of the island's 2 upmarket hotels with 17 rooms, a good restaurant and tours organized.
E-F Iona Hostel, T01681-700781, www.iona.hostel.co.uk. A fabulous hostel with views to the Treshnish Islands. 25-min walk north from the village and ferry. It's best to book ahead in summer. A wee gem of a hostel that also promises the best duck eggs this side of heaven.

🍴 Eating

Craignure to Tobermory p100
♥♥♥-♥♥ Mediterranea, Salen, T01680-300200, www.mull-cuisine.co.uk. Open daily Tue-Sun and Fri, Sat 1830-2100, Sun 1100-1500 in the Winter. An island gem serving Sicilian classics. Beyond the bright yellow door awaits mouth-watering seafood and pasta creations, delightful staff and a cosy ambience. Book ahead.

Tobermory p101, map p102
The best value fish and chips are sold nightly by the mobile vendor at the harbour front.
♥♥♥-♥ Western Isles Hotel, see Sleeping, above. Tasty menu with local seafood and game on the finer dining room menu, or cheaper bar meals in the **Conservatory Bar**.
♥♥ The Café Fish, right on the pier above the TIC, T01688-301253, www.thecafefish.com. Open Mon-Sat. Choose the cosy interior or al fresco for dining on the freshest seafood, including squat lobster. A real delight.
♥♥ MacGochan's, T01688-302350, on the harbour front. Similar good pub grub and live music.
♥♥-♥ Mishnish Hotel, T01688-302009, Main St. Despite its makeover, 'the Mish' retains an element of charm and serves up hearty meals to accompany your real ale.
♥♥-♥ Shmooze Restaurant, Main St, T01688-302203. A recent addition to the seafront, diners will find a frequently changing menu of seafood staples and an emphasis on freshly cooked Scottish fare. Reasonable value.

West coast Mull p103
♥♥ Dovecote Restaurant, Calgary Hotel, by Dervaig, T01688-400256, www.calgary.co.uk. Open Mar-Nov. This is where to enjoy delicious fish and locally sourced meats in an informal atmosphere.
♥ Old Byre Heritage Centre, Dervaig, see Sights, page 103. Open Apr-end Oct. Simple, home-made delights offered all day. Not a huge menu but a worthwhile lunch stop.

🎭 Entertainment

Mull p100, map p101
Mishnish Hotel, see Eating, above. Despite the 'themed' old-world decor it wins over **MacGochan's** for its ambience. Both pubs run live music events and attract a healthy numbers of revellers.

There are also music events at **An Tobar**, see Sights, page 103.

⊛ Festivals and events

Mull *p100, map p101*

Apr **Mull Music Festival**, known as the **Whisky Olympics**, for details T01688-302383. Held on the last weekend of the month, it is a great time to be on Mull. You can enjoy a feast of Gaelic folk music and, of course, whisky. The focus of the festival is the bar of the **Mishnish Hotel**, Tobermory.

Jul **Mendelssohn on Mull Music Festival**, held over 10 days in early Jul, is another great festival. It commemorates the famous composer's visit here in 1829. **Tobermory Highland Games**, is held annually on the 3rd Thu of the month.

Sep **Mull and Iona Food Festival**. This mid-Sep festival showcases the wealth of outstanding produce cultivated on the island.

Oct **Tour of Mull Rally**, held in early Oct for over 30 years. This should not be missed by rally enthusiasts, though book early as the island becomes extremely busy.

○ Shopping

Mull *p100, map p101*

From the local butcher and baker to the chocolate-maker, Tobermory is foodie-heaven. It's also where to pick up fishing tackle, camping and bike spares.

A Brown and Son Ironmonger, Main St, Tobermory, T01688-302020. First opened in 1897, this shop is now under new ownership but rest assured it has everything. In addition to trout-fishing permits, this is where to stock up on everything from camping gas to tent pegs. They'll even change your watch battery.

Island Bakery and deli, Main St, T01688-302223. Try their award-winning organic lemon melts, oat crumbles and chocolate gingers with huge pieces of stem ginger.

Isle of Mull Cheese, on the edge of town, 500 yds off the Dervaig Rd, at Sgriob-Ruadh Farm, T01688-302235. Open Apr-Sep Mon-Fri 1000-1600. Here you can savour their

award-winning, traditionally made cheese and admire their wonderful glass barn.

Mull Pottery, southern edge of Tobermory enroute to Salen, T01688-302347. Tasteful hand thrown pots in different shapes and sizes. Good café-bistro upstairs with views across Sound of Mull.

Tobermory Chocolate Company, Main St, T01688-302526. Open Mon-Sat 0930-1700, Sun 1000-1600. Here you can try out their speciality – chocolate made with the local whisky and delicious Staffa Cake.

○ Activities and tours

Mull *p100, map p101*
Boat trips

Alternative Boat Hire, Mark Jardine, Sailing Trips & Boat Hire, Lovedale Cottage, T01681-700537, www.boattripsiona.com. Trips around the coastline and handline fishing on a traditional wooden boat. You can hire by the hour or for an afternoon, May-Oct, from Fionnphort and Iona.

Silver Swift, Raraig House, Raeric Rd, Tobermory, T01688-302390, www. tobermoryboatcharters.co.uk. Boat charter and wildlife cruises, £40, not recommended to children under 12. Spend a day cruising from Tobermory, passing Ardna- murchan lighthouse and spotting basking sharks and seals as you head for the island of Rùm. Picnic on the island before heading back. Trips run from Apr-Oct, call for days.

Turus Mara, Penmore Mill, Dervaig, T0800-858786, www.turusmara.com. Birdwatching and wildlife trips to Staffa, Iona and the Treshnish Isles costing from £25 (from Mull) and £48 (from Oban). Chance to spot seals, puffins and visit the classic Fingal's Cave on Staffa. There's also a special day tour from Oban that includes visits to Ulva (Mull) and Staffa (£35).

Fishing
Sea Angling Trips, Tackle and Books, Main St, Tobermory, T01688-302336. Fish

for mackerel, pollock and dogfish aboard *Amidas*. Trips last approximately 3 hrs and include equipment. £25, children £15. Min 6 people. The shop also sells trout fishing permits (from £5) for inland lochs. Ask the shop for its small leaflet with destinations. Also well stocked with walking maps and equipment.

Wildlife tours

You can find out about the sea-life around Mull by visiting the **Hebridean Whale and Dolphin Trust**, 28 Main St, Tobermory, T01688-302620, www.hwdt.org, Apr-Oct daily 1000-1700, Nov-Mar Mon-Fri 1100-1600. This charity aims to protect the marine environment through education.

Acclaimed wildlife documentaries have further fuelled demand for wildlife tours on the island. Visit www.wildisles.co.uk, for a list of operators.

Island Encounter Wildlife Safaris, Salen, T01680-300441, www.mullwildlife.co.uk. A full-day wildlife safari with local guide Richard Atkinson costs £37, including lunch. You'll see golden eagles, white-tailed sea eagles, hen harriers, divers, merlins, peregrine falcons, seals and porpoises, to name but a few.

Isle of Mull Landrover Wildlife Expeditions, Ulva Ferry, T01688-500121, www.scotland wildlife.com. David Woodhouse runs these excellent day-long tours with lunch £42.50, children £39.50, and the chance to spot golden eagles, otters, seals and porpoise.

Sea Life Surveys, Ledaig, Tobermory, beside McGochan's pub, T01688-302916, www.sealifesurveys.com. Everything from whale, dolphin and shark-watching trips to gentle 'Ecocruz's' (£15) in sheltered waters to Full day Whale watch explorer (£60) can be booked with this operator.

⊖ Transport

Craignure to Tobermory *p100*

Bus There are daily buses from **Craignure**, which coincide with ferry arrivals.

The **Craignure** to **Tobermory** via **Salen** service runs 6 times a day Mon-Fri, 4 times on Sat and 4 times on Sun, Bowman's Coaches, T01680-812313. There's a Bowmans bus from **Craignure** to **Fionnphort** (for Iona) 4 times a day Mon-Fri, 3 times on Sat and 1 on Sun.

Car Tobermory is a 30- to 40-min drive (2-hr cycle) north from the ferry pier at Craignure.

Cycle hire On Yer Bike, Salen, T01680-300501. Daily rental £9, weekly £35. Also has a shop by the ferry terminal in Craignure, T01680-812580.

Ferry To **Oban** from **Craignure**, 5-7 times daily Mon-Sat and 5 times on Sun, 45 mins, £4.90 one way per passenger, £43.50 per car, 5-day return £8.25 and £59, CalMac Oban, T01631-566688, CalMac Craignure, T01680-812343. To **Lochaline** on the Morvern Peninsula (see page 240) from **Fishnish**, Mon-Sat every 45 mins, 9 times on Sun, 15 mins, £2.90 per passenger, £12.80 per car. There are also ferries to **Kilchoan** on the Ardnamurchan Peninsula (see page 241) from **Tobermory**, 7 times daily Mon-Sat and 5 times daily on Sun (May-Aug).

Tobermory *p101, map p102*

Bus There's a bus from **Tobermory** post office to **Dervaig** and **Calgary**, 4 times a day Mon-Fri and twice on Sat, RN Carmichael, T01688-302220.

Cycle hire A Brown and Son Ironmonger, Main St, T01688-302020, bike hire for £15 per day; Tobermory SYHA, Main St, T0870-004 1151.

West coast Mull *p103*

Ferry A small bicycle/passenger-only ferry, makes the 2-min crossing on demand from **Ulva Ferry**, all year for Mon-Fri sailings 0900-1700, Sun sailings Jun-Aug only. From Easter-Sep show signal at the pier to cross.

Oct-Easter best to call the ferryman on T01688-400352, or T01688-500241. Note there's no bus to Ulva Ferry. Either cycle or take the bus to **Salen** and jump on a pre-booked bike, see Cycle hire, above.

South Mull *p104*
Ferry To **Iona**, a passenger-only ferry leaves from **Fionnphort** on Mull frequently Mon-Sat 0815-1815, and Sun hourly 0845-

1800, 5 mins, £4.50 return, bicycles free. In summer, **G MacCormick** runs a late (2000) ferry crossing, T01681-700362.

ⓘ Directory

Mull *p100, map p101*
Banks Clydesdale Bank, Main St, Tobermory, is Mull's only permanent bank. There's also a mobile bank which tours the island.

Coll, Tiree and Colonsay

Just 13 miles long and 4 miles wide, the trickle of visitors who come to explore low-lying, windswept Coll step onto one of the best-kept secrets in Scotland. Here, on lands where the likes of the mysterious Na Sgeulachan standing stone has stood for over 3000 years, tourism remains almost invisible, the 150 islanders enjoying a natural playground where families can picnic on deserted pearl-white beaches with views towards Mull and the Inner Hebrides. Idyllic neighbouring Tiree or Tir-lodh (land of corn) also boasts stunning beaches caressed by the waters of the Gulf Stream. Statistically one of the sunniest and windiest locations in the UK, Tiree's billiard-flat hinterland teems with rare birdlife and excited wildlife enthusiasts, whilst offshore, windsurfers, surfers and kitesurfers play in towering waves that since the 1980s have earned Tiree the nickname of 'mini-Hawaii' – in 2007 it even hosted a round of the PBA Windsurfing World Cup. Little wonder Tiree now offers a healthy numbers of B&Bs! Colonsay too is remote, tranquil and undemanding; an island brimming with wildlife, flowers and even a miniature mountain range. Like Tiree, Colonsay has also steadily embraced tourism and in particular self-catering accommodation. It may not be the easiest island to reach but clearly its magic has already been discovered. ▸▸ *For listings, see pages 116-117.*

Coll → *For listings, see pages 116-117. Colour map 3, B3. Phone code 01879. www.visitcoll.co.uk.*

The best of Coll's 23 beaches are on the west coast, at **Killunaig**, **Hogh Bay** and **Feall Bay**. The latter is separated from the nearby **Crossapol Bay** by giant sand dunes managed by the RSPB, the islands largest landowner, to protect the resident corncrake population. The **CalMac** ferry from Oban calls in at Coll's only village, **Arinagour**, where half of the island's population live and where you'll find the post office (and bike hire opposite), petrol station, general store, and cosy **Island Café**. There's no public transport but a taxi is available. If it's not too windy, it's best to explore by bike. It's worth taking a walk up **Ben Hogh** (341 ft), the island's highest point, overlooking Hogh Bay on the west coast, to get a terrific view of the island. Tired of beaches? Try some fishing or the nine-hole golf course at Cliad 2 miles west of Arinagour.

Tiree → *For listings, see pages 116-117. Colour map 3, B2.*

Ins and outs → *Phone code 01879.*
Getting there and around   CalMac car and passenger ferries sail to the island from Oban, via Coll once daily. The **ferry port** ① *T01879-220337*, is at Scarinish. From 0700-1800 (Monday to Saturday) the whole island is covered by a **Ring n' Ride service** ① *T01879-220419*, a bus/taxi service which operates standard fares and is ideal for exploring the island. Pick-up a copy of the *Area Transport Guide to Tiree and Coll* from Oban TIC (see page 67). Tiree **airport** ① *T01879-220309*, where the flight from Glasgow arrives, is at The Reef.

Sights
Tiree is a low, flat island, only about 11 miles long and 6 miles across at its widest, and is also known by the nickname 'Tir fo Thuinn', or 'Land below the waves'. It is one of the best places to surf in the British Isles. When seen from a distance most of it disappears below the horizon, save its two highest hills, **Ben Hynish** (462 ft) and **Beinn Hough** (390 ft), on the west coast. Though flat, remember that Tiree's fierce winds can make cycling hard

work. Campervans laden with surf-gear are a reminder that this is a windsurfing paradise and each October Tiree hosts the week-long **Tiree Wave Classic**. Scores of world-class windsurfers come to compete and party, putting accommodation at a premium.

The ferry port is at **Scarinish**, at the western edge of the sweep of **Gott Bay**. The main village of Scarinish is also where to find the Co-op supermarket, the post office and the bank, there's also a garage at the pier head. About 4 miles from Scarinish, past the delicious locally sourced shellfish and meats served for dinner at the excellent **Elephants End restaurant** above Gott Bay(see Eating, page 117), is Vaul Bay, where aside from golf, there are the well-preserved remains of **Dun Mor**, a Pictish Broch built around the first century AD and standing on a rocky outcrop to the west of the bay.

The island's main road runs northwest from Scarinish, past the beautiful beach at **Balephetrish Bay** to **Balevullin**, where you can see some good examples of restored traditional thatched houses. Just to the south, at Sandaig, is the **Sandaig Museum** ① *open all year around, but the summer exhibition is open Jul-Sep, Tue and Sat afternoon*, a thatched croft inside which displays tell of the island's social history.

In the southwestern corner of the island is the spectacular headland of **Ceann a'Mara**, or Kenavara. The massive cliffs are home to thousands of sea birds. East from here, across the golden sands of **Balephuil Bay**, is the island's highest hill, Ben Hynish, topped by a radar-tracking station resembling a giant golf ball. It's worth the climb to the top for the magnificent views over the island and to the distant Outer Hebrides. Below Ben Hynish, to the east, is the village of **Hynish**, where you'll find the **Signal Tower Museum**, which tells the story of the building of the **Skerryvore Lighthouse** (1840-1844) by Alan Stevenson, an uncle of Robert Louis Stevenson. This incredible feat of engineering was carried out from Hynish, where a dry dock/reservoir was built for shipping materials by boat to the Skerryvore reef, 11 miles to the southwest.

Colonsay → *For listings, see pages 116-117. Colour map 3, C3.*

Ins and outs → *Phone code 01951.*
Getting there and around There are ferry sailings from Oban arriving at Scalasaig on the east coast. From Kennacraig and Port Askaig there is one sailing a week on Wednesday. Ferries need to be booked well in advance during the summer months. For those on the island without their own transport, there's a limited bus and postbus service around the island from Monday to Saturday. ▸ *For further information, see Transport, page 117.*

Sights
Colonsay's population of around 120 lives in the three small villages, the largest of which is **Scalasaig**, the ferry port. A few miles north of the ferry, in the middle of the island, is **Colonsay House**, dating from 1772. It was sold, along with the rest of the island, in 1904 to Lord Strathcona, who had made his fortune in Canada with the Hudson Bay Company and went on to found the Canadian Pacific Railway. The house is not open to the public but the lovely **gardens** ① *Wed and Fri 1200-1700, £2, children £1*, and woods, full of rhododendrons, giant palms and exotic shrubs, are worth a stroll. There's also the chance to buy home-baking and a cup of coffee near the house.

There are several standing stones, the best of which are **Fingal's Limpet Hammers**, at Kilchattan, southwest of Colonsay House. There are also Iron Age forts, such as **Dun Eibhinn**, next to the hotel in Scalasaig. Colonsay is also home to a wide variety of wildlife and over 190 species of birds have apparently been recorded. You can see choughs, one of Britain's rarest birds, as well as corncrakes, buzzards, falcons, merlins and perhaps even the odd golden eagle or sea eagle. There are also otters, seals and wild goats (said to be descended from the survivors of the Spanish Armada ships wrecked in 1588). The jewel in the island's crown, though, lies 6 miles north of Scalasaig, past Colonsay House, at **Kiloran Bay**. The beach here is described as the finest in the Hebrides. Just a glimpse of this magnificent half mile of golden sands, backed by tiers of grassy dunes, with massive breakers rolling in off the Atlantic, is worth the two-hour ferry crossing alone.

Just off the southern tip of Colonsay is the island of **Oronsay**, 2 miles square with a population of six, and one of the highlights of a visit to Colonsay. The name derives from the Norse for 'ebb-tide island', which is a fitting description as Oronsay can be reached on foot at low tide, across the mud flats known as 'The Strand'. It takes about an hour to walk from the south end of Colonsay to the ruins of a 14th-century **Augustinian Priory**. This was home of some of the most highly skilled medieval craftsmen in the Western Highlands. A surviving example of their work is the impressive Oronsay Cross and the beautifully carved tombstones, on display in the **Prior's House**. Make sure you take wellies for the walk across the Strand and check on the tides. Tide tables are available at the hotel or shop. Spring tides (new and full moon) allow about three to four hours to walk across and back, which is just enough time to see the priory but little else. An alternative is to time one way to coincide with the postbus.

◉ Coll, Tiree and Colonsay listings

For Sleeping and Eating price codes and other relevant information, see Essentials pages 38-45.

● Sleeping

Coll *p114*
B-D Coll Hotel, Arinagour, T01879-230334. A comfortable, 6-bedroom family hotel overlooking the village and serving very good food (ΨΨ-Ψ).
D Caolas House, T01879-230438. A friendly, cosy farmhouse B&B south of Arinagour, by the beach, with terrific home-cooking. Both also available for let.

Tiree *p114*
D Glebe House, Scarinish, T01879-220758. Comfortable accommodation with sea views across Gott Bay. Also dinner if requested.
D-E Scarinish Hotel, Scarinish, T01879-220308. Located right by the old harbour, this modest hotel has fabulous views across the bay from its dining area where the simply served local beef, lamb and shellfish (ΨΨ-Ψ) will tickle your tastebuds.

F Mill House Hostel, Cornaigmore, T01879-220435. Fantastic bunkhouse accommodation close to Loch Bhasapol. Bike hire available.

Colonsay *p115*
Accommodation on Colonsay is limited and must be booked well in advance. Even self-catering options are hard to come by, because the same families return year after year. For details on 20 self-catering options see **Colonsay Cottages**, T01951-200312, www.colonsay.org.uk/estate.
B-C Isle of Colonsay Hotel, a few 100 yds from the ferry, T01951-200316. A cosy 18th-century inn with 9 rooms, a friendly bar, open fire and excellent food. They also arrange island tours.
D-E The Hannahs, 4 Uragaig, T01950-200150. 3 rooms. Cosy and friendly, with renowned home-cooking including a breakfast that will 'blow your socks off'. Also offer ferry pick-up.
F Colonsay Keeper's Lodge, 2 km from the ferry, T01951-200312, www.colonsay.org.uk. Open all year. A comfortable backpackers'

hostel, which sleeps 16. Phone for a lift from the ferry.

🍴 Eating

Coll p114
♥♥-♥ Island Café, Arinagour, T01879-230262. Licensed and great for daytime snacks, coffee and soups. Its Sun lunch is popular, including a roast, shortbread, cheese and oatcakes (from £12.50). Whilst adults dine or laze on the sofas enjoying the sea view, there are toys, books and even table football for the kids.

Tiree p114
♥♥ Elephants End, above Gott Bay, T01879-220694. Serves excellent lunches and dinners in a snug restaurant (BYO).
♥♥ The Glassary Restaurant, Sandaig T01879-220684. Mon-Sat 1700-2100. Delicious dinners and Sun lunch.
♥ An Talla Café and Gift Shop, Crossapol, T07801-435599. Mon-Sat 1030-1600. Coffees, home-baking and light lunches.
♥ The Cobbled Cow, by the airport. Terrific home-baking, good for a snack.

⛰ Activities and tours

Tiree p114
Atlantic Trekking, Jane Isaacson, T01879-220881. Pony trekking.
Skipinnish Tours, Skipinnish, Ruaig, www.skipinnish-sea-tours.co.uk, T01879-220009. From £15-40 per person for trips (Apr-Oct) that include shark and whale spotting and trips to Staffa, Lunga and out to Skerryvore Lighhouse (4 hrs).
Tiree Sand Yachts, 16 Crossapol, T01879-220317. Sand yachting.
Wild Diamond Watersports, Burnside Cottage, Cornaig, T07712-159205, www.surfschoolscotland.co.uk. Offers surfing, windsurfing, kitesurfing and kayaking equipment hire and courses.

Colonsay p115
For wildlife, archaeological and sightseeing tours of the island by bus or on foot, call T01951-200320. On Wed there's also the chance to do a whistle-stop tour of the island before the ferry departs for Kennacraig, from £10.00, children £5, www.colonsay.org.uk.

🚌 Transport

Coll p114
Cycle hire An Acarsaid, Arinagour, T01879-220421. Hires bicycles.
Ferry CalMac, car/passenger ferries leave for **Oban**, daily Fri-Wed, 2 hrs 40 mins, £17.30 return per passenger, £89 per car. The ferry from **Coll** to **Tiree**, 50 mins, costs £5.50 return per passenger, £26.40 per car.
Taxi Barritts, T01879-230402. Taxi service.

Tiree p114
Air Tiree has an airport with 1 flight daily Mon-Sat, all year round to **Glasgow**, 45 mins.
Cycle hire Millhouse Hostel, Cornaigmore, T01879-220435. Hires bikes.
Ferry CalMac car/passenger ferries sail to **Oban**, via **Coll** once daily, 3 hrs 50 mins, see above under Coll for prices.
Taxi John Kennedy Taxis, T01879-220419. Shared and private taxi hire.

Colonsay p115
Cycle hire As the island is only 8 miles long by 3 miles wide, you might consider hiring a bicycle. Bike hire from **A McConnel**, T01951-200355.
Ferry There are ferry sailings to **Oban**, once daily Mon, Wed, Thu, Fri and Sun, 2 hrs, £22.80 per passenger for 5-day return, £114 per car. To **Kennacraig**, 1 sailing on Wed, 3 hrs 35 mins. To **Port Askaig**, 1 sailing on a Wed, 1 hr 15 mins, £5.10 one way per passenger, £26 per car. Ferries need to be booked well in advance during the summer months (Apr-Sep).

Islay and Jura

Islay (prono`unced eye-la), the most southerly of the Hebridean islands and one of the most populous, with around 4000 inhabitants, enjoys a rich farming and crofting heritage but it has one particular claim to fame – single malt whisky. Aside from whisky, people also come here to watch birds. The island is something of an ornithologists' wonderland, and from October to April plays host to migrating barnacle and white-fronted geese flying down from Greenland in their thousands for the winter. The short ferry crossing from Islay takes you to Jura, a primeval and uncompromising place; a lost world, pervaded by an almost haunting silence. The words 'wild' and 'remote' tend to get overused in describing the many Hebridean islands, but in the case of Jura they are, if anything, an understatement. Jura has one road, one hotel, six sporting estates and 5000 red deer, which outnumber the 117 people by 25:1, the human population having been cleared to turn the island into a huge deer forest. Rather appropriately, the name Jura derives from the Norse 'dyr-ey', meaning deer island. Yes, Jura is beautiful – but arguably at a price. For whilst it may be heaven for the landed gentry who control the vast estates, the distinct lack of development ensures affordable housing for the locals remains beyond the grasp of many. ▸▸ *For listings, see pages 124-126.*

Islay → *For listings, see pages 124-126. Colour map 5, A1. Phone code 01496.*

In addition to innumerable tea shops, Islay offers the unique opportunity to visit several of Scotland's most impressive distilleries in one day. The island has eight working distilleries in total (see box, page 123) and their distinctive peaty malts are considered to be among the finest. At the end of May each year, the island hosts the **Islay Malt and Music Festival** for which the distillers produce their special edition malts (see Festivals and events, page 125).

Ins and outs

Getting there and around The airport is at Glenegedale, a few miles north of Port Ellen on the road to Bowmore. The ferry from Kennacraig to Port Ellen sails twice daily on Mondays, Tuesdays, Thursdays, Fridays and Saturdays and once on Wednesdays and Sundays. A ferry also sails from Kennacraig to Port Askaig once daily on Monday, Wednesday and Friday. The ferry from Oban to Port Askaig sails on Wednesdays. For those without their own transport, there's a regular bus service around Islay, with **Islay Coaches** ⓘ *T01496-840273*. There are buses from Portnahaven to Port Ellen, via Port Charlotte, Bridgend, Bowmore and the airport; from Port Askaig to Port Ellen via Ballygrant, Bridgend, Bowmore and the airport; from Port Ellen to Ardbeg, Bowmore, Port Askaig and Portnahaven; and also a postbus to Bunnabahain. Buses run regularly from Monday to Saturday, but only once on Sunday. ▸▸ *For further information, see Transport, page 126.*

Tourist information Islay's TIC ⓘ *Bowmore, T01496-810254, Apr-Sep Mon-Sat 1000-1700, Sun 1400-1700, Oct-Mar Mon-Fri 1000-1600,* will find accommodation for you. Islay can be reached by air from Glasgow (for details, see page 66).

Port Ellen and around

Port Ellen is the largest place on Islay and the main ferry port, yet it still has the feel of a sleepy village. There are many day trips from Port Ellen. A road runs east out to **Ardtalla**, where it ends. Along the way, it passes three distilleries, first **Laphroaig**, then **Lagavulin** and lastly **Ardbeg**, all of which offer guided tours, see page 123. Between the Lagavulin and Ardbeg distilleries is the dramatically sited 16th-century ruin of **Dunyvaig Castle**, once the main naval base and fortress of the Lords of the Isles. Five miles further on is the impressive **Kildalton Cross**, standing in the graveyard of the ruined 13th-century chapel. The eighth-century cross is well preserved and is one of Scotland's most important Early Christian monuments, and the carvings depict biblical scenes.

Southwest of Port Ellen a road runs out to a small, rounded peninsula known as **The Oa**, an area of varied beauty, both wild and pastoral, and with a wonderful coastline. The road runs as far as **Upper Killeyan**, from where it's about a mile uphill to the spectacular headland at the **Mull of Oa**. Here you'll see the strange-looking **American monument**. The obelisk commemorates the shipwrecks offshore of two US ships, the *Tuscania* and the *Ontranto*, both of which sank in 1918 at the end of the First World War. There's a great walk north from the Mull of Oa up to Kintra, but it's best to start out from Kintra.

A turn-off from the road to The Oa leads north to **Kintra**, at the south end of The Big Strand at Laggan Bay, with 5 miles of sands and dunes. There's a restaurant and accommodation here, and it's a great place for camping. The restaurant is at the end of the road, with the beach on one side and, on the other, a wild and spectacular coastal walk incorporating caves and the impressive **Soldier's Rock** sea-stack. Ask at the TIC for the *Explore Islay* walking trail leaflet. Just to the north of Kintra is the **Machrie golf course**, a golfing experience not to be missed.

Bowmore and the Rinns of Islay

The A846 runs north from Port Ellen, straight as a pool cue, to Bowmore, the island's administrative capital and second largest village. Founded in 1768 by the Campbells, it retains a sleepy air. The village is laid out in a grid plan with the main street running straight up the hill from the pier to the unusual round church, designed to ward off evil spirits, who can hide only in corners. Thankfully, the good spirit stayed behind and can be found at the **Bowmore Distillery**, just to the west of Main Street. This is the oldest of the island's distilleries, founded in 1779.

North of Bowmore, **Bridgend**, is the site of the tiny **Islay Ales Brewery**. Here too the A846 joins the A847 which runs west to the hammerhead peninsula known as the **Rinns of Islay** (*rinns* is derived from the Gaelic for promontory). A few miles west of Bridgend the B8017 turns north to the **RSPB Reserve** at **Loch Gruinart**. The mudflats and fields at the head of the loch provide winter grazing for huge flocks of barnacle and white-fronted geese from Greenland, arriving in late October. There's an excellent RSPB visitor centre at **Aoradh** (pronounced *oorig*), which houses an observation point with telescopes and CCTV, and there's a hide across the road. There are about 110 species of bird breeding on Islay, including the rare chough and corncrake.

The coastal scenery around the Rinns is very impressive, particularly at **Killinallan Point**, a beautiful and lonely headland at the far northeast of Loch Gruinart. Also impressive is **Ardnave Point**, west of Loch Gruinart, and further west along the north coast, **Sanaigmore**. The best beaches are at **Saligo** and **Machir Bay** on the west coast, past Loch Gorm. Both are lovely, wide, golden beaches backed by high dunes but swimming is ill-advised due to dangerous undercurrents. Less than a mile behind Machir Bay you'll also find **Kilchoman Distillery and Visitor Centre** ① *T01496-850011, Mon-Fri Nov-Mar, Apr-Oct Mon-Sat 1000-1700, tours 1100 and 1500*, the isle's newest working distiller of the water of life. If you fancy a canter along the sands, this is also where to find the **Rockside Farm Trekking Centre** ① *T01496 850231*.

Islay & Jura

To Oban

Kiloran Bay

Colonsay House

Kilchattan

Colonsay

Scalasaig

Oronsay

Priory

Shian Bay

Loch
Tarbert

Killinallan
Point

Ardnave
Point

*Glen
Batrick*

Beinn Bhre
(1441ft)

Bunnahabhain

Beinn an Òir
(2571ft)

Loch
a'Chnuic Bhric

Killinallan

Paps of Jura

Corran

Sanaigmore

Loch
Gruinart

Beinn a'
Chaolais (2408ft)

Caol Ila

RSPB
Reserve

Visitor Centre

Feolin
Ferry

Gleann Astaile

Glas Bhein
(1841ft)

Saligo Bay

Aoradh
Visitor
Centre

Loch Finlaggan

Port
Askaig

*Gleann
Uillish*

Jura
Brat Bheinn
(1122ft)

Craighou

Loch
Gorm

B8018

Ballygrant

Sound of Islay

Jura Hous

Kilchoman

Kilchoman

Bruichladdich

Bridgend

Loch
Ballygrant

A846

Machir Bay

Bowmore

Port
Charlotte

Bowmore

Beinn
Bheigier
(1612ft)

Rinns of Islay

A847

Laggan

A846

Islay

Ardtalla

Portnahaven

*Laggan
Bay*

B8106

Port
Wemyss

The Big Strand

Glenegedale

Machrie Golf Course

Kildalton Cross

Kintra

Lagavulin

Ardbeg

The Oa

Laphroaig

N

Upper
Killeyan

Laphroaig

Dunyvaig

Port
Ellen

American Monument

*Loch
Kinnabus*

Mull of Oa

5 km
5 miles

Luing

Cruach Scarba
(1474ft) ▲

Scarba

Whirlpool
Gulf of
Corryvreckan

Kinuachdrach

Glengarrisdale Bay

Kinuachdrach
Harbour

Barnhill

Glendebadel Bay

Ben Garrisdale
▲ (1198ft)

Corpach
Bay

Beinn Bhreac
▲ (1533ft)

Ardlussa

Rainberg Mór
(1487ft)

To Tayvallich

Jura

Inverlussa

Keillmore

Lagg
Loch
Lesgamaill

Danna
Island

Beinn
Shiantaidh
▲ (2476ft)

Kilmory

Low Landman's Bay

Point of Knap

Leargybreack

Loch Caolisport

Sound of Jura

Kilberry

Ardpatrick Point

To Kennacraig

Gigha

Sound of Gigha

Ardminish

Tayinloan

Cara Island

Killean

KINTYRE

Port Charlotte is without doubt the most charming of Islay's villages, with rows of well-kept, whitewashed cottages stretched along the wide bay. Here, below the comfortable youth hostel is the **Islay Natural History Trust** ① *T01496-850288, Easter-Oct, Mon-Fri 1000-1600, Jun-Aug Mon-Sat 1000-1600, £3.00, concessions £2.00, children £1.50. All tickets are valid for a week.* It's a must for anyone interested in flora and fauna, with good displays on geology and natural history, a video room and reference library. Housed 300 yds away in a former Free Church, the compact **Museum of Islay Life** ① *T01496-850358, Easter-Oct open every day 1000-1630, £3, concessions £2, children £1*, is especially worth a visit with photographs and over 1600 exhibits, including an illicit still found on the island, highlighting the rich past and culture of the native Ileach's (*ee-lach's*). Close-by there's bike hire, whilst just south of the village you'll find the pleasant **Port Mor Campsite** and **Bon Appetit Café** (T01496-850441). At the southern end of the Rinns, 7 miles south of Port Charlotte, is the picturesque fishing and crofting village of Portnahaven, its Hebridean cottages rising steeply above the deeply indented harbour and where the cosy **An Tigh Seinsse bar** by the harbour serves delicious meals including Queen Scallops and mains of Islay beef.

Port Askaig and around

Port Askaig is Islay's other ferry port, with connections to the mainland and to the islands of Jura and Colonsay. It's little more than a dock, a car park and a pub huddled at the foot of a steep, wooded hillside. A short walk north along the coast is the **Caol Ila distillery**, and a couple of miles further north, at the end of the road which branches left before you enter Port Askaig, is the beautifully situated **Bunnahabhain Distillery**.

The A846 runs east from Bridgend out to Port Askaig passing through **Ballygrant**, just to the south of **Loch Finlaggan**. Here, on two *crannogs* (artificial islands), were the headquarters of the Lords of the Isles, the ancestors of Clan Donald. The MacDonalds ruled from Islay for nearly 350 years, over a vast area covering all of the islands off the west coast and almost the whole of the western seaboard from Cape Wrath to the Mull of Kintyre. To the northeast of the loch, there's the **Finlaggan Centre** ① *T01496-810629, Apr-Sep Mon-Sat 1030-1630, Sun 1300-1630, £3, concessions £2, children £1*, which was recently expanded to accommodate more objects from the ancient site. You can walk across the fen to **Eilean Mor**, where you'll find a medieval chapel and several ornately carved gravestones. On neighbouring, **Eilean na Comhairle** (The Council of the Isle) the Lords of the Isles decided policy.

Jura → *For listings, see pages 98-126. Colour map 5, A1-2.*

Ins and outs → *Phone code 01496.*

Getting there and around A small car and passenger ferry makes the regular five-minute crossing daily to Port Askaig on Islay. For times, contact **Argyll & Bute Council** ① *T01496-840681*. There's also a handy passenger-only ferry between Tayvallich and Craighouse that runs from June to the end of September. There is a bus service on Jura, which runs from Feolin Ferry to Craighouse several times a day, Monday to Saturday. A few buses continue to Lagg and Inverlussa and return to Craighouse. Note that some journeys are by request only and must be booked the day before. Contact **Alex Dunnichie** ① *T01496-820314*. Alternatively, hire a bike. ▸▸ *For further information, see Transport, page 126.*

Sights

Three things bring people to sparsely populated Jura, where in early August locals and visitors participate in the open water rowing competitions of the grandly titled Jura Regatta. First there's the scenery. This is one of the last, true wildernesses in the British Isles and perfect for some real off-the-beaten-track walking. The appealingly named **Paps of Jura**, are three breast-shaped peaks that dominate not only the island itself but also the view for miles around. From Kintyre, Mull, Coll and Tiree, and from the mountains of mainland Scotland from Skye to Arran, they can be seen on the horizon. The Paps provide some tough hillwalking and require good navigational skills, or a guide. It takes a good eight hours to cover all three peaks, though during the Paps of Jura fell race they are covered in just three hours. A good place to start is by the three-arch bridge over the Corran River, north of Leargybreack. The first pap you reach is **Beinn a'Chaolais** (2408 ft), next is the highest, **Beinn an Oír** (2571 ft) and the third is **Beinn Shiantaidh** (2476 ft). To find out about guides, ask at **Jura Stores** (T01496-820231) in Craighouse that has provided much needed provisions since the 1890s.

Next there's wildlife. Aside from the thousands of red deer, there are sea eagles and golden eagles in the skies above and the surrounding seas are full of seals, dolphins and porpoises, with the elusive otter making an occasional appearance. And finally, there's whisky. The island's only road leads from the ferry to the only village, Craighouse, 8 miles away on the southeast coast. Here you'll find the **Jura distillery** ① *T01496-820240, www.isleofjura.com, open all year, tours by appointment, free*, which produces 1½ million litres annually and offers a snifter of the stuff at the end of a friendly and informative tour.

Another of the island's draws is the **Corryvreckan whirlpool** at the very northern tip, between Jura and the uninhabited island of **Scarba**. The notorious whirlpool, the second largest in the world, is in fact a tidal race that creates an action like a gigantic washing machine. It is seen at its awesome best during spring tides, especially with a westerly gale,

Islay's malts distilled

Ardbeg, T01496-302244, www.ardbeg. com, hourly tours Sep-May Mon-Fri 1000-1600, Jun-Aug daily 1000-1700, £3. Describes itself as the peatiest malt whisky in the world. This may be a robust and powerful malt but in 1981 all operations were sadly mothballed. In 1997 it was bought by Glenmorangie and reopened to ensure the malt first distilled in 1815 continued to flow from within the white-washed walls on Islay's eastern shoreline.

Bowmore, T01496-558 9011, www. bowmore.com, mid-Sep to Easter Mon-Fri 0900-1700, Sat 0900-1200, tours Mon-Fri 1000, 1100, 1400, 1500, Sat 1000, £4, concessions £2. Bowmore is the oldest distillery on Islay. Its flagship is the 12 year-old single malt. The Craftsman's Tour (£22) is highly recommended and offers the chance to savour many a single malt during an informative tour behind the scenes. Established in 1779, It has visitor centre with additional information on the history of the distillery and also rents luxuriously appointed former workers cottages just yards from the shore and distillery. Call for details.

Bruichladdich, T01496-850190, www. bruichladdich.com, Mon-Fri 0900-1700, Sat 1000-1600, 45-min tours Oct-Easter Mon-Fri 1130 and 1430, Sat 1130, Easter-Sep additional tour 1030. Mon-Fri 1030, 1130, 1430, Sat 1030 and 1430 only, £5 including dram. Produces a range of innovative malts including Mood Malts, Multi-Vintage and Single Vintage. Claims to produce different Bruichladdich's by drawing upon its maturing stocks that date back to 1964 (pronounced 'brook-laddie').

Bunnahabhain, T01496-840646, www. bunnahabhain.co.uk, Easter-Oct Mon-Fri, tours 1030, 1400, 1515, winter tours by appointment only, you are strongly advised to call ahead to double check all tour times and distillery opening hours. Started in 1881 (and pronounced 'bun-a-havan'), this is known as the 'gentle giant' of Islay because it's the least peaty of the Islay malts. The distiller produces a 12, 18 and 25 year-old malt and also a 34 year-old malt.

Caol Ila, T01496-302760, www.discovering-distilleries.com, Apr-Oct Mon-Fri 0915-1600, tours 0930, 1045, 1345, 1500, £5. Pronounced 'coal-eela', this distillery was founded in 1846 and lies close to Port Askaig, with great views across the Sound of Islay to Jura. Unlike most of its island peers, this single malt is best before dinner.

Kilchoman, Rockside Farm, Bruichladdich, T01496-850011, www.kilchomandistillery. com, visitor centre open Apr-Oct Mon-Sat 1000-1700, Nov-Mar Mon-Fri 1000-1700. Islay's newest distillery (established 2005) will release its first single malt in 2009. It already produces almost 100,000 litres of alcohol per year. Kilchoman claims to be one of only half-a-dozen distilleries in Scotland that carries out traditional floor maltings. All its barley is grown in the fields next door.

Lagavulin, T01496-302730, www. discovering-distilleries.com/lagavulin, tours Mon-Fri by appointment only at 1000, 1130, 1430, £5. Their 16-year-old single malt is one of the classics and also makes the ideal after-dinner tipple. A very interesting tour.

Laphroaig, T01496-302418, www. laphroaig.com, tours all year by appointment only 1015 and 1415, free. The closest to Port Ellen, and its wonderful setting is summed up by its name, meaning 'The beautiful hollow by the broad bay' in Gaelic. According to many this is the ultimate in malt whisky and is at its best after dinner. This distillery has a reputation for one of the best whisky tours on Islay.

when this most treacherous stretch of water creates oar falls of 25 ft and the terrible roar can be heard for up to 10 miles away. A two-hour tidal difference between the sound on the east and the Atlantic flood tides combine with the gulf of Corryvreckan's steep sides and underwater pinnacle, the Hag, to create the vortex. The Royal Navy officially says it's unsailable, but that doesn't stop several local boat tours actually going over the top of it. It is named after a Viking, Bhreacan, who anchored his boat here for three days and nights with a rope woven from the hair of virgins. Unsurprisingly, the rope parted under the strain, casting doubt on the status of one of the contributors, and Bhreacan drowned. To get there, follow the rough track from **Ardlussa** to **Kinuachdrach**, or get someone to drive you, then it's a 2-mile walk. Before setting out, ask at the hotel for information and directions.

In 1947, the Corryvreckan nearly claimed the life of one Eric Arthur Blair – aka George Orwell – who had come to Jura to finish the novel that would later become *Nineteen Eighty-Four*. Despite being diagnosed with TB, Orwell went to live on Jura with his three-year-old adopted son, Richard, in spartan conditions at **Barnhill**, a cottage in the middle of nowhere and 25 miles from the nearest doctor. That summer he invited his niece and nephew to stay, and one day took them out into the Corryvrekan in a tiny boat. When the outboard motor was ripped off by the force of the tide and the boat capsized, Orwell and the others only just escaped with their lives by clambering onto a small island; they were later rescued by a passing lobster boat. Today, Barnhill attracts literary pilgrims and, though closed to the public, can be rented for a week's stay (see Sleeping, below).

Also on the island, 3 miles south of Craighouse village, at Ardfin, is the beautiful **walled garden** ① *daily 0900-1700, £2.50*, at Jura House, which is filled with wild flowers and Australasian plants and trees. There's also a tea tent open in summer and plenty of good walks through the surrounding woods or down to the nearby beaches. See Sleeping, below, for details of self-catering accommodation in Jura House.

⦿ Islay and Jura listings

For Sleeping and Eating price codes and other relevant information, see Essentials pages 38-45.

● Sleeping

Islay *p118, map p120*

B Glenegedale, Port Ellen, T01496-300400, www.glenegedalehouse.com. 5 rooms. The owner of this guesthouse has every right to boast about her breakfasts – in 2006 at another island address she won the Best Breakfast in Britain Award. She's taken the same recipe for success to her new place, which offers a peat fire and the chance for guests to enjoy nature and distillery tours.
B-A Harbour Inn, Main St, Bowmore, just yards from the shore, T01496-810330, www. harbour-inn.com. 7 tastefully furnished en suite bedrooms, but the real treat is the

fabulous restaurant complete with cosy bar (see Eating, below).
B-A Kilmeny Country House, Ballygrant, 4 miles from Port Askaig, T01496-840668, www.kilmeny.co.uk. With wonderful views, this is a stylish rural option with 4 comfortable rooms and highly rated food (dinner £36). Serves locally caught shellfish and reared beef in a friendly atmosphere. Recommended.
B-C Port Charlotte Hotel, on the seafront, Port Charlotte, T01496-850360. 10 rooms. Restored Victorian inn with gardens and conservatory, serving good food (see Eating, below). One of the best around.
C Sornbank, Bridgend, T01496-810544, www.sornbank.co.uk. B&B close to amenities, with excellent breakfast. Lets 2 self-contained flats on a weekly or fortnightly basis.

F Port Charlotte Youth Hostel, Port Charlotte, T01496 850385. Open Apr-Oct. Highly recommended, this very comfortable, spacious hostel is close to the ales, malts and tasty meals served by the **Port Charlotte Hotel** and **Lochindaal Hotel**.

Self-catering
Coull Farm Cottage, Bruichladdich, T01496-850317. Sleeps 5 in a cosy cottage with panoramic views and excellent nearby walks. From £200 per week.
Drumlanrig, Carnduncan, Gruinart, T01496-850503. Sleeps 1-6 people in ~a well equipped and byre cottage and farmhouse cottage, located close to the renowned RSPB bird- spotting reserve and handy for the likes of beaches and pony trekking. From £250-550 per week.

Jura *p122, map p120*
B-C Jura Hotel, Craighouse, T01496-820243, www.jurahotel.co.uk. Open all year. 18 bedrooms. The island's one and only hotel, overlooking the Small Isles Bay. The hotel bar is the island's social hub, and hosts Steve and Fiona Walton, who have been here for 25 years, can provide information on walks as well as arranging tours to the Corryvreckan and fishing trips. The restaurant serves good food, see Eating, below. Great place to relax after a hike and enjoy banter with the locals. Gets very busy in summer. Camping is also possible in the hotel grounds.
C-D The Manse, Craighouse, T01496-820384. Friendly, 3-bedroom option in the village.
E-F Kinuachdrachd Farm and Bunkhouse, T07899-912116. Located to the north of the island. Friendly, comfortable B&B (sleeps 4) and bunkhouse (sleeps 6) run by Mike Richardson. Also offers wildlife tours.

Self-catering
Barnhill, contact Kate Johnson, T01786-850274. Sleeps 7. Very remote – 14 miles north of the nearest pub and shop. For more ascetic souls, and devotees of George Orwell. From £550 per week.
Jura House, contact Mirjam Cool in Craig-house, T01496-820315, mirjamcool@aol. com. Sleeps up to 15. At the top end of the comfort scale. £900-1400 per week.
Jura Lodge, T01496-820240, www.isleofjura. com. The most salubrious choice. Housed inside the distillery grounds, the refurbished lodge was reopened in 2006 and is available for private use at certain times of the year. It sleeps up to 8. They also run residential whisky appreciation courses. From £1500 for the week.

🍴 Eating

Islay *p118, map p120*
Ⅷ Harbour Inn, Main St, Bowmore, T01496-810330, www.harbour-inn.com. Serves outstanding seafood, in a stylish setting.
Ⅷ Kilmeny Country House, Ballygrant, 4 miles from Port Askaig, T01496-840668, www.kilmeny.co.uk. Serves locally caught shellfish and reared beef in a friendly atmosphere. Highly rated food, recommended.
Ⅷ-Ⅶ Port Charlotte Hotel, on the seafront, Port Charlotte, T01496-850360. Serves tasty, locally sourced dishes.
Ⅶ-Ⅵ Lochindaal Hotel, Port Charlotte T01496-850202 You'll find locally caught shellfish, including mussels and scallops on the menu, and beef or lamb sourced from Hebridean farms.

Jura *p122, map p120*
Ⅶ-Ⅵ Jura Hotel, see Sleeping, above. Currently the only option for either a bar meal or evening dining. Try the fresh langoustines or famed venison pie.

🎉 Festivals and events

Islay *p118, map p120*
May Islay Festival of Malt and Music, www.feisile.org. Annual Folk Music festival, for which the distillers produce their own special edition malts.

Sep Islay Jazz Festival, www.islayjazz festival.co.uk.

Jura *p122, map p120*
Aug Jura regatta

⊙ Activities and tours

Jura *p122*
Islay Birding, The Old Byre Main St, Port Charlotte, contact Jeremy Hastings, T01496-850010, www.islaybirding.co.uk. Discover the nature of Islay with Jeremy on his award winning dawn or dusk, £30; ½-day and £60 day wildlife safaris. Recommended.
Mike Richardson, T07899-912116. Guides hill walks and Orwell trails (Easter-Oct) from £30 per person (minimum charge of £75 if fewer than 3 people) and runs a landrover taxi service on Jura.

⊙ Transport

Islay *p118, map p120*
Cycle hire Mountain Bike Hire, 33 Main St, Port Charlotte, T01496-850488. Bike hire available for £10 per day.

Ferry CalMac offices in Kennacraig, T01880-730253, and Port Ellen, T01496-302209, £16.25 per passenger for 5-day return, £88 per car. **Kennacraig** from **Port Askaig,** once daily Mon, Wed, Fri. To **Oban** from Port Askaig, Wed, 4 hrs 15 mins, £13.75 per passsenger, £68 per car. To **Colonsay** from Port Askaig, Wed. Note that ships will sail to **Port Askaig** only during summer 2011 due to major construction work on Port Ellen pier.

Jura *122, map p120*
Cycle hire Jura Bike Hire, Keils, just beyond Craighouse, T07092-180747.
Ferry A small car and passenger ferry makes the regular 5-min crossing daily to **Port Askaig** on Islay, £2.50 return per passenger, £14 per car, **Feolin Ferry.** For times, **Argyll & Bute Council,** T01496-840681. There's also a handy passenger-only ferry between **Craighouse** to the mainland, **Tayvallich** (off B841), that runs Jun-Sep, £15 one-way with bus connections.

Contents

Footprint features

At a glance

⊖ **Getting around** Regular buses, and single-track roads in more remote areas for cycling and walking.
⟡ **Time required** A day trip from Glasgow or Edinburgh, but several days will enable you to include Loch Lomond, Speyside and Perthshire.
☼ **Weather** Snow on the higher peaks of Speyside in winter. May-Sep is the most settled time.
✖ **When not to go** Something to enjoy all year round, but if you're a skier don't come until Jan.

★ Don't miss ...
1 Fortingall, page 139
2 Glen Lyon, page 139
3 Duke's Pass, page 149
4 Drover's Inn, page 154
5 Boat of Garten, page 176

N

10 km
10 miles

The vast swathe of Central Highlands is not a distinct region but rather the sum of disparate parts of other regions, including Perthshire, the Trossachs, Angus Glens, Deeside, Don Valley, the Grampians, Speyside, Strathspey and Loch Lomond.

The historically important regions of Perthshire and Stirling straddle the Highland Boundary Fault, the dividing line between the heavily populated Central Lowlands and the wild and empty Highlands. Just across this 'border' is the Trossachs, a picture-postcard area of mountains, forests and lochs that stretches west from Callander to the eastern shore of Loch Lomond, and the glens of Perthshire, whose atmospheric lochs and mountains are rich in history.

The spectacular and varied landscape ranges from the gentle pleasures of Loch Tay to the rugged peaks of the Grampian Mountains, where there are Munros aplenty for the bagging and decent winter skiing. On the eastern shores of Loch Lomond is the West Highland Way, Scotland's most popular long-distance hike. In the northeast, in the Spey Valley, are the tasty staples of a Highland tourist diet – whisky and salmon – while, nearby, stand many of Scotland's most notable castles, one of which is the holiday home of the most famous family in the UK.

Perthshire

Perth, where the rural and urban intertwine, is the main gateway to the eastern side of the Highlands and the A9, the road north, is a gentle introduction to the wild northern reaches of Scotland. The Perthshire Highlands may lack the sheer magisterial grandeur of the northwest but they have their own serene beauty. Numerous remnants from the highland's troubled past are scattered around the glens of Perthshire, including Blair Castle and Scone Palace.
▶▶ *For listings, see pages 140-145.*

Ins and outs

Getting there
Perth is accessible from almost anywhere in the country. It's only 1½ hours from Edinburgh or Glasgow, and half an hour from Dundee by road, and is on the main train lines to these cities, as well as on the main lines north to Aberdeen and Inverness. ▶▶ *For further details, see Transport page 145.*

Getting around
Though the more remote northerly parts of Perthshire are difficult to reach by public transport, much of the region is easily accessible. The main road north to Inverness, the A9, runs through the heart of the region. Dunkeld and Pitlochry are on the Perth–Inverness rail line and there are several daily trains to Perth. **Stagecoach Strathtay** ⓘ *T0871-200 2233*, run hourly buses (less frequently on Sunday) from Perth to Blairgowrie and Glenshee on the A93.

Tourist information
The region, from Kinross in the south to Blair Atholl in the north and from Glenshee in the east to Rannoch Moor in the west, is covered by **VisitScotland Perthshire** ⓘ *www. perthshire.co.uk*, with tourist offices in Aberfeldy, Blairgowrie, Crieff, Dunkeld, Kinross, Perth and Pitlochry.

Perth and around → *For listings, see pages 140-145. Colour map 4, C3. Phone code 01738.*

'The Fair City' of Perth is aptly named. Situated on the banks of Scotland's longest river, the Tay, Perth and its surrounding area boasts some of the most beautiful scenery in the country. A pleasant, compact town with a popular **farmers market** ⓘ *www.perth farmersmarket.co.uk*, on the first Saturday of every month, Perth was once the capital of Scotland. Awash with traditional traders like Kerrigan's Tobacconists where you'll find old world sweeties, and 'scone shops' of which Scottish comedian Billy Connolly would be proud, there are several notable sights to visit, from the ultra-modern, £20 million Concert Hall that stands on the site of a 17th century horse market, to the fascinating jewel in Perth's crown, Scone Palace. For nearly 500 years Scone was the home of the Stone of Destiny and the site where every Scottish king was crowned. It's pleasant to stroll by the river, whilst the city is well placed for outdoor activities such as walking, fishing and cycling.

Ins and outs
Getting around The train and bus stations are almost opposite each other at the west end of town, where Leonard Street meets Kings Place. The town centre is compact and

easy to get around on foot, but Scone Palace and many B&Bs are on the eastern bank of the river, so you may wish to take a bus. Local buses are run by **Stagecoach** ① *T01738-629339*. To reach Scone Palace take the No 3 Strathtay bus service from outside Mountain Supplies on South Street. This service runs every hour on the hour.

Perth

Sleeping ⬤	Salutation **4** *C3*	Delicious Cafe **3** *C2*	Bars & clubs 🍸
Achnacarry Guest	Sunbank House **5** *C3*	Greyfriars Pub **4** *C3*	Sportsters **9** *C2*
House **1** *A2*		Kerachers **5** *C2*	That Bar **10** *C2*
Kinnaird Guest	**Eating** 🍴	No 63 **6** *C3*	
House **2** *D3*	Bothy **1** *C2*	Old Ship Inn **7** *C2*	
Ramada **3** *C2*	Dean's @ Let's Eat **2** *C2*	Redrooms **8** *C2*	

Tourist information For tourist information, go to the Perth **TIC** ① *Lower City Mills, West Mill St, T01738-450600; Apr-Jun, Sep and Oct Mon-Fri 0900-1700, Sat 1000-1600, Sun 1100-1600; Jul -Aug Mon-Sat 0900-1830, Sun 1100-1700; Nov-Mar Mon-Sat 0900-1600.*

Sights

North of the High Street, on North Port, is the **Fair Maid's House** (closed to the public) the fictional home of Sir Walter Scott's virginal heroine in his novel, *The Fair Maid of Perth*. Close by, at the corner of Charlotte Street and George Street, is the **Museum and Art Gallery** ① *T01738-632488, Sep-May Mon-Sat 1000-1700, Jun-Aug Mon-Sat 1000-1700, Sun 1300-1630, free*, with over 500,000 exhibits including displays on local history, art, archaeology, natural history and whisky.

In the 18th century the world-famous Black Watch regiment was raised in Perth, and the **Black Watch Museum** ① *Hay St, T01738 638152, Apr-Oct Mon-Sat 0930-1700, Nov-Mar Mon-Sat 0930-17000, £4, concessions £3, children £2*, housed in the 15th-century Balhousie Castle, is well worth a visit even to the most un-military minded. The museum is on the edge of the North Inch, to the north of the town centre. It's also worth perusing the work of the renowned Scottish colourist, John Duncan Fergusson, within the **Fergusson Gallery** ① *T01738-4755000, Mon-Sat 1000-1700, free* in Perth's historic Round House.

For those with more horticultural leanings, **Branklyn Garden** ① *116 Dundee Rd, T0844-493 2193 (NTS), Apr-Oct daily 1000-1700, £6, concessions £5*, has been described as "the finest two acres of private garden in the country". Started in 1922 and with an impressive collection of rare and unusual plants, it includes superb examples of Himalayan poppies. Well worth a visit at any time of year, many of the plants grown there are on sale in the shop.

Kinnoull Hill Woodland Park is a beautiful wooded area on the outskirts of the city. The trip to the top of Kinnoull Hill (783 ft) itself affords an astounding view across Perth, down to the Tay estuary and through Fife to the Lomond hills. To the north, the views stretch from Ben More in the west to Lochnagar in the northeast. There are four walks through the Woodland Park – Nature Walk, Tower Walk, Jubilee Walk and Squirrel Walk – and each of these is graded according to how difficult it is and what type of conditions the walker can expect. However, none of the walks are extremely strenuous, though the Squirrel Walk is most suitable for the less able. If you're feeling particularly energetic, cycling and horse riding take place in specific zones in the park, principally in the Deuchny Wood area. There is a Countryside Ranger Service in the park and they will be happy to answer any questions you may have about their work or the park itself. Also ask at the tourist office in town for details.

Huntingtower Castle ① *3 miles west of Perth on the A85 to Crieff, T01738-627231 (HS), Mar-Sep daily 0930-1730, Oct-Mar Mon-Wed, Sat-Sun 0930-1630, £4.50, concessions £3.60, children £2.70*, is also worth a visit. It consists of two complete towers dating from the 15th and 16th centuries, linked by a 17th-century range, and features some fine 16th-century painted ceilings. The castle, once owned by the Ruthven family, has some interesting history of its own. Prior to the building of the range, a daughter of the house once leapt between the two towers to avoid being caught in her lover's bedroom.

The **Museum of Abernethy** ① *May-Sep Thu-Sun 1300-1700, free*, provides a further insight into Perthshires history, including the ancient Picts. This museum is just 7 miles south of Perth on the A912.

Scone Palace

① *T01738-552300, www.scone-palace.co.uk, 24 Mar-31 Oct daily 0930-1730 (last admission 1700), £9, concessions £7.90, children £5.50, grounds only £5, concessions £4.50, children*

£350. For £18 'Scotland's Treasure Ticket' also covers admittance to Blair Castle, Glamis Castle and The Famous Grouse (whisky) Experience in Crieff.

Three miles northeast of Perth on the A93 Braemar road, is the not-to-be-missed Scone Palace, one of the most historically important places in the country (though much of the present palace building only dates from the 19th century). The home of the Earls of Mansfield, Scone (pronounced 'scoon') has a long and fascinating history. It was the capital of the Pictish Kingdom in the sixth century and home of the Celtic church. Here, Kenneth MacAlpin united Scotland, and in AD 838, placed the stone of Scone (or 'Stone of Destiny') on Moot Hill, opposite the palace entrance. This became the ancient crowning place of Scottish kings, including Macbeth and Robert the Bruce. The Royal City of Scone became the seat of government, and the kings of Scotland resided at the Palace of Scone before their coronations. The coronation stone was removed to Westminster by that most hated foe, Edward I, in 1296, and only recently returned to Scotland in a desperate, but failed, Conservative attempt to win back support north of the border. The famed stone currently resides in Edinburgh Castle. In 1651, the last coronation in Scotland took place when King Charles II was crowned by the Scots on the Moot Hill. The ceremony was attended by Lord Stormont, forefather of the present occupier, Lord Mansfield. Part of the church where this took place still remains. Today, Scone Palace attracts over 100,000 annual visitors.

Aside from its impressive history, the palace also houses beautiful collections of porcelain, needlework, royal furniture, clocks, ivories and many other absorbing artefacts. You could also spend a few hours walking in the magnificent 100-acre gardens, filled with bluebells, rhododendrons, roses and rare trees, with strutting peacocks and Highland cattle roaming around. There's also a maze, picnic park and children's adventure playground, plus a gift shop and coffee shop with delicious home baking.

Stanley Mills

ⓘ *T01738-828268, www.historic-scotland.gov.uk, Apr-Sep daily 0930-1730, Oct daily 0930-1630, £5.50, concessions £4.40, children £3.30.*

Seven miles north of Perth off the A9 and on the banks of the River Tay stands one of Scotland's newer tourist attractions – the impressive Stanley Mills water mill complex. In 1786, the first water mill was constructed to harness the power of the Tay to support a thriving cotton spinning industry. Though commercial operations ceased in 1989, in 1995 Historic Scotland began the restoration of the mill complex. In 2008 and after a £4.6 million redevelopment, the complex reopened with the lovingly restored Bell Mill and Mid Mill forming a visitor attraction and education resource that through interactive displays, exhibits and even the 'voices' of the long deceased workers reveals how the mill operated and how it impacted on the lives of the community, including its children.

Dunkeld and Birnam

Twelve miles north of Perth is the attractive village of **Dunkeld**, standing right on the Highland line. It's definitely worth making a stop here, if only to admire the **cathedral** ⓘ *Apr-Sep daily 0930-1830, Oct-Apr daily 0930-1600, free*, in the most idyllic situation on the banks of the fast-flowing, silvery Tay. Half of it is still in use as a church and the other half is in ruins. The oldest part of the cathedral is the 14th-century choir, which now forms the parish church, while the 15th-century nave and tower are also still standing. Much of the original was damaged during the orgy of ecclesiastical destruction that accompanied the Reformation. It was damaged again in the Battle of Dunkeld in 1689, fought between supporters of the protestant William of Orange and the Stuart monarch

James VII. Dunkeld offers excellent walking opportunities, details of which are available from the **TIC** ⓘ *The Cross, T01350-727688, Jul-Aug Mon-Sat 0900-1730, Sun 1030-1630, Sep-Oct Mon-Sat 1000-1630, Sun 1100-1600, Nov-Mar Fri-Sun 1100-1600, Apr-Jun Mon-Sat 1000-1630, Sun 1100-1600.*

Across the bridge from Dunkeld is **Birnam**, made famous in Shakespeare's *Macbeth*. Birnam was the inspiration for another famous literary figure, Beatrix Potter, who spent her childhood summers here. Visitors can explore the origins of Peter Rabbit at the **Beatrix Potter Exhibition** ⓘ *T01350-727674, Mon-Sat 1000-1700, Sun 1100-1630 £1, free for under 3s.* There's also a lovely, child-friendly café.

A short distance north of Dunkeld on the A9 is the turning to **The Hermitage**. A marked woodland walk starts from the car park (£2) and follows the River Braan to the Black Linn Falls, overlooked by Ossian's Hall, an 18th-century folly built by the Duke of Atholl. Surrounded by Douglas fir trees as high as 210 ft, it's a beautifully serene spot, which has inspired the likes of Wordsworth and Mendelssohn. Further on is **Ossian's Cave**. It's worthwhile purchasing a copy of the 'Dunkeld and Birnam' walking routes map (£1) from the Dunkeld TIC and from where you can also walk to The Hermitage. Buses to Pitlochry (T01738-629339) will stop on request just south of The Hermitage.

A few miles northeast of Dunkeld, off the A923 to Blairgowrie, is the **Loch of the Lowes Visitor Centre** ⓘ *Apr-Sep daily 1000-1700, £4, concessions £3, family £7.50*, managed by the Scottish Wildlife Trust. There's a hide with binoculars for viewing a pair of breeding ospreys (early April to August), which can sometimes be seen over the loch. Woodpeckers and red deer are also among the wildlife on the reserve with its 'nest-cam' and shop.

Pitlochry and around → For listings, see pages 140-145. Colour map 4, B3. Phone code 01796.

Despite being one of the busiest Highland tourist towns in the summer, Pitlochry's setting on the shores of the River Tummel, overlooked by Ben y Vrackie, makes it a pleasant enough base for exploring the area, especially out of season. The town also has a few attractions of its own.

Sights

Pitlochry's main attraction is the **fish ladder**, part of the power station and dam which formed man-made **Loch Faskally** when it was constructed on the River Tummel. The ladder allows salmon to swim up to their spawning grounds and you can watch them leaping spectacularly in the spring and summer. The best months are May and June. The fish ladder is across the river, a short distance from the **Pitlochry Festival Theatre**, see page 143.

Also here is **Explorers – The Scottish Plant Hunters' Garden** ⓘ *T01796-484600, www.explorersgarden.com, Apr-Oct daily 1000-1700, £3, concessions £2.50.* This fascinating garden containing diverse plant species and trails, pays tribute to the story of Scotland's 18th- and 19th-century botanists and explorers.

There are two whisky distilleries to visit. The larger, though less inspiring, of the two is Bell's **Blair Atholl Distillery** ⓘ *T01796-482003, Easter-Oct Mon-Sat 0930-1700, Jun-Oct Mon-Sat 0930-1700, Sun 1200-1700, Nov-Easter Mon-Fri tours at 1100, 1300 and 1500, £5, redeemable in shop*, at the southern end of town, heading towards the A9 to Perth. A couple of miles east of town, on the A924, is the **Edradour Distillery** ⓘ *T01796-472095, www.edradour.co.uk; Mar-Apr Mon-Sat 1000-1600, Sun 1200-1600; May-Oct Mon-Sat 1000-1700, Sun 1200-1700; Nov-Dec Mon-Sat 1000-1600, Sun 1200-1600; free*, and producing just 12 casks of whisky a week remains the smallest in Scotland – a blessing or a curse, depending on how busy it is.

Local walks

ⓘ *OS Landranger maps Nos 43 and 52 cover all the walks, and the OS Explorer map No 21 (Pitlochry and Loch Tummel) covers them in greater detail.*

The tourist office sells a useful leaflet, *Pitlochry Walks* (£1), which describes several long local walks, and there are many other fine walks in the surrounding area. The greatest walking attraction is **Ben y Vrackie** (2758 ft), a steep 6-mile walk (there and back) from the tiny hamlet of Moulin, a mile north of Pitlochry on the A924 (turn left at the **Moulin Inn**). The path is well trodden and the going is relatively easy, across bleak moorland, until the steep final ascent on scree. On a clear day the views across Perthshire and towards the Trossachs from the summit are wonderful. Don't attempt this on a cloudy day. In spite of its proximity to Pitlochry, you need to be properly equipped and take the usual safety precautions, see page 26.

Another excellent walk from Pitlochry, described in the tourist office leaflet, leaves town on the north road and turns left past the boat station. It then crosses the Cluanie footbridge and follows the road to Loch Faskally and up the River Garry to Garry Bridge over the Pass of Killiecrankie, see below. The path returns to Pitlochry along the west bank of the River Garry, before turning west up the River Tummel, passing close by the Linn of Tummel, then crossing the Tummel and following the west shore of Loch Faskally to the dam and fish ladder.

Pass of Killiecrankie

Four miles north of Pitlochry the A9 cuts through the Pass of Killiecrankie, a spectacular wooded gorge which was the dramatic setting for the Battle of Killiecrankie in 1689, when a Jacobite army led by Graham of Claverhouse, Viscount 'Bonnie Dundee', defeated the government forces under General Hugh Mackay. One government soldier allegedly evaded capture by making a jump of Olympic gold medal-winning proportions across the River Garry at **Soldier's Leap**. The **NTS visitor centre** ⓘ *T0844-493 2192, Apr-Oct daily 1000-1730, free (honesty box £1 donation advised, parking £2)*, tells the story of the battle and features interactive displays on the area's natural history.

The 1½ mile way-marked trail from the centre through the ancient, native deciduous trees to the gorge and Leap is both rewarding and spectacular. There's also another 3-mile waymarked trail around the **Killiecrankie Nature Reserve** that starts from the Balrobbie Farm car park and which may offer sightings of the great spotted woodpecker. Follow the signs for the reserve from Killiecrankie village, take the minor road over the River Garry, then take the left fork up a steep hill. Turn right at the sharp bend into the farm car park. Access to the reserve is free, but there's a cairn for donations and a parking charge.

Head down the driveway, then turn right along the road which climbs uphill below wooded crags. Turn right through a gate, opposite a cottage and follow a grassy track to a gate in a stone wall. Through the gate, the path climbs diagonally under the crags to an iron gate beside a bench. Go through the gate and the path zigzags steeply up to an area of open marsh. The path curves right and continues to climb across a heather moor and past a ruin.

At the crest of the hill, from where there are wonderful views down to Blair Atholl, go downhill, over a stile and enter woodland. Beyond the trees is another bench, then the trail turns to the right. After another two stiles the path heads left downhill, then zigzags down a rocky slope, before heading diagonally downhill to the right to an iron gate. Pick up the path again by a stone wall and follow it back to the car park.

Blair Castle

ⓘ www.blair-castle.co.uk, T01796-481207, mid-Mar to Oct daily 0930-1630, House and Gardens £8.75, concessions £7.50, children £5.25. Gardens only adult and concession £4.75, children £2.25. Note not all trains from Pitlochry stop at Blair Atholl.

Seven miles from Pitlochry, and a mile from the village of Blair Atholl, is Blair Castle, the traditional seat of the Earls and Dukes of Atholl. This whitewashed, turreted castle dates from 1269 and presents an impressive picture on first sight. This is the headquarters of Britain's only private army, the Atholl Highlanders. Thirty rooms in the castle are open for public viewing and are packed full of paintings, furniture, armour, porcelain and much else besides, presenting a startling picture of aristocratic Highland life in previous centuries. The surrounding landscaped grounds are home to peacocks and Highland cattle, and there are woodland walks, pony trekking, Land Rover tours and a walled Japanese water garden to enjoy. Every August, its grounds also host the internationally acclaimed **Blair Horse Trials** ⓘ www.blairhorsetrials. co.uk. A handy camping site is immediately adjacent to the castle grounds. The castle also runs occasional 'Attic Tours', which give access to private areas including the highest vantage point in the castle. These are extremely popular and prior booking is essential.

Falls of Bruar

Eight miles from Blair Atholl, just off the A9, are the dramatic Falls of Bruar. A well-maintained path leads from the lower falls along the deep gorge of the Bruar River to the upper falls and back down the other side. It's a 1½-mile round trip.

From the House of Bruar (see below), turn right by the adventure playground, then left up the river bank. The path passes under a railway arch and through a kissing gate. It then heads through open forest to a rocky outcrop, from where you can see the lower falls. A series of wooden steps leads down from the outcrop, then a path climbs up until it forks. Go right, then cross the bridge, from where there's a good view of the lower falls. From here a clear path leads up the far side until it reaches a deer fence. Climb up to the gate, go through it and continue uphill through trees until the path levels out high above the gorge. Further on there's a picnic area, then the path curves left down to the upper bridge, which is a great vantage point from which to admire the stunning view. The path heads left through more trees. It then crosses a stream before descending to the lower bridge and then back to the car park. Take extreme care with children.

By the car park is the tourist-trap of the **House of Bruar**, a huge shopping emporium designed like a Victorian hunting lodge where you can buy the likes of fine country clothing, artwork and a wide range of Scottish food and drink products. There's also a good, if busy and somewhat pricey restaurant that serves lunches, home-bakes and coffee.

From Blair Atholl to Kinloch Rannoch

The B8019 turns off the B8079 road from Pitlochry to Blair Atholl and runs west along the shores of beautiful lochs Tummel and Rannoch, best seen in the autumn when the trees change their colours. You may also spot capercaillie and red squirrels in the area. At the eastern end of Loch Tummel is **Queen's View**, a spectacular viewpoint which looks down the loch and across to Schiehallion. Here, there's a **Forestry Commission Scotland Visitor Centre** ⓘ T01796-473123, Apr-Oct daily 1000-1800, free, parking £2, with displays and audio-visual programmes about the area and recently updated maps for sale outlining locals walks and climbs. There's also a tea room (T01796-473133).

Schiehallion (3547 ft) is one of Scotland's best-loved mountains, whose distinctive conical peak made it ideal for use in early experiments in 1774 to judge the weight of the earth. These were not an unqualified success, but led to the invention of contour lines as an aid to surveying the mountain. The walk to the summit is fairly straightforward, except for the very rocky final half-mile stretch. You'll need to be properly clothed and equipped and take a map and compass. The route to the summit starts at the car park on the B846 Kinloch Rannoch to Aberfeldy road, near Braes of Foss. OS sheet No 51 covers the route.

Beyond Loch Tummel is the village of **Kinloch Rannoch**, where hikers can stock up on supplies before heading into the hills. At the time of writing, a property developer has plans to create a six-star holiday retreat in the area for the world's mega-rich. Sixteen miles west of the village the road ends at the very remote Rannoch station, where tired hikers can catch trains north to Fort William or south to Glasgow.

Blair Atholl to Glen Fincastle walk

A lovely 3-mile linear walk leads from Blair Atholl village to Glen Fincastle, passing through woodland and across moorland and pasture. Starting in the village, head down past the watermill and stay on the road until it ends at the river. Then follow a path left until it takes you to a footbridge over the River Garry. Cross the footbridge and then over two stiles until you reach the main A9. Cross the road, taking care as it's usually busy, to another stile, then continue through trees to a gate with a footprint sign. On the other side of the gate, the path zigzags up through a wood which thins out as you reach the top of the hill.

Here, the path fords a stream then continues across open moorland to the other side of the hilltop, where there's a gate. Go through the gate and follow the grassy track down to Tomanraid cottage. From here you can see down into Glen Fincastle. Before the cottage go left over a stile and then down to a gate. Through the gate, head straight along the track until you reach a junction. Go through the gate ahead and down a grassy lane to another gate. Then the path curves diagonally to the left down to a metal gate at the end of a public road. To return to Blair Atholl simply retrace your steps. It's worthwhile popping into the rustic 17th century **Watermill Café** ⓘ *T01796-481321*, in the village for a great coffee, freshly baked breads and bagels, or to purchase bags of oatmeal ground on the premises.

Blair Atholl to Glen Fincastle walk

The quaint town of Aberfeldy, Scotland's first Fairtrade Town stands on the banks of the River Tay, on the A827 which runs between the A9 and Loch Tay. Popular with kayakers who brave the rapids in nearby Grantully, the village is well placed geographically for exploring the northern part of Perthshire and less crowded than Pitlochry. The 14-mile- long Loch Tay is surrounded by some of the loveliest scenery in Perthshire and is well worth exploring.

Aberfeldy

The River Tay is spanned by Wade's Bridge, built by General Wade in 1773 during his campaign to pacify the Highlands.

Dewar's World of Whisky ① *T01887-822010, www.dewars.com, Apr-Oct Mon-Sat 1000-1800, Sun 1200-1600, Nov-Mar Mon-Sat 1000-1600, £6.50, concessions £5 children £4*, just outside Aberfeldy, is another of Scotland's many distillery visitor centres offering a tour, dram and history of the water of life.

A mile west of Aberfeldy, across the Tay at Weem, is **Castle Menzies** ① *T01887-820982, Apr to mid-Oct Mon-Sat 1030-1700, Sun 1400-1700, £4, concessions £3.50, children £2*, an impressive, restored 16th-century 'Z-plan' fortified tower house, the former seat of the chief of Clan Menzies. For a great coffee or lunchtime bite, it's also worth popping into the nearby **House of Menzies** ① *T01887-829666, www.houseofmenzies.com, Apr-Oct daily 1000-1700*, at Castle Menzies Farm. In Dull, 3 miles west you'll also find a fabulous café/delicatessen in the same building as **Highland Safaris** ① *T01887-820071, www.highlandsafaris.net*.

A popular local walk is to the **Falls of Moness**, through the famous **Birks of Aberfeldy**, forever associated with the poet Robert Burns whom in 1787 was inspired by the *birks* (birch trees) to write his eponymous song. It's a fairly easy walk along a marked trail lined with oak, elm, ash and birch trees up to the falls where there are lovely views of Strathtay and the surrounding hills. It's about 4 miles there and back.

Loch Tay and around

It's estimated that Scotland's landscape has over 190,000 known landmarks of archaeological significance. In the past decade divers discovered a 2000-year-old wooden canoe in the depths of Loch Tay. Who knows what other ancient artefacts remain to be discovered.

At the northeast end of the Loch is **Kenmore**, a neat little village of whitewashed cottages dominated by a huge archway which stands at the gateway to Taymouth Castle, built by the Campbells of Glenorchy in the early 19th century. Whilst for several years the castle has been undergoing redevelopment (potentially into a luxury hotel) golfers can still enjoy a scenic round at the 18-hole **Taymouth Castle Golf Course** ① *T01887-830228, from £25*. Half a mile from the village on the southern bank of the loch, is the informative **Scottish Crannog Centre** ① *T01887-830583, Apr to Oct daily 1000-1730, Nov Sat-Sun 1000-1600, £6.50, concessions £5.75, children £4.50*, an authentic reconstruction of a *crannog*, a Bronze Age island dwelling that archaeologists believe was built for both defensive and food storage purposes. There are apparently over a dozen ancient crannogs in Loch Tay. At the Crannog Centre experts reveal how our ancestors ate and slept whilst there's also the opportunity to try and make fire with just wood and flint.

For those with their own transport, two of the least-known and loveliest routes in the country are at hand. The first is the spectacular road which winds its way south from Kenmore high up into the mountains, across a bleak and barren plateau and down the other side to the tiny hamlet of **Amulree**. This road and ancient drovers route is often closed in the winter and there are gates at either end. From Amulree you can continue south to Crieff, through the gentler, but equally stunning scenery of the **Sma' Glen**. Alternatively, you could head north to Aberfeldy and then complete the circuit back to Kenmore.

A few miles west of Kenmore a minor road turns off the A827, which runs along the north bank of the loch, and heads to **Fortingall**, a tiny village of classic beauty which features on many a calendar. It's little more than a row of thatched cottages which wouldn't even get a mention were it not for two amazing claims. The 3000-year-old yew tree in the churchyard is said to be the oldest living thing in Europe. Even more astonishing is the claim that this is the birthplace of Pontius Pilate, said to be the son of a Roman officer who was stationed here. Furthermore, it is believed that Pilate returned here to be buried, and a gravestone in the churchyard bears the initials 'PP'. If you have your own transport, make a detour up **Glen Lyon**, one of the most beautiful of all Scottish glens. On a summer's day there can be few lovelier places on earth, as the River Lyon tumbles through corries and gorges and through flowering meadows, with high mountain peaks on either side and eagles soaring overhead. It's no surprise that Wordsworth and Tennyson waxed lyrical over its qualities. The road from Fortingall runs all the way to the head of the glen, at Loch Lyon. This is walking and fishing paradise. There are several Munros to 'bag' and fishing permits are available at the **Fortingall Hotel**, see Sleeping, page 142.

Ben Lawers → *OS sheet No 51 covers the area.*

The highest mountain in Perthshire, Ben Lawers (3984 ft), dominates the north side of Loch Tay. Its massif of seven summits includes six Munros which are linked by an 8-mile ridge which can be walked in one day by fit and experienced hillwalkers. The best access to the ridge is from Glen Lyon. The trek to the main summit starts from the **NTS visitor centre** ① *T01567-820397, Apr-Sep daily 1000-1700*, 2 miles along a track which turns off the main A827 about halfway between Kenmore and Killin. This track continues over a wild pass to Bridge of Balgie in Glen Lyon. Leaflets describing the climb are available from the visitor centre. It's a 7-mile walk there and back, and though the route is straight-forward and easy to follow, it's a very steep, tough climb of 2700 ft from the centre to the summit. Allow five to six hours. You should be fit, properly clothed, see page 26, and have some previous hillwalking experience; but the views from the top on a clear day are amazing, across to the North Sea in the east and the Atlantic Ocean in the west. Information about an easier 1-mile nature trail and the flora and fauna in the area is available from the visitor centre.

Blairgowrie and Glenshee → *For listings, see pages 140-145. Colour map 4, B3. Phone code 01250.*

The other major road running north from Perth is the A93, soon reaching the respectable town of **Blairgowrie**, or Blairgowrie and Rattray to give it its full title. It lies amidst the raspberry fields of Strathmore and is conveniently placed to serve as an accommodation centre for **Glenshee Ski Centre** ① *T01339-741320, www.ski-glenshee.co.uk, adult day lift passes from £25, children £16*, at the crest of the Cairnwell Pass (2199 ft). The most extensive ski area in Scotland, Glenshee is ideal for telemark and alpine skiing. Call the centre to check weather forecast. The only public transport to the ski resort is a daily **postbus** ① *T0845-6000606, www.royalmail.com/postbus*, service (Monday to Saturday) from Blairgowrie (0730) to Spittal of Glenshee, or from Braemar and Ballater.

A quiet agricultural town, Blairgowrie boasts several good restaurants and tea rooms including **Cargills** by the river and the **Ericht Alehouse**, whilst **Strathmore Golf Centre** ① *T01828-633322, www.strathmoregolf.com*, or **James Crockart & Son** ① *28 Allan St,*

T01250-872056, www.jamescrockartandson.co.uk, will appeal to golf and fishing fanatics respectively. There is also a **TIC** ① *26 Wellmeadow, T01250-872960, daily*. However, for many, Blairgowrie is a convenient sandwich stop before driving south towards Perth or following the twisty A93 road north to the Spittal of Glenshee, the ski centre and the stunning scenery of Braemar and Deeside beyond. ►► *For further information on skiing, see Activities and tours, page 144.*

⊙ Perthshire listings

For Sleeping and Eating price codes and other relevant information, see Essentials pages 38-45.

⊜ Sleeping

Perth and around *p130, map p131*
L Hilton Dunkeld, Dunkeld, T01796-727771, www.dunkeld.hilton.com. Luxurious former summer residence for the wife of the 7th Duke of Atholl, now an impressive hotel with full leisure and outdoor activity facilities.
L Kinnaird House, Dalguise, about 7 miles north of Dunkeld via the A9 and the B898, T01796-482831. On a 9000 acre estate, and boasting fine food (♥♥♥-♥♥) and accommodation.
L-A Ballathie House Hotel, Kinclaven, near Stanley, 9 miles north of Perth, just off the A9, T01250-883268, www.ballathie househotel.com. 43 rooms. An elegant, 19th-century former hunting lodge serving up delicious traditional Scottish cuisine in beautiful surroundings. Renowned as a base for traditional field sports, the estate also offers self-catering and B&B options in its **Sportsman's Lodge** (from £95 per person).
A Huntingtower Hotel, 1 mile west of Perth off the A85 to Crieff, T01738-583771, www.huntingtowerhotel.co.uk. Elegant Tudor-style country house hotel in land-scaped gardens, with 34 rooms. Serves good food and is able to organize many outdoor activities.
B Tormaukin Inn, Glendevon, 10 miles south of Crieff. T01259-781252. Atmospheric 250-year-old inn with comfortable rooms, real ales and a terrific restaurant (♥♥♥-♥♥), serving steak and ale pie and baked hare.
B-C The Luncarty Inn, Marshall Way, Luncarty, T01738-827777. It's 3 miles north

of Perth off the A9, this converted 5-bedroom traditional farmhouse serving reasonable food is handy for the River Tay and golf.
B-C Ramada Hotel, West Mill St, Perth, T01738-628281. Almost opposite the TIC, and beautifully converted from its origins as a 15th-century water mill, this comfortable hotel is handy for the key sites in town.
D Sunbank House Hotel, 50 Dundee Rd, Perth, T01738-624882. 9 rooms. A traditional sandstone hotel overlooking the Tay, 10 mins' walk from the city centre and close to Branklyn Garden and Kinnoull Hill.
C-D Salutation Hotel, 34 South St, Perth, T01738-630066, www.strathmorehotels. com. Refurbished, this building claims to be the oldest established hotel (1699) in Scotland. Bonnie Prince Charlie stayed in room No 20.
E Achnacarry Guest House, 3 Pitcullen Cres, on the A94 Coupar Angus road, 10 mins' walk from Perth town centre, T01738-621421, www.achnacarry.co.uk. Comfortable and can provide guests with golf clubs.
F Comrie Croft, Comrie Rd by Crieff, T01764-670140, www.comriecroft.com. Open all year. Comfortable backpackers' hostel, which also offers mountain bike hire.
F Gulabin Lodge, Cairnwell Mountain **Sports**, Spittal of Glenshee, by Blairgowrie. T01250-885255, www.cairnwellmountain sports.co.uk. Excellent hostel handy for the ski area, postbus and outdoor adventure.
E-D Kinnaird Guest House, 5 Marshall Pl, T01738-628 0121, www.kinnaird-guest house.co.uk. Part of an 1806 Georgian terrace, built on the site of an ancient fort and overlooking the South Inch.

F Wester Caputh Independent Hostel, Caputh, 5 miles east of Dunkeld, on the A984 to Coupar Angus, T01738-710449. Open all year. 17 beds and a log stove. A 3-mile walk to the pub but 300 yds from public transport.

Self-catering
Finegand Holiday Cottages, by Blairgowrie, T01250-885234. Offers 4 rustic, modestly equipped cottages (sleep 4-7) on a quiet upland farm with excellent opportunities for fishing. From £228 per week.

Camping
Cleeve Caravan Park, Glasgow Rd, near the ring road, about 2 miles from town, T01738-639521. Open Apr-Oct.
Scone Palace Camping & Caravan Club Site, 5 miles north of Perth, T01738-552323. Apr-Oct. Located within the picturesque estate. 150 pitches and good amenities, including showers.

Pitlochry and around *p134*
The tourist office, T01796-472215, can provide a full list of guesthouses and B&Bs.
A-B The Atholl Palace Hotel, T01796-472400, www.athollpalace.com. With its conical towers, this grand hotel with a small museum, new pool and spa is probably the most distinctive hotel in the area.
B Killiecrankie Hotel, 3 miles north of town, in the village of Killiecrankie, T01796-473220, www.killiecrankiehotel.co.uk. Open Mar-Dec. 10 rooms. A cosy country house, established in 1840 and renowned for its quality of fine wines, malts and evening meals.
B-D Pine Trees Hotel, Strathview Terr, T01796-472121, www.pinetreeshotel.co.uk. Comfortable, large Victorian country house set in 10 acres of gardens away from the tourist bustle.
C-B Craigatin House & Courtyard, 165 Atholl Rd, T1796-472478. Good value B&B.
C East Haugh House, 1 mile southeast of town, off the old A9, T01796-473121. Set in beautiful gardens, this charming hotel offers

a warm welcome and an excellent restaurant (ɪɪɪ-ɪɪ). Can arrange outdoor sports.
D Easter Dunfallandy Country House, T01796-474128, www.dunfallandy.co.uk. 3 en suite rooms, beautifully appointed with complimentary toiletries. Home-made bread and preserves, afternoon tea on arrival and a fine rural location ensure a rewarding stay.
E Roseburn, 15 West Moulin Rd, T01796-470002, www.roseburn.biz. A relatively new and classy addition to Pitlochry's guesthouse scene, offering 3 delightful bedrooms and a tasty breakfast.
C-E Old Stables, 2 Losset Rd, Alyth, Blairgowrie, T01828-632547, www.oldstables.com. Fabulous 3-bedroom B&B in a converted 19th-century steading, with cosy comforts like the log fire and sauna.
E Fasganeoin Country House, Perth Rd, T01796-472387. A lovely 8-bedroom country house in a secluded setting with views towards Loch Tummel yet just mins away from the thoroughfare of town.
E Spittal of Glenshee Hotel, Glenshee, A93, T01250-885215, www.spittalofglenshee.co.uk. A comfortable 48-bedroom hotel with great bar meals and an adjacent bunkhouse for those on a budget.
F Pitlochry Backpackers, 134 Atholl Rd, T01796-470044. Slap bang in the middle of town, accommodation and 'vibe' that will appeal to the younger crowd and 'young at heart' seeking a welcoming, low-budget stay.
F SYHA Youth Hostel, Knockard Rd, set amidst woodland, just ½ a mile from town, T1796-472308. Open Feb-Oct. Great facilities.

Aberfeldy and Loch Tay *p138*
L-B Ardeonaig House Hotel, south Loch Tay by Aberfeldy, T01567-820400. Charming, fantastic location, a terrific (South African) wine list and food to die for in this recently refurbished and extended escape. Recommended.
A-B Macdonald Loch Rannoch Hotel & Resort, Kinloch Rannoch, T01882 632203, www.macdonaldhotels.co.uk. Escape from

the crowds and relax in style with fine dining, malts, a spa and clay pigeon shooting.
A-B Fortingall Hotel, next to the churchyard, Fortingall, T01887-830367, www.fortingall.com. Peaceful hotel dating back to the Victorian era, with 10 tastefully refurbished en suite rooms and a choice of dining.
C Ailean Chraggan, Weem, a mile or so west from Aberfeldy, T01887-820346. A 5-bedroom family-run hotel serving good food in the bar.
C-D Kenmore Hotel, Kenmore, T01887-830205. Claims to be Scotland's oldest coaching inn, dating from 1572. True or not, the snug bar certainly oozes character and serves hearty meals. The modest bedrooms are reasonable, whilst the somewhat characterless main restaurant provides excellent views over the surrounding area.
D Bunrannoch House, Kinloch Rannoch, T01882-632407, www.bunrannoch.co.uk. Open all year. A former Victorian shooting lodge providing a warm welcome, great home-cooking and terrific views of the loch.
E Balnearn Guest House, Crieff Rd, Aberfeldy, T01887-820431. A clean, family friendly, 10-bedroom guesthouse.
F Adventurer's Escape, Weem by Aberfeldy, T01887-820498. Ideal for canoeing and mountaineering instruction.
F The Bunkhouse, Glassie Farm, Aberfeldy, T01887-820265. Cheap and basic.

Self-catering

The Bothy, Tullichettle, Comrie, T01764-670349. Open Mar-Dec. White-washed 1840s stable converted into cottage with expansive rural views. Sleeps 4. £245-410 per week.
Mains of Taymouth Cottages, Kenmore by Aberfeldy, T01887-830226. Acclaimed, luxury cottages set on a 120 acre rolling estate by the Tay, with facilities including hot tubs, BBQ and fishing. £450-3000 per week.

❷ Eating

Perth and around *p130, map p131*
♥♥♥-♥♥ No 63, 63 Tay St, T01738-441451. Tue-Sat 1200-1400, 1830-2100. Stylish restaurant down by the river with a thoughtful dinner and lunch (♥♥) menu that includes crab and Carnoustie pork.
♥♥ The Bothy Restaurant and Bar, 33 Kinnoull St, T01738-449792. Pleasant ambience with tasty steaks and duck amongst the treats.
♥♥ Dean's @Let's Eat, Kinnoull St, T01738-643377. Tue-Sat 1200-1400, 1830-2130. The place to eat in Perth with contemporary Scottish cuisine, cooked fresh to order with a smile.
♥♥ Kerachers, 168 South St, T01738-449777. Good range of seafood, game and vegetarian dishes.
♥♥-♥ Redrooms, Perth Theatre, 185 High St, T01738-472709. Daily 1000-1700 (and theatre nights). Good selection of open sandwiches and full lunches served in a relaxing ambience that attracts an older and post-theatre clientele. Afternoon tea (£3.95) daily from 1400-1700.
♥ Delicious Café, 46 South Methven St, T01738-451617. Mon-Sat 1000-1700. Child friendly and great range of fresh filled sandwiches, wraps, toasties, coffees and smoothies.
♥ Greyfriars Pub, 15 South St, T01738-633036. Cosy pub serving hearty lunches, daily 1200-1430, with great selection of real ales including 'Piddle in the Cellar!'
♥ The Old Ship Inn, Skinners Lane. Est 1665, one of Perth's oldest licensed premises. For hearty pub grub, old-world charm and banter of local worthies.

Pitlochry and around *p134*
House of Bruar (♥♥), see page 136, is a good if pricey place to stop for a bowl of soup or some fudge along the A9.
♥♥♥ East Haugh Country House Hotel & Restaurant, 1 mile south of Pitlochry on

the old A9 road, T01796-473121, www.easthaugh.co.uk. A 17th-century country house renowned for its dining and excellent seafood.

†††-†† Loft, Golf Course Rd, Blair Atholl, T01796-481377. Thoughtfully prepared and tasty menu. Lovely ambience and value for money.

†††-† Killiecrankie Hotel, see Sleeping, above. Excellent evening meals matched by an award winning reputation for its fine wines.

†† Fern Cottage Restaurant, Ferry Rd, Pitlochry, T01796-473840. Within the walls of this lovely stone walled cottage awaits mouth-watering, freshly prepared lunches (1200-1500) and dinners (1730-2100). Recommended.

† Blair Atholl Water Mill, Ford Rd, Blair Atholl, T01796-481321. Open Mar-Oct. Delicious home-bakes, sandwiches, coffee and even freshly milled oats in this charming and rustic tea room. The mill dates back to 1613, £2 entry to view workings. Recommended.

† Moulin Inn and Brewery, a few miles north of Pitlochry, Moulin on the A924, T01796-472196. Aside from sampling the ales brewed next door, sit back and enjoy the ambience of a pub that opened its doors in 1695 and still serves up good value, traditional Scottish bar meals. And after a few tipples you'll find a warm welcome in the Moulin Hotel (see Sleeping, above).

Aberfeldy and Loch Tay *p138*

††† Ardeonaig House Hotel, south Loch Tay by Aberfeldy, T01567-820400. With Michelin and Inn of the Year Awards, this romantic small hotel also boasts a terrific South African wine list, great breakfast and 3 dinner menus, including the owners Signature menu. Recently reopened after a major expansion it now includes a **Cellar Restaurant**, a treat for the gourmet lover and romantic alike. Recommended.

† The Taybank, Tay Terr, Dunkeld, T01350-727340. If you go to no other pub in Perthshire, make sure you come here for traditional stovies, real ale and a terrific atmosphere aided by spontaneous music sessions. Recommended.

† The Watermill, Mill St, Aberfeldy, T01887-822896. Within this 18th-century former mill, you'll find second-hand books, artworks and terrific sandwiches and cakes to be savoured as you relax by the wood-fired stove.

🍸 Bars and clubs

Perth and around *p130, map p131*
Some pubs are listed under Eating, above. The younger crowd head for **That Bar**, South St; and the lively **Sportsters Bar**, South Methven St.
The Loft, County Pl, T01738-634523, www.loftclub.co.uk. One of Perth's more popular nightclubs.

🎭 Entertainment

Perth and around *p130, map p131*
Famous Grouse Experience, Crieff, T01764-656565. Open Mar-Dec from 0930-1630, Jan-Feb 1030-1500 with tours from £6.95. Tour Scotland's oldest distillery and sample the Famous Grouse and several single malts on a 60-min tour incorporating a BAFTA award-winning interactive show. There's even a dancing grouse and a floor of 'ice'. Recommended.
Perth Concert Hall, Mill St, T0845-612 6319. A striking £20 million arts and rock concert venue complete with minimalist café.
Perth Theatre, 185 High St, T01738-621031. Beautiful, Victorian-era theatre with an excellent reputation for high-class productions.
Playhouse, 6 Murray St, T01738-623126. Offers a dose of escapism on the big screen.

Pitlochry and around *p134*
Pitlochry Festival Theatre, across the river from the town centre, T01796-484626, www.pitlochry.org.uk. Stages a different play every night, 6 nights a week May-Oct and other shows throughout the year.

⊛ Festivals and events

Perth and around *p130, map p131*

May Atholl Highlanders Parade Watch soldiers in full highland regalia and as part of Britain's only private army march at Blair Atholl Castle.

Jun Perthshire Archaeology Month Participate in excavations, guided walks, talks and exhibitions held on the subject throughout Perthshire.

Aug Perth Highland Games Held on the 2nd Sun in Aug (1030-1730) the week after the **Perth Show**, which also take place in South Inch.

⊙ Activities and tours

Perth and around *p130, map p131*
Cycling
Three national cycle routes pass through Perthshire using quiet country roads and off-road track. Ask at the local tourist office or see www.sustrans.org.uk for details.

Fishing
Details of all the Perthshire fisheries are available from the TIC.
Gordonian Fishings, Old Carpow, Newburgh, T01738-850757. Open 15 Jan-15 Oct, this facility provides tuition and permits for salmon, trout and grayling fishing on the River Tay. Trout permits are £29 per day, salmon permits £40-95 per day.

Golf
See www.perthshire.co.uk, for a full list of the area's many courses.
King James VI Golf Club, Moncreiffe Island, T01738-632460. An 18-hole golf-course near the town centre.

Horse racing
Perth Racecourse, near Scone Palace, T01738-551597. Has regular jump racing events during the summer.

Leisure centres
Auchingarrich Wildlife Centre, 10 miles from Crieff, Comrie, T01764-679469, www.auchingarrich.co.uk. Daily 1000-dusk. £7.50, children and concession £6.00. Award winning, family-orientated wildlife centre with highland cattle, falconry centre, playbarn (including for U5s) and rare animals to observe within 100 acres of Perthshire countryside.
Bell's Sports Centre, Hay St, T01738-492460. Open daily 0900-2200. Covers virtually every sport and leisure activity imaginable.
Dewar's Centre, Glover St and next door to the pool, T01738-624188. Where you can curl, ice skate or bowl.
Perth Leisure Pool, T01738-492431. Open daily 1000-2200. Claims to have the best leisure swimming pool in Scotland.

Pitlochry and around *p134*
Horse riding
Blair Castle Trekking Centre, Atholl Estates, Blair Atholl, T01796-481568, www.blaircastle trekking.co.uk. Open Apr-Jun Tue-Sun, Jul-Sep Sun-Fri. Offers short treks, 1 hr, £25; 2 hrs, £38 and longer treks for the more experienced.

Walking
Atholl Estates Ranger Service, Atholl Estates Office, Blair Atholl, T01796-481646, www.athollestatesrangerservice.co.uk. Advice, guided walks and leaflets on 9 waymarked walking and bike trails (30 miles) in the Blair Atholl area.

Aberfeldy and Loch Tay *p138*
Tour operators
Highland Adventure Safaris, Aberfeldy, T01887-820071, www.highlandsafaris.net. Wildlife spot from landrovers (from £90), try gold panning or take to the wheel yourself for some memorable off-road adventure.
Loch Tay Boating Centre, Kenmore, T01887-830291. Apr-Oct daily 0900-1900. Rents speedboats, fishing boats and canoes, as well as bicycles.

Watersports

Aberfeldy, Weem and Kenmore boast several notable centres offering river-kayaking, whitewater rafting and canyoning. Try **Nae Limits**, Dunkeld, T01350-727242, www.nae limits.com; **National Kayak School**, Weem, T01887-820498; Splash, White Water Rafting, Aberfeldy, T01887-829706, www.rafting.co.uk.

Blairgowrie and Glenshee *p139*
Skiing

Cairnwell Mountain Sports, Spittal of Glenshee, T01250-885255. Lessons, ski and snowboard rental.

⊖ Transport

Perth and around *p130, map p131*
Bus Regular buses to **Blairgowrie**, **Dunkeld** (No 23), **Aberfeldy** (No 23), **Pitlochry** (No 27), **Alyth**, **Scone** (No 71), and **Kinloch Rannoch** (No 89), Stagecoach Strathtay, T0871-200 2233, www.stagecoachbus.com.

Citylink buses running between **Perth** and **Inverness** stop at the train station by **Birnam** several times daily. Scottish Citylink buses, T08705-505050, run frequently to **Glasgow** (1 hr 25 mins), **Edinburgh** (1½ hrs), **Dundee** (35 mins), **Aberdeen** (2½ hrs) and **Inverness** (2½ hrs).
Car hire Arnold Clark, St Leonard's Bank, Perth, T01738-442202.
Train There are hourly trains to **Stirling** (30 mins), **Dundee** (25 mins) and **Aberdeen** (1 hr 40 mins), and several daily to **Inverness**

via **Pitlochry** (30 mins) and **Aviemore**. There's a train service daily to **Glasgow Queen St** (1 hr); and frequent trains to **Edinburgh** (1 hr 20 mins).

Pitlochry and around *p134*
Bus Elizabeth Yule Transport, T01796-472 290, runs a Mon-Sat service between **Pitlochry** and **Blair Atholl** and **Killiecrankie** with buses leaving *Pitlochry* at the following times; 0750, 1000, 1300, 1540, 1625 and 1740. On Wed there's also a No 89 service from **Perth** to **Kinloch Rannoch** via **Pitlochry** (2100) and **Killiecrankie** (2120).
Car hire Escape Route, 3 Atholl Rd, Pitlochry, T/F01796-473859, www.escape-route.biz. Mon-Sat 0900-1730, Sun 1000-1700.
Cycle hire Basecamp Bikes, The Firs, Blair Atholl, T01796-481256, www.basecamp-bikes.co.uk. Have well-mapped off-road routes and hire bikes from £25 per day.
Escape Route, 3 Atholl Rd, Pitlochry, T/F01796-473859, www.escape-route. biz. Mon-Sat 0900-1730, Sun 1000-1700. Friendly staff in well stocked bike shop that hires kids and adult mountain bikes (including child seat and tandems). Prices from £8 for a full day. Also good selection of waterproof maps of walking and cycle routes around Perthshire.

Blairgowrie and Glenshee *p139*
Bus There's a regular bus service from **Blairgowrie** to **Dundee** and **Perth** (No 57) and a fairly frequent service (No 71) to **Pitlochry**.

The Trossachs and Loch Lomond

Strictly speaking, the Trossachs (derived from the Gaelic, 'Na Troiseachan' meaning 'the crossing place') is the narrow wooded glen between Loch Katrine and Loch Achray, but the name is now used to describe a much larger area between Argyll and Perthshire, stretching north from the Campsies and west from Callander to the eastern shore of Loch Lomond. It's a very beautiful and diverse area of sparkling lochs, over 20 craggy Munros (mountains of over 3000 ft) and deep, forested glens. For this reason, it's often called the 'Highlands in miniature', best visited in the autumn when the hills are purple and the trees are a thousand luminous hues, from lustrous gold to flaming scarlet and blazing orange. The Trossachs was one of the country's first holiday regions, and remains a major tourist destination. Its enduring appeal is due in no small measure to Sir Walter Scott, who eulogized its great natural beauty in his epic poem, Lady of the Lake, *and whose historical novel,* Rob Roy, *immortalized the region's most famous (and arguably infamous) 17th-century clan chief who ruled the lands west of Balquhidder.*

West of the Trossachs is Loch Lomond, Britain's largest inland waterway, measuring 22 miles long and up to 5 miles wide. Though still 'bonnie', its western banks now reverberate to the noise of traffic heading north from nearby Glasgow (20 miles) to Fort William on the busy and notorious (for accidents) A82. As part of the 720-square-mile Loch Lomond and Trossachs National Park, Scotland's first, recent years have seen bylaws introduced to control the speed of jetskis and boats on the loch. The eastern and northern shores are quieter though on any given day of the year you'll find a hardy hill-walker high above the (eastern shores) road end at Rowardennan on the slopes of mighty Ben Lomond (Scotland's most southerly Munro) enjoying spectacular views down the loch. ▸▸ *For listings, see pages 152-155.*

Ins and outs

Getting there

There are regular (Monday to Saturday) buses from Stirling to Aberfoyle and Callander (T0870-608 2608). There are also daily services to Aberfoyle from Glasgow, via Balfron. There's a daily Scottish Citylink service between Edinburgh and the Isle of Skye, which stops in Callander and links with buses to Killin. Scottish Citylink buses also run regularly from Glasgow to Balloch, and on to Luss and Tarbet. Some buses go to Ardlui and on to Crianlarich.

The **Citylink** ① *T08705-505050,* Oban to Dundee bus runs twice daily through Perthshire villages including Comrie, St Fillans, Lochearnhead and Killin. The same operator also runs a once daily service (Monday to Saturday) from Edinburgh via Stirling to Fort William, that passes through Callander, Strathyre, Lochearnhead (the No 25 postbus connects with Killin), Crianlarich and Tyndrum. **Caber Coaches** ① *T01887-820090,* bus No 893 and the postbus (No 213) operate a service Monday to Saturday between Aberfeldy and Killin via Kenmore. There's also a postbus (No 25) between Crianlarich and Tyndrum and Killin (Monday to Saturday). Pick up a free copy of *Loch Lomond and the Trossachs – exploring the park by ferry, bus or train,* from any TIC. First buses run daily (No10 and No 11A) between Glasgow and Aberfoyle via Drymen, and also operate a service to Balloch that stops in Drymen, and an Aberfoyle to Stirling service (No 11 and No 11A), which stops at Port of Menteith.

There are two rail lines from Glasgow to Loch Lomond. One runs regularly every day as a local (Strathclyde Passenger Transport) service to Balloch. The other is First ScotRail's West Highland line to Fort William and Mallaig, with a branch line to Oban. It reaches Loch

Lomond at Tarbet and there's another station further north at Ardlui. ▸▸ *For further details, see Transport, page 155.*

Getting around
The **Trossachs Trundler** ① *T01786-442707*, is an alternative for those wanting to make the journey from Callander to Aberfoyle via the *SS Sir Walter Scott* on Loch Katrine before winding over the Duke's Pass into Aberfoyle. Running four times a day between May and early October, the minibus can carry two bikes and wheelchairs. Current prices are £7 for a day-pass or £14 for a family of four. Contact the local TIC for details, see below. There's a **postbus service** ① *T0845-740740, www.postbus.royalmail.com*, from Aberfoyle to Inversnaid on Loch Lomond. It leaves Aberfoyle post office Monday to Saturday at 0900 and arrives at Inversnaid at 1325. You'd be quicker hiring a bike and cycling the route.

In addition to cruise companies, there are several small ferry operators, which provide a convenient means for (foot passengers only) to cross Loch Lomond. There's a passenger **ferry service** ① *T01360-870273, Apr-Sep 3 times daily, leave Inverbeg 1030, 1430, 1800, return 1000, 1400, 1730*, which runs across the loch between Inverbeg and Rowardennan. Another service crosses the loch between Inveruglas and Inversnaid, operated by **Inversnaid Hotel** ① *T01877-386223 for details*, but there is no fixed timetable. The ferry between Ardlui and Ardleish, operated by **Ardlui Hotel** ① *T01301-704243*, runs on demand between 0900 and 2000. Raise the signal ball at either side to call the ferryman.

Tourist information
The Aberfoyle **TIC** ① *T08707-200604, www.visitscottishheartlands.com, Apr-Oct 1000-1700, Nov-Mar Sat-Sun 1000-1600*, is on the main street. The Callander **TIC** ① *Ancaster Sq, T01877-330342, Apr-Sep daily 1000-1900, Oct-Mar Mon-Sat 1000-1600*, shares the same building as the Rob Roy and Trossachs Visitor Centre. Fifteen miles southwest of Aberfoyle in Balloch, the southernmost end of Loch Lomond and terminus for trains from Glasgow, is a large **Tourist information office** ① *Daily 1000-1700*, which can provide details about ferry and bus transport in the entire park area. In Tarbet the **TIC** ① *T01301-702260*, is open from April to October.

The Trossachs → *For listings, see pages 152-155. Colour map 4, C1-2.*

Walking in the Trossachs → *OS Landranger maps 56 and 57 covers these routes.*
Loch Lomond and the Trossachs is superb walking country. East of Loch Lomond itself, the two most challenging peaks are Ben Venue and Ben A'an, respectively 3 and 5 miles north of Aberfoyle. **Ben Venue** (2385 ft) is a fairly strenuous climb that begins with a steady waymarked ascent (dress and equip yourself appropriately for the climb) from behind the **Loch Achray Hotel**. Allow about four hours for the return trip. Though **Ben A'an** (1520 ft) isn't a giant of a hill, it's a steep, unrelenting climb from the moment you begin at the car park on the north banks of Loch Achray. The woodland car park is located 2 miles west of the lochside **Harbour Café** ① *T01877-330011*, on the shores of Loch Venachar. You should reach the summit within 1½ hours. Whichever ascent you choose, spectacular views await westwards towards Loch Lomond and southwards to the Campsie Hills and Glasgow. Before you go, pack a picnic to enjoy the views over Loch Katrine. On a still day, it's possible to hear the commentary from the deck of the toy-like *SS Walter Scott* far below Ben A'an. All local TICs sell detailed maps of the area.

Better red than dead

As the tourist board never tires of reminding us, the Trossachs is Rob Roy country. Rob Roy ('Red Robert' in Gaelic) was one of Scotland's most notorious outlaws or one of the bravest Highland heroes, depending on your point of view. It is true that he was a freebooter, but he was also defending Highland clan culture and more specifically fighting for the very survival of his own clan against proscription and persecution by the government and its supporters.

Rob Roy MacGregor (1671-1734) was born in Glengyle, to the northwest of Loch Katrine. The MacGregors' lands included those previously owned by the rival Campbells but bestowed on the MacGregors for services rendered to Alexander II in his conquest of Argyll. For a long time the clan kept possession of their lands by right of the sword, but

the constant attempts by neighbouring clans to displace them led to retaliation by the MacGregors and earned them a reputation for being aggressive. Rob Roy did little to change this image, and his bitter feud with the powerful Duke of Montrose led to his being outlawed and eventually captured and sentenced to transportation. He was pardoned and returned to Balquhidder, where he stayed for the rest of his life. He now lies buried in the churchyard.

The Rob Roy story was first popularized by Sir Walter Scott's eponymous 19th-century novel, and his life continues to be romanticized, most recently in the 1995 film starring Liam Neeson and Tim Roth. Like Robin Hood before him, his courage in refusing to bow to the forces of authority seems to strike a chord with people.

Both these mountains lie within the **Queen Elizabeth Forest Park**. This vast and spectacular wilderness of 75,000 acres borders Loch Lomond to the west and incorporates Loch Ard, Loch Achray and Loch Lubnaig, as well as Ben Venue, Ben A'An and Ben Ledi, which overlooks Callander. The park is run by Forestry Commission Scotland and is criss-crossed by a network of less difficult waymarked trails and cycling paths which start from the David Marshall Lodge, **Queen Elizabeth Park Visitor Centre** ① *T01877-382258, Mar daily 1000-1600, Apr-Jun 1000-1700, Jul-Aug 1000-1800, Sep-Oct 1000-1700, Nov-Dec 1000-1600, closed Jan, Feb; Thu-Sun 1000-1600, parking £3*, about half a mile north of Aberfoyle on the A821. The centre incorporates audio-visual displays on the park's flora and fauna, information on the area's numerous walks and cycle routes, a restaurant and children's play area.

Aberfoyle

The sleepy village of Aberfoyle suddenly bursts into life in the summer with the arrival of hordes of tourists. It lies on the edge of the Queen Elizabeth Forest Park and like Callander to the east, is a major tourist hub providing an ideal base for golf, walking and cycling in the surrounding hills. There's an abundance of guesthouse accommodation, though it's advisable to book ahead during the busy summer season.

Three miles east of Aberfoyle is the **Lake of Menteith**, the only lake in Scotland (as opposed to loch). On **Inchmahome Island** in the middle of the lake are the beautiful and substantial ruins of **Inchmahome Priory** ① *T01877-385294 (HS), Apr-Sep daily 0930-1630, Oct 0930-1530, £5, concession £4, children £3*, the 13th-century Augustinian priory where the four-year-old Mary, Queen of Scots was sent in 1547, safe from the clutches of Henry VIII. A ferry takes visitors over to the island from **Port of Menteith**.

To the north of Aberfoyle is Doon Hill, better known as the **Fairy Knowe**. The tree at the top is said to be the home of the 'People of Quietness', and in 1692 a local minister was less than discreet in telling the world of their secrets. As punishment he was taken away to fairyland, and his spirit has languished there ever since. If you go round the tree seven times, your wish will be granted, but go round it backwards and … well, we won't be held responsible. It's about 1½ hours up and back. Follow the road across the bridge south of the car park by the visitor centre, then continue until it forks; take the left fork, a way-marked path, to the hilltop.

Aberfoyle to Callander

The A821 route north from Aberfoyle, through the spectacular **Duke's Pass**, and then east past Loch Achray and Loch Vennachar, is a beautiful route and not to be missed. There are a couple of worthwhile diversions along the way. About 5 miles north of Aberfoyle, a forest track branches to the right and runs through Achray Forest and along the shores of **Loch Drunkie**, before rejoining the A821 further north. A few miles further on, a road turns left to **Trossachs Pier** on the southern shore of **Loch Katrine**. This is the departure point for cruises on the *SS Sir Walter Scott* between April and October (see Activities and tours, page 154). It sails to the remote settlement of **Stronachlachar** on the far western shores of the loch and back. There is also a 1 hour afternoon cruise at 1330 and 1500 (11) that makes a short, non-stop loop of the southern section of the freshwater loch. There's a cycle path around the loch as far as Stronachlachar so it's possible to take the morning cruise and cycle back to the pier. The superb bike hire outfit Katrine Wheelz (page 155), by the pier is the place to get the whole family on bikes. ▶▶ *For further information, see Transport, page 155.*

Callander and around

At the eastern end of the Trossachs and 14 miles northwest of Stirling is Callander, a tourist honey-pot whose Main Street sadly includes a few too many tartan-tat shops. Yet look closely and you'll also find several excellent restaurants, delightful corner shops selling home-

Callander

Sleeping 🛏
Brook Linn Country
  House **1**
Callander Meadows **6**
Leny House **4**

Monachyle Mhor **5**
Roman Camp
  Country House **2**
Trossachs Backpackers **3**

Eating 🍴
Conservatory at Ballachallan **3**
Deli Ecosse **4**
Lade Inn **5**
Mhor Fish **6**

made fudge and at **Deli Ecosse** by the TIC, a superb range of takeaway or eat-in Scottish and continental sandwiches, wines and fresh coffee. Seafood lovers will find it impossible to walk past the door of the award winning **Mhor Fish**, where you'll find oysters, mussels and all types of freshly caught foods from the sea awaiting your plate or carry out box from the 'chippy' next door. It's just as well there are many walks and cycling trails (including Route 7 to Balquhidder) to burn off those holiday calories. The over-worked **TIC** ① *Apr-May and Oct-Mar daily 1000-1700, Jun-Sep daily 1000-1800*, shares the same building and times as the **Rob Roy and Trossachs Visitor Centre** ① *£4.50*. The interactive displays and two film clips provide an entertaining account of the life of Rob Roy MacGregor.

Opened in 1995, Callander's family-run **Toy Museum** ① *111 Main St, T01877-330004, Apr-Oct daily, 1100-1600 £2.50*, is a true Aladdin's Cave, crammed with toys from the past 100 years. Step into the modest shop, and whatever your age, take a trip down memory lane. There are over 100 original Action Men, Victorian-era tin soldiers, Hot Wheels and Dinky Toys from the 1930s. You will also find bisque dolls dating back to the 1880s, 1930s dolls houses and over 100 vintage teddy bears, including the loveable Paddington Bear.

A recommended local walk is to **Bracklinn Falls**, reached by a woodland trail which leads from Bracklinn Road. At the time of writing this is not a circular walk as a wooden bridge has been washed away. Normally, it's about 30 minutes' walk each way. Another trail from Bracklinn Road leads up to **Callander Crags**, from where there are great views of the surrounding area. Allow 1½ hours there and back. The most challenging walk in the area is to the summit of **Ben Ledi** (2857 ft), but it's a tough climb and you'll need to be fit, experienced and prepared. Ask at the TIC for further information and for maps.

Two miles north of Callander, on the A84 route to the Highlands, are the **Falls of Leny**, in the narrow and dramatic Pass of Leny. The falls are accessible from the car park by the roadside or via the **Callander to Strathyre Cycleway** (Route 7), which follows the old train line to Oban, from Callander north along the west bank of **Loch Lubnaig**. This forms part of the **Glasgow to Killin Cycleway**, which runs from the centre of Glasgow, via Balloch, Aberfoyle, Callander, Balquhidder and Lochearnhead, to Killin. For the fit, this is the best way to see the Trossachs.

The A84 heads north from Callander along the east bank of Loch Lubnaig, and beyond towards **Loch Earn**. A few miles further north, a side road branches left to the tiny village of **Balquhidder**, famous as the burial place of Rob Roy. His grave in the churchyard, by his wife and two of his sons, is thankfully understated. In the nearby converted village library, there's a fabulous cosy **tea room** ① *Mar-Oct, times vary*, with delicious sandwiches.

North of Callander to Lochearnhead and Killin

A few miles north of the turning to Balquhidder, where the A84 meets the A85 from Crieff to Crianlarich, is **Lochearnhead**, at the western tip of Loch Earn. The loch is a highly popular watersports centre, see Activities and tours, page 155. Lochearnhead is also a good base for walking in the surrounding hills. In the far northwestern corner of the Stirling region, just to the west of Loch Tay, is **Killin**, a pleasant little village which makes a good base for walkers wishing to explore the wild mountains and glens of the ancient district of **Breadalbane** (pronounced *Bread-albinn*). Killin's picture-postcard setting, with the beautiful **Falls of Dochart** tumbling through the centre of the village and adjacent **Breadalbane Folklore Centre** ① *T01567-820254, daily Apr-Oct,1000-1600, £2.95, children £1.95*, make this a popular destination for tourists. The Folklore Centre is also where the **TIC** ① *Main St, Mar-Oct daily*, can be found.

Twelve miles west of Killin is **Crianlarich**, at the crossroads of the A82 Glasgow–Fort William road and the A85 to Perth, and at the junction of the Glasgow to Fort William and

Oban rail lines. It is a staging post on the West Highland Way. Six miles further north is tiny **Tyndrum**, which shot to prominence almost 20 years ago after the discovery of gold in the surrounding hills. There's a seasonal **TIC** ⓘ *main road, T01838-400246, Apr-Jun and Sep-Oct daily 1000-1700, Jul-Aug daily 1000-1800*. Adjacent to the TIC is the **Real Food Café**, an award-winning organic fast-food stop that's not cheap – but worth it.

Loch Lomond → *For listings, see pages 152-155. Colour map 4, C1.*

Britain's largest inland waterway is one of Scotland's most famous lochs, thanks to the Jacobite ballad about its 'bonnie banks'. These same banks are now one of the busiest parts of the Highlands, due to their proximity to Glasgow (only 20 miles south along the congested A82). Since 2002, the loch has formed the natural 'hub' of the 720-square-mile Loch Lomond and The Trossachs National Park, a designation that by implementing much needed controls has alleviated much of the disturbance by speedboats and jet skis over the summer months.

At the southern end of the loch is the resort town of **Balloch**, packed full of hotels, B&Bs, caravan parks and any number of operators offering boat trips around the loch's southern waters. At the northern end of the town is **Loch Lomond Shores** ⓘ *T01389-751035, year round daily*, a huge visitor centre-cum-shopping mall, adjacent to which is the **TIC** and **National Park Gateway Centre** ⓘ *T01389-722600, www.lochlomond-trossachs.org*, as well as shops and cafés. Here you can pick up all the information you need on the national park, as well as book a loch cruise, hire bikes, kayaks or sailing dinghies, or simply enjoy the views from the café in the Drumkinnon Tower. The tower is home to the **Loch Lomond Aquarium** ⓘ *T01389-721500, daily 1000-1700, £9.95, children £6.95*, with otter feeding at 1100 and 1500, and rays at 1330. It's a fun, educational experience that takes you on an 'underwater journey' to understand the abundant and diverse marine creatures that live in Loch Lomond, the Clyde Estuary and in the ocean. Giant fish tanks, touch pools, a sunken boat, rare otters and interactive displays are all part of the attraction. Nearby you'll find the watersport, walking and cycling operator, **Can You Experience** ⓘ *www.canyouexperince. com*, and a café aboard the restored steamer *Maid of the Loch*.

The west bank of the loch, from Balloch north to Tarbet, is one long, almost uninterrupted development of marinas, holiday homes, caravan parks and exclusive golf clubs. The most picturesque village here is **Luss**, though it is more of a theme park than a real village. It is to the genuine Highland experience what Ozzy Osbourne is to philosophical debate. One-and-a-half-hour boat trips leave from Luss pier. Further north, things begin to quieten down a bit. At Tarbet, it's worthwhile jumping aboard one of the boats run by **Loch Lomond Cruises** ⓘ *T01301-702356, www.cruiselochlomond.co.uk*. There are a number of cruise options (from £8.50) but surely the most innovative is The **West Highland Way Rambler** (£14.50) whereby hikers first enjoy a 45-minute cruise under Ben Lomond before disembarking on the east shore of the Loch at Rowardennan and hiking 6 miles north along the famous West Highland Way to Inversnaid before being picked up again by the boat. Still further north, the loch gets deeper and narrower en route to **Ardlui** and the famously cosy and rustic **Inverarnan Inn**, beyond which the A82 meets the A85 at **Crianlarich**.

The tranquil east bank of Loch Lomond is a great place for walking. The West Highland Way follows the east bank all the way from **Drymen**, through **Balmaha**, **Rowardennan** and **Inversnaid**. Beyond Rowardennan this is the only access to the loch's east bank, except for the road to Inversnaid from the Trossachs. From Rowardennan you can climb

Ben Lomond (3192 ft), the most southerly of the Munros. It's deceptively long though not too difficult and the views from the top, in good weather, are astounding. An easier climb is **Conic Hill**, on the Highland fault line and very close to Glasgow. The route starts from the Forestry Commission interpretative and ranger post in the car park at Balmaha. It takes about 1½ hours to reach the top, from where the views of the loch are stunning. Across the road, it's worthwhile hopping aboard the **MacFarlane & Son** ① *T01360-870214, www.balmahaboatyard.co.uk*, operated mail-boat cruise (£8) that leaves from the pier and delivers post to the offshore islands. Alternatively, there's a ferry to explore the beautiful isle of **Inchcailloch** with its nature trails and ancient ruins. In both cases, times vary so it's best to call ahead.

◉ The Trossachs and Loch Lomond listings

For Sleeping and Eating price codes and other relevant information, see Essentials pages 38-45.

Sleeping

The Trossachs *p147*
L-A Lake Hotel, in Port of Menteith, on the lakeshore overlooking Inchmahome, T01877-385258, www.lake-hotel.com. A discerning hotel in a beautiful location that cooks up many memorable treats in the restaurant (3-course dinner from £34 per person).
L-A Monachyle Mhor Hotel, Balquhidder, on the road to Inverlochlarig, T01877-384622, www.mhor.net. Renowned for its culinary delights and warm welcome, this family-run hotel boasts 14 wonderfully appointed, individually styled bedrooms in a serene, rural setting with terrific views over the loch. One of the UK's top restaurants, the hotel's organic garden provides fresh herbs whilst much of the produce is sourced in the local area. It's fabulous with the 5-course table d'hôte £46 per head. Recommended.
A MacDonald Forest Hills Hotel, Loch Ard, on the B829 from Aberfoyle, T0844-879 9057, www.macdonald-hotels.co.uk/foresthills. 50 bedrooms. Graceful 19th-century country house converted into a family-friendly hotel, offering multitudinous facilities and activities including a brand spanking new luxury health spa with pool, sauna, steam room and fully equipped gym. There's also the chance to mountain bike, sail, hike and

fish. There are lovely views over Loch Ard from the restaurant, where you can expect the menu to include a variety of delicious, locally sourced meats and fish (♥♥♥-♥♥) or enjoy dining in the less formal **Rafters Restaurant**.
A-B The Four Seasons, in the village of St Fillans, a few miles east of Lochearnhead, T01764-685333, www.thefourseasonshotel. co.uk. Spectacular setting on the shores of Loch Earn, this recently refurbished 12 bedroom, 19th-century house boasts 2 fine restaurants, including the **Meall Reamhar** where a 4-course extravaganza of fine Scottish cuisine will set you back £35 per person. There are also chalets (**C**) within the wooded grounds.
A-B Roman Camp Country House Hotel, Callander, T01877-330003, www.roman camphotel.co.uk. An exquisite16th-century former hunting lodge set in extensive grounds by the river, away from the hoi polloi. Oozes character and Queen Victoria was quite taken with the place. Good Scottish cuisine (♥♥♥-♥♥).
C-B Creagan House, at the northern end of Loch Lubnaig, in Strathyre, T01877-384638. An atmospheric family-run 17th-century farmhouse consistently providing award-winning service combined with fine food, an impressive wine list and over 50 drams in its cosy restaurant (♥♥♥-♥♥).
D Creag-Ard House, Milton, 2 miles west of Aberfoyle overlooking Loch Ard, T01877-382297. Open Easter-Oct. Beautiful location, a warm welcome, a hearty breakfast and

even the chance to trout fish on the loch outside your window. Recommended.
E Brook Linn Country House, Callander, T01877-330103, www.brooklinn-scotland.co.uk. Open Easter-Oct. B&B (and dinner) is available in this fine Victorian house where the secluded walled garden and grounds include a small cottage (£200-500 per week).
D Callander Meadows, 24 Main St, Callander, T01877-330181, www.callandermeadows.co.uk. Closed Tue and lunchtime Wed. Simplicity is the key to this 18th-century townhouse offering 3 delightful en suite bedrooms and a wonderful restaurant menu (ŤŤŤ-ŤŤ), including desserts to die for. Recommended.
F Braveheart Backpackers, Lochay Lodge and Steading by the **Killin Hotel**, T01567-829089. Basic 12-bed accommodation in this pretty village. Bike and canoe hire available.
F Trossachs Backpackers, a couple of miles out of Callander, Invertrossachs Rd which turns off the A81, T01877-331200, www.scottish-hostel.co.uk. Over 30 beds, with dorms and family rooms. Relaxed and peaceful independent hostel with bike rental available next door.

Self-catering
Altskeith House, by Loch Ard, T01877-382878, www.altskeith.com. Just 3 miles west of Aberfoyle, this historic, sandstone house, blessed with breathtaking views over Loch Ard towards Ben Lomond, promises and delivers a heavenly luxury stay for the discerning traveller and friends. A home from home: a huge rustic living room with roaring fire, gargantuan dining room, tastefully appointed 10 en suite bedrooms and a kitchen fit for Jamie Oliver. There are also endless outdoor pursuits to enjoy, from windsurfing, biking and kayaking to walking in the nearby Loch Ard Forest. Glasgow is 45 mins' drive away, Edinburgh 60 mins. £2750-5250 per week.
Leny House, Callander, T01877-331078, www.lenyestate.com. Stay in the baronial north wing of historic Leny House and enjoy

5-star self-catering (£930-1240 per week) or 4 guests can enjoy a luxurious stay in the estate cottages (from £560) and chalets.

Camping
Cobeland Campsite, 2 miles south of Aberfoyle on the edge of the Queen Elizabeth Forest Park, T01877-382392. Open Apr-Oct.
Trossachs Holiday Park, 3 miles south of Aberfoyle, off the A81, T01877-382614. Open Mar-Oct. An excellent site set in 40 acres, with mountain bike hire.

Loch Lomond *p151*
L Cameron House Hotel, 2 miles north of Balloch, T01389-755565, www.cameronhouse.co.uk. Exclusive lochside hotel with spa, 3 restaurants and a marina.
C Rowardennan Hotel, Rowardennan, T01360-870273. Comfortable choice, with a cosy, old world bar. Serves good value food.
F Loch Lomond SYHA Youth Hostel, Arden, T01360-870259, www.syha.org.uk. Grand 19th-century turreted mansion complete with obligatory ghost and outstanding loch-side location close to Ben Lomond footpath.

Camping
Lomond Woods Holiday Park, Tullichewan, on the Old Luss Rd, T01389-755000. A good campsite where you can hire mountain bikes.
Milarrochy Bay, Balmaha, 5 miles north of Drymen, T01360-870236. A very good campsite with stunning views over Loch Lomond.

🍴 Eating

The Trossachs *p147*
ŤŤŤ **Monachyle Mhor Hotel**, see Sleeping, above. This renowned restaurant makes stylish and imaginative use of superb local ingredients. Outstanding service and food, as you'd expect for a dinner that starts at £46 per head. Also run the tasty **Mhor Fish** restaurant and takeaway on the main street in Callander. Book ahead. Recommended.

♥♥♥-♥♥ Callander Meadows, Main St,
Callander, T01877-330181. Great restaurant
that prides itself on its imaginative
menu, fresh, locally sourced produce
and irresistible desserts.

♥♥♥-♥♥ The Conservatory at Ballachallan,
1 mile south of Callander off the main road,
T01877-339190. Mar-Oct. A farm-steading
restaurant specializing in Scottish cuisine,
including seafood such as delicious cullen
skink soup and scallops. Welcoming and
reasonably priced. Also lunches and
home-baking.

♥♥♥-♥♥ Roman Camp Country House Hotel,
see Sleeping, above. Lovely restaurant and
reasonably priced for lunch or dinner.

♥♥ Brig O' Turk tea room, Brig O' Turk,
T01877-376267, Callander. Look out for
the shabby green hut with peeling paint
and tired-looking hanging baskets outside.
Inside it's like a scout hut with higgledy-
piggeldy chairs and mis-matching crockery
and tablecloths. Informal and very good
food when it's open.

♥♥ The Lade Inn, Kilmahog, 1 mile north
of Callander, T01877-330152. Enjoy the
realales from the microbrewery and
delicious meals prepared using locally
sourced produce including trout and beef.
Terrific atmosphere.

♥ Deli Ecosse, Callander, T01877-331220.
Thu-Tue 0800-1700. For hearty sandwiches
and freshly brewed coffee.

Loch Lomond p151

♥♥♥ Cameron House Hotel, 2 miles north
of Balloch, T01389-755565, www.cameron
house.co.uk. 3 lovely restaurants and a
beautiful lochside setting. Dress to impress.

♥♥ Inverbeg Inn, a few miles north of Luss,
Inverbeg, T01436-860678. Good food,
including grilled venison sausages and
seafood chowder. Lacking atmosphere.

♥♥ Oak Tree Inn, Balmaha, on the east side of
the loch, T01360-870357. Excellent pub food
served with a touch of finesse. Busy in summer,
great atmosphere. Has double rooms for B&B
(**D**), should lunch become dinner.

♥ Tarbet Tea room, Tarbet, T01301-702200.
Daily 0830-1700. Tucked just off the main
road as the road forks to Arrochar, this
humble dwelling that served as a school in
The Second World War is where weekend
walkers and cyclists still come in their droves
for a hearty cooked breakfast, toasties or
cream tea (£3.50). Fantastic value and very
friendly; just don't expect silver service.
Recommended.

🍷 Bars and clubs

Loch Lomond p151

The Clachan Inn, Drymen, T01360-660824.
Established in 1734, this whitewashed, croft-
like, cosy pub serving heart bar meals (**♥♥-♥**)
and fine ales may well be Scotland's oldest
registered pub.

Drover's Inn, Inverarnan, T01301-704234.
The famous Highland watering hole, with
smoke-blackened walls, low ceilings, bare
floors, open fires, a hall filled with stuffed
animals, a barman in a kilt and a great
selection of single malts. The perfect place
for a wild night of drinking in the wilderness.
The **Drovers Lodge**, opposite is a handy
place to stay if you can't get far.

🎫 Activities and tours

The Trossachs p147

For detailed advice on the many cycling,
fishing, walking and hiking possibilities
within the Loch Lomond and Trossachs
National Park, contact the **National Park
Gateway Centre**, T01389-722600, www.
lochlomond-trossachs.org. Alternatively, call
T08707-200642 and ask for the *GO Outdoors*
leaflet, www.gosmileoutdoors.co.uk.

Go Ape, David Marshall Lodge Visitor Centre,
1 mile north of Aberfoyle on A821, T0845-643
9215, www.goape.co.uk. Offers adrenaline
junkies the opportunity to swing through
the trees on a high wire aerial course. Thrills
include flying 150 ft above a waterfall. From
£30, children (over 10) from £20.

Lochearnhead Watersports, Watersports Centre, Lochearnhead, T01567-830247, www.lochearnhead-water-sports.co.uk. Offers waterskiing, canoeing, kayaking and wakeboarding on the loch.

SS Sir Walter Scott, Loch Katrine, 5 miles north of Aberfoyle over the Duke's Pass, you'll find a turn-off to the Trossachs pier, T01877-332000. Open Apr-Oct daily. At 1030 the cruise boat sails to Stronachlachar and back (£10.50 return). There is also a 1 hour afternoon cruise (£9) that makes a short, non-stop loop of the southern section of the freshwater loch.

Loch Lomond *p151*

Can You Experience, beside Lomond Shores, Balloch, T01389-756251, www.canyou experience.com. This operator offers guided walks around Loch Lomond, including excursions to the offshore islands, and guided canoe trips. Hires mountain bikes kayaks and even pedalos (£12 for 30 mins).

Cruise Loch Lomond, Tarbet, T01301-702356, www.cruiselochlomond.co.uk. Operating from Tarbet since 1973, its modern cruise boats run a host of excellent year-round excursions with commentary, including the West Highland Way Explorer (from £14.50), Inversnaid Explorer (from £8) and Rob Roy Discovery (from £12.50).

Lomond Adventure, Balmaha, T01360-870218. Easter-Oct. Offers instruction and hire for kayaks, canoes, power boats, dinghy sailing and waterskiing.

Loch Lomond Waterski Club, by Balloch, T01436-860632. Offers tuition and waterski hire (Apr-Sep).

Sweeney's Cruises, Balloch, T01389-752376. Open daily 1030-1930, call to confirm times. Runs cruises from Balloch and Luss.

⊖ Transport

The Trossachs *p147*

Bus The Citylink, T08705-505050, **Oban** to **Dundee** bus runs twice daily through Perthshire villages including **Comrie**, **St Fillans**, **Lochearnhead** and **Killin**. The same operator also runs a once daily service (Mon-Sat) from **Edinburgh** via **Stirling** to **Fort William** that passes through **Callander**, **Strathyre**, **Lochearnhead** (No 25 postbus connects with **Killin**), **Crianlarich** and **Tyndrum**. Caber Coaches, T01887-820090, No 893, and the postbus (No 213) operate a service (Mon-Sat) between **Aberfeldy** (0900) and **Killin** (arrives 1205) via **Kenmore** (arrives 0935). There's also a postbus service (No 25) between **Crianlarich** and **Tyndrum** and **Killin** (Mon-Sat). First run leaves Tyndrum 1110 and arrives Killin 1200.

Cycle hire Katrine Wheelz, by the pier, Loch Katrine, T01877-376316. Apr-Oct daily 0900-1700. £10 per ½ day. Trailer £9 and tandem £28 per day. Recommended. **Wheels**, Invertrossachs Rd, Callander, T01887-331100.

Loch Lomond *p151*

Bus For further details on bus travel from Loch Lomond, see Ins and outs, page 146.

Cycle hire Can You Experience, beside Lomond Shores, Balloch, T01389-602576, www.canyouexperience.com. Rents mountain bikes by the day for £17.

Lomond Activities, Drymen, T01360-660066. Individual and family bike hire, including child seats and helmets.

Deeside

→ *Colour map 4, A4-6.*

The River Dee rises in the Cairngorms and flows down through the surrounding hills, eastwards to the sea at Aberdeen. The valley of the Dee is known as Deeside, or rather Royal Deeside, for its connections with the royal family who have holidayed here, at Balmoral, since Queen Victoria first arrived in 1848. Originally, Queen Victoria and Prince Albert were looking for an estate further west, but were advised that the Deeside climate would be better for Albert's delicate constitution. The queen fell in love with this area and its people, and following Albert's death she sought out the company of straight-talking northerners, preferring their down-to-earth honesty to the two-faced toadies she endured at court.

Today, Deeside's royal associations have made it the tourist honeypot of the northeast, but the royal presence has also saved it from mass development. There's an air of understated affluence and refinement in the villages strung out along the A93 that runs along the north bank of the Dee and, as well as the obvious attraction of Balmoral, there are many other fine examples of baronial castles. Deeside is also a great area for outdoor activities, such as hiking in the surrounding mountains, fishing, stalking, mountain biking, canoeing and skiing. ▶ *For listings, see pages 161-163.*

Ins and outs

Getting there

Aberdeen airport ① *airport information T0844-481 6666*, is 7 miles northwest of the city centre, at Dyce, off the A96 to Inverness. There are regular domestic flights from Scottish and UK destinations, including Orkney and Shetland, as well as international flights from several European destinations. There's car hire and currency exchange at the airport. **First Aberdeen** ① *T01224-650065*, buses run regular daily services to the city centre (35 minutes, £1.30 single). Alternatively, take a bus or taxi to Dyce station and then a train. A **taxi** ① *T01224-353535*, from the airport to Dyce railway station costs around £10, and £19 to the city centre. ▶ *For further details see Transport, page 163.*

Aberdeen is linked to Lerwick in Shetland and Kirkwall in Orkney by **Northlink ferries** ① *T0845-600 0449, www.northlinkferries.co.uk*. There are regular sailings from the passenger terminal in the harbour, a short walk east of the train and bus stations.

Getting around

From Aberdeen, all the main tourist attractions in Deeside can be reached by bus. To reach Balmoral by bus from Aberdeen catch the daily No 201 service destined for Crathie and Braemar. Contact **Scottish Bluebird** ① *T01224-212266*. Buses No 502 and No 503 from Aberdeen leave Banchory at 0938 (May to September only, Monday to Saturday) and travel via Ballater and Braemar on their way to Perth.

If you wish to explore Deeside along a less popular route (though even in the summer, crowds are never great) take the B976 along the south bank of the River Dee. Fortunately, the Heather Hopper, operated by **Stagecoach Bluebird** ① *T01224-591381*, and **Coopers Tourmaster Travel** (same phone number), provides the link between the many rural outposts of Deeside and key Speyside destinations (see also www.cairngorms.co.uk).

Tourist information

The regional **VisitScotland website** ① *www.aberdeen-grampian.com*, is a good starting point. For details of the Castle Trail, Victorian Heritage Trail and Deeside Tourist Route, contact the TIC in Aberdeen, or in any of the towns along the way. Banchory **TIC** ① *in the local museum, Bridge St, behind the High St, Apr-Oct*, can provide information on walking and fishing in the area. T01339 822000, Ballater **TIC** ① *T01339-755306, www.ballaterscotland. com, Oct-May daily 1000-1700, Jun-Sep daily 0900-1800*, is in the Old Royal Station and unsurprisingly is complemented by a small, informative railway museum (same opening hours as the TIC). Braemar also has a **TIC** ① *Balmoral Mews, Mar Rd, T01339-741600, Nov-May Mon-Sat 1030-1330, 1400-1700, Sun 1300-1600, Jun-Oct daily 0900-1700.*

Around Deeside → *For listings, see pages 161-163.*

Aberdeen to Banchory → *Colour map 4, A5-6.*

The first sight of interest heading west from Aberdeen is **Drum Castle** ① *T0844-493 2161, www.nts.org.uk, Castle, tearoom and shop open Apr-Jun and Sep Thu-Mon 1100-1645. Last admission 45 mins before closing. Garden open Apr-Oct daily 1100-1700, Castle and gardens £9, concessions £6.50.* Three miles west of **Peterculter** (pronounced 'Petercooter'), Drum Castle is a combination of a 13th-century square tower, Jacobean mansion house and later Victorian additions. It was given to one William de Irvine by Robert the Bruce for service rendered at Bannockburn and was in the family's hands for over 650 years, until it was taken over by the National Trust for Scotland in 1976. There's a beautiful walled garden and a trail through the 100-acre ancient **Wood of Drum** which forms part of the castle grounds.

A few miles southeast of Peterculter is its sister village, **Maryculter** (pronounced 'Marycooter'), where you'll find **Storybook Glen** ① *T01224-732941, www.storybookglen aberdeen.co.uk, Mar-Oct daily 1000-1800, Nov-Feb daily 1000-1600, £5.40, concession £4.05, children £3.85*, the northeast's answer to Disneyland. This very attractive and tasteful 'theme park' is a great place to take the kids. There are over 100 nursery rhyme and fairytale characters, secret waterfalls and even fairytale castles.

Fifteen miles west of Aberdeen, where the A93 meets the A957 from Stonehaven, is **Crathes Castle** ① *T0844-493 2182, Castle open Nov-Mar Sat/Sun 1030-1545; Apr-Oct daily 1030-1645. Garden and estate all year daily 0900-sunset. Castle and garden £11, concessions £8.* It's a perfect 'fairytale' castle built over 40 years in the mid-16th century. The turreted tower house is still furnished with many period pieces and wall hangings, and is notable for its superb painted ceilings. There are narrow spiral staircases leading to tiny rooms, one of which is said to be inhabited by a ghost. The castle is well worth exploring but is almost overshadowed by the exceptional gardens, which shouldn't be missed. There are no fewer than eight of them, so take your time. There's also a visitor centre, restaurant and shop. It's also worth taking one of several waymarked trails into surrounding countryside inhabited by roe deer and red squirrels.

Banchory to Alford → *Colour map 4, A5. Phone code 01330.*

Banchory, with the River Dee burbling through, makes a very pleasant base for exploring Deeside though aside from salmon and trout fishing in the area, there's little in the town itself to hold the visitor. You can watch salmon leaping spectacularly at the Bridge of Feugh, to the south of town. There is a sad tale, though, of a lady-in-waiting who was staying at Balmoral when the royal family were in residence some years ago. She was standing fishing in the river, in quite deep water, and wearing chest-height waders, when the sovereign rode by. Seeing the king, she curtsied, whereupon the water flowed quickly into her waders and she sank beneath the water and drowned.

From Banchory, head northwest on the A980 to Alford, in the Don Valley, see page 165. Roughly halfway is the village of **Lumphanan**, once thought to be the burial place of Macbeth, the Scottish king so misrepresented by Shakespeare (he is actually buried on Iona). Macbeth's Cairn is instead a prehistoric cairn. Just to the south of the village is the **Peel Ring**, a 12th-century Motte, and one of Scotland's earliest medieval sites.

West of Banchory → Colour map 4, A5.
The attractive little village of Aboyne is 30 miles west of Banchory on the A93. A few miles further on is Dinnet. In the Muir of Dinnet National Nature Reserve you can explore the Burn o' Vat, a sheltered valley which attracts many butterflies and dragonflies. During the walk, you'll come to a huge circular stone chamber and, in nearby Loch Kinord, there are crannogs, which are ancient man-made islands.

Ballater and Balmoral → Colour map 4, A4.
The neat little town of Ballater is proud of its royal connections. You can buy meat from the butcher with his 'By Royal Appointment' sign, or clothes from royal outfitters. This is where Lizzie and Phil pop down to the shops for a pint of milk or perhaps to choose a DVD for a quiet night in. Ever since Queen Victoria first arrived by train from Aberdeen in 1848, the royal family have been spending their holidays here in their summer residence, Balmoral. She was not amused at the prospect of having an unsightly rail station on her doorstep, so the line ended 8 miles east, at Ballater. The line has been closed for some time, but you can still visit the TIC which is within the old train station.

The royals are not the only famous summer visitors. The poet Byron (who attended Aberdeen Grammar School) spent many childhood summer holidays at Ballaterach, a few miles east of Ballater. He had a narrow escape when he slipped and nearly fell into the fast flowing stream at the Linn of Dee, beyond Braemar. He was rescued just in time and went on to wax poetic about the beautiful hills which are Ballater's other great attraction. The town makes the ideal base for hiking (see below) as well as a number of other outdoor activities. Many of the walks set off from within the 6000 acre **Loch Muick** (pronounced 'Mick') and **Lochnagar Wildlife Reserve**, 9 miles southwest of Ballater, at the head of Glen Muick. There's a visitor centre and car park at Spittal of Glenmuick. From here a track leads along the west shore of the loch to the lodge where Queen Victoria met John Brown. You may spot birds of prey and deer. For guides and equipment for canoeing, climbing, mountain biking and skiing, contact **Adventure Scotland** ① T01479 811411, see page 163.

Balmoral Castle → Colour map 4, A4.
① T01339-742534, www.balmoralcastle.com, Apr-Jul daily 1000-1700, £8, concessions £7.50, children £4.50.
Eight miles west of Ballater is the area's main attraction, Balmoral Castle. The 16th-century tower house, formerly owned by the local Gordon family, was bought for Queen Victoria by Prince Albert in 1852 and converted into today's baronial mansion. It has been the royal family's summer retreat ever since. Only the ballroom and the grounds are open to the likes of you and me, and only for three months of the year. Pony trekking and pony cart rides are available around the grounds and are favourite ways of enjoying the wonderful scenery. Opposite the castle gates is **Crathie Church**, which is used by the family when

We are most certainly amused

There has been a gathering of some sort at Braemar for 900 years, ever since Malcolm Canmore set contests for the local clans so that he could pick the strongest and bravest of men for his army. These events take place up and down the country throughout the summer, but none is as famous, or well attended, as Braemar's. Queen Victoria attended in 1848 and the gathering is still patronized by the royal family. Crowds come from all over the world to proclaim the monarch as Chieftain of the Braemar Gathering.

At the gathering the visitor will see contests in traditional Scottish events, such as tossing the caber, Highland dancing and bagpipe competitions and displays. There is an inter-services tug o'war championship, a medley relay race and a hill race up Morrone. The sound of the massed pipes echoing around the encircling heather-clad hills and a plethora of tartan also help to make this a real tourist highlight. The royal connection (and the crowds) apart, many other local communities hold similar games.

they're in residence. There's a small souvenir shop next to the main gates and a visitor centre which gives a lot of information on the castle and its owners.

Braemar → Colour map 4, A3.

Nine miles west of Balmoral, is Braemar, the final town on Deeside, lying at the foot of the awesome, brooding **Cairngorm Massif**, which dominates the Eastern Highlands. Even at the height of summer you can see a dab of snow still lying in a hollow in the surrounding mountains, and Braemar is an excellent base for hiking, see below, and winter skiing at Glenshee, see page 139. It's an attractive little place, much loved by Queen Victoria and much visited during its annual Braemar Gathering (or games, see box above), which attracts tens of thousands of visitors each year, amongst them members of the royal family. **Braemar Highland Heritage Centre** ① *Balmoral Mews by the tourist office, T01339-741944, Apr-Oct daily 0900-1700, Nov-Mar daily 1000-1600, free*, with a small exhibition including a 12-minute audio-visual presentation.

Just north of the village is **Braemar Castle** ① *T01339-741219, May-Oct Sat-Sun 1100-1600 July-Aug Sat, Sun and Wed, £5, concessions £4 and children £3*, dating from 1628. This impressive fortress was used by Hanoverian troops after the Jacobite Rising of 1745. It is L-shaped, with a star-shaped defensive wall and a central round tower with a spiral stair. There are barrel-vaulted ceilings and an underground prison. Its owner also possesses the world's largest cairngorm – a semi-precious stone, a variety of quartz, which is yellow, grey or brown in colour – weighing 52 lbs. Thanks to an inspired restoration project spearheaded by the local community, it's now possible to visit this atmospheric castle.

A very scenic side trip from Braemar is to the **Linn of Dee**, 6 miles west of the village, at the end of the road. Here, the river thunders through a narrow gorge to spectacular effect. There are numerous walks from here along the river, or for the more adventurous, the famous **Lairig Ghru**, which runs through the Cairngorms to Aviemore, see page 173. Between the Linn of Dee and the tiny settlement of **Inverey**, a mile to the east, there's a very basic youth hostel (open early May to end September), which has no showers and no phone, so book through **Braemar Youth Hostel**, see page 162. Unfortunately, there's now no postbus from Ballater post office for Linn of Dee so you'll need to walk or cycle.

Ballater and Braemar are ideal bases for walking in the surrounding Grampian Mountains, and if you feel like 'bagging a Munro' (ie climbing a mountain over 3000 ft), there are some close at hand. All of this area, that's also reportedly home to 25% of Britain's endangered species, is included in the new **Cairngorms National Park** ① *www.cairngorm.co.uk*, which opened in 2003. This is the largest national park in Britain, covering a vast 4500 sq km, from Aboyne in the east to Dalwhinnie in the west, and from Blair Atholl north to Grantown-on-Spey.

Lochnagar → *OS Landranger No 44.*

The best walk in the area is to the summit of Lochnagar (3786 ft), made famous by Prince Charles in the book he wrote for his brothers when young, *The Old Man of Lochnagar*. The noble and mysterious mountain dominates the **Royal Forest of Balmoral** and takes its name from a small loch at its foot (it's also known as the White Mounth). This fine granite mass is approached from the car park by the Rangers' visitor centre at Spittal of Glen Muick. The path to the top is well trodden and well marked, though steep as you near the summit. It's 10 miles there and back, so allow a full day for the climb. You'll need to be properly equipped and take a map.

Cambus o' May and Morrone → *OS Landranger No 43.*

An easier walk is to Cambus o' May, on the river, about 4 miles east of Ballater. It's a great spot for a picnic, or to swim in the river, or to enjoy a stroll along the riverbank. A good walk from Braemar is to the summit of Morrone (2818 ft), the mountain to the southwest. The walk takes about four hours in total.

Glen Tanar to Glen Esk → *OS Landranger No 44.*

Another good climb is the route up Mount Keen (3077 ft), the most easterly Munro, which lies between Deeside and Glen Esk, the loveliest of the Angus glens. Again, you should allow a whole day for this expedition. It can be approached from the visitor centre in Glen Tanar, at the end of the little road that runs southwest off the B976, across the river from Aboyne. You can climb to the summit and return by the same route but, if your party has two cars, it is well worth walking over to Glen Esk, 14 miles away. Drive around to the Invermark car park at the head of Glen Esk and park your car there. From Glen Tanar follow the old drove road which at times runs with the Mounth road. Skirting the **Home Farm** with its Arboretum and its dammed lake, the fairly flat track winds along Glen Tanar through the forest for about 4 miles. Then comes the Halfway Hut, used for rest by former shooting parties. You pass shooting butts en route. The next stretch is through open country with the **Clachan Yell** (626 ft) on the left.

The walk proper then begins to take shape. Cross the stone bridge of **Etnach**, and then the path begins to lead up to the **Shiel of Glentanar**. The second bridge forks left and the track heads for the summit. The rough path continues along a ridge, the shoulder of Mount Keen. From the summit with its stone marker, **Dinnet**, see page 158, and its two lakes are visible to the north, and the River Esk glints its way down the valley to the south. Watch out for adders. On the descent, you'll pass the **Queen's Well**, used by Queen Victoria when she and her party went down to Fettercairn posing as a wedding party. The well is decorated with a graceful granite crown which was erected in 1861. The royal party covered much of the climb on hill ponies. The stone arch at Fettercairn commemorates this visit.

For Sleeping and Eating price codes and other relevant information, see Essentials pages 38-45.

● Sleeping

Banchory to Alford *p157*
There are some very fine places to stay in and around Banchory.

A-B Banchory Lodge Hotel, Dee St, Banchory, T01330-822625, www.banchory lodge hotel.co.uk. The roaring open fires, 4-poster beds and views over the River Feugh and Dee whilst fine dining (ŦŦŦ-ŦŦ) on locally sourced beef and salmon make this one of Deeside's rewarding escapes.

B Raemoir House Hotel, 3 miles north of town on the A980, T01330-824884, www.raemoir.com. This fabulous, Georgian country mansion hotel is set in acres of stunning wood and parkland. Boasting award-winning cuisine including its specially reared Tamworth pork, the Raemoir is a popular lunch stop whilst, for £35 per head, guests are treated to a 3-course formal dinner. Alternatively, pop in for a traditional afternoon tea (£6.50).

B-C Tor-na-Coille Hotel, outside town on the Inchmarlo Rd, T01330-822242, www.tornacoille.com. This tastefully furnished 23-bedroom Victorian country house hotel is set in lovely grounds and boasts a considerable reputation for its modern Scottish cooking (ŦŦŦ-ŦŦ).

D The Old West Manse, 71 Station Rd, T01330-822202. Set in an acre of mature gardens, this is a well-appointed, friendly, 3-bedroom guesthouse where golf, or even a babysitting service, can be arranged.

E June Little, 73 High St, T01330-824666. A good choice with a great breakfast.

Self-catering
Mill of Tilquhillie, Banchory, T01330-844616. A charming self-catering option. A 2-bedroom, granite stone, former watermill complete with wood-burning stove and wildlife pond nearby. Sleeps 4. From £300 per week.

Camping
Feughside Caravan Park, Strachan, by Banchory, T01330-850669. Close to the**Feughside Inn** and just off the B976. Tourers and campers (£15 per tent) are welcome at this well equipped facility.

Ballater and Balmoral *p158*
There's plenty of accommodation in Ballater, from expensive hotels to reasonable B&Bs.

A Darroch Learg Hotel, ½ mile from town, off the A93 heading west to Braemar, T01339-755443, www.darrochlearg.co.uk. Open Feb-Dec. 12 rooms. Friendly country house hotel with fine views, award-winning for superb food (ŦŦŦ) and a notable fine wine list.

A Balgonie Country House Hotel, on the western outskirts of town, off the A93, T/F01339-755482. Open Feb-Dec. 9 rooms. Friendly and comfortable country house hotel with a very good restaurant (ŦŦŦ).

A-B Hilton Craigendarroch, Braemar Rd, T01339-755858, www.hilton.com. Victorian country house converted into a modern resort hotel with full leisure and sports facilities. Lovely restaurants.

C-A Glen Lui Hotel, Invercauld Rd, T01339-755402, www.glen-lui-hotel.co.uk. 19 rooms. Comfortable hotel serving fine food and with good views over the golf course to Lochnagar.

D The Green Inn, town centre, Ballater, T/F01339-755701. Renowned for its cuisine but there are also 3 well-appointed bedrooms upstairs.

B Deeside Hotel, set back from the A93 heading out of town towards Braemar, T01339-755420, www.deesidehotel.co.uk. Friendly, good value and good food, with a terrific selection of malt whiskies.

E Inverdeen House, 11 Bridge Sq, T01339-755759, www.inverdeen.com. Among the many B&Bs, this one is recommended.

Antiques in the house, French, German and Polish spoken. Great breakfasts.

Self-catering
Royal Deeside Holiday Cottages, Ballater, T/F01339-885341. Managed by the Dinnet Estate, there are 4 traditional stone cottages in peaceful surroundings. Sleep 4-6. £295-450 per week.

Camping
Anderson Road Caravan Park, Anderson Rd, Ballater, T01339-755727. Open Apr-Oct.

Braemar p159
Accommodation is hard to find before and during the **Braemar Gathering**, but at other times of the year there's plenty to choose from, including many B&Bs and guesthouses.
A-F Braemar Lodge Hotel, on the outskirts of the village on the road south to Glenshee and Blairgowrie, T01339-741627, www. braemarlodge.co.uk. A lovely hotel with the option of log-cabin (**C-D**) and bunkhouse accommodation (**F**) in the hotel grounds.
E-D Callater Lodge Hotel, Glenshee Rd, T01339-741275, www.hotel-braemar.co.uk. Charming and comfortable 6 bedroom guesthouse where the local visitors include woodpeckers and red squirrels.
D Clunie Lodge, Cluniebank Rd, T01339-741330. Offering 5 rooms, 3 en suite. Good-value guesthouse with fine views.
D Schiehallion House, Glenshee Rd, T01339-741679. Open Jan-Oct. 6 rooms, 5 en suite. Traditional Highland welcome in this friendly guesthouse.
F Braemar Lodge Bunkhouse, 6 Glenshee Rd, T01339-741627, www.braemar lodge.co.uk. A 12-bed bunkhouse that's a good choice for budget travellers. Transport, shops and a pub are just 500 m away.
F Rucksacks, 15 Mar Rd, T01339-741517. A cheap and friendly bunkhouse complete with sauna that's popular with hikers and rents out mountain bikes.

F SYHA Youth Hostel, Corrie Feragie, Glenshee Rd, T01339-741659. Open all year. Terrific former shooting lodge with good range of facilities and reasonably close to the shops and bus stop.

Camping
Invercauld Caravan Site, Glenshee Rd, T01339-741373. Open Dec-Oct.

🍴 Eating

Banchory to Alford p157
🍴🍴 **The Falls of Feugh Restaurant and Tea Room**, Bridge of Feugh, T01330-822123. Open Apr-Sep daily 1000-1700, Oct-Mar Wed-Sun 1000-1600. For terrific home-cooking including traditional soups and home-baking, nip into this eatery nestled above the banks of the river.
🍴-🍴 **Burnett Arms Hotel**, High St, T01330-824944. Aside from the hotels listed above, this former coaching inn is one of the better eateries in Banchory.
🍴 **The Shieling Coffee Shop**, 18 Dee St, T01330-823278. Mon-Sat 0915-1630. A terrific stop for a traditional tea and scone.

Ballater and Balmoral p158
See also Sleeping, above.
🍴🍴🍴 **The Green Inn Restaurant**, 9 Victoria Rd, Ballater, on the green in the town centre, T/F01339-755701. You'll find many a local dining in what remains one of the best restaurants for lunch or dinner (1900-2100) in the area. It's not the cheapest option but the food is thoughtfully prepared and tasty to boot. Also 3 comfortable bedrooms (**C**).
🍴🍴🍴 **Inver Hotel**, Crathie, T01339-742345. An 18th-century inn with a roaring fire and views over the Balmoral Estate, which serves good, honest food. Also accommodation (**B**).
🍴🍴🍴 **La Mangiatoia**, Bridge Sq, Ballater, T/F01339-755999. Serves primarily Italian fare in its family-friendly restaurant.
🍴🍴🍴 **Rowan Tree**, T01339-755191, Bridge St, Ballater. Good coffee and fresh home-baking or pop in for home-made soup, open

sandwiches and a range of mains, including locally sourced beef. Good value.

Braemar *p159*
A quiet town, Braemar isn't teeming with café-bars and restaurants.
₸₸₸-₸₸ Braemar Lodge, see Sleeping, above. Serves daily lunches and dinners, with the dinner menu including staples such as Aberdeen Angus beef and game.
₸₸-₸ The Gathering Place, Invercauld Rd, T01339-741234. Tucked beside **Braemar Mountain Sports** and close to the bank, this lovely, cosy restaurant boasts fine Scottish cuisine with a Mediterranean twist, a roaring open fire and walls adorned with Scottish artwork. Recommended.
₸₸-₸ Taste Coffee Shop and Restaurant, Airlie House, T01339-741425. Thu-Mon 1000-1700. Bright café/restaurant serving good value, wholesome lunches and light bites, including delicious butternut and ginger soup or try the locally sourced venison burger.

✹ Festivals and events

Around Deeside *p157*
Sep Braemar Games, www.braemar gathering.org, or contact the Secretary, BRHS, Coilacreich, Ballater, T01339-755377. Held on the 1st Sat in Sep. Booking is highly recommended.

⓸ Activities and tours

Braemar *p159*
Skiing
Braemar Mountain Sports, 5 Invercauld Rd, Braemar, T01339-741242. For ski and telemark rental and advice.

Deeside *p156*
Fishing
Between Feb-Sep there are many places to fish for salmon on the River Dee. For a full reference of locations and operators visit www.fishdee.co.uk, or T01573-470612, to request a booklet.

Horse riding
Glen Tanar Equestrian Centre, south of Aboyne, in Glen Tanar (see page 160), T01339-886448. Offers riding in the forests and hills.

Tour operators
Adventure Scotland, Croft House, Croftside, Aviemore, T01479-811411, www.adventure-scotland.com. Offers a wide range of adventure activities, including whitewater rafting, mountain biking, skiing and hiking.

⊙ Transport

Around Deeside *p157*
Bus From May-Sep the morning Scottish Bluebird bus No 501 runs from **Ballater** via Strathdon and **Tomintoul** to **Grantown** on Spey. The afternoonCoopers Tourmaster Travel bus runs a daily service from **Ballater** that, include stops at **the Lecht**, **Tomintoul**, **Inverness**, **Aviemore** and **Kingussie** before terminating at **Newtonmore**.

Alternatively, buses No 502 and No 503 from Aberdeen, leave **Banchory**, May-Sep Mon-Sat, 0938 and travel via **Cairnwell** and **Pitlochry** (No 502 only) to **Perth**.

The Don Valley

→ Colour map 4, A4-5.

North of Royal Deeside is the lesser-known valley of the Don, Aberdeen's second river and regarded by enthusiasts as one of the finest trout-fishing rivers in Europe. This relatively little-visited corner of the northeast is a historian's and archaeologist's dream, littered with medieval castles, Pictish stone circles and Iron Age hillforts. A quarter of all Britain's stone circles can be found here. Local tourist offices have free leaflets on the region's archaeological sites, with background information and details of how to find them. The main sites are included in the tourist board's 'Stone Circle Trail'. There's also a well-signposted 'Castle Trail', which includes the area's main castles. One of these castles, Corgarff, stands at the southern end of the notoriously steep Lecht Road, which runs from Cock Bridge to Tomintoul. This area, which will test the mettle of even the fittest cyclist, is known as the Lecht and incorporates Scotland's smallest ski centre. ▶▶ *For listings, see page 167.*

Ins and outs

Getting there There are regular trains and buses to Inverurie from Aberdeen and Inverness. **Bluebird Northern** ① *T01224-212266*, bus No 220 runs from Aberdeen to Alford (1¼ hrs), and from July to September the No 501 Aberdeen to Perth bus stops in Strathdon and Tomintoul after leaving Ballater. There is also a bus (No 362) from Dufftown on a Tuesday and Saturday to Tomintoul, call **Roberts of Rothiemay** ① *T01466-711213*.

Getting around Travelling around the Don Valley without your own transport is not easy but bus No 219 runs from Alford to Strathdon Bellabeg Monday to Saturday. The Heather Hopper, operated by **Stagecoach Bluebird** ① *T01343-544222*, and **D&E Coaches** ① *T01463-222444*, provides the link between the many rural outposts of Deeside.

Inverurie and around → *Colour map 4, A5.*

The solid farming town of Inverurie is 17 miles northwest of Aberdeen on the A96 to Inverness. It makes a useful base for visiting the numerous castles and ancient relics dotted around the area. The **Thainstone Mart** ① *Mon, Thu and Sat 1000*, south of town just off the A96, is one of the largest livestock markets in the country. There's a TIC ① *18 High St, T01467-625800, Apr-Sep 0900-1300, 1400-1700*.

About 6 miles southwest of Inverurie, off the B993 (turn first left after the village of Kemnay), is **Castle Fraser** ① *T0844-493 2164, castle, shop and tearoom open Apr-Jun and Sep-Oct Wed-Sun 1200-1700; Jul-Aug daily 1100-1700. Last admission 45 mins before closing. £9, £6.50.* Built in 1575 by the Sixth Earl of Mar, it is similar in style to Crathes and Craigievar. The interior was remodelled in 1838 and many of the furnishings date from that period. There's a walled garden and trails through the estate. A 'Woodland Secrets' area has been created where children can play amongst wooden sculptures, and there are tepees and even a tree-house.

Close by, and signed off the B993, is the 4000-year-old **Easter Aquhorthies Stone Circle**. This archaeological site is overshadowed by Bennachie (1732 ft), by far the best hill in the area and thought to be the site of Mons Graupius, in AD 83, when the Romans defeated the Picts. It's a straightforward two-hour walk to the summit and the views are great. There are various trails, though the most commonly used route starts from the **Bennachie Centre** ① *1 mile beyond Chapel of Garioch, signposted off the A96 at Pitcaple,*

5 miles northwest of Inverurie, T01467-681470, Nov-Mar Tue-Sun 0930-1600, Apr-Oct daily 1030-1700, free. Near here is the **Maiden Stone**, a 10-ft-high Pictish gravestone with relief carvings showing what looks like an elephant.

A few miles west of the turn-off to Chapel of Garioch, the B9002 heads west off the A96 to the village of Oyne, site of the **Archaeolink Prehistory Park** ① T01464-851500, www. archaeolink.co.uk, Apr-Oct daily 1000-1700, Nov-Feb 1000-1600 (last entry 1500), £6.10, concessions £5.20, children £3.95. In just one day this fantastic, state-of-the-art interpretative centre takes you on a 10,000-year journey back in time. It's a great introduction to the ancient sites in the area and explains why the stone circles were built and what the various carved symbols mean. The 40-acre park includes various interesting features such as a reconstructed Iron Age farm, Stone Age settlement and Roman camp, as well as a hilltop Iron Age fort. The Archeodrome features audio-visual presentations which bring to life the ancient history of the area. There are even prehistoric craft workshops.

Near the village of Daviot, north of the A96 off the B9001 from Inverurie, or via the A920 west of Oldmeldrum, is the **Loanhead of Daviot Stone Circle**. This impressive 6000-year-old site is 500 yds from the village and consists of two stone circles, the smaller of which encloses a cremation cemetery dating from 1500 BC. Thirteen miles north of Inverurie is **Fyvie Castle** ① off the A947 between Oldmeldrum and Turriff, T01651-891266 (NTS), Apr-Jun, Sep-Oct Sat-Wed 1200-1700, Jul-Aug daily 1100-1700, grounds open all year daily 0900-dusk, £11, concessions and children £8. This grandest of Scottish baronial piles is a major feature on the 'Castle Trail'. The oldest part of the castle dates from the 13th century, although the extravagantly opulent interior is mostly Edwardian. Each of the castle's five towers is named after one of the five families who have lived here over the centuries. The landscaped grounds and Fuyvie Loch are also worth exploring and even the tea room is great.

Alford → Colour map 4, A5.

The main tourist centre on Donside is the little country town of Alford (pronounced 'Ah-ford'), 25 miles west of Aberdeen. The principal point of interest in town is the **Grampian Transport Museum** ① T01975-562292, Mar-Sep daily 1000-1700, £6, £5 concessions, £3 children, which features a comprehensive display of transport history, with collections of cars, buses, trams, steam engines and some more unusual exhibits. Almost next door is the terminus for the **Alford Valley Railway** ① T01975 563942, Apr-Jun and Sep Sat-Sun, 30-min service 1300-1630, Jul-Aug daily 1300-1630, £2.50, children £1.50. Pulled along a narrow-gauge railway line between Haughton park and back (one hour) this family-orientated attraction run by train enthusiasts boasts restored diesel loco- motives, a 50-seat 'Silver Jubilee' carriage and a restored 1895 former Aberdeen tram car; double check timetable and prices. The railway station is also where you'll find the TIC ① T01975-562052, Apr-Sep Mon-Sat 0930-1700, Sun 1245-1700. Also in town is the **Alford Heritage Centre** ① Mart Rd, T01975-562906, Apr-Dec Mon-Sat 1000-1700, Sun 1300-1700, Sep-Mar closed on Sun £3, concessions £2, children £1, a charitable organization run by volunteers with a large display of the area's agricultural past and bygone era including a school-room, farmhouse and shoemakers. Alford is close to **Lecht Ski Centre**, see page 171, but you can ski year round on the local dry ski slope at **Alford Ski Centre** ① Greystone Rd, T01975-563024.

Craigievar Castle

① T0844-493 2174. Castle open Easter Fri-Mon 1100-1700; May-Jun and Sep Fri-Tue 1100-1700; Jul-Aug daily 1100-1700. Gardens all year daily. £11, concessions £8.

Six miles south of Alford is one of the northeast's most gorgeous castles, the classic tower house of Craigievar, with its impressive turrets, balustrades and cupolas. The castle remains much as it was when it was built in 1626 by wealthy local merchant, William Forbes. The castle was recently reopened after extensive renovation. The beautiful parkland remains open and is worthwhile for a woodland walk.

Kildrummy Castle
ⓘ T01975-571331, Apr-Sep daily 0930-1730, £4, concessions £3.20, children £2.40.
Six miles west of Alford, the A944 meets the A97 which heads north towards the town of Huntly on Speyside, see page 169. A few miles south of the junction stand the extensive and impressive ruins of Kildrummy Castle, Scotland's most complete 13th-century castle. Amongst the most infamous events in the castle's long and bloody history was the treacherous betrayal of Robert the Bruce's family to the English during the Wars of Independence. It was the seat of the Earls of Mar and used as a headquarters for the Jacobite rebellion of 1715, after which the Sixth Earl of Mar ('Bobbing John') fled to exile in France and the castle fell into ruin. The Kildrummy Castle Gardens are also worth a visit.

Strathdon and Corgarff Castle
The tiny village of Strathdon, 10 miles southwest of Kildrummy, is famous for the **Lonach Highland Gathering**. Held on the third Saturday in August, it has a healthy blast of authenticity in comparison to the more glitzy affair in Braemar on Deeside.

Five miles west of Strathdon the A944 meets the A939 Ballater–Tomintoul road. A few miles beyond the junction is the austere **Corgarff Castle** ⓘ Apr-Sep daily 0930-1730, Oct-Mar Sat-Sun 0930-1630, £5, concessions £4, children £3, a 16th-century tower house, later turned into a garrison post, with an eventful and gruesome history. Here Margaret Forbes and her family were burned alive by the Gordons in 1571 during the bitter feud between the two families. In the wake of the ill-fated 1745 rebellion the government remodelled the castle, building a star-shaped defensive wall, and garrisoned 60 men to maintain order and communications in this part of the Highlands. Corgarff continued in use into the 19th century when English Redcoats were stationed here in order to try and prevent whisky smuggling.

Tomintoul → Colour map 4, A4. Altitude 1600 ft.
Beside Corgarff is the hamlet of **Cock Bridge**, standing at the end of one the most beautiful and notorious stretches of road in the country. In winter, the Tomintoul to Cock Bridge road is almost always the first road in Scotland to be blocked by snow (you have been warned). From Cock Bridge the A939 rises steeply to the Lecht Pass (2089 ft) before dropping dramatically to Tomintoul, the highest village in the Highlands. Tomintoul is well placed for both the Whisky and Castle Trails. It is also the nearest settlement of any size to the Lecht, one of Scotland's top five ski resorts (see below), and it marks the end of the long-distance Speyside Way (see page 170), so is popular with walkers and skiers. The TIC ⓘ T01807-580285, Apr-Jun, Sep-Oct Mon-Fri 1000-1700, Sat 1000-1600, Jul-Aug Mon-Fri 1000-1900, Sat 1000-1700, Sun 1100-1500, is on the village square, as is the **museum and visitor centre** ⓘ T01807-673701, Apr-Aug Mon-Sat 0930-1200, 1400-1630, Sep Mon-Sat 0930-1200, 1400-1600, Oct Mon-Fri 1400-1600, free, which has a display of local history, wildlife, landscape and outdoor activities. Ten miles north of Tomintoul on the B9008 is the **Glenlivet Crown Estate** ⓘ T01479-870070, www.crownestate.co.uk/glenlivet, with a net- work of hiking paths and cycle trails, as well as lots of wildlife, including reindeer. There are several good eating options around here, including **The Clockhouse** (ⓘⓘ). For home-baking pop into the **Whisky Castle Highland Coffee Shop**.

For Sleeping and Eating price codes and other relevant information, see Essentials pages 38-45.

● Sleeping

Inverurie and around *p164*

L-B Thainstone House Hotel, to the south of Inverurie off the A96, T01467-621643. A luxurious country mansion offering excellent cuisine and leisure facilities.

A-B Macdonald Pittodrie House Hotel, near Chapel of Garioch, T0844-879 9066, www.macdonaldhotels.co.uk. 27 rooms. The opulent surroundings of this magnificent baronial mansion are matched by superb cuisine and very comfortable, tastefully furnished bedrooms. After dinner, relax with a dram by the roaring fire, explore the bar or venture down to the wonderful billiard room.

D Breaslann Guest House, Old Chapel Rd, T01467-621608. Offers 2 en suite rooms in a modern bungalow equipped with Wi-Fi.

D Fridayhill, Kinmuck, Inverurie, T01651-882252. A small, comfortable B&B.

Alford *p165*

B-C Carriages Hotel, Commercial Rd, Insch, T01464-820604. Comfortable with good food.

D Forbes Arms Hotel, 1 mile west of town, Bridge of Alford, T01975-562108. Comfortable B&B with dinner option and good bar food (♔♔-♔).

Self-catering

Frog Marsh, Mossat, Alford, T01975-571355. Open year-round. 2 beautifully appointed self-catering cottages, which sleep 2-6. From £385 per week. Recommended.

Kildrummy Castle *p166*

L-A Kildrummy Castle Hotel, Kildrummy, Alford, T01975-571288, www.kildrummy castlehotel.co.uk. Set in beautiful grounds across the river from the castle ruins. 4-poster beds in the master bedrooms. In the restaurant you'll find a great menu (♔♔♔-♔♔).

Strathdon and Corgarff Castle *p166*

D-F Allargue Arms Hotel, by Corgarff, T01975-651410. B&B and bunkhouse accommodation.

F Jenny's Bothy, just before the castle, turn onto an old military road for about 1 mile, T01975-651449, www.jennysbothy.co.uk. Basic but wonderfully remote bunkhouse.

Tomintoul *p166*

C Glenavon Hotel, T01807-580218. There are a few hotels around the main square, the best is this family-run one. Popular with après-skiers, tired walkers and locals.

D Argyle Guest House, 7 Main St, T01807-580766. Lovely, friendly B&B by all amenities.

F SYHA Hostel, Main St, T01807-580364, www.syha.org.uk. Apr-Sep. 20 beds. Handy for food, the pub, the bus and the Speyside Way.

Self-catering

Livet House, Main St, T01807-580727. Small cottage near the pub and outdoor pursuits. £340-570 per week.

● Transport

The Don Valley *p164*

Jul-Sep the morning No 501 bus stops in **Strathdon** and **Tomintoul** on its way to **Grantown**. The afternoon bus continues on to **Dulnain Bridge**, **Carrbridge** and **Inverness**.

Bus No 502 leaves **Strathdon**, Jul-Sep Mon-Sat 1035 and travels via **Ballater**, **Crathie**, **Braemar** and **Cairnwell** to **Pitlochry**.

Bus No 362 leaves from **Tomintoul**, Tue and Sat to **Keith**, Roberts of Rothiemay, T01466-711213. From **Tomintoul**, Central Coaches run a bus to **Glenlivet**, Sat only. No 363 runs via **Tomintoul** and **Aberlour** to **Elgin**, Thu, Central Buses, T01542-882113.

Speyside

→ *Colour map 2, C3-4.*

The River Spey is Scotland's second longest river, rising in the hills above Loch Laggan and making its way northeast to where it debouches at Spey Bay, on the Moray Coast. Speyside is one of Scotland's loveliest valleys and is synonymous with two of Scotland's greatest products, salmon and whisky. The upper part, Strathspey, is equally famous for its hiking, skiing and watersports. It is covered later in this chapter. This section covers the lower part of the valley and comprises the famous Malt Whisky Trail. There are more malt whisky distilleries in this small area than in any other part of the country, including some famous brands such as Glenlivet and Glenfiddich. However, it's not all whisky in these parts: there's also some fine walking along the Speyside Way which runs from Spey Bay south to Tomintoul. ➤➤ *For listings, see pages 171-172.*

Ins and outs

Getting there and around Bluebird Buses ① *T01224-212266*, runs a daily service from Elgin (No 336) to Dufftown.

There's a bus service (No 360 and No 361), which connects Dufftown with Keith and Aberlour (Monday to Friday), and the No 230 connects Dufftown with Huntly (Monday to Saturday). For details call Bluebird Buses. A restored old **train** ① *T01340-821181 (Sat, Tue, Thu only), May and Sep Sat-Sun, Easter, Jun-Aug Fri-Sun, £9, concessions £7, children £5*, powered by a diesel engine runs from Dufftown to Drummuir (5 miles) and on to Keith (10 miles). Call ahead or visit the website for the timetable.

Dufftown and around → *Colour map 2, C4.*

A good place to start your whisky tour is Dufftown, founded in 1817 by James Duff, the fourth Earl of Fife, and the self-proclaimed 'Malt Whisky Capital of the World'. There's more than a grain of truth in that assertion, for there are no fewer than seven working distilleries here. This is indeed the town that was built on seven stills.

Just outside of town, on the A941 to Craigellachie, is the **Glenfiddich Distillery** ① *free*, the town's most famous distillery and one of the best known of all malt whiskies, see box, page 169. Behind the distillery are the 13th-century ruins of **Balvenie Castle** ① *T01340-820121, www.historic-scotland.gov.uk, Apr-Sep Sat-Wed 0930-1700, £4, concessions £3.20, children £2.40*, built by Alexander 'Black' Comyn, then added to in the 15th and 16th centuries, and visited by Mary, Queen of Scots in 1562. Four miles north of Dufftown, at the junction of the A941 and A95, is the little village of Craigellachie, site of the Speyside Cooperage (see box, opposite), and where you can see Thomas Telford's beautiful bridge over the River Spey.

The nearby village of **Aberlour** is the home of the famous **Walkers Shortbread** ① *T01340-871555*. Also here is the expensive but superb **Aberlour Distillery** ① *T01340- 881249, www.aberlour.com, Apr-Oct daily, Jan-Mar, Nov-Dec Mon-Fri 0900-1700, tours at 1000 and 1400, £10*. Close by and in the Easter Elchies Estate is the exclusive **Macallan Distillery** ① *T01340-872280, www.themacallan.com, Mar-Oct Mon-Sat 0930-16230, tours every hour, £5*. Only accompanied children over the age of 8 are permitted on the guided tours.

About 8 miles southwest of Craigellachie, on the A95 to Grantown-on-Spey, is the 'pearl of the north' **Ballindalloch Castle** ① *T01807-500205, Easter-Sep Sun-Fri 1030-1730, £8, concessions £6, children £4*, a mile west of the village of **Marypark**. The castle is one of the loveliest in the northeast and has been lived in continuously by its original family, the

Whisky-a-go-go

Speyside is Scotland's most prolific whisky-producing region and the Malt Whisky Trail is a well-signposted 70-mile tour around seven of the most famous distilleries, plus the Speyside Cooperage. Most of the distilleries offer guided tours, and most (with the exception of Glenfiddich) charge an entry fee, which can then be discounted, in full or in part, from the cost of a bottle of whisky in the distillery shop. Tours also include a free dram. Those listed below are the most interesting. See also www.maltwhiskytrail.com.

Strathisla, *Keith, T01542-783044. Apr-Nov Mon-Sat 0930-1600, Sun 1200-1600, £5, under 18s free.* The oldest working distillery in the Highlands (1786) and perhaps the most atmospheric, in a beautiful setting on the River Isla. This is a relatively rare malt, which is also used in the better-known Chivas Regal blend.

Speyside Cooperage, *near Craigellachie, 4 miles north of Dufftown, T01340-871108, all year Mon-Fri 0900-1600, £3.20, concessions £2.60, children £1.90.* You can watch the oak casks for whisky being made.

Cardhu, *7 miles west of Craigellachie, at Knockando on the B9102, T01340-872555, Easter-Jun Mon-Fri 1000-1700, Oct-Easter Mon-Fri 1100-1500, Jul-Sep Mon-Sat 1000-1700, Sun 1200-1600, £4, under 18s free.* This lovely little distillery is the only malt distillery pioneered by a woman. Their fine malt is one of many used in the famous Johnnie Walker blend.

Glen Grant, *in Rothes, on the A941 to Elgin, T01340-832118, Apr to mid-Dec Mon-Sat 0930-1700, Sun 1200-1700, £3.50, under 18s free.* Stroll through the garden to the heather-thatched dram pavilion.

Glenfiddich, *just north of Dufftown, on the A941, T01340-820373, www. glenfiddich. com, early Jan to mid-Dec Mon-Fri 0930-1630, Easter to mid-Oct Mon-Fri 0930-1630, Sat 0930-1630, Sun 1200-1630, original tour free, connoisseurs' tour £20 (with tastings).* Probably the best known of all the malts and the most professionally run operation. It's the only distillery where you can see the whisky being bottled on the premises, and the only major distillery that's free, including the obligatory dram. It's also one of few Scotch whisky companies still to be in the hands of its founding family.

Glenlivet, *10 miles north of Tomintoul on the B9008, T01340-821720, www.the glenlivet.com, Apr-early Nov Mon-Sat 0930-1600, Sun 1200-1600, free.* This was an illicit whisky until it was licensed in 1824. The distillery was later founded in 1858 and this malt has gone on to become one of the world's favourites.

Macpherson-Grants, since 1546. It houses a fine collection of Spanish paintings and the extensive grounds are home to the famous Aberdeen-Angus herd of cattle, which have been bred here since 1860. Also in Ballindalloch is the **Glenfarclas Distillery** ① *T01807-500257, www.glenfarclas.co.uk, tours Apr-Jun Mon-Fri 1000-1700, Jul-Sep Mon-Fri 1000-1700, Sat 1000-1600, Oct-Mar Mon-Fri 1000-1600, £3.50, children free,* which, despite the relatively high entrance fee, is a worthwhile experience.

Dufftown **TIC** ① *clock tower, centre of the main square, T01340-820501, Apr-Oct 1000-1300, 1400-1700,* has maps and information on the Whisky Trail.

Huntly and around → *Colour map 2, C5.*

Ten miles east of Dufftown is the pleasant little town of Huntly. Close to the Whisky Trail and on the main Aberdeen to Inverness train route, it makes a convenient base from which to explore this area and there is a **TIC** ① *T01466-792255, Apr-Oct Mon-Sat 1000-1300, 1400-*

1700, for further information. The town also boasts a lovely little castle all of its own. The 16th-century **Huntly Castle** ① *T01466-793191, Apr-Sep daily 0930-1730, Oct-Mar Sat-Wed 0930-1630, £5, concessions £4, children £3*, stands in a beautiful setting on the banks of the River Deveron, on the northern edge of town. It was built by the powerful Gordon family and is notable for its fine heraldic sculpture and inscribed stone friezes, particularly over the main door. Near the castle is the **Nordic Ski Centre** ① *T01466-794428*, the only year-round cross-country ski centre in the UK. It also hires ski equipment and mountain bikes.

Seven miles south of town, near the village of Kennethmont, is **Leith Hall Gardens** ① *T01464-831216, garden and grounds open all year; 0900- dusk*, are extensive and include a 6-acre garden, 18th-century stables and ice house, two ponds, a bird observation hide and countryside walks. The Hall is closed to the public but pre-booked tours for groups can be arranged, or the Hall can be hired for functions and weddings; contact T0844-493 2164 or leithhall@nts.org.uk.

The Tap o' Noth walk → *Colour map 4, A5. OS Landranger No 37.*
Eight miles south of Huntly on the A97 is the village of Rhynie, where you turn off for one of the best walks in the northeast. The Tap o' Noth (1851 ft) dominates this part of rural Aberdeenshire and the panoramic views from the top make it a worthwhile climb. It's also a fairly easy walk to the conical summit, where there's a vitrified fort. The total distance is of this walk is 3 miles. Allow at least two hours there and back. It is believed that the name, Tap o' Noth, derives from Gaelic taip o'nochd, which translates as 'look-out top'. But there's also a local legend that the hill's giant, Jack o'Noth, stole the his neighbour's sweetheart. In retaliation, the cuckolded neighbour, Jack o'Bennachie, hurled a huge boulder and flattened Jack on his own hilltop.

Start the walk from the car park at **Scurdargue**, a few miles west of Rhynie, off the A941. Leave the car park and head straight up the track to a gate. Go through the gate and cross some rough pasture into woodland. At the northwest corner of the wood, go through another gate and turn left onto a track. Follow this grassy track uphill beside a fence until you see another area of forestry ahead, with rough pastureland on the right. Follow the faint track across the pasture to the broad track which then climbs up the Tap's western slopes. Follow this all the way to the top, up the tight zigzag on the southern flank and through the eastern entry to the hillfort, into a large enclosure. On the way back down look out for a subsidiary path under the fort's western ramparts. This path descends steeply to the left, south of the main track. It then joins the main track and you can retrace your steps back to the car park.

The Speyside Way → *www.moray.gov.uk.*
The Speyside Way follows the River Spey from its mouth at Spey Bay inland as far as Ballindalloch, then crosses high moorland to Tomintoul and Aviemore. Currently, there is a public consultation on plans to extend the route southwards from Aviemore to Newtonmore. The 84-mile route takes five to seven days to complete. Much of it is on an old railway line and passes close to several small villages, meaning that it can easily be broken down into shorter walks. It also passes several distilleries along the way.

Rucksack Reader produce a guide to the Speyside Way and there is also a very good Harvey map of the route (£11.95) available from TICs, good bookshops and **Moray Council Ranger Service** ① *Boat of Fiddich, Craigellachie, T01340-881266.*

Lecht Ski Centre → *Colour map 4, A5.*

ⓘ *Day ticket £25, children £16, ½-day ticket £14.50, children £11. There's a ski school and equipment (adult ski and snowboard £17) and tubing (for £10 per hr scoot down the piste on a super-fast tyre-like sledge) hire available at the base station, T01975-651440, www.lecht. co.uk. Phone or check website for latest weather conditions.*

The Lecht is a ski resort for all seasons. It offers dry-slope skiing throughout the year and its snowmaking facilities mean that the winter season can be extended beyond January and March. The Lecht's gentler slopes make it ideal for beginners and intermediates and the emphasis is on family skiing. There's a snowboard fun park with half pipe, log slide, gap jump and table top. However, there are also more difficult runs for the more experienced skier, and extensive off-piste skiing. In addition, there's a summer activity area with quad bikes and fun-karts.

⊙ Speyside listings

For Sleeping and Eating price codes and other relevant information, see Essentials pages 38-45.

⊜ Sleeping

Dufftown and around *p168*
A Craigellachie Hotel, Craigellachie, T01340-881204, www.craigellachie.com. 25 en suite rooms are to be found in this superb country hotel, which oozes style and comfort and has a commendable Ben Aigen restaurant (♛♛♛).
A Minmore House Hotel, 10 miles southwest of Dufftown, in the village of Glenlivet, T01807-590378, www. minmorehouse hotel.com. May-Jan. Beside the distillery in 4 acres of grounds, this is the former home of the owner. Whether scoffing the delicious afternoon tea (♛) or tucking into award- winning lunch and dinner (♛♛♛) it's a delight to eat here. Shooting, walking and cycling can be arranged – or choose from a selection of over 100 malt whiskies. Recommended.
C-D Highlander Inn, Victoria St, Craigellachie, T/F01340-881446. Modest accommodation with a reputation for serving hearty bar meals.
D Mrs Souter's B&B, 43 Fife St, T01340-820408. Provides a warm welcome, fine hospitality and an excellent breakfast.
D Tannoch Brae, Dufftown, T01340-820541, www.tannochbrae.co.uk. 6 en suite rooms

in a very comfortable guesthouse with a reputation for fine food (♛♛).

Self-catering
Pitchroy Cottage, Ballindalloch Castle Estate, T01807-500205, www.ballindalloch castle.co.uk. Captain WE Jones, the creator of Biggles, wrote his novel here. Aside from the open fire and peace, guests can enjoy many activities on the estate including stalking, fishing, golf (£20 for 18 holes) and a kids 00 gauge railway. £300-670 per week.

Huntly and around *p169*
A-B The Castle Hotel, Huntly, T01466-792696, www.castlehotel.uk.com. Standing in extensive private grounds, this former home of the Duke of Gordon is now an impressive hotel with tastefully furnished rooms complemented by delicious food (♛♛♛-♛♛).
D-E Greenmount Guesthouse, 43 Gordon St, T01466-792483. Welcoming B&B in this modest, former 1854 townhouse.
E New Marnoch, 48 King St, T01466-792018. Reasonable guesthouse.
E Strathlene, MacDonald St, T01466-792664. Well located near town centre, this is a friendly and comfortable B&B in a traditional granite house.

Camping
Huntly Castle Caravan and Camping Park, T01466-794999. Clean with good facilities.

🍴 Eating

Dufftown and around *p168*
In addition to the restaurants in the hotels, it's worthwhile considering the following in a small town with it share of good food stops.
₮₮-₮₮ La Faisandarie, 2 Balvenie St, Dufftown, T01340-821273. Open Thu-Mon. This lovely restaurant combines locally sourced Scottish flavours with French finesse. Depending on the season you may find partridge, duck, pheasant and venison on the menu, with every lunch and dinner option cooked to order. Has a good reputation if a little pricey. Book first.
₮₮ A Taste of Speyside, Balvenie St, Dufftown, T01340-820860. Superb, simple food at its best. The Taste of Speyside platter includes local smoked salmon accompanied by whisky chicken liver pâté, local farmhouse cheeses, smoked venison, cured herring and oatcakes. The menu will also tickle your tastebuds with the likes of rabbit and cullen skink. A good choice.
₮₮-₮ Glenfiddich Restaurant, Church St, Dufftown, T01340-820363. Fabulous little place with flags, antiques and walls adorned with images of old Hollywood movie stars. Food's pretty good too.
₮₮-₮ The Mash Tun, 7 Broomfield Sq, Aberlour, T01340-881771. Best known for its superb real ales, but also serves fine pub grub. Sits on the banks of the Spey and has a play-ground to keep the saucepan lids entertained.

🍸 Bars and clubs

Huntly and around *p169*
Auld Pit, Bogie St, Huntly. Lively pub with some great folk music nights.

🎭 Entertainment

Dufftown and around *p168*
Commercial Hotel, Church St, T01340-820313. Ceilidhs during the summer.

🎉 Festivals and events

Speyside *p168*
May Spirit of Speyside Whisky Festival, T01343-542666, www.spiritofspeyside.com, www.eventscotland.org. A celebration of 'the water of life' with various whisky-related events taking place throughout the region.

🚌 Transport

Dufftown and around *p168*
Bus To reach **Aberlour** from **Dufftown** (15 mins), take the No 361 operated by Maynes Coaches, T01542-831219, that runs once daily Mon-Fri to **Keith**. From **Aberlour** there are 2 buses Mon-Fri to **Grantown-on-Spey** where you can continue to **Aviemore**.
Alternatively, on Mon **Deveron** coaches, T01542-836363, run from Keith via **Dufftown** to Inverness (2 hrs 40 mins), departing **Keith** at 0915 and **Dufftown** at 0940.
Stagecoach Bluebird, T01343-544222, run at least 5 buses (No 10) daily from **Inverness** to **Aberdeen**, and **Aberdeen** to **Inverness**, 3 hrs 55 mins, with stops in **Huntly** and **Keith**.

Strathspey and the Cairngorms

One of Scotland's busiest tourist areas is Strathspey, the broad valley of the River Spey, Scotland's second longest river, which rises high in the hills above Loch Laggan and flows northeast to its mouth on the Moray Firth. The lower reaches are famous for salmon fishing and whisky, and are covered in the Speyside section of this guide (see page 168), while the upper reaches attract outdoor sports enthusiasts. Hemmed in between the mighty Monadhliath Mountains to the north and the magnificent Cairngorms, Britain's second highest range, to the south, this is an area which offers excellent hiking, watersports, mountain biking and winter skiing. In September 2003, the Cairngorms were officially declared a national park, the largest in Britain.
▸▸ *For listings, see pages 178-182.*

Ins and outs

Getting there This part of the Highland region is easily accessible by public transport as Aviemore is one of the main hubs, with regular buses and trains from Inverness, Perth, Edinburgh and Glasgow. There are several buses (Monday to Saturday) from Inverness to Grantown-on-Spey, Boat of Garten and Aviemore with **Highland Country Buses** ⓘ *T01479-811211*. They also operate several buses a day from Inverness to Newtonmore via Carrbridge, Aviemore, Kincraig and Kingussie. ▸▸ *For further details, see Transport, page 181.*

Tourist information Aviemore **TIC** ⓘ *Grampian Rd, about 400 yds south of the train station, T01479-810930, Sep-Jun Mon-Sat 0900-1700, Jul-Aug Mon-Sat 0900-1900, Sun 0900-1700, phone to check times*, will book accommodation as well as provide free maps and leaflets on local attractions and change foreign currency. The train station, banks, supermarket, restaurants, guesthouses and a couple of excellent outdoor shops are all to be found along the main thoroughfare of Grampian Road. Buses, including those to the ski centre and **Scottish Citylink**'s Inverness/Glasgow/Edinburgh services, stop here too.

Aviemore and around → *Colour map 4, A3. Phone code 01479. Population 2500.*

The main focus of the area is the tourist resort of Aviemore, a name synonymous with winter sports. In the 1960s Aviemore was transformed from a sleepy Highland village into, until very recently, a jumble of concrete buildings, tacky gift shops and sprawling coach parks. Today, the creation of the **Macdonald Aviemore Highland Resort** ⓘ *www.aviemorehighlandresort.com*, complete with retail complex, food court, restaurants, golf course, swimming pool and beauty spa has significantly helped Aviemore rectify the worst excesses of its early mistakes. Still, Aviemore remains a 'tourist honey-pot' with a rash of 'trendy' bars that are a magnet for the stag, hen and après-ski crowds. It's certainly heaven for the outdoor enthusiast, discerning diner, whisky lover or real ale drinker, as this bustling town now boasts several notable restaurants and watering holes. ▸▸ *For further information, see Sleeping and Eating, pages 178 and 179.*

Unless wishing to soak up the luxury and leisure facilities of the Macdonald Aviemore Highland Resort, hang loose on the Extreme Dreams indoor **climbing wall** ⓘ *Tue-Thu 1700-2200, Sat-Sun 0900-1700*, at Dalfaber or hop on the Strathspey Railway (see page 181), you'll find Aviemore is the only staging post for the places of interest in and around the surrounding mountains, forests, rivers and villages. A great place for kids is the **Cairngorm Reindeer Centre** ⓘ *Glenmore Forest Park, on the road from Coylumbridge, 7 miles from Aviemore, T01479-861228, www.reindeer-company.demon.co.uk, hill visits May-*

Sep 1100 and 1430, Oct-Apr 1100, £9.90, children £5, concession £7, where you can observe reindeer at the centre or join the reindeer herder on the hillside, and even feed the stags and hinds of the glen.

Families will also enjoy the **Cairngorm Sled-dog Adventure Centre** ⓘ *T07767-270526, www.sled-dogs.co.uk, year-round, kennel visit 1 hr, £8, children £4, 20-min trip £60, children £40*, just 3 miles east of Aviemore on the 'ski road' and 500 yds past the Clay Pigeon Shooting range in Rothiemurchus Estate. A range of daily tours are offered, including a kennel visit where visitors can see the 30 huskies being fed and trained and also learn about the history of dog-sledding. There are short daytime and evening trips, where you can experience being pulled by the dogs, and for the more adventurous there's a three-hour sled-dog safari (£150 per person) that includes helping to prepare the dogs, 'mushing' through the forest in a specially adapted buggy and enjoying a brew deep in the woods. Whichever you choose, prepare to get wet, muddy and/or snowy. It can be cold so wrap up warmly.

The **Rothiemurchus Visitor Centre** ⓘ *Inverdruie, www.rothiemurchus.net, T01479-812345*, is definitely worth a visit. In addition to being packed with information on the walks, nature trails, stalking, fishing, pony trekking and cycling options on the huge estate, the centre boasts a fantastic delicatessen and high-quality arts and crafts shop, whilst directly next door in Ord Ban await delicious lunches, dinners and day-time snacks.

The area around Aviemore is blessed with an abundance of craggy peaks, lochs, rivers and acres of forest, including pockets of the ancient and native Caledonian pine forest. Subsequently, much of Speyside is home to rare wildlife including pine martens, wildcats, red squirrels, ospreys and capercaillie, and Britain's only herd of wild reindeer. Most of upper Strathspey is owned by Forestry Commission Scotland and Rothiemurchus Estate, which has been in the possession of the Grant family since the 16th century. Fortunately, the owners enthusiastically support access to these lands that form part of the Cairngorms National Park and which, among the opportunities for outdoor adventure and inhaling fresh air, boast miles of waymarked trails. Thanks to an undulating forest cycle trail completed in 2008, it's now possible for families to pedal off the road from Aviemore all the way to Glenmore and picturesque (9 miles east) at the bottom of the Cairngorm Mountain access road.

An easy circular walk of about two hours around **Loch an Eilein** in Rothiemurchus Estate starts from the end of the side road which turns east off the B970, 2 miles south of Aviemore. From the car park at the end of the road head for the lochside. The route around the loch is clearly marked and it's difficult to lose your way as it follows the loch shore. It's a very pleasant walk through woodland with views of a 14th-century castle ruin on an island in the middle of the loch. The views and change of light here are breathtaking, whilst it's a magical experience to hear one's call echo across the loch and through the silent forest. It's a romantic spot too, highlighted by the fact locals sometimes marry in the forest by the lochside. You can extend the walk by around a mile by including the circuit around **Loch Gamhna**. The paths around Loch an Eilein are also connected with the massive network of trails around Rothiemurchus. OS Sheet 36 covers the route. There are toilets by the car park (£3), and in a small croft, postcards, ice-cream and information about the walks and wildlife in the area are available.

Cairngorms National Park

The area around Aviemore is only a small part of the Cairngorms National Park, whose boundaries extend from Grantown on Spey to the heads of the Angus Glens, and from

Ballater on Deeside to Loch Laggan. Scotland's second national park is also the UK's largest at 1400 square miles. It is home to 25% of Scotland's native woodland and is a refuge for many rare plants and animals, including 25% of the UK's threatened species. Probably the most famous of the park's wild residents is the osprey, but you'll also see golden eagles, ptarmigan, the extremely rare crossbill, red deer, red squirrel and pine marten. As well as the park's natural attractions, there are also countless outdoor activities on offer, as the Cairngorms is one the UK's prime climbing and hiking areas and now home to an increasing number of outdoor adventure operators. Unsurprisingly, it's also where several of Scotland's most gifted Winter Olympic athletes train and whether you're looking for excellent mountain biking, watersports, winter sports (see pages 139 and 171), horse riding, fishing or stalking, this is the place to come.

Cairngorm is Scotland's longest-established ski resort and remains Scotland's largest ski area, with almost 30 runs and over 20 miles of pistes. This is where many of Britain's leading ski racers have first learnt the arts of skiing and snowboarding. When the sun shines, the snowfall is good and the crowds are few it can be a very satisfying experience. The season normally runs from January until the snow disappears, which was May in 2008. **Cairngorm Ski Area** ① www.cairngormmountain.org.uk, is 9 miles southeast of Aviemore and starting over 2500 ft above Loch Morlich, is reached by a frequent bus service (No 34 and No 36) from Aviemore. One of Scotland's most extensive ski areas, visitors can rent skis and snowboards, book lessons and purchase day and half-day ski passes from the busy **Day Lodge** ① T01479-861261, at the foot of the ski area. Aside from dozens of pistes, Cairngorm also boasts Scotland's only **funicular mountain railway** ① *during ski season daily 0900-1600, every 20 mins, out of season 1000-1600, £9.75, concessions £8.45, children £6.15*. This runs to the **Ptarmigan restaurant/café** and gift shop near the summit of Cairn Gorm. The Aviemore TIC and the Cairngorm Day Lodge ticket office provide free piste maps of the Cairngorm ski area. The **Cairngorm Ranger Service** ① T01479-861703, by the Day Lodge, post up a daily mountain weather forecast, advise on the local wildlife and run occasional guided walks.

The Cairngorms provide some of Scotland's most challenging walking, with no fewer than 49 Munros and half of Britain's eight mountains over 4000 ft (Ben Macdrui, Braeriach, Cairn Toul and Cairn Gorm). These mountains come into their own in winter, providing experienced climbers with a wide range of classic ice climbs and fantastic opportunities for ski touring. However, in light of the sub-Arctic weather conditions, which can descend in minutes to produce frightening and disorientating white-outs, forays onto these summits should not be taken lightly. They require a high degree of fitness, navigational experience and preparation (see page 26).

Walking in the Cairngorms

The summit of **Cairn Gorm** (4084 ft) is readily accessible as you take the mountain railway up to the **Ptarmigan restaurant**. However, the railway cannot be used to access the high mountain plateau beyond the ski area and mountain walkers may not use the railway for their return journey.

There are over 50 miles of footpath through this area, including many peaceful walks through the **Rothiemurchus Forest**. There are also ranger-led guided walks. You can find out more at the excellent **Rothiemurchus Estate Visitor Centre** ① T01479-810858, *daily 0900-1730*, which is a mile from Aviemore along the ski road and can provide a free *Visitor Guide and Footpath Map*.

Another good area for walking is around **Glenmore Forest Park**. The **visitor centre** ① *T01479-861220*, near Loch Morlich produces a very good *Glen More Forest Guide Map* which details the many local walks. The centre also has a lovely café, a great interpretative display about the wildlife, and panels/photographs that offer insights into the role Glenmore played in training the Norwegian resistance and commandos during WWII.

The best known of the long-distance trails is the famous **Lairig Ghru**, a 25-mile hike from Aviemore over the Lairig Ghru Pass to Braemar. The trail is well marked but can easily take over eight hours and is very tough in parts. Note that the weather in this part of the world can be very unforgiving for the ill-equipped and unprepared. Do not underestimate this walk. You can check the weather forecast at the likes of the friendly and experienced outdoor retailer **Mountain Spirit** on on Grampian Road.

An easier proposition is a 12-mile loop which leads to the start of the Lairig Ghru pass, starting from Loch Morlich. To reach **Loch Morlich** take the B970 east from the southern end of Aviemore, beyond Coylumbridge. The route starts at the western end of Loch Morlich where a forestry track runs south from the road. It leads to a bridge over the River Luineag. Cross the bridge and continue along the track, keeping straight on where another track heads off left. About a mile further on, another track heads off to the right, but keep to the left fork, signposted for **Rothiemurchus Lodge**.

The track climbs up towards the lodge. Just before it, turn right on to a clear track which leads up to a reservoir. Soon another track heads off to the right, signposted for the Lairig Ghru. Follow this path through heather moorland. The path then heads left, climbing up through open moorland to the lip of the glen. The entrance to the Lairig Ghru is straight ahead.

After about a mile, as the hills begin to encroach on either side, a rough path almost doubles back to the left. Follow this path up the slope to the gap between Creag a' Chalamain and Creag an Leith-Choin. The deep gully, the Chalamain Gap, is filled with huge boulders and requires great care when clambering through it. Beyond the gully a path leads through heather and pine saplings, dropping down to the side of a burn, then climbing up on its other side. Continue on this path, which then drops steeply down to the side of the burn. Cross the footbridge and climb the slope beyond to reach the main road. Turn left along the road to return to the start of the route.

Boat of Garten → *Colour map 4, A3 Phone code 01479.*

① *The most unusual way to get here is on the Strathspey Steam Railway (see page 181), which runs regularly Apr-Sep from Aviemore. Loch Garten is not easy to reach without your own transport, check with TICs for tours.*

Eight miles northeast of Aviemore is the quiet village of Boat of Garten, home to breeding pairs of rare ospreys on Loch Garten, 2 miles east of the village. **Abernethy Forest RSPB Reserve** ① *T01479-831476, Apr-Aug daily 1000-1800, £3, concessions £2, children 50p*, on the shore of Loch Garten, can be visited during the nesting season when the RSPB opens an observation centre. This is also one of few places in the world to see Scottish crossbills. You may also see ospreys at the Rothiemurchus trout loch at Inverdruie, and maybe even on Loch Morlich and Loch Insh. The Abernethy reserve is home to several other rare species such as capercaillie, whooper swans and red squirrels. 'Caperwatch' takes place from April to mid-May (0530 to 0800).

Carrbridge → *Colour map 4, A3. Phone code 01479.*

At Carrbridge, a pleasant little village 7 miles north of Aviemore, is the **Landmark Forest Theme Park** ① *T01479-841613, www.landmark-centre.co.uk, Apr to mid-Jul daily 1000-*

1800, mid-Jul to Aug 1000-1900, Sep-Mar 1000-1700, £11.55, concessions £9.25, children £8.70, a woodland park which combines entertainment, education and shopping. This is where kids can really let off steam as they explore the raised Treetop Trail for viewing wildlife, a maze, fire tower and the highly popular Water Coaster. It's far from tacky and it's great fun. In the village itself is the decidedly fragile-looking 17th-century stone arch of the **Bridge of Carr**, which is definitely not for vertigo sufferers. The nine-hole, 2623-yd **Carrbridge Golf Course** ① *T01479-841623*, is also worth a hit.

Kingussie → *Colour map 4, A2. Phone code 01540. Population 1500.*
The quiet village of Kingussie (pronounced *King-yoosie*) lies 12 miles southwest of Aviemore and makes a pleasant alternative as a place to stay. Kingussie is on the main Inverness to Perth/Glasgow/Edinburgh routes and all Perth to Inverness trains stop here as do most Citylink buses. There are also several services (run on schooldays only) by Highland Country Buses between Kingussie, Glenmore, Laggan Bridge and Dalwhinnie. For further information, see www.rapsons.co.uk.

The main attraction here and in the village of Newtonmore, 2 miles south, is the excellent **Highland Folk Museum** ① *T01540-661307, Apr-Aug daily 1030-1730, Sep-Oct daily 1100-1630, free*, which offers an insight into highland life in the 17th century. The traditional, re-created blackhouse and collection of highland artefacts is in Kingussie, whilst the 17th century 'township' in Newtonmore includes actors in traditional dress 'working' on a farm, in an old smokehouse and a water mill. During the summer there are also demonstrations of spinning, woodcarving and peat-fire baking. The **TIC** ① *T01540-661297*, is housed in the museum and has the same opening hours.

Another worthwhile attraction is **Ruthven Barracks**, standing on a hillock across the river. This former barracks was built by the English Redcoats as part of their campaign to tame the Highlands after the first Jacobite rising in 1715. It was destroyed by the Jacobites in the wake of defeat at Culloden to prevent it from falling into enemy hands, and it was from here that Bonnie Prince Charlie sent his final order which signalled the end of his doomed cause. Access is free and the ruins are particularly attractive at night when floodlit.

At nearby Kincraig village, between Kingussie and Aviemore, is the **Highland Wildlife Park** ① *T01540-651270, Apr-Oct daily 1000-1700, Nov-Mar daily 1000-1600, park tours £13.50, concessions £11.50, children £10*, which has a captive collection of rare native animals, including wildcat, European bison and over 60 red deer.

Fifteen miles south of Kingussie down the A9 in the village of Dalwhinnie is the **Dalwhinnie Distillery** ① *T01540-672219; Jan-Easter Mon-Fri 1100-1400; Easter-May Mon-Fri 0930-1700; Jun-Sep Mon-Sat 0930-1600; Jul-Aug Mon-Sat 1000-1600; Oct Mon-Sat 1100-1600; tours £6, children over 8 £4*, established in 1898. Take a tour and sample its 15 year-old malt.

Grantown-on-Spey → *Colour map 4, A3. Phone code 01479. Population 3250.*
This genteel Georgian holiday town is 15 miles northeast of Aviemore and attracts the more mature tourist by the coach load. Everything here is geared towards fishing, and anyone wishing to get kitted out in proper style should get themselves down to either **Mortimers** or **Ritchies** on the High Street. The **TIC** ① *T01479-872773, Apr-Oct daily 0900-1800*, is also here.

For Sleeping and Eating price codes and other relevant information, see Essentials pages 38-45.

◉ Sleeping

Aviemore and around *p173*

L-B Hilton Coylumbridge Hotel, Coylumbridge by Aviemore, T01479-810661, www.hilton.co.uk/coylumbridge. Set in 65 acres of woodland by Rothiemurchus Estate, the family-friendly credentials of this luxury hotel include a dedicated Fun House, dry ski slope and climbing wall, whilst parents can relax by the pool and enjoy fine dining (♛♛-♛♛). 15 mins' walk from Aviemore centre.

A-D The Macdonald Aviemore Highland Resort, T0845-608 3734, T01479-815300, T01479-811244 (for the country club). www.aviemorehighlandresort.com. Huge leisure and conference complex featuring 4 hotel options: the luxurious **Macdonald Highland Hotel** (**A**), the family-orientated **Academy Hotel** (**B**), the **Four Seasons** (**A**) and the **Aviemore Inn** (**B**). The resort features a fine-dining restaurant **Aspects** (♛♛♛-♛♛), whilst its nearby Dalfaber Golf and Country Club boasts the popular **Steakhouse Restaurant** (♛♛♛-♛♛). This Macdonald village within a village also comes complete with 1st-class leisure facilities, including the 18-hole **Spey Valley Golf Course** (£70 a round), and swimming pool . There are regular buses daily between Cairngorm Mountain and the resort (No 34), via Glenmore and Coylumbridge.

B-C Corrour House Hotel, Inverdruie, 2 miles southeast of Aviemore, T01479-810220, www.corrourhouse.co.uk. Open Dec-Oct. This Victorian country house enjoys wonder- ful views and offers thoughtfully prepared dinners using local produce (♛♛♛-♛♛). With breathtaking views over the Rothiemurchus Estate towards the Lairig Ghru and Cairngorm massif, this arguably remains the best small hotel in the area.

B-D Glenmore Lodge, Glenmore, T01479-861256, www.glenmorelodge.org.uk.

Britain's top outdoor training centre, patronized by many British Winter Olympians. Equipped with a pool, gym and even a roller-ski cross-country track within the forest, there's twin-room and chalet accommodation available. This is an ideal base for those seeking a rural retreat with top-class instruction in climbing, mountaineering and kayaking.

D Cairngorm Hotel, Grampian Rd, T01479-810233, www.cairngorm.com. Slap bang in the midst of Aviemore, this is where to combine a comfortable stay with good craic in the bar among the locals whilst dining on hearty bar meals and freshly prepared game and seafood in the restaurant (see Eating).

D-C Mackenzie Highland Inn, Grampian Rd, T01479-810672. Rooms and reasonable bar meals (♛) available.

D Rowan Tree Restaurant & Guest House, Loch Alvie, 1½ miles south of Aviemore on the B9152, T01479-810207, www.rowantreehotel.com. Like the **Corrour**, this is a tasteful, friendly hotel that goes the extra mile for guests. One of the oldest hotels in the area, it seves excellent food.

D International Starters, Grampian Rd, T01479-810941, www.internationalstarters.co.uk. 14 rooms. This restaurant offers stylish en suite rooms just 5 mins walk from the main thoroughfare and train station.

D-F Happy Days Hostel, 65 High St, Kingussie, T01540-661175 www.cairngormhighlandhostel.com. A budget option, and with a handy chippy downstairs.

F-E Aviemore Independent Bunkhouse & Backpackers Hostel, Dalfaber Rd, T01479-811137. 40 beds. Very cosy and high-quality facilities, with the excellent **Old Bridge Inn** pub and restaurant next door. Recommended.

F The Laird's Bothy, High St, Kingussie next to **Tipsy Laird** pub, T01540-661334, www.thetipsylaird.co.uk. A decent hostel with the Be@Home internet café just a few doors up.

F The Pottery Bunkhouse, Laggan Bridge T01528-544231, www.potterybunkhouse. co.uk. A spacious, clean, 34-bed escape with a hot-tub. Doesn't accept credit cards. Pop to the **Monadhliath Hotel** for breakfast.
F SYHA hostel, Grampian Rd, T01479-810345. Open all year. Very good hostel, just mins from all amenities and transport links.

Grantown-on-Spey *p177*
As you'd expect, there's a wide range of upmarket accommodation. Some of the best places in town are on Woodland Terr.
A Muckrach Lodge Hotel & Restaurant, a few miles southwest of town at Dulnain Bridge, T01479-851257, www.muckrach.com. A delightful, high-class, small hotel and one that retains its reputation for fine cuisine (ꟷꟷꟷ).
B Culdearn House, Woodlands Terr, T01479-872106, www.culdearn.com. With 6 beautifully appointed bedrooms, this country house is a fine place to stay, with its attention to detail, fine dining (ꟷꟷꟷ) and even finer collection of malt whiskies.
C-D The Garth Hotel, Castle Rd, T01479-872836. This is where to combine a comfortable stay with freshly prepared dinners (ꟷꟷꟷ-ꟷꟷ) before choosing from among the hotel's excellent selection of whiskies.
F Ardenbeg Bunkhouse & Outdoor Centre, Grant Rd, T01479-872824, www.ardenbeg.co.uk. A good-value budget option, geared up to quickly have you enjoying the outdoors.

Self-catering
Muckrach Castle, 3 miles from Grantown-on-Spey, T01738-477521. With views towards the Cairngorms, this provides a rare opportunity to relax in your own 15th century castle. 5 bedrooms, sleeps 8-10. From between £930 and £3000 per week.

⚹ Eating

Aviemore and around *p173*
The **Macdonald Aviemore Highland Resort**, has a food court for guests.

ꟷꟷꟷ-ꟷꟷ **Steakhouse**, Dalfaber Golf & Country Club, T01479-815300, www.aviemore highlandresort.com. Less formal than **Aspects**, and the place to enjoy tender Scotch beef.
ꟷꟷꟷ-ꟷ **Aspects**, T01479-815300, www. aviemore highlandresort.com. Daily 1930-2130. Within the resort complex, Aspects prides itself on offering freshly produced Scottish-based cuisine in a stylish setting.
ꟷꟷꟷ-ꟷ **Cairngorm Hotel**, see Sleeping, above. Continues to deserve its reputation for serving up tasty Scottish dinner classics, as well as your favourite pub-grub.
ꟷꟷ **International Starters**, see Sleeping, above. Opened in Jun 2008, this polished restaurant is all leather and wood with attentive staff and fine food.
ꟷꟷ **Old Bridge Inn**, Dalfaber Rd, T01479-811137. Tucked away on the old road below the main street, this atmospheric inn remains a high-quality eating establishment favoured by many a local. Ceilidhs and Highland dinner dances are hosted and, for less formal eating, diners can sit by the bar to enjoy a pint of real ale with some hearty pub-grub. Recommended.
ꟷꟷ-ꟷ **Mountain Café**, 111 Grampian Rd, Aviemore, T01479-812473. Daily 0830-1700. It's not the cheapest breakfast or lunch in town but with choices like porridge (£5.50), fresh fruit and zuchini pancakes, and a menu to suit vegan, gluten free and vegetarian diners, this café combines memorable eating with style.
ꟷꟷ-ꟷ **The Winking Owl**, Grampian Rd, T01479-810646. The wooden interior, mountain views, and steak and stag pie (£8.95) make this a worthwhile stop for a drink or bite.

Around Aviemore
ꟷꟷꟷ-ꟷ **Ord Ban,** Inverdruie, 2 miles along the 'ski road' at Rothiemurchus visitor centre, T01479-810005, www.ordban.com. This is where to bite into wonderfully fresh, appetizing daytime snacks or enjoy a tasty wholesome lunch or dinner (Mon-Sat 1830-2100) with meats and fish sourced from

the local area. Sun host Sliverscreen night. Recommended.

†¶-¶ Loch Insh Watersports Centre, T01540-651272, Kincraig, between Aviemore and Kingussie. A good lochside restaurant which doubles as a café during the day.

Kingussie *p171*

†¶¶-¶¶ The Cross, Tweed Mill Brae, a private drive leading off Ardbroilach Rd, T01540-661166. This is a good place to eat freshly prepared local produce. They also have rooms (**A-C**).

¶¶ Osprey Hotel, Ruthven Rd, T01540-661510, www.ospreyhotel.co.uk. Like the nearby **Scot House Hotel** (see below), expect appetizing seasonal produce, including locally sourced lamb and venison. There's also a great range of beers and single malts behind the bar.

¶¶ Scot House Hotel, Newtonmore Rd, T01540-661351, www.scothouse.com. The emphasis here is on using the best local produce. In season, expect venison from the nearby estates and salmon. The bar also offers a wide range of single malt whiskies.

¶¶-¶ Monadhliath, just south of Newtonmore at Laggan Bridge, T01528-544276. Serves up great value breakfasts, bar-lunches (1200-1400) and dinners (1800-2100).

¶ The Pottery Bunkhouse, 2 miles east of the mountain bike centre at Laggan Wolftrax, Laggan Bridge, T01528-544231. Serves up excellent home-baking, soup and filled sandwiches. You can also buy pottery and knitwear here.

¶ Tipsy Laird pub, High St, T01540-661334. Hearty bar meals and real ales. Also has a beer garden.

¶ Gilly's Kitchen, High St, T01540-662273. Tasty home-made soups, open sandwiches and fresh home-baking in a cosy dining area.

🕐 Bars and clubs

Aviemore and around *p173*
Two Hoots, 123 Grampian Rd. Fri-Sat 2200-0300. Recently opened nightclub.

🕐 Activities and tours

Strathspey and the Cairngorms *p173*
Fishing
Fishing is a major pursuit in the area. Armed with a permit, you can fish for trout and salmon on the River Spey (from £43 per day). Rothiemurchus Estate also offers rainbow trout fishing and equipment hire for its stocked loch (daily 0900-1700) at Inverdruie (day £25 and £5 tackle hire). There's even a 'novice loch' where, with rod and tackle provided, beginners can benefit from an hour's instruction with one hour fishing for £35. For further information about fishing at Rothiemurchus and on the Spey, call T01479-810703 or the local fishing secretary on T01479-831274. Alternatively, log onto www.fishspey.co.uk, fishfindhorn. co.uk, or www.visitscotland.com/ fish, for a full listing of stockists and hire outlets in the Speyside area.

Cairngorm Mountain Sports, Grampian Rd, Aviemore, T01479-810903. Permits, rods and tackle can be bought here.

Horse riding
Horse riding and pony trekking are on offer at various places throughout Strathspey.
Alvie Stables, Alvie, near Kincraig, T01479-831409, T07831-495397. Excellent, offering rides for adults and children (over 4 years). From 20 min mini-rides to 1½-hr canters and hacks for the more experienced.
Carrbridge Trekking Centre, Station Rd, Carrbridge, T01479-841602. Offer 1- and 2-hr treks with 30 min treks for young children. Ideal for families, but advanced notice of arrival recommended. From £15 for 30 mins.

Mountain biking
From Rothiemurchus Estate and Glenmore Forest to the tough 'Burma Road' connecting Carrbridge with Aviemore and the Ryvoan route, Cairngorms National Park and outlying areas make perfect mountain bike country for novices and experts. Strathspey is teeming with mountain bike routes for all levels.

Tour operators

As one of Scotland's primary outdoor adventure locations, there are a host of operators offering all kinds of adrenaline activities and professional coaching.
G2 Outdoor, Dalfaber Industrial Estate Aviemore, T07946-285612, T01479-811008, www.g2outdoor.co.uk. From gorge walking to mountaineering, telemark skiing and river kayaking (£50), this is a highly professional, fun-orientated outfit.
Glenmore Lodge, Aviemore, T01479-861256, www.glenmorelodge.org.uk. Arguably Britain's top outdoor training centre with a rash of expert mountain and kayaking guides available to coach those who want to learn or improve their kayaking, winter mountaineering and/or rock climbing skills.
Highland Wildlife and Birdwatch Safaris, Aviemore, T01479-811169, T07974-151503, www.highlandwildlifesafaris.co.uk. Run great value guided wildlife tours in and around Cairngorms National Park.
Rothiemurchus Estate, T01479-812345. Amongst its host of outdoor activities the estate runs an excellent 'Behind the Scenes' tour (£15 per person, 3 hrs, max 7 people) designed to provide photo opportunities and an insight into the wildlife, ancient Caledonian forest and history of the land as you explore the vast estate by 4WD. Over 12s can also try quad-biking at Alvie Estate and Rothiemurchus with **Highland Venture**, T01479-810330, www.highlandventure. co.uk, £40, 1 hr.
Strathspey Steam Railway, Aviemore Station, Dalfaber Rd, Aviemore, T01479-810725, www.strathspeyrailway.co.uk. £10.50, children £5.25, family £26. A round trip from Aviemore through Boat of Garten to Broomhill, 1½ hrs. A fabulous 'old world' experience. Apr-Oct and 'Santa' and 'New Year' (Mince Pie) specials. The station is just to the east of the main train station.

Skiing

For information on skiing in the Cairgorms, see page 175. High above Loch Morlich and Rothiemurchus Estate, those with a guide or highly competent in self-navigation can enjoy fantastic ski mountaineering and cross-country terrain if there's sufficient snow. Contact **Mountain Spirit**, T01479-811788, and **G2 Outdoor** for expert advice.

Walking

The walks around Strathspey are covered by OS Landranger map No 36 (1:50,000 scale) or OS Outdoor Leisure Map No 3 (1:25,000 scale). See page 175.

Watersports

In summer, the main activities are water-sports, and there are 2 centres which offer sailing, canoeing and windsurfing tuition and equipment hire.
Loch Insh Watersports Centre, Kincraig by Kingussie, T01540-651272, www.lochinsh. com. Open year-round. The centre has been running for 40 years and offers a host of activities, including kayaking, sailing, wind-surfing in addition to mountain bike hire and boat trips to spot wildlife on the loch. There's also a fabulous boathouse café/ restaurant, a guesthouse and alpine style self-catered chalets with loch views.
Loch Morlich Watersports Centre, 8 miles east of Aviemore, T01479-861221. Open May-Sep. Windsurfing, kayaking and sailing.

✪ Transport

Aviemore and around *p173*
Bus To **Inverness**, 45 mins; **Kingussie**, 20 mins; **Pitlochry**, 1 hr 15 mins; **Perth**, 2 hrs; **Glasgow**, 3½ hrs; and **Edinburgh**, 3 hrs 30 mins. For **Aberdeen**, change at Inverness. **Scottish Citylink**, T08705-505050, www.citylink.co.uk.
Car hire Northern Vehicle Hire, agents for **Europcar**, T01463-235337.
Cycle hire Bothy Bikes, Ski Rd, Rothiemurchus, T01479-810111. Daily

0900-1730. Friendly, highly knowledgeable operator and guide located in the wooden cabin behind the tennis courts at Inverdruie. Buy and hire high quality mountain bikes, £15 for ½-day, £20 for a day; clothing; and trail maps, £2.50. Kids' bikes can be hired for £6 for a ½ day and £8 for a day. **Loch Insh Watersports Centre**, T01540-651 272, www.lochinsh.com. Hires bicycles.

Train There are direct trains to **Glasgow** and **Edinburgh**, 3 hrs; and **Inverness**, 40 mins.

Carrbridge p176

Bus The easiest means of travelling south from the village of Carrbridge is by catching the 15X bus that runs 4 times a day Mon-Fri between **Inverness** and **Aviemore** via **Carrbridge**, **Boat of Garten** and **Nethy Bridge**. This service also runs 4 times daily in the opposite direction, for example leaving Carrbridge at 0912, arriving in Inverness at 0947. Alternatively, there's a service to **Aviemore** (No 33) from **Carrbridge** 3 times daily Mon-Sat.

Kingussie p177

Bus There are also several services run on schooldays by **Highland Country Buses** between **Kingussie**, **Glenmore**, **Laggan Bridge** and **Dalwhinnie**. See also www.rapsons.co.uk.

From **Kingussie**, at least 2 buses (No 35 and No 38) run Mon-Sat to **Aviemore** via **Kincraig**, 20 mins. On schooldays only, the No 37 leaves Kingussie High School at 1535 and travels via **Insh**, Loch an Eilean Rd and **Rothiemurchus** to Glenmore, 1 hr 15 mins. The easiest way to head north to **Aviemore** and **Inverness** bus station is by catching the M91 Citylink service that runs 4 times a day between **Edinbugh** and **Inverness**. Also catch this service to travel south from **Kingussie** to **Edinburgh** via **Dalwhinnie**, **Pitlochry** and **Perth**.

Grantown-on-Spey p177

Bus Buses Mon-Sat to **Aviemore**, 35 mins; 2-3 buses a day, Mon-Sat to **Inverness**, 1 hr 15 mins.

Contents

North & Northwest

At a glance

⊖ **Getting around** There are public
buses and good train links but a car
is necessary to explore remote areas.
⏱ **Time required** At least 1 week.
☼ **Weather** Be prepared for bad
weather on the mountains.
⊗ **When not to go** Oct-Mar some
tourist facilities are closed.

★ Don't miss ...
1 **The Moray Firth**, page 198
2 **West Highland Railway**, page 228
3 **Glen Coe**, page 230
4 **Glenelg**, page 250
5 **The Applecross Inn**, page 262
6 **Sandwood Bay**, page 274

20 km
20 miles

Atlantic Ocean

Orkney Islands

Rousay
Birsay
Marwick · Evie
Mainland
Stromness
Greamsay · Houton
Cava
Hoy · Cara
Flotta

Cape
Wrath
Sandwood
Bay 6
Durness · Whiten
Head

Pentland Firth
Dunnet Head
Scrabster · John o'Groats
Thurso
Keiss

Kinlochbervie
Handa
Island
Rhiconich · Tongue
Skerray · Strathy
Bettyhill
Roadside · Westerdale
A882
Wick

A838
Scourie
Allnabad
Forsinard
Achavanich
A9 · A99
Latheron

Dail Bho
Thuath
Isle of Lewis
(Eilean Leòdhais)
Griais
Port nan Giúran
Steòrnabhagh
(Stornoway)

Clashnessie · Kylesku
Clachtoll
Lochinver
Rubha
Coigeach
Achiltibuie

Inchnadamph
A837
Inverpolly
Nature Reserve
Ullapool

Crask Inn
Kildonan Lodge
Kinbrace
Borgue · Dunbeath
Berriedale
North Sea

Lairg
A839
Brora
Golspie
Dornoch
Helmsdale

Shiant
Islands

Cove
Melvaig
Poolewe
Gairloch
Redpoint
Torridon

Gruinard
Bay
Dundonnell
A835
Inverlael

Braenta
Boath
Evanton
Dingwall
Fortrose
A949
Dornoch Firth
Edderton · Tain
A9 · Hill of Fearn
Cromarty 1
Fortrose
Fort
George
Moray Firth
Portmahomack
Lossiemouth
Hopeman · Elgin
A941
Brodie
Castle
Nairn · Forres
Rothes

Sound of Raasay
Loch Torridon
Kinlochewe
A832
Achnasheen
A890
Craig

Applecross 5
A896
Lochcarron
Raasay
Scalpay

Rona
Beauly
A833
A831
Drumnadrochit
Dores
Inverness
Croy
A940 · A939
Dava
Strathspey
Marypark
A941

Skye
Plockton
Stromeferry
Dornie
Breakish
Elgol
Teangue
Ardvasar
Rùm
(Rhum)

Glenelg 4
Shiel Bridge
Invermoriston
Fort Augustus
A887
Loch Ness
Errogie
Grantown
on Spey
Carrbridge
Boat of
Garten
Aviemore
A939 · A944
Lynemore

Soay
Kinloch
Hourn
Knoydart
Invergarry
Garvamore
Monadhliath Mountains
Cairngorm Mountains
Kingussie
Crathie · Ballater
Inverey · Auchallater

Eigg
Arisaig
Muck
Ockle
Lochailort 2
Morar
Mallaig
Morar
Glenfinnan
A830
Loch
Arkaig
Spean
Bridge
Loch
Laggan
Grampian
Mountains
A9
Clova

Ardnamurchan
A861
Moidart
Polloch
Fort William
Ben Nevis
(1344m)
Onich · Kinlochleven
Glen
Coe 3
Glencoe
Kinloch
Rannoch
Blair Atholl
A93
Blacklunans
Alyth

Tobermory
Lochaline
Morvern
Portnacroish
A828
Bridge of
Balgie
Coshieville
Pitlochry
A924
Dunkeld
A923

Mull
Craignure
Lismore
A82
Tyndrum
Killin
Kenmore
Milton
Bankfoot
Dundee

Oban
Kerrera
Lochearnhead
St Fillans
A822
A85
Perth

The Northwest Highlands is the part of Scotland that best reflects the romantic image of the country. Wild, rugged, and sparsely populated after the infamous 17th- to 18th-century Highland Clearances, this is the Scotland of mist-shrouded glens, towering mountain peaks, windswept purple heather hillsides, brooding lochs, ghostly ancient castles and quaint coastal ports.

Inverness is the 'Capital of the Highlands'. It lies at the northeastern end of the Great Glen, which cuts diagonally across the southern Highlands to Fort William like a surgical incision, linking deep and mysterious Loch Ness with the west coast and giving access to Lochaber, the self-proclaimed 'outdoor capital of the UK'. Still further south is Glencoe, another climber's paradise and one of the Highland's most evocative Highland glens. Inverness is also ideally situated for exploring the northeast coast, dotted with charming fishing ports and archaeological sites, while the storm-battered, remote northern coastline, running west from John o'Groats to Cape Wrath, attracts surfers and those probing the history of the Clearances.

The main town on the northwest coast is Fort William, which lies in the shadow of Britain's highest mountain, Ben Nevis. Northwest from here stretches a dramatic shoreline of deep sea lochs and sheltered coves of pure white sand backed by towering mountains and looking across to numerous Hebridean islands. West of Fort William, via the lyrical Road to the Isles, is work-a-day Mallaig, the main departure point for ferries to Skye and the Small Isles. Further north is Ullapool, a key ferry port for the Outer Hebrides and the ideal base from which to explore Assynt and the wild and near-deserted far northwest.

Ins and outs

Getting there

There are daily flights to Inverness airport from London, Edinburgh and Glasgow. Inverness is linked to the south by the notorious A9 from Edinburgh and Perth, to Aberdeen by the A96 and to Fort William by the A82, and is well served by buses. Wick, Thurso, Ullapool, Portree (Skye), Fort William and Aberdeen all enjoy regular bus connections with Inverness. Daily trains from Glasgow and Edinburgh run to Inverness with subsequent connections north to Wick and Thurso, west to Kyle of Lochalsh and east to Aberdeen. Fort William is easily reached from Glasgow by bus, whilst the train (via Fort William) terminates at Mallaig for the ferry to Skye (Armadale). ▸▸ *For further details, see Transport, page 195.*

Getting around

Exploring the Northwest Highlands is undeniably easier if you have your own transport, though the main tourist centres, including Ullapool and Wick, are easily accessed by bus or train. Getting off the beaten track requires patience but is worthwhile and easily achieved with a little forward planning. Some of the time you'll need to rely on the, sadly, ever-reducing local **postbus service** ⓘ *T08457-740740, www.royalmail.com/postbus*, which travels countless single-track roads to deliver post to villages and hamlets scattered across the Highlands. Ask local tourist offices and post offices for timetables. Excellent online sources of travel information, including timetables and operators, are www.travelinescotland.com, and www.rapsons.co.uk. Tourist offices throughout the Highlands also carry leaflets on their local and regional transport network. Details of ferries from the mainland ports to Skye, the Outer Hebrides and Orkney are given in the respective island chapters, but by far the most scenic route to the Highlands is the spectacular West Highland Railway, one of the world's great rail journeys, particularly the section from Fort William to Mallaig (see box, page 228).

Tourist information

Roughly speaking, this chapter includes the northern half of mainland Scotland. It's covered by **VisitScotland**'s highland region ⓘ *T0845-225 5121, www.visithighlands.com,* whose tourist offices can provide free information and book local accommodation (for a small fee). From November to March smaller TIC offices may be closed or have restricted opening hours.

Climate

The Northwest Highlands suffers from notoriously unpredictable weather and that ever-present travelling companion, the midge. The midge is the scourge of many a Highland holiday: a ferocious, persistent and unbelievably irritating little beast that thrives in damp, humid conditions and who will drive you to the edge of sanity. For details on how best to combat this little terror, see page 51.

The only predictable thing about the weather is its unpredictability. You can have blazing sunshine in April, pouring rain in July and a blizzard in May. So, you'll need to be prepared for everything. Climbers and walkers especially must take heed of all weather warnings. It can be hot enough for bikinis in the car park at the foot of a 2000-ft mountain, and two hours later near the summit you're faced with driving, horizontal hail, rain or snow and unable to see further than the end of your nose. People die every year on the Scottish mountains simply because they are ill-prepared; it is essential to take proper precautions, see page 26.

Inverness

→ Colour map 2, C2. Phone code 01463. Population 70,000.

Inverness is the only city in the Highlands and as the busy and prosperous hub of the region, its population has trebled over the past 30 years. All main routes through the Highlands pass through here at some point, so it's a hard place to avoid. The town's position at the head of the Great Glen and on the shores of the Moray Firth have made it a firm favourite with tourists, who flock here in their legions during the summer months to look for the evasive Loch Ness Monster. Although Inverness city itself holds few major sights, it's a buzzing, attractive place to base yourself as you explore the other attractions in the surrounding area, including the possibility of spotting pods of dolphins in the Moray Firth. The city, however, is not without its own appeal, particularly the leafy banks of the River Ness, which runs through its heart, linking Loch Ness with the Moray Firth, and its fair share of fine accommodation and restaurants.
▶▶ For listings, see pages 190-197.

Ins and outs

Getting there

There are daily flights from London Gatwick, Edinburgh, Stornoway and Kirkwall with British Airways (Loganair), and daily flights from London Gatwick, London Luton and Bristol with easyJet. There are regular flights from Stornoway, Birmingham, Exeter, Manchester, Southampton and Belfast with Flybe, whilst Ryanair flies from Nottingham (East Midlands) and Aer Arann from Dublin. The **airport** ① *T01667-464000, www.hial.co.uk*, is 7 miles east of the town at Dalcross. There's a daily **airport bus** ① *T01463-710555*, every 30 minutes to the town centre, which takes 20 minutes and costs £2.90. A taxi from the airport costs around £14. The **bus station** ① *just off Academy St, T01463-233371*, and the **train station** ① *east end of Academy St, T01463-239026*, have left-luggage lockers charging a maximum of £5 per item per day. ▶▶ *For further details, see Transport, page 195.*

Getting around

Inverness town centre is compact and easy to explore on foot, and most of the hotels and guesthouses are within a 15-minute walk of the TIC. Loch Ness is not within walkable distance, so you'll either need your own transport, or you'll have to book a tour. ▶▶ *For further information, see Activities and tours, pages 194 and 215.*

Tourist information

The very busy **TIC** ① *T0845-225 5121, Easter-Oct Mon-Sat 0900-1800, Sun 0930-1600, call for winter opening hours*, is in an unattractive building at the foot of Castle Wynd, near Ness Bridge, a five-minute walk from the train station. It stocks a wide range of literature on the area, can book accommodation and transport, and gives out free maps of the town and environs. There's also a bureau de change and internet access. Information (and possibly tickets) for the tours listed on the next few pages are available from the TIC. It's also worth visiting www.inverness-scotland.com.

Background

One of the old town's first visitors was that much-travelled cleric, St Columba, who came in AD 565 to confront the Pictish King Brude, whose fortress was reputedly at Craig Phadraig, a few miles west of Inverness. Around the mid-12th century King David I built the original castle and made Inverness a royal burgh on the strength of its growing importance as a trading port. Furs, hides, wool and timber were all exported as far afield as the Mediterranean. The town's economic prosperity and status as the most important northern outpost, however, made it a prime target for marauding Highland clansmen, and during the Wars of Independence in the 13th century Inverness was also a regular target for both English and Scots armies.

The town's renaissance came with the completion of the Caledonian Canal and rail links with the south in the 19th century. These improved communications heralded something of a tourist boom amongst the wealthy and fashionable who came north to the Highlands to shoot anything that moved in the name of sport. In the mid-19th century Queen Victoria decided to embrace all things Scottish, which only boosted the town's popularity. Over recent decades Inverness has grown rapidly, not only as a prime base for visiting tourists, but also as the main administrative and commercial centre for the Highlands. Since being conferred city status in 2000, Inverness has continued to enjoy a boom period. In 2006, the 750 seat **Ironworks** (see Entertainment, page 193) opened its doors, the Highland capital's first ever purpose-built live concert venue, and in 2008, the beloved **Eden Court Theatre** reopened after a £23 million refurbishment.

Sights

The city is dominated by its red sandstone **castle** which now houses the **Sheriff Court**. Built in 1834, this Victorian edifice is very much the new kid on the block in terms of Scottish castles. The original castle dates from the 12th century and was built on a ridge to the east of the present structure. Nothing remains of the old castle, which is unsurprising given its bloody and eventful history. It was here that King Duncan of Scotland was slain by Macbeth, an event dramatically (and erroneously) portrayed in Shakespeare's eponymous work. The castle was occupied three times during the Wars of Independence in the 13th century, and when Robert the Bruce recaptured it in 1307 he destroyed it. In the mid-17th century Cromwell ordered his men to build a stone version on the same site. In 1715 James Francis Edward was proclaimed king there, but not long after it was destroyed by the Jacobites to prevent it from falling into enemy hands following the defeat of Bonnie Prince Charlie at Culloden, see box, page 199. On the castle terrace is a statue of Flora MacDonald, a poignant memorial to her role in helping the prince to escape (see box, page 311). Directly across the road, is the **Castle Tavern**, beloved by real ale drinkers.

Below the castle, on Castle Wynd by the TIC is **Inverness Museum and Art Gallery** ① *Mon-Sat 1000-1700, free.* In recent years this interesting museum, complete with café, has undergone a £1 million refurbishment and now includes a wealth of exhibits that outline the social history of the Highlands, its wildlife, and ancient artefacts from the times of the Vikings and the Picts. Among the interactive displays is an opportunity to try your hand at speaking Gaelic. Just around the corner, on High Street, is the Gothic-style **Town House**, where Prime Minister Lloyd George held an emergency cabinet meeting in 1921, the first ever to be held outside London.

Inverness

To Moray Firth Cruises, Black Isle, Wick & Edinburgh (A9)

To 2 3 10, Airport, Black Isle (A9), Nairn & Aberdeen (A96)

Library

Leakey's Bookshop

Old High Church

Dunbar's Hospital

Footbridge

Abertarff House

Eastgate Shopping Centre

Highland House of Fraser Kiltmaker Centre

Ness Bridge

Bank La Tolbooth Steeple

Town House

Museum & Art Gallery

St Andrews Cathedral

Eden Court Theatre

Footbridge

To Bught Park & Ness Islands

To 4 13, Loch Ness, Fort William & Jacobite Cruises (A82)

To Beauly (A862)

To 17

To 11

To 7 & Culloden Moor

200 metres
200 yards

N

Sleeping
Columba **1** B1
Culloden House **2** A3
Drumossie **3** C1
Dunain Park **4** C1
Eastgate Backpackers Hostel **5** B3
Glenmoriston Town House & Abstract Restaurant **6** C1
Glenruidh House **7** C3
Highlander Hostel **8** B2

Inverness Student Hotel **9** C2
Inverness Tourist Hostel **10** A2
Kingsmills Inverness **11** B3
Kinkell House **12** C3
Melness Guest House **13** C2
Moyness Guest House **14** C1
Rocpool Reserve **15** C2
SYHA Youth Hostel **16** A3
Trafford Bank **17** A1
Winston **18** B1

Eating
Café No 1 **1** B2
Castle Tavern **2** B2
Kitchen **3** B1
Leakey's Bookshop **4** A1
Lemon Tree **5** A2
Mustard Seed **6** A1
Peat **7** B2
Riva **8** B1
River Café & Restaurant **9** A2
Rocpool Rendezvous **10** B1

Shapla **11** B2

Bars & clubs
Bakoo **12** B2
Blackfriars **13** A1
Gellions **14** B2
Hootananny **15** A2
Johnny Foxes **16** B2
Pivo **17** A2

Opposite, on the corner of Bridge Street and Church Street, is the **Tolbooth Steeple**, which dates from 1791 and which had to be repaired after an earth tremor in 1816. Apparently, a (now blocked off) tunnel once led from the castle to a prison located below the Tolbooth. Among the cafés and bars to be found on historic Church Street – a fascinating part of the city local 'culture vultures' aim to steadily rejuvenate – is the town's oldest building, **Abertarff House**. Built around 1592, it is now a contemporary art and jewellery gallery. Almost opposite is the much-restored **Dunbar's Hospital**, built in 1688 as an almshouse for the town's poor. At the end of Church Street, where it meets Friar's Lane, is the **Old High Church** founded in the 12th century and rebuilt in 1772, though the 14th-century vaulted tower remains intact. In the adjoining atmospheric graveyard, prisoners taken at Culloden were executed, and you can still see the bullet marks left by the firing squads on some of the gravestones. At the far end of Church Street you'll also find **Leakey's Bookshop**, housed within a former church. Jam-packed with second-hand books, and with a delightful café upstairs, the owners estimate their towering shelves contain over 100,000 books.

The **Highland House of Fraser Kiltmaker Centre** ① *4-9 Huntly St, T01463-222781, www.highlandhouseoffraser.com, daily 0900-1700, factory tour Mon-Fri, £2, concessions and children £1*, still has a working kilt factory upstairs. In addition to watching kilts being made, two informative videos provide insights to the history of highland dress (including what Scotsmen wear under their kilts). In addition to mannequins dressed in period outfits, there are props used in the making of *Braveheart*. Nearby, directly opposite the castle, is the neo-Gothic **St Andrews Cathedral** which dates from 1869, and is worth a peek if you're passing by. Continuing south along Ness Bank, past the impressive glass frontage of the refurbished **Eden Court Theatre** (see Entertainment, page 193) you reach **Bught Park** (see Sleeping, page 192), which overlooks the Ness Islands, joined by footbridge to both banks. The islands are attractively laid out as a park and are a favourite with local anglers. This also happens to be a lovely place for a peaceful evening stroll.

◉ Inverness listings

For Sleeping and Eating price codes and other relevant information, see Essentials pages 38-45.

◉ Sleeping

Inverness *p187, map p189*
With an abundance of guesthouses, B&Bs and several good-quality hotels in and around Inverness, you shouldn't have much trouble finding somewhere to stay, though it does get very busy in Jul and Aug. Ideally, reserve ahead or consider booking through the TIC.

The best places to look are along both banks of the river south of the Ness Bridge, Old Edinburgh Rd and Ardconnel St (east of the castle) and around Bruce Gardens, Ardross St, Kenneth St and Fairfield Rd (the

west bank). There are also several budget hostels in and around the centre, and a couple of campsites.

L Culloden House Hotel, Milton of Culloden, 3 miles east of town near the A9, T01463-790461, www.cullodenhouse.co.uk. Within this delightful Georgian mansion where Bonnie Prince Charlie prepared for battle at Culloden, you'll discover 1st-class accommodation and award-winning fine dining (¶¶¶).

L Rocpool Reserve Hotel, Culduthel Rd, T01463-240089. Inverness doesn't lack stylish, luxurious hotels and this boutique hotel, 10 mins' walk from the centre, is no exception. For those with deep pockets, its restaurant also offers exceptional food, including lunch (£15.50 2 courses).

L-A New Drumossie Hotel, 3 miles southeast of the town centre, Old Perth Rd, T0844-879 9017, www.drumossiehotel. co.uk. 44 rooms. Views over the Moray Firth and handy for Culloden Moor, this is a deluxe hotel in a rural setting with all the creature comforts including a lovely restaurant (ﾔﾔﾔ-ﾔﾔ).

L-A Dunain Park Hotel, about 3 miles southwest of the town centre, just off the A82 Fort William Rd, T01463-230512, www.dunainparkhotel.co.uk. 11 rooms. An elegant Georgian mansion house within extensive gardens, with Victorian 4-poster beds, luxurious marble bathrooms and an excellent restaurant (see Eating, below). Can also arrange fishing, golf and riding.

L-A Glenmoriston Town House Hotel, 20 Ness Bank, T01463-223777. With 30 individually styled rooms, this is a classy establishment. Its **Abstract** restaurant and more informal **Contrast Brasserie**, have both picked up notable awards and there are more than 25 malts available in the piano bar.

A-C Kingsmills Hotel Inverness, Culca-bock Rd, 1 mile south of the city centre near A9, T01463-257100. Another higher end hotel, with 82 rooms. Parts of the building date back to the 17th century. Comfortable rooms and superb leisure facilities, including spa and a guest discount at the adjacent Inverness Golf Club.

A-C Trafford Bank, 96 Fairfield Rd, T01463-241414, www.traffordbankguesthouse.co.uk. 5 en suite rooms. Owners Lorraine Feel and Koshal Pun continue to delight and win awards for their sumptuous guesthouse, which assures guests comfort, style and a very warm welcome.

B Kinkell House, 11 Old Edinburgh Rd, T01349-861270, www.kinkellhouse.co.uk. Clean, comfortable Victorian family home with spacious rooms close to all amenities.

B-C Columba Hotel, 7 Ness Walk, T01463-231391, http://columba-inverness.hotel-rv. com. Overlooking the river, this hotel from 1881 has recently been refurbished, and offers 76 comfortable rooms in a very central location.

B-C Glenruidh House Hotel, Old Edinburgh Rd South, 2 miles from the town centre and adjacent to Loch Ness Golf Course (phone for directions), T01463-226499, www. cozzeenessie-bed.co.uk. 5 rooms. Packed with history and character, this peaceful, friendly 'boutique' hotel serves organic, fresh produce in a secluded setting … and has over 40 species of birds in its garden.

C Moyness Guest House, 6 Bruce Gardens, T/F01463-233836, www.moyness.co.uk. Fine Victorian villa in a quiet area near the theatre, with 7 very comfortable en suite rooms and nice touches like Botanics products in the bathrooms. During the 1920s this was the home of acclaimed Scottish author, Neil M Gunn.

D Highland Voyages, Eala Bhan tall ship, T07786-106960, www.highlandvoyages. co.uk. When moored at Seaport Marina, this place offers on board B&B accommodation in 5 (bunk-bed) cabins. Also offers sailings, see Activities and tours, page 194.

D Melness Guest House, 8 Old Edinburgh Rd, T01463-220963, www.melnessie.co.uk. 4 rooms that include en suite and family. Clean and comfortable accommodation in an 18th-century building that long-ago was the 'Craigneish School for Young Ladies'.

D Winston, 10 Ardross Terr, T01463-234477, www.winstonguesthouse.com. Friendly and comfortable guest- house overlooking the river and minutes walk from the **Eden Court Theatre**.

F Eastgate Backpackers Hostel, 38 Eastgate, T/F01463-718756, www.eastgateback packers.com. 38 beds including 2 twins and 4 (6-bed) dorms. Secure, clean and central.

F Highlander Hostel, 23a High St, T01463-221225, www.highlanderhostel.com. The new kid on the hostel block, with impressive facilities.

F Inverness Student Hotel, 8 Culduthel Rd (at the top of Castle St), T01463-236556. Ok, hotel is pushing it but this is a great, lively hostel, close to the centre and just yds away from great food at the **Castle Tavern**.

F Inverness Tourist Hostel, 2 mins from bus station, 24 Rose St, T01463-241962, www.invernesshostel.com. Don't let the dingy entrance fool you. This is an excellent backpacker rest stop with facilities including satellite TV, internet access, friendly staff, terrific cooking facilities and complimentary tea and coffee. The budget traveller's dream.

F SYHA Youth Hostel, Victoria Drive, off Millburn Rd, T01463 231771. 166 beds. Huge hostel in former school hall of residence. Good amenities, quieter location than many hostels but further from the city centre.

Self-catering

Easter Dalziel Farm Cottages, 7 miles east of Inverness, T01667-462213, www.easter dalzielfarm.co.uk. 3 comfortable, traditional cottages (sleep 4-6) on a 210 acre family farm. A 3-bedroom farmhouse B&B (**D**) is also available from £180-520 per week.

Camping

Bught Caravan and Camping Site, Bught Park, on the west bank of the river near the Inverness Aquadome, T01463-236920. Open Easter-Oct. The largest and most centrally located campsite, with good facilities, £7 per tent and £7 per head thereafter; £16 per caravan pitch with electricity; £3 for laundry.

Bunchrew Caravan and Camping Park, 3 miles west of Inverness, T01463-237802. Open Mar-Nov. Excellent campsite with views towards Ben Wyvis and the Beauly Firth and with good hot showers. 2 people can pitch a small tent for £14.50.

❶ Eating

Inverness *p187, map p189*

As you'd expect in a major tourist centre, there's the usual plethora of pubs, cafés and restaurants serving cheap and basic food for the non-discerning palate, but those looking for a high standard of cuisine won't be disappointed either.

Takeaways and chain restaurant options are plentiful, particularly on Academy St, Eastgate, around the train station and on Young St, just across the Ness Bridge.

♥♥♥ Abstract, Glenmoriston Town House Hotel, 20 Ness Bank. Tue-Sat 1800-2200. The award-winning French- inspired cuisine from the à la carte menu comes at a price but for those who seek fine-dining in style, it's definitely worth it. 8-course tasting menu £50. Book ahead.

♥♥♥ Dunain Park Hotel, see Sleeping, above. Fine combination of elegance and Scottish cuisine, including fresh Scottish seafood. Take a post-dinner stroll in the lovely gardens.

♥♥♥ Rocpool Reserve, see Sleeping, above. The decor oozes style and chic. Just like the boutique hotel, the lunch and dinner cuisine here hits the mark – albeit at a price.

♥♥♥-♥♥ The Kitchen, 15 Huntly St, T01463-259119, www.kitchenrestaurant.co.uk. One of the city's newer food haunts and the sister restaurant of **The Mustard Seed** (see below) across the river. Thoughfully prepared menu and lovely ambience for an evening meal. Good value set lunch (£5.95) and early bird (1700-1900) dinner (£10.95) offers.

♥♥♥-♥♥ The Mustard Seed, 16 Fraser St, T01463-220220. Daily 1200-1500, 1730-2200. Cheery, stylish interior, and a lunch and dinner menu packed with local, freshly prepared produce.

♥♥♥-♥♥ Peat, 20 Bridge St, T01463-701900, www.peat-by-the-bridge.co.uk. Overlooking the river, this trendy restaurant specializes in all things seafood. Look out for the fresh crab, lobster and langoustines at the entrance, which are destined for your plate.

♥♥♥-♥♥ Riva, 4-6 Ness Walk, T01463-237377, www.rivainverness.co.uk. A stylish and good value riverside eatery that specializes in Italian food.

♥♥ Contrast Brasserie, Glenmoriston Town House Hotel, see Sleeping, above. Daily 1200-1430, 1700-2100. A treat on a (slightly) more modest budget. Delicious food.

♥♥ Rocpool Rendezvous, 1 Ness Walk T01463-717274. Stylish interior with attentive staff and fabulous food. Family friendly. Book ahead.

Shapla, 2 Castle Rd, T01463-241919. Daily 1200-2330. Good Indian restaurant with Tandoori and Balti menu and good views of the river in the upstairs lounge.

Café No 1, 75 Castle St, T01463-226200, www.cafe1.net. Mon-Sat 1200-1400, 1800-2130. Central location with reasonable selection of meat and vegetarian dishes. Early bird dinner offer (Mon-Fri 1730-1845).

The River Café and Restaurant, 10 Bank St, T01463-714884. Mon 1000-2030, Tue-Sat 1000-2130, Sun 1730-2030. Popular for lunches and delicious high tea.

The Castle Tavern, 1 View Pl, T01463-718178. Recently bought by renowned publican George MacLean, you can feast on hearty, good value and freshly prepared pub grub. There's a great selection of real ales downstairs and a beer garden. This is a CAMRA rated establishment, with a food menu (available until 2200) that changes daily and great views of the castle and river from upstairs.

Leakeys Bookshop, Church St, T01463-239947. After browsing through over 100,000 second-hand books and old maps, where better to sup on some home-made soup, a sandwich or simply a coffee before stocking up on your book collection.

The Lemon Tree, 18 Inglis St. Located in the pedestrianized town centre, this family-run café offers good home-baking and basic but filling meals. Popular with older visitors.

Bakeries

Ashers, Church St. A good bakery that prides itself on its famous whisky cakes.

🍷 Bars and clubs

Inverness *p187, map p189*
Bakoo, High St. Where the young clubbers let their hair down.

Blackfriars, Academy St. A decent pub that runs ceilidhs and live music for the backpacker fraternity on most nights.

Castle Tavern, View Pl. Excellent choice of real ales, good atmosphere and bar food.

Gellions, Bridge St. Claims to be the oldest pub in the highland capital. Good to try 'neeps and tatties' (£4.95) and for ceilidh's on a Wed and Sat.

Hootananny, 67 Church St. A great bet for all things Scottish, has live music including ceilidhs most nights. Don't be surprised if you find yourself dancing on the tables with the backpacker crowd. Probably the best pub atmosphere in Inverness.

Johnny Foxes, 26 Bank St. Irish folk music most nights in summer and great bar food.

Love 2 Love, Castle St. Another venue for the younger clubber.

Pivo, 38-40 Academy St. Enjoyed by those in search of the real Czech brews and a trendier atmosphere.

🎭 Entertainment

Inverness *p187, map p189*
Cinema
The cinema attached to **Eden Court Theatre**, see below, shows a programme of art house and newly released movies. Prices vary depending on the performance.

Warner Village, A96 Nairn Rd, 2 miles from town centre. 7 screens, tickets cost from £6.

Live music
The Ironworks, 122b Academy St, T08717-894173, www.ironworksvenue.com. The 1st purpose-built live music venue.

Theatre
Eden Court Theatre, Bishops Rd, overlooking the River Ness, T01463-234234. This renowned theatre and cinema re-opened in 2008 after a multimillion pound refurbishment. Diverse theatre and arthouse productions. Also has a small café-bar.

⊛ Festivals and events

Inverness *p187, map p189*
There are numerous events held in and around Inverness throughout the year. These range from a humble pub ceilidh and a food festival to a full-blown Highland Games and the Baxters Loch Ness Marathon (Oct). With 2009 heralded as the Year of Homecoming, drawing the Scottish diaspora to these shores from around the world, the Highlands will stage many diverse events. For details contact the TIC or log onto www.eventscotland.org.
Feb/Mar Inverness Music Festival, T01463-716616.
Mar/Apr Folk festivals, T01738-623274. Local folk festivals held over Easter weekend.
Jun Rock Ness, www.rockness.co.uk. Live big bands play at Dores on the northern shores of Loch Ness.
Jul Inverness Highland Games, held in the 3rd week of the month.

⊙ Shopping

Inverness *p187, map p189*
Inverness is a good place to buy a kilt, or practically anything else in tartan. To find your own clan tartan, head for the **Highland House of Fraser Kiltmaker Centre**, see page 190. The **Eastgate Shopping Centre** has all the usual high-street shops such as Gap and Marks & Spencer.

Bookshops
Leakey's Bookshop, Church St. Mon-Sat 1000-1700. A brilliant second-hand bookshop, with a huge wood-burning stove in the middle of the shop and a café upstairs.

Highland dress and traditional gifts
Chisholm's Highland Dress, 47-51 Castle St, T01463-234599; **Highland House of Fraser**, Bridge St, T01463-222781; **James Pringle Weavers of Inverness**, 21 Bridge St, T01463-236517.

Market
Victorian Market, accessed off Church St and Academy St. Established in the 18th century, this market has a wide range of interesting and quirky shops although there is also the inevitable tartan tat.

ⓐ Activities and tours

Inverness *p187, map p189*
Boat tours
Caley Cruisers, Canal Rd, Inverness, T01463-236328, www.caleycruisers.com. If you fancy skippering your own power boat down Loch Ness and through the Caledonian Canal, you can do it in style with friends and family start from £410 to £2050 for the bigger boats.
Highland Voyages, Eala Bhan tall ship, T01667-404441, www.highlandvoyages. co.uk. Aboard this converted wooden herring drifter, enjoy day sails from £48-£68. Five day week living onboard from £380-£480.
John o'Groat's Ferries, contact the Inverness TIC, T01955-611353, www.jogferry. co.uk. For the ultimate day-trip, Orkney Islands Day Tours leave from Inverness every day throughout the summer, Jun-Sep (depart 0900, return 1945), £49, under 16s ½-price. Ancient sites include Skara Brae (older than the Egyptian pyramids) and the Ring of Brodgar. Booking essential. For tours from John o'Groats, see page 194.

Bus tours
Citysightseeing Inverness, leave from Bridge St outside the TIC, T01667-459849, www.city-sightseeing.com. Open-topped bus tours around the city, mid-Jun-Sep daily 1015-1700. Tickets valid for 24 hrs from the time of travel, and can be bought online or onboard. £6, concessions £4.50, children £3.
Exquisite Scotland, Cala na Sithe, Kirkhill, T01463-831643, www.exquisitescotland. com. Able to carry up to 8 passengers, this operator offers bespoke tours to suit your needs, whether it's visiting Culloden, Skye or finding a river to fish or a fairway to putt.

The Hebridean Explorer, Elmbank, Lewiston, Drumnadrochit, T07943-863292, www.the hebrideanexplorer.com. This family-run operator offers personal (for up to 5 people) and private (from £160 per day) tours to destinations including Loch Ness, upto £45 per person; Isle of Lewis, £125 per person; and Skye.

Highland Taxis, Farraline Park, T01463-222222, www.highlandtaxis.co.uk. Offers a highly personalized tour service (18 different tours), from exploring the far northwest for a day, £220 per person or £47.50 per person if 4 travel; Culloden Battlefield, £17.50 per person based on 4; and as far as the Cuillins of Skye, £55 per person based on 4 travelling.

Jacobite, Tomnahurich Bridge, Glenurquhart Rd, T01463-233999, www.jacobite.co.uk. Operates all kinds of informative tours that leave at 1030 from Inverness Bus Station. Also runs a courtesy bus from Inverness TIC to connect with their Loch Ness cruises. Offer a 6½-hr packed day-long tour (£37, concessions £34, children £25), which will see you sail on the dark waters of Loch Ness for 30 mins, pop into the Loch Ness Monster Exhibition Centre and visit atmospheric Urquhart Castle, before entering the 18th century engineering marvel that is the Caledonian Canal. Contact the operator for specific pick-up/drop-off points.

Puffin Express, tours leave from Castle Wynd, the narrow street between the Town House and the TIC, T01463-717181, www.puffinexpress.co.uk.

Cycling

Opened in 2002, the 73-mile-long Great Glen Way can be cycled. The stretch alongside the Caledonian Canal is flat and good for families. For a free leaflet, T01320-366322. To read about the Way, visit www.greatglenway.com.

Golf

There's an 18-hole public course at Torvean, 2 miles from town on the A82 to Fort William, T01463-711434.

History and ghost tours

Davey the Ghost, leaves from outside the TIC, T0845-2255121. Nightly 1900, £8, concessions £7. Tales of ghosts and ghouls.

Happy Tours, tours begin outside the TIC, T07828-154683, www.happy-tours.biz. Apr-Sep Mon-Sat, tours at 1100, 1300, 1500, 1700 and 1900. £10, children £5.Try the new Riverside Rickshaw tour £30.

Iceskating

Ice Centre, Bught Park, T01463-235711, www.inverness-ice-centre.org.uk. Daily 1400-1630, 1900-21.30. £4.50, children £3.50.

Swimming

Aquadome Leisure Centre, Bught Park, T01463-667500. Mon-Fri 1000-2000, Sat-Sun 1000-1700. Competition-sized pool with flumes, wave machine and kiddies' pool. Also gym and other indoor sports facilities.

Ten-pin bowling

Roller Bowl, 167 Culduthel Rd, T01463-235100. Mon-Fri 1200-late, Sat-Sun 1100-late.

Tennis and squash

Inverness Tennis and Squash Club, Bishop's Rd, T01463-230751.

⊖ Transport

Inverness p187, map p189

Bus

Bus timetables and even operators on some routes change frequently. If in any doubt and for the latest information, call **Traveline Scotland**, T0871-200 2233, www.traveline scotland.com, or www.rapsons.co.uk.

There are regular daily buses to **Glasgow** and **Edinburgh** (via **Aviemore**), **Pitlochry** and **Perth** with Scottish Citylink, T08705-505050. Change at Perth for **Dundee**. There are regular daily Citylink buses to **Ullapool**, connecting with the ferry to **Stornoway**; also to **Fort William** and **Oban**. There are daily Citylink buses to **Kyle of Lochalsh**, **Portree** and **Uig** (connecting with ferries to **Tarbert** and **Lochmaddy**), and regular, daily Citylink buses to **Fort Augustus** via **Drumnadrochit** and **Urquhart Castle** (also with Rapsons, T01463-710555), and to **Scrabster**, for the ferry to **St Margaret's Hope**, via **Wick** and **Thurso**.

To **Ullapool** via **Dingwall** and **Braemore Junction**, there are 2 buses, Mon-Sat, Highland Country Buses, T01463-710555, in addition to the regular service operated by Citylink. **Scotbus**, T01463-224410, operate 1 bus daily, Jun-Oct, between **Inverness** and **Inverewe Gardens**, via **Achnasheen**, **Kinlochewe**, **Loch Maree**, **Gairloch** and **Poolewe**. To **Tain** there is a daily service with Citylink, but to reach **Lairg** there's an irregular service with MacLeods and Royal Mail, T08457-740740. To **Tain** and **Helsmdale**, via **Dornoch** there are regular daily buses with Citylink. To **Lochinver** from **Ullapool** there's 1 bus, Mon-Sat, operated by Tim Dearman, T01349-883585, that departs Ullapool Ferry Terminal at 1055 and arrives in **Lochinver** at 1154. This bus continues to **Durness** via **Kylesku** and **Rhiconich** (for Sandwood Bay). Dearman Coaches carry a bike trailer on this route.

Between **Applecross** and **Inverness**, Skyeways, T01599-555477, operate a bus Mon, Wed and Sat via Lochcarron and Kishorn that also stops on request (Wed and Sat only) in **Shieldaig**. To **Grantown-on-Spey**, daily service with Highland Country Buses, T01463-710555. Stagecoach Inverness T01463-239292, run services to places around **Inverness**, including **Beauly**, **Muir of Ord** and **Dingwall**. To reach **Tomich** (and **Glen Affric**) via Beauly use the Ross Minibuses service, T01463-761250. **Fort George** (No 11) and **Cawdor Castle** (No 12) are reached from Inverness with Highland Country Buses, T01463-710555. Stage-coach runs daily services to **Aberdeen** via **Nairn**, whilst the battle scene of Culloden and Cawdor Castle can both be reached using a Tourist Trail Rover ticket (from £6)

with Highland Country Buses. It's worth noting that Rapsons, T01463-710555, www.rapsons.com, operate a 'Rack and Ride' scheme for some cyclists on certain routes including **Inverness** to **Aviemore**.

Car hire
Arnold Clark, 47 Harbour Rd and at the airport, T01463-236200 or T0845-6074500; Enterprise, Harbour Rd, T01463-235525; Focus, an office at the airport, T01667-461212; Turner Hire Drive, office on Lotland St, T01463-716058, T0870-902 0200. Prices vary but expect to pay from £35 per day.

Cycle hire
Highland Cycles, Telford St, T01463-234789. Mon-Sat 0900-1730.

Ferry
For details of connections to **Stornoway** (Lewis) and **Lochmaddy** (North Uist), contact **CalMac**, T0870-565000, T08000-665000, www.calmac.co.uk. For **Scrabster** to **Stromness**, Northlink Ferries, T01856-851144, T08456-000449. For **John o'Groat's** to **Burwick** (Orkney), John o'Groat's Ferries, T01955-611353, www.jogferry.co.uk; or for **Gill's Bay** to **St Margarets Hope** (Orkney) aboard a superfast catamaran (1 hr sailing), **Pentland Ferries**, T01856-831226, www.pentlandferries.co.uk.

Taxi
Tartan Taxis, T01463-222777. Around £16 from the city centre to the airport.

Train
For more information, T0845-748 4950. There are direct trains to **Aberdeen**, **Edinburgh** (via **Aviemore**) and **Glasgow**. There are several daily services to **London King's Cross** (via **Perth**) and **Edinburgh**, and a Caledonian Sleeper service to **London Euston** or from London Euston to **Fort William** via **Inverness**, ScotRail, T08457-550033, www.firstscotrail.co.uk. There is also a regular service to **Wick** and **Thurso**,

via **Tain**, **Lairg** and **Helmsdale**. The journey from Inverness to **Kyle of Lochalsh** (for Skye) is one of the most scenic in Britain. There are 2-3 trains Mon-Sat.

⊙ Directory

Inverness *p187, map p189*
Banks Most of the major banks can be found in the town centre around Inglis St. **Bank of Scotland**, opposite the Town House on the High St; **Clydesdale**, opposite the train station; **Lloyds TSB**, Church St. **Royal Bank**, High St. **Currency exchange** Money can be changed at the TIC at 2.5% commission; **Thomas Cook**, 9-13 Inglis St, T01463-711921, Mon-Fri 0900-1700. **Internet** Inverness Library; Mail Box Etc, 24 Station Sq; TIC. Several of the backpacker hostels also provide internet access. **Library** Inverness library, opposite the bus station, with excellent genealogical research unit. Consultations with the resident genealogist cost around £14 per hr, T01463-236463. The library also houses the Highland archives, where you can research the history and culture of the region, Jun-Sep Mon-Fri 1000-1300, 1400-1700, Oct-May 1400-1700. **Medical services Hospitals**: Raigmore Hospital, southeastern outskirts of town near the A9, T01463-704000, for accidents and emergencies. **Pharmacies**: Boots, 14-16 Queensgate, T01463-233295, Mon-Wed and Fri 0845-1800, Thu 0845-1900, Sat 0830-1800, Sun 1100-1700; also at **Eastgate Shopping Centre**, Fri-Wed 0900-1730, Thu 0900-1900.

Around Inverness

→ *Colour map 2, C2.*

East of Inverness along the Moray Firth stretches a long coastline of clifftop walks, fine beaches, attractive old towns and many historic sites and castles. The Moray Firth is perhaps best known for its large resident population of dolphins. Scores of these beautiful and intelligent mammals live in the estuary, the most northerly breeding ground in Europe, and there's a very good chance of seeing them, particularly between June and August. The Moray Firth dolphins have become a major tourist attraction and several companies run dolphin-spotting boat trips. You can also see them from the shore. Two of the best places are on the southern shore of the Black Isle, see page 289, and Fort George, on the opposite shore, see below. The Kessock Bridge, which crosses the Moray Firth to the Black Isle, is another good dolphin-spotting location and also has a visitor centre, where you can listen in to their underwater conversations.

West of Inverness, the Moray Firth becomes the Beauly Firth, a relatively quiet little corner despite its proximity to Inverness, as most traffic heading north crosses the Kessock Bridge on the main A9. The A862 west to Beauly offers a more scenic alternative, and the chance to visit a 13th-century priory and a distillery. South of Beauly, the A831 leads to two of Scotland's most beautiful glens, Glen Strathfarrar and Glen Affric. ▸▸ *For listings, see pages 203-205.*

The Moray Firth → *For listings, see pages 203-205. Colour map 2, C2.*

Culloden → *Colour map 2, C2.*

ⓘ *T0844-493 2159, www.culloden.org.uk. Site open daily all year, visitor centre open daily Feb-Mar 1000-1600, Apr-Oct 0900-1800, Nov-Dec 1000-1600, £10, concessions and children £7.50. Café/restaurant, educational rooms and a shop.*

The eerie and windswept Culloden Moor, 5 miles to the east of Inverness on the B9006, was the site of the last major battle fought on the British mainland. In 2007, the £8.5 million National Trust for Scotland visitor centre was opened, complete with its rooftop walk (10 minutes) with views over the restored battlefield, where on 16 April 1746 the Jacobean dream to place a Stuart, Prince Charles Edward Stuart (Bonnie Prince Charlie) back on the Scottish throne was brutally crushed by Hanoverian (largely English) forces amidst the heather and tussocky grass of Culloden Moor. This fateful battle was not simply Scotsmen fighting Englishmen but tragically, saw Scottish clan pitched against clan, whilst the Jacobean side included Irish and even English soldiers. Though the battle lasted barely an hour, the Hanoverian soldiers led by the Duke of Cumberland went on to commit appalling bloodshed across the Highlands, earning Cumberland the name, 'the Butcher.' Even to this day, his name is despised by many for the murderous post battle rampage he oversaw in a bid to forever stamp out sympathy for the Jacobites.

Fashioned from natural timbers and stone, the interior of the spectacular new visitor centre combines artefacts and displays (including Jacobite swords and the Princes unfinished waistcoat) with cutting edge interactive displays (including a 'Battle Immersion Theatre' and 'voices' from witnesses of the battle) to provide visitors with an evocative and stirring account of the build up to the battle, the fateful day and the brutal consequences of a Jacobite/Hanoverean showdown that changed the face of Scottish history. From the visitor centre, walk along the paths (35 minutes), past clan graves marked by simple headstones. Next to the visitor centre, the restored cottage of Old Leanach – which was used by the Jacobites as a headquarters, and where 30 Highlanders were

Battle of Culloden

The second Jacobite rebellion of 1745 was ill-fated from the start. Bonnie Prince Charlie's expedition south lacked sufficient support and was turned back at Derby. After their long and dispiriting retreat north, the half-starved, under-strength army – exhausted after an abortive night attack on Hanoverian forces at Nairn – faced overwhelmingly superior forces under the command of the ambitious Duke of Cumberland at Culloden.

The open, flat ground of Culloden Moor was hopelessly unsuitable for the Highlanders' style of fighting, which relied on steep hills and plenty of cover to provide the element of surprise for their brave but undisciplined attacks. In only 40 minutes the Prince's army was blown away by the English artillery, and the Jacobite

charge, when it finally came, was ragged and ineffective. Cumberland's troops then went on to commit the worst series of atrocities ever carried out by a British Army. Some 1200 men were slain, many as they lay wounded on the battlefield. Prince Charlie, meanwhile, fled west where loyal Highlanders protected him until he made his final escape to France.

But the real savagery was to come. Cumberland resolved to make an example of the Highlands. Not only were the clans disarmed and the wearing of Highland dress forbidden, but the Government troops began an orgy of brutal reprisals across the region. Within a century the clan system had ended and the Highland way of life changed forever. For further information, see page 444.

burnt alive – is arranged as it would have been at the time of the battle. A memorial cairn, erected in 1881, is the scene each April of a commemorative service organized by the Gaelic Society of Inverness.

Clava Cairns

This impressive and important Bronze Age site lies only a mile southeast of Culloden and is well worth a short detour. The 5000-year-old site consists of three large burial cairns encircled by standing stones, set in a grove of trees. The less imaginative visitor may see it as merely a pile of stones but no one can fail to be affected by the spooky atmosphere of the place, especially if no one else is around. To get there, continue on the B9006 past Culloden Moor, then turn right at the **Culloden Moor Inn** and follow the signs for **Clava Lodge**. Look for the sign on the right of the road.

Fort George → *Colour map 2, C2.*

ⓘ *T01667-460232, Apr-Sep daily 0930-1730, Oct-Mar daily 0930-1630, £6.90, concessions £5.50, children £4.10, wheelchair access, café.*

Standing proudly on a sandy spit that juts out into the Moray Firth is Fort George, Europe's finest surviving example of 18th-century military architecture. In today's money it's estimated the mightiest artillery fortification in Britain would cost over £1 billion to build. Begun in 1748, it was the last in a chain of three such fortifications built in the Highlands – the other two being Fort Augustus and Fort William – as a base for George II's army to prevent any potential threats to Hanoverian rule. It was completed in 1769, by which time the Highlands were more or less peaceful, but it was kept in use as a military barracks. Today it remains virtually unchanged, and as a functioning military base don't be surprised to find armed sentries at the main gate. You can walk along the ramparts to get an idea of the sheer scale of the place and also enjoy the sweeping views across the Moray Firth. You may even be lucky enough to see a school of dolphins. Within the fort are the barracks, a chapel, workshops and the Regimental Museum of the Queen's Own Highlanders, which features the fascinating Seafield Collection of arms and military equipment, most of which dates from the Napoleonic Wars.

Cawdor Castle → Colour map 2, C2.
① T01667-404401, May to early-Oct daily 1000-1730, £8.30 concessions £7.50, children £5.20. Highland Country Bus No 12 runs Mon-Sat to Cawdor Church from Inverness. It's a 10-min walk from there to the castle.

Though best known for its legendary association with Shakespeare's *Macbeth*, Cawdor Castle post-dates the grisly historical events on which the great Bard based his famous tragedy. The oldest part of the castle, the central tower, dates from 1372, and the rest of it is mostly 16th or 17th century. But despite the literary disappointment, the castle is still one of the most appealing in Scotland. It has been in the hands of the Cawdor family for over six centuries and each summer they clear off, leaving their romantic home and its glorious gardens and Big Wood of native trees species open for the enjoyment of ordinary folks like us. There's also a nine-hole golf course and self-catering accommodation (£550 per week) on the estate at Banchor Cottage.

According to family legend, an early Thane of Cawdor, wanting a new castle, had a dream in which he was told to load a donkey with gold, let it wander around for a day and watch where it lay down, for this would be the best spot for his new castle. He duly followed these instructions and the donkey lay down under a thorn tree, the remains of which can still be seen in the middle of a vaulted chamber in the 14th-century tower.

Just to the west of Cawdor is **Kilravock Castle** ① T01667-493258, www.kilravockcastle. com. This 14th-century stately home (pronounced *Kilrawk*) is still the seat of the Rose family. In recent years Kilravock has opened its doors as a castle B&B and self-catering experience (see Sleeping, page 203). Guests can enjoy a guided tour of the castle at 1000 Monday to Saturday. From April to September there's delicious home-baking in the castle tea room.

Nairn and around → Colour map 2, C2. Phone code 01667. Population 11,190.
With two championship golf courses, the seaside town of Nairn also claims to have the driest and sunniest climate in the whole of Scotland. This alone should be reason enough visit, but there are other attractions besides the sunshine for there are miles of sandy beach stretching east to the Culbin Forest and two of the best castles in the country are within easy reach – Cawdor Castle, see above, and Brodie Castle, see below. Nairn is also only 5 miles from the airport and makes a pleasant alternative to staying in Inverness.

Nairn Museum ① Viewfield House, Viewfield Dr, www.nairnmuseum.co.uk, Apr-Oct Mon-Fri, 1000-1630, Sat 1000-1300, £3, concession £1.50, gives an insight into the area's history and includes the Fishertown Room, highlighting the lives of the hardy men and women who in the 18th and 19th century made their living from the herring trade.

About 2 miles east of Nairn, in the little village of **Auldearn**, is a 17th-century *doocot* (dovecote). Nearby the Boath Doocot information boards record the 1645 Battle of Aldearn in which the victorious troops of Charles I, led by the Marquess of Montrose, defeated and killed almost 2000 Covenanters.

From Nairn, Harbour **Phoenix boat trips** ① T01667-456078, www.phoenix-boat-trips.co.uk, offer enjoyable wildlife cruises out onto the Moray Firth to spot the seals off Ardersier and possibly dolphins.

Ten miles south of Nairn on the A939 to Grantown is **Dulsie Bridge**, a very popular local beauty spot which is a great place for a summer picnic or to swim in the River Findhorn. On the southern shores of the Moray Firth, just east of Nairn, is **Culbin Sands**, a stretch of sand home to a variety of birdlife and managed by the RSPB. The best time to visit is from autumn to spring when bar-tailed godwits, oystercatchers, knots, dunlins, ringed plovers, redshanks, curlews, shellducks, red-breasted mergansers, greylag geese and snow buntings, to name but a few, come here in their droves.

Brodie Castle → Colour map 2, C3.
① T0844-493 2156, castle open Apr daily 1030-1630, May-Jun Sun-Wed 1030-1630, Jul-Aug daily 1030-1700, Sep-Oct Sun-Thu 1030-1630. Grounds open all year. £9, concessions £6.50.
Brodie Castle, 8 miles east of Nairn, just off the main A96 to Forres, is one of Scotland's finest castles. The oldest part of the castle, the Z-plan tower house, is 16th century, with additions dating from the 17th and 19th centuries, giving it the look of a Victorian country house. The interior of the house is the epitome of good taste, with fabulous ceilings, and you can look round several rooms, including the huge Victorian kitchen. The collections of French furniture and Chinese porcelain are wonderful but most notable are the outstanding paintings, which include Edwin Landseer and Scottish Colourists. The grounds, too, are a delight, especially in spring when the daffodils are in bloom and there are specially constructed hides to observe the wildlife.

The Beauly Firth → For listings, see pages 203-205. Colour map 2, C1-2.

Beauly and around → Colour map 2, C1-2. Phone code 01463.
① The train station at Beauly has the shortest platform in the UK, so take care getting off.
The sleepy little market town of Beauly is 10 miles west of Inverness, where the Beauly river flows into the Firth. It's a lovely wee place – hence its name. According to local legend, when Mary Queen of Scots stayed here, at the priory, in 1564, she was so taken with the place that she cried (in French, of course) "Ah, quel beau lieu!" (What a beautiful place!).

At the north end of the marketplace is the ruin of **Beauly Priory** ① daily 1000-1800, free, founded in 1230 for the Valliscaulian order but, like so much else of Scotland's ecclesiastical heritage, it was destroyed during the Reformation. Close by, the **Beauly Centre** ① T01463-783444, daily 1000-1800, provides information on the area, a genealogy service, web access, café, gifts, clan history and even contains a reconstructed 1920s village shop to highlight how locals lived in the last century.

Four miles east of Beauly, at Balchraggan just off the main Inverness road, is **Moniack Castle Winery** ① Apr-Sep Mon-Sat 1100-1700, Oct-Mar 1100-1600,, where you can try a range of wines, including elderflower and birch. Four miles to the north and just off the A832 is the **Glen Ord Distillery** ① T01463-872004, www.discovering-distilleries.com Jan-Mar, Oct-Dec Mon-Fri 1100-1600, Apr-Sep Mon-Fri 1000-1700, Jul-Sep Mon-Fri 1000-1700, Sat-Sun 1000-1600, £5 (including a dram), which was established in 1838. The malt tour is enjoyable – particularly the dram. If travelling by bus it's a 10-minute walk after taking the Nos 17, 18 or 19 Stagecoach bus from Inverness to Muir of Ord.

The River Beauly is one of Scotland's best salmon-fishing rivers, and 5 miles south of Beauly, at **Aigas**, is a **fish lift** ① Mon-Fri 1000-1500, where you can watch salmon bypass the dam with the aid of technology. Nearby, on the A831 Cannich road, golfers will love the picturesque and challenging nine-hole **Aigas Golf Course** ① T01463-782942.

Dolphin cruises

The waters in this area are renowned for their populations of that well-loved mammal, the dolphin. Buckie is the home of the **Moray Firth Wildlife Centre**, which houses a dolphin exhibition and where you can find out everything you ever wanted to know about them. Spey Bay (one hour east of Inverness) is the home of the **Whale and Dolphin Conservation Society (WDCS)**, T01343-820339. Its wildlife centre, complete with shop and café, is packed with information about the dolphins and their latest sightings. There's also a WDCS centre at North Kessock, from where you can try to observe dolphins in the Beauly Firth from the viewing window.

There are various dolphin-spotting cruises around the Moray Firth, but there is a code of conduct for boat operators. Before you choose a cruise, make sure the company is signed up to the **Dolphin Space Programme (DSP)**, www.dolphinspace.org.

Moray Firth Dolphin Cruises, Inverness, T01463-717900, www.inverness-dolphin-cruises.co.uk, Mar-Oct daily 1030-1800, £12.50, concessions £10, children £9. Boat departs from Shore Street Quay, Inverness harbour. Take the courtesy bus from the tourist office. Throughout the 90-minute tour, this professional operator provides a chance to spot the bottlenose dolphins while also pointing out common and grey seals and abundant birdlife. Take warm clothes. **Dolphin Trips Avoch**, Harbour office, Pierhead, Avoch, T01381-622383, £10, children (three to-12 years) £7, under 3s free. Run informative 60-minute wildlife cruises up to six times a day from April to October. **Ecoventures**, The Dolphin Centre, Cromarty, Black Isle, T01381-600323, www.ecoventures.co.uk, £22, concessions £16. Leave daily subject to weather conditions. Just 40 minutes north of Inverness by car over the Kessock Bridge (A9) and A832, this experienced operator uses a high-speed RIB boat for a thrilling ride out to spot the bottlenose dolphins and possibly minke whale.

Glen Strathfarrar → *Colour map 1, C6.*

Southwest of Beauly are glens Affric and Strathfarrar. Glen Strathfarrar, the lesser known of the two, is unspoiled and considered by some to be the more beautiful. To get there, take the A831 9 miles south from Beauly to Struy and follow the signs. Access to the glen is restricted by the estates in the area to 25 cars at a time. As a general rule there's gate access from Easter to late summer but it's best to call (T01738-493942) for advice. Once you're in, there is a tremendous feeling of peace, and there's good climbing, fishing and walking. The little ungraded road runs for 14 miles all the way to the impressive **Monar Dam** at the head of the glen. Glen Strathfarrar can also be reached from Drumnadrochit, via Cannich (see below). Most of the walks and cycle routes here are covered by OS Landranger Nos 25 and 26.

Glen Affric → *Colour map 3, A6. OS Landranger Nos 25 and 26.*

The A831 continues south from Struy through Strathglass to the village of **Cannich**, gateway to glorious Glen Affric, a dramatic and beautiful gorge, with the River Affric rushing through it, and surrounded by Caledonian pine and birch forest – in fact this is one of the few places where you can still see the native Scots pine. There are few, if any, more stunning sights in the Scottish Highlands and it's perfect for walking, or even just to drive through and stop for a picnic on a sunny day. Thanks to Rapson's and Ross's Minibus, it's possible to reach the beautiful and remote inner reaches of Glen Affric. The best departure point is Inverness Bus Station (stand seven) where **Ross's minibus** ① *T01463-761250, T07801-988491*, departs at 0845 on a Monday, Wednesday and Friday (July-September) and travels via Beauly and Cannich to the upper car park in Glen Affric. Alternatively, catch the **Rapson's** ① *T01463-710555*, bus from Inverness that picks up passengers at Drumnadrochit Post Office and heads 10 miles west into Glen Affric via Balnain and Tomich Post Office. On a Monday, Tuesday, Wednesday and Friday in summer, Ross's minibus goes back down the glen to meet passengers off the Rapsons bus at Cannich (around 1210) and drives back up Glen Affric to the road end.

Beyond Loch Affric the serious walking starts. From **Affric Lodge**, 9 miles west of Cannich, begins a 20-mile trail west to **Morvich**, near Shiel Bridge, on the west coast near Kyle of Lochalsh, see page 252. This strenuous walk is for experienced hikers only, and takes around 10 hours. You can stop off halfway at one of the most remote youth hostels in Scotland, **Glen Affric Youth Hostel** at Allt Beithe, see Sleeping, below.

There are also many shorter, easier walks around Glen Affric. There are some short, circular marked trails at the end of the road which runs west from Cannich almost to Loch Affric, and also from the car park at the impressive **Dog Falls**, 4½ miles from Cannich and a great place to stop for a picnic and swim. Cycling in the forests around Cannich is good too – you can hire bikes at the friendly **Cannich Caravan and Camping Park** (see Sleeping, below). The owner's a keen cyclist.

Glen Affric can also be reached from **Drumnadrochit** (see page 206), by heading west on the A831 through Glen Urquhart to Cannich. Just before Cannich, on the road from Drumnadrochit, a single-track road leads left (south), past the Caravan and Camping Park, to the tiny village of **Tomich**. From here, it's a 3-mile hike up a woodland trail to a car park. A few hundred yards down through the trees takes you to the 70-ft plunging **Plodda Falls**. An old iron bridge affords a spectacular view of the waterfall.

◉ Around Inverness listings

For Sleeping and Eating price codes and other relevant information, see Essentials pages 38-45.

◉ Sleeping

Nairn and around *p200*
L The Boath House Hotel and Spa, Aldearn T01667-454896, www.boath-house.com. Apparently once described as the most beautiful regency house in Scotland, this stunning hotel with 6 tastefully appointed bedrooms combines award-winning dining with luxury spa treatments
B-F Kilravock Castle, 7 miles west of Nairn, Croy, T01667-493258, www.kilravock castle. com. Just like Mary Queen of Scots, you can be a guest of what has been described as a historical gem housing artefacts from

Culloden. Beautiful garden and spooky dungeons in this atmospheric 14th-century castle. Also offers backpackers a budget stay.
C-D Greenlawns, 13 Seafield St, T01667-452738, www.greenlawns.uk.com. A friendly, 7 bedroom guesthouse where you'll tuck into the likes of kedgeree, smoked salmon and scrambled eggs for breakfast, in a dining room crammed with antiques.
D-E Bracadale House, Albert St, T01667-452547, www.bracadalehouse.com. Very fine B&B.

Camping
Nairn Camping and Caravanning Club, Delnies Wood, Nairn, T01667-455281. Open Apr-Oct. Clean with good amenities in a secluded spot, but it's 3 miles to the pub.

Beauly and around *p201*

C Lovat Arms Hotel, opposite end of the main street from **The Priory Hotel**, T01463-782313, www.lovatarms.com. A wonderful 22-bedroom country house with a relaxed air and a tartan touch. Try the terrific Scottish game and seafood in the restaurant (♥♥♥-♥♥) or relax with a dram or cup of tea beside the log fire. Terrific Sun lunch (1230-1400).
B-C The Priory Hotel, the Square, on the main street, T01463-782309, www.priory-hotel.com. Delightful hotel (**A** with dinner).

Glen Affric *p202*

C The Tomich Hotel, Tomich, T01456-415399, www.tomichhotel.co.uk. You'll find a friendly welcome and good food at this former Victorian hunting lodge that will appeal to the visitor in search of walking, stalking and fishing alike. There's even haggis on the breakfast menu.
D-F Bearnock Country Centre, 6 miles west of Drumnadrochit, Glen Urquhart, T01456-476296, www.bcclochnesshostel.co.uk. Opened in 2007, it's beautifully furnished with solid oak furniture and provides free tea, coffee and bed linen. Ideal for mountain biking, fishing and hiking in the area.
F Cougie Lodge, near Tomich, T01456-415459, www.cougie.com. Open Apr-Sep. It's a long walk from Tomich but call ahead and the owners of this delightful independent hostel will pick you up.
F Glen Affric Backpackers, Cannich, T/F01456-415263. Closed Christmas and New Year. 70 beds and a great open fire. Owner has extensive contacts for local activities and walks.
F Glen Affric Youth Hostel, Allt Beithe, T0845-293 7373. Apr to mid-Sep.

Self-catering

Culligran Cottages, Glen Strathfarrar, T01463-761255. Enjoy your own cottage or chalet along 15 miles of private road, where you can spot deer, fish or ride bikes.

Camping

Cannich Camping and Caravan Park, Cannich, T01456-415364. Mid-Mar to Oct. Just 5 mins' walk from the Spar shop. Handy campsite with caravans for rent. Very friendly and bike hire available.

🍴 Eating

Cawdor Castle *p200*
♥♥-♥ **Cawdor Tavern**, close to the castle, T/F01667-404777. A very popular, traditional country pub serving excellent food in a friendly atmosphere. Perfect for lunch or dinner after visiting the castle.

Nairn and around *p200*
♥♥♥-♥♥ **The Boath House Hotel and Spa**, see Sleeping, above. Dripping with awards for their cuisine, this delightful rural retreat is well worth a visit.
♥ **Asher's tea room**, 2 Bridge St. It is recommended for a hot snack. Run by the same folk as the one in Inverness.
♥ **Classroom**, Cawdor St. Great for coffee, tasty home-baking and sandwiches.

Beauly and around *p201*
♥♥♥-♥ **Lovat Arms Hotel**, see Sleeping, above. Serves up terrific food in the restaurant or relax in the bar with tasty snacks.
♥ **Beauly Tandoori**, the Square, T01463-782221. Good for a cheap curry.

⛰ Activities and tours

Nairn and around *p200*
Cycling
If you have a mountain bike, bring it to Lochaber and Glen Affric. Glen Urquhart Forest has fantastic trails outside Cannich.

Golf
Aigas Golf Course, the best golf course in the area, see page 201.

Horse riding
Heatherfield Riding Centre, Lochloy Rd, T01667-456682. Offer pony trekking.
Highland Trekking and Trail Riding, Cougie, Tomich by Cannich, T01456-415323, www.cougie.com, www.glenaffric.org. Open all year. Ride in the stunning wilds of Glen Affric.

Mountain biking
Moray Monster Trails (southeast of Nairn); Balnain Bike Park in Urquhart Forest east of Cannich; and Learnie Forest (Black Isle) provide miles of forest/trail cycling for all standards on state-of-the-art tracks. See www.forestry.gov.uk, for details.

⊖ Transport

Culloden *p198*
Bus Highland Country Bus (Rapsons) No 12 runs to **Inverness**, daily.

Fort George *p199*
Bus Highland Country Bus No 11 to **Inverness**, several daily Mon-Sat. Also buses to **Nairn**.

Cawdor Castle *p200*
Bus Highland Country Bus No 12, Mon-Sat to **Inverness**.

Nairn and around *p200*
Bus There are regular daily buses to **Inverness**, 30 mins, Highland Country Buses and Stagecoach/Bluebird, see page 195. There are also buses to **Fort George**. To

Cawdor Castle there's an infrequent service, Mon-Fri, No 252, **Forres Taxis**, T0800-834233.
Cycle hire Rafford Cycles, Forres, T01309-672811. Bikes for hire from £16 per day.
Train Nairn is on the **Aberdeen** to **Inverness** rail line, and there are several trains daily to Inverness, 20 mins.

Brodie Castle *p201*
Bus Bluebird/Stagecoach buses run to **Inverness** via **Nairn**, 45 mins.

Beauly and around *p201*
Bus To **Inverness**, daily, No 19, Stagecoach, T01463-239292. To **Muir of Ord** and **Dingwall**, take the **Inverness** bus.
Train You can take the train to **Inverness** from here, it stops on its way from **Thurso**.

Glen Affric *p202*
Bus To **Inverness** from **Cannich** and **Tomich** via **Drumnadrochit**, Mon-Sat, Highland County Buses, T01463-710555 (No 17); Ross's Minibus, T01463-761250, T07801-988491.
    Ross's Minibus service leaves from Glen Affric car park Mon, Wed and Fri at 1700 and returns via **Cannich** and **Drumnadrochit** to **Inverness**. It is strongly recommended to call ahead to confirm the timetable. You only other option is to walk out of the glen to the village of Cannich and catch the No 17 **Rapson's** bus that runs 4 times Mon-Sat. On a Tue only, **Ross's Minibus** also runs from Cannich Post Office at 0945 to **Dingwall** via **Beauly** and **Muir of Ord**, arriving at 1039.

Loch Ness and around

One of Scotland's biggest attractions is the narrow gash of Loch Ness, Britain's deepest body of fresh water, stretching 23 miles from Fort Augustus in the south almost to Inverness in the north. The loch is scenic in its own right, with rugged hills rising steeply from its wooded shores, but visitors don't come here for the views. They come every year, in their hundreds of thousands, to stare across the dark, cold waters in search of its legendary inhabitant, the Loch Ness Monster. A huge tourist trade has grown up around 'Nessie', as the monster is affectionately known, and every summer the main A82, which runs along its western shore, is jam-packed with bus-loads of eager monster-hunters, binoculars trained on the loch surface, desperate for one glimpse of the elusive beast. If you do see it, bear in mind your photograph could be worth a fortune! ▸▸ *For listings, see pages 212-217.*

Ins and outs

Getting around
The best way to see the loch is on a cruise from Inverness (page 194). There are also boat trips from Drumnadrochit and Fort Augustus (see page 216). Most of the tourist traffic uses the congested A82, built in 1933 and which offers few decent views of the loch. By far the best views of are from the quiet and picturesque B862/852, which runs along the eastern shore from Fort Augustus up to Inverness. It's possible to make a complete circuit of the loch, which is best done in an anti-clockwise direction heading south from Inverness on the A82, but you'll need your own transport (or take a tour), as there are no buses between Fort Augustus and Foyers. There are regular daily bus services between Inverness and Fort William, with additional buses between Invergarry and Fort Augustus. Fort Augustus is a convenient stopover between Fort William and Inverness. Citylink buses between Inverness and Kyle of Lochalsh stop at Urquhart Castle, Loch Ness Youth Hostel, Invergarry and Invermoriston. ▸▸ *For further details, see Activities and tours, page 215, and Transport, page 217.*

Around the loch ➜ *For listings, see pages 212-217.*

Drumnadrochit ➜ *Colour map 2, C1. Phone code 01456.*
The Nessie tourist trade is centred on the village of Drumnadrochit, 15 miles south of Inverness, where the canny locals have cashed in on the enduring popularity of the monster myth. The monster hype is almost overpowering, with two rival Monster exhibitions and the inevitable souvenir shops selling all manner of awful tartan tat, including those scary-looking tartan dolls with flickering eyelids, the 'See-You-Jimmy' tartan bonnet, complete with ginger 'hair', and not forgetting the Loch Ness Monster novelty hat. Fortunately, the very friendly **TIC** ① *in the car park, T01456-459076, Apr-Sep Mon-Sat 0900-1730, Sun 1000-1600, call ahead for winter hours,* can offer alternative suggestions, such as exploring peaceful Glen Affric (see page 202). There are also toilets a beside the TIC (daily 0700-1800).

One of the two Monster Exhibitions is the **'Original' Loch Ness Monster Visitor Centre and Lodge Hotel** ① *T01456-450342, www.lochness-centre.com, Jul-Aug daily 0900-2100, Sep-Jun daily 0900-1700, £5.50, concessions £4.35, students £4.50, children £4,* features a wide-screen cinema documenting the 'latest' facts and 'sightings' of Nessie. There's also a gift shop, but the most authentic experience of all is the restaurant's tasty home-

The Great Glen Way

The Great Glen Way is a waymarked walking trail that runs for 73 miles between Inverness and Fort William. Panoramic views of Loch Ness can be seen at many of the sections between Fort Augustus and Inverness. Although a relatively easy walk, there are some fairly tough sections around Loch Ness and you'll need to be properly equipped and have a good map. OS Landranger Nos 26, 34 and 41 cover the entire route. It should take 4-5 days to complete, depending on your level of fitness. It is probably better to walk it in 'reverse', from Fort William to Inverness, as the easiest section is then at the start. The Great Glen Way also has its own website, www.greatglenway.com.

baking. **Loch Ness Cruises** (*MV Nessie Hunter*) operates from here, see page 194. The rival exhibition is **Loch Ness 2000 Exhibition** ⓘ *T01456-450573, Feb-May daily 0930-1700, Jun and Sep daily 0900-1800, Jul-Aug daily 0900-1830, Oct daily 0930-1700, Nov-Mar daily 1000-1530, £6.50, concessions £5, children £4.50*. This Nessie exhibition also details eye-witness accounts, but more pertinently provides a more elaborate audio-visual experience.

If it all gets too much, then fear not, for Drumnadrochit gives easy access to one of the most beautiful corners of Scotland. The A831 heads west from the village through Glen Urquhart to Cannich, about 12 miles away, at the head of Glen Affric, a great place for walking or enjoying a picnic. ▶▶ *For further information, see page 202.*

Castle Urquhart

ⓘ *T01456-450551, Apr-Sep daily 0930-1800, Oct-Mar daily 0930-1630, £7.20, concessions £5.70, children £4.30. Citylink bus (No919) stops at Urquhart Castle.*
A few miles south of Drumnadrochit are the ruins of Castle Urquhart. The castle bears the scars of centuries of fighting but its setting, perched on a rocky cliff on the loch's edge, is magnificent and, not surprisingly, one of the most photographed scenes in Scotland. Dating from the 14th century, the castle was a strategic base, guarding the Great Glen during the long Wars of Independence. It was taken by Edward I, held by Robert the Bruce against Edward II, and was then almost constantly under siege before being destroyed in 1692 to prevent it from falling into Jacobite hands. Most of the existing buildings date from the 16th century, including the five-storey tower, the best-preserved part of the complex, from where you get great views of the loch and surrounding hills. The entire complex is accessed via the stunning new visitor centre that in addition to the obligatory café includes an informative short-film about the history of the castle.

Invermoriston → *Colour map 4, A1. Phone code 01320.*

Between Drumnadrochit and Fort Augustus is the tiny village of Invermoriston, probably the most tranquil spot on the entire Inverness to Fort Augustus stretch of the A82. It's a beautiful little piece of Highland scenery, with a photogenic old stone bridge over foaming river rapids and with marked woodland trails leading off into the hills past some lovely waterfalls. There's an interesting **Clog and Craft Centre** ⓘ *T01320-351318*, where high quality clogs and leather goods are made to measure. Just along the road is the **Glenmoriston Arms**, where in addition to a resident ghost in the fabulous accommodation, the new owner tempts the palette with fine food and a vast selection of malts.

Great Monster Hunt

In a country full of myths and legends, the Loch Ness Monster is the greatest of them all. As elusive as a straight answer from a politician, Nessie has single-handedly sold more tins of tartan-wrapped shortbread to foreign visitors than Edinburgh Castle.

Tales of Nessie go way back to the sixth century, when St Columba is said to have calmed the beast after she had attacked one of his monks. But the monster craze only really took off with the completion of the A82 road along the loch's western shore in 1933. Since then there have been numerous sightings, some backed up with photographic evidence, though the most impressive of these – the famous black-and-white movie footage of Nessie's humps moving through the water, and the classic photograph of her head and neck – have been exposed as fakes.

In recent decades determined monster hunters have enlisted the help of new technology, such as sonar surveys but have failed to come up with conclusive evidence. Enter Cyber Nessie, the latest attempt to end the years of rumours, hoaxes and speculation. Nessie's very own website, www.lochness.co.uk, is a 24-hour real-time video watch of Loch Ness, and has already produced a couple of claimed sightings.

At Invermoriston the A887 heads west through **Glen Moriston** to meet the A87, which runs from Invergarry (see page 209) all the way through the rugged and dramatic Glen Shiel and under the shadow of the Five Sisters of Kintail en route to Kyle of Lochalsh and Skye.

Fort Augustus → Colour map 4, A1. Phone code 01320.

At the more scenic southern end of Loch Ness stands the village of Fort Augustus, the former clan village of Kilchuimen until set up as a garrison after the Jacobite rebellion of 1715 to serve as the headquarters of General Wade's campaign to pacify the Highlands. Today, Fort Augustus is a very busy little place, full of monster-hunting tourists and boats using the flight of five locks to enter or leave Loch Ness on their journey along the Caledonian Canal. The TIC ① T01320-366779, Apr-Oct, is in the car park next to the petrol station and cashpoint.

Like many visitors, you may find yourself drawn to the canal side, watching yachts and cruise boats negotiate the first of many locks to access/leave Loch Ness. Alternatively, pop into **The Clansman Centre** ① T01320-366444, Easter-Oct daily 1000-1800, £4.50, concessions £3.50, where young guides in traditional dress provide a lively and entertaining presentation of 17th-century Highland family life in an old turf house. If you've time, pop into the **Caledonian Canal Heritage Centre** ① Jun-Sep daily, free, with its history of the impressive canal system. Nearby, children may also enjoy the **Highland and Rare Breeds Croft** ① T01320-366433, £2, concessions £1.50, where Highland cattle, red deer, Shetland sheep, ducks and rabbits can be spotted.

Fort Augustus to Dores → Colour map 4, A1-2.

A very worthwhile detour from Fort Augustus is to take the B862/852 up the east shore of Loch Ness, a mostly single-track road that skirts the loch for much of its length to the village of Dores. It's a much quieter and more scenic route than the busy A82 and follows General Wade's original (and very straight) military road which linked Fort Augustus with Fort George. Though it makes a more interesting alternative to the more popular A82 route from Inverness to Fort Augustus, it's best done from south to north, if you have the time. Today, this road also attracts runners from around the world for the annual (October) Baxters Loch Ness Marathon. This route is only possible if you have your own transport. There are buses south from Inverness, but they only run as far as Foyers. If you're feeling very fit, it can be done by bike, as a tough trip from Fort Augustus or from Inverness, possibly using the one way bike hire service offered by **Off Beat Bikes** in Fort William (see Activities and tours, page 228).

From Fort Augustus, the road winds its way up into rugged hills past Glendole where the largest hydro electric scheme to be built in Scotland in 50 years recently became operational. Nearby is the good real ale house of the historic Whitebridge Hotel and the nearby 1732 White Bridge. The road then drops back to the lochside at **Foyers**. It's worth stopping here to see the impressive waterfall where the River Foyers plunges into Loch Ness or to enjoy an overnight stay at **Foyers House** (see Sleeping, page 213). To get there, follow the steep (and slippery) track down from opposite the shops. Three miles further north, at **Inverfarigaig**, is **Boleskine House**, once home of Alastair Crowley, who is said to have practised devil worship here. In the 1970s the house was bought by Jimmy Page of Led Zeppelin, but sold some years later after the tragic death of his daughter. Those of a nervous disposition may wish to pass on quickly and continue to the little village of **Dores**, at the northeastern end of the loch, where you can enjoy some fine forest walks or reasonable pub grub at the **Dores Inn**.

You can then continue to Inverness, or return via the beautiful hill road that leads up to **Loch Mhorand** back to Fort Augustus via the **Stratherrick Valley**. From **Errogie**, at the northern end of Loch Mhor, there's a dramatic section of road that winds down to the loch through a series of tight, twisting bends, reminiscent of an Alpine pass, and great for cyclists. There are also interesting marked woodland trails around Errogie.

Fort Augustus to Fort William → *For listings, see pages 212-217.*

South of Fort Augustus, the A82 leaves behind Loch Ness and runs along the west shore of Loch Oich and then the east shore of Loch Lochy, until it reaches Spean Bridge. Here the A82 continues south to Fort William, while the A86 branches east through Glen Spean to join the A9 Perth to Inverness road finally at Kingussie. All along this route are many opportunities to get off the beaten track and explore huge chunks of real wilderness, deserted since the Clearances and soaked in the blood of history.

Invergarry and around→ *Colour map 4, A1. Phone code 01809.*
The old village of Invergarry stands where the A82 turns west to meet the A87. There's not much to see or do in the village, but the surrounding area merits some exploring, particularly the route west through Glen Garry, and there are several places to stay.

Inside the entrance to the **Glengarry Castle Hotel**, on the shores of Loch Oich (see Sleeping, page 213) stand the ruins of **Invergarry Castle**, once the stronghold of Clan Ranald of Glengarry and later destroyed by the Duke of Cumberland as he wreaked revenge on the Highlands in the aftermath of Culloden (see box, page 199). The hotel was later built as the main house of the Ellice family, who made their fortune from the Hudson Bay Company in Canada and who were the main driving force behind the creation of the Victorian planned village.

A mile or so south of the village, at **North Laggan**, is a monument by the side of the road standing over **The Well of the Seven Heads**. This tells the grisly story of the Keppoch Murders, one of the most infamous clan murders which took place at **Roy Bridge** (see page 212) in the 17th century. It all began when the chief of the clan MacDonnell

Old as the hills

The Great Glen, which splits the Scottish mainland from Fort William in the south to Inverness in the north, is one of the world's major geological fault lines. The Glen was formed millions of years ago when the northern part of the Caledonian mountains 'slid' more than 60 miles south, leaving behind a massive glen with four freshwater lochs – Loch Linnhe, Loch Lochy, Loch Oich and Loch Ness.

The most famous of these is Loch Ness, which attracts hordes of visitors eager to catch a glimpse of its elusive monster. The renowned engineer, Thomas Telford, succeeded in connecting all these lochs when he built the impressive Caledonian Canal. The canal took 22 years to complete, and when it was opened in 1822 was the first in Britain to take ships from one coast to the other. It remains

the only canal in the country capable of carrying ships of up to 500 tons. The best way to appreciate the glen is by boat, through the 38 miles of natural lochs and rivers and the 22 miles of canal, and every summer pleasure craft of all shapes and sizes ply its length. The main A82 runs from Inverness south to Fort William. The southern section, from Fort Augustus, follows the original line of the road constructed in 1727 by General Wade to link the military garrisons at Fort William and Fort Augustus (hence their names).

Another way to travel through the Great Glen is along the excellent cycle route, which follows the canal towpaths, forest trails and quiet minor roads to avoid the busy main road. The route is outlined in the Forestry Commission leaflet, available from most TICs.

died, leaving two young sons, who were sent away to complete their education before returning to Roy Bridge to celebrate the elder brother's accession to chieftainship. Another branch of the clan present at the celebrations started a fight in which both brothers were killed. Believing they had been murdered, one of their cousins persuaded a fellow clan member to raise 50 men and march on the murderers' house at nearby Inverlair. The accused murderers – a father and his six sons – were duly slaughtered and their heads cut off, to be displayed before the local laird at Glengarry. On the way to his lodge, the heads were washed here in this well.

A few miles further south, at **Laggan**, where the A82 crosses to the east bank of Loch Lochy, is the site of the **Battle of the Shirts**. The A87 leads west from Invergarry through Glen Shiel to Shiel Bridge, on the way to Kyle of Lochalsh on the west coast, see page 252. About 7 miles along the A87, past the turning for Kinloch Hourn (see below), is the **Glen Garry viewpoint**, from where you get one of the most stunning, and famous, of all Highland views. From this angle Loch Garry looks uncannily like a map of Scotland, so get out the camera for that classic holiday snap.

Glen Garry to Kinloch Hourn → *Colour map 3, A5-6.*

A mile or so before the Glen Garry viewpoint, where the A87 begins to leave the shores of Loch Garry, is the turning left for the road through Glen Garry, described as the longest and most beautiful cul-de-sac in Britain. The little single-track road turns and twists for 22 glorious miles along the shores of Loch Garry and Loch Quoich all the way to Kinloch Hourn at the head of Loch Hourn. Known as 'the loch of the devil' this sea loch forms part of the wonderful wilderness area of Knoydart aptly dubbed the 'Rough Bounds.'

Glen Garry is now virtually deserted but was once home to some 5000 people who were driven out during the infamous Highland Clearances in the 19th century. The road passes the tiny hamlet of **Tomdoun**, once the junction of the main road to Skye, until the massive post-Second World War hydroelectric schemes changed the landscape. Experienced hillwalkers can still follow the old route to Skye, through Glen Kingie, along Loch Hourn and then across the wild Knoydart Peninsula until they reach the tiny but welcoming settlement of **Inverie**. From here a little ferry ① T01687-462320, Apr-Sep, Mon-Fri, Oct-Mar, Mon,Wed and Thu, runs to Mallaig, see page 243.

Beyond Tomdoun the road passes a huge dam, built in the 1950s, which raised the waters of **Loch Quoich** by over 100 ft, flooding many of the old settlements. Also flooded was **Glen Quoich Lodge**, which can count Edward VII and Sir Edward Landseer among its notable guests. It was reputedly Glen Garry that gave Landseer the inspiration for his famous painting *The Monarch of the Glen*. The road then reaches its highest point, at 1200 ft, before descending to **Kinloch Hourn**, once a thriving crofting and fishing village.

Spean Bridge → Colour map 3, B6. Phone code 01397.
The main A82 runs down the east shore of Loch Lochy to the village of Spean Bridge, at the head of Glen Spean, beneath the towering Lochaber Mountains. The village gets its name from Thomas Telford's bridge across the River Spean. Two miles west are the remains of the old 'Highbridge', built in 1736 by General Wade, and the site of the first clash between Government troops and the Jacobites, three days before Prince Charles raised his standard at Glenfinnan.

Spean Bridge is only 8 miles north of Fort William so gets busy in the summer, but it still makes a more peaceful and attractive alternative base for exploring this astoundingly beautiful part of the Highlands. There's a **TIC** ① T01397-712576, Easter-Oct, just off the main road behind the **Spean Bridge Hotel**. This hotel, complete with its **Shinty Bar** watering hole, also houses the excellent **Commando Exhibition** ① free. The area is also the starting point for the excellent **Grey Corries ridge walk** (OS Landranger Map No 41).

Loch Arkaig and around → Colour map 3, A5-6. Phone code 01397.
A mile north of Spean Bridge on the A82 is the striking **Commando Memorial**, which commemorates the men who trained in the area from their secret base at Achnacarry during the Second World War and the 1700 commandos who lost their lives. It's worth lingering for a few moments to appreciate the fantastic views including (on a clear day) the summit of Ben Nevis. From here the B8004 branches west to **Gairlochy**, crossing the Caledonian Canal, then the B8005 heads north to Loch Arkaig, a long, deep and mysterious loch stretching west through the mountains. Bonnie Prince Charlie passed this way, before and after Culloden, through an area which has, for centuries, been the seat of the Camerons of Lochiel. The Camerons were fervent supporters of the Jacobite cause and when Prince Charles landed at Loch nan Uamh, on the road from Fort William to Mallaig, he called on Cameron of Lochiel to join him at Glenfinnan.

In the tiny township of **Achnacarry**, nestled between the shores of Loch Lochy and Loch Arkaig, you can find out about the Camerons and their involvement in the Jacobite rebellion of 1745 at the **Clan Cameron Museum** ① T01397-712480, Easter to mid-Oct daily 1330-1700, Jul-Aug 1100-1700, £3.50 concessions £2, children free. This interesting museum is housed in an old cottage, rebuilt after being burned by government troops in 1746.

Beyond the turn-off to Achnacarry, the single-track road runs through the Clunes Forest and The Dark Mile, a long line of beech trees which completely cuts out daylight. At the east end of Loch Arkaig, a stone bridge crosses the Caig Burn. Beside the bridge is a car park, from where a path leads up to the spectacular **Cia-Aig Falls** which tumble into a deep, dark pool known as **The Witch's Cauldron**. It was here that an old hag was accused of casting her evil eye over Lochiel's cattle, causing them to fall ill and die. But when she fell into the pool and drowned, the cattle miraculously began to recover from their illness. The road runs along the north shore of Loch Arkaig all the way to the head of the loch, from where experienced and well-equipped hill walkers can hike through the glens to Loch Nevis, 'the loch of heaven', and Knoydart.

Glen Roy and Loch Laggan → Colour map 4, A-B1. Phone code 01397.

From Spean Bridge the A86 runs east through dramatic Glen Spean to meet the A9 Perth to Inverness road which leads to Aviemore, see page 173. The road (and railway) passes through **Roy Bridge**, which is the turn-off for Glen Roy, noted for its amazing 'parallel roads'. These are not in fact roads, but three gravel ledges etched on to the mountains at different heights. The 'roads' marked the shorelines of a glacial lake formed during the last Ice Age. Roy Bridge was also the site of the infamous Keppoch Murders, see page 209.

The road continues east towards Loch Laggan. After a couple of miles it passes **Cille Choirille**, an ancient church built by a 15th-century Cameron chief as penance for a life of violence. The church fell into disrepair but was restored and reopened in 1932 and now attracts people of all creeds as it's said to inspire peace and spiritual healing. Further east, at the eastern end of Loch Laggan, is the massive **Laggan Dam**, built in 1933 to provide water for the aluminium smelter at Fort William. The water is piped through tunnels up to 15 ft in diameter carved through the core of Ben Nevis. The road runs along the north shore of the loch, past the **Creag Meagaidh National Nature Reserve**, where you can see herds of red deer right by the reserve car park. A recently repaired path leads from here up to **Lochan a' Choire** (about four hours). Note that there are no bus or postbus services between Spean Bridge and Laggan.

◉ Loch Ness and around listings

For Sleeping and Eating price codes and other relevant information, see Essentials pages 38-45.

◉ Sleeping

Drumnadrochit *p206*

B Loch Ness Inn, Lewiston, T01456-450991, www.staylochness.co.uk. Fabulously new and beautifully appointed accommodation and restaurant, 1½ miles south of the TIC in Drumnadrochit, and with connections to the acclaimed **Applecross Inn**. In addition to 12 comfortable bedrooms, this former rustic brewery, just off the main road, has a **Brewery Bar** serving the likes of Isle of Skye real ale and a menu (ŦŦŦ-ŦŦ), of hand-dived scallops, Applecross Bay prawns and all manner of locally sourced produce.

C The Benleva Hotel, T01456-450080, www.benleva.co.uk. A former manse, this small, atmospheric hotel prides itself on a fine range of real ales and its use of freshly prepared local produce. Each Sep, it helps host the **Loch Ness Beer Festival** so book ahead. The 400-year-old chestnut tree outside the front door was the former hanging tree.

D Gillyflowers, T/F01456-450641, gillyflowers@cali.co.uk. Good-value guesthouse in converted croft.

D-E Loch Ness Backpackers Lodge, Coiltie Farmhouse, Lewiston, T01456-450807, www.lochness-backpackers.com. A terrific, low-budget option run by friendly, helpful owners who can arrange boat trips and walks in the area.

E-F Bearnock Country Centre (Loch Ness Hostel), 6 miles west of Drumnadrochit towards Cannich, T01456-476296, www.bcc lochnesshostel.co.uk. This new backpackers oozes quality and style. Beautifully furnished, fully en suite and with great facilities, this place is within reach of both Loch Ness and Glen Affric. Highly recommended.

Invermoriston *p207*

B Glenmoriston Arms Hotel, T01320-351 206, www.glenmoristonarms.co.uk. Formerly a 17th-century drovers inn, this comfortable, 8 bedroom hotel on the route of the Great Glen Way is proud of its freshly prepared cuisine that draws on local produce (♛♛♛-♛♛) and there are 150 malt whiskies behind the bar. Johnson and Boswell were guests during their 18th century tour of the Highlands and it's said there's a resident ghost.
F SYHA Loch Ness Youth Hostel, a few miles north, on the main A82, T01320-351274. Mid-Apr to end Oct. Fantastic views across Loch Ness.

Self-catering
Lann Dearg B&B and Studios, Invermoriston, T01320-351353, www. lanndearg.com. Right by the the Great Glen Way, this delightful B&B (C) with adjoining, fully equipped self- catering studios (£60 per studio per night) offers a luxurious stay after a hard days hike by the lochside. There's even the option of a 'breakfast basket' if you can't be bothered rolling out of bed.

Camping
Loch Ness Caravan & Camping Park, 1½ miles south of Invermoriston, and 6 miles north of Fort Augustus, T01320-351207. Open Mar-Jan. On the shores of the loch with great views and excellent facilities.

Fort Augustus *p208*

A-C Lovat Arms Hotel, T01463-782313. Beautiful, family-run mansion house, which in recent years has been refurbished at considerable expense to ensure you enjoy a luxurious stay and delicious food (♛♛♛-♛♛). They also run the acclaimed Loch Torridon Hotel.
B-C Caledonian Hotel, T01320-366256. Directly opposite the Lovat, this is another lovely place to dine (♛♛♛-♛♛) and enjoy a comfortable sleep (10 en suite rooms).
D Auchterawe House, Fort Augustus T01320-366228. Open all year. 6 en suite rooms. Comfortable and friendly.
D Sonas, on the Inverness Rd, T01320-366291. Run by Mrs Service who certainly lives up to her name.
E-F Morag's Lodge, Bunoich Brae, T01320-366289, www.moragslodge.com. Open all year. Friendly, good value – another excellent option along Loch Ness.

Fort Augustus to Dores *p208*

D Evergreen Guest House, Inverfarigaig T01456-486717, www.evergreenlochness. co.uk. The very friendly owners of this east-shore guesthouse also offer dinner, B&B and innovative car and walking tours around the Loch Ness area (see Activities and tours, below).
D Whitebridge Hotel, 3 miles south of Foyers, T01456-486226. Old world hotel with comfortable accommodation. Also serves good real ales and bar food.
D Foyers House, Foyers, T01456-486405. Small guesthouse that prides itself on its view of Loch Ness from the decking and tasty evening treats such as game pie. They do not accommodate children or babies. (♛♛).

Camping
Fort Augustus Caravan and Camping, at the southern end of the village, T01320-366618. A good option for campers.

Invergarry and around *p209*

B Glengarry Castle Hotel, T01809-501254, www.glengarry.net. Mar-Nov. 26 tastefully appointed bedrooms set in 60 acres of woodland running down to Loch Oich. The hotel prides itself on its traditional Highland hospitality with the daily changing dinner menu (♥♥♥-♥♥) serving up the best of local Scottish produce.

D Forest Lodge, South Laggan, south of Invergarry and 24 miles north of Fort William, T01809-501219, www.flgh.co.uk. A welcoming and comfortable B&B that can also rustle-up a 4-course Scottish dinner (£17 per person), whilst you enjoy the scenery.

F Invergarry Lodge, Mandally Rd, Invergarry, T01809-501412, www.invergarrylodge.co.uk. Open all year. Independent hostel sleeping up to 26 in 4-6 bed rooms. Fully equipped kitchen and safe cycle shed.

Self-catering

Faichmard Farm Chalets, Invergarry, T01809-501314, www.glengarryselfcatering. co.uk. Rustic, secluded, cosy and peaceful. Sleeps 3 at a modest price. £220 plus per week.

Camping

Faichem Park, Ardgarry Farm, lodge and cottages, 15 mins' walk from the village, T01809-501226, www.ardgarryfarm.co.uk. There's a fabulous double room in the farmhouse offering B&B (**D**), and options for 4-6 people to enjoy self-catering (£290-560 per week) in well equipped lodges with spectacular views.

Glen Garry to Kinloch Hourn p210

The **Cluanie Inn** (see page 252 for details), sits in an isolated spot before the road presses further westward into Glen Shiel under the mighty Sisters of Kintail. 30 mins further west is the turn-off towards Loch Hourn and the remote, roadless wilds of the beautiful Knoydart Peninsula. With the lodge at Skiary now closed, call the Knoydart Foundation rangers office at Inverie (T01687-462242) for details of accommodation options near Loch Hourn and around the peninsula.

Spean Bridge p211

There's no shortage of accommodation in Spean Bridge.

L Corriegour Lodge Hotel, 9 miles north of Spean Bridge on the A82, T01397-712685, www.corriegour-lodge-hotel.com. Open Feb-Dec. 9 rooms. Lovely Victorian hunting lodge on the shores of Loch Lochy, with fine views and an excellent restaurant, £49 for a 5-course candlelit dinner.

L Old Pines Hotel and Restaurant, just past the Commando Memorial on the B8004, T01397-712324, www.oldpines.co.uk. This delightful boutique hotel is where discerning guests will experience a truly personal touch. Each of the 8 rooms is individually appointed to a very high standard. The warm scones and tea on arrival are just a hint of the treat in store at dinner where venison, local lamb, prime beef and shellfish feature. It's not inexpensive but for a touch of class in an unpretentious manner this could be a fine choice for an overnight stay or just for dinner (♥♥♥).

D Corriechoille Lodge, 2 miles north of Spean Bridge, T/F01397-712002, www. corriechoille.com. Apr-Oct. This secluded former fishing lodge offers a very comfortable stop for the night and a roaring open fire.

D Invergloy House, T01397-712681. A friendly, comfortable former coach house converted into a B&B, which is set in 50 acres of gardens and offers 2 en suite rooms.

E Smiddy House, T01397-712335. A comfortable guesthouse with a small restaurant (♥♥). Self-catering also available in the adjacent **Old Smiddy**.

Camping

Gairlochy Holiday Park, west towards Gairlochy, T01397-712711. Open Apr-Oct. Camping and self-catering chalets from £250-620 per week.

Stronaba Caravan & Camping, north of the village, T01397-712259. Apr-Oct.

Glen Roy and Loch Laggan p212

F Aite Cruinnichidh, Achluachrach, 1½ miles from the village, T01397-712315. This comfy bunkhouse even has a sauna.

F Grey Corrie Lodge, Roy Bridge, T01397-712236. Very handy for the nearby pub, transport and local shop.

F Station Lodge, 5 miles east at Tulloch train station, T/F01397-732333. Ideal if arriving by train or planning to hike in the hills. The friendly owners will even cook very early breakfasts to accommodate walkers and climbers. The trains stop practically at the door.

🍴 Eating

Drumnadrochit p206
The hotels all tend to serve decent bar food and some B&Bs offer evening meals.
¶¶¶-¶¶ The Loch Ness Inn, 1 mile north of Urquhart Castle, T01456-450991. Lovely setting and offering fresh seafood, locally sourced produce and a good range of real ales.
¶¶-¶ Karasia, Balmacaan Rd, T01456-450003. Scotland's love-affair with curry has recently even reached the shores of Loch Ness. Great food.

Fort Augustus p208
¶¶-¶ Bothy Bite, down by the canal bridge, T01320-366710. A cosy choice serving simple but tasty bistro-style meals.
¶¶ Lock Inn, by the canal. A good place for a drink and serves good pub food.
¶¶ Poachers, Richmond House Hotel, Main St. For a drink and good pub grub.

Spean Bridge p211
There's a chip shop and the **Spean Bridge Mill Coffee Shop**, T01397-712260, around the back of the Spean Bridge Hotel.
¶¶¶-¶¶ Old Station Restaurant, Station Rd, T01397-712535, www.oldstationrestaurant. co.uk. Sep-Jun Thu-Tue, Jul-Aug daily. As long ago as 1894, trains on the West Highland Railway Line puffed up to its door, and now the railway station has been converted it serves delicious evening meals from 1800 in a fascinating interior.
¶¶-¶ Spean Bridge Hotel, T01397-712250, www.speanbridgehotel.co.uk. Aside from its Commando Museum and reasonable food, it's also worth popping into the refurbished **Shinty** bar. Here you can share a real ale or some pub grub with the locals whilst admiring the local shinty team's silverware.

Glen Roy and Loch Laggan p212
¶¶¶-¶¶ Best Western Glenspean Lodge Hotel, 1½ miles east of Roy Bridge, T01397-712223. For those in search of sustenance, this tastefully modernized hunting lodge rustles up a tasty bar lunch (1200-1400) and dinner.
¶¶-¶ Stronlossit Inn, Roy Bridge, T01397-712 253, www.stronlossit.co.uk. Serves reasonable meals and a good range of real ale and malts. Also has rooms (**C**)
F Bunroy Caravan Park, in a secluded spot, Roybridge, T07909-850724. Directly opposite the **Stronlossit Inn**, handy for the train station.

🎪 Festivals and events

Fort Augustus p208
Jun-Sep Highland Gatherings. Late Jun and Jul, mid-Aug and early Sep is the period when Fort Augustus hosts the Highland Gatherings, featuring traditional dancing and piping competitions, tossing the caber and sheep dog trials.

🎯 Activities and tours

There are various monster-spotting tours of Loch Ness which leave from the tourist office in Drumnadrochit or Fort Augustus.

Drumnadrochit p206
Boat trips
Castle Cruises Loch Ness, Temple Pier, T01456-450695, T01456-450205, www.loch nesscruises.com. Offers 60-min cruises (£10) on Loch Ness, leaving from Drumnadrochit aboard the MV Morag.
Jacobite, Tomnahurich Bridge, Glenurqu-hart Rd, Inverness, T01463-233999, www.jacobite. co.uk. Tours depart from the Clansman Hotel, about 5 miles north of Drumnadrochit. Loch

Ness cruises that incorporate Castle Urquhart, the Caledonian Canal and a visit to the Loch Ness Monster 2000 Exhibition. Its Discovery tour includes a 3½-hr cruise on the loch (£26); its Temptation option offers a 30-min cruise and 60-min tour of the castle (£21). Contact the operator for specific pick-up/drop-off points.

Horse riding
Highland Riding Centre, Borlum Farm, Drumnadrochit, T01456-450220, www. borlum.com. Children must be over the age of 4 to ride.

Fort Augustus to Fort William *p209*
Boat trips
Cruise Loch Ness, Knockburnie, Inchnacardoch, Fort Augustus, T01320-366277, www.cruiselochness.com. Sailing out of Fort Augustus by the Caledonian Canal for the past 40 years, this renowned operator has catered for Hollywood and Scottish stars alike and uses onboard 3D underwater imaging to relay 'real time' information about what is lurking in the peaty depths of Loch Ness. Mar-Nov hourly, 1000-1600, Jul-Aug 1000-2000, 1 hr, £11, children £6.50.
Fingal of Caledonia, The Slipway, Corpach, Fort William, T01397-772167, www.fingal-cruising.co.uk. Runs all-inclusive 4- and 6-day cruises in a converted Dutch 'spitz' barge that gently ploughs its way through the 60-mile waterway of the Great Glen. In addition to sailing the length of the loch, and wildlife tours of Loch Linnhe, its Great Glen Way tour allows guests to walk up to 14-mile sections of the route each day before meeting the barge each evening at prearranged points. On board, guests can make use of mountain bikes, canoes, sailing dinghies and wind-surfers lashed to the deck. Guides and instructors are included. Cruises operate Apr-Oct and cost from £350-725 per person.
George Edwards, contact Castle Cruises Loch Ness, T01456-450395, www.lochness-cruises.com, or 'Original' Loch Ness Monster

Visitor Centre, see page 206. George takes would-be monster-spotters out on the loch in his boat, Nessie Hunter, which is based near Drumnadrochit. He not only once caught a glimpse of Nessie but also discovered the deepest part of the loch (812 ft), now known as Edward's Deep. Cruises run hourly Apr-Oct 1000-1800. Trips last 1 hr, £10, children £6.

Climbing
Nevis Guides, Bohuntin, Roy Bridge, T01397-712356.

Mountain biking
Laggan Wolftrax Mountain Bike Centre, 20 miles west of Roy Bridge, T01528-544786, www.laggan.com. Has miles of purpose-built trail in Strathmashie Forest, bike hire from £18 plus and an excellent café.

Fishing
Loch Arkaig in particular is renowned for its trout fishing.
Fishing Scotland, Roy Bridge, T/F01397-712812, T07737-627907, www.fishing scotland.co.uk. Jimmy Coutts runs professional fly-fishing courses for the expert and novice alike, giving them the opportunity to learn to fly fish or fish for wild salmon and trout on select lochs and rivers.

Horse riding
Old Pier House , Fort Augustus, T01320-366418. Offers guests 2-hr horse riding for around £50 and the chance to hire canoes. Non-guests can ride if they phone and request in advance.

Tour operators
Evergreen B&B and Car Tours, see Sleeping, above. Fiona and Graeme Ambrose run fabulous car tours to some of the Highlands' most beautiful locations. Even if you're not staying at their guesthouse, you can arrange to be picked up in Fort Augustus. Depending on the season and conditions, trips explore around Loch Ness,

as far south as Fort William and Glencoe and even northwest to romantic Plockton and Loch Carron. From £45 for a ½-day tour of southern Loch Ness to £160 for a full blown odyssey to the far northwest of Scotland complete with your own chauffeur and guide. (FOR GUESTS ONLY)

Highland Activities, Keepers Cottage, Inverlair, Tulloch near Roy Bridge, T0845-094 5513, T07850-323267, www.highland activities.co.uk. Offer the chance (from £45) to go canyoning, quad biking, mountain biking, fun yakking and rafting.

Watersports

Monster Activities at Great Glen Water Park, east shore of Loch Oich, near South Laggan, T07710-540398. An outdoor activities centre, with hostel accommodation nearby, offering adventure sports including whitewater rafting, canoeing, mountain biking, rock climbing, sailing, windsurfing, hillwalking and water skiing. Self-catering lodges for rent too.

⊖ Transport

Drumnadrochit p206
Bus Citylink buses between **Inverness** and **Fort William** stop here several times daily in either direction. There are also buses (No 17 and No 306) from Inverness to **Cannich** and **Tomich**, via **Drumnadrochit**.

Fort Augustus p208
Bus Several buses daily (No 919) to **Fort William** or **Inverness**, 1-hr. The same service stops at **Invergarry** daily.

Cycle hire Monster Activities, 25 miles north of Fort William at the southern edge of Loch Oich, T01809-501340. You can hire bikes (and boats).

Invergarry and around p209
Bus Invergarry is on the **Fort William** to **Inverness** bus route, which stops in **Fort Augustus**. It is also on the main **Fort William** to **Kyle of Lochalsh** (and Skye) Citylink route (Nos 915, 916) and a couple of buses pass through daily in both directions. For times T08705-505050.

Unfortunately, there's no longer a postbus service that runs from **Invergarry** to **Kinloch Hourn**. Your best option is to catch the Scottish Citylink (No 915, No 91 and No 917), which runs 4 times daily and request to be dropped off at the turn-off for the long walk into the glen.

Spean Bridge p211
Bus There are regular buses to **Fort William** and **Inverness**. Spean Bridge is also on the **Fort William** to **Glasgow** railway line.

Loch Arkaig and around p211
Bus At least 1 bus per day (Mon-Sat) travels the route to **Fort William** via **Banavie** and **Gairlochy**, T01397-702373, for details.

Glen Roy and Loch Laggan p212
Bus There is a No 40 bus to **Fort William** from **Roy Bridge**, 3 times daily Mon-Fri, 1 on Sat. **Roy Bridge** is also on the **Fort William** to **Glasgow** railway line.

Fort William and around

Fort William, the self-proclaimed 'Outdoor Capital of the UK', is also the gateway to the Western Highlands and one of the country's main tourist centres. It stands at the head of Loch Linnhe, with the snow-topped mass of Ben Nevis towering behind. You could be forgiven for assuming that it's quite an attractive place, but you'd be wrong. Despite its magnificent setting, Fort William has all the charm of a motorway service station. After passing a string of B&Bs on the southern outskirts the visitor finds a dual carriageway running along the lochside past uninspiring 1960s- to 1970s-era concrete boxes masquerading as hotels. Unsurprisingly, the majority of Fort William's attractions are out of town. The surrounding mountains and glens are amongst the most stunning in the Highlands and attract hikers and climbers in their droves: Ben Nevis – Britain's highest peak at 4406 ft – and also the very beautiful Glen Nevis, which you may recognize from movies such as Braveheart *and* Rob Roy. *There are also snowsports on the slopes of nearby Aonach Mor, one of Scotland's top ski areas. Here, in and above, Leanachan Forest, you'll find world-class cross-country and downhill mountain biking. Since 2002, Fort William has hosted the annual Mountain Bike World Cup.* ▶▶ *For listings, see pages 223-229.*

Ins and outs

Getting there
Fort William is easily reached by bus, from Inverness, Glasgow and Oban, and by train, direct from Glasgow via the wonderful West Highland Railway, see box, page 228. The train and bus stations are at the north end of the High Street, next to the supermarket. If you're driving, parking can be a problem. There's a big car park beside the loch at the south end of town, and another behind the tourist office. You can also walk to Fort William, if you have a week to spare, from just north of Glasgow, along the 95-mile-long West Highland Way, see box, page 228.

Getting around
The town is strung out for several miles along the banks of Loch Linnhe though the centre is compact and easy to get around on foot. Many of the B&Bs and several backpacker hostels and camping options are within Glen Nevis or around Corpach, 1½ miles to the north. Both areas are serviced by frequent buses from the town centre. There are buses every 20-30 minutes to and from Caol and Corpach, and every hour on Sunday and in the evening. Monday to Saturday there is a two-hourly service (No 42) to Glen Nevis Youth Hostel (fewer on Sunday). Buses No 41 and No 42 run daily to Nevis Range during the summer. During the ski season there are at least three daily buses (from 0745) to Nevis Range with the last return journey at 1630. ▶▶ *For further details, see Transport page 227.*

Tourist information
The very busy **TIC** ① *Cameron Sq, just off the High St, T0845 2255121, Apr, May Mon-Fri 0900-1700, Sun 1000-1700, May-Jun Mon-Sat 0900-1800, sun 0930-1700 Jun-Sep Mon-Sat 0900-1860, Sun 09300-18300, Sep- Nov Mon-Sat 0900-1700, Sun 1000-1600,* stocks a good range of books, maps and leaflets covering local walks. Staff will also help arrange transport to more remote Highland parts.

Fort William

Sleeping
6 Caberfeidh **1**
Alexandra **2**
Bank Street Lodge **3**
Calluna **4**
Crolinnhe **5**
Distillery House **6**
Fort William Backpackers **7**
Glenlochy Guesthouse **8**

Grange **9**
Lime Tree **10**
Mrs Johnalda Macleod **11**

Eating
Café Chardon **1**
Crannog Seafood **2**
Grog & Gruel **3**

Fort William

→ *For listings, see pages 223-229. Colour map 3, B6.*
Phone code 01397.

Though it's not a pretty sight, Fort William is the largest town hereabouts and has all the services and facilities you'd expect. There are banks with ATMs on the pedestrianized High Street, as well as a supermarket, a good bike shop and outdoor-equipment outlets.

Sights

There's little of real interest in the town, although the **West Highland Museum** ⓘ *Cameron Sq by the TIC, T01397-702169, Jun and Sep Mon-Sat 1000-1700, Oct-May Mon-Sat 1000-1600, Jul-Aug Mon-Sat 1000-1700, Sun 1400-1700, £3.50, concessions £2.50, children £1, under 12s free*, is a worthwhile exception. It contains excellent exhibits of Jacobite memorabilia, including a 'secret' portrait of Bonnie Prince Charlie which is revealed only when reflected in a cylindrical mirror. There are also fine displays of High- land clans and tartans, wildlife and local history. The fort from which the town gets its name was built in 1690 by order of William III to keep the rebellious Scottish clans in order. The garrison fought off attacks by Jacobites during the rebellions of 1715 and 1745 but was then demolished to make way for the railway line. Remnants of the forts outer walls are all that remain and can be seen by the lochshore.

Ben Nevis Distillery ⓘ *T01397-700200, www.bennevisdistillery.com, Mon-Fri 0900-1700, Easter-Sep Mon-Sat 1000-1600, Jul- Aug Mon-Fri 0900-1800, Sat 1000-1600, Sun 1200-1600, tours £4, children £2*, is at Lochy Bridge, at the junction of the A82 to Inverness and the A830 to Mallaig, about a mile north of the town centre. It's a bit too polished for some though the imaginative audio-visual display that features the mythical giant Hector McDram provides light amusement. There's also a pleasant café and restaurant. Just before the distillery, on the left, are the 13th-century ruins of **Inverlochy Castle**.

Three miles from the town centre along the A830 to Mallaig, in the suburb of Banavie, is **Neptune's Staircase**, a series of eight linked locks on the Caledonian Canal. The locks lower the canal by 90 ft in less than 2 miles between Loch Lochy and Loch Eil and comprise the last section of the canal which links the North Sea with the Irish Sea. It's a pretty dramatic sight, with equally dramatic views of Ben Nevis and its neighbours behind Fort William. In fine weather, **The Moorings Hotel** (see page 223) by the canal is great for watching boats come and go as you enjoy a midday bite. You can also walk or cycle along the canal towpath from here. For details on the new **Great Glen Way** ① www.great glenway.fsnet. co.uk, which links Fort William with Inverness, see box, page 208.

Further along the A830 to Mallaig, in the village of Corpach, is **Treasures of the Earth** ① T01397-772283, Oct-Jun 1000-1700, Jul-Sep daily 0930-1900, £4.99, concessions £3.99, children £3.99, an exhibition of crystals, gemstones and fossils displayed in a huge simulated cave.

Glen Nevis → For listings, see pages 223-229. Colour map 3, B6.

Only 10 minutes' drive from Fort William is one of Scotland's great glens, the classic Glen Nevis. If you can forget the sight of streams of campervans on the road and distant figures threading their way up the steep track towards the summit (dress appropriately) you could almost be mesmerized by the sparkling Water of Nevis as it tumbles through a wooded gorge, closed in by the steep, bracken-covered slopes of the magnificent hulk of Ben Nevis. The whole scene is both rugged and sylvan, and some may say the nearest you'll get to a Himalayan valley in the Scottish Highlands. It's not surprising, then, that this is a favourite with movie directors and has featured in films such as *Rob Roy*, *Braveheart*, *Highlander III* and *Harry Potter and the Philosopher's Stone*.

There are many walks in and around the glen, not least of which is the return trek up to the summit of Britain's highest mountain. Aside from the walks described below, there are several easy, marked forest walks which start from the car park at the **Glen Nevis Visitor Centre** ① open daily, about half a mile up the Glen. Here, you'll also find toilets and an interesting interpretive display. Pick up a leaflet here or at the TIC (£1) for scenic walks around the area or check out www.forestry.gov.uk. There are buses into Glen Nevis, as far as the youth hostel, from Fort William bus station.

Ben Nevis → OS Landranger No 41.

Every year many thousands of people make the relatively straightforward ascent of Ben Nevis, and every year a frighteningly high percentage end up injured, or lost, or dead. Don't let the infamous ascent by a Ford Model T car in 1911 fool you. It's reported an average of four people perish on the mountain every year. Whatever the figure, it's vital that anyone venturing up the Ben is appropriately dressed and equipped for the hike. It should be remembered that the weather in Scotland's mountains can change at an alarming speed. Though it may be 20°C in the Glen Nevis car park when you set off, even far from the summit you may quickly find yourself in a disorientating blizzard or hill fog. It goes without saying that you need to be well prepared. You will need a good, strong pair of boots, warm clothing, waterproofs, food and drink. You should also take a map and a compass. Allow six to eight hours for the return trip. In the winter months the top part of the mountain is covered in snow. You should not attempt the walk unless you are an experienced hill climber.

The main tourist path, built as a pony track to service the long-gone observatory on the summit, starts from the car park at Achintee Farm, on the north side of the river, reached by the road through Claggan. It climbs gradually at first across the flank of Meal an t-Suidhe, before joining the alternative path from the youth hostel. This latter route is shorter but much steeper.

The trail continues to climb steadily as it begins to follow the Red Burn, until it reaches a junction, with Lochan Meal an t-Suidhe down to the left. Here, an alternative route down from the summit heads left under the north face of the mountain (see below). This is the halfway point of the main route. The path crosses the Red Burn and then climbs by a series of long and seemingly never-ending zigzags up to a plateau. If you're tired, consider that the record for the annual 10-mile run from Fort William to the summit and back is one hour 25 minutes! The path splits in two, but both paths take you up to the summit, marked by a cairn and emergency shelter, on the ruins of the old observatory. Note that on the upper sloping plateau the path can 'disappear' in mist and snow, and some cairns and beacons have been removed by vandals masquerading as purists. If conditions deteriorate, a compass is a life-saver. There is a form of shelter on the summit but ensure you're carrying extra clothes.

To return simply retrace your steps all the way. If the weather is settled enough and you have time, you can follow the alternative route below the north face. This leads right round the mountain to the Charles Inglis Clark mountain hut, then heads down into the Allt a' Mhuilinnglen which leads all the way down to the distillery on the A82, a mile north of the

Ben Nevis

To Inverness
A830 to Mallaig
Ben Nevis
A82
Aluminium Factory
Claggan
To Fort William
Allt a' Mhuilinn Glen
P 1 2 P
Visitor Centre
start
4
Lochan Meal an t-Suidhe
2
3
P 1
Red Burn
Charles Inglis Clark Mountain Hut
North Face
Glen Nevis
River Nevis
Observatory Ruins & Shelter
Ben Nevis (4406ft)
To Steall Falls walk

N
1 km
1 mile

Sleeping
Achintee Farm Guesthouse **1**
Ben Nevis Inn **2**

Glen Nevis Caravan & Camping Park **4**
SYHA Youth Hostel **3**

Eating
Café Beag **1**
Glen Nevis **2**

town centre. Note that this route adds an extra 3 or 4 miles to the descent and should only be attempted by fit and experienced hillwalkers.

Steall Falls → OS Landranger No 41.

A fairly easy low-level walk is to the spectacular 300 ft-high Steall Falls at the head of the glen. It's a popular walk, especially in the summer but this doesn't detract from its stunning natural beauty.

The path starts at the end of the twisty road, at the second car park. Before setting off you might like to note the sign by the steep waterfall that cascades down to the edge of the car park. It reads 'Warning! This is not the path to Ben Nevis'. If you need to be warned against attempting to climb up Ben Nevis through a waterfall, you probably shouldn't be left alone in possession of this book, never mind let loose on the Scottish mountains. Once you've shaken your head in disbelief at the apparent mind-numbing stupidity of some of your fellow travellers, follow the track alongside the Water of Nevis. The path climbs steadily through the woods and becomes rocky, with the river thundering below through the steep gorge. It runs close to the river before emerging from the gorge and opening up into a wide, flower-filled meadow, with a high waterfall at the far end. It's a beautiful, tranquil place and ideal for a picnic. Follow the path across the valley floor until it crosses the river via a precarious bridge that consists of three ropes of thick wire in a V-shape. The path then leads to the bottom of the falls. You can also head left at the bridge and continue up the valley to some ruins. From here the path leads to Corrour station, 14 miles away. However, it's for fit, well prepared and experienced hillwalkers only. You can then catch a train back to Fort William. It's a very popular route, and there's even accommodation at the end of it, near the train station.

Steall Falls walk

Nevis Range

ⓘ T01397-705825, www.nevis-range.co.uk. Gondola Sep-Oct, mid-Dec to Jun 1000-1700, Jul-Aug 0930-1800. Gondola prices: £10.50 return, concessions £9, children £6, under 5s free; day ticket £13, children £7.50. There is wheelchair access and guide dogs ride free.

Nevis Range, 3 miles north of Fort William at Torlundy, just off the A82 to Inverness, is situated on the mountain of **Aonach Mhor** (4006 ft) and is Scotland's highest skiing and snowboarding resort. The ski area is reached by Scotland's only gondola lift system and in a good season it permits skiing between Christmas and May. The 1½-mile (15-minute) ride is a popular attraction, not only with wintersport enthusiasts, but also with summer hillwalkers keen to gain easy access to the mountains. A couple of easy walks lead from the gondola station to Sgurr Finnisgaig (40 minutes) and Meal Beag (one hour), both of which offer stunning views from the top. Beside the top gondola station there's a small shop and a large self-serving **Snowgoose restaurant** (♛♛-♛) providing fantastic vistas across Lochaber. Mountain bikers come for some truly world-class riding (see page 227).

◉ Fort William and around listings

For Sleeping and Eating price codes and other relevant information, see Essentials pages 38-45.

◉ Sleeping

Fort William *p219, map p219*

Fort William has an abundance of accommodation, ranging from large luxury hotels to modest guesthouses and B&Bs. You'll find B&Bs and hostels on the road north towards Corpach and Banavie whilst the southern entrance to Fort William on Achintore Rd is truly packed with B&Bs and hotels. Running parallel is Grange Rd, which is also lined with B&B accommodation. Nearer to the town centre, Fassifern Rd and Alma Rd are also a hive of hostel and B&B activity. Wherever you search for a pillow, remember that as a tourist hub Fort William gets extremely busy in the high season and during key events (see Festivals and events, page 226). Ideally, book ahead or through the tourist office for a small fee. The TIC carries copies of the *Fort William and Lochaber Accommodation Guide*.

South of Fort William, on the A82, the villages of Onich and North Ballachulish, make an attractive alternative.

L Inverlochy Castle Hotel, 3 miles north of town on the A82 to Inverness, T01397-702177, www.inverlochy.co.uk. This is your castle in the Highlands. A luxurious stay is

assured; unsurpassed elegance, impeccable service and superb food (see Eating page 225), all set in 500 acres of grounds.

B The Grange, Grange Rd, T01397-705516, www.grangefortwilliam.com. Delightful 4 bedroom escape in a Victorian town house with views over Loch Linnhe.

B The Lime Tree, Achintore Rd, T01397-701806. Offers 9 beautifully appointed bedrooms – hardly surprising as its co-owned by a resident artist and includes an art gallery. In addition, fabulous lunches and dinner are served. It's fantastic and deserves its growing reputation for a quality stay. Recommended.

B The Moorings Hotel, 3 miles out of town in Banavie, on road to Corpach and Mallaig, T01397-772797, www.moorings-fortwilliam.co.uk. Overlooks Neptune's Staircase; well situated and comfortable with a reasonable Jacobean restaurant (♛♛♛-♛♛).

B-C Crolinnhe, Grange Rd, T01397-702709. Mar-Nov. 10 mins' walk from town, this grand Victorian villa is a luxurious B&B. The welcome is friendly and the food delicious but don't dare take those muddy boots into the hall! If you opt for the luxury double your room includes a jacuzzi.

C 6 Caberfeidh, Fassifern Rd, T01397-703756. A friendly B&B that will prepare packed lunches after you've slept in your 4-poster bed.

C Alexandra Hotel, The Parade, T01397-702241. Recently refurbished, this large sandstone hotel provides a reasonable standard of accommodation and food (♔). Very handy for the town centre.

C Distillery House, Nevis bridge, T01397-700103, www.visit-fortwilliam.co.uk/distillery-house. Situated between the Glen Nevis and Achintee turn-offs, this smart, comfortable guesthouse will appeal to those who seek a touch of class close to the town centre. Also offers self-catering in nearby cottages for £200-490 per week.

D Glenlochy Guesthouse, Nevis Bridge, North Rd, T01397-702909. Almost directly opposite Distillery House. This substantial villa with 10 (including family) rooms is another smart choice for those in search of a friendly welcome, good food and relaxation.

D Mrs Johnalda Macleod, 25 Alma Rd, T01397-703735. Open all year. Unpretentious and comfortable.

D Rhiw Goch, Banavie, T01397-772373. Unbeatable views of Ben Nevis (when not shrouded in mist) and overlooking the Caledonian Canal. Owners are welcoming and serve a terrific breakfast in this small B&B about 500 yds north of the **Moorings Hotel**. Also hire kayaks.

E-F Bank Street Lodge, Bank St, T01397-700070, www.bankstreetlodge.co.uk. 42 beds. Open all year. Independent, centrally located backpackers' hostel with family/double rooms and en suite.

F Fort William Backpackers, Alma Rd, 500 yds from the train station, T01397-700711, www.scotlandstophostels.com. Packed with information and young backpackers.

F Snowgoose Mountain Centre & Smiddy Bunkhouse, Station Rd, next to the Corpach train station, 4 miles west of Fort William on A8309 to Mallaig, T01397-772467, www.highland-mountain-guides.co.uk. Alpine-style bunkhouse accommodation for up to 12, plus hostel for 14, fully self-catered.

Self-catering

Calluna, Heathercroft, about a 15-min walk from the TIC, T01397-700451, www.fortwilliamholiday.co.uk. Open all year. 2 modern, semi-detached apartments have been configured to suit groups or families, whilst the ground-floor will suit a wheelchair-bound visitor and carer. Run by experienced mountain guide, Alan Kimber. 6-bed apartment from £300 per week, 8-bed apartment from £400 per week. **The Old School Chalet**, Duisky, 16 miles from Fort William, T01397-722227. Perfect peace and quiet assured in this basic (centrally heated) log cabin by the sea loch of Loch Eil. Forget shops, think nature. Sleeps 6. From £195-275 per week.

Glen Nevis p220, map p221

Glen Nevis is excellent for camping, whilst Achintee at the start of the Ben walk has several excellent guesthouses and accommodation options.

E Achintee Farm Guesthouse, by the start of the path to Ben Nevis, T01397-702240, www.achinteefarm.com. Lovely setting and terrific welcome. Recommended.

F Ben Nevis Inn, above Achintee Farm; across the river and up the steep steps from the visitor centre, T01397-701227, www.ben-nevis-inn.co.uk. An independent hostel where you'll find walkers and climbers enjoying banter, a real ale and hearty food (♔-♔) beside a roaring fire in this 17th-century inn. The hostel's a little cramped, but upstairs you'll find the best atmosphere in Fort William. Worth the walk.

F-E Farr Cottage Lodge and Activity Centre, Corpach, T01397-772315, www.farrcottage.com. This lively set-up can accommodate individuals or groups in bunkhouse or self-catering style. Terrific facilities, including internet and laundry, and hearty breakfast and dinners. Can organize everything from hillwalking and mountain biking trips to sea- fishing, kayaking, go-karting and canyoning.

F SYHA Youth Hostel, 3 miles out of town, near the start of the path up Ben Nevis, Glen Nevis, T0870-0041120, www.syha.org. uk. Though remote, this popular hostel is an excellent choice if you plan to hike on the Ben. Book ahead.

Camping
Glen Nevis Caravan & Camping Park, 2 miles up the Glen Nevis Rd, T01397-702191, www.glennevisholidays.co.uk. Mid-Mar to late Oct. Good facilities. With option to rent cottages.

🍴 Eating

Fort William *p219, map p219*
Finally, Fort William and its environs can boast several real culinary gems ready to reward your taste buds. Be wary though, for there are also those still earning a crust off run-of- the-mill bar lunches and uninspiring dinners. Note that many places stop serving after 2200 – in which case it's a chippy dinner at the likes of **Sammy's** in Caol, Fort William, Mon-Sat 1700-2300. A 10 mile taxi ride from Fort William is the **Lochleven Seafood Café** (🍴🍴), which serves excellent seafood. See page 237 for details.

🍴🍴🍴 **Crannog Seafood Restaurant**, Town Pier, T01397-705589. Great seafood by the pier with views across Loch Linnhe. Based in an old smokehouse it has a great ambience, delicious food and there's a good wine list to help wash down delicious lobster or salmon. Book ahead.

🍴🍴🍴 **The Eagle Inn**, Laggan Locks, northern end of Loch Lochy. The original owner has moved on but this lovingly restored Dutch barge, complete with a clean, cosy galley and fabulous wooden bar is the perfect place to enjoy a light bite or evening meal.

🍴🍴🍴 **Inverlochy Castle Hotel**, see Sleeping, above. Here you'll experience exquisite fine dining – at a price. Will it be the black pudding with white truffles and scrambled eggs? Perhaps the saddle of rabbit or poached loin of venison? The food and wine list is 1st class – and so is the view out the window. Dress to impress. Built in 1863, it's regarded as one of Scotland's and indeed Europe's best country house/castle hotels.

🍴🍴-🍴🍴 **The Lime Tree**, see Sleeping, above. In addition to its beautifully appointed bedrooms, this relative newcomer to Fort Bill's gastro scene promises to serve up a flavoursome, freshly prepared dinner (including slow cooked aromatic lamb) and a hearty lunch. Recommended.

🍴🍴-🍴🍴 **The Moorings Hotel**, 3 miles out of town, Banavie, on road to Corpach and Mallaig, T01397-772797, www.moorings-fortwilliam.co.uk. Good-value bar meals, whilst the more formal Jacobean restaurant serves up reasonable evening treats.

🍴🍴-🍴🍴 **Old Pines**, by the Commando Monument, Spean Bridge, T01397-712324, www.oldpines.co.uk. Enjoys a lovely wooded setting, where guests are pampered and can feast on organic, freshly prepared dinners made using local seafood and game. Book ahead.

🍴🍴 **The Grog & Gruel**, 66 High St, T01397-705078. Open until 2400. There's a good atmosphere in this traditionally styled bar that serves a range of cask ales, a good selection of malt whiskies and bar meals. The younger crowd may prefer the **Ben Nevis Bar** across the road.

🍴 **Café Chardon**, just off High St. The best freshly prepared sandwiches in town.

Glen Nevis *p220, map p221*
🍴🍴-🍴 **The Ben Nevis Inn**, Achintee, T01397-701227, www.ben-nevis-inn.co.uk. Yes, it's a long walk into the glen but many of the lunch and dinner treats, including venison, are filling and freshly prepared. There's often live music and a generally great atmosphere. Best in the area.

🍴🍴-🍴 **Glen Nevis Restaurant**, 200m from the SYHA hostel, T01397-705459. Apr-Oct daily 1200-2200. Serves a standard 2-course lunch and 3-course dinner.

🍴 **Café Beag**, down from the SYHA, T01397-703601. Sep-Jun Tue-Sun 1000-1700, Jul-Aug daily. A cosy place with a fire, home-baking, baked potatoes and organic ice-cream.

⊛ Festivals and events

Fort William p219, map p219

As the self-proclaimed Outdoor Capital of the UK, Fort William annually hosts a number of high profile events.

May/Jun UCI Mountain Bike World Cup, www.ridefortwilliam.co.uk. Since 2002, this has been held annually at Nevis Range, 6 miles north of town. Watched by over 20,000 spectators, the downhill riders descend the 2-mile long course at an electrifying speed.

Jul Lochaber Highland Games. Caber tossing and Highland dancing.

Sep Ben Nevis Race, www.bennevisrace. co.uk. 500 runners undertake the gruelling 10-mile run from Fort William to the summit of Ben Nevis and back. Staged for over 100 years, the record stands at 1 hr 25 mins.

○ Shopping

Fort William p219, map p219

Nevisport, High St, T013967-704921. Has a huge selection of books, maps and guides, a bureau de change and good café-bar.

West Coast Outdoor Sports, High St, T01397-705777. A good outdoor activity equipment shop.

○ Activities and tours

Fort William p219, map p219
Adventure sports

There are several good whitewater rivers around Fort William ranging in difficulty from Grade I-VI, or you can paddle the Caledonian Canal. For advice on operators and lessons, see www.canoescotland.com. There's also an indoor climbing wall at the Lochaber Leisure Centre, Belford Rd, T01397-704359.

Rhiw Goch, Top Locks, Banavie, T01397-772373, www.rhiwgoch.co.uk. Close to

Neptune's Staircase. Hires out sea kayaks for £25 per day.

Snowgoose Mountain Centre, Station Rd, next to the Corpach train station, 4 miles west of Fort William on A8309 to Mallaig, T01397-772467, www.highland-mountain- guides.co.uk. Offers lessons in mountaineering, canoeing, kayaking, skiing and mountain biking. Also hires equipment.

Vertical Descents, Inchree, 8 miles south of Fort William, T01855-821593, www.vertical descents.com. There are many excellent outdoor adventure operators in Scotland – this is one of them. Offers canyoning, whitewater rafting, mountain biking and fun yakking, amongst others.

Boat trips

Crannog Cruises, Town Pier, T01397-700714, www.crannog.net. Run trips of 1½ hrs from Mar-Oct, £10, children £5. Board the *Souter's Lass* in Fort William (daily 1000, 1200, 1400, 1600) for a chance to spot local marine wildlife including seals, otters and seabirds.

Sea Ventures, 3 Kincardine Pl, T07766-138538, www.seaventuresscotland.com. Thrilling fast-boat trips from 60 mins to 1 week in search of dolphins, whales, seals and birdlife or simply to explore the Isles of Staffa and Mull. Cruises start from £15 for the Loch Linnhe experience and they'll be happy to arrange a customized itinerary subject to sea conditions.

Hiking and climbing

Fort William is a mecca for hikers and climbers and boasts one of the highest concentrations of guides and instructors in the land. For information on the climb up Ben Nevis and walks around Glen Nevis, see page 220. Nevis Range offers some of the most accessible winter climbs in the country for experienced climbers. For details of the gondola ride, see page 223. If you want to hire a guide, note that the information board/staff in Nevisport (see Shopping, above) can provide useful advice.

Abacus Mountaineering, www.abacus
mountaineering.com, T01397-772466; Alan
Kimber at West Coast Mountain Guides,
T01397-700451; Alpha Mountaineering,
T07748-275825, www.alphamountaineering.
co.uk; Mountain Motion, T01397-701731;
Snowgoose Mountain Centre, see
Adventure sports, above.

Mountain biking
It's easy to see why Scotland is now
regarded as one of the world's top mountain
biking destinations. The Leanachan Forest,
below Aonach Mhor, 3 miles north of town,
covers a huge area with over 25 miles of
mountain bike trails, ranging from easy
to demanding and including the (world-
class) Witch's Trail. These are free cross-
country routes run by the Forestry
Commission (www.forestry.gov.uk,
or www.ridefortwilliam.co.uk).

Nevis Range is also home to the 2-mile-
long World Cup downhill mountain
bike course. Not for the faint-hearted or
inexperienced. Bikers (over 12s) and bikes
reach the top of this steep descent using
the resort's gondola system (see page 223).
Adult single £12, multi-trip £28, single youth
£8, multi-trip £19. Track open May-Sep daily
1015-1600 (subject to weather).

A more gentle alternative is the new Great
Glen Cycle Route, mainly off-road, running
from Fort William to Inverness. See box,
page 207. If you want to cycle this long-
distance route, Off Beat Bikes in Fort William
(see Cycle hire, below) offer an excellent
one-way bike hire service.

Sea kayaking
Rockhopper Scotland, 2 Montrose
Mansions, Corpach, Fort William, T07739-
837344, www.rockhopperscotland.co.uk.
Whether a beginner or expert, the friendly,
fully qualified guides at Rockhopper are
available for a ½-day (£40), full day (£70) or
even overnight sea kayaking adventure in
Ardnamurchan. Paddle down Loch Sheil,
across the narrows to Ardgour or along
the remote northern coastline off Glenelg
with the chance to spot eagles and basking
sharks. Highly recommended.

Skiing
Nevis Range Ski Centre, see page 223.
Nevis Range hires all the snowboard and
ski equipment required. You can also try
Nevisport, High St, T013967-704921.

Swimming
Lochaber Leisure Centre, Belford Rd,
T01397-704359. Mon-Fri 0930-0900, 1230-
2000 Sat-Sun 1230-1600.

Tour operators
Jacobite SteamTrain, contact West Coast
Railway Company, T01524-737751, T01524-
737753, www.steamtrain.info. Runs from Fort
William to Mallaig, Jun to mid-Oct Mon-Fri,
Jul-Aug daily, departing Fort William at 1020,
arriving in Mallaig at 1225, departing Mallaig
at 1410 and arriving back in Fort William at
1600. Day return £31, children £17.50, 1st-class
return £49, children £25 (see box, page 228).

⊖ Transport

Fort William p219, map p219
Bus For the Fort William area contact
Highland Country Buses, T01463-710555,
www.rapsons.co.uk.

Long-distance services include several
daily Citylink buses to Inverness, 1 hr 50
mins, £7.20; to Oban, 1 hr 30 mins, £10.40,
via Glencoe, 30 mins; and to Uig, 3½ hrs, via
Portree and Kyle of Lochalsh, 1 hr 50 mins,
£19. Citylink buses several times daily to
Glasgow via Glencoe and Tyndrum, 3 hrs,
£17.80; and to Edinburgh, 4 hrs, £25.20, via
Stirling, 3 hrs. There is a bus to Mallaig via
Lochailort (for Ardnamurchan), Mon-Sat,
1 hr 10 mins, £5, Shiel Buses, T01967-
431272. To Kinlochleven, via Glencoe,
daily, 50 mins, Highland Country Buses.
Unfortunately, there's no longer a postbus
service to Glen Etive so you'll need to
walk or cycle in.

Riding the rails

Running from Glasgow to Mallaig via Fort William, the **West Highland Railway** is only 164 miles long but is widely acknowledged as one of the most scenic railway journeys in the world. The great thing about this journey is its variety, taking you from the distinctive red tenements of Glasgow and the former ship-building areas of the River Clyde, to the windy wilderness of Rannoch Moor and the chilly splendour of the hills. It's about an hour after leaving Glasgow that you get your first taste of Highland scenery when the train hugs the eastern bank of sinewy Loch Long. Then it's on past the 'bonnie banks' of Loch Lomond, Britain's largest body of inland water. It's impossible not to pass this serene loch without thinking of the famous ballad about two Jacobite soldiers captured after the '45 rebellion. The soldier taking 'the low road' is due to be executed, his companion taking the 'high road' is due to be released.

After Ardlui, at the top of Loch Lomond, the countryside gets more rugged. Wherever you look you see something of interest: a waterfall, a buzzard surfing on the breeze, perhaps a herd of Highland cattle wallowing in a river.

The **West Highland Way**, the long-distance footpath from Glasgow to Fort William, is close to the line now and at stations such as Crianlarich, Upper Tyndrum and Bridge of Orchy you can often spot footsore walkers with muddy boots – who get on the train looking slightly guilty and collapse on their seats with sighs of relief.

The landscape gets wilder and bleaker as the railway crosses the lonely, peaty wastes of Rannoch Moor and on to Corrour, which featured in the film version of Irvine Welsh's cult book *Trainspotting*. Then you descend to the lusher country around Tulloch, before pulling in to Fort William. This is a popular visitor centre as it's close to Ben Nevis, Britain's highest mountain, and beautiful Glen Nevis, which has featured in films such as Braveheart and Rob Roy. Now comes the most spectacular part of the journey. Leaving Fort William, the train crosses Thomas Telford's Caledonian Canal – where you can see an impressive series of eight locks known as 'Neptune's Staircase' – hugs the shore of Loch Eil, then crosses the magnificent Glenfinnan Viaduct, a masterpiece in concrete. You soon get superb views of the evocative Glenfinnan Monument that commem- orates the start of the 1745 rebellion, before pulling in to Glenfinnan Station. The train now takes you through a landscape of craggy hills and glacial lochs etched with birch and pine trees. You pass Loch nan Uamh, from where Bonnie Prince Charlie fled for France after his defeat at Culloden, then draw in to Arisaig, the birthplace of the man who inspired RL Stevenson's Long John Silver. Next is beautiful Loch Morar, Britain's deepest inland loch and home – so legend has it – to a mysterious monster. Soon you get great views across the water to the craggy islands of Eigg and Rùm, before finally pulling in to the port of Mallaig.

Car hire Hawco Volkswagen Rental, Caol Industrial Estate T01397-700900. **Practical Car & Van Hire**, Slipway Autos, Corpach, T01397-772404, www.practical.co.uk. Prices from around £35 per day.
Cycle hire Off Beat Bikes, 117 High St, T01397-704008, www.offbeatbikes.co.uk.

Offer an excellent one-way bike hire service (including panniers and spares) from £40 per day, including the option to start your ride in Inverness. Also offer bikes sales, repairs and advice. Bikes from £17 per day to £110 for a full-on downhill bike to tackle the World Cup course at Nevis Range. Kids and tandem bikes, helmets and armour also available.

Rhiw Goch, Top Locks, Banavie, T01397-772373, www.rhiwgoch.co.uk. Close to Neptune's Staircase, hires out bikes (£12).

Ferry There is a passenger-only ferry service to **Camusnagaul**, on the opposite bank of Loch Linnhe, from the Town Pier. It sails Mon-Sat 0745-1740 and takes 10 mins, £1.50, children 75p. The **Corran Ferry**, T01855-841 243, to **Ardgour** (see page 239) is 8 miles south of Fort William, just off the A82. Throughout the year the ferry makes the 5-min crossing every 20-30 mins from 0710 and every hr thereafter until 2100 (Fri-Sat until 2130). Single £6.40, pedal bikes free. Slight timetable variation in winter. For further details contact Corran Ferry, ask the TIC or look at www.lochabertransport.org.uk.

Taxi Al's Tour and Taxi Service, T01397-700700.

Train There are 2-3 trains daily to **Glasgow**, 3 hrs 45 mins, via **Crianlarich**. To **Mallaig**, 1 hr 20 mins, to connect with ferries to **Armadale** on Skye (see page 319). To **Oban**, daily, occasionally changing at Crianlarich. There is a sleeper service to **London Euston** (see page 30), but you'll miss the views.

● Directory

Fort William *p219, map p219*
Banks Plenty of ATMs on the High St. Note that if you planning to travel into remoter areas such as Ardnamurchan or Knoydart, banks are few and far between.
Internet Library, High St.

Glen Coe

→ Colour map 3, B6. Phone code 01855.

There are many spectacular places in the Scottish Highlands, but few, if any, can compare to the truly awesome scenery of Glen Coe. No-one could fail to be moved by its haunting beauty, with imposing mountains, their tops often wreathed in cloud, rising steeply on either side from the valley floor. The brooding atmosphere of the landscape is only enhanced by the glen's tragic history. Once you've heard of the Glen Coe Massacre it sends a shiver down the spine every time you pass this way. Scotland's most famous glen is also one of its most accessible, with the A82 Glasgow to Fort William road running through it. Much of the area is owned by the National Trust for Scotland and is virtually uninhabited, leaving huge tracts of glen and mountain which provide outstanding climbing and walking. There's also skiing at the Glencoe Mountain Resort and canoeing on the rivers Coe and Etive. ►► For listings, see pages 235-238.

Onich, North Ballachulish and Kinlochleven

The A82 south from Fort William passes through tiny Onich and the car ferry for Ardnamurchan at Corran before the B863 turns east at North Ballachulish and heads past the excellent **Lochleven Seafood Café** (see Eating, page 237) to Kinlochleven, at the head of Loch Leven. It can also be reached on the same road from Glencoe village, 7 miles west. Until the late 1990s a huge, unsightly aluminium factory dominated and was the lifeblood of the community. Fortunately, the entrepreneurial ingenuity of a Lochaber climber has since transformed the defunct factory into **Ice Factor**, the world's largest indoor ice-climbing facility (see Activities and tours, page 237) and there's even the **Atlas micro-brewery** next door. Industrialists can find out all about the history of aluminium-working in Kinlochleven at **The Aluminium Story** ① *Linnhe Rd, T01855-831663, Apr-Sep Mon-Fri 1000-1300, 1400-1700, free.*

The West Highland Way passes through the village and many walkers spend the night here before setting out on the last stretch before Fort William. There are also good walks in the surrounding hills and glens of the Mamores, a few of which are described below.

Walks near North Ballachulish

Five miles north of the village of North Ballachulish and having turned off the road for Inchree and **Vertical Descents** (see Activities and tours, page 238) a moderate one-hour circular walk up to Inchree Waterfall begins at the car park just 100 yds past the Vertical Descents bothy. A clearly marked trail, the huge waterfall is very dramatic to the eye, particularly when it's in spate. So too are the views back towards Loch Linnhe. The path continues up past the waterfall to the forest road which leads back downhill to the car park.

Walks around Kinlochleven → OS Landranger No 41.

There are some relatively easy short walks from Kinlochleven up the glen of the River Leven, including the one to the impressive **Grey Mare's Tail waterfall**. It's a short walk of under an hour, signposted from the village.

Dressed for the outdoors, a rewarding half-day walk is to follow the West Highland Way south from the village to the top of the **Devil's Staircase** (named by the 400 soldiers who had to endure severe hardship while building it in the 17th century), where it meets the A82 at the eastern end of Glen Coe. The well-signposted route begins at the wooden bridge north of Ice Factor and climbs gradually on a dirt jeep-track up to Penstock House,

A stab in the back

Glen Coe is probably best known as the scene of one of the most shameful and notorious incidents in Scottish history.

Following his succession to the throne, William III wanted all the clans to swear an oath of allegiance by 1 January 1692. After much hesitation, the Jacobite clans of the West Highlands agreed to do so. However, Maclain of Glencoe, chief of a small branch of the MacDonalds, was not only late in setting off on the journey, but mistakenly went to Fort William to sign, instead of Inveraray. By the time he reached Inveraray it was 6 January and the deadline had passed.

The government decided that the rebellious clan be punished, in order to set an example to other clans, some of whom had not taken the oath. A company of 120 soldiers, under the command of Campbell of Glenlyon, were sent to Glen Coe and, since their leader was related by marriage to Maclain, the troops were billeted in MacDonald homes, in keeping with the long-standing Highland tradition of hospitality.

There they stayed for almost two weeks, until the cold-blooded order came through to "... put all to the sword under seventy". And so, on a cold winter's night, in the early hours of 13 February 1692, the Campbells ruthlessly slaughtered their hosts. Maclain and 37 men, women and children were slain in their beds, while many others fled into the hills, only to die of hunger and exposure. It was a bloody incident which had deep repercussions and proved to be the beginning of the end of the Highland way of life. For further information, see box, page 444.

There's a monument to the fallen MacDonalds in the village of Glencoe, where members of the clan still gather on 13 February each year. For a powerful and evocative account of the Massacre, read *Glencoe* by John Prebble (Penguin, first published 1966).

at 1000 ft. At the top, near the house, the track forks to the right and continues on a rough but well maintained footpath to the Devil's Staircase. The path is marked with the West Highland Way thistle sign, so it's easy to follow uphill to the top of the pass (1804 ft), from where you get great views of Loch Eilde Mór and the Mamores to the north. The path then descends down the staircase to Glen Coe, with breathtaking Buachaille Etive Mór in front of you all the way. You'll have to return to Kinlochleven by the same route, or you could carry on to the **Kingshouse Hotel** (see Sleeping, page 236). The return trip from Kinlochleven should take four or five hours, or you can start out from Glencoe (see below). Before leaving, ensure you are properly equipped. This section of the West Highland Way was once part of the old military road which ran from Fort William to Stirling.

Another good hike, though more strenuous, is to **Beinn na Callich** (2507 ft). You'll need to be fairly fit as it's a steep climb; allow around six to seven hours for the return trip. The route is well marked and starts from the West Highland Way footpath opposite the school, which is on the road heading northwest out of the village towards Fort William. The path climbs steeply at first, crosses the tarmac road to **Mamore Lodge**, then continues until it joins General Wade's old military road, which takes the West Highland Way on its final 11 miles to Fort William. From here, you'll see the path zigzagging up the mountain. Continue along the old military road for about 400 yds until you cross a wooden bridge. Then follow a path down to another wooden bridge, where the ground is quite boggy. Cross the bridge and the path begins to zigzag uphill until it levels out on to a plateau, before continuing relentlessly upwards through a long series of zigzags to the summit, marked by a couple of cairns and a commemorative plaque. The views from the top make the tiring climb worthwhile. You can see down on to Loch Leven, over to Glen Coe and across the magnificent Mamores.

Fit and experienced hillwalkers can access the **Mamores** from the **Mamore Lodge** road. Once you're up there you have the opportunity to bag several Munros, via a series of excellent ridge walks connecting **Am Bodach** (3386 ft) with **Stob Coire a' Chairn** (3219 ft), **Na Gruagaichean** (3461 ft), **An Gearanach** (3222 ft), **Sgor An Iubhair** (3285 ft), **Sgurr a'Mhaim** (3606 ft) and **Stob Ban** (3278 ft). These peaks and ridges can also be reached from Glen Nevis, see page 220. As well as the proper equipment, take a map and a compass.

Ballachulish
On the southern shore of Loch Leven, a mile or so west of Glencoe village on the A82, is the old slate quarrying village of Ballachulish. Aside from interpretive panels at the TIC, there's 550 yds of wheelchair accessible path to view the quarry and its history where for 300 years Gaelic speaking locals toiled to excavate the slate. There are a few B&Bs and a

Glen Coe & Loch Leven

Sleeping [bed]	Clachaig Inn **3**	Isles of Glencoe **4**
Ballachulish **1**	Glencoe Independent	Kingshouse **5**
Ballachulish House **2**	Hostel **8**	Red Squirrel Campsite **7**

couple of hotels close by. In the car park just off the main road is the **TIC** ① *T01855-811866, Mar-May Mon-Sat 0900-1700, Sun 1000-1700, May-Oct Mon-sun 0900-1800,* with a good coffee shop. Here, you can also find out all about the quarries.

Glencoe village

At the western entrance to the glen, on the shores of Loch Leven, is Glencoe village, 16 miles south of Fort William just off the A82. There are several places to stay in and around the village, as well as a post office and in stark contrast to the Spar general store next door there's also the thatched **Glencoe Folk Museum** ① *late May-Sep daily 1000-1730, £2.50,* which has collections of 17th- to 18th-century costumes, military memorabilia and, according to the owner, a chair that once belonged to none other than the Young Pretender. The most significant development in recent years has been the revamped and impressive **National Trust for Scotland Visitor Centre** ① *1 mile south of Glencoe village, T0844-493 2222, Jan-Mar Thu-Sun 1000-1600, Apr-Oct daily 0930-1730, Nov-Dec Tue-Sat 1000-1600, £6, concessions £5.* There are interesting interpretive displays, information about the area's history (including the massacre), geology, fauna and flora. During the summer, the ranger service organizes guided walks and Landrover safaris. This eco-friendly building also boasts a lovely café.

Climbing and hiking in Glen Coe → OS

Landranger No 41. www.glencoemountain.com.
Glen Coe offers some of Britain's most challenging climbing and hiking, with some notoriously treacherous routes and unpredictable weather conditions that claim lives every year. The routes described below are some of the least strenuous, but you'll still need a map, good boots, warm clothing, food and water, and you should take the usual precautions, including checking on the weather forecast, see page 26.

One of the most popular walks is the relatively straightforward hike up to the **Lost Valley**, a secret glen where the ill-fated MacDonalds hid the cattle they'd stolen. Allow around four hours for the return trip. Start from the car park by the large boulder (see map), opposite the distinctive **Three Sisters**. Head down to the valley floor and follow the gravel path which leads down to a wooden bridge across the River Coe. Cross the bridge and follow the path up and over the stile. From here there's a choice of two routes. The less obvious route heads right and offers an easier climb into the valley. This eventually meets the lower, well-worn track, which involves a bit of scrambling but

Scorrybreac Guesthouse **10**
Signal Rock Cottage **9**
SYHA Youth Hostel **6**

Eating 🍴
Lochleven Seafood Cafe **1**

is more exciting as it follows the rushing waters of the **Allt Coire Gabhail**. The upper and lower paths meet a few miles further up and here you cross the river by some stepping stones. Proceed up the steep scree slope until you reach the rim of the **Lost Valley**, where many of the MacDonalds fled on the night of the infamous massacre. Once in the valley there are great views of Glencoe's highest peak, Bidean nam Bian ('pinnacle of the mountains') at 3776 ft, Gearr Aonach and Beinn Fhada and you can continue for a further 50 minutes to the head of the valley. From here it's possible to climb Bidean, but you'll need to be fit, experienced and well equipped.

Glen Coe also offers one of Scotland's classic ridge walks, the **Aonach Eagach**. With potentially fatal drops it's not for the inexperienced or faint-hearted as there are some very exposed pinnacles you must climb around. The exposed ridge runs almost the entire length of the glen, starting at **Am Bodach** and ending at **Sgor nam Fiannaidh**. Don't make the mistake of descending from the last summit straight down to the **Clachaig Inn**. Instead, take the safer marked route.

Another difficult route is to the summit of **Buachaille Etive Mór**, one of the most photographed mountains in Scotland and one you'll probably recognize immediately the first time you see it from the A82, especially on the road north up to Glencoe. The mountain is best viewed from the **Kingshouse Hotel** and the route starts from Altnafeadh, a couple of miles west of the hotel. This is also the start or finish point for the fairly easy half-day walk over the **Devil's Staircase**, which is part of the West Highland Way. For a description of the route, see page 230. **Glen Etive** runs southwest from the hotel. It's a very beautiful and little-visited place, and great for wild camping. Unfortunately, there's now no postbus so you'll need to walk in or cycle.

Finally, there are some short, pleasant walks around **Glencoe Lochan**, an artificial loch created in the mid-19th century by Lord Strathcona for his homesick Canadian wife. Take the left turning off the minor road to the youth hostel just beyond the bridge over the River Coe. There's a choice of three walks of between 40 minutes and an hour, all detailed at the car park (or see www.forestry.gov.uk).

Glencoe Mountain Resort
① *T01855-851226, www.glencoemountain.com. Chairlift Dec-Oct daily 0930-1700, £10, during the winter ski season an adult day pass is £25, children £20.*
The **Glencoe Ski Centre** is just over a mile from the **Kingshouse Hotel**, on the other side of the A82, on **Meall A'Bhuiridh** (3636 ft). Established in 1956, it is Scotland's oldest ski centre and remains one of the best. The aptly titled Flypaper is the steepest 'black' marked piste in Scotland. In the summer months, for £20 mountain bikers can enjoy all day (lift) access to its downhill course.

For Sleeping and Eating price codes and other relevant information, see Essentials pages 38-45.

Sleeping

Onich, North Ballachulish and Kinlochleven *p230, map p232*

There's a wide selection of places to stay in the villages of Onich and North Ballachulish, mostly with good views of the loch. They make an attractive alternative to Fort William and you may catch sight of gannets, seals, porpoises, and even sea otter in and around Ballachulish Bay and Loch Leven.

L The Lodge on the Loch Hotel, Onich, T01855-821237, www.lodgeontheloch.com. For guests who expect that little bit extra (at a price), with some rooms (including 4-poster beds) giving views over the sea loch. Handy for Glencoe and Fort William. Reasonable dinners from daily 1830-2100.

A-C Allt-nan-Ros Hotel, Onich, T01855-821210, www.allt-nan-ros.co.uk. James and Fiona Macleod's Victorian country house overlooks Loch Linnhe with views across to Appin and the hills of Ardgour and Morvern. There are pretty gardens, great food (👑👑-👑👑👑), and even a 10% discount on the new 'Dragon's Tooth' Ballachulish 9-hole golf course.

B Cuilcheanna House, Onich, T01855-821226. Easter-Oct. A comfortable guesthouse just off the main road with a reputation for a warm welcome and tasty food.

B Onich Hotel, Onich, T01855-821214. Standard hotel rooms, some with loch views and a great panorama over Loch Linnhe from the conservatory. Good range of meals (👑👑), including hot sandwiches (1200-1700) in its busy bar.

C MacDonald Hotel, Fort William Rd, Kinlochleven, T01855-831539. Year-round. A welcoming, 10 bedroom hotel with a Bothy bar and restaurant serving reasonable food (👑👑), open to residents and campers alike. Round the back of the hotel the owners have added several modern but small bunk bed- based cabins (from £22 per person) and space for 11 camp pitches £6 per night. Campers can also enjoy a full Scottish breakfast (£7).

D Camus House, Onich, T01855-821200. Mar-Oct. Lovely guesthouse with sea views.

D The Inn at Ardgour, Ardgour, T01855-841225. This historic watering hole that also serves good value lunches and dinners is just 300 yds across the water from the Corran Ferry.

D Woolly Rock B&B, North Ballachulish, T01855-821338. Open all year. 4 rooms with sea views over Loch Linnhe. Good-value guesthouse.

D-E The Corran Inn, 6 miles south of Fort William, right by the Corran ferry slipway off the A82, T01855-821235. A warm welcome is assured in this small hotel that also serves up great value hearty lunches and dinners (👑-👑). Nip into its wee (former Temperance) bar, complete with tin roof for a dram or real ale. Behind the hotel is the 32-bed **Corran Bunkhouse** (**F**), T01855-821000.

E Tigh-na-Cheo Guest House, Garbhein Rd, Kinlochleven, T01855-831434. Friendly, with a superb outlook over Loch Leven and the Mamores. Very close to **Ice Factor** and the West Highland Way.

F Blackwater Hostel, Lab Rd, Kinlochleven, T01855-831253, www.blackwaterhostel. co.uk. Based in a row of old stone cottages, this is a friendly, well-run backpackers' hostel. 30 camping pitches outside the door (beware of the midges). The **Ice Factor** is only 200 yds away and the West Highland Way is at your feet.

F Inchree Hostel, Inchree, on the A82 to Fort William, T01855-821287, T0800-3101536, www.inchreecentre.co.uk. Buses stop 100 yds from the hostel. Dorms, and twin and double rooms. Good facilities and on-site bistro and bar (👑👑-👑). **Vertical Descent** is just up the road.

Ballachulish *p232, map p232*

As well as one of the most historic hotels in Scotland, there's a wide selection of cheaper B&Bs and guesthouses in the village.

L Ballachulish House, some 200 yds beyond the **Ballachulish Hotel** on the A828 to Oban, T01855-81126. 8 rooms. This is a beautiful hotel, oozing style and an eclectic history, including an alleged role in inspiring RL Stevenson's *Kidnapped* classic and possibly once host to the treacherous officers who slaughtered the MacDonald's in Glencoe. Today, the fine bedroom decor is complemented by personal touches such as the home-made shortbread and Arran Aromatics toiletries. The recipient of a Michelin star, this retreat's style and taste extends seamlessly to the restaurant (♥♥♥).

L-C Ballachulish Hotel, South Ballachulish by the bridge, T01855-831500, www.ballachulishhotel.com. 54 rooms. With a touch of tartan, the rooms are tasteful with some affording stunning loch views. However, it's the **Bulas Bar & Bistro** (♥♥♥-♥♥) that attracts many, try its daily *bulas* (Gaelic pot) creations, including venison and seafood pie using fresh, locally sourced produce.

A-B The Isles of Glencoe Hotel, T01855-811602, www.islesofglencoe.com. 39 rooms. A modern hotel and leisure complex adjacent to **Lochaber Watersports** on the shores of the loch. Lovely sea views from the 'top-deck' bedrooms whilst families will enjoy the excellent facilities, including heated pool, sauna and outdoor adventure play area. The restaurant is open for lunch from 1200 (♥) and dinner (♥♥) from 1830-2130. Non guests can swim and use the sauna after a minimum spend of £7.50 on the premises.

D Fern Villa, T01855-811393. A good-value guesthouse.

Glencoe village *p233, map p232*

There are several B&Bs and guesthouses in the village and quite a few options around.
C Clachaig Inn, about 3 miles south just off the A82 on the old 'B' road that winds back to the village, T01855-811252, www.clachaig.com. Though more highland twee than its rustic beginnings of yesteryear, this remains a popular haunt for walkers. There's good-value accommodation and self-catering in chalets (from £485 per week) but it's the real ales from Kinlochleven's Atlas Brewery, live music and hearty pub grub (♥♥-♥), including wild boar sandwiches, that attracts people.

C Kingshouse Hotel, east end of the glen, almost opposite the turn-off to the **Glencoe Ski Centre**, T01855-851226. From Glencoe village you'll need to walk 15-20 mins to the road entrance of the White Corries (Glencoe) ski area where Citylink buses pull over. This is Scotland's oldest established inn and, judging by the decor it feels like it. However, thanks to the congenial, cosy **Climber's Bar** and the West Highland Way which passes its door, it's little wonder that this historic hotel is popular with the many who camp across the old stone bridge. The sign on 'The Kingy' hotel door is telling: it advises non patrons there's a toilet in the village (10 miles away!).

D Scorrybreac Guesthouse, 1 mile from Glencoe village, T/F01855-811354, www.scorrybreac.co.uk. Dec-Oct. Pleasant guesthouse.

E Signal Rock Cottage, 1½ miles from Glencoe village down the old road, T01855-811295. This newly built, timber clad B&B is set amidst the trees in 50 acres of land. Secluded but worth the walk.

F Glencoe Independent Hostel, near the SYHA Youth Hostel, T01855-811906, www.glencoehostel.co.uk. This is a basic but friendly bunkhouse complete with open fire. It's a 10- to 15-min walk for food or a pint at the **Clachaig Inn**.

F SYHA Youth Hostel, on the same road as Clachaig Inn, about 2 miles from the village, T01855-811219. Excellent hostel very popular with cyclists and climbers. Book ahead.

Camping
Glencoe Camping and Caravanning Club Site, T01855-811397. Mar-Oct. At the westernmost edge of Glencoe village with views down the loch towards Ballachulish.

Footprint Mini Atlas
Scotland Highlands & Islands

Altitude in feet
1800
900
500
200
0

Motorway
Primary Route, A Road
B Road
Other Road
Rail

7 Unst
Yell Fetlar
Mainland
Foula Lerwick
Shetland Islands

Fair Isle

7 Orkney Islands
Mainland
Hoy
Pentland Firth

1 Outer Hebrides
Lewis
Harris
The Minch
North Uist Ullapool
The Little Minch
Benbecula Uig
Skye Portree

Durness Thurso John o'Groats **2**
Wick

North Sea

Moray Firth
Fraserburgh
Inverness Peterhead

South Uist
Kyle of Lochalsh
Barra Rùm
Inner Eigg
Hebrides Mallaig
Coll Fort William
Tiree
Aviemore Aberdeen

Atlantic Ocean

Mull Oban
Colonsay
3
Crianlarich Crieff Perth Dundee
Pitlochry
Stirling
St Andrews **4**
Firth of Forth

Jura Greenock Glasgow
Islay Bute EDINBURGH
Campbeltown Arran Prestwick
Ayr
Jedburgh

NORTHERN IRELAND Stranraer Dumfries
5 **6**
Solway Firth ENGLAND

N

50 km
50 miles

Map 1

Atlantic Ocean

Cape Wrath

Faraid Head

Whiten Head

Tongue Bay

Kyle of Tongue

A

Sandwood Bay

Kyle of Durness
Balnakeil
Durness
Sangobeg
Rispond

Portnacon
Cranstackle (2632ft) ▲
Loch Eriboll
Loch Hope
Eriboll

Tongue

Oldshoremore

Kinlochbervie
Loch Inchard
Achriesgill
Rhiconich

A838

Foinaven (3003ft) ▲

Ben Hope (3042ft) ▲

Ben Loyal (2507ft) ▲

Fanagmore
Tarbet
Loch Laxford
Laxford Bridge
Arkle (2583ft) ▲

Allnabad
Loch Meadie

Loch na...

Handa Island
Scourie

Loch Stack
Loch More

Strathmore

Altnaharra

Ben Klibre (3154ft) ▲

Eddrachillis Bay
Point of Stoer
Drumbeg
Kylestrome
Kylesku
Unapool

A838

Loch Leod
Loch More

Beinn Leoid (2599ft) ▲

Ben Hee (3335ft) ▲

SUTHERLAND

Clashnessie
Stoer
Clachtoll
Quinag (2562ft) ▲
Glas Bheinn (2547ft) ▲

Achmelvich
Loch Assynt
Inchnadamph

Rubha Coigeach

Lochinver
Inverkirkaig
Sullven (2399ft) ▲

Ben More Assynt (3275ft) ▲

Loch Shin

Enard Bay

Canisp (2777ft) ▲
Cul Mor (2786ft) ▲

A837

Inchnadamph National Nature Reserve

Ledmore

Achiltibuie
Loch Sionascaig
Stac Pollaidh (2012ft) ▲
Elphin
Knockan
Inverpolly Nature Reserve

A837

B

Lairg

Summer Isles

Loch Lurgainn

Culnacraig

A835

Ardmair

Meall Liath Choire (1799ft) ▲

Oykel Bridge
Oykel

Invercassley
Linesidemore

Glen Oykel
Cassley

Glen Einig
Einig

Minch

Loch Broom

Ullapool

Leckmelm

Carron

Ardgay

Bon Brid

Greenstone Point
Opinan
Mellon Udrigle
Gruinard Bay
Laide
Coast
Cove
Rubha Reidh
Aultbea

Badcaul

Dundonnell

An Teallach (3485ft) ▲
Loch na Sealga

A832

Inverlael

A835

Beinn Dearg (3558ft) ▲

Carn Chuinneag (2947ft) ▲

EASTER ROSS

Braentra

Boath
Dalr

Melvaig
Midtown
Poolewe
Inverewe Gardens

Fionn Loch

Mullach Coire Mhic Fhearchair (3344ft) ▲

Corrieshalloch Gorge

Sgurr Mor (3643ft) ▲

Big Sand
Loch Gairloch
Gairloch
Port Henderson
Redpoint

Loch Maree

Slioch (3216ft) ▲

WESTER ROSS

Loch Fannich

A832

2

Evanton

C

Culb...

Fearnmore
Lower Diabaig
Talladale

A832
Beinn Alligin (3233ft) ▲
Beinn Eighe Nature Reserve
Beinn Eighe (1010ft) ▲
Kinlochewe

Loch Luichart

Loch Garve

Strathpeffer
Contin

Conon Bridge
Tore

Inner Sound

Inveralligan
Torridon
Liathach (3459ft) ▲

A896

Achnasheen

A890

Sgurr a'Mhuillinn (2885ft) ▲

Orrin Reservoir

Redcastle

Beauly Fir

na

Shieldaig
Loch Damh
Sgorr Ruadh (3151ft) ▲

Craig

Beauly

Dochgarroch
Lochend

Dor

Applecross
Beinn Bhan (2941ft) ▲

A896

Balnacra
Achintee

Sgurr a'Chaorachain (3456ft) ▲

Sgurr a'Choire Ghlais (3554ft) ▲

Glen Strathfarrar
Farrar

Strathglass

Toscaig

Lochcarron
Attadale
Loch Monar

Glen Urquhart

A831

Milton

Drumnadrochit

Crowlin Islands

4
Kyle of Lochalsh
Balmacara

Plockton
Duirinish
Stromeferry

Loch Kishorn
Loch Carron

Aonach Buidhe (2951ft) ▲

3

5
Loch Mullardoch

Glen Cannich
Cannich

6
A831

Dornie
Carn Eighe (...)

Glen Affric
Affric

Map 2

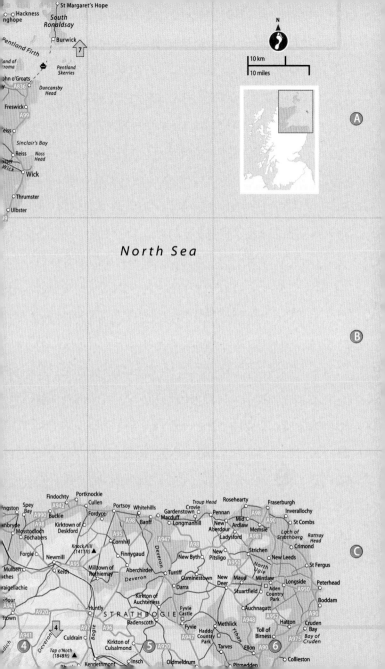

Hackness
nghope
St Margaret's Hope
South
Ronaldsay
Burwick

Pentland Firth
7

land of
roma
hn o'Groats
A836
Duncansby
Head
Pentland
Skerries

Freswick
A99
eiss
Sinclair's Bay
Reiss
Noss
Head
ter
Wick
Wick
Thrumster
Ulbster
9

A

N

10 km
10 miles

North Sea

B

Findochty
Portknockie
ngston
Spey
Bay
A942
Cullen
Buckie
A990
Portsoy
Whitehills
Troup Head
Crovie
Rosehearty
Fraserburgh
anbryde
A98
Fordyce
Kirktown of
Deskford
Mosstodloch
Fochabers
A98
Banff
Gardenstown
Macduff
Longmanhill
Pennan
New
Aberdour
Mid
Ardlaw
Inverallochy
St Combs

Forgie
Newmill
Knock Hill
(1411ft)
Cornhill
Finnygaud
A95
Milltown of
Rothiemay
Aberchirder
Deveron
Turriff
Deveron
A947
New Byth
Cuminestown
New
Pitsligo
Ladysford
A981
A950
Strichen
North
Ugie
Loch of
Strathbeg
Crimond
Rattray
Head
New Leeds
St Fergus

Mulben
athes
Keith
A95
Darra
New
Deer
Maud
Stuartfield
Aden
Country
Park
Longside
Peterhead
A950
raigellachie
flour
A941
Forgie
Huntly
STRATHBOGIE
Bogie
Badenscoth
Fyvie
Castle
Methlick
Haddo
Country
Park
Auchnagatt
A948
Hatton
Cruden
Bay
Bay of
Cruden
Boddam
A90

ttown
A941
4
Culdrain
Tap o'Noth
(1848ft)
A96
Kirkton of
Auchterless
Fyvie
A947
Toll of
Birness
Ellon
A90
A952
A975
Colliestone

A920
Kirkton of
Culsalmond
5
A920
Oldmeldrum
Tarves
6

Kennethmont
Insch
Pitmedden

C

Map 3

Bheag (1602ft)

Bracadale

Stadhlaigearraidh ○ ○ Loch Sgioport

Uibhist a'Deas (South Uist)

Sky

Tobha Mór ○

Portnalong ○ ○ Portnalong
Carbost ○

A863

Rubha Ardvule

Talisker ○

Gearraidh
Bhailteas ○

Loch Eynor

Beinn Bhreac ▲ Mingini (1460ft)

Dalabrog ○

Glen Brittle ○

Lochboisdale
(Loch Baghasdail) ○

Loch Brittle
Cui Sc
Ala (32

Cille Bhrighde ○
Pol a'Charra ○

Loch Baghasdail
Ludag ○

Cuillin Sound

So

A

○ Eiriosgaigh
(Eriskay)

Scurrival Point

Canna

Eo'laigearraidh ○ _Fuday_

Sanday

Sound of Canna

○ Kilmory

Greian Head **Eilean Barraigh**
(Barra)

Rum (Rhum)

Borgh ○

Kinloch ○

Hallival

A888

Sound of Barra

Askival ▲
(2665ft)

Castlebay
(Bagh a'Chaisteil) ○ ○ Earsairidh

Castlebay to
Mallaig
(summer only)

Ainshval ▲
(2553ft)

Bhatarsaigh
(Vatersay) ▲

Rubha nam
Meirleach

Cleac
E

Sanndraigh

An Sg
(129(

Miughalaigh
(Mingulay)

Galmis
or
Muck

Eilean
nan Each

Bearnaraigh

Wiay

Sea of the Hebrides

Sanna
Point

Achosnic
Point of
Ardnamurchan

Eilean Mor

B

○ Sorisdale

Clabhach ○ ○ **Coll**

○ Arinagour
Loch
Eatharna

Caliach
Point

Calgary ○ Derva

Gunna

Calgary Bay

○ Caolas

Kilninian ○

Hough Bay

Tiree

Scarinish ○

Loch Tuath

Barrapoll ○
Balephuil ○

Hynish Bay
Balemartine ○

Gometra

Ulva

Treshnish Isles

Staffa

Little
Colonsay

Atlantic Ocean

N

Iona Abbey ▲ □○ Fionnphort

Loch Scr

10 km

Baile Mor ○ _Iona_

Bunessan ○

10 miles

○ Fidden

Ross of Mu

Soa Island

Sound of Iona

Ardchiavaig ○

C

Rub
Geo

Kiloran Bay
Colonsay

○ Kiloran

Kilchattan ○
Scalasaig ○

Loch
Staosnai

Garvard ○

Dubh
Eilean

Oronsay

1 **2** **3**

Rubh a'
Mhoil

Sgarbh
Bre

Map 4

Map 5

Atlantic Ocean

NORTHERN IRELAND

10 km
10 miles

Garvard
Dubh Eilean
Oronsay
Shian Bay
Loch Righ Mor
Jura
Ardlussa
Tayvallich
Cairnbaan
Lochgilphead
Ardrishaig
Otter Ferry
Clachan of Glendaruel
Craigandaich
Auchenbreck

Rubh' an t-Sailein
Loch Tarbert
Tarbert
Keillmore
Kilmory
Point of Knap
Loch Caolisport
Druimdrishaig

Nave Island
Sgarbh Breac (1195ft)
Rubh a' Mhail
Ben an Oir (2576ft)
Danna Island
Small Isles

Sanalgmore
Port Askaig
Feolin Ferry
Kilfinan
Port Driseach
Tighnabruaich
Kames
Millhouse
Colintra

Loch Gorm
Aoradh
Ballygrant
Kilberry
Tarbert
West Tarbert
Port Bannatyne
Rothesay
Bute

Rinns of Islay
Bridgend
Islay
Rubha na Traille
Ardpatrick Point
West Loch Tarbert
Kennacraig
Ardlamont Point
Meikle Kilmory

Bowmore
Beinn Bheigeir (1611ft)
Claggain Bay
Ardminish
Kilberry
Clachan Claonaig
Skipness
Sound of Bute
Kingart

Glenegedale
Kintour
Gigha
Ballachroy Crossaig
Cock of Arran
Lochranza
Garroch He

Kintra
Port Ellen
Eilean a'Chairn
Sound of Gigha
Tayinloan
Killean
Kintyre
Pirnmill
Casteal Abhail (2819ft)
Corrie
Goat Fell (2868ft)

The Oa
Lower Killeyan
Texa
Cara Island
Carradale
Dippen
Dougarrie
Arran
Brodick
Brodick Castle & Garden

Mull of Oa
Rubha nan Leacan
Glenacardoch Point
Glenbarr
Saddell
Tormore
Ard Bheinn (1680ft)
Lamlash

Bellochantuy Bay
Lussa Loch
Blackwaterfoot

Kilchenzie
Peninver
Ardnacross Bay
Whiting Bay

Machrihanish Bay
Campbeltown
Davaar Island
Lagg
Bennan Head
Pladda

Machrihanish
Conie Glen
Macharioch
Southend
Sanda Island
Ailsa Craig

Ballantrae
Milleur Point
Cairnrya
Kirkcolm
Leswalt
Loch Ryan
Cairnryan to Larne (Northern Ireland)
Stranraer
Stranraer to Belfast
Castle Kenned
Portpatrick
Stoneykirk
Sandhead
Galloway
Port Logan
Mull o Gallow

Map 7

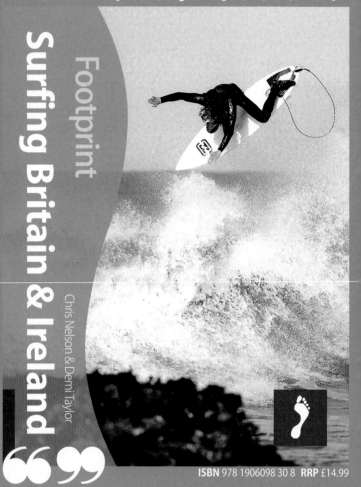

Live. Surf. Travel.

Footprint

Surfing Britain & Ireland

Chris Nelson & Demi Taylor

ISBN 978 1906098 30 8 **RRP** £14.99

In praise of the Footprint surf series

Wavelength *A guide to Britain which every surfer should own*
Surfer Magazine *A one stop guide to surfing across the continent*
Extreme Sports Channel *Hailed as 'the new surfer's bible'*
Carve *An indispensable guide to any Euro jaunt*

Distance chart

Aviemore																	
190	**Campbeltown**																
95	107	**Crianlarich**															
90	142	35	**Crieff**														
132	298	226	222	**Durness**													
126	189	88	65	258	**Edinburgh**												
61	129	51	86	169	132	**Fort William**											
140	138	56	49	272	46	107	**Glasgow**										
31	193	116	121	104	157	65	170	**Inverness**									
148	313	242	237	93	273	185	286	119	**John o'Groats**								
100	171	93	128	179	174	43	149	104	223	**Mallaig**							
105	87	41	76	213	122	44	97	109	228	86	**Oban**						
85	160	52	18	217	43	104	59	116	232	143	93	**Perth**					
142	238	160	195	187	236	109	216	113	212	48	153	192	**Portree**				
138	303	232	227	74	263	175	276	110	20	213	219	220	201	**Thurso**			
157	252	175	210	202	251	124	231	128	227	63	217	168	207	16	**Uig**		
85	240	162	175	67	210	111	224	57	130	112	155	167	119	120	134	**Ullapool**	
131	297	219	221	94	257	168	271	103	16	207	212	216	196	21	209	114	**Wick**

Distances in miles 1 mile = 1.6 kilometres

Map symbols

- □ Capital city
- ○ Other city, town
- ⊂⊃ International border
- ⁓⁓ Regional border
- ⊖ Customs
- ◯ Contours (approx)
- ▲ Mountain, volcano
- ⤵ Mountain pass
- ⊥⊥⊥ Escarpment
- ⟋ Glacier
- ▦ Salt flat
- ⬚ Rocks
- ⩗ Seasonal marshland
- ⬚ Beach, sandbank
- ⑆ Waterfall
- ⌁ Reef
- ═══ Motorway
- ━━ Main road
- ── Minor road
- ═ ═ ═ Track
- ⋯⋯ Footpath
- ── Railway
- ▬⊣ Railway with station
- ✈ Airport
- ⛍ Bus station
- Ⓜ Metro station

- ‑ ‑ ‑ ‑ Cable car
- ++++ Funicular
- ⚓ Ferry
- ▭▭▭ Pedestrianized street
- Σ ⊂ Tunnel
- → One way-street
- ▥ Steps
- ⥿ Bridge
- ▟▟ Fortified wall
- ⬚ Park, garden, stadium
- ● Sleeping
- ● Eating
- ♪ Bars & clubs
- ▬ Building
- † Sight
- † ♁ Cathedral, church
- ⛩ Chinese temple
- ⩎ Hindu temple
- ⚲ Meru
- ☪ Mosque
- ⌂ Stupa
- ✡ Synagogue
- ⓘ Tourist office
- ⏦ Museum
- ✉ Post office
- Ⓟ Police

- Ⓢ Bank
- @ Internet
- ♪ Telephone
- ⚑ Market
- ✚ Medical services
- Ⓟ Parking
- ⛽ Petrol
- ⛳ Golf
- ∴ Archaeological site
- ◆ National park, wildlife reserve
- ⚘ Viewing point
- ⛺ Campsite
- ⌂ Refuge, lodge
- ⛫ Castle, fort
- ⚓ Diving
- ⭝⭝ Deciduous, coniferous, palm trees
- ⌂ Hide
- ⚘ Vineyard, winery
- ⚗ Distillery
- ⚓ Shipwreck
- ⚔ Historic battlefield
- ▣ Detail map
- ◁ Related map

Index

Red Squirrel Campsite, T01855-811256.
Open year-round. If walking south from
Glencoe village on the 'B' road you'll reach
this modest campsite before the hostels
further along the road.

❶ Eating

Onich, North Ballachulish and
Kinlochleven *p230, map p232*
❦❦❦ **Ballachulish House**, some 200 yds
beyond **Ballachulish Hotel**, just off the A828
to Oban, T01855-811266, www.ballachulish
house.com. Mar-Oct. 8 rooms. Steeped in
history, delicious game and seafood are just
some of the tempting dishes. Book ahead.
❦❦ **Inchree Bistro and Bar**, Inchree, T01855-
821393. Open daily. A friendly and informal
place that produces good food and attracts
a fun-loving outdoor crowd.
❦❦ **Lochleven Seafood Café**, 4½ miles along
the B863 from North Ballachulish, Onich,
T01855-821048, www.lochlevenseafood
cafe.co.uk. May-Aug 1200-1430, 1800-
2100 and snack menu 1430-1600. Superb,
mouth- watering and excellent. The seafood
at this simple but stylish restaurant is
unrivalled. Feast on caught oysters, scallops,
langoustines and a gargantuan seafood
platter. There are non fishy treats too but
as the latest catch in the tanks highlights,
affordable tasty seafood is the star attraction.
Book ahead. Recommended.
❦❦-❦ **Bothan Bar and Bistro**, Ice Factor,
Kinlochleven, T01855-831100. Daily 1100-
late. A hip post-climb gathering place with a
delicious restaurant menu, including venison
and Loch Leven shellfish, tasty bar snacks,
and refreshing real ales from Kinlochleven's
own Atlas microbrewery on tap; Blizzard,
Sisters and Latitude. There is a wonderful
wood-burning stove, the chance to watch
fellow climbers on the walls and enjoy the
view of Loch Leven and the Mamores.
❦ **Fishnet fish and chip shop**, Kinlochleven,
opposite the **Tail Race Inn**. Open all year.
Proudly proclaims to be the West Highland
Way's only chip-shop. Great portions.

Glencoe village *p233, map p232*
For Eating options, refer to Sleeping, above.

❶ Bars and clubs

Onich, North Ballachulish and
Kinlochleven *p233, map p232*
Bothan Bar, Ice Factor, Kinlochleven
and the **Tail Race Inn** (the local worthies'
haunt) both serve beer from the local
Atlas microbrewery. It's also worth
popping into the cosy bar in the
MacDonald Hotel along the road.

❶ Shopping

Glen Coe village *p233*
Crafts
Crafts and Things, in a delightful old whitewashed croft at the northern end of Glencoe
village. Has expanded to offer both an array
of woollens, crafts and excellent home-
baking and light bites (❦) in its homely café.

❶ Activities and tours

Onich, North Ballachulish and
Kinlochleven *p230, map p232*
Brewery Tours
Atlas Brewery, Kinlochleven, T01667
404555, www.atlasbrewery.com. Easter-
Sep. Free tour of the microbrewery at 1730.
Formerly the carbon bunker for the massive
aluminium smelter, Atlas microbrewery
produced its first beers in Feb 2002 and
now sells its finest tipples far and wide.

Climbing
For advice, contact the Mountaineering Council
of Scotland (MCofS) on T01738-493942,
www.mountaineering-scotland.org.uk.
Ice Factor, Kinlochleven, T01855-831100,
www.ice-factor.co.uk. Tue-Thu 0900-2200,
Fri-Mon 0900-1900. Housed in a former
aluminium smelter, the world's largest indoor
ice-climbing facility is truly spectacular.
A giant refrigerated toy-box for anyone in
search of vertical fun, over 500 tons of snow

are packed onto the 15-m-high vertical walls. Novice (under instruction) or expert, the ice wall simulates as closely as possible outdoor conditions. There are also 15-m-high rock-climbing walls, a bouldering area, a well-stocked equipment shop and even a sauna and steam room, before you reflect on your day in the **Bothan Bar and Bistro** upstairs (see Eating, above). Annual membership £10, £5 for14-17 year olds. Daily rates vary according to the activity, with beginners only permitted to climb under instruction or expert supervision. Call for rates and times. A competent climber can enjoy all-day rock climbing for £9; or 2 hrs ice-climbing for £20, children £17.50. It's £5 for the sauna and steam room, £3.50 if also climbing.

Climbing Guides
Ice Factor's professional climbing staff also run outdoor mountaineering and climbing courses.

Alan Kimber, West Coast Mountain Guides, Calluna, Heathercroft, T01397-700451, www.westcoast-mountainguides.co.uk. Recommended professional climbing guide.
Mike Pescod, Abacus, 6 Hillview Dr, Corpach, www.abacusmountainguides.com. Recommended professional climbing guide.

Mountain biking
Vertical Descents, see Watersports, below. Mountain bikes, £15 for ½-day, £20 for full-day.

Golf
Ballachulish House, T01855-811695. This challenging and scenic 9-hole golf course (from £15 per round) is open to the general public.

Glencoe Mountain Resort *p234*
Snowsports
Glencoe Ski Centre is the oldest resort in Scotland and has pistes suitable for beginners and experts. The Flypaper is reportedly the steepest black-marked run in Scotland and is definitely for experts only. It affords stunning views southwards over Glencoe. There is also a small café (winter only) above the first chairlift.

Watersports and other activities
Lochaber Watersports, next door to the Isles of Glencoe Hotel, North Ferry View, Old Ferry Rd, Onich T01855-811931, T07760-793894, www.lochaberwatersports.co.uk. Double open kayak, £30 for 3 hrs; 2-person dinghy, £35 for 3 hrs; and fast (RIB) powerboat two day course £230 per person.
Vertical Descents, Inchree Falls, Onich, T01855-821593, www.verticaldescents.com. Yes, it can rain in Scotland but who cares if you've a wetsuit on and are having fun experiencing the thrills and spills of fun-yakking (£50, a mix of rafting and kayaking) or the adrenaline-pumping activity of canyoning (from £50). After a day climbing (or jumping off) waterfalls or blasting through the water in a kayak you're certain to come back refreshed.

⊖ Transport

Onich, North Ballachulish and Kinlochleven *p230, map p232*
Bus Highland Country Buses, T01397-702373, run Mon-Sat 6 times a day, Sun 3 times, between **Kinlochleven** and **Fort William**, 50 mins. En route these (No 44) buses stop at **Onich** and **Corran Ferry**. They also stop at **Glencoe Junction** (the southern edge of the village). You can also catch the **Scottish Citylink** service to **Glasgow**, which leaves Fort William 4 times a day and stops at **Glencoe village**.

Glencoe village *p233, map p232*
Bus There are daily Citylink buses to **Glasgow** and **Fort William**, 2½ hrs.

West of Fort William

West of Fort William lie some of the Britain's most extravagantly scenic landscapes and some of its most remote places. From southernmost Morvern, through the ruggedly handsome Ardnamurchan Peninsula, across the evocatively named 'Road to the Isles', through the haunting and tragic 'Rough Bounds' and on to the hopelessly isolated and utterly wild lands of Knoydart, this is serious wilderness, with little pockets of accessible and user-friendly Highlands thrown in for good measure.➤➤ *For listings, see pages 245-249.*

Ardgour, Ardnamurchan and Morvern → *For listings, see pages 245-249. Colour map 3, B4-5.*

This lonely, southwestern corner features a dramatic landscape of rugged mountains, ancient forest, wild moorland and near-deserted glens, fringed by a coastline of sparkling white beaches and clear turquoise seas with wonderful views across to the isles of Mull, the Small Isles and Skye. This is one of the least-populated areas in Britain, mainly due to the legacy of the Highland Clearances in the mid-19th century, when whole communities were evicted by landlords in favour of more profitable sheep. Today, the issue is more finding people willing to stay year-round instead of leaving villages like Kilchoan with all too many homes run only as seasonal self-catering or second home hideaways. With so few people around, the whole peninsula is a haven for wildlife with a huge variety of birds and animals, such as deer, pine martens, wildcats and eagles. If you have both the time and the energy, it's worth exploring by car, foot or even kayak (see Activities and tours, page 248) and there's a myriad of (Forestry Commission Scotland) footpaths to explore. However, distances can be deceptive and if driving, ensure you've enough fuel.

Ins and outs

Getting around Once you leave the A830 Fort William to Mallaig road, buses are few and far between, so it's not easy to get around quickly without your own transport. You'll need your own transport to reach Ardnamurchan Point and Sanna Bay as there are no buses beyond Kilchoan. If driving, note most of the roads are single-track. If you're travelling by car, access is via the A861, leaving the A830 before Glenfinnan or at Lochailort. You can also make the five-minute ferry crossing to Ardgour from the Corran Ferry, about 8 miles south of Fort William on the A82, see page 239. From Corran, the ferry sailings are frequent and leave daily from around 0700-1800. The journey costs £6.40 for a car and driver, pedestrians and cyclists travel free.➤➤ *For further details, see Transport page 248.*

Tourist information The website www.ardnamurchan.com, has lots of information on walks, as well as local events and attractions. Some 40 walks in the area are listed in a local guidebook, *Great Walks* (£4), available at tourist offices. OS Explorer Maps 383, 390 and 391 cover the entire region. See also Activities and tours, page 248.

Ardgour → *Colour map 3, B5. Phone code 01967.*

The name Ardgour means 'height of the goats', and you can still see feral goats in this huge, sparsely populated wilderness bordered by Loch Shiel, Loch Eil, Loch Linnhe and Loch Sunart. Access is via the A861 south from Kinlocheil, or on the Corran Ferry to the tiny lochside villages of **Corran** and **Clovulin**.

The attractive little village of **Strontian** on the shores of Loch Sunart gave its name to the element strontium, which was first discovered in the nearby lead mines in 1790. These now-abandoned mines also produced most of the lead shot used in the Napoleonic wars. Strontian is the largest settlement in these parts and has a small grocery shop, post office, petrol pumps and a **TIC** ① *T01967-402131, Mar-Jun Mon-Sat 1000-1600, Jun-Aug Mon-Sat 1000-1700, Sun 1000-1600, Sep-Oct Mon-Sat 1000-1600*. One mile north of the village is the **Ariundle Nature Reserve**, which offers a pleasant two-hour nature trail through the glen and a 40-minute forest walk. It's all well signposted and there's a café/bistro.

Morvern → *Colour map 3, B4. Phone code 01967.*

Just east of Strontian the A884 leads south through the dramatic, wildlife rich landscape of Morvern to the tiny remote community of **Lochaline** on the Sound of Mull, departure point for the CalMac ferry to Fishnish. About 3 miles before Lochaline is the turning left for the track which leads down the side of Loch Aline to the 14th-century ruins of **Ardtornish Castle**. First you'll come to **Kinlochaline Castle** (keys available at the cottage) and **Ardtornish House**. This house stands on the site of the original house, which was visited on several occasions by Florence Nightingale, who was a family member of the original owners. The author John Buchan spent many summers here in the 1930s. There's a path which leads from the estate office uphill across open moorland for an hour until it reaches **Loch Tearnait**. In the centre of the loch is a 1500-year-old crannog, an artificial island built for defensive purposes. This walk is detailed in the tourist board's leaflet, along with the Ariundle Nature Trail (see above). During the stalking season (1 July to 20 October) check at the estate office before setting out on the walk to the Loch.

Ardnamurchan Peninsula and Moidart → *Colour map 3, B4. Phone code 01972 and 01967.*

The main places of interest in this area are to be found on the rugged Ardnamurchan Peninsula (from the Gaelic *Aird nam Murchan*, meaning 'Point of the High Seas'), the end of which is the most westerly point on the British mainland. The winding A861 runs west from Strontian along the north shore of Loch Sunart to **Salen**, where the single-track B8007 branches west and runs all the way out to the tip of the peninsula. The A861 meanwhile turns north and twists and turns along a spectacular single-track road to Acharacle.

The first settlement you head west out to Ardnamurchan Point is **Glenborrodale**. Before you reach the tiny hamlet look out on the left for the castellated late-Victorian towers of **Glenborrodale Castle**, once the property of a certain Jesse Boot, who founded a chain of chemist shops which you may have heard of. Just west of Glenborrodale is the excellent **Glenmore Natural History Centre** ① *T01967-500254, Apr-Oct Mon-Sat 1030-1730, Sun 1200-1730*, should be on the list of everyone with the faintest interest in the peninsula's wildlife and nature – for which Ardnamurchan is renowned. The 'Living Building' with turf on the roof and bark on the floor ensures you will see birds and animals (including pine martens) up close, whilst the interactive displays are both fun and informative for all ages. It's a good place for kids, and a life-saver when the weather is just too bad to venture outside. There's a good little **Antler Tearoom** (⑪) serving home-baking and light lunches, and a decent gift shop. In addition, this is the base of the wonderful **Sunart Suppers** ① *T07772-850133*, frozen gourmet food, made to order and available to collect or be delivered. It's self-caterers and campers heaven with the likes of highland venison and fish pie. A mile to the east is the **RSPB Reserve** where you can see golden eagles, otters and seals. You can take a two-hour wildlife trip to the seal colonies – or further afield to Tobermory on Mull or Staffa and the Treshnish Islands (see Activities and tours, page 248).

A few miles west of the centre, the B8007 turns away from the coast. Here you'll see the beautiful bay of **Camas nan Geall** (Bay of the stranger or pledge, the precise meaning is unclear). It's worth stopping at the car park to admire the fantastic views, or take the path down to the beach. Between Glenborrodale and Kilchoan, a road runs to the north coast of the peninsula and the beautiful beaches at **Fascadale**, **Kilmory** and **Ockle**.

The straggling crofting village of **Kilchoan** is the main settlement on Ardnamurchan. Shortly after passing the sign for the village, you can turn left to the scenic ruin of **Mingary Castle**, built around the 13th century. There's a TIC ① *T01972-510222, Easter-Oct daily*, which provides information on local scenic walks and will help with accommodation. Beyond Kilchoan the road leads to the lighthouse at mainland Britain's most westerly point, with stunning views (on a clear day) across to the small isles of Rùm, Eigg, Muck and Canna, with the Cuillins of Skye rising behind Rùm. The former (36 m high) lighthouse was designed by Alan Stevenson, father of Robert Louis, and built in 1849. The buildings have been converted into the **Ardnamurchan Lighthouse Visitor Centre** ① *T01972-510210, www.ardna murchan.u-net.com, Apr-Oct daily 1000-1700, £5.50*, where you can learn about the history and workings of lighthouses. There's self-catering accommodation, a café and gift shop.

A mile northwest of Kilchoan a road branches to the right to the beautiful long, white beach at **Sanna Bay**. It's worth making the trip here just to walk on the beach, but this is also a good place to spot whales and dolphins. On the road to Sanna Bay is the tiny settlement of **Achnaha**, which is famed for its rare 'ring-dyke' system, a huge, natural rock formation which is the crater of an extinct volcano.

North of Salen on the A861 is the scattered crofting township of **Acharacle**, at the western end of Loch Shiel surrounded by rolling hills. The village has several shops, a post office, garage and plenty of places to stay. A couple of miles to the west a road leads to beautiful **Kentra Bay**. Cross the wooden bridge, follow the footpath round the side of Kentra Bay and then follow the signs for Gortenfearn, where you'll find the famous 'singing sands'. Not only is the beach music to the ears as you walk its length, but the view across to Skye and the small isles is a feast for the eyes.

Three miles north of Acharacle is **Loch Moidart**. Here, perched on a rocky promontory in the middle of the loch, is the 13th-century ruin of **Castle Tioram** (pronounced 'Cheerum'), one of Scotland's best-loved castle ruins. This was the seat of the MacDonalds of Clanranald, until it was destroyed by their chief in 1715 to prevent it from falling into Hanoverian hands while he was away fighting for the Jacobites. There are plans to restore the castle, but you can visit it (free) via the sandy causeway that connects it to the mainland at low tide. You can paddle the seal rich, crystal clear waters in the Sound of Arisaig with **Rockhopper Seakayaking** ① *www.rockhopperscotland.co.uk*. The A861 follows the shores of Loch Moidart, into the region of the same name, before joining the A830 Fort William to Mallaig road at Lochailort.

The Road to the Isles → *For listings, see pages 245-249. Colour map 3, A4-B6.*

The Road to the Isles, the 46-mile stretch of the A830 from Fort William to Mallaig, runs through a series of magnificent glens before emerging on a coastline of vanilla-coloured beaches and sinuous bays backed by machair and washed by turquoise seas, with views across to Rùm, Eigg and the Cuillins of Skye. This is also the route followed by the West Highland Railway (see box, page 228), frequently hailed as one of the great railway journeys in the world. Either way – by road or rail – this is a beautiful journey, through

Raising standards

It all started on 19 August 1745 at Glenfinnan, 19 miles west of Fort William at the head of Loch Shiel. Less than a month earlier, Prince Charles Edward Stuart had landed on the Scottish mainland for the first time, on the shores of Loch nan Uamh, between Lochailort and Arisaig. He had come to claim the British throne for his father, James, son of the exiled King James VII of Scotland and II of England.

The clan chiefs had expected French support, but when the Prince arrived with only a handful of men they were reluctant to join the cause. Undeterred, the prince raised his standard and his faith was soon rewarded when he heard the sound of the pipes and Cameron of Lochiel, along with 800 men, came marching down the valley to join them. It must have been an incredible moment.

a landscape that resonates with historical significance. For this is Bonnie Prince Charlie country, where the ill-fated Jacobite Rising began, and ended, with the Prince's flight to France.

Glenfinnan → *Colour map 3, B5. Phone code 01397.*

Some 17 miles west of Fort William, at the head of Loch Shiel, is Glenfinnan, a kind of single-malt distillation of Highland beauty. A grand monument marks the spot where Bonnie Prince Charlie raised the Jacobite standard in 1745. It was erected in 1815 by Alexander MacDonald of Glenaladale in memory of the clansmen who fought and died for the Prince. You can climb to the top (mind your head, though) for even better views down the loch. There's a powerful sense of history here and as you gaze across eerie Loch Shiel stretching into the distance, veiled by steep mountains, you can almost hear the wail of the bagpipes in the distance, through the mist. On the other side of the road is the **National Trust for Scotland Visitor Centre** ① *T01397-722250, Apr-Jun, Sep-Oct daily 1000-1700, Jul-Aug daily 0930-1730, £3.50, concessions £2.50*, which has displays and an audio programme of the Prince's campaign, from Glenfinnan to its grim conclusion at Culloden. The Glenfinnan Games are held here in mid-August.

A mile away, in Glenfinnan village, is the **Station Museum** ① *T01397-722295, Jun-Oct daily 0900-1700, other times by appointment, £1*, which is housed in the railway station on the magnificent Fort William to Mallaig railway line. It has displays of memorabilia from the line's 100-year history. You can also sleep and eat here (see below). The 1000-ft span of the **Glenfinnan Viaduct**, between the visitor centre and the village, is one of the most spectacular sections of the famous West Highland Railway, see box, page 228.

About 10 miles west of Glenfinnan the road passes through the tiny village of **Lochailort**, complete with the pleasant Lochailort Inn and where the A861 branches south to the remote Ardnamurchan Peninsula, see above. A couple of miles further on, is **Loch nan Uamh**, where Prince Charles first landed on the Scottish mainland (he first landed on Eriskay in the Outer Hebrides) and from where, a year later, he fled for France following the disastrous defeat at Culloden, see box, page 199. A path leads down from the car park to the Prince's Cairn, which marks the beginning and the end of the Jacobite cause. A few years ago, scientific imaging proved that contrary to reports, a horse and cart were not entombed in the concrete foundations of the Glenfinnan Viaduct following an accident during its building. However, it did prove the horse and cart lie encased under the Loch nan Uamh Viaduct.

Arisaig and Morar → *Colour map 3, A4. Phone code 01687.*

At the western end of the Morar Peninsula is the little village of Arisaig, scattered around the head of a sheltered bay with An Sgurr's knobbly peak peering above the narrow mouth. The village has sleeping and eating options, as well as a post office, general store (with ATM) and doctor's surgery and is a useful service centre for the many self-catering cottages and caravans that line this stretch of coastline. There are some nice beaches around, and the road west from the village out to the **Rhue Peninsula** is great for seal spotting. You can also take a cruise from Arisaig to the islands of Rùm, Eigg and Muck, see Transport, page 248.

Arisaig was the birthplace of Long John Silver, who worked on the construction of the nearby lighthouse at Barrahead, one of many designed by the father of Robert Louis Stevenson who met Silver and was so impressed that he immortalized him in his classic *Treasure Island*.

The main A830 bypasses Arisaig on its way to Mallaig, while a wiggly single-track road hugs the coast and heads north, past the golf course and on past beautiful Camusdarach beach (which featured in the film *Local Hero*) before joining the main road by the tiny village of Morar. A single-track road leads up behind the village of Morar to dark, mysterious **Loch Morar,** the deepest inland loch in the country and home of Morag, Scotland's other, lesser-known, but more attractive (according to the locals) monster. Two locals reported seeing her in August 1969 and a scientific investigation two years later uncovered a remarkable number of eye-witness accounts. You could always try to elicit further information from the locals over a wee dram in the bar of the **Morar Hotel**. The road runs along the north shore of the loch for 3 miles until it reaches the pretty little hamlets of **Bracora** and **Bracorina**. Here the road stops, but a footpath continues all the way to **Tarbet** on the shores of Loch Nevis, from where it's possible to catch a boat back to Mallaig, see Transport, page 248. It takes about three hours to walk to Tarbet – where there's now a bothy – and you'll need to get there by 1530 for the boat.

Mallaig → *Colour map 3, A4. Phone code 01687.*

The end of the road – and railway line – is Mallaig, a busy fishing port and main departure point for ferries to Skye. It's a no-nonsense, workmanlike place, with little in the way of worthwhile diversions, but there are decent facilities and at least the train and bus stations and CalMac ferry office are all within a few yards of each other. Also close by are banks with ATMs and the post office. The TIC ① *by the harbour, T01687-462170, Apr-Oct daily, Nov-Mar Mon, Tue and Fri*, has a café.

Beside the train station is the **Mallaig Heritage Centre** ① *T01687-462085, Apr-Jun and Oct Mon-Sat 1100-1600, Jul-Sep Mon-Sat 0930-1630, Sun 1230-1630, Nov-Mar Wed-Sat 1200-1700, £2, concession £1.50 under 16s free*, with interesting descriptions of the local Clearances, the railway line and the fishing industry.

Knoydart Peninsula → *For listings, see pages 245-249. Colour map 3, A5. Phone code 01867.*

The Knoydart Peninsula, the most remote and unspoilt region in Britain and one of Europe's last great wildernesses, literally lies between Heaven and Hell, for it is bordered to the north by Loch Hourn (Loch of Hell) and to the south by Loch Nevis (Loch of Heaven). Knoydart is not for wimps. It can only be reached on foot, or by boat from Mallaig, and consequently attracts walkers, who can wander for days around a network of trails without seeing another soul. If you've time and love the outdoors it's worth the trip.

Ins and outs

Bruce Watt Sea Cruises ① *T01687-462320, www.knoydart-ferry.co.uk*, run trips to the remote village of Inverie (45 minutes), and Tarbet on Loch Nevis. They sail on Monday, Wednesday and Friday all year and from Monday to Friday in summer. On a Monday and Friday the boat calls in at Tarbet (all year, also on a Wednesday in summer). If you intend to catch the boat at Tarbet you must contact them in advance to confirm numbers There's also a ferry service from Arnisdale, on the north shore of Loch Hourn, to Barrisdale To arrange a crossing, contact Billy Mackenzie in Arnisdale, T01599- 522247. It's a passenger only fast boat (also takes bikes) that sails subject to sea conditions and that can also be hired for wildlife spotting.

If approaching Knoydart from the Glenelg road, there's a **MacRae Kintail bus** ① *on request, T01599-511384*, that runs Monday to Friday from Shiel Bridge to Glenelg (see page 250), from where you can take a ferry across to Kylerhea on Skye. Note: if planning to explore the Knoydart Peninsula it's advisable to call **Knoydart Foundation** ① *T01687-462242*, for travel and accommodation advice, including information on stalking activity.

Walking on the Knoydart Peninsula

A two-day hiking route starts from Kinloch Hourn, reached by bus from Invergarry, see page 209. The trail winds its way around the coast to Barrisdale and on to Inverie. Another route into Knoydart starts from the west end of Loch Arkaig, and runs through Glen Dessarry. Both are tough hikes and only for fit, experienced and well-equipped hillwalkers. An easier way in is by boat (see Transport, page 248).

The peninsula's only settlement of any size is tiny **Inverie**, with just 60 inhabitants, one of only a few villages in Scotland which can't be reached by road, but still has a post office, a shop, a few places to stay and Britain's most remote pub. Much of the peninsula is mountain, with four peaks over 3000 ft. Its 85 square miles is a mix of private sporting estate, conservation trust and community partnership. Almost a decade ago one chunk of the peninsula, the 17,000-acre **Knoydart Estate**, was rescued from a succession of indifferent landlords by a community buy-out, funded by public money and individual donations. The Knoydart Foundation's trustees include the conservationist Chris Brasher and impresario Cameron Mackintosh, and if you sit outside the **Old Forge** long enough, one of them might pass by, or stop for a chat. Equally possible is the sighting of otters in the Sound of Sleat or golden eagles soaring overhead.

West of Fort William listings

For Sleeping and Eating price codes and other relevant information, see Essentials pages 38-45.

Sleeping

Ardgour *p239*

L-A Kilcamb Lodge Hotel, Strontian, T01967-402257, www.kilcamblodge.com. Mid-Feb to Dec. This luxurious Victorian country house standing in its own grounds just north of Strontian on the shores of Loch Sunart has its own private beach. The perfect bolthole, with only the occasional otter or eagle to disturb the peace, also serves superb food.

B-C The Inn at Ardgour, Ardgour, next to Corran Ferry, 9 miles from Fort William, T01855-841225, www.ardgour.biz. 12 en suite rooms. Small hotel dating from 1746. Cosy, lively bar with a fine selection of malts and good value lunches and dinners. Good choice for walkers, with lovely views. Recommended.

C Ben View Hotel, 1 mile west of Strontian, T01967-402333, www.benviewhotel.co.uk. In addition to its 9 comfortable bedrooms, enjoy views over Loch Sunart, a dram in the bizarre pine panelled bar and delicious locally sourced food. Also has 2 self-catering cottages by the hotel that sleep 2 (from £220 per week).

C Strontian Hotel, Strontian, T01967-402029, www.thestrontianhotel.co.uk. You can't miss this 6-bedroom hotel, right by the shores of Loch Sunart and with breathtaking views over the sea loch from its restaurant (ɪ̈ɪ). Dinner until 2100.

E Heatherbank, Upper Scotstown, Strontian, T01967-402201, www.heatherbankbb.co.uk. Open Easter-Oct. 3 en suite rooms. Modern house with great views to the Ardgour hills. Spacious guest lounge with log fire. Discounts for longer stays.

Ardnamurchan Peninsula and Moidart *p240*

A-B Meall Mo Chridhe, Kilchoan, T/F01972-510238. Year-round. A beautiful 3-bedroom

17th-century converted manse set in over 40 acres with great sea views and fine cooking. Dinner available for non-residents (ɪ̈ɪ̈ɪ), but booking essential.

B-C Strontian Hotel, by Strontian, T01967-402029. Fabulous 18th-century inn that looks right down Loch Sunart. Opportunities to spot seals and otters, fish, dine or simply relax in one of 6 comfortable bedrooms.

B-F Glenuig Inn, Glenuig, by Loch Ailort, T01687-470219, www.glenuig.com. 18th-century inn that changed ownership in 2008 and is undergoing extensive renovation until Easter 2009. Offers comfortable bunkhouse accommodation for £25 (plus £10 breakfast) per person. Also en suite accommodation for families or groups. Reasonable lunches and dinners (including lamb and fish) served in the restaurant (until 2100). Good bar and terrific views of loch. Owner is a keen sea-kayaker and has links with local operators. Great area to spot seals and basking sharks.

D Cala Darach, Glenmore by Glenborrodale, T01972-500204. Open Mar-Oct. 3 en suite rooms. Lovely country house with views across Loch Sunart.

C Kilchoan House Hotel, Kilchoan, T01972-510200, www.kilchoanhotel.co.uk. 7 en suite rooms. Comfortable option with views of Mull from most of the rooms. Also good meals served 1200-1400 and 1800-2030, in the bar or dining room. 3-course dinner from £15.95.

D Loch Shiel House Hotel, Acharacle, T01967-431224. 8 en suite rooms. Comfortable hotel serving decent bar meals (ɪ̈ɪ-ɪ̈). Contact them for details of cruises on Loch Shiel.

D Salen Inn, Salen, T01972-431661, www. salenhotel.co.uk. Open all year. Decent hotel accommodation and good food (ɪ̈ɪ), with the likes of seafood, lamb and venison on the menu. Cosy bar and information on walks.

C-F Sonachan Hotel, a few miles beyond Kilchoan, on the road to Ardnamurchan

Point, T/F01972-510211, www.sonachan. u-net.com. Open all year. The most westerly hotel on the UK mainland, close to the lighthouse and beaches and surrounded by 1000 acres of grounds with walking and fishing opportunities. Good food available and children welcome. Also has a 4-bedroom self-catering house and 2 rooms.

Self-catering
Glenmore House and Cottage, Port An Aiseig, Glenborrodale, T01972-500263, www.holidayardnamurchan.co.uk. Luxury self-catering cottage and lodge on shores of Loch Sunart, facilities include whirlpool baths and sauna. Available all year, £400-£1500 per week.
Shoreline Cottages, Glenborrodale, T01972-500248. Great views out to sea from 2 lovely, secluded cottages set in 13 acres of grounds. Fabulous opportunities to spot wildlife and enjoy a true escape from the daily stresses of urban life. From £545 per week.

Camping
Branault Croft Caravans, Achateny by Acharacle, T01972-510284. Apr-Oct. Offers 3 static (luxury) caravans on a working croft at the northern edge of the peninsula. A peaceful escape and ideal for young children, with acres of space to play in and explore. Lovely views across the sea towards Eigg and Skye. £110-170 per week.
Resipole Farm Caravan Park, 1 mile or so east of Salen, Resipole, T01967-431235, www.resipole.co.uk. Self-catering chalets, caravan and tent pitches, and caravans for rent. Also has a restaurant and bar on site. Fantastic views over the sea. Gets busy but highly recommended.

Glenfinnan p242
A The Prince's House, main road, ½ mile past monument on the right, heading west, T01397-722246, www.glenfinnan.co.uk. Mar-Nov. 9 en suite rooms. Comfortable old coaching inn which offers good food (¶¶).

A-B Glenfinnan House Hotel, off the main road, T/F01397-722235, www.glenfinnan house.com. Mar-Oct. 17 en suite rooms. Charming house dating back to mid-1700s with fabulous bedrooms, lovely meals (1800-2030) and a bar that serves the likes of venison sausages (1200-2100). Great place to hear local folk music, fish or relax over an intimate dinner (¶¶¶). Recommended.
F Glenfinnan Sleeping Car, at the train station, T01397-722400. Bunkhouse accommodation for 10 people. Also offers mountain bike hire and you can eat here in the **Glenfinnan Dining Car** (¶¶-¶).

Arisaig and Morar p243
B Arisaig Hotel, Arisaig, T01687-450210, www.arisaighotel.co.uk. Open all year. 18th-century former coaching inn with 13 en suite rooms and good sea views. Meals (¶¶) served in the restaurant and 2 bars (¶). Child-friendly, with separate playroom,10% off green fee at Traigh golf course (3 miles away).
B The Old Library Lodge, Arisaig, T01687-450651. Apr-Oct. 6 en suite rooms. Lovely food in restaurant (¶¶¶), with well-furnished rooms. Recommended.

Mallaig p243
B West Highland Hotel, T01687-462210, www.westhighlandhotel.co.uk. Apr-Oct. Centrally located with 40 reasonable rooms. The restaurant is proud of its seafood dishes and this is the place to order a 'West Highland Coffee' liqueur prepared to the hotels secret recipe (¶¶).
D Western Isles Guesthouse, follow the road round the harbour to East Bay, T/F01687-462320. Jan-Nov. Excellent-value guesthouse which serves dinner to guests.
D-E Glencairn House, East Bay, T01687-462359, www.glencairn-house.co.uk. Apr-Sep. 2 en suite rooms. Comfortable rooms with TV and DVD.
F Sheena's Backpackers' Lodge, Station Rd, T01687-462764, www.mallaigbackpackers. co.uk. The cheapest place to stay is this friendly, easy-going independent hostel,

with dorm beds, double rooms and
kitchen facilities.

Knoydart Peninsula *p243*

There's a growing number of options, see
www.knoydart-foundation.com. Other
than those listed below, there are 3 or 4
additional great value (**E-F**) backpacker
options on the peninsula, including the
Kilchoan Barn, T01687-462724; and
The Old Byre, T01687-460099.
A Doune Stone Lodge, 3-4 miles up the
peninsula's only road, standing in splendid
isolation, T01687-462667, www.doune-
knoydart.co.uk. 3 en suite rooms, all with
bunk beds for 2 children. Minimum stay 3
nights. Price includes breakfast, packed lunch
and dinner. The food is superb and cannot
be praised highly enough. Guests are picked
up by boat from Mallaig (around £20), where
you can leave your car. The owners also run
the nearby **Doune Bay Lodge**, with shared
facilities, for parties of up to 14 (from £575
per person). Can be self-catered, fully catered,
or somewhere in between. Also the option to
charter the *TSMV Mary Doune* boat for £2940.
Highly recommended.
B The Gathering, Knoydart, T01687-
460051. A fabulous B&B, only opened a few
years ago, offers stylish rooms and great
breakfasts. Friendly host. Recommended.
B Pier House, Inverie, T01687-462347,
www.thepierhouseknoydart.co.uk. 4 rooms,
2 en suite, 2 with extra beds for children.
Price includes dinner. Good, old-fashioned
hospitality and wonderful local seafood (♥♥).
F Knoydart Foundation Backpackers,
15 mins' walk from the pier and pub,
T01687-462242. Basic but good value
at only £14 per bunk.
F Torrie Shieling, Inverie, T01687-462669.
It's a bit more expensive than most
other hostels, but is very comfortable,
and popular with hikers. They also have
their own transport for trips around the
peninsula and will collect guests from
Mallaig by arrangement.

🍴 Eating

Ardgour *p239*

♥♥♥-♥♥ **The Inn at Ardgour**, Corran, T01855-
841225, www.ardgour.biz. Family-run,
atmospheric inn serving good value bar food,
full à la carte menu and takeaway snacks.
Dogs and children welcome. Informal dining
with fantastic sea views. Recommended.
♥♥ **Ariundle Centre**, Strontian, T01967-402279,
www.ariundle.co.uk. Daily 0900-1730. Licensed
tea room/restaurant serving soups, salads
and snacks. Also does candelit suppers
during the summer, phone for details.

Morvern *p240*

♥♥ **Lochaline Hotel**, Lochaline, T01967-
421657. Hotel serving decent bar meals.
♥♥ **Whitehouse**, Lochaline, T01967-421777.
Open Mon-Sat for lunch and dinner (till
2100). Local organic produce.

Ardnamurchan Peninsula and Moidart *p240*

All the hotels listed under Sleeping serve
good food.
♥♥ **Glenuig Inn**, 5 miles from Loch Ailort and
tucked back from the shoreline of the Sound
of Arisaig, T01687-470219. Undergoing
extensive refurbishment, will re-open in
Apr 2009. Hearty lunches and dinners
in a friendly, simple setting with a couple
of real ales on tap. Dinner until 2100.
♥♥-♥ **Clanranald Hotel**, at Mingarry, T01967-
431202. Tasty food is also available here.

Arisaig and Morar *p243*

Very good meals can be found at the **Arisaig
Hotel**, although the **Old Library Lodge and
Restaurant** definitely has the edge – see
Sleeping, above.
♥ **Café Rhu**, Arisaig, next door to the Spar
store, T01687-450707. Open daily 1000-
1800. Snacks, soups, filled rolls and burgers,
also offers takeaway. Internet available £1
per hr. Friendly and good with kids.

Mallaig p243

If you're heading across to Skye you could buy some delicious peat-smoked salmon from **Andy Race**, by the harbour, T01687-462626, www.andyrace.co.uk, and eat it on the ferry with some brown bread. Alternatively, grab some excellent fish and chips or freshly caught scallops at the Cornerstone chippy.

¶¶ Cabin Seafood Restaurant, by the harbour. Serves decent meals and a great value 'teatime special'.

¶ Tea Room, below Sheena's Backpackers (see Sleeping, above). Great value meals, including a print of prawns and all manner of daytime hearty snacks.

Knoydart Peninsula p243

¶¶¶-¶¶ The Old Forge, Inverie, T01687-462267. The most remote pub on mainland Britain, where you can enjoy some tasty local seafood and a pint of real ale in front of an open fire. The craic among the locals and visitors also produces a terrific atmosphere. There's even the occasional impromptu ceilidh. Mercifully devoid of wannabe city slickers, this isn't the place to dress to impress – think more walking boots, waterproofs and midge cream'. Recommended.

⚙ Activities and tours

Ardgour, Ardnamurchan and Morvern p239
Boat trips
Ardnamurchan Charters, T01972-500208. Offers a 2-hr wildlife trip to the seal colonies – or further afield to Tobermory on Mull or Staffa and the Treshnish Islands.

Sea kayaking
Rockhopper Scotland, based in Fort William (see page 227). Offer sea-kayaking adventures in Ardnamurchan. Highly recommended.

Glenfinnan p242
Loch Shiel Cruises, Jim Michie, Marnoch, Roshven, Lochailort, T/F01687-470322, www.highlandcruises.co.uk. Runs a variety of cruises down Loch Shiel, from Glenfinnan to Acharacle. Sailings most days from Apr-Oct. Parking available at the **Glenfinnan House Hotel**, see Sleeping, page 246. Prices from £8 for 1 hr and £22 for a full loch cruise, with the possibility of spotting golden eagles. Cyclists can also join a cruise and disembark at the Polloch Pontoon to cycle back along the banks of the loch to Glenfinnan.

Arisaig and Morar p243
Arisaig Marine, The Harbour, Arisaig, T01687-450224, www.arisaig.co.uk. Trips to Eigg, Muck or Rùm aboard *MV Sheerwater*. Varied wildlife and spectacular scenery.

Mallaig p243
MV The Grimsay Isle, Ewen Nicholson, 6 Gillies Park, T01687-462652, T07880-815158, www.road-to-the-isles.org.uk/grimsayisle.html. Available for fishing charters and ferry service.

⊖ Transport

Ardgour, Ardnamurchan and Morvern p239
Bus Shiel Buses, T01967-431272, run most of the bus services. There's a bus once a day on Tue, Thu and Sat to **Fort William** from **Lochaline**, 2 hrs. There's a bus (No 500) once a day, Mon-Sat to **Fort William** from **Acharacle**, 1½ hrs, via Lochailort. The No 500 and No 502 also runs Mon-Sat from **Mallaig**, 1½ hrs, to Fort William. There's a bus, if you are very patient and super organized (to **Fort William** from **Kilchoan**, Mon-Sat, 2 hrs 25 mins, via **Glenuig**, 1 hr; **Acharacle**, 1 hr 20; and **Glenborrodale**, 2 hrs. There's also one service (No 506), Mon-Fri to **Fort William** from **Kilchoan**, 2½ hrs, via **Ardgour** and **Salen**.
Ferry For details of the ferry from Lochaline to Fishnish on Mull and from Kilchoan to Tobermory, see page 112.

Arisaig and Morar p243
Ferry Arisaig Marine, T01687-450224, www.arisaig.co.uk, sails from Arisaig pier to

Rùm, Eigg and Muck daily Mon-Fri all year and also Sat-Sun from Jun-Aug. The islands are visited on different days, though there is a boat to Eigg every day except Thu in summer. You can visit all 3 islands in a day, allowing 2-5 hrs ashore. Fares range from £18 return to Eigg, £19 to Muck and £24 return to Rùm (children 2 and under free to all islands, 3-10 years £10, 11-16 years £13). See also page 334. These trips cater for the island's residents as much as tourists, so don't expect a running commentary, though hot and cold drinks are served on board.

Mallaig p243

Bus Shiel Buses, T01967-431272, runs 2 buses daily Mon-Sat from **Mallaig** to **Fort William,** Jul-Sep, 1½ hrs, £5, and on Mon, Thu and Fri the rest of the year. The West Highland Flyer, T07780-724248, runs daily, Mar-Oct between **Oban** (0945) and **Mallaig** (1215) via Fort William (1100) and connects with the ferry to Skye and the Small Isles. It's possible to get off and on at **Onich, Fort William** and **Glenfinnan** but book in advance and call for the latest prices (from around £17 one way).

Ferry CalMac, T01687-462403, ferries run throughout the year to **Armadale** on Skye (see page 319), to **Lochboisdale** and Castlebay (see page 369), and to the **Small Isles** (see page 328).

Train There are several services daily (1 on Sun) to **Fort William**, with connections to **Glasgow**. There's also a steam train which runs in the summer months (see box, page 228).

Knoydart Peninsula p243

There are no roads through Knoydart so the only means of accessing and leaving the area is on a (very) long walk north from **Inverie** via the hamlet of **Barrisdale** to the road end at **Kinloch Hourn**. Alternatively, call Billy Mackenzie in Arnisdale, T01599-522247, to arrange for a passenger only (and bikes) pick-up from **Barrisdale**, across **Loch Hourn** to **Arnisdale** from where you can walk out to the bus at **Glenelg**.

Ferry To return to **Mallaig** from **Inverie**, contact **Bruce Watt Sea Cruises**, T01687-462320, www.knoydart-ferry.co.uk, which runs passenger only sailings on Mon, Wed and Fri Oct-Apr and Mon-Fri May-Sep. On a Mon and Fri the boat calls in at **Tarbet** on Loch Nevis and returns to Mallaig 1745. The Wed sailing to Tarbet only takes place from mid-May to mid-Sep. Though billed as a wildlife cruise, this is essentially a working ferry and fares are £11 return, and £16 for the afternoon sailing.

Great Glen to Kyle of Lochalsh

The A87 is one of the main Highland tourist routes, connecting the Great Glen with the west coast and the Isle of Skye. It runs west from Invergarry between Fort Augustus and Fort William, through Glen Moriston and Glen Shiel to Shiel Bridge, at the head of Loch Duich, and on to Kyle. At Shiel Bridge a road branches off to Glenelg, from where you can enjoy a magical and short ferry crossing to Skye. It's a beautiful journey and by far the best way to reach the island.
‣ *For listings, see pages 252-255.*

Ins and outs

Getting there Unfortunately, there's no longer a postbus service between Kyle and Glenelg so you'll need to call **MacRae Kintail** (No WR61) ⓘ *T01542-836363*, which runs one trip (Monday and Friday only) from Kyle of Lochalsh to Glenelg via Ratagan Youth Hostel. On demand it will continue to Arnisdale and Corran. There's also a bus (No 62 and No 64) to Plockton from Dornie via Kyle of Lochalsh, which runs three times a day, starting at 0830 from Kyle.

Glen Shiel → *Colour map 3, A5. OS Landranger No33.*

The journey from Invergarry to **Shiel Bridge** is worth it for the views alone. Glen Shiel is a sight to make the heart soar as high as the 3000-ft peaks that tower overhead on either side. This is one of the most popular hiking areas in Scotland, with the magnificent and much-photographed **Five Sisters of Kintail** on the north side of the glen, and the equally beautiful South Glen Shiel Ridge on the other.

There are several excellent hiking routes in Glen Shiel, but these mountains are to be treated with great respect. They require fitness, experience and proper equipment and planning. None of the routes should be attempted without a map, compass and detailed route instructions. You should be aware of the notoriously unpredictable weather conditions and also check locally about deer stalking. The season runs from August to October, but for more details contact the local stalkers (T01599-511282). A good trekking guide is the *SMC's Hill Walks in Northwest Scotland*.

The **Five Sisters Traverse** is a classic ridge route. It starts at the first fire break on the left as you head southeast down the glen from Shiel Bridge and finishes at Morvich, on the other side of the ridge. Allow a full day (eight to 10 hours). You can also hike from Morvich to **Glen Affric Youth Hostel** at Cannich. It's a strenuous 20-mile walk, but you can stop off midway at the remote **Allt Beithe Youth Hostel**. For details, see Glen Affric, page 202.

The magnificent **South Glen Shiel Ridge** is one of the world's great hikes. It starts from above the **Cluanie Inn**, see Sleeping, page 252. From here, follow the old public road to Tomdoun; it then meets up with a good stalking path which climbs to the summit of the first Munro, Creag a' Mhaim (3108 ft). The ridge then runs west for almost 9 miles and gives you the chance to pick off no fewer than seven Munros. Allow a full day for the walk (nine to 10 hours), and you'll need to set off early.

Glenelg and around → *Colour map 3, A5. Phone code 01599.*

One of the most beautiful journeys in Scotland and certainly overlooked by the majority of tourists is the road from Shiel Bridge to the sublime little outpost that is Glenelg; a tiny village on the shores of the Sound of Sleat, only a short distance opposite Kylerhea on Skye (for transport details see page 255). The unclassified single-track road, constructed by 17th-century Hanoverian forces to link the ruin of Bernera Barracks (see below) with Fort Augustus, turns off the A87 and climbs steeply and dramatically through a series of sharp switchbacks to the top of the **Mam Ratagan Pass** (1115 ft). From here the view back across Loch Duich to the Five Sisters of Kintail is simply amazing, and the all-time classic calendar shot.

The road then drops down through Glen More to Glenelg, the main settlement on the peninsula. Known until the 18th century as Kirkton (it's believed a church stood here as far back as the 13th century), Glenelg lies on the old drovers' route that ran from Skye to the cattle markets in the south. This little-known corner of the Western Highlands is Gavin Maxwell country and was featured in *Ring of Bright Water*, his much-loved novel about otters. He disguised the identity of this beautiful, unspoiled stretch of coastline, calling it Camusfearna, and today it remains a quiet backwater.

You can see the famous otters at **Sandaig**, on the road running from Glenelg, where Gavin Maxwell lived. The site of his cottage is now marked with a cairn. As well as otters, you can see numerous seabirds, seals and porpoises in the Sound of Sleat, and around the peninsula you may be lucky enough to catch a glimpse of wildcats, pine martens, golden eagles and the recently reintroduced sea eagles. The village itself consists of a row of whitewashed cottages surrounded by trees and overlooked by the ruins of the 18th-century **Bernera Barracks**. Just before the village the road forks. The right turning leads to the Glenelg-Kylerhea ferry, which makes the 10-minute crossing to Skye, see page 255.

A road runs south from Glenelg to Arnisdale. About 1½ miles along this road, a branch left leads to the **Glenelg Brochs** – Dun Telve and Dun Dun Troddan – two of the best-preserved Iron Age buildings in the country. Dun Telve, excavated in 1914, stands to a height of over 30 ft and the internal passages are almost intact. The road south from Glenelg continues past Sandaig Bay and runs along the north shore of unearthly Loch Hourn, with great views across the mountains of Knoydart. The road ends at little fishing hamlet of **Arnisdale**, from where you can take a boat across the loch to Barrisdale on the Knoydart Peninsula. For details, see page 244. A bit further along the coast, the road ends at the even tinier hamlet of **Corran**.

Eilean Donan Castle → *Colour map 3, A5. Phone code 01599.*
① *T01599-555202, www.eileandonancastle.com. Mar-Nov 1000-1800, £5, concessions £4.50. Citylink buses between Fort William and Inverness and Skye stop by the castle.*
Some 10 miles west of Shiel Bridge on the A87 is the little village of Dornie, home to the one of Scotland's most-photographed sights, the stunningly located Eilean Donan Castle. It stands on a tiny islet at the confluence of Loch Duich and Loch Alsh, joined to the shore by a narrow stone bridge and backed by high mountains. This great calendar favourite and tourist honeypot has also featured in several movies, including *Highlander*, which starred Sean Connery.

The original castle dates from 1230 when Alexander III had it built to protect the area from marauding Vikings. It was destroyed by King George in 1719 during its occupation by Spanish Jacobite forces sent to help the 'Old Pretender', James Stuart. It then lay in ruins, until one of the Macraes had it rebuilt between 1912 and 1932. Inside, the Banqueting Hall with its Pipers' Gallery is most impressive, and there's an exhibition of military regalia and interesting displays of the castle's history. The views from the battlements are also worthwhile. However, to escape the tourist hordes, don't forget about that fantastic winding road to Glenelg across the mountains to the south.

Kyle of Lochalsh → *Colour map 3, A5. Phone code 01599.*

Before the coming of the controversial Skye Bridge a mile to the north, see page 316, the little town of Kyle, as it is known, was the main ferry crossing to Skye and consequently a place which attracted a busy tourist trade. Now though, the tourist traffic bypasses Kyle, which notwithstanding tremendous views to Skye, suffers from a workaday feel. There are a couple of banks with ATMs, two small supermarkets and a post office in the village. The TIC ① T01599-534276, Apr-late Oct Mon-Fri 0930-1700, Sat-Sun 1000-1630, is at the main seafront car park. There are also toilets here (daily 0800-2100).

Plockton → *Colour map 3, A5. Phone code 01599.*

If there were a poll taken of visitors' favourite Highland villages, then you can bet your sporran that Plockton would come top with most folk. If you look for a definition of picturesque in your dictionary, it'll say 'see Plockton'. Well, maybe not – but it should. Actually, the name is derived from Am Ploc that roughly translates as blunt promontory.

Plockton's neat little painted cottages, built in the early 18th century by the landowner to provide fishing employment after clearing traditional crofting lands for sheep, are ranged around the curve of a wooded bay, with flowering gardens and palm trees. Yachts bob up and down in the harbour and there are views across the island-studded waters of Loch Carron to the hills beyond. Even on the telly Plockton's charms proved irresistible, and millions of viewers tuned in each week to watch the TV series *Hamish Macbeth*, which featured Robert Carlyle as the local bobby. Plockton's a popular place with artists who are drawn by the village's setting and the wonderful light. A good place to find some of their work, as well as other souvenirs, is **The Studio Craft Shop**, on the corner of the seafront and the road leading out of town.

There are lots of good walks around the village. One of the best ways to appreciate it is to head up to **Frithard Hill**, from where there are great views of the bay. Another good walk is along the beach, starting from the High School playing fields at the top of the village. The craft shop (and newsagent) sells a booklet (£3) of local walks.

◉ Great Glen to Kyle of Lochalsh listings

For Sleeping and Eating price codes and other relevant information, see Essentials pages 38-45.

● Sleeping

Glen Shiel *p250*
B-C Cluanie Inn, Glenmoriston, some 9 miles east of Shiel Bridge, T01320-340238, www.cluanieinn.com. 10 en suite rooms including 2 with jacuzzi and 1 with a 4-poster bed. Also offers more modest Clubhouse (£35 per person) accommodation. This is one of the Highlands' classic hotels. It's a firm favourite with hikers and climbers and it's easy to see why. After a hard day's ridge walking, what could be better than jumping into the

jacuzzi, then having a hot dinner, bar meal and a good real ale or malt beside a log fire. Recommended.
B-F Kintail Lodge Hotel, T01599-511275, www.kintaillodgehotel.co.uk. Open all year. 12 rooms. Small, cosy hotel beautifully located by the shores of Loch Duich, dinner also available. Wee Bunkhouse attached with 12 beds. You can also hire bikes.
B-C Grants at Craigellachie, Ratagan, T01599-511331, www.housebytheloch. co.uk. Open all year. About 1 mile along the road to Glenelg/Kylerhea ferry is the turn-off to tiny Ratagan and this genuine hidden gem of a place. 4 en suite rooms, 2 in the main house and 2 in the newly refurbished Butt and Ben. Hosts Tony and Liz Taylor have

created a little haven of peace, comfort and fine cuisine. It's a restaurant with rooms and the rave reviews for the former (🍴🍴🍴) are matched by the style and comfort – and superb views – of the latter. The rooms in the But and Ben can be booked on a self-catering basis. Recommended.

F Ratagan Youth Hostel, just past Shiel Bridge, T01599-511243. Open Feb-Dec. One of the great hikers' hostels.

Camping
Morvich Caravan Club Site, 1½ miles past Shiel Bridge in direction of Kyle, T01599-511354. Open late Mar-late Oct. Large site with full facilities.
Shiel Shop and campsite, Shiel Bridge, T01599-511221. Small pub/restaurant, with groceries and fuel all close at hand.

Glenelg and around p250
B-C Glenelg Inn, Glenelg, T01599-522273, www.glenelg-inn.com. Open all year. It's worth stopping in Glenelg, if you've got the time, to experience a night in this wonderfully cosy place. Even if you can't spend the night, at least spend an hour or 2 enjoying the atmosphere, good ale and superb food, either in the dining room (🍴🍴🍴) or the bar (🍴🍴). If you're really lucky, you may even chance upon an impromptu folk jam. Rooms are spacious and inviting. Warmly recommended.
E Mrs Chisholm, Glenelg, T01599-522287. Open all year. Cheaper B&B option in the village.

Eilean Donan Castle p251
There are several places to stay in the nearby village of Dornie.
B Conchra House Hotel, Ardelve, T01599-555233, www.conchrahouse.co.uk. Open all year. 5 en suite rooms. To get here, cross the bridge in Dornie and turn right for Killilan, a tiny hamlet at the head of Loch Long, the hotel is ¾ mile up this road. This historic 18th- century hunting lodge is peaceful, has lovely views and a reputation for good food.

D Glomach House, Aullt-Na-Chruinn, T01599-511222, www.glomach.co.uk. Open all year. 3 en suite rooms. Tidy and comfortable B&B on the shores of Loch Duich at Shiel Bridge. Self-catering cottage also available for rent, comprising 2 double bedrooms. No pets.
C-D Loch Duich Hotel, across the bridge from **Dornie Hotel**, T01599-555213, www.lochduichhotelco.uk. Open all year. 11 en suite rooms. Offers comfortable accommodation, meals (seafood restaurant and bar meals) and live music in the bar on a Sun evening. Wide selection of malt whiskies.
D Dornie Hotel, Dornie, T01599-555205, www.dornie-hotel.co.uk. Open all year. 12 rooms, many en suite. A good option and serves very good food (🍴🍴).
E Caberfeidh House, Ardelve, by Dornie, T01599-555293, www.caberfeidh.plus.com. Open all year. 5 rooms, 4 with views of the castle. Friendly and comfortable guesthouse. Very good value.
F Silver Fir Bunkhouse, Carndubh, T01599-555264. A 6-bed bunkhouse.
F Whitefalls Retreats, near Cochra House Hotel, at Camasluinie, T01599-588205, www.holidayhighlands.co.uk. A 10-bed independent hostel. 1 room sleeps 6 and 1 room sleeps 4.

Kyle of Lochalsh p252
It's a good idea to get the TIC to book a room for you, as there's not much choice in Kyle itself.
C-D Kyle Hotel, Main St, T01599-534204, www.kylehotel.co.uk. Open all year. 31 en suite rooms. Reasonable food (🍴🍴) in restaurant and adjacent **Nor-West Café** (🍴).
B-C Tingle Creek Hotel, Erbusaig, T01599-534430, www.tinglecreek-hotel.co.uk. Open all year. Small hotel with a big, friendly welcome. Lovely setting and great views. Good food in restaurant and guests can enjoy a drink in the **Galleon** bar before dinner.
F Cuchulainn's, Station Rd, T01599-534492. Cheap hostel accommodation and standard restaurant fare (🍴).

Camping

Reraig Caravan Site, 4 miles east of Kyle, at Balmacara, T01599-566215.

Plockton *p252*

B The Haven Hotel, Innes St, T01599-544223, www.havenhotelplockton.co.uk. Open all year. 15 en suite rooms. Serves good Scottish food in the restaurant (¶¶). Dogs welcome.

A-B Plockton Hotel, Harbour St, T01599-544 274, www.plocktonhotel.co.uk. Open all year. 11 en suite rooms. Comfortable and tastefully furnished rooms above a perenially busy wee bar. All have views across the bay. There area few places along the waterfront and this is among the best. If you eat in the front restaurant (¶¶¶-¶¶) you'll enjoy views out over the bay. Recommended.

C Plockton Gallery@the Manse, Innes St, T01599-544442. Open all year. 3 en suite rooms. Part gallery, part guesthouse, this place offers something different. A bit more expensive than the average but worth it for the quality and service. Veggie options available with a bit of notice, disabled access and parking. Recommended.

B Plockton Inn, Innes St, T01599-544222, www.plocktoninn.co.uk. Open all year. 14 rooms. Small hotel with 7 bedrooms added in an annexe across the road. Very good seafood in restaurant or in lively bar where you can also hear live folk music twice a week (usually Tue and Thu). Open log fires and there's also a great little beer garden at the front where you can sit and enjoy a drink on a balmy summer evening.

D An Caladh, beside the shore T01599-544356. This is a lovely option right by the shore from where the owner occasionally goes out fishing in the bay.

D-E Heron's Flight, Cooper St, T01599-544220, www.heronsflight.org. Open Mar-Oct. 3 rooms. Friendly and welcoming B&B run by Ann Mackenzie and her dog, Ruah. Veggie and continental options for breakfast, no cards accepted. No single occupancy or single night bookings.

E Shieling, Harbour St, T01599-544282. At the far end of the harbour. There are lots of B&Bs to choose from on the seafront and this is one of the nicest.

F Nessun Dorma, Burnside, T01599-544235. Bunkhouse 1 mile out of Plockton at the railway station, run by Mick and Gill Coe. Cheapest option. Packed lunches available on request.

❶ Eating

Eilean Donan Castle *p251*

Aside from the hotels listed above, there are a couple of places in Dornie serving decent food, the best of which is probably the **Clachan Pub** where you can enjoy a good-value 3-course evening meal (¶¶).

Kyle of Lochalsh *p252*

¶¶ The Waverley Restaurant, Main St, T01599-534337. Daily 1730-2130. Daily specials including vegetarian dishes. Good value.

Plockton *p252*

There are several good eateries in Plockton with the **Plockton Inn**, **Haven Hotel** and **Plockton Hotel**, all serving memorable seafood dishes including huge bowls of mussels. Also try:

¶¶ Plockton Shores, Harbour St, T01599-544263. Open all year. Fabulous choice of scallops, locally sourced beef and vegetarian options. Recommended.

¶ Grumpy's, Innes St, right by the harbour. Open all year. A fantastic chippy with a difference, where you'll find the local catch of the day and prawns among the bargain bites for those on a budget.

❶ Activities and tours

Kyle of Lochalsh *p252*
Boat trips

There are a couple of interesting boat trips from Kyle.

Seaprobe Atlantis, T0800-9804846, www.seaprobeatlantis.com. The *Seaprobe Atlantis*, is a unique sailing craft fitted with underwater windows, providing an amazing view of seals, kelp forests and even a Second World War wreck. A 60-min trip is £9.50, children £4.75.

Plockton *p252*
Boat trips
Calum's Plockton Seal Trips, 32 Harbour St, T01599-544306, www.calums-sealtrips.com. Run 1-hr seal-spotting trips from the harbour, £8, children £5. In addition to seals you may spot otters and rare birdlife. The operator even offers your money back if you don't spot any seals.

⊖ Transport

Glen Shiel *p250*
Bus Citylink buses between **Fort William**, **Inverness** and **Skye** pass through Glen Shiel several times daily.

Glenelg and around *p250*
Ferry The community owned **Glenelg** to **Kylerhea** ferry provides the most scenic connection to **Skye**, www.skyeferry.com. 10-min crossing Easter-Oct daily 1000-1800;

Jun-end Aug until 1900. Per car with up to 4 passengers, £12, day return £16.

A more scenic route would be to take the passenger ferry from **Arnisdale** to **Kinlochhourn**, year-round, daily by arrangement, T01599-522247. Expect to pay from £15 per single trip, www.arnisdaleferryservice.com.

Kyle of Lochalsh *p252*
Bus Scottish Citylink buses, T0990-505050, run from Kyle to **Inverness**, 3 daily, 2 hrs; to **Glasgow** via **Fort William**, 4 daily, 5 hrs; and to **Edinburgh** via **Fort William**, 1 daily, 6½ hrs. **Scottish Citylink** buses run to **Portree**, 1 hr, and **Uig**, 1½ hrs, for ferries to **Tarbert** on Harris and **Lochmaddy** on North Uist. There's also a regular shuttle service across the bridge to **Kyleakin**, every 30 mins. **Train** The train journey to **Inverness** from Kyle, though not as spectacular as the West Highland line, is very scenic. It runs 3-4 times Mon-Sat, 2½ hrs, and once or twice on Sun from May-Sep. There's also an observation car and dining car in the summer.

Plockton *p252*
Cycle hire Gordon Mackenzie, T01599-544255. Hires bikes for £15 per day.

Wester Ross

From Loch Carron north to Ullapool, is the region of Wester Ross, an area of dramatic mountain massifs, fjord-like sea lochs and remote coastal villages. Here lies some of Europe's most spectacular scenery, from the isolated peninsula of Applecross to Tolkien-esque peaks of Torridon, which offer some of Scotland's best climbing and hillwalking. There are also gentler attractions such as the vast, sprawling gardens at Inverewe and the beguiling pink sands of Gruinard Bay. >> *For listings, see pages 262-267.*

Loch Carron and around → *For listings, see pages 262-267.*

Ins and outs

Getting there and around   There's a postbus service (Monday to Saturday) from Shieldaig to Kishorn and Lochcarron. The first bus leaves Shieldaig at 0900 and the second at 1020. It's possible to reach Applecross by public transport, but only just. If you catch the 1130 from Shieldaig you can reach Applecross by 1300, via the beautiful and winding coast road. You can also use the railway to enter the region by catching the train to Lochcarron (excluding Sunday). Another option is to catch the Skyeways (No WR87) bus from Inverness to Applecross at 1500 (Monday and Wednesday) and 1600 on a Saturday, which stops at Lochcarron en route.

Along Loch Carron

East of Plockton, just before the road meets the A890 at **Achmore**, is the **West Highland Dairy** ① *T01599-577203*, where you can pick up some good local cheese for a picnic – weather permitting of course. The road passes the turn-off for Stromeferry and continues along the east shore of Loch Carron to **Strathcarron** at its northeastern end, on the Inverness to Kyle of Lochalsh rail line.

Lochcarron village → *Colour map 1, C4. Phone code 01520. Population 870.*

Lochcarron village consists of little more than a main street along the shore of the loch, but it has more facilities and services than most other places in these parts. Here you should take the opportunity to withdraw cash at the Bank of Scotland ATM, fill up with petrol and buy some supplies at the small self-service store. The TIC ① *within the local post office/grocers, T01520-722357*, is very friendly and has details of some excellent walks in the surrounding hills.

Two miles south of the village on the road to the 15th-century ruins of **Strome Castle** is Lochcarron Weavers, where you can see tartan being made and also buy from a vast range of woven goods.

Loch Kishorn to Applecross → *Colour map 1, C4.*

There are many scenic routes in the Highlands but the road from Kishorn, west of Lochcarron to Applecross beats them all. The **Bealach na Ba** ('Pass of the Cattle') is the highest road in Scotland and is often closed during the winter snows. It climbs relentlessly and dramatically through a series of tortuous switchbacks – both spectacular and terrifying in equal measure. The high plateau, at 2053 ft, is cold and desolate, but from here you have the most amazing views: from Ardnamurchan Peninsula to Loch Torridon, taking in Eigg, Rùm, the Cuillins of Skye, the Old Man of Storr and the Quirang.

The narrow, single-track road then begins its gradual descent to the isolated little village of **Applecross**, site of one Scotland's first Christian monasteries, founded in AD 673. The village consists of a row of whitewashed fishermen's cottages looking across to the island of Raasay and backed by wooded slopes. It's a beautifully tranquil place where you can explore beaches and rock pools or enjoy a stroll along sylvan lanes – and then of course there's the very wonderful **Applecross Inn**, see Sleeping, page 262.

Torridon and around → *For listings, see pages 262-267. Colour map 1, C4. Phone code 01445.*

Torridon is perhaps the most striking skyline in the Scottish Highlands. The multi-peaked mountains of **Beinn Alligin**, **Liathach** (pronounced *Lee-ahakh*) and **Beinn Eighe** (*Ben-eay*) form a massive fortress of turrets, spires and pinnacles that provides an awesome backdrop to Loch Torridon, as well as the most exhilarating walking and climbing on the Scottish mainland. The straggly little village of Torridon makes the ideal base from which to tackle these mountains.

Ins and outs
Torridon may offer some of the best walking on the Scottish mainland but it also presents some of the most serious challenges. You need to be fit, experienced and well prepared and also be aware of the notoriously unpredictable weather. You should have a compass and the relevant map. OS Outdoor Leisure series No 8 covers the area. For recommended mountain guides, see page 266.

Around Loch Torridon
The coast road from Applecross meets the A896 from Lochcarron at the lovely little village of **Shieldaig** on the southern shore of Loch Torridon. There's a shop, a post office, a campsite and a couple of B&Bs. Several miles east, a side road turns off the A896 by **Torridon village** and winds its way along the northern shore of the loch, then climbs through dramatic scenery before dropping to the beautiful little village of **Diabaig** (pronounced *Jee-a-beg*), 10 miles from Torridon village. It's a worthwhile side trip, as the views across to the Applecross peninsula and Raasay are fantastic. There's also a great 7-mile coastal walk from Diabaig to Redpoint (see below).

Much of the Torridon massif is in the care of the National Trust for Scotland, and just before Torridon village is the **NTS Countryside Centre** ① *T01445-791221*, where you can get information and advice on walks in the area, as well as books and maps. About 400 yds past the centre is the **Deer Museum**, which has a small display describing the management of red deer in the Highlands as well as some live specimens outside.

Beinn Alligin
Beinn Alligin (3232 ft) is the most westerly of the Torridon peaks and probably the least demanding. The **Allt a'Bhealaich Walk** is a steep but short walk of about two hours. It starts from the car park just beyond the stone bridge that crosses the Abhainn Coire Mhic Nobuil. Follow the path that runs beside the river gorge until you reach the first bridge, cross it and follow the east bank of the Allt a' Bhealaich burn. Higher up, cross the second bridge and continue to follow the track up to the 380-m contour line, then turn back retracing your steps. This walk doesn't include the ascent of the peak but the views are magnificent. Those who wish to climb the three **Horns of Beinn Alligin** can continue from the 380-m contour line above the second bridge. The track that follows their ridge is exposed and requires rock scrambling experience.

Liathach

Seven-peaked Liathach (3460 ft) stretches over 5 miles, and the magnificent ridge walk is considered by many to be the most impressive in Britain. This walk requires a high level of stamina and will take at least seven to eight hours. It also helps if you have a car waiting at the end.

A good place to start this long and strenuous challenge is about half a mile or so east of Glen Cottage, which is just over 2 miles east of the Countryside Centre. A steep climb takes you to a point just west of **Stuc a'Choire Dhuibh Bhig** (3000 ft). Then retrace your route to climb the twin tops of **Bidein Toll a'Mhuic** (3200 ft), linked by a narrow ridge. The path from here descends to the head of a deep ravine and keeps to the crest of the ridge around the rim of **Coireag Dubh Beag** which plunges steeply to the north. The ridge then rises across a field of huge and unstable boulders to the highest peak – **Spidean a'Choire Leith**. The view from this point is stunning, with Coire na Caime before you, surrounded by 2000-ft sheer cliffs. From here, the path follows a narrow exposed ridge for over a mile towards **Mullach an Rathain** (3358 ft). Unless you are an experienced scrambler with a good head for heights, the best way from here is to take the path to the south, below the sharp pinnacles. Beyond the pinnacles the climb to Mullach an Rathain is straightforward. The track from here to **Sgorr a'Chadail** is a long but fairly easy walk and ends on the path in Coire Mhic Nobuil, see Beinn Alligin, above.

Coire Walk

A less difficult walk, but still requiring a fair degree of fitness and taking most of the day, is the Coire Walk. It follows the River Coire Mhic Nobuil to its watershed and down again by the **Allt a'Choire Dhuibh Mhoir** to the main road in Glen Torridon. Again, two cars will shorten the distance considerably.

The walk starts at the same point as the Beinn Alligin walk (see above). It follows the path up to the first bridge then branches east and continues on the path that runs north of the river, all the way to its source in the pass between Liathach and Beinn Dearg. Here the ground is boggy between the string of pools and lochans and the path is less distinct, but it becomes clear again in the upper reaches of the Coire Dubh Mor, a huge gully that separates Liathach from Beinn Eighe. A little further on, the path joins a stalkers' path which curves round Sail Mhor to the famous **Coire Mhic Fhearchair**, considered to be the most spectacular corrie in Scotland (see Beinn Eighe, below). The Coire path leads to a ford, which is crossed by stepping stones, then descends following the west side of the burn down to the car park on the Torridon road, from where it's about 4½ miles to Torridon village.

Diabaig to Red Point Walk → OS Landranger No 19.

An excellent low-level coastal walk is from Diabaig to Red Point. It is far less strenuous or daunting than the others described above and there is a clear path. It starts at the wooden gate to the right of the post office in Diabaig and ends at Red Point Farm, 7 miles away.

After 4 miles the coastal path reaches the derelict croft houses in the Craig Valley. There are two possible routes from here. You can follow the footpath above the coastline, or leave the footpath after crossing the wooden bridge over the Craig river and climb through an area of woodland. Take a reference from your OS map and you'll reach the highest point, **Meall na h-Uamha**, from where there are superb views. You can then descend to rejoin the coastal path and continue until you reach the glorious golden sands of Red Point, with wonderful views across to Skye and Raasay. Keep to the path through the farm until you reach the car park. Unless you've arranged your own transport here, you'll have to walk back the way you came, or catch the schoolbus to Gairloch, see page 260.

Beinn Eighe National Nature Reserve

While most of the Torridon massif is managed by the National Trust of Scotland, Beinn Eighe (which means 'File Peak' in Gaelic) is under the control of Scottish Natural Heritage. It is Britain's oldest National Nature Reserve, set up in 1951 to protect the ancient Caledonian pine forest west of Kinlochewe. It has since been designated an International Biosphere Reserve and extended to cover 30 square miles. The reserve is the home of a great variety of rare Highland wildlife, including pine martens, wildcats, buzzards, Scottish crossbills and golden eagles. There's also a wide range of flora which can best be appreciated on the excellent mountain trail described below which climbs from the ancient pine woods through alpine vegetation to the tundra-like upper slopes.

About half a mile northwest of Kinlochewe on the A832, is the Beinn Eighe visitor centre, which has excellent interactive audio visual displays about the flora and fauna in the reserve and sells pamphlets on the trails described below.

Beinn Eighe (3309 ft) has nine peaks and is the largest of the Torridon Mountains. To traverse its ridge is a mighty undertaking and can take two days. A much shorter and easier walk around the base of the mountain is described here. The mountain and woodland trails both start and end in the car park at the side of Loch Maree, about 2 miles beyond the visitor centre. The woodland trail heads west along the lochside then crosses the road and climbs for about a mile up to the Conservation cabin before descending back to the starting point. It should take about an hour and is easy to follow, though quite steep in parts, and you'll need a good pair of walking boots. The mountain trail is 4 miles long and rough and steep in parts. You should be well equipped with good walking boots, waterproofs, food and warm clothing. It should take three to four hours. The route is well marked with cairns and you should not stray from the path. The trail heads south from the car park and begins a gentle ascent through woodland to a boggy area and then begins to zigzag up a very steep and rugged section, climbing to over 1000 ft in less than half a mile. This is the steepest section of the trail, but the views back across Loch Maree to Slioch are fabulous. The summit of the mountain trail is **Conservation cairn** (1800 ft) from where you can see the tops of 31 Munros on a clear day and enjoy a close-up view of the impressive Beinn Eighe ridge a few miles to the south. The trail now begins to descend as it heads northwest towards **An t-Allt** (1000 ft), turns northwards down to a small enclosure, then heads east to the deep Allt na h-Airidhe gorge. From here the trail continues down to the treeline and runs through woodland to join up with the top of the Woodland Trail. Follow the path to the right to get back to the car park.

Kinlochewe and Loch Maree → *Colour map 1, C5. Phone code 01445.*

On the north side of the Torridon Mountains is the sprawling village of Kinlochewe, at the southeastern end of beautiful Loch Maree. It's a good base for walking in and around Loch Maree, and has a hotel, post office within the village shop/café and one of the area's scarce **petrol stations** ① *Apr-Oct Mon-Sat 0830-1800, Sun 0900-1700*. The loch is dotted with islands and bordered by the mass of Slioch (3215 ft) to the north and ancient Caledonian pine forest to the south. Running along its northern shore, from **Slioch** almost as far as **Poolewe**, is the remote **Letterewe Estate**, one of Scotland's great deer forests. The A832 skirts the south shore of the loch, running northwest from Kinlochewe, and passes the **Victoria Falls**, a mile or so beyond Talladale. The falls commemorate Queen Victoria's visit in 1877. To find them, look for the Hydro Power signs.

Gairloch and around → *For listings, see pages 262-267. Colour map 1, C4. Phone code 01445.*

Gairloch consists of a string of tiny crofting townships scattered around the northeastern shore of the loch of the same name. It's a beautiful place, attracting a large number of visitors who come for the many sandy beaches, excellent walks, golf and fishing, and the chance of seeing seals, porpoises, dolphins and whales in the surrounding waters.

Ins and outs

Getting there and around There are buses from Inverness three times a week, also buses to Kinlochewe and a local postbus service. From June to October a daily **Scotbus** *① T01463-224410*, leaves Inverness for Gairloch at 0800, and travels via Kinlochewe to arrive in Gairloch at 0954. The bus continues to Inverewe Garden. ▸▸ *For further details, see Transport page 266.*

Tourist information There is a **TIC** *① T01445-712130, Apr-Sep Mon-Sat 0930-1700, Sun 1100-1500, Oct Mon-Sat 1000-1600*, at the car park in Auchtercairn, where the road branches to Strath. They book accommodation and sell books and maps. There are shops and takeaways in Strath and Auchtercairn, a petrol station in Auchtercairn, and a bank near the harbour at Charleston.

Gairloch Heritage Museum

① T01445-712287, Apr-Oct Mon-Sat 1000-1700, Oct 1000-1330, £4, concessions £3, children £1. If you are interested in local history, or the weather is bad – not unknown – then this museum may entertain for a hour or so. Included are archaeological finds, a mock-up of a crofthouse room, schoolroom and shop, the interior of the local lighthouse and an archive of old photographs. It is found beside the tourist office on the A832 to Poolewe, a few yards beyond the turn-off to Strath.

Big Sand, Melvaig and Midtown

The beach by the golf course at Gairloch is nice, but the beach at Big Sand, a few miles northwest of Strath, is better, and quieter. Further north is Melvaig, from where you can walk to **Rubha Reidh Lighthouse**, see Sleeping, page 264. Around the headland from the lighthouse is the beautiful, secluded beach at **Camas Mor**. This is a good place for spotting sea birds, and there's a great walk from here on a marked footpath to Midtown, 4 miles northwest of Poolewe. You'll have to walk or hitch from here or try and catch a ride with the community ring and ride bus.

The waters around Gairloch are home to a wide variety of marine mammals such as seals, otters, porpoises, dolphins, minke whales and even killer whales. For details of wildlife cruises, see page 266.

Destitution Road

Many of the roads in the area were built during the Potato Famine of 1840 in order to give men work, with funds supplied by Dowager Lady Mackenzie of Gairloch. These became know as the 'Destitution Roads', and one of these is the narrow B8056 which runs west for 9 miles to Red Point from the junction 3 miles south of Gairloch, at Kerrysdale. This is a lovely little side trip and well worth it, especially on a clear evening to enjoy the magnificent sunsets at **Red Point beach**. The beach itself is extremely seductive, backed by steep dunes and looking across to the Trotternish Peninsula on Skye. So romantic is this spot that some people (naming no names) have been known to plight their troth here. Red Point is also the start or finish point for the excellent coastal walk to or from Diabaig, see page 257. On the road to Red Point is the picturesque little hamlet of **Badachro**, tucked away in a wooded, sheltered bay with fishing boats moored in its natural harbour. It's worth stopping off here on the way back from Red Point for a wee dram at the **Badachro Inn**.

There are many other good walks in the area, including to **Flowerdale Falls**, the **Fairy Lochs** and the **USAAF Liberator**. The TIC has a selection of walking guides and OS maps.

Poolewe → Colour map 1, B4. Phone code 01445.

Five miles east of Gairloch on the other side of the peninsula is the neat little village of Poolewe, straddling the mouth of the River Ewe, where it cascades into sheltered Loch Ewe. There are some good walks around Poolewe, including the one around Loch Kernsary described below. There's also a nice little drive up the side road running along the west shore of Loch Ewe to Cove. You can walk from Midtown, midway along the road, to Rubha Reidh, north of Gairloch (see above).

Loch Kernsary → OS Landranger Map No 19.

This straightforward but rewarding walk covers 6 miles and should take around 2½ to three hours. The track is very boggy underfoot in places, especially after rain, so you'll need good boots.

Start in Poolewe, from the car park by the school near the bridge over the Ewe. Head up the single-track road with the river on your right. Go through the gate, then the track heads away from the river and up into woodland. At the Letterewe Estate gate cross the stile and continue to the next fork. Turn left here to Kernsary Estate, with views of Loch Maree and Beinn Eighe to the south. Follow the track to the next gate, go through and cross the wooden bridge. Continue along the track and you'll see Loch Kernsary on your left. At the next fork, turn left over the bridge and pass Kernsary Cottage on the right. Beyond the cottage, go through the gate and immediately head left down towards the burn, where the ground may be boggy. There's no path here, but cross the wooden footbridge and continue straight on, past the piles of stones on your left. Cross the stile, and the path follows the length of Loch Kernsary. At the head of the loch, the path climbs to give you views down to Poolewe. Follow the path down until it eventually takes you to the main road. Turn left and follow the road back to the car park.

Inverewe Garden

ⓘ T0844-493 2225. Garden open Jan-Mar and Nov-Dec daily 1000-1500; Apr-Oct daily 1000-1600. Visitor Centre and restaurant Apr-Oct daily 1000-1600 (restaurant 1100-1600). £9, concessions £6.50, family £22

The reason most people come this way is to visit Inverewe Garden where you'll find an astonishing collection of exotic subtropical plants growing on the same latitude as Siberia, thanks to the mild climate created by the North Atlantic Drift. This wonderful 50-acre oasis of colour is a mecca for garden lovers, but even those who flinch at the mere sight of a lawn-mower will be bowled over by the sheer scale and diversity of plants and flowers on view. The garden was created from a treeless wilderness by Osgood Mackenzie, starting in 1862. By the time of his death in 1922 he had produced an internationally renowned walled and woodland garden. His work was continued by his daughter, who then gave the garden to the National Trust for Scotland in 1952. Since then, the plant collection has diversified even more and an intricate maze of paths leads you through ever-changing displays of Himalayan rhododendrons, Tasmanian eucalyptus, many Chilean and South African species, together with a large collection of New Zealand plants.

The garden is well worth visiting in any weather and at any time of the year, but especially from the end of April through the summer when the rhododendrons are in bloom. You should allow at least a couple of hours to do it justice. The garden is about a mile north of Poolewe on the main A832. There's a visitor centre and gift shop and a good restaurant, which serves snacks and hot meals.

Gruinard Bay → *Colour map 1, B5. Phone code 01445.*

North of Poolewe the A832 passes Aultbea on its way to Laide, where it then skirts the shores of Gruinard Bay, with its lovely coves of pink sand. From Laide Post Office a side road branches north to **Mellon Udrigle** and **Opinan**, both with great beaches. It's worthwhile following the signs left to the hamlet of **Mellon Charles**. Here you'll find the fabulous **Perfume Factory** ⓘ *T01445-731618, Apr-Oct daily 1000-1700 (closed on Mon), Nov-Dec Thu-Sat 1100-1600*, with its abundance of natural fragrances derived from the likes of wildflowers. There's also a very good café with lovely views over Loch Ewe. Between Laide and Mellon Udrigle, at **Achgarve**, a road branches left for about mile. From the end of this road you can walk all the way to **Slaggan**, a ruined village on the other side of the peninsula. It's a nice spot for a picnic but don't be tempted to swim in the sea as the tidal race makes it dangerous.

Gruinard Bay is a very beautiful part of the northwest coast but will always be synonymous with **Gruinard Island**, standing ominously in the middle of the bay. The island was used as a testing ground for biological warfare during the Second World War and was contaminated with anthrax spores. The Ministry of Defence finally agreed to decontaminate it in 1990 and it has now been declared 'safe'.

◉ Wester Ross listings

For Sleeping and Eating price codes and other relevant information, see Essentials pages 38-45.

● Sleeping

Loch Carron and around *p256*
B Applecross Inn, Applecross, T01520-744262, www.applecross.uk.com. 7 rooms. There are, sadly, too few authentic Highland hostelries where you could quite happily while away a few hours, or even days, but if you have to be holed up somewhere to escape the rotten weather, then this place is as good as any and better than most. Owner Judith Fish ensures you receive a warm welcome, the atmosphere is friendly and the seafood is so fresh you can almost see it swimming past as you order. Bar food served 1200-2100, children welcome until 2030,

ceilidhs on Fri evening. Sit outside in the beer garden on a summer's eve. The rooms upstairs have been refurbished to a high standard and downstairs now includes a bedroom adapted for guests with a disability. Excellent value and highly recommended.
C Rockvilla Hotel, Main St, T01520-722379, www.rockvilla-hotel.co.uk. Open all year. 4 rooms. Small, family-run hotel offering very good food (ⴌⴌ).
D Clisham Guest House, Main St, T01520-722995, www.clishamguesthouse.co.uk. Open all year. 3 en suite rooms. Friendly and comfortable accommodation, tea room out front serves home-baked cakes.
C Little Hill of my Heart, Applecross, T01520-744432. Open all year. 3 rooms. Lovely wee B&B overlooking Camursterrach Bay. Rooms tastefully furnished and

breakfasts are a bit out of the ordinary with kedgeree, smoked haddock and salmon fishcakes alongside more familiar staples.
D The Old Manse, Lochcarron, T01520-722208, www.theoldmanselochcarron. com. 5 rooms. Comfortable, old world style guesthouse with views across the loch.

Self-catering
Callakille, 8 miles north of Applecross, T01456-486358, www.wildernesscottages. co.uk. A beautifully converted 2-bedroom croft house that's tastefully furnished and an idyllic bolt-hole from the stresses of urban life. Unwind by the roaring fire and enjoy the panoramic views over the Inner Sound of Raasay. In addition to fantastic walking and wildlife spotting opportunities, there's also good trout and sea fishing in the area. From £420 per week. Highly recommended.

Camping
Applecross Campsite, 1 mile from the village, T01520-744268. Open Mar-Oct. Decent facilities, upgraded in 2006. Family friendly and lots to do, with its own café on site (see Eating, below).

Torridon and around p257
L-B The Torridon, 1 mile south of the turn-off to Torridon village, T01445-791242, www. thetorridon.com Whatever your budget, this is an excellent option. The 12 recently tastefully refurbished en suite rooms at the Inn (**B-C**) form part of this fairytale Gothic pile on the lochside. There's also the Boathouse self-catering option with it own private jetty and beautifully appointed bedrooms (£820 per week). However, it's the dining experience for which The Torridon is renowned (♯♯♯-♯♯), with the option to fine dine on the freshest locally sourced seafood and game.
A The Old Mill Highland Lodge, on Loch Maree at Talladale, halfway between Kinlochewe and Gairloch, T01445-760271, www.theoldmillhighlandlodge.co.uk. Open Mar-Oct. 6 rooms. The best accommodation

around here, this converted mill is set in its own gardens. It's friendly and comfortable, offers great food (price includes dinner), seclusion and views.
A Tigh-an-Eilean Hotel, Shieldaig, Loch Torridon, T01520-755251. End Mar-Nov. 11 rooms. Great wee, upmarket hotel overlooking the loch, so views are wonderful. Terrific food in the restaurant and also occasional impromptu bursts of folk music. Recommended.
C-D Kinlochewe Hotel, Kinlochewe, T01445-760253, www.kinlochewehotel. co.uk. Open all year. 9 rooms. Offers B&B as well as 12 cheaper (£10 per person per night) bunkhouse beds and cheap bar meals.
C Ferroch, Achnasheen, T01445-791451. Open all year. 3 en suite rooms. Superior B&B in former crofthouse. Beautiful location, (**B** including dinner).
D Hillhaven B&B, Hillhaven, Kinlochewe, T01445-760204, www.kinlochewe.info. Open all year. 3 en suite rooms. Good-value B&B catering for walkers and cyclists.
D The Rivendell Guesthouse, Shieldaig, T01520-755250, A relative newcomer to the scene, close to the **Tigh an Eilean Hotel** and with views across to Shieldaig Island.
F SYHA hostel, on the easternmost fringe of Torridon village, T01445-791284. This 44 bed hostel is ideal for exploring the surrounding Torridon hills. It's about a 20-25 min walk from here to the **Torridon Inn** and a well earned pint. Note that at the time of writing, the village store remains closed, a sad reflection perhaps of the areas increasing number of absent landlords – an issue that also affects the likes of Ardnamurchan further south.

Camping
There is a basic campsite at **Taangan Farm**, at the head of Loch Maree.

Gairloch and around p260
There are numerous B&Bs scattered through-out the area. Most of the owners will provide maps and information on local walks.

L Pool House Hotel, Poolewe, T01445-781272, www.poolhouse.co.uk. Open all year. 7 en suite rooms, all with Royal Navy names reflecting the former use of the house as the Royal Naval headquarters for directing Second World War North Atlantic convoys. On the Cove Rd by the lochside, this former home of Osgood Mackenzie (who designed the nearby gardens) has been transformed into one of the very best hotels in the country (witness the numerous awards and accolades on their website). A stay here does not come cheap, but if you've got the money then look no further, for there is, quite simply, no better place to stay in this category. The dishes created by chef Daniel Hall on the **North by Northwest** dining room are worthy of such luxurious surroundings (¶¶¶). Very highly recommended.

B-C The Creel Restaurant & Charleston House, Gairloch, T01445-712497. Open Mar-Dec. 4 en suite rooms. Guesthouse/restaurant with a reputation for high-quality food (¶¶), especially local seafood. Also delicious home-made bread and ice cream. **A-B** including dinner.

B-C The Old Inn, Gairloch, T01445-712068, www.theoldinn.net. Open all year. 17 rooms. This venerable old pub/restaurant with rooms is constantly winning awards for its fine ales and superb seafood (¶¶). Located by the harbour, it makes an excellent base for exploring the area and staying here gives the advantage of not having to move far after enjoying the best pint of real ale for miles around. Recommended for those who don't turn in too early.

C Myrtle Bank Hotel, Gairloch, T01445-712004, www.myrtlebankhotel.co.uk. 12 rooms. Modern hotel in the centre of Gairloch overlooking the loch, very good food and service in the restaurant (¶¶¶-¶¶).

C-D Old Smiddy Guest House, in Laide, near Gruinard Bay, T01445-731696, www.oldsmiddy.co.uk. Mar-Oct. 3 rooms. Superior guesthouse in great location, with lavish breakfasts and an excellent restaurant (¶¶¶

for 4-course dinner, BYOB), which is open to non-residents, but book well in advance. Highly recommended.

D Burnside B&B, 48 Mellon Charles, 3 miles west of Aultbea, T01445-731270. This small, 3-bedroom guesthouse is a real gem. Very welcoming host with a fund of stories, large breakfast and lovely views. Recommended.

D Dry Island, Badachro, T01445-741263. Open all year. 1 en suite room, 2-night minimum stay May-Sep. Here's a chance to stay in a B&B on a private island, accessed from the mainland by a floating bridge or on foot at low tide. Beautiful surroundings and all the peace and tranquility you can handle. Also nice touches such as dressing gowns and slippers. For couples there's the chance to get away from it all by hiring the Old Curing Station (built 1785), from £200 per week.

C Gairloch View Guest House, Auchtercairn, Gairloch, T01445-712666, www.gairlochview. com. A pleasant 2-bedroom option close to all amenities.

D Kerrysdale House, Gairloch, T01445-712292, www.kerrysdalehouse.co.uk. Open all year. 3 rooms. Charming B&B in a building that dates back to 1793, with the added benefit of a garden to enjoy in summer.

D-F Rubha Reidh Lighthouse, 11 miles north of Gairloch, at the end of the road, T/F01445-771263, www.ruareidh.co.uk. Open all year. This comfortable B&B and hostel has 5 double, twin or family rooms (4 are en suite) and 2 dorms with 4-6 beds (**F** per person). Rooms are fairly plain but it's the wonderful setting you're paying for, and the history (it was built in 1910 by RL Stevenson's cousin). Breakfast is £6 extra and dinner is £13.50 and served at 1900. It's essential to book well ahead in the high season. The whole lighthouse can also be rented on a self-catering basis for parties of 20+ (£1100 for 3 nights in high season). To get here without your own transport, try cycling, hiking or give the Westerbus community bus service (T01445-712255) a call in advance and expect to pay around £2.50 for the journey.

E Duisary, Gairloch, T01445-712252, www.
duisary.freeserve.co.uk. Apr-Oct. 3 rooms.
Cosy B&B run by Isabel Mackenzie. This
modernized crofthouse is on the road that
turns off to the right by the **Millcroft Hotel**,
beyond the fire station.

E Mrs A MacIver, Charleston, by the
harbour, T01445-712388. Mar-Nov.
3 en suite rooms. Friendly, comfortable B&B.

E Stratford House, Strath, Gairloch, T01445-
712183, www.stratfordhouse.btinternet.
co.uk A very welcoming 2-bedroom option
that also offers the chance to enjoy some
lovely home-baking in the lounge.

F Carn Dearg Youth Hostel, 3 miles
beyond Gairloch, on the road to Melvaig,
T01445-712219. Open 15 May-3 Oct.

F Sail Mhor Croft Independent Hostel,
south of Ullapool in Camusnagaul by
Dundonnell, T01854-633224, www.sailmhor.
co.uk. 16 beds, clean and cosy. Try and call
ahead to say you're coming.

Camping

Badrallach Bothy & Camp Site, near
Gruinard Bay, T01445-633281, www.
badrallach.com This campsite is situated in
the tiny, remote hamlet of Badrallach. A few
miles east of Dundonnell, take a side road
which branches left and runs for 7 miles.
The bothy (it's a lovely backpackers) has
a peat fire and 12 beds.

Camping and Caravan Club Site, between
Poolewe Village and Inverewe Garden,
T01445-781249. An excellent site.

Gairloch Caravan & Camping Park, Strath,
T01445-712373. With full facilities and close
to all amenities.

Gruinard Bay Caravan Park, in Laide near
Gruinard Bay, T01445-731225. Open Apr-Oct.

Big Sands Holiday Centre, Big Sand, about
a mile beyond Strath, T01445-712152.
Open Easter-Oct. Fabulous facilities and
truly gobsmacking views.

🍴 Eating

Loch Carron and around *p256*

♥♥♥-♥♥ Walled Garden Restaurant,
Applecross, T01520-744440. Open Mar-Nov.
This rustic option prides itself on locally
sourced produce, including the use of
vegetables grown and picked from the
garden. It's quite an informal place to eat
but the food is exquisite. Definitely worth
booking ahead at weekends.

♥♥ Applecross Inn, see Sleeping, above.
The food here is fantastic, with starters that
can include seafood chowder and locally
collected oysters. For mains there's the likes
of locally reared venison and Applecross
Bay prawns.

♥♥ Carron Restaurant, about 5 mins' drive
from the village, across the loch on the A890,
T01520-722488. Open Apr-Nov Mon-Sat
1030-2100. An excellent option.

♥♥-♥ Kishorn Seafood Bar, on the road
to Lochcarron from Applecross, after the
Bealach na Ba Pass, T01520-733240. Open
Apr-Oct. This oasis of culinary excellence
must not be missed. The seafood is very
fresh and at around £4 for half a dozen
Queen Scallops (you read that correctly)
is there anywhere in the UK offering such
amazing value? More standard fare also on
offer for those unfortunate souls who can't
eat seafood. Highly recommended.

♥ Flower Tunnel, at Applecross campsite
(see Sleeping, above). Mar-Nov daily from
0900, meals from 1200. Serves pizza, steak
pie, fish and chips, etc, in a large flower-filled
plastic tunnel.

Gairloch and around *p260*

Hotels are often the best options for eating
out, see Sleeping, above. Of particular note
are the **Old Inn**, the **Creel Restaurant** and
the **Myrtle Bank Hotel**.

♥♥♥-♥♥ Badachro Inn, Badachro, T01445-
741255, www.badachroinn.com. Good food
in this handily placed hotel on the road to
Red Point. Nice views from the dining room

and beloved by the yachtie fraternity.
A great place for a pint and seafood.
ŸŸ-Ÿ Blueprint Café, on main road through
Gairloch, opposite **Mountain Lodge**, T01445-
712397. Open Mar-Nov until 1600 for lunch
and snacks and later for dinner. Food is fairly
standard but good value nonetheless.
ŸŸ-Ÿ Inverewe Garden, Poolewe, T01445-
781200. Mar-May and Sep daily 1000-1700,
May-Aug daily 1000-17.30, Oct daily
1000-1600. The best place to eat cheaply
around Poolewe.
ŸŸ-Ÿ Melvaig Inn, Melvich, on road north
of Gairloch towards lighthouse, T01445-
771212, www.melvaig-inn.co.uk. Open all
year 1200-2300. This café-bar/restaurant
leans heavily towards meat and chicken
though there's also local seafood. All mains
are under a tenner, so very good value and
there are lovely comfy sofas to enjoy the
views over the sea. In truth, with the pool
table and juke box, it's more the sort of place
you'd expect to find in a city centre – not
amidst the splendid solitude of Rua Reidh.
ŸŸ-Ÿ Mountain Lodge, Strath Sq, Gairloch,
T01445-712316. Open Mar-Nov until 1800,
later in Jul-Aug. Good veggie options in this
very friendly restaurant with outside terrace
overlooking Gair Loch and mountains
beyond. It is run by mountaineers and also
has an adjacent bookshop. Little pricey for
its home-baking but can't deny the views
are fantastic.

⊙ Activities and tours

Torridon and around *p257*
Climbing and hillwalking
For those who are not experienced
hillwalkers, there's a Ranger Service for
visitors. Jul-Aug the ranger takes guided
walks up into the mountains 3 times a
week. For more details, call T01445-791221.
Island Horizons, Kirkton Rd, T01520-722238.
For guided walks around Lochcarron.
Martin Moran, T01520-722361.
A recommended local mountain guide.

Quad biking
Highland Trails, book at The Anchorage
post office/craft shop at the harbour
or at Flowerdale Estate office, T01445-
712378. Quad bike tour of the Flowerdale
Deer Forest

Gairloch and around *p260*
Fishing
For information on sea-angling trips,
contact the chandlery shop at the
harbour, T01445- 712458.

Wildlife cruises
Gairloch Marine Wildlife Centre, by the
pier, T01445-712636. You can take excellent
wildlife-spotting boat trips aboard, *MV
Starquest* that leaves from the Charleston
Pier, Mar-Oct, book at the recently revamped
Wildlife Centre. 2-hr cruise, 1000, 1230 and
1500, £20 (subject to weather conditions).
You may spot minke whales, seals, porpoise
and even killer whales as you explore
the coastline.

⊙ Transport

Loch Carron and around *p256*
Bus There's a postbus service to **Shieldaig**
from **Kishorn** and **Lochcarron**, Mon-Sat.
It's possible to leave **Applecross** by public
transport, but only just. A postbus service
leaves **Applecross** at 0920 to arrive in
Shieldaig at 1015.
  Another option is to catch the Skyeways
(No WR87) from **Applecross** post office
(Wed and Sat, 0800; call to request on
T01599-555477) to arrive in **Shieldaig** at
0900, **Lochcarron** at 0930 and **Achnasheen**
station at 1015. If you stay on the bus
you'll reach **Inverness** by 1125.
Train Don't forget you can also use the
railway to leave the region by catching the
train from Lochcarron (Mon-Sat).

Torridon and around *p257*
Bus A postbus journey leaves **Shieldaig**
at 1025 and arrives in **Torridon** at 1045

(Mon-Sat only). A postbus service leaves **Shieldaig** for **Applecross**.

For buses between **Gairloch** and **Shieldaig**, **Lochcarron Garage** (No 705) run a service on schooldays that leaves **Shieldaig** at 1400, reaches **Torridon** at 1415, **Kinlochewe** post office at 1435 and **Gairloch** at 1515.

Gairloch and around *p260*
Bus From Jun-Oct there's a daily bus to **Inverness** with Scotbus, T01463-224410. The bus leaves **Inverewe** daily at 1020, 1430 and 1750 respectively, with the first 2 buses

terminating at **Achnasheen station** in time to connect with the FirstScotRail train from **Inverness** to **Kyle of Lochalsh**.

Westerbus, T01445-712255, also run a service from **Gairloch** (0745) to **Inverness** (1025), Mon, Wed and Sat via **Mellon Charles/Aultbea** (0820), **Laide** (0835), **Dundonnell** (0850), **Braemore Junction** (for connections to **Ullapool**), and **Strathpeffer** (0952). The same bus company also run a service, Tue, Thu and Fri, between **Laide** (0745) and **Inverness** (1025) with stops including **Poolewe** (0805) and **Loch Maree**.

Ullapool and around

The attractive little fishing port of Ullapool, on the shores of Loch Broom, is the largest settlement in Wester Ross. The grid-pattern village, created in 1788 at the height of the herring boom by the British Fisheries Society, is still an important fishing centre as well as being the major tourist centre in the northwest of Scotland and one of the main ferry terminals for the Outer Hebrides. At the height of the busy summer season the town is swamped by visitors passing through on their way to or from Stornoway on Lewis, heading north into the wilds, or south to Inverness. It has excellent tourist amenities and services, and relatively good transport links, making it the ideal base for those exploring the northwest coast and a good place to be if the weather is bad.

North of Ullapool you enter a different world. The landscape becomes ever more dramatic and unreal – a huge emptiness of bleak moorland punctuated by isolated peaks and shimmering lochs. A narrow and tortuously twisting road winds its way up the coast, past deserted beaches of sparkling white sand washed by turquoise seas. There's not much tourist traffic this far north and once you get off the main A835 and on to the backroads, you can enjoy the wonderful sensation of having all this astonishingly beautiful scenery to yourself. ▶▶ *For listings, see pages 275-280.*

Ins and outs

Getting there and around

Ullapool is the mainland terminal for ferries to Stornoway (Lewis). **Scottish Citylink** ① *T08705-505050*, buses from Inverness (twice daily Monday to Saturday, just under 1½ hours, £13.10 return) connect with the ferry to Stornoway. The local **CalMac office** ① *Shore St, opposite the pier, T01854-612358*, also has details. There are buses to places further north, and south along the coast, they stop at the pier near the ferry dock. Monday to Friday the first bus from Ullapool to Achiltibuie leaves at 1040 and if requested by the passenger will stop in Reiff and Altandhu (1130) before continuing to Achiltibuie and Badenscallie. There's a **Tim Dearman Coach** ① *T01349-883585*, service once a day Monday to Saturday (April to the end of September) from Inverness bus station via Ullapool, Lochinver and Kylesku to Scourie. ▶▶ *For further details, see Transport page 280.*

Tourist information

The **TIC** ① *6 Argyle St, T01854-612135, Easter-Oct daily, Nov-Easter Mon-Fri 1300-1630*, is well run, helpful and provides an accommodation booking service as well as information on local walks and trips. It also has a good stock of books and maps. To find out what's on, tune in to Loch Broom FM (102.2 and 96.8) or pick up a copy of the *Ullapool News* on Fridays.

Ullapool → *For listings, see pages 275-280. Colour map 1, B5. Phone code 01854. Population 1800.*

Ullapool's attractions are very much of the outdoor variety and include the Falls of Measach, Achiltibuie and Stac Pollaidh. However, whilst in town it's worth taking a stroll around the harbour to watch the comings and goings of the fishing fleet, and you might even see the occasional seal or otter swimming close to the shore. The only real 'sight' as such is the **Ullapool Museum and Visitor Centre** ① *T01854-612987, www.ullapoolmuseum.co.uk, Apr-Oct Mon-Sat 1000-1700, Nov-Mar by prior arrangement only, £3, concessions £2, children 50p,* in a converted church in West Argyle Street. It has some interesting displays on local history, including the story of those who set sail from here in 1773 on board *The Hector*, the first ship to carry emigrants from the Highlands to Nova Scotia in Canada.

Walks → *All routes are covered by OS Maps Nos 15, 19 and 20.*

There are several good walking trails which start in Ullapool. One of these is to the top of **Ullapool Hill**, or **Meall Mhor** (886 ft). Starting from the tourist office, head to the end of Argyle Street, turn left on to North Road. Walk down the lane between Broom Court and the Hydro sub-station and then follow the path which zigzags up the hillside. There's a good cairned path up to the top of the hill. The views from the top over Glen Achall, and on a clear

Ullapool

To Daley's Deals Car Hire

To Rhue Lighthouse

To Stornoway

To Ullapool Hill

Highland Stoneware

Morefield Pl
Morefield Cres
Kanachrine Pl
Old Moss Rd
Broom Hill
Moss Rd
North Rd

Ullapool

Castle Terr
Riverside Terr
Fraser Ct

St Valery Place
Leisure Centre Swimming Pool
Ladysmith
Custom House St

West Terr
Latheron La
Quay St
Market St
Pulteney St
Mill St
Royal Pk
Garve Rd A835

Ullapool Museum & Visitor Centre
Seaforth Rd
Argyle St
Captain's Shore Cabin
Jetty

West Argyle St
Mountain Man Supplies
West La
West Shore St

Pier

Loch Broom

N

200 metres
200 yards

Sleeping
Broomfield Holiday Park **1**
Ceilidh Place **2**
Dromnan Guest House **3**
Ferry Boat Inn **4**
Harbour Lights **5**
Point Cottage Guest House **6**
Shieling Guest House **7**

SYHA Youth Hostel **8**
Tanglewood House **9**
Ullapool Tourist Hostel **10**

Eating
Frigate **1**
Mariner's at Morefield
Hotel **2**

Seaforth Inn **3**
Tea Store **4**

Bars & clubs
Arch Inn **5**

day, the mountains of Sutherland, are superb. You can return by traversing the hillside to the top of the Braes, or take a track leading to Loch Achall and follow the Ullapool river through the quarry road back to the village. The return trip takes one to two hours.

A relatively easy, but much longer walk, of five to six hours, is to **Rhidorroch Estate**. Take the A835 north out of Ullapool. Opposite the petrol station and before the bridge, take the road on the right signed 'Quarry'. Go through the quarry keeping to the left, and follow the Ullapool river until you see Loch Achall. Continue along the north bank of the loch for another 6 miles. East Rhidorroch Lodge is on the right; cross the bridge to get there, then skirt the lodge fences and cross to the track which leads up the southwestern hill. This brings you out to Leckmelm, about 4 miles south of Ullapool on the A835. This last section offers wonderful views across Loch Broom to An Teallach. From Leckmelm you can also climb **Beinn Eilideach** (1837 ft).

A good coastal walk is to **Rhue Lighthouse** and back. From the north end of Quay Street go down the steps to the river. Cross the bridges and head left by the football field. Follow the path to the left by the duck pond and cross in front of the bungalow. Then follow the shoreline north for about 2 miles, climbing up the hillside when the tide is high. Follow the path until you reach the little white lighthouse at Rhue Point. To return, take the single-track road out of Rhue back to the main road and up over the hill to Ullapool. It's about 6 miles in total.

There are many more strenuous hiking routes around Ullapool. The A835 south of town gives access to **Beinn Dearg** (3556 ft) and the **Fannichs**, a range of hills on the southern side of Dirrie More. There's also **An Teallach**, a favourite with Scottish climbers, see page 270. North of Ullapool are the mountains within the Inverpolly National Nature Reserve (see below).

All routes require hillwalking experience and you should be well prepared for the unpredictable weather conditions. A good guidebook is *The Northern Highlands, SMC District Guide*, by Tom Strang. ▸▸ *For details of tour operators offering trips, see Activities and tours, page 279.*

South of Ullapool → *For listings, see pages 275-280. Colour map 1, B5.*

On the southern shore of Little Loch Broom is the village of **Dundonnell**, from where there are spectacular views of awesome **An Teallach** (3483 ft), a mountain of almost mythical status amongst Scottish climbers and spoken of in hushed, reverential tones. The path to the highest of its summits is clear and begins southeast of the **Dundonnell Hotel**. It will take a full day and you'll need to be well prepared (OS map No 19) and heed the usual advice.

The A832 coastal road meets the A835 Ullapool to Inverness main road at Braemore junction, 12 miles south of Ullapool. Before heading on to Ullapool it's worth stopping at the very impressive **Falls of Measach**, just by the junction. The falls plunge 150 ft into the spectacular **Corrieshalloch Gorge** (or 'ugly/fearsome gorge' in Gaelic) and can be crossed by a distinctly wobbly suspension bridge (not for vertigo sufferers). The falls can be reached from the A835, but the most dramatic approach is from the A832 Gairloch road.

North of Ullapool → *For listings, see pages 275-280. Colour map 1, A5/B5-6.*

The region immediately north of Ullapool is called Assynt, and is heaven for serious hillwalkers and climbers. Though most are not Munros, they offer a stiff climb. The views from the summits are truly breathtaking, including across to Skye but it's vital you dress for the mountains and prepare for harsh weather conditions that can materialize at a moments notice from the Atlantic. Amongst the most spectacular of Assynt's distinctive 'island peaks' are **Suilven** (2398 ft), **Ben More Assynt** (3275 ft), **Quinag** (2650 ft) and **Canisp** (2775 ft). Much of this region is protected in the Inverpolly and Inchnadamph National Nature Reserves, home to an extremely rich and diverse wildlife.

Inverpolly National Nature Reserve → *Phone code 01854. OS Landranger No 15.*

About 12 miles north of Ullapool on the main A835 is the exceptional **SNH Visitor Centre** ① *T01854-666234, open all year 24 hrs a day*, at Knockan Crag. It's an interactive display of the geology, flora and fauna of an area that marks some of the world's oldest geological rock formations (www.northwest-highlands-geopark.org.uk). From the visitor centre there's a marked trail which leads up to the **Crag**, and the views from the clifftop are excellent, across to Inverpolly's 'island' peaks of Cul Mór, Cul Beag and Stac Pollaidh.

A few miles north of here is the village of **Knockan**. Nearby, at **Elphin**, is the **Highland and Rare Breeds Farm** ① *mid-May to Sep daily 1000-1700*. Elphin has a great tea room offering fabulous home-baking, it's on the left as you drive towards Ullapool. Beyond Elphin is **Ledmore**, where the A837 branches east towards Lairg and Bonar Bridge. There's a good craft shop at Ledmore where you can buy hand-knitted jumpers.

Between Ullapool and Knockan Crag is the turn-off west (left) to the distinctive craggy peak of **Stac Pollaidh**. A path has been established by the John Muir Trust, which takes you on a circular walk around the peak from the car park. Take the right-hand path and go round at the same level, or climb up the rear to the top, go around the summit and descend by the same path. You'll need a head for heights to reach the summit, as much of the route is exposed, but the stunning views are worth it. Be careful not to stray from the path; it's been put there because of the damage inflicted by tens of thousands of pairs of boots each year, resulting in serious erosion on the south face. It's a fairly easy 2½-hour walk.

Achiltibuie → *Phone code 01854.*

The unclassified single-track road winds its way west past Stac Pollaidh to the turn-off for Achiltibuie. This old crofting village, with whitewashed cottages set back from the sea with views across to the beautiful Summer Isles, is home to a small grocers, post office (excellent for checking out the latest community events on the go) and one of the northwest's best dining options and hotels, the **Summer Isles Hotel**. Look directly south from here and you'll clearly spot the low lying Summer Isles over a mile offshore and a popular destination for experienced sea kayakers.

Another worthwhile attraction is the **Smokehouse** ① *T01854-622353, www.summerisles foods.co.uk, May-Sep Mon-Sat 0930-1700, free*, at Altandhu, 5 miles north of Achiltibuie. Here you can watch the salmon, herring, trout and other fish being cured before buying some afterwards. Close by is the good value **Am Fuaran Bar** ① *Altandhu, T01854-622339*, where you can get a a sandwich, an evening meal or just a pint and game of pool. A few miles further down the road in Polbain, is the **Coigach Craft and Gift Shop** ① *T01854-622346*, a good place for a cuppa and the chance to buy some local crafts or a fishing permit.

Lochinver and around → *Phone code 01571.*

The road from Achiltibuie north to Lochinver is known locally as the 'wee mad road', and you'd be mad to miss this thrilling route which twists and winds its way through some the northwest's most stunning scenery. A mile south of the village is the magnificent **Achins Bookshop**, a friendly place packed with second-hand books. The village of Lochinver is a working fishing port and the last sizeable village before Thurso. It has a good tourist office, lots of accommodation, a bank with ATM, post office, petrol station and several good eating options. Pick up fishing permits at the post office or Assynt Visitor Centre.

The best place to start is the Assynt Visitor Centre ① *T01854-844654, Apr-Oct Mon-Fri 1000-1700, Sun 1000-1600*, which houses the TIC. It has displays on the local geology, history and wildlife and there's also a ranger service with guided walks throughout the summer. Those looking for high quality hand-crafted, earthenware gifts should head for **Highland Stoneware**, see page 279.

A few miles south of Lochinver, beyond Inverkirkaig, is the trail along the river to the **Kirkaig Falls**. The path starts near the Achins Bookshop. Follow the path for about 2 miles until it branches right to the falls in the gorge below. Continue along the main path for about another ¾ mile until you reach Fionn Loch, with superb views of mighty Suilven. The walk up to the falls and back should take around 1½ hours. This is one of the main approaches to the foot of the mountain.

Loch Assynt and Inchnadamph → *Phone code 01571.*

The area east of Lochinver is a remote wilderness of mountains and moorland dotted with lochs and lochans. As well as being a favourite haunt of hardy climbers and walkers (ask at the Lochinver TIC for the leaflet about local walks), Assynt is a paradise for anglers. Most of the lochs are teeming with brown trout, and fishing permits are readily available throughout the area from the TIC in Lochinver or at local hotels, guesthouses and B&Bs. There's also salmon fishing on the River Kirkaig, available through the **Inver Lodge Hotel** and on Loch Assynt through the **Inchnadamph Lodge**, see Sleeping, page 275.

The A837 Lochinver to Lairg road meets the A894 to Durness 10 miles east of Lochinver at Skiag Bridge by Loch Assynt. Half a mile south of here, by the loch, are the ruins of **Ardvreck Castle**. The castle dates from 1597 and was the stronghold of the Macleods of Assynt until a siege in 1691, when it was taken by the Seaforth Mackenzies. Before that, the Marquess of Montrose had been imprisoned here following his defeat at Carbisdale in 1650. Access to the castle is free, but the ruins are in a dangerous state and should be approached with care.

To the east of the road lies the **Inchnadamph National Nature Reserve**, dominated by the massive peaks of Ben More Assynt and Conival, which should only be attempted by experienced hillwalkers. A few miles south of the village of Inchnadamph, at the fish farm, is a steep, but well-marked footpath up to the **Bone Caves**. This is one of Scotland's oldest historical sites, where the bones of humans and animals such as lynx and bear were found together with sawn-off deer antlers dating from over 8000 years ago.

Lochinver to Kylesku → *Phone code 01571.*

The quickest way north from Lochinver is the A837 east to the junction with the A894 which heads to Kylesku. But by far the most scenic route is the B869 coast road that passes moorland, lochs and beautiful sandy bays. It's best travelled from north to south, giving you the most fantastic views of the whale-backed hump of **Suilven**, rocky talisman of the great poet, Norman MacCaig. Untypically, most of the land in this part of Assynt is owned by local crofters who, under the aegis of the Assynt Crofters' Trust, bought 21,000 acres of the North Assynt Estate, thus setting a precedent for change in the history of land ownership in the Highlands.

The trust now owns the fishing rights to the area and sells permits through local post offices and the tourist office in Lochinver. It has also undertaken a number of conservation projects, including one at **Achmelvich**, a few miles north of Lochinver, at the end of a side road which branches off the coast road. It's worth a detour to see one of the loveliest beaches on the west coast, with sparkling white sand and clear turquoise waters straight out of a Caribbean tourist brochure. A terrific place for a family picnic. There's a great youth hostel here, though the caravan site jars with the beauty of the surrounding landscape.

From the beach car park below the hostel a path leads northwest along the coast. Bear left off the sandy path shortly after the white cottage on the hill ahead comes into view, and follow the footpath until the road is reached at Alltan na Bradhan, where there are the remains of an old meal mill. Continue north from here along the coast for about a mile until you reach a small bay just before Clachtoll and its **campsite** ① *T01575-855373, www.clachtollbeachcampsite.co.uk*, the **Split Rock**. Close by are the remains of an Iron Age broch, but don't cause further damage by clambering over the ruins. Return to the beach by the same path. The walk there and back should take about 1½ hours.

Old Man of Stoer
① *Check access locally during the deer-stalking season which runs from mid-Aug to mid-Oct.* A side road turns left off the B869 north of Stoer and runs out to **Stoer lighthouse**. From here you can walk across the Stoer Peninsula to the **Old Man of Stoer**, a dramatic rock pillar standing offshore, surrounded by sheer cliffs. Allow about three hours for the circular walk which starts and ends in the lighthouse car park. There is no public transport to the lighthouse, but the Lochinver to Drumbeg postbus runs to Raffin, 1 mile away. A clear path runs from the car park to the cliffs then follows the line of the cliffs northwards. The path heads inland for a short distance as it bypasses a deep gully then meets the clifftop again, and after a mile or so you can see the Old Man tucked away in a shallow bay, battered by huge waves. Beyond the Old Man the path continues to the head- land, the **Point of Stoer**, from where it turns back on itself and climbs **Sidhean Mór** (532 ft). The views from here are fantastic, across to Harris and Lewis and south to the mountains of Assynt. From here, follow the faint path south, back towards the lighthouse, passing a small loch below Sidhean Beag on your left and an obvious cairn on your right. Then you pass a radio mast and follow the clear track back to the lighthouse car park. OS Landranger Map No 15 covers the route. Nine miles further on, in beautiful **Eddrachillis Bay**, is **Drumbeg**, a popular place for anglers who come to fish in the many lochs of North Assynt.

Kylesku → *Colour map 1, B5. Phone code 01971.*
The road runs east from Drumbeg, under the shadow of towering **Quinag** (2654 ft), to meet the A894 heading north to Kylesku, site of the sweeping modern road bridge over Loch a'Cháirn Bháin. From Kylesku you can visit Britain's highest waterfall, the 650-ft high **Eas a'Chùal Aluinn**, near the head of Loch Glencoul. Cruises leave from the old ferry jetty below the **Kylesku Hotel** to the falls, see Activities and tours, page 280.

There's also a trail to the top of the falls. It starts at the south end of Loch na Gainmhich, about 3 miles north of Skiag Bridge. Skirting the loch, follow the track in a southeasterly direction up to the head of the Bealach a Bhuirich (the Roaring Pass). Continue until you meet a stream, with several small lochans on your right. Follow this stream until it plunges over the Cliffs of Dubh (the Dark Cliffs). You can get a better view of the falls by walking to the right about 100 yds and descending a heather slope for a short distance. Allow about three to four hours for the round trip.

Scourie and Handa Island → Colour map 1, A5. Phone code 01971.

Ten miles north of Kylesku is the little crofting community of Scourie, sitting above a sandy bay. Anyone remotely interested in wildlife is strongly advised to make a stop here to visit Handa Island, a sea bird reserve run by the Scottish Wildlife Trust, and one of the best places in the country for bird life. The island is now deserted, except for the warden, but once supported a thriving community of crofters, until the potato famine of 1846 forced them to leave, most emigrating to Canada's Cape Breton. Now it's home to huge colonies of shags, fulmars, razorbills, guillemots and puffins, in season. The best time to visit is during the summer breeding season, from late May to August. There's a footpath right round the island, which is detailed in the free SWT leaflet available at the warden's office when you arrive. You should allow three to four hours. There's a **ferry service** ① T01971-502077, Mon-Sat 0930-1700, £10 return, children £5, to the island from Tarbet Beach, 3 miles northwest off the A894, about 2 miles north of Scourie. It sails continuously, depending on demand, from April to September, and the crossing takes 15 minutes. It's no longer possible to take the postbus from Scourie to the jetty for Handa Island so you'll need to walk, cycle, drive or take a taxi. It's worth it though. There is also an excellent wildlife boat trip that leaves from Fanagmore, a mile from Tarbet on the other side of the peninsula. ▶▶ For further information, see Activities and tours, page 280.

Kinlochbervie and around → Colour map 1, A5. Phone code 01971.

The road north from Scourie passes Laxford Bridge, where it meets the A838 running southeast to Lairg, see page 293. The A838 also runs north to Durness, on the north coast (see page 281). At Rhiconich, the B801 branches northwest to Kinlochbervie, a small village with a very big fish market. This is one of the west coast's major fishing ports, and huge container lorries thunder along the narrow single-track roads carrying frozen fish and seafood to all corners of Europe. Right by the quayside is the no frills Fisherman's Mission that serves hearty, cheap meals – if they let you in!

A few miles beyond Kinlochbervie is **Oldshoremore**, a tiny crofters' village scattered around a stunning white beach, and a great place to swim. The less hardy can instead explore the hidden rocky coves nearby.

At the end of the road is **Blairmore**, from where a footpath leads to **Sandwood Bay**, one of the west coast's most wonderful beaches and on protected land managed by the John Muir Trust conservation charity. It's a 4-mile walk in each direction but because of its isolation you'll probably have this glorious mile-long stretch of white sand all to yourself. At one end is a spectacular rock pinnacle and it is said to be haunted by the ghost of an ancient shipwrecked mariner. Allow three hours for the walk there and back, plus time at the beach. Romantic souls may wish to take a tent and watch the sunset with a loved one and a bottle of their favourite single malt. Sandwood Bay can also be reached from Cape Wrath, a hard, long day's hike to the north, see page 274.

For Sleeping and Eating price codes and other relevant information, see Essentials pages 38-45.

◉ Sleeping

Ullapool *p268, map p269*

There is no shortage of places to stay in and around Ullapool, ranging from one of the very finest hotels in the UK to guesthouses and B&Bs, a couple of good youth hostels and a campsite. Garve Rd, heading south out of town, has several guesthouses, and there are lots of B&Bs along Seaforth Rd and Pulteney St. Unfortunately the famous **Altnaharrie Inn** has closed, though the ferry from Ullapool to the other side of Loch Broom is running; for details T01854-612656.

B The Ceilidh Place, 14 West Argyle Pl, T01854-612103, www.theceilidhplace.com. 13 rooms and each named after a 'famous' visitor who has recommended books to be read – and which are left in each of the different, tastefully furnished rooms. Let's face it, this former boat shed that grew from the inspirations of one man is not one of your run of the mill hotels. It's different and refreshingly so, with a cosy lounge, bookshop, restaurant, bar and café. It also hosts a varied programme of arts events such as live music, plays, poetry readings, exhibitions and ceilidhs. It's a great place to relax and soak up some local culture. Recommended.

B Tanglewood House, T01854-612059, www.tanglewoodhouse.co.uk. Open all year. 3 en suite rooms. Chalet-style house in stunning location overlooking Loch Broom, with its own private beach. Part of the **Wolsey Lodge** scheme, so you dine with the hostess, Anne Holloway, who offers superb cooking (4-course dinner £33) in a civilized atmosphere. All rooms have their own balcony and wonderful views across the loch. Highly recommended.

C The Shieling Guest House, Garve Rd, T01854-612947. 6 rooms. Purpose built, charming house on the edge of Ullapool and set within an acre of it own grounds with views over the loch and mountains. Even has its own sauna.

C-D Harbour Lights Hotel, Garve Rd, on the left, heading into Ullapool on the A835, T01854-612222, www.harbour-lights.co.uk. Open Mar-Oct. 22 rooms. Modern hotel offering good service with comfortable rooms.

D Braemore Square Country House, Braemore, T01845-655357, www.braemore square.com. Open all year. 3 rooms. 11 miles south of Ullapool and set in 46 acres of grounds is the former estate house of Victorian engineer Sir John Fowler, who designed the Forth Rail Bridge. B&B, with comfortable and tastefully furnished rooms, all in splendid isolation. Guests have use of the kitchen. Self-catering also available (£390 per week in summer). Recommended.

D Dromnan Guest House, Garve Rd, T01854-612333. Open all year. 7 rooms. Very pleasant and friendly guesthouse that also offers free access to the local swimming pool.

D Ferry Boat Inn, Shore St, T01854-612366, www.ferryboat-inn.com. On the lochside, decent accommodation and food and though cramped, the best pub in town.

D Point Cottage Guest House, 22 West Shore St, T01854-612494, www.point cottage.co.uk. Open Feb-Nov. 3 en suite rooms. Lovely old fishing cottage at the quieter end of the loch-front.

F SYHA youth hostel, Shore St, T01854-612254. Mar-Dec. A very good hostel. You can pick up some information on local walks and it also offers bike hire, internet and laundry facilities. Recommended.

F Ullapool Tourist Hostel, West House, West Argyle St, T01854-613126. Open all year. This independent hostel has the full range of facilities, including free internet for guests and mountain bike hire. Also runs local bus tours.

Camping

Broomfield Holiday Park, Shore St, T01854-612 0020. Open Easter-Sep. At the west end of the village, this campsite has great views across to the Summer Isles and a laundrette on site.

South of Ullapool *p270*

B Dundonnell Hotel, in Dundonnell, south of Ullapool, T01854-633204, www.dundonnell hotel.com. Open Feb-Dec. Good-value hotel and good food, including vegetarian options, in their refurbished **Claymore Restaurant** (ꭨꭨꭨ-ꭨꭨ) and **Broombeg Bar**. Worth the stop.

Achiltibuie *p271*

L Summer Isles Hotel, T01854-622282, www.summerisleshotel.com. 3 en suite rooms, 2 suites and 1 cottage. Open Easter to mid-Oct. This relaxing, civilized hotel changed hands recently and is now under the ownership of the Mackays, who also own a hotel on Barra. The hotel enjoys magnificent views across to the SummerIsles and boasts a fabulous restaurant, see Eating, below.

F SYHA Youth Hostel, a few miles south at Achininver, T01854-622254. Mid-May to early Oct. Basic and very cheap.

Lochinver and around *p271*

L The Albannach Hotel, Baddidaroch, T01571-844407, www.thealbannach.co.uk. Open Mar-Nov. 6 en suite rooms. This wonderful 18th-century house overlooking Loch Inver is one of the very best places to stay in the northwest and everything a romantic Highland hotel should be. Rooms are tall, dark and handsome and the food in the award-winning restaurant is imaginative and generous, featuring only the freshest of local fish, fowl and game. The price includes dinner. Non-residents are also welcome (£50 for dinner) but booking is essential. Highly recommended.

L Inver Lodge Hotel, Iolaire Rd, T01571-844496, www.inverlodgehotel.co.uk. The spacious, luxuriously appointed rooms,

each named after a local mountain or loch, look out over the hills and sea whilst head chef Peter Cullen cooks up a storm in the restaurant (ꭨꭨꭨꭨ-ꭨꭨ). This is a fabulous retreat in the northwest of Scotland. Recommended.

D-E Veyatie Lochinver, 66 Baddidarroch, T01571-844424, www.veyatie-scotland.co.uk. Open all year. 3 rooms. Superior B&B, welcomes pets and hill walkers.

E Polcraig, T01571-844429, cathelmac@aol.com. Open all year. 5 en suite rooms. Large modern house offering a friendly welcome and good value B&B.

Loch Assynt and Inchnadamph *p211*

B-C Inchnadamph Hotel, Assynt, T01571-822202, www.inchnadamphhotel.co.uk. An old-fashioned Highland hotel on the shores of Loch Assynt, catering for the hunting and fishing fraternity, see page 272.

D-E Inchnadamph Lodge, Assynt Field Centre, T01571-822218, inch-lodge.co.uk.co.uk. Open all year, but phone ahead Nov-Mar. Great hostel accommodation in bunk rooms, as well as twin, double and family rooms. Continental breakfast is included. It's ideally situated for climbing Ben More Assynt and guides are available.

Lochinver to Kylesku *p272*

There's not much accommodation around here other than self-catering cottages.

Camping

Clachtoll Beach Campsite, 6 miles north of Lochinver, T01571-855377. May-Sep. Good facilities, friendly owners and in a superb location. Recommended.

Kylesku *p273*

A-B Kylesku Hotel, T01971-502231, www.kyleskuhotel.co.uk. 6 en suite, tastefully furnished rooms with views across the sea lochs and neighbouring mountains. This is a great place simply to relax, enjoy a malt and dine on great value pub meals and restaurant fare that draws on the best of the region's lamb, beef and seafood. Enjoy.

B-C Newton Lodge, T/F01971-502070, www.newtonlodge.co.uk. Mid-Mar to mid-Oct. 7 en suite rooms. Great views, especially if you use the telescope in the conservatory. Keep an eye out for wildlife, including eagles, and enjoy a chance to really unwind with delicious home-cooking. Another fine example of hospitality that rewards those who make the effort to explore Scotland's landscape beyond Inverness.

Self-catering
Kylesku Lodges, T01971-502003. Beautifully appointed lodges with a patio and delightful wood finishings that overlook sea lochs. Great option for couples and families who wish to escape, fish (wild brown trout), spot wildlife or simply relax. From £395 per week.

Scourie and Handa Island *p274*
There are lots of options in this area, including the following:
B-C Eddrachilles Hotel, Badcall Bay, T01971-502080, www.eddrachilles.com. Mar-Oct. 12 en suite rooms. This charming 200 year-old building stands in 300 acres of grounds overlooking the bay. The food on offer is superb and there's an excellent range of malt whiskies behind the bar.
B-C Scourie Hotel, Scourie, T01971-502396, www.scourie-hotel.co.uk. Open Apr-Oct. 20 rooms. A 17th-century former coaching inn popular with anglers, which is also an excellent place to eat (lunch ₶, dinner ₶₶₶).
C Scourie Lodge, Scourie, T01971-502248. Open Mar-Oct. 3 rooms. There are several B&Bs in the village, but none better than this welcoming lodge. Also does good evening meals and dinner, B&B option from £55.

Camping
There's a campsite on Harbour Rd, T01971-502060.

Kinlochbervie and around *p274*
B Rhiconich Hotel, Rhiconich, T01971-521224, www.rhiconichhotel.co.uk. Open all year. 10 en suite rooms. Modern functional

hotel with good facilities and surrounded by superb scenery. Good value lunch and dinner (1800-2100), whilst you enjoy fine views over Loch Inchard and try to spot the otters, seals and myriad of the wildlife in the area.
D Old School Hotel, Inshegra, halfway between Kinlochbervie and the A838 at Rhiconich, T/F01971-521383, www.oldschoolhotel.co.uk. Open Apr-Oct. 6 en suite rooms. This is the best place to stay in the area, with great food served in an intimate former classroom that dates back to the 1800s. Recommended.
E Benview, T01971-521242. Open Apr-Sep. A friendly B&B.

Camping
There's a small campsite at Oldshoremore, T01971-521281.

❶ Eating

Ullapool *p268, map p269*
₶ **The Ceilidh Place**, see Sleeping, above. Open 1100-2300. One of those places that tourists seem to hang around for hours or even days. It exudes a laid-back, cultured ambience. The self-service coffee shop does wholefood all day during the summer, while the restaurant serves more expensive full meals, with an emphasis on vegetarian and seafood at night. There's even outdoor seating. Also hosts live music and various other events, see Bars and clubs, below. Not the cheapest in town but one of the best.
₶ **Mariner's Restaurant**, Morefield Hotel, North Rd, T01854-612161. May-Oct. On the edge of town heading north, in the middle of a housing estate. The setting may be alittle incongruous but the seafood is sensational, which is why people travel from miles around. Good value.
₶-₶ **The Frigate**, Shore St, T01854-612969. Open daily 0900-2130. Whether you want porridge for breakfast, a mid-morning bagel, kids meals or steak pie, this bright café bistro caters for all tastes. It's also a good place to stock up on picnic items. Try the ice-cream.

♦♦-♦ **Seaforth Inn**, Quay St, T01854-612122.
Popular and award winning pub serving
delicious seafood, and other staples to suit
all pockets. Bar meals downstair are good
value. Their chippy next door is also an award
winning eatery Gets busy at weekends.
♦ **Tea Store**, 27 Argyll St, T01845-612995.
Daily 0800-2000. No-nonsense café serving
all day breakfasts, etc, and home-baked
goodies. Recommended for a hearty breakfast and to meet the local prawn fishermen.

Achiltibuie p271

♦♦♦ **Summer Isles Hotel**, see Sleeping, above.
This hotel boasts a great restaurant serving
some of the best seafood on the planet. A
fine seafood lunch will cost you around £25,
whilst a sublime 5-course set dinner will set
you back around £52 a head but you can
enjoy delicious bar lunches for a fraction of
the price. Even if you're not staying or eating
here, it's worth stopping to have a drink on
the terrace and watch the sun set over the
islands. Recommended.

Lochinver and around p271

♦♦ **Culag Hotel**, Lochinver, T01571-844270.
Sitting by the harbour, this hotel doesn't
impress from the outside but as many locals
know this is a great place for a pint, banter
and a reasonably priced lunch.
♦♦ **Riverside Bistro**, Main St, on the way into
town on the A837, T01571-844356. Apart
from the hotel listed above, the best food
is here. Try their famous pies which use
the best in local venison, beef, poultry and
seafood, and there are also vegetarian and
sweet options available. Eat in or takeaway.
Not cheap but tasty, with views over the sea.
♦ **Caberfeidh**, Main St, T01571-844321. Near to
the bistro, this is the cheap and cheerful option.

Scourie and Handa Island p274

♦♦ **Old School Hotel & Restaurant**, see
Sleeping, above. Daily 1200-1400, 1800-
2000. Serve really good, home-cooked food
to grateful souls who have ventured this far
north. The best for miles around.

♦♦ **Seafood Restaurant**, Tarbet, just above
the tiny jetty, T01971-502251, www.seafood
restaurant-tarbet.co.uk. Run by Julian Pearce
who also runs Laxford Cruise, see Activities
and tours, below. If you're up this way,
don't miss a visit to this restaurant which
serves the latest catch from the boats. It's a
wonderful, if unexpected, place to find, with
views across the sea inlets. Recommended.

◑ Bars and clubs

Ullapool p268, map p269

Arch Inn, 11 West Shore St, T01854-612454.
If you want reasonable bar food, a pool table
and a jumping atmosphere as you down
your pint, then this is the place to be.
The Ceilidh Place, see Sleeping, above. For
something bit more sedate and civilized than
the other choices, head here where you can
enjoy a quiet drink in the cosy **Parlour Bar** or
take advantage of their varied programme of
events. There's live music Mon-Sat throughout
the summer, and on a Mon in winter there
are also ceilidhs and poetry readings. The
clubhouse opposite stages plays.
Ferry Boat Inn (or 'FBI' as it's known locally),
Shore St. Ullapool's favourite pub though
very cramped. It has a Thu night live music
session year round, and during the summer
you can sit outside on the sea wall and
watch the sun go down as you drain your
pint of superb real ale.
Seaforth Inn, see Eating, above. Gets busy
at weekends and has a barn-like feel, but
it's a great place to eat and hear live music.

◉ Festivals and events

Ullapool p268, map p269

Sep Loopallu Festival, www.loopallu.co.uk.
Big music festival held over a weekend in late
Sep. Only started in 2005 but already seizing
the imagination of music lovers around the
country. Held in various venues around town.

O Shopping

Ullapool p268, map p269
There's no major supermarket but the town is well supplied with shops.
The Captain's Cabin, on the corner of Quay St and Shore St. Sells books, as well as crafts and souvenirs.
The Ceilidh Place, see Sleeping, above. Has a good bookshop if you don't plan to head for **Achins** by Lochinver.
Highland Stoneware, Mill St, heading north towards Morefield, T01854-612980, www. highlandstoneware.com. Look no further than here for high quality, hand turned and painted pottery. You can wander round the studios before browsing in their gift shop, which is pricey, but you may have luck in their bargain baskets.
Mountain Man Supplies, opposite the museum, West Argyle St. A good outdoor equipment shop.
On The Rocks, 114 Achmelvich, by Lochinver, T01571-844312. Mon-Sat 1000-1700. Craft shop and gallery, including original paintings of the beautiful sands at Achmelvich.
Unlimited Colour Company, 28 Argyle St, T01854-612844. Mon-Sat 0900-1700. An excellent option for all manner of brightly coloured, hand-dyed natural weaves, scarves, hats, cushions and throws.

Lochinver and around p271
Highland Stoneware, above the northern shore of the bay, Lochinver, T01571-844376, Nov-Mar Mon-Fri 0900-1800, Easter-Oct Mon-Fri 0900-1800, Sat 0900-1700, www. highlandstoneware.com. The main 'factory' for this high quality, hand turned and painted pottery.

O Activities and tours

Ullapool p268, map p269
Boat tours
Seascape Expeditions, T01854-633708, www.sea-scape.co.uk. 2-hr trips that leave from Ullapool harbour daily in summer aboard a fast-rib (£28.50 per person). It's an exhilarating 40-mile sea-trip around the Summer Isles with the chance to spot wildlife.
Summer Queen Cruises, 1 Royal Park, T01854-612472, www.summerqueen.co.uk. During the summer, the *MV Summer Queen*, runs 4-hr cruises to the Summer Isles, with a 45-min landing on Tanera Mór with its café and post office. Leave Mon-Sat at 1000 from the pier and costs £26, £13 child. There are also 2-hr wildlife cruises around Loch Broom, Annat Bay and Isle Martin, which leave daily at 1415. Both options offer opportunities to wildlife watch, including possibly seals, dolphins and even minke whales. From £18. Cruises can be booked at the booth by the pier or by calling the number above.

Deer stalking
North Assynt Estate, T01571-855298, www. sportingassynt.co.uk. For deer stalking from late Jul-Oct.

Fishing
With over 150 lochs filled with wild trout and salmon, Assynt is also excellent for fishing. **Assynt Angling Group**, www.assyntangling. co.uk; **Assynt Crofters Trust**, T01571-855298, www.assyntcrofters.co.uk.

Tour operators
Cape Adventure, Ardmore, Rhiconich, T01971-521006, www.capeadventure.co.uk For multi-adventures, including walking weeks and weekends, and sea kayaking, contact this excellent outdoor operator.

Achiltibuie p271
I Macleod, Achiltibuie Post Office, T01854-622200, or at home T018754-622315. For cruises to the Summer Isles from Achiltibuie pier on board the *Hectoria*. Cruises leave Mon-Sat at 1100 and 1430 during Jul and Aug, 1100 only for the rest of year and last approx 3 hrs, with 1 hr ashore on the islands. They cost £22 per person (½-price for children).

Kylesku p273

On board the MV Statesman, T01971-502345, cruises go to Eas a'Chùal Aluinn waterfall leaving from the old ferry jetty below the Kylesku Hotel. You can also see porpoises, seals and minke whales en route. The 2-hr round trip runs Apr-Oct Mon-Thu and Sun 1100-1500. Costs £15, children £5. You may be able to get closer to the falls by getting off the boat and walking to the bottom, then getting on the next boat.

Scourie and Handa Island p274

Laxford Cruises, Seafood Restaurant, Tarbet, T01971-502345. Sail around beautiful Loch Laxford, where you can see lots of birds from nearby Handa Island, as well as seals, porpoises and otters. Trips leave Easter-Sep Sun-Fri 1000, 1200 and 1400. The trips last 1 hr 45 mins and cost £16. For bookings contact Julian Pearce at the restaurant just above the jetty.

⊖ Transport

Ullapool p268, map p269

Bus Scottish Citylink buses run Mon-Sat between Ullapool and **Inverness**. There are also buses Mon-Sat to **Inverness** with Rapson's Coaches, T01463-710555, and Spa Coaches, T01997-421311. There are buses Mon-Sat from Inverness to **Lochinver** via Ullapool with Spa Coaches and Tim Dearman Coaches, T01349-883585. The bus continues to **Achmelvich Youth Hostel**. From Mon-Sat (Sun only in Jul and Aug) there's a daily bus from Inverness via **Ullapool**, **Lochinver**, **Kylesku**, **Scourie** and **Rhiconich** to **Durness** with Tim Dearman coaches (carries a bike trailer too). There's a bus Mon, Wed, Thu and Sat to **Gairloch**, operated by **Westerbus**, T01445-712255.

Car hire Daley's Deals, Morefield Industrial Estate, T01854-612848.

Cycle hire Available at hostels (see page 275).

Achiltibuie p271

Bus D&E Coaches, T01463-222444, run Mon-Sat between **Ullapool** and Achiltibuie.

There is 1 bus that leaves Achiltibuie on a Sat at 0751, reaching Polbain Stores at 0755, **Altandhu** at 0800, and **Ullapool** at 0900.

Another possibility Mon-Sat is to take the Spa Coaches or Dearman Coach (No 67) from **Ullapool ferry terminal** (1637) to Drumbeg shop via **Elphin** (1656), **Inchnadamph** (1711), **Lochinver** (1730) and **Achmelvich Youth Hostel** before requesting a stop at **Stoer** (1758), **Clashnessie** (1803) or **Drumbeg** (1813).

Lochinver and around p271

Bus There's a postbus service from **Lochinver** to **Lairg**, Mon-Sat, that runs along the main road via **Elphin**. However on its 3d run from Lochinver post office (1355) it will (on request) detour to **Drumbeg** (1439) via **Clashnessie** (1429) and **Stoer** (1414).

Scourie and Handa Island p274

Bus There's a Tim Dearman Coach service, T01349-883585, once a day Mon-Sat (Apr-Sep) from **Inverness bus station** (0850) via **Ullapool**, **Lochinver** and **Kylesku** to **Scourie** that continues to **Laxford Bridge** (1307), **Kinlochbervie** (1327) and **Rhiconich** (1340) to arrive in **Durness** at 1405.

Kinlochbervie and around p274

Bus George Rapson and IP Mackay, T01971-511343, run Mon-Sat between **Balnakiel Craft Village** (0800) and **Durness** to the train station at **Lairg** (1035) for connections to **Inverness** via **Rhiconich** (0830) and **Kinlochbervie** (0845). On Wed, IP Mackay, T01971-511343, buses travel from **Kinlochbervie Ceilidh Place** (1600) and past the Rhiconich Hotel to **Durness**, (35 mins). To travel between **Sheigra** and Kinlochbervie, call **Allan Bruce Taxis**, T01971-521477.

❶ Directory

Ullapool p268, map p269

Bank Royal Bank of Scotland, Ladysmith St; Bank of Scotland, West Argyle St, with ATM.

North coast

Scotland's rugged north coast is not for the faint hearted: over 100 miles of storm-lashed cliffs, sheer rocky headlands and deserted sandy coves backed by a desolate and eerily silent wilderness of mountain, bog and hill loch; the only place on mainland Britain where arctic flora and fauna come down to sea level. This is Britain's most spectacular and undisturbed coastline, a great place for birdwatching, with vast colonies of seabirds, and there's also a good chance of seeing seals, porpoises and minke whales in the more sheltered estuaries.
▸▸ *For listings, see pages 285-288.*

Ins and outs

Getting there and around
Getting around the far north without your own transport can be a slow process. Getting to Thurso, the main town, by bus or train is easy, but beyond that things get more difficult. Highland Country Buses run a regular service between Thurso train station and John o'Groats from Monday to Saturday, with at least three daily stopping en route at Gill's Bay. They also run a daily service from Thurso train station to Scrabster (at least three times daily) but it's strongly advised to call ahead (T01463-710555) to confirm times in order not to miss your ferry connection.▸▸ *For further details, see Transport page 288.*

Tourist information
Durness **TIC** ① *T01971-511259, Apr-Oct Mon-Sat, Jun-Aug daily*, arranges guided walks and has a small visitor centre with displays on local history, flora and fauna and geology. The Thurso **TIC** ① *Riverside Rd, T01847-893155, Mar-May, Mon-Sat 0930-1600, 31 May-4 Jun Mon-Sat 0930-1630, Sun 1000-1600, Jul-5 Sep 0930-1730, Sun 1000-1600, Sep-31 Oct Mon-Sat 0930-1630, Oct-Mar closed*, has a leaflet on local surfing beaches.

Durness and around → *For listings, see pages 285-288. Colour map 1, A6. Phone code 01971.*

Durness is not only the most northwesterly village on the British mainland, but also one of the most attractively located, surrounded by sheltered coves of sparkling white sand and machair-covered limestone cliffs. It's worth stopping here for a few days to explore the surrounding area. One of the village's most famous visitors was John Lennon, who used to spend childhood summers here with his Aunt Elizabeth, a local resident. This unlikely relationship was marked in 2002 with the creation of the **John Lennon Memorial Garden**. Beatles fans can now visit this lovely spot which features sculptures by local artist Lotte Glob, as well as standing stones bearing the lyrics to the fab four's classic *In My Life*.

Smoo Cave
A mile east of the village is the vast 200-ft-long Smoo Cave. A path from near the youth hostel leads down to the cave entrance which is hidden away at the end of a steep, narrow inlet. Plunging through the roof of the cathedral-like cavern is an 80-ft waterfall which can be seen from the entrance, but the more adventurous can take a boat trip into the floodlit interior.

A few miles east of the Smoo Cave are a couple of excellent beaches, at **Sangobeg** and **Rispond**, where the road leaves the coast and heads south along the west shore of stunning **Loch Eriboll**. Eriboll is Britain's steepest sea loch and was used by the Royal Navy during the Second World War as a base for protecting Russian convoys.

Balnakeil

About a mile northwest of Durness is the tiny hamlet of Balnakeil, overlooked by a ruined 17th-century church. In the south wall is a grave slab with carved skull-and-crossbones marking the grave of the notorious highwayman Donald MacMurchow. If you're looking for souvenirs, or an escape from the rat race, then head for the **Balnakeil Craft Village** ① *Apr-Oct daily 1000-1800*, an alternative artists' community set up in the 1960s in a former RAF radar station. Here you can buy weavings, pottery, paintings, leatherwork and woodwork in the little prefab huts. The Chocolatier and 'Chocolate Bar' café, **Cocoa Mountain**, is a must visit, specializing in fresh handmade truffles, hot chocolates, coffees and organic teas. You can watch the chocolates being made on the premises. Balnakeil has also become well known in golfing circles. The nine-hole **golf course** ① *T01971-511364*, is the most northerly in mainland Britain, and its famous ninth hole involves a drive over the Atlantic Ocean. The beach here is glorious, especially in fine weather when the sea turns a brilliant shade of turquoise. Even better, walk north along the bay to Faraid Head, where you can see puffin colonies in early summer. The views across to Cape Wrath in the west and Loch Eriboll in the east, are stupendous.

Cape Wrath

There are several excellent trips around Durness, but the most spectacular is to Cape Wrath, Britain's most northwesterly point. It's a wild place and the name seems entirely appropriate, though it actually derives from the Norse word *hwarf*, meaning 'turning place'. Viking ships used it as a navigation point during their raids on the Scottish west coast. Now a lighthouse stands on the cape, above the 1000 ft-high Clo Mor Cliffs, the highest on the mainland, and breeding ground for huge colonies of seabirds.

You can walk south from here to **Sandwood Bay**, see page 274. It's an exhilarating but long coastal walk, and will take around eight hours. It's safer doing this walk from north to south as the area around the headland is a military firing range and access may be restricted, which could leave you stranded.

To get to Cape Wrath, first take the passenger **ferry** ① *T01971-511343 or 511287, May-Sep daily, £5 return*, across the Kyle of Durness from Keoldale, 2 miles south of Durness. The ferry then connects with a **minibus** ① *T01971-511343, £8*, for the 11 mile journey to the cape (40 minutes).

Tongue to Thurso → *Colour map 2, A1-2.*

The road east from Durness runs around **Loch Eriboll** on its way to the lovely little village of **Tongue**. A causeway crosses the beautiful Kyle of Tongue, but a much more scenic route is the single-track road around its southern side, with great views of **Ben Hope** (3041 ft) looming to the southwest. The village of Tongue is overlooked by the 14th-century ruins of **Varick Castle**, and there's a great beach at **Coldbackie**, 2 miles northeast.

The A836 runs south from Tongue through Altnaharra to Lairg, see page 293. It also continues east to the crofting community of **Bettyhill**, named after the Countess of Sutherland who ruthlessly evicted her tenants from their homes in Strathnaver to make way for more profitable sheep. The whole sorry saga is told in the interesting **Strathnaver Museum** ① *T01641-521418, Apr-Oct Mon-Sat 1000-1300, 1400-1700, £2, concessions £1.50, students, £1, children 50p*, housed in an old church in the village and tells the story of crofting life at the time of the Strathnaver Clearances. There are also Pictish stones in the churchyard behind the museum.

The museum sells a leaflet detailing the many prehistoric sites in the Strathnaver Valley which runs due south from Bettyhill. There are a couple of great beaches around Bettyhill, at **Farr Bay** and at **Torrisdale Bay**, which is the more impressive of the two and forms part of the **Invernaver Nature Reserve**. There's a small **TIC** ① *T01641-521244, Easter-Sep Mon-Sat 1015-1700*, in Bettyhill.

East from Bettyhill the hills of Sutherland begin to give way to the fields of Caithness. The road passes the turn-off to **Strathy Point** before reaching **Melvich**, another small crofting settlement overlooking a lovely sandy bay.

South from Melvich the A897 heads to Helmsdale, see page 296, through the **Flow Country**, a vast expanse of bleak bog of major ecological importance. About 15 miles south of Melvich at Forsinard is an **RSPB Visitor Centre** ① *T01641-571225, www.rspb.co.uk, Easter-Oct daily 0900-1730*, the guided walks through the nature reserve leave from here. These peatlands are a breeding ground for black- and red-throated divers, golden plovers and merlins as well as other species. Otters and roe deer can also be spotted.

Thurso and around → *For listings, see pages 285-288.*

Thurso is the most northerly town on the British mainland and by far the largest settlement on the north coast. In medieval times it was Scotland's chief port for trade with Scandinavia, though most of the town dates from the late 18th century when Sir John Sinclair built the 'new' extension to the old fishing port. The town increased in size to accommodate the workforce of the new nuclear power plant at nearby Dounreay, but the plant's demise has threatened the local economy. Today Thurso is a fairly nondescript place, mostly visited by people catching the ferry to Stromness in Orkney, or the occasional hardcore surfer.

Thurso → *Colour map 2, A3. Phone code 01847. Population 9000.*

There's little of real interest in the town centre, but the train station is at the south end of Princes St. Near the harbour are the 17th-century ruins of **Old St Peter's Church**, which stand on the site of the original 13th-century church founded by the Bishop of Caithness. The **Heritage Museum**, which features some Pictish carved stones, now forms part of the new **Caithness Horizons** ① *www.caithnesshorizons.co.uk*, development which is situated in the town hall on the High Street. There may be little in the way of activity in the town, but 10 miles west of Thurso there's plenty of radioactivity at the **Dounreay Nuclear Power Station**. Though its fast breeder reactors were decommissioned in 1994, the plant is still a major local employer and now reprocesses spent nuclear fuel. The **Dounreay Visitor Centre**, previously situated at the power station, is now part of the Caithness Horizons development and offers the opportunity to learn more about nuclear power.

Strathmore to Braemore → *OS sheet No 11 covers the route.*

This walk gives a flavour of the bleak but beautiful landscape of the Caithness hinterland. The 16-mile linear route starts from **Strathmore Lodge**. To get there, head south from Thurso on the B874. After a short distance turn on to the B870 and follow it for 10 miles to the little hamlet of Westerdale, which stands on the River Thurso. Turn right here on to an unnumbered road and follow this road for about 5 miles. Just past the white Strathmore Lodge the road splits. Follow the right-hand track which runs through commercial forestry, before emerging on to open moor with Loch More on the left.

Where the forestry begins again on the right, the track swings left across an arm of the loch and heads southwards. At the southern end of the loch a track runs left to **Dalnaha**, but keep going straight ahead, along the valley of the River Thurso. You then reach a cluster of buildings at **Dalnawillan Lodge**. Ignore the track which heads off to the right and carry straight on, past the house at **Dalganachan**, over Rumsdale Water and on to the junction before **The Glutt**, which is a series of buildings. Turn left here and follow the track for a further 4 miles until you reach the junction beside Lochan nan Bò Riabach. Continue down the valley of Berriedale Water to Braemore. There is no public transport from here, so you'll have to arrange your own transport if you don't want to retrace your steps.

Dunnet Head → *Colour map 2, A3. Phone code 01847.*
About 10 miles northeast of Thurso is the most northerly point on the British mainland. No, not John o'Groats, but Dunnet Head. It's reached by turning off the Thurso to John

Thurso

Sleeping 🛏
Annandale **1**
Forss Country House **2**
Murray House **3**

Park **4**
Sandra's Backpackers **5**
Station **6**
Thurso Camping Site **7**

Eating 🍴
Charlie Chan **1**
Tempest Café **2**

o'Groats road at Dunnett, at the east end of Dunnett Bay, a 3-mile-long sandy beach that's popular with surfers who come to tackle the gigantic waves of the **Pentland Firth**, the wild and treacherous strait between the mainland and Orkney. Dunnet Bay has an excellent reef break and there's another good reef break at Brims Ness to the west. Further west still, at Strathy Bay, you'll find rollers that can match anything in Hawaii (though the water's obviously a lot colder). Dunnett Head is a much nicer place than John o'Groats, with marvellous views across to Orkney and along the entire north coast (on a clear day). There's a Victorian lighthouse out at the point, and the dramatic seacliffs are teeming with seabirds. There's also a great little café, see Eating page 287.

Some 15 miles east of Thurso are the **Castle and Gardens of Mey** ⓘ *T01847-851473, www.castleofmey.org.uk, May-Jul, mid-Aug to Sep daily 1030-1600, £9.50, concessions £8.50, children £4, under 5s free, family £23, visitor centre, tea room and shop open daily 1000-1700.* Built by the 4th Earl of Caithness, the castle's future was under threat until the intervention of the late Queen Mother who bought it in 1952 and who holidayed here every year. The castle still welcomes royal visitors in the shape of Prince Charles who holidays here each summer.

John o'Groats → *Colour map 2, A4. Phone code 01955.*
Let's be honest, John o'Groat's isn't the most inspiring place to visit. It's beloved by tourists who think they've reached the northernmost point of the UK mainland (it's actually Dunnet Head) and charity walkers, runners and cyclists who've made the admirable long haul from Land's End over 700 miles to the south. But with the notable exception of the excellent **Northcoast Marine Adventures** fast rib tours at the harbour, there's little here to persuade you to prolong your stay. It gets its name from the Dutchman Jan de Groot, who was commissioned by King James IV to run a ferry service to Orkney in 1496. Ferries still operate from here to Burwick in Orkney, see Transport, page 288. There's a **TIC** ⓘ *T01955-611373, Apr-Oct Mon-Sat,* as well as a post office, craft shops and a chippy.

Two miles east of John o'Groats is **Duncansby Head**, which is far more rewarding. South of the headland a path leads to the spectacular **Duncansby Stacks**, a series of dramatic rock formations. The 200-ft cliffs are home to countless seabirds and you can see the narrow, sheer-sided inlets known locally as *geos*.

◉ North coast listings

For Sleeping and Eating price codes and other relevant information, see Essentials pages 38-45.

● Sleeping

Durness and around *p281*
B Mackays Rooms & Restaurant, Durness, T01971-511202, www.visitmackays.com. Easter-Oct. 7 en suite rooms. The modern, uninspiring exterior hides one of the best hotel experiences in the north of Scotland. Rooms are spacious and tastefully furnished with not a hint of tartan cheesiness on display. Staff are efficient and the food in the restaurant a revelation. Excellent value. Recommended.

C Ben Loyal Hotel, Tongue, T01847-611216, www.benloyal.co.uk. Open all year. 11 en suite rooms. Friendly, hospitable small hotel and a good choice for the area. Food is recommended and the bar is a good place to while away an evening or 2.
B-C Tongue Hotel, Tongue, T01847-611206. Open all year (except Christmas week). 19 en suite rooms. This former hunting lodge of the infamous Duke of Sutherland has great views across the Kyle of Tongue and the staff are extremely accommodating. Catering mostly for anglers it can arrange impromptu fishing trips and the restaurant does good food.

D Bighouse Lodge, Melvich, T01641-531207, www.bighouseestate.com. Open May-Oct. 12 recently refurbished rooms. 18th-century mansion converted into a small hotel at the mouth of the Halladale river in 4 acres of its own grounds. Mainly aimed at the huntin' shootin' an' fishin' brigade.

D Rhian Cottage, Tongue, T01847-611257, www.rhiancottage.co.uk. Open all year. 5 rooms. Good value B&B with comfortable rooms and conservatory. Great breakfasts (cater for vegans) with lovely touches that include filling your thermos flask and preparing a packed lunch (£6.50).

C-D Farr Bay Inn, Bettyhill, T01641-521230, www.farrbayinn.co.uk. 4 good en suite rooms and decent bar food too. Note that the property is for sale at the time of writing, as a going concern.

E Cloisters, Talmine, T01847-601286, www.cloistertal.demon.co.uk. Open all year. 3 en suite rooms, 1 with disabled facilities. B&B in 19th-century converted church.

D Glengolly B&B, Durness, T01971-511255, www.glengolly.com. Open all year. 3 rooms, all with en suite or private facilities. Good value B&B in a working croft.

F Durness SYHA Youth Hostel, Smoo, to the east of the village, T01971-511264, www.syha.org.uk, Mid-Mar to early Oct. Basic but comfortable, and handy for the beach and Smoo cave.

F SYHA Youth Hostel, Tongue, T01847-611789, T08701-553255. Mid-Mar to late Oct. Beautifully situated at the east end of the causeway, with views towards Ben Loyal and the sea lochs. Great value.

Camping
Talmine, T01847-601225, 5 miles north of Tongue. By the beach.

Thurso and around *p283, map p284*
Thurso has a wide variety of accommodation, most of it fairly average.
B-C Forss Country House Hotel, 4 miles out of Thurso at Bridge of Forss, T01847-861201, www.forsshousehotel.co.uk. The nicest place to stay by far around Thurso, if not the entire north coast. This small, family-run hotel is set in 20 acres of lovely woodland and has an excellent restaurant (ŦŦŦ-ŦŦ), open to non-residents (but pre-book). Rooms are spacious (the en suite bathrooms are bigger than many other hotel rooms), the attention to detail is impressive and the service is spot on. Nothing is too much trouble for the staff here. Highly recommended.

C-D Station Hotel & Apartments, 54 Princes St, Thurso, T01847-892003, www.stationthurso.co.uk. Open all year. 38 en suite rooms. Central with decent food. Friendly and welcoming, good value.

C Park Hotel, Oldfield, at the south end of town, 10 mins' walk from train station, T01847-893251, www.parkhotelthurso.co.uk. Open all year. 21 en suite rooms. Modern and rather functional building but clean, comfortable and extremely hospitable with good food at reasonable prices. Rooms at the front have best views.

B Borgie Lodge Hotel, Skerray, by Thurso, T01641-521332, www.borgielodgehotel. co.uk. Open all year. 8 rooms (7 en suite). Fine, small country hotel with appeal for gun sports and fishing types but also very fine food.

E Annandale, 2 Rendel Govan Rd, T01847-893942, thomson@annandale2.freeserve. co.uk. Open all year. 3 rooms. Very good-value B&B.

D Bencorragh House, Upper Gills in Canisbay, a few miles west of John o'Groats, T01955-611449, www.bencorraghhouse. com. Mar-Oct. Very decent B&B in farmhouse.

D Murray House, 1 Campbell St, T01847-895759, www.murrayhousebb.com. Open all year. 5 en suite rooms. Friendly and welcoming B&B, dinner also available by prior arrangement. Good value.

D Sharvedda, Strathy Point, by Thurso, T01641-541311, www.sharvedda.co.uk. 3 rooms. Good quality B&B also offering evening meals by prior arrangement.

F Sandra's Backpackers, 24-26 Princes St, T01847-894575, www.sandras-backpackers. co.uk. Probably the best option at the very cheapest end of the scale and right beside a good chip shop.

Camping
There are a couple of campsites at John o'Groats and further west by the beach at Huna. Ask at the TIC.
Thurso Camping Site, north of town on the road to Scrabster, T01847-892244. The nearest campsite to Thurso.

🅞 Eating

Durness and around *p281*
⑪ The Seafood Platter, Durness, T01971-511224. Open Mar-Oct Mon-Sat 1000-1700 (till 2100 peak season), Sun 1200-1700. Fresh, local seafood cooked at its best. Recommended.
⑫ Cocoa Mountain, Balnakeil Craft Village, Durness, T01971 511233, www.cocoa mountain.co.uk. Easter-Sep 0900-1800, Oct-Easter 1000-1700. Very popular, high quality chocolatier and café.

Thurso and around *p283, map p284*
The **Forss Country House Hotel** (see Sleeping, above), is the best place to eat in the area; the other hotels listed are good options in town for a decent meal.
⑪⑪⑪ The Bower Inn, between Thurso and Wick, turn off the coast road at Castletown and follow the B876 until you see the sign for Gillock, T01955-661292. A close second to the **Forss** for upmarket places to eat in the area.
⑪⑪⑪ The Captain's Galley, Scrabster, T01847-894999, www.captainsgalley.co.uk. Open for dinner Tue-Sat 1900-2100. Small restaurant so booking a must. Top-notch seafood restaurant in unpretentious surroundings, just the freshest of food brought to you within mins of being landed (or so it seems). Best choice hereabouts.

⑪⑪ Charlie Chan, 2 Sinclair St, T01847-890888. Best of the ubiquitous Chinese restaurants in town.
⑫ Dunnett Head Tearoom, Dunnett Head, a few miles from the lighthouse, T01847-851774. Apr-Oct daily 1500-2000. Serves snacks and meals to hardy surfers.
⑫ Tempest Café, by the harbour next to the surf shop of the same name (see Activities and tours, below), T01847-892500, www. tempestsurf.co.uk. Open Tue-Sun 1000-1800. Good, chilled vibe. Menu features typical surfer-type fare (ie loads of carbs).

🅔 Entertainment

Thurso and around *p283, map p284*
Viking Bowl, Ormlie Rd, T01847-895050. Compex with bowling and cinema.

🅞 Activities and tours

Thurso and around *p283, map p284*
Boat trips
John o'Groats Ferries, Ferry Office, John o'Groats, T01955-611353, www.jogferry. co.uk. Operate **Orkney Islands Day Tours**, which leave daily May-Sep at 0900, return at 1945 (£46, children £23, under 5s free). A shorter day tour goes daily from Jun-Sep at 1030, returns at 1800 (£42, children £12, under 5s free). There's also a wildlife cruise Jun-Aug, which departs at 1430 (£15, children £7.50, under 5s free, family £37.50).
Northcoast Marine Adventures, John o'Groats harbour, T01955-611797, www. northcoast-marine-adventures.co.uk. Mar-Oct daily 1000-1930. Whether you want to spot seals, explore sea caves or zip across the huge waves of the Pentland Firth, you'll have fun aboard this high powered rigid inflatable boat that leaves every 2nd hour from the harbour. £20, children £12.

Surfing
The best break in the region, indeed, one of the best breaks in the world, is Thurso East. For a detailed description of the wave

and how to access it, see Footprint's *Surfing Britain*, which describes all the breaks along this coast. A good surf shop is Tempest Surf, by the harbour in Thurso, T01847-892500, www.tempestsurf.co.uk. Daily 1000-1800.

⊖ Transport

Durness and around *p281*
Bus On the 2nd and 4th Sat of every month there's 1 bus from **Durness post office**, via **Tongue** and **Bettyhill** to **Thurso** with IP Mackay, T01971-511343. There's a postbus service from **Tongue** to **Lairg** via **Altnaharra**, Mon-Sat, departing Tongue at 0815 Mon-Fri and 0745 on a Sat.

From Mon-Sat (Sun Jul-Aug only) there's a daily bus from **Durness** to **Inverness** via **Rhiconich, Scourie, Kyleskuand, Lochinver, Ullapool** with Tim Dearman coaches, T01349-883585, it carries a bike trailer too. On a Wed only, IP Mackay buses, T01971-511343, (No 807) runs between **Durness** (1635), and **Kinlochbervie**.

Thurso and around *p283, map p284*
Bus Citylink buses, T0870-5505050, run to **Inverness** 4 times daily, 3½ hrs. Those from Inverness continue to **Scrabster** to connect with ferries to **Stromness** in **Orkney**. Citylink buses to **Inverness** connect with buses to **Edinburgh**.

Highland Country Buses, T01463-710555, run local services to **Bettyhill**, 3 times daily Mon-Fri, 1 hr 10 mins, on a route that includes **Reay**. There are regular daily buses to **Wick** via **Halkirk** or **Castletown**.
Car hire William Dunnett & Co, T01847-893101, www.dunnets.co.uk.
Cycle hire The Bike & Camping Shop, the Arcade, 34 High St, T01847-896124. Rents mountain bikes for £10 per day.
Ferry Northlink Ferries, www.northlink ferries.co.uk, to **Stromness** in (Orkney) leave from **Scrabster**, 2 miles north of Thurso. John o'Groats Ferries sail to **Burwick** (Orkney) twice daily from May-Sep, 40 mins, £18 one way, £28 return. A connecting bus takes passengers on to **Kirkwall**, 40 mins, price included in ferry ticket.
Train 3 trains leave daily from **Inverness** (3½ hrs), 2 of them connecting with the ferries from **Scrabster** to **Stromness** (Orkney). Trains continue to **Wick** (30 mins) and trains to **Inverness** leave from here.

East coast

The east coast of the Highlands, from Inverness north to Wick, doesn't have the same draw as the west coast and attracts far fewer visitors, but it has its own, gentler appeal, and there are many lovely little seaside towns to explore, especially the singular former sea port of Cromarty. The main attraction in these parts, though, is undoubtedly the resident pod of bottlenose dolphins, which can be seen along the Moray coast between May and September.
➤➤ *For listings, see pages 298-302.*

The Black Isle → *For listings, see pages 298-302. Colour map 2, C2. Phone code 01381.*

Across the Kessock Bridge from Inverness is the Black Isle, which is neither an island nor black. It enjoys long hours of sunshine and low rainfall, and is an attractive landscape of rolling acres of barley and stately woods of oak and beech dropping down to the Moray coast. It also has a compelling atmosphere – a combination perhaps of its soft microclimate, lush vegetation and attractive architecture. Its main attractions are the picturesque town of Cromarty and Chanonry Point, on the southern side near Rosemarkie, which is one of the best dolphin-spotting sites in Europe.

North Kessock to Tore
On the north side of the Kessock Bridge, just north of the village, is the North Kessock **TIC** ① *T0845 2255121, Easter-Oct daily.* Next door is the **Dolphin and Seal Visitor Centre**, which gives details of accredited dolphin cruises. You can see dolphins from the village of North Kessock just to the south.

One of the many sacred wells (and caves) in the area is the unmissable **Clootie Well**, on the verge of the main road between Tore and Munlochy Bay Nature Reserve. It was once blessed by St Curitan (see below) and is thought to cure sick children. Thousands of rags still flutter from the surrounding trees, though well-worshippers are in danger of being mown down by traffic. Despite the presence of cars, it's an eerie place.

Fortrose and Chanonry Point
Further east on this road, beyond Munlochy and Avoch (pronounced *Och*) is the village of Fortrose, on the east shore. The magnificent cathedral at Fortrose is now largely a ruin; rainwashed carved faces of rose-coloured sandstone peer down from roof bosses, and snapped-off stumps of window tracery are a reminder of Reformation vandalism. On the golf course at **Chanonry Point**, overlooking the Moray Firth, a plaque marks the spot where the Brahan Seer was boiled in a barrel of tar. Chanonry Point is also a great place for seeing dolphins. They come close to shore at high tide and there's a good chance of seeing them leaping above the waves.

Rosemarkie
A few miles from Fortrose on the north side of Chanonry Point is the tiny village of Rosemarkie. Celtic saints Curitan and Boniface selected this sheltered spot on the southern shore for their Christian mission in the seventh century. St Boniface is remembered at nearby St Bennet's Well. **Groam House Museum** ① *T01381-620961, www.groamhouse. org.uk, May-Oct Mon-Sat 1000-1700, Sun 1400-1630, Mar, Apr, Nov-early Dec Sat-Sun 1400-1600, free,* houses a huge collection of Pictish sculptured stones found locally, imaginatively

displayed alongside contemporary artwork inspired by them. A year-round programme of events and lectures is devoted to the study of Pictish culture. A lovely marked trail leads into Fairy Glen, now a nature reserve, from the top end of the High Street, through a wooded gorge where you may spot woodpeckers and treecreepers. The name obviously derives from the fairies that live here, though the last sighting was in the 1970s.

Cromarty → Phone code 01381.

On the northeastern tip of the Black Isle Peninsula, at the mouth of the Cromarty Firth, is the gorgeous wee town of Cromarty, one of the east coast's major attractions. Its neat white-harled houses interspersed with gracious merchants' residences are almost unchanged since the 18th century when it was a sea port thriving on trade as far afield as Russia and the Baltic. Many emigrants bound for the New World embarked here. The town's prosperity, based on textiles and fishing, turned to decline and dereliction. Although restored and fully populated, Cromarty now has the atmosphere of a backwater, though a very attractive one at that, where you feel as if you're stepping back in time, in stark contrast to the numerous oil rigs moored on the opposite shore in Nigg Bay.

For an insight into the history of the area, visit the 18th-century **Cromarty Courthouse** ① *Church St, T01381-600418, www.cromarty-courthouse.org.uk, Apr-Sep daily 1000-1700, Adults £2, includes loan of headset for recorded tour of the town's other historic buildings,* which houses the town's museum. Next to the courthouse is the thatch-roofed **Hugh Miller's Cottage** ① *T08444-932158, www.nts.org.uk, Mar-Sep daily 1300-1700, Oct Sun and Tues only 1300-1700, £5.50, concessions £4.50, family £15,* birthplace of the eminent local geologist and author. Also worth seeing is the elegant 17th-century **East Church**.

There's a good walk along a coastal path from the east end of the village through woodland to the top of the South Sutor headland, one of the two steep headlands guarding the narrow entrance to the Cromarty Firth. There are excellent views from here across the Moray Firth. Leaflets describing this and other local walks are available at the Cromarty Courthouse.

One of Cromarty's main attractions is its dolphins. They can be seen from the shore, or with a boat trip, see Activities and tours, page 301. To the west, the mudflats of **Udale Bay** are an RSPB reserve and a haven for wading birds and wintering duck and geese, which can be viewed from a hide.

Poyntzfield Herb Garden is an organic plant nursery specializing in rare and native medicinal herbs. Worth visiting if only for a glimpse of the house, and the view from the car park over the Cromarty Firth through massive beech trees.

The Cromarty Firth → For listings, see pages 298-302. Colour map 2, C1-2.

Dingwall and around → Phone code 01349.

Dingwall, at the head of the Cromarty Firth, has two major claims to fame. Not only is it believed to be the birthplace of Macbeth, it was also the home for many years of Neil Gunn (1891-1973), perhaps the Highlands' greatest literary figure, see also page 296. It's a fairly dull, though functional town, with good shops and banks lining its long main street. **Dingwall Museum** ① *T01349-865366, May-Sep Mon-Sat 1000-1630, nominal entry fee payable,* tells the history of this Royal Burgh.

East of Dingwall, before Evanton, is **Storehouse of Foulis** ① *T01349-830038, www.storehouseoffoulis.co.uk, Mon-Sat 0900-1800, Sun 1000-1700, free,* which has history and wildlife exhibitions, and offers the chance to see the local seal population. Standing on a hill above **Evanton** is the **Fyrish Monument**, a replica of the Gate of Negapatam in India, built by local men and funded by local military hero, Sir Hector Munro, to commemorate his capture of the Indian town, in 1781. To get there, turn off the B9176 towards Boath. It's a stiff two-hour climb up to the top.

The Cromarty Firth is a centre for repairing North Sea oil rigs, and many of the villages along its north shore have benefited from the oil industry. One of these is **Invergordon**, just west of Nigg Bay, which has suffered in recent years due to the closure of the local aluminium factory. Beyond Invergordon, a road branches south to Nigg Ferry. The ferry from Cromarty to **Nigg** was once a major thoroughfare, and now a tiny two-car ferry makes the 20-minute crossing in the summer months (every 30 minutes from 0800-1815). From the ferry you get a good view of **Nigg Bay**, a vast natural harbour used in both world wars by the Royal Navy. Its entry is guarded by the dramatic headlands of the Sutors, identified in folklore as friendly giants. The oil rigs ranged along the firth and the oil terminal at Nigg, are a dramatic and not unpleasant contrast with Lilliputian Cromarty.

Strathpeffer and around → *Phone code 01997.*

Just along from the Cromarty Firth is Strathpeffer, which gets busy in the summer with coach parties, but it's a pleasant place and there are some excellent walks in the surrounding hills. The little village gained recognition in 1819 when Doctor Morrison, a physician from Aberdeen, bathed in its sulphur springs and cured himself of rheumatoid arthritis. He quickly spread the word and Strathpeffer became a fashionable spa resort attracting thousands of visitors. Two world wars intervened and the town's popularity declined. Today the only reminder of its past is the **Water Sampling Pavilion** in the square where you can test the waters. There's a seasonal **TIC** ① *main square, T01997-421415.*

Just outside Strathpeffer on the road to Dingwall is the **Highland Museum of Childhood** ① *T01997-421031, Mar-Oct Mon-Sat 1000-1700, Sun 1400-1700, Jul-Aug Mon-Fri 1000-1900, Sat 1000-1700, Sun 1400-1700, £2.50, concessions £2, children £1.50, family £6,* which has historical displays on childhood in the Highlands, as well as collections of dolls, toys and games.

A fine walk is to **Knock Farrel** and the **Touchstone Maze**, site of an Iron Age vitrified fort which lies at the north end of a ridge known locally as the **Cat's Back**. A marked trail starts from Blackmuir Wood car park. Head up the hill from town, turn left up a road immediately before the youth hostel, and the car park is on the left. The walk is 6 miles in total and takes about three hours. Aside from OS Landranger sheet 26, the route is also described in a Forestry Commission leaflet *Forests of Easter Ross*, available from tourist offices.

Another excellent side trip is to **Rogie Falls**, near Contin, which is 3 miles southwest of Strathpeffer on the main A835 Inverness to Ullapool road. The short walk up to the falls starts from the car park 3 miles north of Contin on the A835. There are also some pleasant woodland walks around here. Experienced hikers can tackle magnificent **Ben Wyvis** (3432 ft). The route to the summit starts 4 miles north of Garve, 7 miles northwest of Contin.

Tain and around → *For listings, see pages 298-302. Colour map 2, B2-C2.*

Squeezed between the Cromarty Firth to the south and the Dornoch Firth to the north is the Tain Peninsula, whose largest town is Tain, a place with a 1950s time-warp feel. It has an impressive historical portfolio: its backstreets are an intriguing jigsaw of imposing merchants' houses, steep vennels, secret gardens and dormer windows. The town serves a vast hinterland. Among the hills are little-visited backwoods and farm towns, narrow valleys lined with crofts where cattle graze in boggy haughs and, to the west, glens and moorland. Along the seaboard are the windswept fields of the Tarbat Peninsula. Good sea angling is to be had from the harbours of the otherwise dull coastal villages such as Balintore, and at Shandwick is a massive Pictish stone. It is said that unbaptized children were buried near the stone which is now in the Museum of Scotland in Edinburgh.

Tain

The **Collegiate church** is on Castle Brae, just off the High Street, and inside is a 17th-century panel painted with the badges of the trade guilds, a reminder of the town's busy international trade. Another reminder is the imposing 16th-century **Tolbooth** in the High Street. Next to the church is **Tain through Time** ① *T01862-894089, www.tainmuseum.org. uk, Apr-Oct Mon-Sat 1000-1700, £3.50, children over 6 and concessions £2.50, family (up to 2 adults and 4 children) £10*, a museum housed in the Pilgrimage which charts the town's medieval history. One of Tain's main attractions, just off the A9 to the north of town, is the very fine **Glenmorangie whisky distillery** ① *T01862-892477, www.glenmorangie.com, Mon-Fri 0900-1700, Jun-Aug Sat 1000-1600, Sun 1200-1600, tours (45 mins) from 1030-1530, approx £2.50*, where you can see how the world-famous whisky is made and try a sample. Famous for its various wood finishes, Glenmorangie remains Scotland's best-selling single malt whisky. You can now stay here, in some considerable style and comfort, at **Glenmorangie House** (see Sleeping, page 298).

Just to the south of town, off the A9, is the **Aldie Water Mill**, a restored 16th-century mill in working order, with various high-quality craft shops attached. Nearby is the **Tain Pottery** ① *T01862-894112, www.tainpottery.co.uk, Apr-Oct Mon-Fri 0900-1800, Sat-Sun 1000-1700, Nov-Mar Mon-Sat 0900-1730*, which you can also visit.

Portnahomack

The seaside village of Portnahomack, or 'port of Colman', is named after the missionary who was keen as mustard to found a religious settlement here. Archaeological work is revealing the importance of this area in Pictish times. The **Tarbat Discovery Centre** ① *T01862-871351, www.tarbat-discovery.co.uk, Easter-Apr and Oct daily 1400-1700, May-Sep daily 1000-1700, £3.50, under 12s free, concession £2*, in Tarbat Old Church, displays recently discovered Pictish stonecarving. From the harbour, with its 18th-century girnals (grain warehouses) and sheltered sandy beach, you can see a huge stretch of the Sutherland coast, and the great sandbanks – the 'gizzen brigs' – at the mouth of the Dornoch Firth. Boat trips are available from the harbour for sea angling. A worthwhile trip is out to Tarbat Ness lighthouse, about 3 miles north.

Hill of Fearn

South from Portnahomack, just west of the junction of the B9165 and the B9166, is Hill of Fearn. Fearn Abbey was moved here around 1250 from its original site near Edderton, where it was too vulnerable to sea raiders. It later became the parish church, but one Sunday in 1742 lightning struck the roof which fell in, killing 38 worshippers. This tragedy was preceded by a fairy harbinger sighted at nearby Loch Eye. In Hill of Fearn is the excellent **Anta Factory Shop** ① *www.anta.co.uk, Mon-Sat 0930-1730, Sun 1000-1700*, one of the very best places in the country for classy tartan furnishing fabrics, as well as tartan rugs and throws, and pottery.

Fairies were said to cross the Dornoch Firth on cockle shells and were once seen building a bridge of fairy gold, perhaps a forerunner of the Dornoch Bridge which carries the A9 across the firth just north of Tain. A more pleasant and interesting route is to follow the A836 along the south shore. From The Struie, reached by the B9176 which branches south at Easter Fearn, there's a panoramic view over the Dornoch Firth and the Sutherland hills.

Edderton to the Kyle of Sutherland

In the churches of Edderton and Kincardine are Pictish stones. Another stands in a field northwest of Edderton (but don't disturb the crops or livestock). A quartz boulder at **Ardgay**, the 'Clach Eiteag', commemorates the cattle tryst and fair which once took place locally.

Ten miles from Ardgay, at the end of lovely Strathcarron, is the isolated **Croick church**, one of the most poignant reminders of the infamous Clearances. Here, in 1845, 90 local folk took refuge in the churchyard after they had been evicted from their homes in Glencalvie by the despicable Duke of Sutherland to make way for his sheep flocks. A reporter from *The Times* was there to describe this "wretched spectacle", as men, women and children were carted off, many never to return. His report is there to read, but far more evocative and harrowing are the names and messages the people scratched in spidery copperplate in the window panes.

North of Ardgay is the **Kyle of Sutherland**, where several rivers converge to flood into the sea through lush water meadows. Montrose was defeated here, at Carbisdale, in 1651. Overlooking the Kyle, at **Culrain**, is the 19th-century **Carbisdale Castle**, once home of the exiled King of Norway. It now houses a youth hostel, see Sleeping, page 299. After the Dornoch Ferry disaster of 1809, a bridge was built over the Kyle at **Bonar Bridge**, from where the A949 runs eastwards to join the main A9 just before Dornoch, while the A836 continues north to Lairg (see below). A few miles north of Invershin are the **Falls of Shin**, an excellent place to watch salmon battling upstream on their way to their spawning grounds (best seen June to September). The visitor centre has information about six easy walks in the immediate area; all are under an hour long. It also boasts an excellent café/shop (see Eating, page 300) and a shop described as 'Harrods of the north' (Mohammed Al Fayed's estate is close by, which explains the goods on offer).

Lairg → *Phone code 01549.*

Eleven miles north of Bonar Bridge is the uninspiring village of Lairg, the region's main transport hub. Lairg is best known for its annual lamb sale, when young sheep from all over the north of Scotland are bought and sold. It is said that all roads meet at Lairg, and it's certainly a hard place to avoid. From here, the A839 heads east to meet the A9 between Dornoch and Golspie, and west to meet the A837 which runs out to Lochinver. The A836 heads north to Tongue, and south to Bonar Bridge. The A838 meanwhile heads northwest to Laxford Bridge and on to Durness, near Cape Wrath. There's a **TIC** ① *T01549-402160, Apr-Oct daily.*

There are several interesting walks around the village, some of which lead to prehistoric sites, such as the Neolithic hut circles at nearby **Ord Hill**. These walks, and many others in the region, are described with maps in the Forestry Commission's leaflet *Forests of the Far North*, which is available at the Ferrycroft Countryside Centre and the TIC.

Dornoch and around → *Colour map 2, B2. Phone code 01862.*

Dornoch is another architectural delight, with its deep, golden sandstone houses and leafy cathedral square. Bishop Gilbert of Moravia (Moray) built the cathedral circa 1245. His family's success in gaining a foothold in northeast Scotland against the Norsemen was rewarded with the Earldom of Sutherland. It was trouble with the Jarls which prompted Gilbert to move his power base here from Caithness, mindful that his predecessor had been boiled in butter by the locals (proof that too much of the stuff can kill you). The TIC ① T08452-255121, Oct-May Mon-Fri 0900-1700, Jun and Sep Sat 1000-1600, Jul-Aug Mon-Fri 0900-1700, Sat 1000-1600, Sun 1000-1600, is on Castle Street.

The 13th-century **cathedral** ① *Mon-Fri 0730-2000, has volunteers welcoming visitors to the Cathedral from 1000-1600 from mid-May to mid-Sep*, was badly damaged in 1570, then subjected to an ill-conceived 'restoration' by the Countess of Sutherland in 1835. Among the few surviving features is a series of gargoyles, including a green man, and the effigy of an unknown knight. Opposite the cathedral is the 16th-century Bishop's Palace, now a hotel, see Sleeping, page 299.

Nowadays Dornoch is famous for its links golf course, one of the world's finest and relatively easy to get on. It overlooks miles of dunes and a pristine sandy beach. A stone near the links marks the spot where the last witch in Scotland was burned, in 1722. Folklore recounts a bloody battle against raiding Vikings in 1259 on the beach at Embo, just to the north, in which Sir Richard Murray was killed. The battle is commemorated at the Earl's Cross. Trout fishing is available on Dornoch Lochans; enquire locally.

Straggling crofting townships such as **Rogart** are scattered through the glens and around the coast, all occupied and worked vigorously. The coastal population was swollen in the 19th century by tenants evicted from the inland glens; they were resettled here and encouraged to try fishing at such villages as Embo. Others joined the eager flood of emigrants to the New World already under way. Crofting tenancies still exist, but crofters now enjoy more protection, see box, page 345.

North of Dornoch is **Loch Fleet**, a river estuary with a ferocious tidal race at its mouth and an SNH reserve protecting rare birds and plants. The rotting skeletons of the fishing fleet abandoned in the First World War lie in the sand on the south shore west of the car park. Nearby is **Skibo Castle**, where the couple formerly known as "Mr and Mrs Madonna" tied the knot, in relative secrecy. It is home to the very, very exclusive **Carnegie Club** ① *www.carnegieclub.co.uk*, for envious voyeurs or those with too much money. There are several walks in the forestry plantations in the area.

Far northeast coast → *For listings, see pages 298-302.*

North of Dornoch, the A9 follows the coast of Sutherland into the neighbouring county of Caithness through a series of straggling villages, still haunted by the memories of the Duke of Sutherland, one of Scotland's most odious landowners. The chief town in these parts is Wick, once the busiest herring port in Europe.

Ins and outs

Getting there and around A few miles north of Wick, is the airport. There are direct flights here from Kirkwall (Orkney), Sumburgh (Shetland) and Aberdeen, Stornoway, Durham, Bristol, Newcastle, Edinburgh and Southampton. For the most up to date information on the taxi, car hire and bus service options available to you on arrival at Wick airport, it's recommended to contact airport information on T01955-602215. The train and bus

The light fantastic

Due to the absence of light pollution, Scotland offers some of the best areas of inky dark sky in Europe. Visit www.darkskyscotland.org.uk. A feature of visiting the far north of Scotland in winter is the chance of seeing the Aurora Borealis, or Northern Lights, which decorate the night skies like a gigantic laser show. The best time to see them is between October and March – especially during December and January. Try to get as far north as you can, though there are no guarantees of a sighting as cloud cover can obscure visibility. Any of the north-facing coastal villages are a good bet.

stations are next to each other behind the hospital. If you don't fancy flying, don't forget there are regular trains from London to Inverness, with **ScotRail** ⓘ *T0845-601 5929, www.firstgroup.com/scotrail*, trains travelling north to Thurso and Wick.

Golspie → Colour map 2, B2. Phone code 01408. Population 1650.

The picturesque little village of Golspie (around 1800 inhabitants) offers more than just a couple of banks and a supermarket. For half a mile from here are the **Highland Wildcat Trails** ⓘ *www.highlandwildcat.com*, Scotland's most northerly purpose built mountain bike tracks with over 20 miles of trail to suit every level of rider. What's more, after you've hired a bike at Square Wheels in Strathpeffer the forested trails are free to explore.

In Golspie there's also an 18-hole golf course, and the **Orcadian Stone Company** has a large display of fossils and geological specimens from the Highlands and beyond. The town lives in the dark shadow of the Sutherlands: on **Beinn a'Bhraggaidh** (1293 ft), to the southwest, is a huge, 100 ft-high monument to the Duke of Sutherland. Those who make it up to the monument and who know something of the Duke's many despicable acts may find the inscription risible, as it describes him as "a judicious, kind and liberal landlord". There's no reference to the fact that he forcibly evicted 15,000 tenants from his estate. Not surprisingly, locals would like to see this eyesore removed from the landscape, broken into tiny pieces and then scattered far and wide. Unfortunately, and most surprisingly, they have thus far been unsuccessful.

A mile north of the village is the grotesque form of **Dunrobin Castle** ⓘ *T01408-633177, Mar-May, Sep-Oct Mon-Sat 1030-1630, Sun 1200-1630, Jun-Aug Mon-Sat 1030-1730, Sun 1200-1730, £8.50, concessions £7, children £5*. This is the ancient seat of the Dukes of Sutherland, who once owned more land than anyone else in the British Empire. Much enlarged and aggrandized in the 19th century, with fairytale turrets, the enormous 189-room castle, the largest house in the Highlands, is stuffed full of fine furniture, paintings, tapestries and objets d'art. The whole unedifying spectacle is a legacy to obscene wealth and unimaginable greed, on a par with Nicolae Ceausescu's palace in Bucharest. The hideous confection overlooks admittedly beautiful gardens laid out with box hedges, ornamental trees and fountains. The museum is an animal-lover's nightmare and almost a caricature of the aristocracy, with a spectacular Victorian taxidermy collection. There are also local antiquities, some from ancient brochs, and Pictish stonecarvings.

Brora → Colour map 2, B2. Phone code 01408. Population 1860.

Brora sits at the mouth of the River Brora which, as everywhere on this coast, is the site of a once-lucrative salmon netting industry. At the harbour, the ice house is a relic of the herring boom. Coal mines, opened in the 16th century, salt pans and a brickworks are all defunct. Still very much alive, however, is **Hunter's**, the local weavers of heavyweight traditional tweeds, and a good place to invest in some natty headwear. A mile or so north of town is the interesting **Clynelish distillery** ① *T01408-623000, www.malts.com, Easter-Sep Mon-Fri 1000-1700, Oct Mon-Fri 1000-1600, Nov-Easter by appointment only*. Tour £5. Something of a cult amongst whisky lovers, this malt is distinctive for its briny flavour. **Castle Cole** in lovely Strath Brora, 8 miles northwest, is one of several ruined brochs. Another, **Carn Liath** (signposted), is by the main road, 3 miles south of Brora.

Helmsdale → *Colour map 2, B3. Phone code 01431.*

North of Brora is the former herring port of Helmsdale, which gets busy in the summer. The village is most notable for its excellent **Timespan Heritage Centre** ① *T01431-821327, Easter-Oct Mon-Sat 1000-1700, Sun 1200-1700, £4, concessions £3, children £2, Family £10*, which brings the history of the Highlands to life through a series of high-tech displays, sound effects and an audio-visual programme. There's also a café and shop on site. The **TIC** ① *T01431-821402, www.helmsdale.org*, is situated within Strath Ullie Crafts on the harbour next to the river side car park.

North from Helmsdale the A9 climbs spectacularly up the **Ord of Caithness** and over the pass enters a desolate, treeless landscape; an area devastated during the Clearances. To get some idea of the hardships people had to endure, stop at the ruined crofting village of **Badbea**, just beyond Ousdale. At **Berriedale**, a farm track leads west to the Wag, from where you can climb **Morven** (2313 ft), the highest hill in Caithness, with amazing views across the whole county.

Dunbeath → *Colour map 2, B3. Phone code 01593.*

The A9 coast road then drops down into Dunbeath, a pleasant little village at the mouth of a small *strath* (or glen). This was the birthplace of one of Scotland's foremost writers, Neil Gunn (1891-1973). His finest works, such as *The Silver Darlings* and *Highland River*, reflect his experiences of growing up in the northeast and are fascinating accounts of life here during the days of the herring boom, though the sleepy harbour of today is barely recognizable as the erstwhile bustling fishing port. The villages of Dunbeath, and Latherton to the north, are included in the **Neil Gunn Trail**, as is the beautiful walk up the glen, described in the leaflet available at the **Dunbeath Heritage Centre** ① *T01593-731233, www.dunbeath-heritage.org. uk, Easter-Oct daily 1000-1700, other times by arrangement, £2, concessions £1, children free.* Here, in Neil Gunn's former school, you can learn all about the life and works of the famous novelist as well as the history of Caithness. Just outside the village is the **Laidhay Croft Museum** ① *T01593-731244, Easter-Oct daily 1000-1700, £2, children 50p*, a restored traditional longhouse with stable, house and byre all under the same roof. It also has a tea room.

Wick and around → *Colour map 2, A4. Phone code 01955.*

A century ago Wick was Europe's busiest herring port, its harbour jam-packed with fishing boats and larger ships exporting tons of salted fish to Russia, Scandinavia and the West Indian slave plantations. The fishing industry has long since gone, and the demise of the nearby nuclear power station at Douneray has only added to the tangible sense of ennui. There are, however, some interesting archaeological sites in Caithness, as well as the dramatic landscapes, and Wick makes a useful base for exploring the area. There is a **TIC** ① *T01955-602547, Sep-Jul Mon-Sat 0900-1730, Aug Mon-Sat 0900-1730, Sun 1100-1600*, in McAllans menswear shop on the High Street.

After the goldrush

A short drive from Helmsdale, up the Strath of Kildonan (or Strath Ullie), is Baile an Or (Gaelic for 'goldfield'), site of the great Sutherland Gold Rush of 1869. It all started after local man Robert Gilchrist returned home from the Australian gold fields only to discover gold here, on his doorstep. His success brought others rushing to Kildonan, and soon a shanty town had sprung up to accommodate them.

Within a year the gold rush was over, but small amounts are still found today. Anyone who fancies their luck can try a bit of gold panning in the Kildonan Burn at Baile an Or, about a mile from Kildonan train station. You can rent out gold panning kits at Strath Ullie Crafts & Fishing Tackle, opposite the Timespan Heritage Centre in Helmsdale, for £2.50 per day, and licences are free.

Wick is actually two towns. On one side of the river is Wick proper and on the other is Pulteneytown, the model town planned by Thomas Telford for the British Fisheries Society in 1806 to house evicted crofters who came to work here. Now it's one great living museum of fishermen's cottages and derelict sheds and stores around the near-deserted quays. It gives a good idea of the scale of the herring trade during its heyday in the mid-19th century, when over 1000 boats set sail to catch the 'silver darlings'. Here, on Bank Row, is the superb **Wick Heritage Centre** ① *T01955-605393, www.wickheritage.org, Easter-Oct Mon-Sat 1000-1545, £3, children 50p.* The highlight of the centre is its massive photographic collection dating from the late 19th century.

Three miles north of Wick are the impressive 15th-century clifftop ruins of **Sinclair and Girnigoe Castle**. There is a good walk along the rocky shore east of town to The Trinkie, a natural rock pool fed by the sea, and about a mile further on to the Brig o' Trams. Ask for details at the TIC. Before Wick, at Ulbster, is another archaeological site, the **Cairn o' Get**. Opposite the sign are the precipitous **Whaligoe Steps**, which lead to a picturesque harbour.

Archaeological sites around Caithness

Caithness may lack the impressive henges of other parts of the UK but it does boast a number of stone rows: areas covered by large numbers of small stones arranged in geometric patterns. These are thought to date from circa 2000 BC. The best and most easily accessible is the **Hill o' Many Stanes**. To get there, drive 9 miles south of Wick. On the A9 and turn right onto a minor road where you see the signpost. A short way up this road is a signposted gate into the field, on the left-hand side. A path leads to the curious fan-shaped configuration of Bronze Age standing stones; 200 of them in 22 rows. No one yet knows their precise purpose but studies have shown that there were once 600 stones here.

There are also a couple of Pictish Brochs in Caithness. These were almost entirely unique to the north and northwest of Scotland and were windowless, dry-stone towers, between 10 and 45 ft in height, with a circular ground plan. The walls were hollow in places to allow staircases and small chambers. These were built between 2000 BC and AD 200, though they continued in use after that time, and were used for both domestic and defensive purposes. There are remains of a broch at **Nybster**, 7 miles south of John o'Groats on the A9. Look out for the sign for the harbour and broch on the right heading north. Turn onto the minor road which leads down to a small car park. Follow the path along the clifftop to the broch, which stands on a headland surrounded by steep cliffs on three sides. Just to the south of here, at Keiss, are the remains of another broch.

One of the most interesting archaeological sites in the north are the well-preserved **Grey Cairns of Camster**. These chambered cairns, dating from the third and fourth millenia BC, are burial mounds of stone raised around carefully structured circular chambers with narrow entrance passages. To get there, head a mile east of Lybster on the A9, then turn left on to the minor road leading north to Watten. The cairns are 5 miles along this road, on the left-hand side. They comprise two enormous prehistoric burial chambers dating from 2500 BC. They are amazingly complete, with corbelled ceilings, and can be entered on hands and knees through narrow passageways.

⊙ East coast listings

For Sleeping and Eating price codes and other relevant information, see Essentials pages 38-45.

⊜ Sleeping

Cromarty *p290*
For such an appealing place, there's precious little accommodation, so it's advisable to book ahead during the summer months.
D-E Braelangwell House, Balblair, T01381-610353, www.btinternet.com/braelangwell. Mar-Sep. 3 rooms. Superior standard of B&B in elegant Georgian house. Recommended.
C-D Royal Hotel, Marine Terr, T01381-600 217, www.royalcromartyhotel.co.uk. Open all year. 10 rooms. The best place to stay, with a good restaurant (♛-♛), and cheaper meals available in the bar.

Dingwall and around *p290*
A The Dower House, 2 miles north of Muir of Ord on A862 to Dingwall, T01463-870090, www.thedowerhouse.co.uk. Open all year. 3 en suite double rooms and 1 suite. Very comfortable small hotel set in 5 acres of woodland and gardens, excellent food (dinner ♛). Worth the money. It won the Good Hotel Guide 2008 Cesar Award. Recommended.
B Kinkell House Hotel, Easter Kinkell, Conan Bridge, by Dingwall, T01349-861270, www.kinkellhousehotel.com. 9 en suite rooms. Lovely country hotel in farmland. Style, comfort and attention to detail, as well as superb cooking.
B Tulloch Castle Hotel, Tulloch Castle Dr, T01349-861325, www.tullochcastle.co.uk. Open all year. 19 en suite rooms. This 12th-

century castle is the smartest place around, 4-poster bed costs a bit more. No pets. Children under 3 free.
D Fairfield House, Craig Rd, Dingwall, T01349-864754. Open all year. 4 en suite rooms. Better-than-average B&B.

Strathpeffer and around *p291*
B-C Coull House Hotel, Contin, 3 miles southwest of Strathpeffer, T01997-421487, www.coulhousehotel.com. Open all year. 20 rooms. Top of the list is this elegant 19th-century country house offering fine food. Excellent choice.
D-E White Lodge, the Square, T01997-421730, www.the-white-lodge.co.uk. Open all year. 2 en suite rooms. Another very good B&B. Self-catering cottage available.
E Brunstane Lodge Hotel, Golf Course Rd, T01997-421261, www.brunstanelodge.com. Open all year. 6 en suite rooms. Good little hotel serving decent cheap bar meals.
E Craigvar, the Square, Strathpeffer, T01997-421622, www.craigvar.com. Open all year. 3 en suite rooms. Elegant Georgian house offering considerable style and comfort at this price, one of the best B&Bs in the region. Recommended.

Tain *p292*
A-L Glenmorangie House at Cadboll, Fearn, by Tain, T01862-871671, www.theglenmorangiehouse.com. 6 en suite rooms. Owned by the whisky people, this place oozes style. Accommodation in the main house is supplemented by 3 cottages which sleep a total of 6. Price includes a

lavish 5-course dinner and afternoon tea as well as breakfast. Recommended.

B Morangie House Hotel, Morangie Rd, T01862-892281, www.morangiehotel.com. 26 rooms. Now part of the Swallow chain, this Victorian hotel still serves excellent food in its restaurant. Very good value.

B-C Mansfield House Hotel, Scotsburn Rd, T01862-892052. 19th-century baronial splendour and superb cuisine. Restaurant also open to non-residents (♕♕♕). Highly recommended.

E Golf View House, 13 Knockbreck Rd, T01862-892856, www.golf-view.co.uk. Open Feb-Nov. 3 en suite rooms and 1 suite. Substantial house offering very fine B&B.

Lairg p293

D Highland House, 88 Station Rd, T01549-402414, www.lairghighlandhouse.co.uk. Open all year. 3 en suite rooms. Good B&B.

E Lairg Highland Hotel, Main St, T01549-402243, www.highland-hotel.co.uk. Open all year. 6 en suite rooms. Decent value, also does bar meals.

F Sleeperzzz.com, Rogart Station, Rogart, T01408-641343, www.sleeperzzz.com. The most interesting place to stay, where you can get cheap hostel accommodation in the 3 old rail carriages that have been converted to sleep 20 people. There's a 10% discount for bike or train users and children under 12 receive a 25% discount.

Edderton to the Kyle of Sutherland p293

F Carbisdale Castle Youth Hostel, Culrain, T08700-0041109, www.carbisdale.org. Mar-Oct (except the 1st 2 weeks in May). The largest and most sumptuous hostel in Scotland, and possibly anywhere else, is ½ mile up a steep hill from the station. Staying here is an amazing experience and will charm any frustrated would-be aristocrat. Available Nov-Feb for exclusive hire.

Dornoch and around p294

There are lots of good B&Bs.

B 2 Quail Restaurant and Rooms, Castle St, T01862-811811, www.2quail.com. Open Apr-Oct Tue-Sat for dinner, Nov-Mar Fri-Sat only. 3 rooms above 1 of the very best (and smallest) restaurants in the region, run by Michael and Kerensa Carr. Rooms are not huge but the magnificent set 3-course menu using Scottish produce (♕♕♕) more than compensates. Highly recommended.

B-D Dornoch Castle Hotel, Castle St, T01862-810216, www.dornochcastlehotel. com. Open Apr-Oct. Formerly the Bishop's Palace, this 16th-century building is full of character and boasts excellent food (♕♕♕). Good special offers.

C Auchlea Guest House, Auchlea, T01862-811524, www.auchlea.co.uk. Open all year. 3 en suite rooms in a modern bungalow run by Mrs Garvie. Serves a full, traditional Scottish breakfast with porridge.

Camping

Dornoch Caravan Park, by the golf course and the beach, T01862-810423.

Brora p295

A-B Royal Marine Hotel, Golf Rd, T01408-621252, www.royalmarinebrora.com. Open all year. Early 20th-century country house designed by Robert Lorimer, this fine golf hotel boasts an indoor pool, spa and gym. Has an excellent reputation for its food.

E Glenaveron, Golf Rd, T/F01408-621601, www.glenaveron.co.uk. 3 en suite rooms. Among the many B&Bs here, this is an excellent choice and good value. Under 6s free.

Helmsdale p296

D Navidale House Hotel, Navidale, T01431-821258. Open Feb-Nov. 10 rooms. Most upmarket choice, a good place to eat.

E Broomhill House, T01431-821259, www.blancebroomhill.com. Open all year. 2 en suite rooms. Good-value B&B with a distinctive turret, run by Sylvia Blance. Evening meals served on request.

F SYHA Youth Hostel, Stafford St, T01431-821636. Offers 24 beds, some private rooms.
E Torbuie, Navidale, T01431-821424.
Open Apr-Oct. Good value B&B. En suite rooms with sea views.

Wick and around *p296*
C-D Portland Arms Hotel, 15 miles south, Lybster, T01593-721721, www.portlandarms.co.uk. Open all year. 22 rooms. Best around, a 19th-century coaching inn, full of character serving great food in both formal and informal settings (ᵀᵀᵀ-ᵀᵀ).
D-E Wellington Guest House, 41-43 High St, T01955-603287. Open Mar-Oct. Worthwhile choice if **The Clachan** is full.
D The Clachan, 13 Randolph Pl, South Rd, TT01955-605384, www.theclachan.co.uk. Open all year. 3 en suite rooms. Best B&B in town in our opinion.

🍴 Eating

Cromarty *p290*
ᵀᵀ **Cromarty Arms**, opposite Cromarty Courthouse, T01381 600230. Cheap home-made bar food. Also has live music some nights.
ᵀᵀ **Sutor Creek**, 21 Bank St, T01381-600855, www.sutorcreek.co.uk. Wed-Sun 1100-2100. Cooperative café/restaurant that's famous for its superb wood-fired pizzas, but also other dishes using local ingredients in season. Recommended.
ᵀᵀ **Thistle's Restaurant**, Church St, T01381-600471. Has an imaginative menu, including interesting vegetarian dishes.
ᵀ **Binnie's Tearoom**, Church St. A great place for tea and scones.

Portnahomack *p292*
ᵀᵀᵀ-ᵀᵀ **The Oyster Catcher**, Main St, T01862-871560, www.the-oystercatcher.co.uk. Open Mar-Oct Wed-Sun. A great place to eat out here is this small café/restaurant serving a wide variety of snacks and lunches, and dinner from 1930 (if booked). Crêpes are a speciality, but it also does pasta, soups, seafood and fish.

Edderton to the Kyle of Sutherland *p293*
ᵀᵀ-ᵀ **Falls of Shin Restaurant**, Achany Glen, by Lairg, T01549-402231. Open Jun-Sep from 0930, Oct-May from 1000. A gastronomic oasis housed in the most unlikely of places. Simple food cooked to perfection, probably better than your mum makes. Good value.

Brora *p295*
ᵀᵀᵀ-ᵀᵀ **Il Padrino**, Station Sq, T01408-622011. Tue-Sun for lunch and dinner (open from 1100 for coffee, from 1200 for meals). Good italian food, if a bit pricey.

Helmsdale *p296*
ᵀᵀ **La Mirage**, Dunrobin St, opposite the TIC, T0143-821 615, www.lamirage.org. Daily 1100-2100. Famous tea room whose erstwhile proprietress, the inimitable Nancy Sinclair, modelled herself, and her tea room, on Barbara Cartland, queen of romantic novels. The whole effect is pure kitsch. Good food though, especially the fish and chips.

Wick and around *p296*
The best places to eat are out of town at the **Portland Arms Hotel** (see Sleeping, above) and the **Bower Inn**, see page 287.
ᵀᵀ **Bord de L'Eau**, Market St, T01955-604400. Open Tue-Sat for lunch and dinner. French bistro-style cooking. Very popular with locals.
ᵀᵀ **Queen's Hotel**, Francis St, T01955-602992. Probably the next best place in town.
ᵀ **Cabrelli's**, 134 High St. Great café serving large portions of carbs to locals.

🛍 Shopping

Tain *p292*
Bannerman Seafoods, The Burgage, T01862-892322, www.bannerman-seafoods.co.uk. A fish and seafood wholesalers, sells local mussels.
Brown's Gallery, Castle Brae, www.brownsart.com. Showcases work by Highland artists.

Dornoch and around *p294*
The Dornoch Bookshop, High St, T01862-810165. The only bookshop in the area and stocks local books.

✪ Activities and tours

Cromarty *p290*
Boat trips
Dolphin-spotting boat trips leave from Cromarty, but go with an accredited operator. **EcoVentures**, Harbour Workshop, Victoria Pl, T01381-600323, www.ecoventures.co.uk. ½-day and full-day trips leave from the harbour to see porpoises, seals, dolphins, and perhaps even killer whales further out. Accredited operator.

Mountain biking
The challenging tracks of Learnie Red RockTrails are just 3 miles from Rosemarkie village. See also www.HiMBA.org.uk and www.forestry.gov.uk/mtbscotland.

☉ Transport

Cromarty *p290*
Bus Highland Bus & Coach, T01463-233371, runs a service to **Inverness** from **Fortrose** and **Cromarty**, up to 12 times daily Mon-Sat, once on Sun. There is also a once daily Mon and Fri service from **Dingwall**.

Dingwall and around *p290*
Bus There are hourly buses between **Inverness** and **Invergordon**, via Dingwall. There are also hourly buses between **Inverness** and Dingwall via **Muir of Ord**. There are buses between Dingwall and **Rosemarkie**, Mon and Fri, and between Dingwall and **Cromarty**, Mon and Fri. **Train** Dingwall is on the rail line between **Inverness** and **Kyle of Lochalsh** and **Thurso**. There are several trains daily in each direction, 30 mins to Inverness.

Strathpeffer and around *p291*
Bus There are regular buses between Strathpeffer and **Dingwall**.
Cycle hire Square Wheels, the Square, T01997-421000. The place to buy or hire your mountain bike kit (from £15) for a fantastic day in the hills.

Tain *p292*
Bus Citylink buses between **Inverness** and **Thurso** pass through Tain Mon-Fri. There are also buses to **Portmahomack**, Mon-Fri; **Balintore**, Mon-Sat; **Lairg** via **Bonar Bridge**, Mon-Sat; and **Dornoch** via **Bonar Bridge**, once a day Mon-Thu with Inverness Traction, T01463-239292, and Rapson's of Brora, T01408-621245.
Train Tain is on the **Inverness** to **Thurso** rail line. There are 3 trains daily in each direction.

Lairg *p293*
Bus Inverness Traction buses, T01463-239292, run from here to **Ullapool**, with connections to **Lochinver** and **Durness**, from May to early Oct, Mon-Sat. Lairg is also the central point for several postbus routes, T01463-256228.
Train Trains between **Inverness** and **Thurso** stop at Lairg and Rogart stations 3 times daily.

Dornoch and around *p294*
Bus Hourly buses run daily between **Inverness** and **Lairg** stop in **Ardgay** and **Bonar Bridge**. Citylink buses between **Inverness** and **Thurso** also stop in Dornoch up to 8 times daily.
Train Services between **Inverness** and **Thurso** stop at **Ardgay** and **Culrain**.

Helmsdale *p296*
Bus and train Buses and trains are the same as for Wick (see below). Helmsdale is on the **Inverness** to **Wick/Thurso** rail line.

Wick and around *p296*

Air Direct flights to **Kirkwall** (Orkney), **Sumburgh** (Shetland) and Mon-Fri to **Aberdeen**, **Stornoway**, **Durham**, **Bristol** and **Newcastle** with Eastern Airways, T01652-680600. Destinations with Flybe, T0871-700 0535, www.flybe.com, include **Edinburgh** and Southampton.

Bus Scottish Citylink, T08705-505050, buses between **Inverness** and **Thurso** stop en route in **Wick** (3 daily). There are also regular local buses to **Thurso**, via **Halkirk** or **Castletown**, and buses to **Helmsdale**, daily, and **John o'Groats**, Mon-Sat.

Car and cycle hire Richard's Garage, Francis St, T01955-604123.

Train Trains leave for **Inverness**, daily, 4 hrs, via **Thurso**, **Helmsdale**, **Golspie**, **Lairg** and **Dingwall**.

Contents

Footprint features

Skye & the Small Isles

At a glance

☺ **Getting around** The main roads
are well served by public transport
but you'll need a car or bike to
explore further off the beaten track.
✪ **Time required** Allow several
days to tour Skye, longer if including
the Small Isles.
☀ **Weather** The Cuillins attract
heavy weather off the Atlantic,
from Apr-Oct you'll maximize your
chance of enjoying fine weather.
✖ **When not to go** During Oct-
Mar, the weather is less settled.

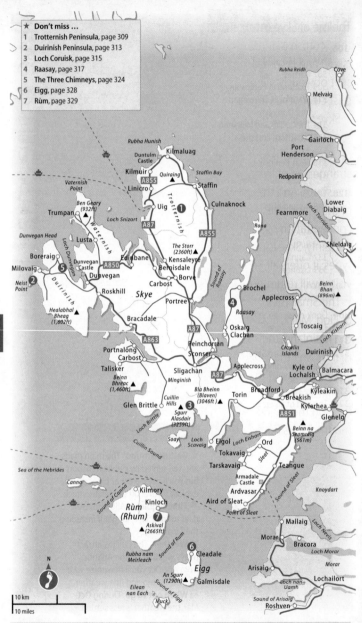

Cove
Rubha Reidh
Melvaig
Gairloch
Port
Henderson
Rubha Hunish
Kilmaluag
Duntulm
Castle
Kilmuir   Quiraing   Staffin Bay
Kilmuir   Staffin
Linicro   Culnaknock
Vaternish   Uig   Trotternish ❶
Point
Ben Geary
(932ft)
Trumpan   Loch Snizort
Waternish   Rona
Dunvegan Head   Lusta   The Storr
Boreraig   Loch Dunvegan Edinbane   (2360ft)
Milovaig   Dunvegan Castle Bernisdale
Milovaig   Dunvegan   Borve   Sound of Raasay Brochel
Neist   Duirinish   Roskhill   Carbost
Point ❷   Skye   Portree
Healabhal
Bheag   Bracadale
(1,602ft)
Portnalong   Peinchorran
Carbost   Sconser
Talisker   Sligachan
Beinn   Minginish   Bla Bheinn
Bhreac   (Blaven)
(1,460ft)   Cuillin   (3046ft)   Torin
Glen Brittle   Hills ❸
Sgurr
Alasdair
(3259ft)   Loch Scavaig
Cuillin Sound   Soay   Elgol   Loch Eishort
Sea of the Hebrides
Canna
Sound of Canna
Kilmory
Kinloch
Rùm   Askival
(Rhum) ❼   (2665ft)
Rubha nam
Meirleach
Cleadale ❻
Eigg
An Sgurr
(1290ft)   Sound of Eigg
Eilean
nan Each   Muck

Fearnmore   Loch Torridon
Lower
Diabaig
Shieldaig
Applecross   Beinn
Bhan
(896m)
Toscaig
Crowlin
Islands   Duirinish
Applecross   Kyle of
Lochalsh   Balmacara
Breakish   Kyleakin
Broadford   Kylerhea
Beinn na   Glenelg
Seamraig
(561m)
Ord   Knoydart
Tokavaig   Sleat   Teangue
Tarskavaig   Armadale   Sound of Sleat
Castle
Aird of Sleat   Ardvasar
Point of Sleat   Mallaig   Loch Nevis
Morar   Bracora
Loch Morar
Morar
Arisaig   Loch nan   Lochailort
Uamh
Galmisdale   Roshven   Sound of Arisaig

Raasay ❹
Oskaig
Clachan
A87
A863
A855
A850
A87
A851
A855

N
10 km
10 miles

The Isle of Skye (An t-Eilean Sgitheanach), the best known of all the Scottish islands, gets its name from the Norse word for cloud (skuy) and is commonly known as Eilean a' Cheò (the Misty Isle), so it obviously rains a lot here. But when the rain stops and the mist clears, the views make the heart soar.

Skye's spectacular combination of mountains and sea creates some of Britain's most breathtaking scenery. There are the surreal rock formations of the Trotternish Peninsula, the hummocky strangeness of Fairy Glen and the gentler pleasures of Sleat in the south. And then there are the Cuillins. Standing in the centre of the island, these implacable mountains are the greatest concentration of peaks in Britain and among the most challenging. Certainly, Skye is one of the best places in Scotland for outdoor types: it offers air, sea, land and light in their purest form and any visitor will return home physically refreshed and spiritually uplifted.

The Small Isles is the collective name given to the four islands of Eigg, Muck, Rùm and Canna, lying south of Skye. Seen from the mainland, they look a very tempting prospect. Visiting the islands isn't the logistical nightmare of yesteryear, though sailings are less frequent than on many routes and accommodation and facilities remain limited. However, the determined traveller, with time on their hands, will be well rewarded, particularly on Eigg and mountainous Rùm, with its superb walking and abundant wildlife.

Isle of Skye

Aside from swooning at the island's natural beauty, the most popular destination is Dunvegan Castle, stronghold of the Macleod clan, while their old enemies, the MacDonalds hail from the Sleat Peninsula in the south of the island. The most famous Macdonald, Flora, who helped Bonnie Prince Charles flee to France, was born at Milton on South Uist but latterly moved to Skye and was buried at Kilmuir in 1790. ▶▶ *For listings, see pages 319-327.*

Ins and outs

Getting there

The quickest route to Skye is across the bridge (no toll) from Kyle of Lochalsh to Kyleakin. Coach services run to Skye from Glasgow (via Fort William) and Inverness (bus No 917), with connections to all main cities in the UK (**Scottish Citylink**, T0871-266 3333; **National Express**, T0871-781 8178). The Citylink bus service from Inverness runs three times daily and the journey takes three to four hours. The Glasgow service runs to Kyleakin, Portree and Uig, three to four times daily and it takes three hours to reach Portree from Fort William. Winter services are less frequent with only a few buses in each direction each day.

There is also a train service from Kyle of Lochalsh to Inverness, see page 255. Eyed from the south, the high arch of Skye Bridge is certainly dramatic. A still more scenic approach to the island is by ferry from Mallaig to Armadale, on the southern Sleat Peninsula. The car and passenger ferry makes this 30-minute crossing eight times each way Monday to Saturday, and six times on Sunday (reduced sailings in winter). Booking is recommended, call T08000-665000 or visit www.calmac.co.uk. The one-way trip costs £4.05 per passenger and £21.20 per car. A five-day saver return is £6.80 and £36.50. Trains from Fort William and Glasgow Queen Street connect with some of the ferries, see www.firstscotrail.co.uk.

The best way to Skye is from Glenelg to Kylerhea, south of Kyleakin. The tiny community-owned car ferry makes the 10-minute crossing every 20 minutes, daily from Easter to October between 1000 and 1800. Between June and the end of August it sails until 1900. The cost per car is £12 or £15 return (with up to four passengers), see page 255 for details. Information and ticket bookings can be found at www.skyeferry.co.uk. ▶▶ *For further details, see Transport page 326.*

Getting around

Skye is the second largest Hebridean island (after Harris and Lewis), at almost 50 miles long and between seven and 25 miles wide. It is possible to run up a hefty mileage as the extensive road system penetrates to all but the most remote corners of its many peninsulas. It is possible to get around by public transport midweek, with postbuses supplementing the normal services, but, as everywhere in the Highlands and Islands, buses are few and far between at weekends, especially Sunday, and during the winter. Buses run between Portree, Broadford, Uig (for ferries to the Western Isles), Kyleakin, Armadale (for ferries to Mallaig), Dunvegan and Carbost, and a more limited service runs from Broadford to Elgol and Portree to Glen Brittle. Getting around by public transport is more time consuming in winter (October to March) as bus services are less frequent on some routes. ▶▶ *For further details, see Activities and tours page 326, and Transport page 326.*

Tourist information

Skye is well served by all types of accommodation: B&Bs, guesthouses, hostels, bunkhouses, campsites and some very fine hotels. During the peak summer months advance bookings are recommended. These can be made directly or through the island's tourist information centres in Portree, Broadford, Uig and Dunvegan. See www.visithighlands. com, and www.isleofskye.com. For local tourist information centres see individual sections.

Portree → *For listings, see pages 319-327. Colour map 1, C3. Phone code 01478.*

Portree is Skye's capital and, as such, is a functional kind of place with all the attendant facilities and services you'd expect to find in the island's main settlement. That said, it's

Portree

Sleeping	Portree Independent	Harbour View Seafood 2
Bayfield	Hostel 6	Sea Breezes 3
Backpackers 1	Torvaig Campsite 7	
Bosville 2	Viewfield House 8	**Bars & clubs**
Cuillin Hills 3		Isles Inn 4
Marmalade 4	**Eating**	Pier Hotel 5
Otterburn 5	Cafe Arriba 1	Royal Hotel 6

N

100 metres
100 yards

fairly attractive; a busy fishing port built around a natural harbour, with a row of brightly painted houses along the shorefront and the rest of the town rising steeply up to the central , the centre of which is now dominated by a public car park (pay and display).

Ins and outs
Getting there and around Portree is ideally placed for trips to all but the most south-westerly parts of the island. Buses leave from the bus station in Somerled Square to Dunvegan, Uig, Broadford, Kyleakin, Armadale, the Talisker Distillery and Glenbrittle. There are also services to the mainland. The town is compact enough to get around easily on foot, though there is a regular town bus service for those needing to get into the centre from the outskirts.

Tourist information The helpful **TIC** ① *Bayfield Rd, T01478-612137, year-round Mon-Sat*, has bus timetables, a good selection of books and maps, internet access and several (20p) leaflets outlining local walking routes including the 2-mile-long Portree Forest walk.

Sights
Aros Experience ① *Viewfield Rd, ½ a mile from town centre on the road to Broadford, T01478-613649, www.aros.co.uk, Easter-Oct daily 0900-1800, Nov-Dec daily 0900-1730, £4.50, concessions £3.50, children under 12 free*, provides a 20 minute audio-visual display of the island's history and cultural heritage, and a birds-eye 'live cam' view of a sea eagles nest. The island's only theatre is housed here and features a varied programme of events, including drama, traditional music, comedy and films (see Entertainment, page 325). There's also a restaurant with reasonable snacks and a shop selling tartan souvenirs, which seems to dominate the Aros experience. Certainly, culturally this place is no replacement for the much missed An Tuireann Arts Centre further up the road which closed in 2008 after failing to satisfy the bean counters.

A nice, gentle introduction to walking in the area, and an opportunity to stretch your legs before tackling more strenuous routes such as the Old Man of Storr or the Quiraing, starts out from Bosville Terrace. Follow the street as it curves round, then take the right fork at the first junction, down towards the shore. Just after the car park to the right the road splits: follow the path to the right along the northern shore of the bay. The path follows the shore and passes a viewpoint and flagpole. It then becomes rougher as it swings round the headland and reaches a gate in a dyke. Go through the gate and cross the muddy field, then follow the fence up to the left until you reach another gate. Climb over the gate and continue along the edge of the next field, then cross a stile at the top. Walk up the slope to the clear track and follow this left as it heads uphill. You'll then see some houses; take the track beyond the house on the left and follow it down between two large farm buildings. The path heads down across rough moorland towards Portree. Cross the stile and continue downhill through some woods; then you'll see a hotel on your left before rejoining the original road near the car park. It's about two and a half miles and takes about one and a half hours at an easy pace. The path can get very muddy in places. Details of several local walks can be found in the TIC.

North from Portree is the 30-mile-long Trotternish Peninsula, sticking out like a giant thumb hitching a lift from a passing ferry. The interior of the peninsula is a basaltic lava wilderness full of bizarre rock formations. A 20-mile-long escarpment of sheer cliffs and towering pinnacles dominates the landscape. The best known of these strange formations, the **Quiraing** and **Old Man of Storr**, can be explored on foot (see below and page 310). The A855 and A87 roads follow the coast around the peninsula, and a spectacular minor road bisects the ridge from Staffin Bay to Uig. Trotternish is best explored with your own transport, but there are a few daily buses covering the circular route from Portree.

Uig

The A87 runs northwest from Portree to the tiny ferry port of Uig, dramatically set in a horseshoe bay and the departure point for ferries to **Tarbert** (Harris) and **Lochmaddy** (North Uist). The island's busy and helpful **Caledonian MacBrayne** ① *T0800-665000, www.calmac.co.uk*, ferry booking office is here whilst just 20 yds past CalMac's door you'll also find the production nerve centre (and shop) of the acclaimed **Skye Brewery** ① *T01470-542477, www.skyebrewery. co.uk*, which exports its ales around the world. Alternatively, also by the CalMac office, kids will enjoy painting their own earthenware pot at the **Uig Pottery** ① *May-Sep Mon-Sat*.

Just outside the village is the magical **Fairy Glen**. Turn right just before the **Uig Hotel** coming down the hill from the Portree direction. About a mile up the single track road you enter an eerie, mysterious world of perfect conical hills, some up to 60-ft high. It's almost inconceivable that these are natural formations, and the inevitable mist only adds to the spooky strangeness of the place.

Uig to Duntulm

At **Kilmuir** is the **Skye Museum of Island Life** ① *T01470-552206, Easter-Oct Mon-Sat 0930-1700, £2.50, children £2.* The group of thatched houses give a fascinating insight into a crofting community's way of life of at the end of the 19th century, and is the most authentic of several such museums on Skye. Behind the museum, at the end of the road, is **Flora MacDonald's Monument**, which marks the grave of Skye's most famous daughter, with her husband buried alongside. The rather austere memorial is inscribed with Dr Johnson's poignant tribute, see box, page 311. Indeed, so highly regarded was 'Flory' that it's said her funeral was the largest ever seen in the Highlands. Apparently, her cortege stretched for 1½ miles whilst over 300 gallons of whisky were drunk at her wake!

At the northwest tip of the peninsula, 15 minutes' drive from Uig, is **Duntulm Castle**, a dramatic ruin perched atop a steep cliff, haunted by keening winds and the ghosts of its tragic past: according to local legend, the castle was abandoned around 1732 when a nursemaid accidentally let the baby heir fall from a window onto the cliffs below. The 15th-century structure, built on the site of an ancient Norse stronghold, became the chief Skye residence of the powerful MacDonalds and was the most imposing castle in the Hebrides.

The Quiraing walk

Beyond Duntulm the A855 heads across the tip of the peninsula to the east coast, where the famous bizarre rock scenery is found. At the north end of **Staffin Bay**, a minor road cuts across the peninsula to Uig. This road is the access point for the Quiraing, the famous jumble of strangely shaped hills and rocks that is one of the island's classic walks. This four-mile walk is quite demanding, but the dramatic scenery more than compensates. To get

Take no prisoners

Violent conflict between neighbouring clan chiefs was so commonplace on Skye and in the rest of the Western Highlands that it was almost accepted as part of the very fabric of society. One particularly gruesome example took place on Eigg in 1577. The Macleods had taken refuge in a cave but their presence was discovered by the MacDonalds, who piled brushwood at the entrance and set fire to it, burning alive the 395 people sheltering inside, almost the entire population of the island. Revenge came the following year, at Trumpan church in Ardmore Bay on Skye. The Macleods landed under cover of the early morning fog and set light to the church, burning the congregation inside.

to the starting point, drive 19 miles north from Portree on the A855. At Brogaig, just north of Staffin, take the single-track road to Uig. Follow it and, just after the road has zigzagged its way up the face of the ridge, park in the car park to the left. Cross the road and follow the well-defined path along the base of the cliffs, with a steep grassy slope down to the right. After about one mile you'll start to see some of the well-known rocky features on the far side of a rough valley. The most imposing of these is **The Prison**, a huge, tilted square block. On the left, among the towering cliffs, is **The Needle**, a shaft of rock about 120-ft high. Scramble up the narrow gully to the left of The Needle to reach **The Table**, an area of flat grassland surrounded by high cliffs (local shinty teams used to play here). From The Table continue along the path at the foot of the cliffs, past a small lochan on the right and through a stone dyke, until you reach the lowest point of the ridge on your left. Scramble up on to the ridge and make your way back along the tops of the cliffs (take care at this point). There's a hard climb up the slopes of Meall na Suirmamach, but the views from the top are spectacular. Continue along the top of the cliffs for just over a mile and you'll see the car park. Even if you don't attempt the walk, the road over the back of the Trotternish ridge from Uig makes a worthwhile detour.

Kilt Rock

A few miles south of Staffin Bay is Kilt Rock, an impressive 60-m sea cliff which gets its name from the vertical columnar basalt strata overlying horizontal ones beneath. A rather tenuous comparison perhaps, but the cliffs south of Staffin are particularly spectacular, as are the **Lealt Falls**, a torrent of mountain water at the head of a gorge, a few miles south of Kilt Rock. The falls are signposted by the road, so all you have to do is park the car and peer over. Just before the turn for Kilt Rock at Ellishadder is the wee **Staffin Museum** ① *May-Oct*, sporting such finds as a dinosaur bone and Bronze Age artefacts.

Old Man of Storr walk

A few miles further south, and seven miles north of Portree, is a car park which is the starting point for another of Skye's famous walks: up to the Old Man of Storr, the distinctive pinnacle which has detached itself from the cliffs of the Storr behind. This basalt finger of rock, 165 ft high, stands beneath the steep cliffs of **The Storr** (2360 ft) and is visible from the A855. The starting point for the three and a half mile walk up and back (1½ hours) is the car park on the left, just over six miles north of Portree, near the northern end of Loch Leathan, which can be reached by bus from Portree. Cross the stile over the wall by the Forestry Commission sign and follow the clear track up through the conifer plantation.

Faithful Flora

In Kilmuir graveyard is the memorial which marks the grave of Flora MacDonald, one of the most famous characters in Skye's long history. The memorial bears Dr Johnson's fitting epitaph: A name that will be mentioned in history, and if courage and fidelity be virtues, mentioned with honour.

It was Flora MacDonald who helped Bonnie Prince Charlie to escape capture following the Jacobite defeat at Culloden in 1746. Pursued by government troops, the prince fled from South Uist 'over the sea to Skye' aboard Flora's boat, disguised as an Irish servant girl by the name of

Betty Burke. He then made his way to Portree, where he bade farewell to the young woman who had risked her own life to protect his.

When Flora's part in the prince's escape became known, she was immediately arrested and sent to the Tower of London. She was released a year later, married a Skye man and then emigrated to North Carolina where she spent the next 12 years of her life. They returned to her husband's house in Kingsburgh in 1786. Flora died in Skye in 1790, and it is said that her funeral was the largest ever witnessed in the Highlands.

The track is a gradual uphill climb until you come out into open grassland. Go through the gate in the fence and then it's a steep climb up the grassy slope with the massive pinnacle towering overhead. Once at the top you enter an area of weird and impressive rock formations. You can follow any of the dozens of paths that lead between the rocks, or just enjoy the fantastic views across to Raasay and the mainland beyond. You can follow the same path back down to the car park.

Waternish, Dunvegan and Duirinish

→ *For listings, see pages 319-327. Colour map 1, C2-3. Phone code 01470.*
In the northwest of Skye the peninsulas of Waternish (or Vaternish) and Duirinish point out into the Minch towards the Western Isles. The larger Duirinish Peninsula holds more interest for the visitor, featuring the beautiful green valley of **Glendale**, an area brimming with history, the dramatic walk to **Neist Point** and **Dunvegan Castle**, Skye's most famous landmark.

Edinbane
The turn-off to this much-visited part of the island is four miles northwest of Portree. The A850 swings west towards Dunvegan but eight miles before the castle and at the head of Loch Greshornish is the tiny village of Edinbane, where there's a campsite, two hotels, several B&Bs, a petrol station and the renowned **Edinbane Pottery** ⓘ *T01470-582234, www. edinbane-pottery.co.uk, 0900-1800 Nov-Easter weekdays and Easter-Oct daily. workshop and showroom*, which is a must for hunters of imaginative hand-crafted souvenirs.

Waternish Peninsula
The A850 continues west. Those with their own transport and time on their hands might wish to make an interesting little detour at the **Fairy Bridge**, where the B886 runs north to **Trumpan**, near the tip of the Waternish Peninsula. If the weather's good (and it is, occasionally), this is the best place to watch the sun set in a blaze of red over the Outer

Things to do on Skye when it's raining

Just in case you didn't know, it can rain quite often on Skye and, unless you're one of those hardy souls who's prepared to brave the elements, you'll need to know about the island's main indoor attractions. There are numerous opportunities to shelter from the rain, but most of them cost money and many will leave you regretting it, so here's our list of the top 10 things to do. Details of opening times and admission prices are given under each relevant destination.

Beginning in Portree, there's the **Aros Experience** (page 308), which gives a good introduction to the island's history. North of Uig, at Kilmuir on the Trotternish Peninsula, is the **Skye Museum of Island Life** (page 309), which pretty much does what it says on the sign. Northwest from Portree is **Dunvegan Castle** (see below), home of the Clan Macleod and top of most visitors' itineraries. On the road to Dunvegan is **Edinbane Pottery** (page 311), where you can buy pots of every shape and size and watch them being made.

Travelling south from Dunvegan, you'll reach the turn-off to the **Talisker Distillery** (page 315), the island's only whisky distillery, where you can sample the distinctive peaty taste. While you're there you can visit nearby **Carbostcraft Pottery** (page 325), in the village of Carbost, and indulge in some more gift buying. If you're in need of some refreshment after all that culture and shopping, you could do a lot worse than the bar at the **Sligachan Hotel** (page 322), which boasts an impressive array of whiskies and climbers' beards. In the southern peninsula of Sleat, near the Armadale ferry terminal, is **Armadale Castle** (page 319), with a visitor centre that is worth visiting. Nearby is one of the branches of **Skye Batiks** (page 325), with a huge selection of these 'new age' style fabrics in a range of original Celtic designs (the other branch is in Portree). And for that final drink before boarding the ferry to Mallaig, pop into the cosy bar of the **Hotel Eilean Iarmain** (page 323), which serves wonderful food.

Hebrides. If there's no sunset, then you could always visit **Skyeskyns** ⓘ *T01470-592237, www.skyeskyns.co.uk, daily 0900-1800*, in Loch Bay, the country's only traditional exhibition tannery. While here, you could also pop into the island's oldest pub, the **Stein Inn** (see Sleeping, page 324). Close by, you can buy high quality handspun Scottish merino wools and cashmere at **Shilasdair** ⓘ *T01470-592297, daily 1000-1800.*

The ruined church at Trumpan, at the end of the road, has some grisly skeletons in its cupboard (see box on page 310). In the graveyard is the 'trial stone'. A hole in the stone was used to test whether or not an accused person was telling the truth. If they could quickly find the hole and stick their arm through it while blindfolded, they were found innocent, but if not, they were guilty. The church is also the starting point for the strenuous 8-mile walk out to **Waternish point** and back.

Dunvegan

A few miles further on from the turn-off to Waternish is the little village of Dunvegan. Just to the north of the village is proud **Dunvegan Castle** ⓘ *T01470-521206, www.dunvegan castle.com, Apr-mid Oct daily 1000-1730, mid Oct -Apr daily 1100-1600, castle and gardens £9, concessions £7, children £4.50, gardens only £7, concessions £6, children £3.50*, the island's most important tourist attraction. The no. 56 Stagecoach bus serves the castle, running from Glendale to Portree via Dunvegan, and back

The castle is the home of the chiefs of the Clan Macleod who have lived here for over seven centuries, making it the oldest continuously inhabited castle in Britain. The present structure dates from the 15th and 16th centuries and, though the Victorian restoration has left it looking more like a baronial house, a look inside reveals its true age. Among the few genuinely interesting relics on display is Rory Mor's horn, a huge drinking vessel which the chief's heir must drain 'without setting down or falling down', when filled with claret (about one and a half bottles). There's also a lock of Bonnie Prince Charlie's hair, clipped from his head by Flora MacDonald as a keepsake, but pride of place goes to the Fairy Flag. The flag has been dated to between the fourth and seventh centuries and is made of Middle Eastern silk. It is said to have been given to the clan chief by a fairy, and has the power to ensure victory in battle for the clan on three occasions. It has been used twice so far. The lovely castle gardens lead down to the lochside jetty, from where you can take a **seal-spotting cruise** ① *T01470-521500, May-Oct daily, £7, children £4*. These shores are reportedly inhabited by 35% of Skye's seal population. Nevertheless, you'll get a refund if you fail to spot one. There's also a busy restaurant and gift shop by the castle gates.

In the village of Dunvegan is **Giant Angus MacAskill Museum** ① *T01470-521296, Easter-Oct daily 0930-1800, £1.50, concessions £1, children free*, housed in a thatched, whitewashed cottage, which relates the life story of the tallest ever Scotsman, Angus MacAskill, born on the Outer Hebridean island of Berneray and who grew to 7 ft 9 ins tall. He emigrated to Novia Scotia and toured the United States with the midget General Tom Thumb, who is said to have danced on his outstretched hand. More interesting than the museum though, are the stories of its owner, Peter MacAskill, in particular the one about the replica coffin, which is worth the admission fee alone. Peter is a descendent of Angus and also runs the museum at Colbost (see below).

Duirinish Peninsula

West of Dunvegan is the Duirinish Peninsula. The northern half is populated along the western shores of **Loch Dunvegan** and in the beautiful and green **Glendale**, an area brimming with history but with hardly an island family left. Glendale is now dubbed 'Little England', owing to the large number of incoming settlers from the south. The area is famed throughout the Highlands and Islands, for it was here in 1882 that local crofters, spurred on by the **Battle of the Braes**, see box, page 315, resisted the cruel and petty tyranny of their estate manager. The authorities sent a gunboat to deal with the uprising and arrested the ringleaders, some of whom were imprisoned in Edinburgh and became known as the 'Glendale Martyrs'. This episode sparked a radical movement throughout the Highlands and led to the Crofter's Holdings Act of 1886, which gave the crofters a more secure tenure and fair rent, see box, page 345. The uninhabited southern half of the peninsula is dominated by Healabhal Bheag (1601 ft) and Healabhal Mhor (1538 ft), a pair of decapitated hills known as **Macleod's Tables**. They are so named because legend has it that the clan chief held a huge open-air feast for King James V on one of the hilltops.

The **Glendale Visitor Route** is signposted from just before Dunvegan village and leads westwards along the shores of the loch and across the peninsula. There are several interesting little sights along the way. Those interested in finding out more about the region's history, and crofting on the island, should head for the **Colbost Folk Museum** ① *T01470-521296, Easter-Oct daily 0930-1800, £1.50, concessions £1, children free*, housed in a restored blackhouse, with a peat fire burning and an illicit still out the back. The museum is adjacent to the **Three Chimneys** restaurant and four miles from Dunvegan on the B884 to Glendale. A little further on is **Skye Silver** ① *T01470-511263, Mar-Oct daily 1000-1800,* where you can buy silver jewellery in traditional Celtic designs. Further north is the studio of **Diana Mackie** ① *T01470-511795 (phone for appointment), www.diana-mackie.co.uk*, who designed the interior of the renowned Three Chimneys restaurant (see above) and whose landscape artwork is inspired by the dramatic coastal scenery just beyond her door.

Borreraig was home to the famous MacCrimmons, hereditary pipers to the Macleod chiefs and the first composers, players and teachers of *piobaireachd* (pibroch), which can be heard at an annual recital at Dunvegan Castle in early August. The ruins of the ancient piping college can still be seen. Moving from the sublime to the ridiculous, in the village of **Glendale** is a **Toy Museum** ① *T01470-511240, www.toy-museum.co.uk, all year Mon-Sat 1000-1800, £3, concessions £2, children £1*, which should appeal to kids of all ages.

The B884 continues west, then a road turns off left for Waterstein. At the end of this road (just over two miles) is a car park which is the starting point for the walk out to the lighthouse at **Neist Point**, the most westerly point on Skye and one of the most pleasant walks on the island. It's about 1½ miles there and back and well worth the effort. The path is easy to follow and the views of the sea cliffs are wonderful. There are lots of nesting seabirds around and you might even spot whales offshore. The **lighthouse**, built in 1909, is now unmanned.

The Cuillins and Minginish

→ *For listings, see pages 319-327. Colour map 3, A3. OS Landranger No 32 & OS Outdoor Leisure No 8.*
The district of Minginish is the wildest and least-populated part of the island, but for many it is the greatest attraction, for this is where the Cuillins are to be found. This hugely impressive mountain range, often shrouded in rain or cloud, is the spiritual heartland of the island, and when it's clear their heart-aching grandeur can be appreciated from every other peninsula on Skye. Though officially called the Cuillin 'Hills', these present some of the toughest climbing in Britain. Indeed, the magnificent scenery and vast range of (high and low level) walks and scrambles have attracted climbers and walkers for centuries, but have also claimed many lives. It cannot be stressed too strongly that the Cuillin ridge, whilst famous and spectacular is also an exposed and demanding route that should only be attempted by experienced climbers and/or with a qualified guide. For further information, see page 26.

Walks into the Cuillins
There are three routes into the Cuillins: from the Sligachan Hotel, from Glen Brittle, and from Elgol. The eastern part of the range is known as the **Red Cuillins**. Their smoother, conical granite peaks contrast sharply with the older, darker gabbro of the jagged-edged **Black Cuillins** to the west. The latter are particularly suitable for rock climbing and best approached from Glen Brittle, while the former are accessed from the Sligachan Hotel. There are 20 'Munros' (mountains over 3000 ft in height) in the Cuillins, with the highest being Sgurr Alasdair, at 3251 ft. Though the sheer majesty of the mountains can only be appreciated at close quarters by the climber, there are impressive views from Elgol, from the road into Glen Brittle and, more distantly, from the west coast of Sleat. **Glen Sligachan** is one of the most popular routes into the Cuillin range and the main access point for the more forgiving Red Cuillins, the walk to **Loch Coruisk**, or the ascent of **Marsco**.

Glen Brittle → *Phone code 01478.*
Six miles along the A863 to Dunvegan from Sligachan is a turning left to Portnalong, Carbost and the Talisker Distillery (see below), which soon leads to the entrance to

Law of the land

One of the most significant incidents in the island's history took place in April 1882, when a group of around 100 local crofters and their families fought a pitched battle against a force of 60 police sent by the government from Glasgow. The 'Battle of the Braes', as it became known, was caused, like many other such uprisings throughout the Highlands and Islands, by threatened evictions. The local crofters were so incensed by the injustice of the eviction notices served on them that they destroyed the offending documents, leading the government to dispatch its police force. The defeat of the government forces of law and order by a bunch of men, women and children with sticks and stones is often described as the last battle fought on British soil, and led eventually to the establishment of a Royal Commission to look into the crofters' grievances.

Glen Brittle. To reach Glen Brittle, take the Portree–Carbost–Fiscavaig bus (Stagecoach No 53/54). Get off at the turn-off and then walk the remaining 8 miles.

The road down Glen Brittle affords great views of the western side of the imposing Black Cuillins, until it ends at the campsite and shore at the foot of the glen. From Glen Brittle there are numerous paths leading up to the corries of the Black Cuillins. There are many alternative options for those wishing to continue up to the upper corries or to the main ridge. One of the finest of the Cuillin corries is **Coire Lagan**. This walk starts from the beach at Glen Brittle village and takes you up to the lochan in the upper coire, with Sgurr Alasdair, the most difficult of the Munros, towering overhead. A fine Cuillin sampler is the short walk to the spectacular **Eas Mor** waterfall.

Talisker → *Phone code 01478.*

A recommended trip for whisky drinkers, or if it's raining, is to the excellent **Talisker Distillery** ① *T01478-614308, www.discovering-distilleries.com, Apr-Oct Mon-Sat 0930-1700, Jul-Aug daily 1100-1700, Nov-Mar Mon-Fri 1000-1700, tours, £5*, at **Carbost** on the shores of Loch Harport, on the B8009 (not in the village of Talisker itself, which is on the west coast). This is Skye's only whisky distillery and produces a very smoky, peaty single malt, with a distinctive hot, peppery palate, particularly the 20- and 25-year-old expressions. The entry fee includes a discount voucher on any 70cl bottle of malt whisky sold in the shop.

Elgol → *Phone code 01471.*

One of the most rewarding drives on Skye is the 14-mile single-track road from Broadford to Elgol (Ealaghol), a tiny settlement near the tip of the Strathaird Peninsula, from where you can enjoy the classic view of the Cuillins from across Loch Scavaig and also see the islands of Soay, Rùm and Canna. It was from here, on 4 July 1746, that the Young Pretender finally left the Hebrides. Before leaving, he was given a farewell banquet by the MacKinnons in what is now called **Prince Charlie's Cave**. There's also the added attraction of a dramatic boat trip, to the mouth of **Loch Coruisk**, in the heart of the Black Cuillin. The glacial sea loch, romanticized by Walter Scott and painted by Turner, is over 2 miles long but only a few hundred yards wide, closed in by the sheer cliffs on either side and overshadowed by the towering mountains of black basalt and gabbro. The road to Elgol also gives great views of Bla Bheinn (pronounced Blaven), best seen from Torrin, at the head of Loch Slapin.

Elgol to Camasunary Bay

Elgol is the starting point for the walk to Camasunary Bay. This 9-mile coastal walk is quite demanding, but on a clear day the views of the Cuillins make it well worth the effort. It starts from the car park in Elgol. From here, walk back up the road for a short distance, then turn left along a track behind some houses, signposted for 'Garsbheinn'. Beside the last of these houses is a sign for the path to Coruisk. Follow this path along a steep grassy slope. The views across Loch Scavaig to the island of Soay and the Cuillins behind are marvellous. The slope gets even steeper beneath Ben Cleat, and you'll need a good head for heights to continue across the foot of Glen Scaladal, crossing a burn in the process (which can be tricky if it's in spate). Then it's on along the path beyond Beinn Leacach to Camasunary Bay, with its backdrop of mighty Sgurr na Stri and Bla Bheinn. The shortest way back is to retrace your steps but, as an alternative, follow the clear track from Camasunary up the right side of Abhainn nan Lean over the hills to the east until it joins the B8083 from Broadford. From here it's about three and a half miles back along the road to Elgol.

Broadford and the east coast → *For listings, see pages 319-327. Colour map 3, A4-5.*

Broadford (An t-Ath Leathann), Skye's second-largest village, basically consists of a mile-long main street strung out along a wide bay. The village may be low on charm but it's high on tourist facilities and makes a good base for exploring the south and east of the island. The road north from Broadford to Portree passes through Sconser, departure point for the short ferry ride to the little-visited island of Raasay.

Broadford

Broadford has plenty of accommodation and places to eat. Next to the Esso station is a Co-op, there's a laundrette in the petrol station shop (open 24 hours) and a bank with ATM. There is no tourist office as such, just an information point housed in the Otter Shop in the main car park (with erratic opening hours). Broadford is also home to one of the most incongruous attractions on the island, or elsewhere in the Highlands, the **Skye Serpentarium** ① *The Old Mill, Harrapool, T01471-822209, www.skyeserpentarium.org.uk, Apr-Oct Mon-Sat 1000-1700, Jul-Aug daily 1000-1700, £3.50, children £2,* a rescue centre for all kinds of snakes, lizards and other reptiles, which you can look at or touch: a welcome retreat if it's raining. Housed within the same rustic mill building is the cosy **Old Mill Café** ① *T01471-822800,* where you can feast on home-baking. Whilst just 50 m behind here is the fabulous **Creelers Restaurant** (see Eating, page 324).

Kyleakin

The opening of the Skye Bridge, linking the island with the Kyle of Lochalsh (see page 252), has turned the former ferry terminal of Kyleakin (Caol Acain) into a quiet backwater, though the absence of road traffic and coastal views north and across to Lochalsh make it a pleasant place to stay. It's particularly popular with backpackers. The bridge is supported in the middle on the small islet of **Eilean Ban**, erstwhile home of author and naturalist, Gavin Maxwell, and now home to an otter sanctuary. It can be visited as part of tour from the **Bright Water Visitor Centre** ① *Kyleakin, T01599-530040, www.eileanban.org, Apr-Oct Mon-Fri 1000-1700 (opening times vary so call ahead), free (donations welcome).* The interactive centre is worth a visit, especially if you have kids, and the keepers cottages on Eilean Ban can be rented for between £300-570 per week, which is ideal for wildlife enthusiasts. In Kyleakin, by the pier, history buffs can read up about the ruin of **Castle Maol** on the headland and how in 1263

King Haakon once sailed into the area with 120 ships in preparation for doing battle with King Alexander III of Scotland. The village pub, **King Haakon**, serves good bar meals but if you'd prefer a curry, try the recently opened **Taste of India** ① *T01599-534134*, just past the roundabout on the road to Portree.

Kylerhea
About 4 miles out of Kyleakin a road turns left off the A87 and heads southeast to Kylerhea (pronounced Kile-ray). The bridge may be the most convenient route to Skye, but the best way to cross is on the small car and passenger ferry that makes the 10-minute crossing to Kylerhea from Glenelg. For full details of times and prices, see page 306. Near Kylerhea is the Forestry Commission **Otter Haven** ① *T01320-366322, daily 0900 till 1 hr before dusk, free*. An hour-long nature trail takes you to an observation hide where you can look out for these elusive creatures.

Broadford to Portree
The road north to Portree runs between the fringes of the Red Cuillins and the coast, giving good views across to the **Isle of Scalpay**.

Continuing north, the road then turns west past Luib and along the shores of brooding Loch Ainort until it reaches **Sconser**, the departure point for the ferry to Raasay and then climbs around Loch Sligachan before descending into Portree. On the opposite side of the loch from Sconser are the crofting communities known as **The Braes**, who successfully opposed their landlords' eviction notices and brought the crofters' cause to the public's attention (see box, page 315).

Isle of Raasay → OS Landranger No 24.
The lush and beautiful island of Raasay lies only a few miles off the east coast of Skye, yet despite its attractions it is all too often ignored by the tourist hordes. The island is a nature conservancy, where you may see seals, eagles and otters. Its hilly terrain and superb cliff scenery also offer numerous walking opportunities, the best of which is to the distinctive flat-topped summit of **Dun Caan**, the island's highest point at 1456 ft. The views from the top are amongst the finest in Scotland. Raasay falls away to the sea, with the Cuillins on one side and the peaks of Torridon and Kintail on the other, shouldering past one another, their great blunt heads bumping the clouds. The walk to the top of the extinct volcano, via an old iron mine, is relatively straightforward and one of the most rewarding anywhere in the islands. So much so, in fact, that Boswell was inspired to dance a Highland jig on reaching the top in 1773, during his grand tour with Dr Johnson. Another excellent walk starts from North Fearns, at the end of a road running east from **Inverarish**, to the deserted township of **Hallaig**, down the side of Beinn na Leac and back to North Fearns. The circular route is 5 miles long.

Raasay was for much of its history the property of the Macleods of Lewis, whose chief residence was the ruined **Brochel Castle**, before moving to **Clachan**, where **Raasay House** is now located. The original Raasay House was torched by government troops after Culloden, along with all the island's houses and its boats, as punishment for the Macleods giving refuge to Bonnie Prince Charlie. After the Macleods sold the island in 1843, the Clearances began in earnest and Raasay suffered a long period of emigration, depopulation and poverty. It is not surprising, then, that the island's most famous son, the great poet **Sorley Maclean**, wrote so passionately about this lost society. Born in Oskaig in 1911, he wrote in his native Gaelic as well as in English, and is highly regarded internationally. He died in 1996. Raasay's population now numbers around 150 and the island is a bastion of the Free Church, whose strict Sabbatarian beliefs should be respected by visitors.

Gaelic spread

Outside the Outer Hebrides, Skye is the most important centre of Gaelic culture, with a large proportion of the island's population speaking Gaelic in everyday life. This in itself is remarkable given the significant drop in population during the Clearances and the continued undermining of Gaelic culture ever since, especially through the State education system.

Today, as in other parts of the Hebrides, the native culture is again under threat, this time from the huge influx of 'white settlers' from the south, but there is also a new-found pride and interest in the Gaelic language. This has been helped by the existence of the Gaelic college on Sleat, through Gaelic writers such as the late Sorley Maclean, a radical local newspaper (The West Highland Free Press), economic support from Highlands and Islands Enterprise, and spiritual under-pinning from the Sabbatarian Free Church. Gaelic is being taught again in schools and can be heard on television. The ancient heritage of the Highlands and Islands is fighting back and reasserting itself as a major European culture.

Those who make it to the north of the island may wish to note that the 2 miles of road linking **Brochel** to **Arnish** were the work of one man, Calum Macleod. He decided to build the road himself after the council turned down his requests for proper access to his home. He spent between 10 and 15 years building it with the aid of a pick, a shovel, a wheelbarrow and a road-making manual which cost him three shillings. He died in 1988, soon after its completion, and it continues to be known as 'Calum's Road'. For an account of Calum's Road, read the book of that name penned by the journalist and author, Roger Hutchinson.

Sleat Peninsula → For listings, see pages 319-327. Colour map 3, A4. Phone code 01471.

East of Broadford is the turn-off to the peninsula of Sleat (pronouned 'slate'), a part of the island so uncharacteristically green and fertile that it's known as 'The Garden of Skye'. Sleat is another entry point to the island. Ferries cross from Mallaig on the mainland to Armadale on the southeastern shore of the peninsula. While the rest of the island is the preserve of the Macleods, Sleat is MacDonald country. The MacDonalds of Sleat are one of the major surviving branches of Clan Donald, and have the right to use the title Lord MacDonald (but not Lord of the Isles, which is now used by the heir to the throne).

Isle Ornsay

South of Duisdale is the signed turning for Isle Ornsay, or Eilean Iarmain (pronounced *eelan yarman*) in Gaelic, a very beautiful place in a small rocky bay overlooking the tidal Isle of Ornsay with the mountains of Knoydart in the background. This was once Skye's main fishing port, and the neat whitewashed cottages and tiny harbour are still there. It is also largely Gaelic-speaking, thanks mainly to the efforts of its landlord, Sir Iain Noble, who owns the hotel (see Sleeping, page 323) and his own local Gaelic whisky company as well as the northern half of the peninsula, which is known as Fearan Eilean Iarmain.

A few miles further on is a turn-off to the left which leads to the villages of **Ord**, **Tokavaig** and **Tarskavaig**, on the west coast of the peninsula, from where, on a clear day, there are views across to the Cuillins. Near Tokavaig is the ruin of **Dunsgaith Castle**, home of the MacDonalds of Sleat until the 17th century. Tarskavaig is a typical crofting township.

In the early 19th century the MacDonalds claimed the more fertile glens inland for their sheep farms and evicted the people to coastal townships like Tarskavaig. Just beyond the turn-off to Ord are the remains of **Knock Castle**, yet another MacDonald stronghold.

Ostaig

At Ostaig is the Gaelic College, **Sabhal Mor Ostaig** ① T01471-888000, founded by Sir Iain Noble. All subjects are taught in Gaelic, including full-time courses in business studies and media, as well as short courses in Gaelic music and culture during the summer months. The bookshop has a good selection of books and tapes for those wishing to learn the language. Ostaig is also the beginning or end (depending on which direction you're heading) of the detour to Tarskavaig, Tokavaig and Ord.

Armadale to the Point of Sleat

Just before the ferry pier at Armadale is **Armadale Castle** ① T01471-844305, www. clandonald.com, Apr-Oct daily 0930-1730, £6, concessions £4, Nov-Mar shops and gardens open 1000-1600, which was built in 1815 as the main residence of the MacDonalds of Sleat. Most of the castle is now a roofless ruin but the servants' quarters contain an excellent exhibition and accompanying video explaining the history of the Lordship of the Isles. The Clan Donald Lords of the Isles took over from their Norse predecessors in ruling the Hebrides until their power was broken in 1493. The former stables at the entrance comprise offices, a restaurant and bookshop, while the estate manager's house has been converted to accommodate an extensive library and archives. The castle is surrounded by 40 acres of handsome gardens and woodland, and there are ranger-led walks along nature trails with fine views across to the mainland.

Just beyond Armadale Castle is the tiny village of **Armadale**, which is strung out along the wooded shoreline and merges into the neighbouring village of **Ardvasar** (pronounced Ard-vaa-sar), which has a post office and general store. Armadale's raison d'être is the ferry pier and there's not a huge amount to keep you occupied except for Ragamuffin, T01471-844217, a friendly shop famed for its colourful knitwear and quirky gifts. Also on the ferry pier is the excellent **Seafari** boat trip operator (see Activities and tours, page 326). About four or five miles past the ferry port, at the end of the road, is **Aird of Sleat**, a crofting township, from where you walk out to the lighthouse at the **Point of Sleat**. It's a 5-mile walk on a clear path across moorland with fine coastal scenery.

⊙ Isle of Skye listings

For Sleeping and Eating price codes and other relevant information, see Essentials pages 38-45.

⊜ Sleeping

Skye does not lack quality accommodation to suit every budget, though in the busy summer season it's strongly advised to book ahead. The local TICs have lists of available accommodation and for a small fee will book it for you. See also www.skye.co.uk.

Portree *p307, map p307*
There are several guesthouses on Bosville Terr and many B&Bs on Stormyhill Rd and the streets running off it. Prices tend to be slightly higher in Portree than the rest of the island, though B&Bs on the outskirts of town are usually cheaper. There's also an excellent campsite and two good backpackers.
L Cuillin Hills Hotel, off road north to Staffin, on the edge of town, T01478-612003, www. cuillinhills-hotel-skye.co.uk. Open all year. 28 rooms. Set in 15 acres of gardens overlooking

the bay. Variety of rooms at different rates – ask for front rooms with views of harbour and hills . The highly regarded View restaurant is set in a gallery space, while the informal brasserie hosts jazz concerts

A-L Bosville Hotel, Bosville Terr, T01478-612846, www.bosvillehotel.co.uk. 18 rooms. Comfortable and stylish accommodation in central, upmarket hotel with views across the harbour. Enjoy a malt in the **Merchant Bar** – once the village bank. The **Chandlery Restaurant** is one of the best on Skye (see Eating, page 324).

A-B Viewfield House Hotel, on the road into Portree from the south, T01478-612217, www.viewfieldhouse.com. Open mid-Apr to mid-Oct. 11 bedrooms. A 200-year-old country house full of antiques, set in 20 acres of woodland garden. Good food and old-world hospitality, and the log fire adds to the welcoming atmosphere. Has a charming 5-bedroom cottage suitable for family self-catering, £450-700 per week.

B Marmalade, Home Farm Rd, T01478-611711, www.marmaladehotels.com. Open all year. Recently refurbished, this Georgian period building with views across the harbour boasts seven en suite contemporary styled rooms (including family) and great value restaurant (including Sun roast) and bar food Lovely gardens and family friendly.

C Otterburn, Coolin Hills Estate, T01478-613588. 2 rooms. A cosy B&B with stunning views over Portree and harbour.

F Bayfield Backpackers, T01478-612231, www.skyehostel.co.uk. Another central hostel, with 24 beds. Clean and friendly with all amenities just mins from the door.

F Portree Independent Hostel, Old Post Office, The Green, T01478-613737. 60 beds. Right in the centre of town, 100 yds from the town square. Laundrette, Internet access in the lounge and kitchen.

Camping

There's a well maintained, friendly campsite with great showers at Torvaig, 2 miles north of Portree centre, T01478-611849, Apr-Oct.

Trotternish Peninsula *p309*

A Flodigarry Country House Hotel, a few miles north of Staffin, T01470-552203, www.flodigarry.co.uk. Beautifully located at the foot of the mighty Quiraing and with stunning views across Staffin Bay, this is one of the great country house hotels, with a relaxing old-world atmosphere and restaurant. Flora MacDonald's cottage is in the grounds and has been tastefully refurbished, giving the chance to stay in a place steeped in the island's history. The lively bar is a good place to enjoy a laugh and a jig.

B Uig Hotel, on the right of the road into Uig from Portree, beside a white church, opposite **Frazer's Folly**, T01470-542205, www.uighotel.com. Open all year. 16 en suite rooms. Comfortable accommodation in a traditional country house with great views across the bay, good food and a friendly island welcome.

C Duntulm Castle Hotel, near Duntulm Castle, T01470-552213, www.duntulm castle.co.uk. Open Mar-Nov. Friendly and homely with great views across the Minch to the Outer Hebrides. Idyllic and good value. Also offer 3-night dinner and B&B fishing breaks (£375 per person).

D Woodbine House, Woodbine House, Uig, T01470-542243, www.skyeactivities. co.uk. Open Easter-Oct. 5 rooms. Whitewashed stone cottage renowned for flexible room options (ideal for families) and a warm welcome.

D Cuil Lodhe Guest House, Cuill, Uig, T01470-542216. Open all year. 3 en suite rooms. Cosy B&B set on shore of Uig Bay, all rooms with sea views.

F Dun Flodigarry Backpackers Hostel, 100 yds from the bar of the **Flodigarry Country House Hotel**, T/F01470-552212, www.hostelflodigarry.co.uk. Open Mar-Oct. 40 beds. Clifftop seaviews and adequate facilities including laundry, drying room and kitchen. Camping also available.

F SYHA Youth Hostel, 1 mile from the Uig ferry terminal, T01470-542746. Open mid-Mar to Oct. High above the port on the south side of the village. Offers spectacular views over the bay. Basic but comfortable, with a few family and private rooms. The warden can help arrange bike and canoe hire.

Camping

There's camping at Flodigarry Backpackers Hostel (above) and south of Staffin Bay, T01470-562213. Open mid-Apr to end Sep.

Waternish, Dunvegan and Duirinish p311

There are many places to stay in and around Dunvegan, and the TIC will arrange accommodation for you, T01470-521581.

L The House Over-By, Colbost, Dunvegan, T01470-511258, www.threechimneys.co.uk. A few yards away from the very wonderful **Three Chimneys** (see Eating, below), on Duirnish Peninsula and run by the same folk. Six sumptuous rooms, all with sea views.

L-A Skeabost Country House Hotel, Skeabost Bridge, 6 miles north of Portree on A850 to Dunvegan, T01470-532202, www.skeabostcountryhouse.com. Open all year. 14 rooms. This former Victorian hunting lodge on the shores of Loch Snizort, now part of the Oxford Hotels and Inns group, has a snooker room, guest lounges, a nine-hole golf course and salmon fishing on nearby River Snizort. Grand setting and grounds let down by décor that's a tad tired for the pricetag.

B-A The Spoons, 75 Aird Bernisdale, T01470-532217, www.thespoonsonskye.com. Open all year. 3 rooms. A cosy hotel with luxury touches recently built and designed by owners who cut their cloth running the quality lodgings and kitchen of Eilean Shona House. Superb cooking and baking.

A-L Greshornish House Hotel, Edinbane, T01470-582266, www.greshornishhouse.com. Open all year. 8 rooms. Set in 10 acres of land at the end of a single-track road by the shores of the eponymous loch. If you're after peace and tranquillity then

look no further. Head chef Colin Macdonald produces superb food in the dining room (**L-A** including dinner), and there's also a billiard room, tennis court and croquet lawn for those clement days.

B-C (£80-100) **Shorefield House**, Edinbane, T/F01470-582444, www.shorefield-house.com. Open all year. 4 rooms. Superb B&B in modern home with flexible room options for families and groups, as well as separate self-catering accommodation. Much praised breakfasts served in bright conservatory room.

B Hillside House, 34 Lochbay, T01470-592263, www.bed-and-breakfast-on-skye.co.uk. 3 rooms. Traditional-looking house built in 2007 with clever eco-friendly facilities, light-filled rooms and jaw-dropping loch-side views.

C-B (£85-100) **Lyndale House**, Edinbane, T01470-582329, www.lyndale.net. Quiet, delightful retreat hidden down a private drive off the A850 to Dunvegan. 300-year-old house with lovely views and sunsets from the sitting room. Nice touches, such as fresh flowers and bathrobes, and organic produce for breakfast. Also 3 fabulous, self-catering cottages from around £500 per week.

D-C The Lodge at Edinbane, Edinbane, T01470-582217, www.the-lodge-at-edinbane.co.uk. Open all year. 6 en suite rooms. If it's old-world character you're after, this place has it in spades; there's even a ghost or 2. A 16th-century former hunting lodge by the shores of Loch Greshornish, it's also where to enjoy good value bar meals and restaurant fare over a malt or real ale.

D (£60) **Crossal House**, Glen Drynoch, T01478-640745, www.crossal.co.uk. Open all year. Two rooms. Homely B&B set in gardens and surrounding wilds of Glen Drynoch.

Camping

F Kinloch Campsite, Dunvegan, T01470-521531, www.kinloch-campsite.co.uk. Apr-Oct. Pleasant, small campsite with sea views and bakery, fuel, Wi-Fi and shop nearby.

The Cuillins and Minginish *p314*

C Coruisk House, on the right-hand side just after the Elgol village sign on the road from Broadford, T01471-866330, www.seafood-skye.co.uk. Open Apr-Sep. Restaurant with all rooms en suite. Worth coming here for the freshest of seafood (lunch ♔♔, dinner ♔♔♔), which can be enjoyed al fresco (they have a Midge Master). Also has a self-catering cottage and traditional crofthouse for rent.

B Sligachan Hotel, 7 miles south of Portree, where the A87 Kyleakin–Portree road meets the A863 to Dunvegan, T01471-865 0204 www.sligachan.co.uk. With the Cuillins almost at its back door, this is the legendary rallying point for climbers (though it also has its fair share of more sedentary guests). 21 refurbished bed- rooms, a genteel MacKenzies bar and a rather barnlike though lively **Seamus** bar, which stocks a selection of malts and also serves the island's real ales and hearty (♔♔) meals. There's also a 20-bed bunkhouse (Mar-Oct) and a campsite, although there's superb and free wild camping just up river.

C-D Rowan Cottage, a mile east at Glasnakille, T01471-866287, www.rowan cottage-skye.co.uk. Open mid-Mar to end Nov. Attractive B&B that will also organize a packed lunch and supper tray on request.

F Croft Bunkhouse, Wigwams & Bothies, north of Carbost, near Portnalong, T01471-640254, www.skyehostels.com. Open all year. Sleeps 40 and there's also room for camping. Transport from Sligachan or Portree, rents mountain bikes, there's a pub and shop nearby.

F Skyewalker Independent Hostel, beyond Portnalong on the road to Fiscavaig, T01471-640250, www.isleofskye-hostel.com. Now under new management, this pleasant hostel is in a converted school. Basic and clean 36 bunk accommodation with adjoining lounge area. On site café and shop, live folk music and a giant al fresco chessboard.

Camping
The well run campsite opposite **Sligachan Hotel** is possibly the most popular budget place to stay in the area, clean, central and with hot showers. There's also a campsite by the shore in Glen Brittle, T01471-640404.

Broadford and the east coast *p316*
B-C White Heather Hotel, Kyleakin, T01599-534577, www.whiteheatherhotel. co.uk. Open Mar-Oct. 9 en suite rooms. Friendly and welcoming small hotel overooking the harbour. Hosts, Gilllian and Craig, are very helpful and breakfasts are excellent, with views of the harbour thrown in for good measure.

D Luib House, Luib, by Broadford, T01471-820334, www.luibhouse.co.uk. Open all year. Welcoming, rustic B&B with views over Loch Ainort. Great breakfast and will accept dogs.

D-E Tir Alainn, 8 Upper Breakish, T01471-822366. Open all year. 3 rooms, 2 en suite. Just outside Broadford on road to Kyleakin. Pam and Ron are extremely welcoming and run a cosy B&B, offering exceptional food, good views, comfy guest lounge and expert mountain-guide advice.

F Dun Caan Hostel, near the old ferry quay, Kyleakin, T01599-534087, www.skyerover. co.uk. Open all year. Of all the hostels around this part of the island, this one stands out for the personal service. Clean and cosy and packed with information on the local area and Skye. Bike hire available. Recommended.

F Skye Backpackers Hostel, Kyleakin, T01599-534510, www.scotlandstophostels. com. Another budget option with the pub and ruin of Castle Maol close at hand.

Self-catering
Fossil Cottage, a mile or so south of Broadford, at Lower Breakish off the A87 to Kyleakin, T01471-822297, www.fossil-cottage-skye.co.uk. Has been beautifully converted from a 15-year-old croft (and recently a bothy) to a 1-bedroom, TV-free zone right by the water. From £320-£560 per week.

Isle of Raasay p317

D Borodale House (the original name of the house in 1870), on the Isle of Raasay near to the Outdoor Centre, T/F01478-660222, www.isleofraasayhotel.co.uk. Open all year. Extensively refurbished and formerly known as the Isle of Raasay Hotel, with 12 en suite rooms, a lovely **Cuillin View Restaurant** (ⅲⅲ-ⅱⅱ) serving tasty lunches and dinners that include locally reared venison. Sea views.

D Raasay Outdoor Centre, T01478-660266, www.raasayoutdoorcentre.co.uk. The main settlement on the island is Inverarish, a 15-min walk from the ferry dock. Half a mile further is this centre housed in the huge, 259 year-old Georgian mansion that was Raasay House. Offers basic accommodation for backpackers, families and educational groups. After a day's exertions on sea and land, refuel with the home-baking, hearty fare and real ales served by the good value **Dolphin café/restaurant** (0900-2300, evening meals 1830-2100).

F SYHA Hostel, Creachan Cottage, T01478-660240. Open mid-Mar to end-Oct. Reached via a rough track leading up a steep hill from tiny Oskaig. Basic, rustic 20-bed hostel. 2-mile walk to the nearest shop.

Sleat Peninsula p318

L Hotel Eilean Iarmain, Isle Ornsay, T01471-833332, www.eilean-iarmain.co.uk. 12 rooms. Award-winning Victorian hotel full of charm and old-world character, with wonderful views. It is lovely and romantic, and an absolute must if you're in the area and can afford it. Its award-winning restaurant features local shellfish landed only yds away (open to non-residents). A cheaper option is to eat in the cosy bar next door, which serves pub grub of an impossibly high standard in a more informal atmosphere. The hotel also offers winter shooting on the local estate, and you can enjoy a tasting of the local whisky.

L Kinloch Lodge, at the head of Loch na Dal, T01471-833333, www.claire-macdonald.com. The track that leads to the 19th-century **Sporting Lodge** turns off the A851 about eight miles south of Broadford. Lord and Lady MacDonald's family home oozes comfort and refined style with its antiques, prints and classy touches such as Egyptian cotton sheets. This is also a place to enjoy one of Scotland's finest culinary experiences in the grandest of settings. Lady Claire MacDonald is one of the best-known cooks in Scotland and author of several cookbooks, and if you do decide to treat yourself make sure you leave enough room for their exquisite puddings. The 5-course fixed menu is in our expensive range, but well worth it.

L-B Duisdale Hotel, Duisdale, T01471-833202, www.duisdale.com. Extensively refurbished, this former Hunting Lodge which boasts 17 individually styled rooms (2 with 4-poster beds), tasty lunch, afternoon tea, and dinner that draws on the local seafood. Has a fabulous Chart Room in which to savour a malt. There's also the chance to enjoy a day's sail of the offshore islands aboard its private 42-ft yacht.

L-A Toravaig House Hotel, Knock Bay, Teangue, T01471-820200, www.skye hotel.co.uk. Open all year. 9 plush and contemporary en suite rooms. This was voted Scottish Island Hotel of the Year in 2005 and 2007, and its Islay Restaurant won Highlands and Islands Restaurant of the Year 2009-2010. Perfect for those seeking peace and quiet and a romantic break. It's isolated for those who like a pub within walking distance, but why go elsewhere when you're surrounded by such luxury.

B Ardvasar Hotel, in Ardvasar, near ferry terminal, T01471-844223, www.ardvasar hotel.com. Traditional whitewashed coaching inn with 9 rooms, an excellent restaurant and the liveliest pub in the vicinity.

F Flora MacDonald Hostel, Kilmore, between the turning for Isle Ornsay and Armadale, T01471-844440, www.isle-of-skye-tour-guide. co.uk. Clean and friendly 20-bed hostel, offering free transport to and from Armadale Pier.

❷ Eating

There are notable exceptions, including the magnificent **Three Chimneys** restaurant, but some of the best food on Skye is to be found in hotel dining rooms, so also check the Sleeping section for places to eat. Many B&Bs also provide evening meals on request.

Portree *p307, map p307*

♈♈♈ Chandlery Seafood Restaurant, Bosville Hotel, see Sleeping. Run by chef John Kelly, who trained at the Savoy, this restaurant serves exquisite fine food, drawing on the local larder of fresh meats and fish. Oozes style and ambience. The best in town.

♈♈♈-♈♈ Café Arriba, Quay Brae, T01478-611830. Daily 0700-1700, 1800-late. A cosy, bright place with a slightly bohemian air, serving mouth-watering breakfasts, lunches and dinners to suit vegetarians and meat-eaters alike. A starter can include the eastern Dukkah aromatic spice mix or try a main of venison and apricot, or butterbean and apricot korma.

♈♈♈-♈♈ Harbour View Seafood Restaurant, 7 Bosville Terr, T01478-612069. Apr-Oct 1200-2200. Freshest of seafood in cosy surroundings. Good 2nd choice after **Chandlery** and offering a good selection of fine wines to accompany mouth-watering daily specials.

♈♈♈-♈♈ Sea Breezes Restaurant, right by the pier, T01478-612016. Open daily. This snug, bright restaurant will delight the seafood lover and steak afficianado alike. It's not the cheapest in town but you're assured of quality and ambience. Early bird, 2 course dinner from 1700-1800 (£18). Recommended.

♈ The Chip Shop on the pier and directly next door to the busy **Lower Deck Seafood Restaurant**. Open until 2100 daily. A great option for simple, no frills fast food, with guaranteed fresh fish. On the author's visit it ran out of fish and chips. Now that's popular!

Trotternish Peninsula *p309*

♈♈-♈ Pieces of Ate, in the village of Staffin, T01470-562787. Tue-Thu 1030-1630, Fri-Sat 1030-2030, Sun 1100-1500. A great place for home-made soups, bacon rolls, sandwiches, coffee, home-bakes and deli produce.

♈ Pub an the Pier, Uig. Open until 2300. Cheap bar meals, and the famous Cuillin ales are brewed at the nearby Skye Brewery. You can also change foreign currency here.

Waternish, Dunvegan and Duirinish *p311*

♈♈♈ The Three Chimneys, Duirnish Peninsula, Calbost, T01470-511258, www.threechimneys. co.uk. Mon-Sat 1230-1400, 1830-2130. Savour the creative dishes produced by head chef Michael Smith and his team and you'll appreciate why this remote dining experience is considered one of the best in the country. Indeed, some guests even fly to Skye just to experience it. Also accommodation (**L**).

♈♈♈-♈♈ Lochbay Seafood, Waternish Peninsula, T01470-592235, www.lochbay-seafood-restaurant.co.uk. Open Apr-Oct Sun-Fri for lunch and until 2100. You should finish off the day with a meal at this wonderful restaurant where you can almost see your dinner being landed. Book ahead.

♈♈♈-♈♈ Stein Inn, Waternish, T01470-592362, www.steininn.co.uk. Bar meals Mon-Sat 1200- 1600, 1800-2130, Sun 1230-1600, 1800-2100. Reputedly the oldest inn on Skye, book a table here and enjoy a real ale or malt before feasting on venison or shellfish. If you over indulge, there's accommodation (**C**).

Broadford and the east coast *p316*

♈♈♈-♈♈ Creelers Restaurant, just off main road behind the Serpentarium, T01471-822281. Open Tue-Sat (also some Mon's), 1200-1000. Bright, sea-facing restaurant adorned with artwork. Attentive, friendly staff serve simple, appetizing seafood, memorable desserts and a tapas option, Recommended.

¶¶ Red Skye Restaurant, Breakish, T01471 822180 www.redskyerestaurant.co.uk. Open Mon-Sun, 1200-2100 (last orders). Housed in the handsome old village schoolhouse, this newish addition to the Skye dining scene is proving popular with punters from near and far. Head chef Campbell MacFadyen's creative take on traditional and Mediterranean dishes complements the modern décor and relaxed atmosphere. Expect hearty Scots favourites like Cullen skink and Skye haggis alongside juicy salads.
¶¶-¶ Claymore Bar-Restaurant, south end of Broadford, T01471-822333. Decent bar meals.
Kinloch Lodge, Sleat, T01471-833333. Open daily in high season. Lady Claire Macdonald's renowned restaurant may be pricey but head chef Marcello Tully's inventive, changing menus (from £52 per person) based on seasonal and local produce are perfect for that special dining occasion in the Garden of Skye. Reservations essential.

⊕ Bars and pubs

Portree *p307, map p307*
The town's nightlife is mainly confined to eating and drinking. The **Pier Hotel**, Quay St, T01478-612094, by the harbour, is a real fishermen's drinking den; the refurbished **Royal Hotel**, Bank St, T01478-612525, is also popular; for reasonable bar food (¶¶) until 1000, and a younger crowd, head just past the square to the **Isles Inn** at the end of Wentworth St.

Waternish, Dunvegan and Duirinish *p311*
Stein Inn, see Eating and Sleeping above. There are few pleasures in life equal to sitting outside this venerable old pub with a pint of ale from the local Isle of Skye brewery and tucking into an excellent pub supper (¶¶-¶¶) while watching a Hebridean sunset. On less clement evenings the old peat-burning fire inside provides an alternative feel-good factor.

😊 Entertainment

Portree *p307, map p307*
Aros Experience, see page 308. Call the box office for details of their monthly programme, T01478-613750. Has a theatre which shows drama, movies and live music.
Portree Community Centre, Camanahd Sq, Park Rd, T01478-613736. The place to come if you fancy a wild Fri night ceilidh though pubs like the **Isles Inn** by the town square also hold occasional live music/ceilidh nights.

😊 Festivals and events

Portree *p307, map p307*
Early Aug Highland Games, www.skye-highland-games.co.uk, tickets £8, children £4. A one-day event held in Portree. These games, first held in 1877, include traditional highland dancing and piping competitions.

⊙ Shopping

Portree *p307, map p307*
There's a **Co-op** supermarket, diagonally opposite the Bosville Hotel, and a large **Tesco** supermarket on the road to Uig.
Carbostcraft Pottery, Bayfield Rd. Pottery in a variety of designs. Also have a shop near the Talisker Distillery, see page 315.
Crocks & Rocks, Main St. Hebridean jewellery.
Over the Rainbow, at the top of Quay Brae, T01478-612555. Open 0900-2200 in the high season. A good place to buy woollens.
Skye Batiks, the Green, near the TIC, T01478-613331. Sells handmade 'batiks' (colourful cotton fabrics), which are pricey but unique souvenirs from Skye, see also page 312.
Skye Woollen Mill, Dunvegan Rd, T01478-612889. Knitwear and tartan souvenirs.

The Cuillins and Minginish *p314*
Cioch Direct, 4 Ullinish, Struan, T01470-572307. For mountain gear.
Ragamuffin, T01470 844217, at Armadale's ferry pier in Sleat. Filled with vibrant knitwear and interesting gifts.

Skyeskyns, 17 Lochbay, Waternish, T01470-592237. A fascinating place to learn about a traditional tannery and peruse pelts turned into fabulous rugs and throws.

⚙ Activities and tours

Portree *p307, map p307*
If the weather's good, Portree offers a wide variety of outdoor activities.

Boat trips
MV Stardust boat trips, Portree Harbour, T07798-743858, www.skyeboat-trips.co.uk. Sail daily from the pier, and offer a range of cruises, fishing forays and wildlife trips (£12-25), including the chance to spot the rare white-tailed sea eagle, as well as to see the seals at Griana Sgeir and the birdlife at Holm Island. Trips can also be made to Rona, north of Raasay, £18 per person, children £9.

Trotternish Peninsula *p309*
Whitewave Activities, a few miles north of Uig, on the A855 at Linicrowhere, T01471-542414, www.white-wave.co.uk. Here you can try windsurfing, rock climbing, archery, walking and sea kayaking. There's also a café specializing in vegetarian, seafood and Celtic music, and a B&B.

Uig *p309*
Skye Activities, Woodbine Guest House, Uig, T01470-542243. Boat trips on a nippy 6-m rib, wildlife watching, fishing and charters. Mountain biking, archery and waterskiing too.

The Cuillins and Minginish *p314*
Boat trips
Bella Jane Boat Trips, Elgol, T0800-731 3089, www.bellajane.co.uk. Trips to Rùm or Canna. From £12.50 for a 1½-hr trip.
Fast-Boat, T0845-224 2219, www.fast-boat. net. Private charter along Skye's coastline, Raasay, the Small Isles and even to Harris. From £280 per day including skipper and boat.

Misty Isle Boat Trips, Sealladh na Mara, Elgol, T01471-866288, www.mistyisleboat trips. co.uk. Makes the spectacular trip from Elgol into the gaping maw of Loch Coruisk, One of the highlights of any trip to Skye. 3 hrs, including 1½ hrs ashore, £18, children £7.50. You should be able to see seals and porpoises en route. There's also a one-way trip for experienced walkers/climbers (£12.50 adult, children £7.50) who wish to make the return journey on foot or to explore the Cuillins.

Climbing
Some of the guides who offer climbing on Skye are: **Guiding on Skye**, George Yeomans, T01478-650380, www.guidingonskye.co.uk, also offers bushcraft and survival instruction; **Richard MacGuire**, 4 Matheson Pl, Portree, T01478-613180, www.blavenguiding.co.uk, operating since 1995; **Skye Guides**, Mike Lates, 3 Luib, Broadford, T01471-822116, www.skyeguides.co.uk.

Fishing
Skye Ghillie Fly Fishing, 4 Windsor Cres, Portree, T01478-611533, www.skyeghilliefly fishing.co.uk. Salmon and sea-trout fishing, guiding, and ghillie services and tuition.

Isle of Raasay *p317*
Raasay Outdoor Centre, see Sleeping, above, T01478-660266, www.raasayoutdoor centre.co.uk. This reputable operator runs various adventure courses, from climbing to sailing. Also offers basic accommodation.

Sleat Peninsula *p318*
Seafari, T01471-833316, T01471-844787, www.seafari.co.uk. 1- and 2-hr wildlife trips 3-hr whale-spotting trips and a day trip from the pier at Armadale. £15-£100.

⊖ Transport

Portree *p307, map p307*
Bus There are buses (No 57A) Mar-Oct Mon-Sat around the Trotternish Peninsula, in each direction, via **Uig**. Daily buses to

Kyleakin, and to **Armadale** via **Broadford**. There are buses Mon-Sat to **Carbost** (for the Talisker Distillery). Also use this service to access **Glenbrittle**, alighting at Carbost and walking eight miles. There are buses daily Mon-Sat to **Glendale** via **Dunvegan**, and buses Mon-Sat to **Waternish** via **Dunvegan**.
Cycle hire Island Cycles, the Green, T01478-613121. Mon-Sat 1000-1700, hire mountain bikes. Isle of Skye Trekking and Riding Centre, near Suladale and about 10 miles west of Portree towards Dunvegan, T01470-582419, www.theisleof skyetrekkingcentre.co.uk, friendly and fully trained staff. Trekking and horse riding for all ages and abilities.
Taxis A2B Taxis, T01478-613456; Ace Taxis, T01478-613600.

Trotternish Peninsula *p309*
Bus Scottish Citylink runs a service to **Inverness**, **Fort William** and **Glasgow**. For more information, see Ins and outs, page 306.
Ferry From **Uig** to **Lochmaddy** on **North Uist** (1 hr 45 mins) and to **Tarbert** on **Harris** (1 hr 45 mins). For details see page 306, or contact Uig, T01470-542219.

The Cuillins and Minginish *p314*
Bus To **Portree** via **Sligachan** from **Portnalong**, take the No 53 bus that runs Mon-Sat. The same service stops at the Talisker Distillery, Carbost.

If you've walked into the remote areas of Glenbrittle and Eynort, the only option is to walk out for 8 miles until you meet the B8009, where you can pick-up the No 53 at Carbost to return to Drynoch junction on the A863. Here you can either stay on the No 53 to **Sligachan** and **Portree**, or wait for the No 56B **Portree** to **Dunvegan** service that stops (schooldays only) at **Drynoch** and heads north to **Struan** and Dunvegan Hotel.

Broadford and the east coast *p316*
Bus Daily Citylink buses run from **Broadford** to **Portree**, **Inverness** and **Fort William**. Buses run daily to **Kyleakin**, **Portree** and **Armadale/Ardvasar**. There are buses from **Kyleakin** to **Portree** via **Broadford**, to **Armadale** and **Ardvasar** via Broadford (Mon-Sat) and every 30 mins to **Kyle of Lochalsh**, see page 252, via the Skye Bridge.
Car hire S Morrison Ltd Broom Pl, Portree T01478-612688, www.portreecoachworks. co.uk. From around £40 per day.
Cycle hire Fairwinds Bicycle Hire, 4th house on left past Broadford Hotel, T01471-822270. Mar-Oct. Rents bikes from £10 per day.
Ferry CalMac car and passenger ferry from **Sconser** to **Raasay** several times daily Mon-Sat, twice on Sun, 25 mins, £5.65 per passenger return, £22 per car, bicycles free.

Sleat Peninsula *p318*
No 52/55 Bus Mon-Sat from **Ardvasar** and nearby Armadale Pier to **Portree** (1 hr 20 mins) and **Kyleakin** (1 hr) via **Broadford** (40 mins). 1st bus leaves at 0940.
Ferry For crossings to Mallaig, see page 306.

ⓘ Directory

Portree *p307, map p307*
Banks Clydesdale Bank, Bank of Scotland, Somerled Sq; Royal Bank of Scotland, Bank St. **Internet** Portree Backpacker's Hostel, Dunvegan Rd; Portree Independent Hostel, see Sleeping page 319; the TIC. **Laundry** Portree Independent Hostel, see Sleeping, page319. **Post** Post office, top of Quay Brae.

Broadford and the east coast *p316*
Banks Bank of Scotland, by the shops opposite the road to the new pier, Broadford.

The Small Isles

These four tenacious little siblings are a world away from the Scottish mainland and not for the faint or fickle traveller. It almost takes longer to reach them from London than it does to fly to Australia, so you have to be pretty determined. Those who do make it this far are rewarded with perfect peace and an almost primeval silence and solitude. This is nature in the glorious, unabashed raw; a slow-moving, sepia-tinged counterpoint to the frenetic pace and special effects of 21st-century life. ➨ *For listings, see pages 333-334.*

Ins and outs

Getting there

A CalMac passenger-only ferry sails from Mallaig to at least two of the islands once daily. Saturday is your only opportunity to step ashore on all four of the islands. For the latest seasonal timetable visit www.calmac.co.uk

From April to September the CalMac ferries from Mallaig are supplemented by cruises from Arisaig with **Arisaig Marine** ⓘ *T01687-450224, www.airsaig.co.uk, aboard MV Shearwater.* There's a good chance of seeing dolphins, seals, porpoises and even whales during the bumpy ride. ➨ *For further details, see page 243, and Transport page 334.*

Eigg

Eigg

Sleeping ⬤
Glebe Barn 1
Kildonan House 2

➔ *For listings, see pages 333-334. Colour map 3, A3-B3. Phone code 01687.*

Little Eigg (pronounced *egg*), only 5 miles long by 3 miles wide, has had something of a chequered past. In 1577 it was the scene of one of the bloodiest episodes in the history of clan warfare (see box, page 310). More recently it has been at the heart of a bitter land ownership debate. Having en- dured a succession of absentee landlords, ranging from the merely eccentric to the criminally negligent, the 70 remaining islanders seized the moment in 1997 and bought the island themselves, in conjunction with the Scottish Wildlife Trust. In February 2008, Eigg's own solar, wind and hydro- powered electricity supply was switched on. The island's wildlife includes otters, seals, eagles and many other birds, such as the Manx shearwater, guillemots and black- throated divers. It's worth tagging along on one of the regular walks organized by the Scottish Wildlife Trust warden, John Chester.

The end of an era

George Bullough and his wife, Lady Monica, brought a slice of Belgravia to the tiny Hebridean island of Rùm. Every autumn the family showed up to stalk deer and throw lavish parties for the glitterati and aristocracy of the day. Guests would be met at the pier by chauffeur-driven Albion cars while those arriving by ferry would step into a horse-drawn carriage, or be given a piggy-back by the castle staff when the tide was out. The outrageously wealthy Bulloughs guarded their privacy with a level of ruthlessness that would make even today's pop and film stars blush. Guns were routinely fired at passing boats to warn off any unwanted commoners and discourage the curious.

All this frivolous excess ended suddenly with the outbreak of war in 1914. George Bullough was appointed to a military post, the island's able-bodied staff were sent to the trenches to die for their country and the family's 220-ft steam-yacht, Rhouma, became a minesweeper. After the war, the Bulloughs visited less and less often and the castle began to show signs of neglect. Even the poor humming-birds died when the heating failed. Sir George himself died in 1939 and Lady Monica abandoned the place in 1954 – literally – leaving musical instruments on the stands in the ballroom and wine in the cellar. In 1957 the Bullough family sold Rùm to the Nature Conservancy for £23,000.

The island is dominated by **An Sgurr**, a distinctive 1289-ft flat-topped basalt peak with three vertical sides. It can be climbed fairly easily by its western ridge, though the last few hundred feet are precipitous, and there are superb views of the Inner Hebrides and mountains of Knoydart from the summit. Sitting in the shadow of the Sgurr, at the southeastern corner, is the main settlement, **Galmisdale**. This is where the ferries drop anchor (passengers are transferred to a smaller boat), and there's a post office, shop, craft shop, tea room and bike hire all by the pier. At the northern end is the small township of **Cleadale**, on the Bay of Laig. Just to the north are the 'Singing Sands', a beach that makes a strange sound as you walk across it. At the end of the island's only road you'll find its most famous property, **Howlin' House**, which apparently once belonged to JRR Tolkien. More details on the island are available at www.isleofeigg.org.

Muck → *For listings, see pages 333-334. Colour map 3, B3. Phone code 01687.*

Tiny Muck, just 2 miles long by one mile wide, is the smallest of the four islands and is flat and fertile, with a beautiful shell beach. It has been owned by the MacEwan family since 1879. The island gets its unfortunate name (*muc* is Gaelic for pig) from the porpoises, or 'sea pigs', that swim round its shores. The ferry berths at **Port Mór** close to which there's a range of accommodation, including a bunkhouse and hotel. There's also a tea room and craftshop. The 38 islanders use wind power to generate their own electricity. Visit the island's website, www.islemuck.com, or www.isleofmuck.com, for more information.

Rùm → *For listings, see pages 333-334. Colour map 3, A3. Phone code 01687.*

Diamond-shaped Rùm, known as the Forbidden Island, is the largest of the group and the most wild, beautiful and mountainous. The island is owned and run by Scottish Natural

Heritage as an enormous outdoor laboratory and research station, and most of the 30 or so inhabitants are employed by them. Studies of the red deer population are among the most important areas of their work, and access to parts of the island is restricted. This is not prohibitive, though, and there are many marked nature trails, walks and birdwatching spots. The island is a haven for wildlife and perhaps its most notable resident is the magnificent white-tailed sea eagle, successfully re-introduced on to Rùm in the 1980s and now spreading beyond the island. Rùm is also home to golden eagles, Manx shearwaters and, less appealingly, millions of midges. The island is the wettest of the Small Isles and a haven for the little buggers.

Ins and outs
Ferries are anchored at the new pier, at the mouth of Loch Scresort, from where it's a 15-minute walk to Kinloch Castle. The castle stands at the head of narrow Loch Scresort by the little hamlet of **Kinloch**, where you'll find the one-and-only shop, and the community hall which also operates a tea room.

Rùm

Sleeping ●
Kinloch Castle 1

Kinloch Castle

ⓘ *By daily guided tour only (1 hr), and timed to coincide with the arrival of the ferry, £7 children £3.50, ask at the hostel for details.*

Though it looks like a wilderness, Rùm once supported a population of 300. Most of them were shipped off to Canada in the mid-19th century, leaving behind an uninhabited deer forest for sporting millionaires. One of these, John Bullough, a cotton millionaire from Accrington, bought it in 1888 and passed it on to his son, Sir George Bullough, who built the extravagant and extraordinary Kinloch Castle. No expense was spared on this massive late-Victorian mansion, built in 1900 at a cost of £250,000 (which equates to £15 million today). It took 300 men nearly three years to build Bullough's dream, using red Annan sandstone from Dumfrieshire shipped by puffer from the mainland. For the gardens, 250,000 tons of soil were shipped from Ayrshire and used for planting exotic specimens collected from around the world. A nine-hole golf course and bowling green were laid out, along with a Japanese-style garden and huge walled garden. Hothouses were built to grow tropical fruits, and palm houses were home to hummingbirds, turtles and even alligators. One of these creatures escaped, only to be shot by Bullough to prevent them 'interfering with the comfort of the guests'. As well as the elaborate carvings, wood panelling, furniture and flooring, the castle also incorporated many state-of-the-art features such as an electricity generator, central heating, air conditioning and an internal telephone system (the first private residence in Scotland to do so). Pride of place, however, went to the magnificent Orchestrion, a fantastical mechanical contraption that simulated a 40-piece orchestra and belted out military marches, polkas, operatic excerpts and popular tunes of the day from its position under the main staircase. It is still in working order and visitors today will be treated to a surreal rendition of *The Liberty Bell March* (the Monty Python theme tune to you and me).

In 2003 Kinloch Castle was a finalist in the BBC's first *Restoration* series, though plans to continue its costly restoration have reportedly currently stalled. Note that visitors must take off their shoes as they are escorted round the lavish rooms, many of them fading, peeling or leaking. The castle is testament to Edwardian wealth and extravagance and the tour is worth the boat trip alone. You can even stay at the castle; in the hostel which occupies the former servants' quarters.

Island walks

Rùm's other great attraction is its mountain range, which offers some of the best island mountain treks outside the Cuillins of Skye. The highest point is **Askival** (2664 ft), which can be reached by the main ridge from **Halliva**, though the route involves some rock scrambling and is only advised for fit and experienced walkers. Before setting out, ask permission from the reserve office at the **White House** ⓘ *T01687-462026, Mon-Fri 0900-1230.*

The Bullough family mausoleum, built in the style of a Greek Doric temple, stands incongruously on the west coast at **Harris Bay**. It's an interesting seven and a half mile walk across to the mausoleum from Kinloch. A less strenuous alternative is the **Kinloch Glen Trail**, which is signposted by the stone bridge as you head from the castle to the farmstead. The circular route is two and a half miles and takes a leisurely one to two hours.

Canna is the most westerly of the Small Isles and is owned by the National Trust for Scotland (NTS). It's a small island, five miles long by one mile wide, bounded by cliffs and with a rugged interior, fringed by fertile patches. It's attached to its smaller neighbour, **Sanday**, by a narrow isthmus which is covered, except at low tide. There's now also a bridge linking them. The main attraction for visitors is some fine walking. It's about a mile from the ferry jetty up to the top of **Compass Hill** (458 ft), so called because its high metallic content distorts compasses. The highest point on the island is **Carn a' Ghaill** (690 ft). During the summer, a day trip from Mallaig allows you over nine hours in which to explore Canna and enjoy the fantastic views across to Rùm and Skye.

The population of 20 mostly work on the island's farm. Canna was gifted to the National Trust by its benevolent owner, the late Dr John Lorne Campbell, a notable Gaelic scholar. The island continues to be run as a single working farm and, since it was sold in 1938, has been an unofficial bird sanctuary with 157 recorded bird species, including Manx shearwater and puffins. In 2008, after a £500,000, two-year eradication project to protect the seabird population, the NTS officially declared the entire island rat-free.

Canna & Sanday

⊙ The Small Isles listings

For Sleeping and Eating price codes and other relevant information, see Essentials pages 38-45.

⊜ Sleeping

Eigg *p328, map p328*

In addition to the options below, self-catering cottages and camping are also available. For details, visit www.isleofeigg.org.

B Lageorna, T01687-482405, www.lageorna. com. Green Tourism Scheme B&B offering 2 rooms, self catering options and excellent food in its restaurant (£20 for 4 courses).

F The Glebe Barn, T01687-482417, www.glebebarn.co.uk. Open Apr-Oct (all year for groups). An independent hostel and outdoor centre. Comfortable accommodation in twin, family and bunk rooms. Residential courses and retreats, self-catering or fully catered options for groups. There's a self-contained 2-person apartment (from £230 per week or £45 per night). Groceries can be pre-ordered from the local shop (T01687-482432) and delivered.

Muck *p329*

C Port Mór House Hotel, T01678-462365. The price includes a 3-course dinner, which is also available to non-residents if they book before 1600. The restaurant specializes in seafood and all the food is home-cooked, with the lamb sourced from a local farm and the venison shot on the estate. Open log fires and views across to the Ardnamurchan Peninsula. You can ask permission at the tea room if you want to camp.

D Carn Dearg, Port Mór, T01687-462371. Offers comfortable (2-bedroom) B&B accommodation with an evening meal available for £12.50 per person.

D Godag House, between Port Mór and Gallanach, T01678-462371. Comfortable B&B, dinner is £10 extra. Family friendly.

Rùm *p329, map p330*

E-F Kinloch Castle, T01687-462037. Open all year. 55-bed hostel in the old servants' quarters, with twin (£45), 4-bed and 6-bed dorms (£18) (**F**) with breakfast an additional £7.50, packed lunch £7 and 3-course dinner in the bistro at the rear of the castle, £18.50. Guests can also choose to sleep in greater privacy and comfort on a B&B basis in the castle's Oak Rooms (£55) (**D**). There's a small bar in the castle selling real ale (daily 1700-2300).

Camping

There are 2 bothies (**F**) on Rùm (Dibidal and Guirdal), run by the Mountain Bothy Association. Wild camping is also permitted (no fires) near the pier where a stand pipe provides water. You must inform the reserve manager at the **White House** if camping, T01687-462026.

Canna *p332*

Those wishing to stay can camp rough, with permission from the NTS, www.nts.org.uk.

❶ Eating

The few places to stay on the islands serve food, and there's a tea room and a shop on Muck.

Eigg *p328, map p328*

There's a tea room, and a well-stocked shop at the jetty, T01687-482432, open Mon-Sat.

Rùm *p329, map p330*

The café/tea room on is housed in the village hall (always open as an escape from the rain or midges), and serves hot drinks, cakes, soup and other home-made food. It's open several afternoons a week during summer. There's also the bistro and bar at Kinloch Castle.

The shop has limited opening hours, depending on the islanders requirements, but is always open after 1700. Call the Reserve Office, T01687-462026, to check in advance.

Canna *p332*
There a small tea room but no shop, so you'll need to bring your own supplies.

⚙ Activities and tours

The Small Isles *p328*
The islands are rich in wildlife, with plenty of opportunities to spot seals and possibly basking sharks, porpoise and even orca whilst inter-island hopping aboard the *MV Sheerwater*, see Ins and outs, page 328.

Rùm *p329, map p330*
Visit the old boat shed by the pier, where there's a (very) small exhibition of wildlife and marine life, a reminder that Rùm is a National Nature Reserve with its colony of Manx shearwater, golden- and white-tailed sea eagles and red deer.

⊖ Transport

The Small Isles *p328*
On Eigg Muck and Rùm, walking is the primary means of transport, but you should also be able to hire a bike from the locals.
Ferry On a Mon and Thu from late Mar-late Oct, the ferry departs **Mallaig** at 1015 to arrive at **Eigg** at 1130. The Mon sailing continues to **Rùm** (1245) and **Canna** (1355), before returning to Mallaig (1750) via **Rùm**

and **Eigg**. The Thu morning boat leaves **Eigg** to reach **Muck** at 1220, returns to **Eigg** for 1310 and disembarks at Mallaig at 1435. On a Tue and Fri morning, the boat sails for **Muck** and **Eigg**, whilst the Fri afternoon sailing calls in at **Rùm** and **Canna** only. On a Wed, the boat from Mallaig calls in at **Rùm** (1135), **Canna** (1245) and **Rùm** again (1555) before returning to **Mallaig** at 1725. For more details of latest seasonal timetable, contact the **CalMac** office in Mallaig, T01687-462403. The **Fort William** train is time-tabled to await the Small Isles boats.

An adult return from **Mallaig** to **Eigg** (1 hr 15 mins direct) is £11.35; **Muck** (1 hr 40 mins direct) £17.25; **Rùm** (1 hr 20 mins direct) £16.75; **Canna** (2 hrs 15 mins via Rùm) £21.05. A non-landing cruise ticket that visits all of the islands costs £16. Bicycles now go free. .

Arisaig Marine, T01687-450224, www.arisaig.co.uk, sails daily (1100) Apr-Sep from Arisaig to **Eigg** (£18 return), Muck (£19 return) and **Rùm** (£24 return). Refer to their website for a comprehensive sailings timetable.

Eigg *p328, map p328*
Bus/taxi Davie Robertson, T01687-482494.
Cycle hire Eigg Bikes, close to An Laimhrig at the pier, call Euan Kirk, T01687-482432 (day), T01687-482405 (evening). Hires bikes from £15 per day.
Ferry For ferry information, see above.

Contents

Outer Hebrides

At a glance

⊖ **Getting around** There's an ever-improving public bus service, and regular sailings to the main islands. You'll need a car, bike or hiking boots to explore the more remote areas.

◉ **Time required** 1 week for a whistle-stop tour, longer to explore in depth.

◐ **Weather** From Apr to Sep the weather can be surprisingly warm and settled. In winter, be prepared for storms.

⊗ **When not to go** From Oct to Mar some hotels, restaurants and tourist attractions may be closed.

★ Don't miss ...
1 Calanais, page 348
2 Uig sands, page 349
3 Bays, page 358
4 Barra, page 368
5 St Kilda, page 376

Port Nis
Tabost
Dail Bho Dheas
Siadar
Baile an Truiseil
Arnol
Barabhas
Siabost
Tolastadh Ùr
Cárlabhagh
Newmarket
Stornoway
(Steòrnabhagh)
Griais
Tunga
Leodhais
(Lewis)
Miabhig
Timsgearraidh
Calanais
Crulabhig
Achadh Mór
Crosbost
Breanais
Mealasta Island
Uig
Baile Ailein
Cearsiadar
Ceann a Tuath na Hearadh (North Harris)
Grabhair
Airidh a'Bhruaich
Leumrabhagh
Scarp
Huisinis
Gasker
Abhainnsuidhe
Bun Abhainn Eadarra
Tarasaigh
An Tairbeart (Tarbert)
Rèinigeadal
Caolas Scalpaigh
Ceann a Deas na Hearadh (South Harris)
Eilean Scalpaigh (Scalpay)
Taobh Tuath
Shillay
Pabbay
An t-Ob
Bearnaraigh
Boreray
Ròghadal
To St Kilda

Kilmaluag
Otternish
Baile Mhartainn
Solas
Kilmuir
Loch nam Madadh (Lochmaddy)
Uibhist a'Tuath (North Uist)
Uig
Llinicro
Staffin
Trotternish
Culnacnock
Claghan na Duib
Heisker Monach Islands
Saighdinis
Trumpan
Lùsta
A855
Uachdar
Beinn na Faoghla (Benbecula)
Boreraig
Skye
Kensaleyre
Creag Ghoraidh
Wiay
Milovaig
Colbost
Dunvegan
Carbost
Portree
Roskhill
Stadhlaigearraidh
Loch Sgioport
Bracadale
Oskaig
Peinchorran
Gearraidh Bhailteas
Uibhist a Deas (South Uist)
Portnalong
Talisker
Sligachan
Dalabrog
Loch Baghasdail (Lochboisdale)
Cille Bhrighde
Ludag
Soay
Elgol
Eiriosgaigh Eriskay
Eilean Barraigh (Barra)
Sea of the Hebrides
Canna
Bagh a'Chaisteil (Castlebay)
Earsairidh
Kilmory
Rùm (Rhum)
Kinloch
Bhatarsaigh (Vatersay)
Sanndraigh
Cleadale
Mingulay (Miughalaigh)
Atlantic Ocean
Eilean nan Each
Eigg
Bearnaraigh
Wiay
Galmisdale
Muck

N

10 km
10 miles

Outer Hebrides

Little Minch
Waternish
Duirinish

Sound of Barra

Outer Hebrides

336 · Outer Hebrides

The Outer Hebrides are a narrow, 130-mile-long chain of more than 200 islands lying 40 miles off the northwest coast of the Scottish mainland. Only 10 of these are populated – Lewis, Harris, Scalpay, Berneray, North Uist, Benbecula, South Uist, Eriskay, Barra and Vatersay – giving a total population of just under 30,000.

The main administrative centre and the only town of any size is Stornoway on Lewis. The rest of the population is scattered throughout the islands in much smaller villages, mostly strung out along the coast. Despite the frequency of transport connections with the mainland, the Outer Hebrides remain remote in every sense. Unlike Skye and the Inner Hebrides, tourism is of far less importance to the local economy. In many ways, the islands are the last bastion of the old Highland life. Though newer industries such as fish farming have been introduced, the traditional occupations of crofting, fishing and weaving still dominate and, outside Stornoway, life is very much a traditional one, revolving around the seasons and the tides.

Relentlessly battered by fierce Atlantic winds, the islands can seem a hostile environment and an unappealing proposition. Much of the interior is bleak peat bog, rocks and endless tiny lochs, and the long, straggling crofting communities only add to the feeling of desolation. But anyone who has stood on a clifftop and felt a thrill at the power and potential of all that water should come here. Nowhere else in Britain is there such a sense of emptiness and of the sheer forces of nature. These are islands at the very edge of our imagination.

Ins and outs

Getting there

Air **Flybe/Loganair** fly from Glasgow to Stornoway on Lewis, Barra and Benbecula on North Uist. There are also flights from Edinburgh to Stornoway, Inverness to Stornoway, and from Benbecula to Barra and Stornoway. Eastern Airways fly from Aberdeen to Stornoway (T08703-669100, www.easternairways.com). Weather conditions are so changeable that flights are prone to delay and can be very bumpy. Flights to Barra have an added complication: they land on the beach meaning that the runway disappears twice a day under the incoming tide.

Bus For details of bus connections on Skye and on the mainland, contact **Scottish Citylink** ① *T08712-663 3334.* ⟫ *For further details, see Transport pages 353, 361 and 375.*

Ferry CalMac car and passenger ferries sail to Stornoway (Lewis), Tarbert (Harris), Lochmaddy (North Uist), Lochboisdale (South Uist), Eriskay and Castlebay (Barra). Ferry details are given under each destination, but note that times change according to the day of the week and time of the year. For full details of ferry timetables contact **CalMac** ① *T08705-650000, www.calmac.co.uk. A 'CalMac Status' App can be downloaded free of charge from itunes. Alternatively, look on the website to see how to receive updates by text (but remember a signal is not always possible in some parts of the Islands).* Some routes, including the Stornoway to Ullapool crossing are very busy and if travelling with a car it's strongly advised to book your ticket in advance. A cost-effective and super-flexible way to get around the islands with a car is to purchase a **CalMac Island Rover** ticket. Available for eight and 15 consecutive days of travel respectively, these allow the ticket holder to travel on as many routes as you like without paying any additional fares. An eight-day passenger-only Rover ticket costs £48.50 a 15 day costs £70. An eight-day car ticket is £232, a 15 day is £348. Bicycles are carried free with a Rover ticket. Another option is to purchase the **CalMac Island Hopscotch** ticket, available for use on 26 routes and valid for 30 days unlimited travel on each route. For example, a ticket for the Oban–Lochboisdale–Berneray–Leverburgh–Stornoway–Ullapool route allows you to visit South and North Uist, Harris and Lewis and costs £23.70 per passenger and £111 per car. See the CalMac guide or call the numbers above for full details.

Getting around

You should allow plenty of time to explore the islands fully. With your own transport and travelling from top to bottom, a week would be enough time for a whistle-stop tour but not enough to explore in any depth or scratch beneath the surface. You will need to allow for the lack of public transport on Sundays on most islands (taxi is the only way around), and for the fact that weather conditions (including the tide at Barra airport) can occasionally affect ferry and flight timetables.

Air **Flybe/Loganair** ① *www.flybe.com, T0871-700 2000,* fly daily between Barra, Benbecula and Stornoway.

Bus Bus services have improved and now run regularly to most main towns and villages on the islands (see www.cne-siar.gov.uk).

Never on a Sunday

The islands are the Gaidhealtachd, the land of the Gael. Gaelic culture has remained more prominent here than in any other part of Scotland, and the way of life and philosophy of the islanders will seem totally alien and fascinating to many visitors. Gaelic is the first language for the majority of the islanders – and the only one for the older generation – but the all-pervading influence of the English media has taken its toll and the language is under threat. Though Gaelic is still taught in schools, the younger generation tends to speak to each other in English. Visitors will not have any language problems, as the Gaelic- speaking inhabitants are so polite they will always change to English when visitors are present (though place names and signposts are in Gaelic).

The church is also an important factor in preserving the language, and services are usually held in Gaelic. In fact, religion is one of the most pervasive influences on Hebridean life, and the islanders' faith is as strong as the winds that pound their shores. The islands are split between the Presbyterian Lewis, Harris and North Uist, and the predominantly Roman Catholic South Uist and Barra. Benbecula, meanwhile, has a foot in both camps. On Lewis and Harris the Free Church is immensely powerful and the Sabbath is strictly observed. Don't expect to travel anywhere by public transport; shops and petrol stations will be closed, and you'll be hard pressed to find a place to eat. Even the swings in the playgrounds are padlocked! Things are changing, however, and October 2002 saw the revolutionary move to allow Loganair to fly to Stornoway on a Sunday. Despite a tsunami-like wave of protest from the church, who described the idea as "a breach of God's moral law", Loganair's tourist-friendly flights took to the air.

Car Most of the islands' roads are single track but in good condition and, unlike other parts of the Highlands and Islands, not too busy though you may encounter a road blocked by cattle and wandering sheep! On Sunday you'll barely meet another soul. Petrol stations are few and far between, expensive and closed on Sundays so if low on petrol think carefully before passing a fuel sign. The normal rules for single track roads apply and, as elsewhere in the Highlands, you need to look out for sheep. Distances are greater than most people imagine. For example, the distance from Nis (Ness) at the northern tip of Lewis to Leverburgh in the south of Harris is 85 miles. From Stornoway to Tarbert is 37 miles. And the distance from Otternish in the north of North Uist to Lochboisdale, the main ferry port on South Uist, is 50 miles. Several local car hire agencies offer reasonable rental deals. Expect to pay around £30 per day, depending on the size of engine and age of the car. You cannot take a rented car off the islands.

Cycle Cycling is a great way to explore the islands. You can fully appreciate the amazing scenery around, and it only costs a few pounds to transport a bike by ferry. There is, of course, the major problem of strong winds, which can leave you frustrated and exhausted, especially if cycling into the prevailing south-westerly wind. ► *For further details, see Transport pages 353, 361 and 375.*

Ferry A ferry sails to Berneray from Leverburgh (Harris) at least three times daily. Several ferries sail daily from Barra to the island of Eriskay. There's also a regular passenger ferry from Ludag in South Uist to Eoligarry on Barra.

Tourist information

There are tourist information centres in Stornoway and Tarbert, which are open all year, and also in Lochmaddy, Lochboisdale and Castlebay, which are open early April to mid October. Full details are given under each destination. **Visit Hebrides** ① *www.visithebrides. com*, produces an accommodation brochure and TIC's also stock the free and handy *Explore the Outer Hebrides Guide with Maps*, which details key routes and places of interest. The Visit Hebrides website also provides lots of information on the islands, including accommodation and up-and-coming events. You should invest in a copy of the *Highlands & Islands Travel Guide*, which is available from the local TICs. Accommodation on the islands is generally not difficult to find, except perhaps at the height of the summer when you should book in advance, either directly or through the local tourist office. It's also a good idea to book ahead if you're staying on a Sunday, and if you're staying in the countryside you should check if there's a convenient pub or hotel to eat in. Certainly, as highlighted by the recent formation of the **Outer Hebrides Speciality Food Trail** ① *www.foodhebrides. com*, you won't go hungry on these islands, which are renowned for the quality of their seafood, meat and real ale. There are many excellent self-catering options on the islands and this is a most cost-effective way to get to know one particular island. Check out the Visit Hebrides website, see above.

Activities

Those intent on walking in the islands should visit the excellent website walking. visitscotland.com, which has details of over 18 walks in the Hebrides. Several operators offer guided walking holidays, see Essentials, page 57, for further details. A great way to experience the islands is to get out onto the water, and in addition to excellent wildlife cruises, don't forget that the Outer Hebridean chain is now regarded as one of Europe's best locations for sea kayaking (see **Uist Outdoor Centre (www.uistoutdoorcentre. co.uk)** and **Clearwater Paddling (www.clearwaterpaddling.com)**, page 374). If surfing's your thing then you're also in the right place. The northwest coast of Lewis, especially the stretch between Dalmore Bay and the beach at Barabhas, has some of the best surfing in Britain.

Leodhas (Lewis)

→ Colour map 1, A3. Phone code 01851.

Lewis constitutes the northern two thirds of the most northerly island in the Outer Hebrides. It is by far the most populous of the Outer Hebridean islands and, with over 20,000 inhabitants, makes up two thirds of the total population. Just over 8000 people live in and around Stornoway, the largest town in the Hebrides and the administrative capital of the Western Isles. The majority of the rest of the population live in over 280 crofting townships strung out along the west coast between Port Nis (Ness) and Càrlabhagh (Carloway). The west coast is also where you'll find the island's most interesting sight: the prehistoric remains of Dùn Chàrlabhaigh (Carloway) Broch, the impressive Calanais (Callanish) Standing Stones, the restored blackhouse village of Garenin and the Arnol Blackhouse. These can all be visited as a day trip from Stornoway, either on an organized tour or on the 'West Side Circular' bus service. The interior of the northern half is flat peat bog, hence the island's name which means 'marshy' in Gaelic. Further south, where Lewis becomes Harris, the scenery is more dramatic as the relentlessly flat landscape gives way to rocky hills, providing the backdrop to the sea lochs that cut deep into the coast and the beautiful beaches around Uig. Look out for a free copy of the leaflet Outdoor Hebrides *at TIC's.* For listings, see pages 350-353.

Background

Lewis was controlled by the Vikings and the Norse influence can be seen in many of the place names, such as Uig (which is Norse for 'a bay'). After the end of Norwegian sovereignty in 1266, the island was ruled by the Macleods, said to be descendants of early settlers from Iceland. Control of the island was wrested from them by the Mackenzies, who then proceeded to sell it, in 1844, to Sir James Matheson. The new owner built Lews Castle in Stornoway and began to develop the infrastructure of the island, as well as investing in new industries. Though many crofts were cleared and families sent to Canada, the people of Lewis fared well and certainly much better than their counterparts in the Southern Isles.

The next proprietor was Lord Leverhulme, founder of Lever Brothers, who bought the island (along with Harris) in 1918. He planned to turn Lewis into a major fishing centre and ploughed money into developing the infrastructure. He was forced to abandon his plans, however, partly because of the decline of the fishing industry, and partly owing to the growing conflict between him and the islanders returning from the war who wanted land of their own to farm. As a final benevolent gesture, Lord Leverhulme offered Lewis to the islanders, but only Stornoway Council accepted. The island was then divided into estates and sold, and hundreds of people emigrated.

Today the economy of Lewis is still based on the traditional industries of crofting, fishing and weaving, though there are other economic activities such as fish farming, which is now a major employer, service industries, construction, the controversial wind farm development and increasingly, tourism.

Steòrnabhagh (Stornoway) → For listings, see pages 350-353. Colour map 1, B3. Population 5600.

The fishing port of Stornoway, the only town in the Outer Hebrides, is the islands' commercial capital and, as such, boasts more services and facilities than you might expect in any town of comparable size. It's not a pretty place, dominated as it is by the oil industry, but has the full range of banks, shops, hotels, guesthouses, pubs and restaurants, garages, car hire firms, sports facilities, an airport and ferry terminal, and, for the visiting tourist, it presents a rare opportunity to stock up on supplies.

Stornoway is also the administrative capital and home to the Comhairle nan Eilean (Western Isles Council), which has done much to broaden the local economy and to promote and protect Gaelic language and culture. The BBC is rapidly developing programmes and a digital network dedicated to the Gaelic language. Indeed, every July, Stornoway and the Hebridean islands host the **Hebridean Celtic Festival** ⓘ *www. hebceltfest.com*, an ever expanding and popular celebration of Celtic music and the arts that also attracts international acts.

Ins and outs

Getting there and around Stornoway is the island's transport hub. The airport is 4 miles east of the town centre, a £6 taxi ride away. **Flybe/Loganair** ⓘ *T0871-700 2000, www.fly be.com*, flies from Glasgow to Stornoway twice a day from Monday to Saturday. There is a also a daily flight from Edinburgh and four flights a day from Inverness. The CalMac ferry terminal is just beyond the bus station, which is on South Beach, a short walk from the town centre. CalMac runs a ferry service from Ullapool to Stornoway, two or three times a day in the summer and twice daily in the winter, Monday to Saturday. A one-way ticket costs £7.85 per passenger and £39.50 per car. Contact the CalMac offices ⓘ *T01854-612358*, in Ullapool for further details. Buses leave from Stornoway to all parts of the island, see page 353, for further details. Note that buses do not run on Sunday. It is advisable to pick up a free copy of the comprehensive Lewis and Harris bus timetables at the TIC, or visit www.cne-siar.gov.uk.

The town is compact and most of what you need is within easy walking distance of the tourist office. Some of the B&Bs in the residential areas are quite a distance from the centre, but there's an hourly town bus service, or hire a taxi. ▸▸ *For further details, see Transport, page 353.*

Tourist information The helpful **TIC** ⓘ *26 Cromwell St, T01851-703088, Easter-Sep Mon-Sat 0900-1800, Oct-Easter 0900-1700 (though opening hours vary) and for the arrival of the evening ferry* , stocks maps, bus timetables and various books and brochures. It also sells tickets for minibus tours to Calanais, and wildlife trips around Lewis and Harris.

Sights

Stornoway is short on conventional tourist sights and once you've been to the tourist office and bought the necessities from the local supermarkets, there's not much else to do. The focal point of the town has always been its sheltered deep-water **harbour** and, though the fishing industry has declined since its peak at the end of the last century, there's still a fair amount of activity in the early morning as the latest fresh catch is loaded onto trucks for far-flung European destinations. On a Saturday morning you can buy the latest fresh batch of fish from a market stall on Point Street by the town hall. The harbour is usually full of seals, giving the town its nickname of Portrona (port of seals). There's a good view across the harbour to **Lews Castle**, a 19th-century edifice built by Sir James Matheson with money earned from opium and tea. The castle now houses a college and its real attraction is the wooded grounds, the only place you'll see trees on the islands.

Museum nan Eilean ⓘ *Francis St, T01851-709266, Apr-Sep Mon-Sat 1000-1730, Oct-Mar Tue-Fri 1000-1700, Sat 1000-1300, free*, features a range of temporary exhibitions on island life and history. Anyone remotely interested in Harris Tweed should visit the **Lewis Loom Centre** ⓘ *T01851-704500, Mon-Sat 1000-1700, £2.50*, housed in the Old Grainstore at the northern end of Cromwell Street, just off Bayhead. The 40-minute guided tour includes demonstrations of traditional methods of warping, dyeing and spinning, and offers a detailed history of Harris Tweed. There's also a craft shop.

Stornoway

To Tarbert (A858)

To ②⑤, Hospital, Port Nis & Barabhas

Torquil Terr

Co-op Supermarket

River Bayhead

Westview Terr

MacAulay Rd

Stag Rd

Leverhulme Dr

Kennedy Terr

Bayhead St

MacKenzie St

Matheson Rd

Robertson

Lews

Plantation Rd

Goathill Rd

Lewis Loom Centre

Scotland St

Cromwell St

Kenneth St

Church St

④

Keith St

Lewis St

Museum nan Eilean 🏛

North Beach

ℹ

🅿

①

④

③

Francis St

Quay St

Castle St

Bank St

Public Library

②

✉

An Lanntair Arts Centre

Garden St

⑥

Sandwick Rd

South Beach

James St

Esplanade Quay

Morrisons Supermarket

Shell St

Rigs Rd

Bells Rd

Calmac Ferry Terminal

Inaclete Rd

Newton St

Harbour

To Ullapool

To ① & Airport (A866)

N

200 metres
200 yards

The **An Lanntair Arts Centre** ① T01851-703307, www.lanntair.com, Mon-Sat 1000-late, *free*, is the main venue for social and cultural events on the islands. The light and airy building has exhibition spaces for local, national and international artists, a cinema, and stages for various musical and theatrical events. There's also a very good café (see Eating, page 352).

North to Nis (Ness) → *For listings, see pages 350-353. Colour map 1, A3.*

The A857 leaves Stornoway and runs northwest through barren, treeless and relentlessly bleak moorland to **Barabhas (Barvas)**. The landscape is scarred by deep gashes caused by peat digging, and the unfamiliar smell you detect in your nostrils is peat burning – a strange mixture of burning grass, whisky and coffee. Peat is the main source of domestic fuel used on the islands, and outside most houses you'll see large stacks of peat, or *cruachs*.

The road from Barabhas northeast to Nis runs through a series of forlorn-looking, scrawny settlements that all seem identical and merge into one. They consist of modern, characterless grey pebble-dash cottages with the ubiquitous piles of peat in the gardens; the abandoned cars and vans scattered around everywhere only add to the ugly and depressing scene.

Just beyond Barabhas a sign points left to the **Morvern Art Gallery**, which has a café, making it a welcome refuge in bad weather. A few miles further on is a turning right to **Baile an Trùiseil (Ballantrushel)**, site of the huge **Clach an Trùiseil**, a 20-ft monolith (the largest in Europe), which was the scene of the last major battle on the island, fought between the Morrisons of Nis and the MacAuleys of Uig. This is the first of a number of prehistoric sights between here and **Siadar (Shader)**, which may be of interest to the keen archaeologist. Otherwise there's little of note on the road north to Nis as it passes through the typical crofting townships of **Coig Peighinnean Buirgh (Five Penny Borve)**, **Gàbhsann bho Dheas (South Galson)**, **Dail (Dell)**, **Suaineabost (Swainbost)**, **Tàbost (Habost)** and **Lional (Lionel)**. In saying that, those who are keen to buy souvenirs should look in at the **Borgh Pottery** ① T01856-850345, Mon-Sat 0930-1800, www.borghpottery.com, by the bridge at Coig Peighinnean. Here you'll find a wide range of beautiful and original domestic and decorative ware.

The road continues north, passing through a number of villages that collectively make up **Nis (Ness)**, until it ends at the fishing village of **Port Nis (Port of Ness)**. It's a lovely spot, with a picturesque little harbour, and a golden sweep of beach enclosed by steep cliffs. Each September the locals head out to the island of **Sula Sgeir**, 30 miles to the north, for the annual cull of young gannets (*gugas*), which are considered something of a delicacy by the people of Lewis (but be warned: they're an acquired taste). In Ness, the kids will love the community established play park set amidst the machair and dunes.

Just before Port Nis is Lional, where the B8015 turns off right and leads to the start of the 10-mile coastal trail to **Tòlstadh (Tolsta North)** and the beautiful beaches of Traigh Mhor and Garry. Numerous shielings (basic stone huts where farming communities lived during summer grazings in high pasture) pepper the landscape from an earlier era when local crofters drove their cattle to the summer pastures in the island's interior. The beaches can be reached much more easily by road north from Stornoway. For details of the coastal walk, ask at the tourist information centre in Stornoway.

Another minor road heads northwest to the tiny hamlet of **Eòropaidh (Eoropie)** (pronounced 'Yor-erpee'). By the road junction that leads to Rubha Robhanais is the ancient **Teampull Mholuaidh (St Moluag's Church)**, thought to date from the 12th century and restored to its present state in 1912. It is now used on certain Sundays by Stornoway's Episcopal Church. From Eòropaidh a narrow road runs to the lighthouse at

Croft conversion

The word 'croft' is derived from the Gaelic croit, meaning a small area of land. Crofting has been the traditional way of life in the Scottish Highlands for many centuries. Its emotive hold on the psyche of the Highlander comes from the long, hard struggle for security of tenure, see box, page 444.

A croft is aptly described as a parcel of land entirely surrounded by regulations. Most crofts consist of a few acres of arable land with a proportion of grazing land shared with other crofts. Each crofter is, in effect, a kind of small tenant-farmer, the distinction being that he has almost absolute security of tenure and has the right to assign the croft to a member of his family whether the landlord agrees or not. In fact, over the years, the crofter has managed to acquire most of the rights of ownership with few of the disadvantages.

The croft is the area of land involved and not the house which is called the 'croft house'. Crofts can vary in size, from a quarter of an acre upwards. Those on Lewis are small and relatively unproductive, with an average size of only about 5 acres, while on the Uists, where the land is more fertile, crofts are up to 50 acres or more.

As well as having the sole tenancy of the croft, the crofter usually has a share in a huge area of 'common grazing' along with the other members of the crofting community – commonly called a township. They also work together in such activities as fencing, sheep dipping or cutting peat.

In reality, crofting does not provide a viable means of living. Very few crofters rely solely on their smallholding for an income and most need to have several occupations (including running a B&B) to make ends meet. But without the family croft, whole communities would just pack up and leave, so crofting functions as a means of preventing the depopulation of remote rural areas.

The crofter's lot may change for the better, however, thanks to the Scottish Parliament's new Land Reform Bill, which includes a special right to buy for the crofting communities.

Rubha Robhanais (Butt of Lewis), the most northerly tip of the island. It's a great place for spotting seabirds or whales and dolphins, but also very wild and windy. Half a mile back down the road a path leads to the tiny beach of **Port Sto**, which is more sheltered.

West coast of Lewis → *For listings, see pages 350-353. Colour map 1, A2-3/B2.*

The west coast of Lewis contains most of what you'll want to see and can be covered in a day trip from Stornoway, either with your own transport, by public bus or as part of a minibus tour.

Arnol

At the end of the village of Arnol is the **Blackhouse Museum** ⓘ *T01851-710395 (HS), Apr-Sep Mon-Sat 0930-1730, Oct-Mar Mon-Sat 0930-1630, £4, concessions £3.20, children £2.40* , one of the best surviving examples of an original blackhouse in Scotland and well worth visiting. These traditional thatched houses were once common throughout the Highlands and Islands, and were inhabited until the 1960s. They were built in the tradition of 'longhouses', which can be traced back 1000 years to the time of the Viking invaders. The name 'blackhouse' dates back to the 1850s when modern buildings were introduced. These were known as

Gatliff Trust

The **Gatliff Hebridean Hostels Trust** (GHHT) is a non-profit-making charitable organization run entirely by volunteers, working with the island community to establish, maintain and develop a chain of 'value-for-money' hostels offering clean, cheap, simple, safe, welcoming and traditional croft-style accommodation in dramatic and beautiful locations for visitors to the Outer Hebrides.

The GHHT is independent of the SYHA but has adopted status. Visitors do not have to be members of either organization to use and stay in the hostels. First established in 1961 by Herbert Gatliff, the trust was originally intended to provide young persons of limited means with the opportunity to meet local people and enjoy the unique natural environment and cultural heritage of the islands. However, in recent years, visitors of all incomes, ages, nationalities and interests have been encouraged to use the facilities.

The trust is currently involved in the operation of four hostels situated at Garenin (Isle of Lewis), **Rhenigidale** (Isle of Harris), **Berneray** (North Uist) and **Howmore** (South Uist). Further hostels may be opened on other islands in the future.

The hostels are open all year and looked after by non-resident wardens who live and practise crofting nearby. No advance bookings are accepted but it is very unlikely that visitors will find themselves turned away and without a bed for the night. There is also limited space for camping at the hostels. Hostels provide bunk/camp beds, cooking facilities and cutlery, piped water, toilets and coal/wood fires, but visitors should bring their own food and a sleeping bag is recommended.

Current charges are: £8 per night, under 18s £5.50, camping £4.50, day visitors £1. Annual membership £10, under 18s £7.50. For further information regarding membership, contact details, hostel locations and photographs, a reading list and places of interest to visit in the surrounding area, visit the GHHT website, www.gatliff.org.uk.

'white houses' so the older-style houses were called 'blackhouses'. The blackhouses were well adapted to the harsh local climate. They had no windows or chimney and were built with local materials – stone, turf and thatch of oat, barley or marram grass – with a peat fire burning continually in the central hearth. Attached to the living quarters was the cattle byre. This particular blackhouse was built in 1885 and inhabited until 1964.

Siabost and around

Two miles south of the Arnol turn-off, at **Bragar**, look out for an archway, formed from the jawbone of a blue whale that was washed up on the coast nearby in 1920. A few miles further on is the township of Siabost (Shawbost), where the charmingly ramshackle **folk museum** ① *Apr-Sep Mon-Sat 0900-1800, free*, which was started as a project by local school-children, now contains an interesting collection of Hebridean artefacts.

Just south of Siabost, beside a small loch, is the sign for the recently restored **Norse Mill and Kiln**, which are a half-mile walk over the hill from the car park. There's not much to see as yet, but it's worth getting out of the car if you want to stretch your legs. A little further on is the popular surfing beach at Dalmore before you reach the turning for **Dail Beag** (**Dalbeg**), another lovely secluded beach.

Music to your ears

As the heartland of Gaelic culture, the Outer Hebrides are host to many music events throughout the year ranging from a spontaneous ceilidh to one of the three local mods. Mods usually consist of three days of competition in piping, singing, instrumental music, drama and poetry, and are an opportunity to see the best of the local talent. More information can be obtained from An Comunn Gaidhealach, T01851-703487.

Also listed below are the various Highland Games and agricultural shows, where you can also see piping competitions and Highland dancing.

Late March Feis nan Coisir, Stornoway, Lewis.

First Friday in April Donald Macleod Memorial Piping Competition, Stornoway, Lewis.

May-June Highland Festival, held in various locations.

Early June Harris Mod, Tarbert, on Harris.

Second week in June Lewis Mod, Stornoway, Lewis.

Mid June Uist Mod, Iochdar, on South Uist.

May-June Lochmaddy Boat Festival, Lochmaddy, North Uist.

Mid July Berneray Week, Bearnaraigh (Berneray), North Uist.

July Ceolas Music School, South Uist.

Early July Barra Festival for two weeks.

Early/mid July Feis Tir an Eorna, Paibeil, North Uist; Barra Highland Games, Borgh (Borve), Barra, lasting for a week.

11-14 July Hebridean Celtic Music Festival, Stornoway, Lewis.

Mid July North Uist Highland Games, Hosta, North Uist.

Mid/late July Harris Gala; South Uist Highland Games, Aisgeirnis (Askernish), South Uist; Lewis Highland Games, Tong, Lewis.

Mid July Barra Highland Games.

Third week of July Harris Festival

Late July Barra Live, Barra; West Side Agricultural Show, Barabhas (Barvas), Lewis; South Uist Agricultural Show, Iochdar, South Uist; South Harris Agricultural Show, Leverburgh.

July Feis Eilean an Fhraoich, Stornoway, Lewis.

Late July/early August North Uist Agricultural Show, Hosta, North Uist.

Early August Carloway Agricultural Show, Càrlabhagh (Carloway), Lewis; Fies Tir a Mhurain, Lionacleit, Benbecula; Lewis Carnival, Stornoway; Fish Festival, Stornoway; Twin Peaks Hill Race, North Uist.

Second week August Harris Arts Festival, Tarbert.

Gearrannan (Garenin)

The landscape gradually becomes more undulating and scenically interesting as the road then passes through the village of **Càrlabhagh (Carloway)**, Lord Leverhume's proposed fishing port. Here, a branch road leads to the ruined and deserted blackhouse village of Gearrannan (Garenin). Since 1989, the old village has been extensively renovated, with the aid of EU funding, and several derelict crofts have been painstakingly restored to their original style of stone walls and thatched roofs. One of these is now a **museum** ⓘ *T01851-643416, Apr-Sep Mon-Sat 0930-1730, £3, concessions £2*. There's also a Gatliff Trust hostel (see Sleeping, page 351), called **Garenin Hostel**, a café serving snacks and light lunches, and four self-catering cottages. An old cart track leads down to the bay, from where the sight of the sun setting out at sea really is something to behold. Above the village, a 4-mile coastal footpath can be followed through the lazy beds (see page 358) and above the sea cliffs to reveal a stunning view of beautiful **Dalmore Bay**. The Atlantic waves seem to break relentlessly on golden sands and the beach is, not surprisingly, a favourite haunt of surfers from Stornoway and further afield. Swimmers and bathers should be careful, however, because, as with many of the west coast beaches, there can be a fierce rip-current carrying the unwary into deeper water out at sea. Ask at the Gearrannan village, where you can also stay in unique blackhouse accommodation (see Sleeping, page 351), for a map of this coastal walking route that ends in Dalbeg.

Dùn Chàrlabhaigh (Doune Carloway) Broch
A little further on, standing a few hundred yards from the main road, is the Dùn Chàrlabhaigh Broch (Dun Carloway), the best-preserved building of its type in the Outer Hebrides. The impressive 2000-year-old drystone habitation is beautifully situated on a rocky outcrop, commanding great views across Loch Carloway to the sea beyond. The remaining outer wall is 30-ft high and slopes inwards, with an inner wall which rises vertically, leaving chambers between the walls. Parts of the inner wall have collapsed, revealing the interior stairs and galleries.The **Doune Broch Visitor Centre** ① *T01851-643338, Apr-Oct Mon-Sat 1000-1800, free,* which can be found here, tastefully complements the architectural style of the site, and which gives a good audio-visual description of how life must have been in one of these structures around 50 BC. There's also a small shop and public toilets.

Calanais (Callanish)
① *www.calanaisvisitorcentre.co.uk, T01851-621422 (HS), site open Apr-Sep daily 1000-1900, Oct-Mar daily 1000-1600, free, visitor centre is open Apr-Sep Mon-Sat 1000-1800, Oct-Mar Wed-Sat 1000-1600.*
Five miles south of Dun Chàrlabhaigh is the jewel in the islands' prehistoric crown, and one of the most atmospheric and evocative places in Scotland, if not the UK. The **Calanais Standing Stones** are the equal of Stonehenge in historical value but what sets them apart is their imposing physical presence, which can be appreciated at close quarters, and their spectacularly beautiful setting. The stones are aligned in the form of a Celtic cross and, in the centre, is a main circle of 13 stones, with a central monolith over 12-ft tall, and a chambered burial cairn. The oldest part of this great ceremonial site – probably the stone circle – dates from around 3000 BC (older than Stonehenge) and continued in use until about 800 BC. The full significance of the site is not yet known, though it is thought to be a lunar calendar, built to track the path of the lunar cycle. Every 18.6 years the moon returns to the same point and the stones at Calanais plot its slow progress over the intervening years until the moon 'sets' inside the stone circle. This astounding event – known as a lunar standstill – last occurred in 2006. There are also a number of smaller and more isolated stone circles a few miles south of Calanais on the road to Gearraidh na h-Aibhne (Garynahine). Next to the stones is the **Calanais Visitor Centre**, which features 'The Story of the Stones' exhibition, a very good restaurant (see Eating, page 352) and a shop. Margaret Curtis, who has been studying and excavating the site for over 30 years, offers a guided archaeological tour (see Activities and tours, page 352).

The Uig Peninsula → *For listings, see pages 350-353. Colour map 1, B2.*

From Gearraidh na h-Aibhne the main A858 runs back to Stornoway, while the B8011 forks west to the remote Uig Peninsula in the southwest of the island. Here are some of the Outer Hebrides' finest beaches and most dramatic coastal scenery, and you'll barely see another soul.

Bearnaraigh (Great Bernera) to Cnip

Four miles down this road is a turning to the right onto the B8059, which leads to the island of Bearnaraigh, now connected to the mainland of Lewis by a single-track road bridge. The main settlement on the island is **Breacleit (Breaclete)**, where you can find out about the island's history and the Iron Age village at Bostadh from the **Bernera Museum** ① *T01851-612285, Jun-Sep Mon-Sat 1100-1800, £2*. The rest of the island is fairly interesting with tiny fishing villages, one or two brochs and some standing stones. The nicest part, though, is on the north coast, near the tiny hamlet of **Bostadh (Bosta)**, where a lovely little sandy bay looks out to the nearby island of **Bearnaraigh Beag (Little Bernera)**.

The B8011 continues across bleak moorland, then cuts north to **West Loch Roag**, which is fringed by some fine sandy beaches and backed by a much hillier landscape. Just beyond **Miabhag (Miavaig)** is the turn-off right to **Cliobh (Cliff)**, with its picturesque beach which is unsafe for swimming. A mile further on is the little village of **Cnip (Kneep)**, to the east of which is the beautiful **Traigh na Berie**, a long sandy beach backed by flat machair which is ideal for camping.

Gallan Head

Beyond Miabhag, the eerie peninsula of Gallan Head provides a setting befitting a science fiction drama or Cold War Orwellian novel, with empty, decaying Ministry of Defence buildings battered by the Atlantic storms. Wandering around the abandoned site, it is easy to form ideas of bizarre, top-secret government experiments and early-warning missile tracking in this seemingly edge-of-the-world place, far removed from the unwanted, prying eyes of everyday society.

Mangersta and the Flannan Islands

Beyond Ardroil the road continues to Mangersta where, at Aird Fenish, is some of the most spectacular coastal scenery in the Outer Hebrides. The cliffs plunge dramatically beyond the road to the inaccessible beach below, with a series of crumbling sea stacks battered by the fearsome waves, and seabirds riding the updraughts adding to the sense of natural beauty, energy and sheer power. Further south at **Brenish**, about a 10-minute walk from the road, is a menacing blowhole connected to the sea by an underground passage.

Far out into the Atlantic are the haunting Flannan Islands, scene of an unsolved mystery in 1900 following the disappearance of three lighthouse keepers. Various explanations have been put forward over the years, ranging from a freak wave in stormy weather to a monster sea serpent or even a dispute and fight between the men; whatever the real reason, the legend continues. See page 352 for boat trips.

Timsgearraidh (Timsgarry)

At Timsgearraidh (Timsgarry) are the **Traigh Chapadail (Uig sands)** at the village of **Eadar Dha Fhadhail (Adroil)**. This is the loveliest of all the beaches on Lewis, with miles of sand dunes and machair, but it is famous for an entirely different reason. It was here in 1831 that a crofter dug up the 'Lewis Chessmen', 78 pieces carved from walrus ivory and belonging to at least eight incomplete chess sets from 12th-century Scandinavia. Some are now in the Museum of Scotland in Edinburgh, but most can be found outside their country of origin, in the British Museum in London (where you'll also find the Elgin Marbles). In recent years the Scottish Government has reportedly made several requests to the British Museum for the return of the chessmen.

⊙ Leodhas (Lewis) listings

For Sleeping and Eating price codes and other relevant information, see Essentials pages 38-45.

⊙ Sleeping

For those who want to visit the South Lochs on the east of Lewis, there are a couple of accommodation options: **Tigh Na Bruaich** (**C-D**), 8 Balallan, off the A859 and 14 miles from Stornoway, T01851-830742, T07763-185281, a traditional croft house; and **Kershader Hostel** (**E**), on the south shore of Loch Erisort off the A859 near North Harris, T01851-880236, www.syha.org.uk, cosy community-run 14-bed hostel with great facilities including a café and knitwear shop, ideal for accessing local birdwatching, fishing and walking.

Stornoway *p341, map p343*

As the largest settlement on the islands, Stornoway has a good selection of accommodation from which to choose, though you should book in advance in the peak summer season. The TIC will do this for you, for a small fee. There are many B&Bs in and around the town centre, some of which offer a 'room only' rate, including on Matheson Rd close to the town centre and ferry terminal.

A-B Cabarfeidh Hotel, Perceval Rd South, T01851-702604, www.cabarfeidh-hotel. co.uk. 46 rooms. On the outskirts of town and not as convenient as the **Royal**. Free broadband and all modern trappings.
B Royal Hotel, Cromwell St, T01851-702109, www.royalstornoway.co.uk. 26 rooms. Billed as Stornoway's most historic hotel, great value, central and with views across the marina. Reasonable food in its contemporary, all wood **HS-1 café-bar**, but for atmosphere and a tremendous meal book a table in its **Boatshed** restaurant (see Eating, below).
C Braighe House, 20 Braighe Rd, T01851-705287, www.braighehouse.co.uk. Open all

year. Four en suite rooms. Very comfortable, tastefully furnished accommodation in modern house with sea views. Tasty breakfasts and friendly welcome. A good alternative to the more expensive hotels in town. Recommended.
C-D Park Guest House, 30 James St, T01851-702485. 8 rooms. This Victorian townhouse is comfortable, only 500 yds from the ferry terminal, and is the best of the guesthouses. It also has an excellent restaurant. Price is **B** with dinner, **D** for room only.
D-E Fernlea, 9 Matheson Rd, T01851-702125, www.fernlea-guesthouse.co.uk Open Feb-Dec. Recently upgraded Victorian listed building with 3 en suite rooms. Room only, **C**. Off-street parking.
F Heb Hostel, 25 Kenneth St, Stornoway, T01851-709889, www.hebhostel.com. Centrally located hostel with 26 beds. Clean and friendly.
F Laxdale Holiday Park, Laxdale Lane, about a mile out of town on the road to Barabhas, T01851-703234, www. laxdaleholidaypark.com. Open all year. Bunkhouse has 16 beds and good facilities, including showers and toilets suitable for the disabled. The park also has space for 37 tents (£7 per night), and a 3-bedroom self-catering bungalow (from £350 per week).

North to Nis *p344*

A Broad Bay House, Back, Lewis, T01851-820990, wwwbroadbayhouse.co.uk. About 9 miles north of Stornoway. Modern and recently opened luxurious 4-bedroom guesthouse overlooking the sea. Beautifully appointed rooms and the opportunity to relax over a delicious 4-course evening meal (♦♦♦♦ (£35 per person)).
C Galson Farm Guest House and Bunk-house, Gàbhsann bho Deas (South Galson), halfway between Barabhas and Port Nis, T01851-850492, www.galsonfarm.co.uk. Open all year. Friendly and beautifully

restored 18th-century house with sea views. Dinner available (£25pp) (ɪɪɪ). Owners also have **Galson Farm Bunkhouse (F)**, which is a small welcoming hostel with 8 beds and basic facilities.

E Loch Beag B&B, 19 Fivepenny, Ness T01851-810405 This harled bungalow doesn't look much but it's good value for money and closeness to the Traigh sands.

West coast of Lewis p345

If you want to stay near the stones and visit them at dusk or sunrise, there are several inexpensive B&Bs in and around the village of Calanais.

C Loch Roag and Eshcol Guest House, 21 Breasclete, T01851-621357, www.eshcol. com. Open Mar-Oct. 3 rooms. A few miles from the stones. Comfortable accommodation in modern house overlooking Loch Roag and with the option of a 5-course dinner (ɪɪɪ).

C-D Loch Roag Guest House, T01851-621357, 22a Beascleit, www.lochroag.com. Open Mar-Oct. 6 rooms. Donald owns the house next door to his father (hence the same telephone number). He also offers high-quality accommodation and dinner, whilst the 2 cedar lodges – with spa – can be let for £800+ a week.

C Cean Bodiach B&B, 10 Tolsta Chaolis, T01851-621722, www.hebrideanholiday cottages.co.uk. Located between the stones and the broch,

C Leumadiair Guest House, 7a Callanish, T01851-621706, www.leumadair.co.uk. Has views of the stones which are just 2 mins away. It offers a 3-course dinner (£25 per person)

F Garenin Hostel, Garenin, near Carloway, www.gatliff.org.uk. 1 of 4 Gatliff Trust hostels in the Outer Hebrides (see box, page 346). A renovated blackhouse, situated by a gorgeous beach and with the added benefit of a ground-source heat pump, making it awfully cosy in cold weather. No telephone or TV. Recommended.

Self-catering

B Gearrannan Blackhouse Village, Carloway, T01851-643416, www.gearrannan. com. Open all year. 4 blackhouses have been restored and refurbished as self-catering thatched cottages in a fantastic location. One of the cottages sleeps up to 16. Prices from £89 per night.

Great Bernera to Cnip p349

A Auberge Carnish, 5 Carnish, Uig, T01851-672459, www.aubergecarnish.co.uk. 5-star accommodation and food in a stunning setting, this new venture, run by the couple who formerly owned the acclaimed Bonaventure (now Gallan Head Hotel) opens in May 2011.

B Baile Na Cille Guest House, Timsgarry, T01851-672242, www.bailenacille.co.uk. Open Easter-Oct. 7 en suite rooms. One of the best places to stay around Uig bay, this restored 18th-century manse is beautifully located overlooking a 2-mile stretch of sand. Superb home cooking 4-course dinner for £30) and one of the warmest welcomes in the islands. **B** including dinner.

D Gallan Head Hotel, north of Timsgarry, Aird Uig, T01851-672474, www.gallanhead hotel.co.uk. Open all year (limited in Dec). 5 rooms. This restaurant with rooms is a great place to stay, and eat. Don't be put off by the grim-looking disused military buildings, accommodation here is very comfortable. And the food, with an emphasis on the preparing locally sourced meats and seafish, is excellent.

🍴 Eating

Stornoway p351, map p343

The pubs and hotels serve the usual range of bar meals. Note that pubs are closed on Sun and some hotels cater only for residents.

ɪɪɪ **The Boatshed**, in the **Royal Hotel**, see Sleeping, above. Open daily. Fabulous maritime themed setting with the addition of a roaring open fire, wooden table and stone finishings. Recommended as the best of the hotel options. Less upmarket and offering a reasonably priced menu in a contemporary styled setting, is their **HS-1 Café Bar**.

♥♥♥-♥♥ Sunsets Restaurant, 26 Francis St, T01851-705862. Terrific option for diners seeking a taste of the freshest seafood and shellfish in town.

♥♥ Digby Chick, 5 Bank St, T01851-700026. Open Mon-Sat for lunch and dinner (closes 2100). This contemporary family-run restaurant is a popular local choice and one of the best places in town for seafood.

♥♥-♥ Stornoway Balti House, 24 South Beach, near the bus station, T01851-706116. For your fix of delicious tandoori and balti dishes, pop into this terrific restaurant that also offers takeaway and an express lunch (£6.50).

♥♥-♥ Thai Café, 27 Church St, T01851-701811. Open Mon-Sat until 2300. Few would expect such authentically good Thai cuisine so far north, but it's true. Come and be amazed. The BYO policy also helps keep prices down.

♥ Ann Lanntair Arts Centre, Kenneth St, Stornoway, T01851-703307. Good for snacks and light lunches in airy surroundings.

North to Nis *p344*
♥♥ The Cross Inn, Cross, Nis (Ness), T01851-810151, www.crossinn.com. The Islands' most northerly restaurant serving locally-grazed beef and the catch of the day.

West coast of Lewis *p345*
♥♥ Tigh Mealros, a few miles south of the stones, Gearraidh na h-Aibhne, T01851-621333. Closes at 2100. They serve good local grub in a cosy, relaxed atmosphere, with scallops a speciality.

♥ Calanais Visitor Centre Café, see page 348. The best place to eat near the stones, offering diners reasonably priced, freshly made soups, salads and home-baking.

The Uig Peninsula *p348*
♥♥♥ Gallan Head Hotel , see Sleeping, above. Restaurant and B&B serving food Mon-Fri 1830-2100. A plentiful 3-course set dinner for £32, catering for vegetarian and gluten free diets.

O Shopping

Stornoway *p341, map p343*
There's a **Tesco** supermarket beside the ferry terminal (closed Sun), and a **Co-op** by the 1st roundabout on the road out to Barabhas. However, for a taste of the Hebrides, pop into some of the following outlets in and around Stornoway: **Hebridean Brewing Company**, 18a Bells Rd, www.hebridean-brewery.co.uk, Mon-Fri 0900-1700, for a real ale taste of the Hebrides; **WJ MacDonald**, 5 Francis St, a butcher making the renowned Stornoway black pudding. If you want to catch your own supper **Sportsworld**, 1-3 Francis St, T01851-705464, sells bait and fishing gear all year round.

The Uig Peninsula *p348*
Uig Lodge Smoked Salmon, T01851-672396, www.uiglodge.co.uk. The place to buy smoked salmon.

● Activities and tours

Stornoway *p341, map p343*
Surfing
Lewis Surf Trek, 18a Guershader, T07939-194880, www.lewissurftrek.com. Lewis is excellent for surfing. Whether you want a half- (£25) or full-day (£40) board and wetsuit hire or a full-blown 2-day surf safari (£90 per person), give these guys a call.

Tour operators
Charles Engebret (T01851-702303) leaves from the pontoon next to the Lifeboat station and takes you to the bird colonies of the Shiant Islands.
Galson Motors, T01851-840269, leaves from Stornoway bus station. Day-trips to Calanais. The RSPB (T01851-703296 www.rspb.org.uk) lead a number of guided walks around breeding grounds and migration stop-offs.
Maclennan's Coaches, at the ferry terminal, T01851-706267. Day-trips to Calanais and the Blackhouse.

West coast of Lewis *p345*
Tour operators
Margaret Curtis, Olcote, New Park, Calanish, T01851-621277, http://www.geo.org/callan. htm#tof. The 1-hr tour of the Callanish site gives an insight into the history and purpose of the stones.

The Uig Peninsula *p348*
Island Cruising, 1 Erista, Uig, T01851-672381, www.island-cruising.com. For wildlife, diving, birdwatching and live-aboard boat trips as far afield as the Flannan Islands and St Kilda.
Seatrek, Murray MacLeod, 16 Uigean, Uig, T01851-672469, www.seatrek.co.uk. Aboard a high-speed RIB, this operator offers a host of trips, including a 2-hr (1000-1200) easy cruise off Uig during which you'll also check on the seals and lobster pots (£35); a Sea Stack trip off Little Bernera (1300-1500 £35); an island trip with ruins and sea caves (£45); and a full- blown day (£95) that includes the chance to see the isle of Scarp, famous for the film The Rocket Post (see Scarp page 356).

⊖ Transport

Stornoway *p341, map p343*
Air Flybe/Loganair, T0871-700 2000, www.flybe.com, flies to **Glasgow**, Mon-Sat, 2 daily, 1 hr. There is a also a daily flight to **Edinburgh**, 1 hr, and flights from **Inverness** Mon-Sat, 4 daily, 40 mins. Eastern Airways T08703-669100, www.easternairways.com, flies daily to Aberdeen Mon-Fri 55 mins.
Bus From Stornoway to **Port Nis (Ness)** via **Barabhas (Barvas)**, 4-6 times daily; to **Arnol**, **Siabost (Shawbost)**, **Càrlabhagh (Carloway)**, **Calanais (Callanish)**, and back to Stornoway, 'West Side Circular', 4-6 times

daily; to **Bear-naraigh (Great Bernera)** via **Gearraidh na h-Aibhne (Garynahine)**, 4 daily; to **Uig District**, 3-4 daily; to **Ranais (Ranish)**, 6-8 times daily. Contact the tourist office in Stornoway, T01851-703088, or the bus station, T01851-704327, for further details.
There are also buses from Stornoway to **Tarbert** and **Leverburgh** on Harris (for the ferry to North Uist), T01851-705050, 4-5 times daily, Mon-Sat. Bus timetables are available from the tourist office.
Ferry CalMac runs a ferry service to **Ullapool**, 2 times Mon-Sat (Mar-mid Jun) 3 times on Wed (Mid Jun-Aug) and 1 daily Nov-Feb. It also now runs once on a Sun all year round (2 hrs 40 mins). Contact **CalMac** offices in Stornoway, T01851-702361, for further details.
Car and cycle hire Car and bike rental is available at good rates from **Lewis Car Rentals**, 52 Bayhead St, T01851-703760; **Mackinnon Self Drive**, 18 Inaclete Rd, T01851-702984, hires cars; **Alex Dan's Cycle Centre**, 67 Kenneth St, T01851-704025. Mon-Sat 0900-1800, rents bikes for £14 per day and £45 per week.
Taxi Central Cabs, T01851-706900.

West coast of Lewis *p345*
Car hire/taxi Arnol Car Rentals, Arnol, T01851-710548. Free airport and ferry delivery.

ⓘ Directory

Stornoway *p341, map p343*
Banks Bank of Scotland, directly opposite the tourist office, has an ATM. Other major banks are also in the centre and also have ATMs. **Internet** Public library, 19 Cromwell St. **Post** Main post office, 16 Francis St.

Na Hearadh (Harris)

→ Colour map 1, B2-3. Phone code 01859.

Harris is not an island but, together with Lewis, forms the largest of the Outer Hebrides, with Harris taking up the southern third. The two parts are divided by the long sea lochs of Loch Seaforth in the east and Loch Resort in the west, though this division is rarely shown on maps. Though joined, the two are very different in terms of geography. Harris is largely mountain and rock, whereas Lewis is flat moorland. The largest town and site of the ferry terminal is An Tairbeart (Tarbert). To the north are the highest peaks in the Outer Hebrides, surrounded by some of the finest unspoilt wilderness in the whole country. To the south are miles of wonderful beaches; sands and stunning seascapes that will convince you it's the Caribbean. For it's not just the flawless white sand but the gin-clear water that breaks over them. When the sun comes out, it's as if someone had been fiddling with the colour control: cool greens mutate to psychedelic shades of turquoise and blue. The east coast is not so much a contrast as a shock to the system; a preternaturally strange lunar landscape straight out of a science fiction film. With your own transport you could 'do' Harris in a day quite comfortably, but why just spend a day? Whatever the weather, you'll want to spend more time here and appreciate its precious natural beauty. ▸▸ *For listings, see pages 359-361.*

Ins and outs

Getting there
There's a regular bus service between Stornoway and Tarbert (four to five times a day) Monday to Saturday, which continues to Leverburgh, via the west coast of South Harris. Ferries sail from Uig (Skye) to Tarbert (one hour 35 minutes), once or twice a day, Monday to Saturday. A one-way ticket costs £5.35 per passenger, £24.20 per car. Contact Uig, T01470-542219, or Tarbert, T01859-502444.

Background

The separation of Harris and Lewis dates back to Norse times, when the island was divided between the two sons of Leod, progenitor of the Macleods. Harris remained in Macleod hands until 1834. The recent history of Harris is closely bound up with that of Lewis. Both were bought by the soap magnate, Lord Leverhulme, see page 341, whose grandiose schemes for Lewis came to nothing. Leverhulme then turned his attentions to Harris, where the peaceful little village of An t-Ob (Obbe) was renamed Leverburgh and transformed into a bustling port with all manner of public works programmes under development. His death in 1925 brought an end to all his plans for Harris and, instead of becoming a town with a projected population of 10,000, Leverburgh reverted to being a sleepy village, with only the harbour, the roads and the change of name to show for it all.

Since the Leverhulme era there has been no main source of employment for the population of 2400 on Harris, though a successful fishing industry continues on Scalpaigh (Scalpay). There is still some crofting supplemented by the acclaimed but financially precarious Harris Tweed industry (www.harristweed.org) though most of the estimated 130 plus Hebridean weavers reside on Lewis. In addition to public services and crafts, tourism is increasingly important to the island. Indeed, with its wealth of Caribbean-like beaches, diversity of wildlife, excellent walking terrain and fabulous accommodation and eating options, this compact Hebridean 'island' is now establishing itself as a year-round destination. The community launched Winter Harris (www.winterharris.com) in 2007 and as a result it's reported that some hoteliers have already seen a 15% rise in profits over the winter months.

Ceann a Tuath na Hearadh (North Harris)

→ For listings, see pages 359-361. Colour map 1, B2. Phone code 01859.

North Harris is the most mountainous part of the Outer Hebrides and its wild, rugged peaks are ideal for hillwalking. In 2003, 135,900 acres of the wildlife (including deer) rich former North Harris Estate were purchased for the community for around £8 million to be managed by the North Harris Community Trust. The A859 south from Lewis gets progressively more scenic as it skirts **Loch Siophort (Seaforth)**, and the mountains rise before you like a giant barrier. The road then climbs past **Bogha Glas (Bowglass)** and **Aird a Mhulaidh (Ardvourlie)** with Clisham (2619 ft), the highest peak in the Outer Hebrides, and **Sgaoth Aird** (1829 ft) towering overhead on either side. Clisham in particular, though not a Munro, is a very staisfying peak to bag: steep, spectacularly craggy and the views from the top will break your heart.

Just off the A859 near Ardvourlie is **Ardvourlie Castle Guest House**. If you can't afford such luxury but still crave the isolation, then carry on south until you reach the turn-off to **Reinigeadal (Rhenigidale)**, which was the most remote community on Harris and accessible only by sea or by a rough hill track until the access road was built. Here you'll find a **Gatliff Trust Youth Hostel**, see Sleeping, page 359. From Reinigeadal an ascent of shapely **Toddun** (528 m) provides exhilarating exercise rewarded with fine views east across the Minch to the mainland and, in the other direction, to the mountain wilderness of North Harris.

The A859 continues west across the crest of the craggy hills then drops down to the turn-off for the single-track B887, which winds its way all the way out to Huisinis (Hushinish) between the impressive mountains of the Forest of Harris on one side and the northern shore of West Loch Tarbert on the other, with views across to the Sound of Taransay and the beaches of South Harris. Immediately beyond the turn-off, you pass through **Bun Abhainn Eadarra (Bunavoneadar)**, which was a thriving whaling station until 1930 and one of Lord Leverhulme's many schemes for the island. The old whaling station is worth a visit even though the site has not been developed as a tourist attraction.

Just before the village of **Miabhag (Meavaig)**, a defined footpath heads north into the hills up Glen Meavaig to Loch Voshimid. Further on, though, is a better opportunity for walking. Just before the gates of **Amhuinnsuidhe Castle** (pronounced 'Avan-soo-ee') is a signpost for Chliostair Power Station. From here you can walk two miles up to the dam, then follow the right-hand track round the reservoir and the left-hand track round the upper loch, before you arrive in a wild and remote glen.

Just beyond the castle gates you'll see a beautiful waterfall spilling straight into the sea. The road then runs right past the front door of the castle, built in 1868 by the Earl of Dunmore, and still a private residence, before passing through an archway and continuing to the tiny crofting township of **Huisinis (Hushinish)**, beautifully situated in a sandy bay. This is where the road ends; next stop the USA. Follow the track to the right across the machair, where a footpath above the jetty and rocky beach can be followed to the old fishing lodge at **Cravadale** and Loch Cravadale beyond. Make a detour to the golden sands and turquoise waters of **Traigh Mheilein**, overlooking Scarp. From the coast, strong walkers can follow Glen Cravadale inland, eventually rejoining the main road near Amhuinnsuidhe Castle.

Right to buy

The Forest of Harris is a vast mountain wilderness extending north from West Loch Tarbert to Loch Resort and forming the de facto boundary with Lewis. It is one of the most isolated and unspoilt upland landscapes in Scotland and, because of its remoteness, receives very few visitors. For experienced hillwalkers, however, it is a paradise, offering rugged mountains, dramatic escarpments, airy ridges and desolate glens. There are endless walking possibilities, including a horse- shoe walk around Clisham and a long walk through Glen Ulladale to Kinloch- resort, a former crofting community now abandoned, but

once described as the remotest habitation in Britain. Known as the North Harris Estate, this 22,000-acre tract of land was owned and managed by the family of the Bulmer cider empire – until 2003. In a move that had Scottish lairds incandescent with rage, the 800 residents of the estate were granted the right to take over the land on which they live, for more than £2 million, and finally throw off the shackles of feudal rule. Now that they have become masters of their own destiny, the community can relish the thought of a prosperous future, with energy development plans, sporting rights and tourism top of the agenda.

The rocky island of **Scarp** supported a population of more than 100 as late as the 1940s but was abandoned in 1971, and now the crofters' cottages are used as holiday homes. The island was the scene of a bizarre experiment in 1934, when a German rocket scientist, Gerhard Zucher, tried to prove that rockets could be used to transport mail and medical supplies to remote communities. His theory went up in smoke, however, when the rocket exploded before it even got off the ground, with 30,000 letters on board.

An Tairbeart (Tarbert) and around

→ *For listings, see pages 359-361. Colour map 1, B2. Phone code 01859. Population 500.*
Tarbert, the largest settlement on Harris, lies in a sheltered bay on the narrow isthmus that joins North and South Harris. It's a tiny 'capital' but still the main ferry port for the CalMac ferry from Harris to Uig on Skye. Tarbert is also where to find groceries, **Harris tweed** ⓘ *www.harristweedandknitwear.co.uk*, a post office, petrol, and a range of eating and accommodation options. The **TIC** ⓘ *T01859-502011, Apr-Oct Mon-Sat 0900-1700 and for the arrival of the evening ferry, in winter check times*, is close to the ferry terminal.

An interesting little excursion from Tarbert is the 10-mile return route that runs east through the tiny villages of **Urgha** and **Caolas Scalpaigh** to **Carnach** at the end of the road. Just beyond Urgha, on the north side of the road, is a path which leads across the hills, part of the land managed by the North Harris Community Land Trust, to the remote settlement of **Reinigeadal**. The twisting path was originally used by the community in Reinigeadal; hardy children would make the daily journey across the hills to Tarbert before the village was connected to the A859 by the new road. The zigzagging, exposed path, on which several people are known to have perished, passes through enchanting scenery above **Loch Trollamarig** in a setting more reminiscent of Scandinavia's fjordland. A visit can easily be made to the deserted village of **Molinginish**, nestled snugly in a small glen above the loch and reputedly where the royal family once anchored for a picnic. Ensure you are properly equipped with boots and rainwear for the 6-mile walk.

The island of **Scalpaigh** (**Scalpay**), now connected to Harris by a road bridge opened by Tony Blair in 1998, is a thriving fishing community with a population of over 400. It's a pleasant three-mile walk across the island to **Eilean Glas Lighthouse**, built by the Stevensons and the first ever on the Outer Hebrides.

Ceann a Deas na Hearadh (South Harris)

→ *For listings, see pages 359-361. Colour map 1, B2.*

An absolute must while you're in the Outer Hebrides is the 45-mile circular route around South Harris. If you only do one thing while you're here, then make sure this is it, for the change in scenery from the west coast to the east is utterly astounding. One thing you're sure to puzzle over as you travel round is the fact that most people live on the harsh and inhospitable east coast, known as Na Baigh (Bays), while the beautiful west coast with its miles of glorious golden sands is scarcely populated. This is not through choice. The fertile west coast housed most of the population until the end of the 18th century when they were cleared to make way for sheep farms. Some emigrated to Cape Breton, while others were 'resettled' by landowners, forced to farm the infertile, rocky soil of the east side.

West coast of Harris

The main road from Tarbert runs south, skirting East Loch Tarbert, then cuts inland and heads west through a dramatic lunar landscape of rocks dotted with tiny lochans. It then begins to descend towards the sea revealing to your right the vast golden expanse of **Losgaintir** (**Luskentyre**) beach. A single-track road turns off to the right and runs out to the tiny settlement of Losgaintir where in his tiny workshop overlooking the machair and azure sea, weaver Donald John Mackay is among the dozen or so Hearrachs (indigenous inhabitants from Harris) who produce the world famous hand-crafted Harris tweed using his loom. The weaver, whom once famously supplied cloth to Nike for a range of training shoes, sells hats (from £12) and hand-woven tweed jackets (from £160) from his workshop at 6 Luskentyre. The road cuts through the rich machair as it follows the magnificent stretch of bleached white sand that fills the entire bay, washed by turquoise sea and backed by steep dunes. All this set against the backdrop of the mountains to the north. This is paradise refrigerated.

A short distance offshore is the island of **Tarasaigh** (**Taransay**), which was well populated at the beginning of the 1900s but was recently abandoned. The island gained national prominence in 2000 as the setting for the popular BBC television series *Castaway*, in which an assortment of supposedly normal people from a variety of backgrounds were challenged to pit their wits against the elements and each other for a period of a full year. You can enjoy a day trip to the island (see Activities and tours, page 361).

The road follows the coast, passing through the tiny settlements of **Seilebost**, **Horgabost** and **Burgh** (**Borve**), Norse names highlighting the Vikings once plundered these lands. At **Horgabost** it's worthwhile making the brief 10-minute stroll above the white sands to marvel at the roughly hewn MacLeod's Stone that overlooks the sea and which dates back to the Bronze Age. There's B&B accommodation at Seilebost and Horgabost, while, a few miles further on, is another beautiful stretch of white sands at **Sgarasta Bheag** (**Scaristabeg**), perfect for surfing, golf and with a couple of stunning places to stay (see Sleeping, page 359).

Beyond Sgarasta Bheag, the village of **An Taobh Tuath** (**Northton**) provides access to the scenic promontory of **Toe Head**, almost cut off from the rest of Harris by the huge expanse of the golden sands at Sgarasta. At the excellent **Seallam Centre** ① *T01859-520258, www.seallam.com, Mon-Sat 1000-1700, £2.50*, you can learn all about the history and natural environment of Harris and take the chance to determine if you have ancestral links to the Hebrides. There's also a lovely café here. Nearby, a ruined chapel of 16th-century origin is situated on the machair below **Chaipaval** (365 m), whose heathery slopes can be climbed for one of the best views out to sea towards St Kilda, some 40 miles distant.

Ant-Ob (Leverburgh)

The road then runs along the south shore until it reaches An t-Ob (formerly Obbe, now Leverburgh), site of Lord Leverhulme's ambitious plan to turn a sleepy crofting township into a major fishing port, see page 354. A tiny, unremarkable village where some of the original buildings can still be seen, this is also the base of the excellent **Am Bothan Bunkhouse** (see Sleeping, page 360) and the departure point for CalMac's car ferry to Berneray. ▶▶ *For further details, see Transport page 361.*

Ròghadal (Rodel)

Three miles east of Leverburgh, at the southeastern tip of Harris, is Ròghadal (Rodel), dominated by the beautiful 12th-century **St Clement's Church**, something of an unusual sight in such a remote spot and one of the most impressive religious building in the Hebrides. (Only the Benedictine abbey on Iona is larger.) The church stands on a site that dates back 1500 years and was built by Alastair Crotach (Hunchback) Macleod of Harris in the 1520s. Though impressive from the outside, particularly the huge tower, the real interest lies in the silent, chilly atmosphere of the interior, where you'll find a collection of remarkable carved wall tombs, some blackened by fire that once ravaged these walls. There are three tombs, the most notable of which is that of the founder, Alastair Crotach. The one in the south wall of the choir is also worth a close look.

Na Baigh (Bays)

Running north from Ròghadal up the east coast of South Harris is the **Golden Road**, so named by the locals because the of the huge cost of building it. This twisting, tortuous single-track road runs through a bizarre and striking moonscape, and driving through it is a unique experience (but keep your eyes on the road or you'll end up in one of the many narrow sea lochs). It seems inconceivable that anyone could survive in such an environment, but the road passes through a string of townships, including picturesque **Geocrab**, all created in the 19th century by the people evicted from the west coast. People here have spent years eking a meagre living from the thin soil by building 'lazy beds' (thin strips of piled-up earth between the rocks) for planting potatoes. Weaving and fishing also provide much-needed income.

At **Lingreabhagh** (**Lingarabay**) the road skirts the foot of **Roinebhal**, which was, until recently, the proposed site of one of the largest super-quarries in Europe. This would have demolished virtually the entire mountain over many decades. Local people and environmentalists fought a successful campaign to prevent the proposal going ahead, thus protecting a precious natural asset (see box, above). Today, it's not quarries but wind farm developments that threaten to blight the landscape of the Outer Hebrides. The road passes through a succession of tiny settlements before joining the A859 just south of Tarbert.

For Sleeping and Eating price codes and other relevant information, see Essentials pages 38-45.

◉ Sleeping

North Harris p355

B Ardhasaig House, Aird Asaig, 4 miles northwest of Tarbert off A859, T01859-50200, www.ardhasaig.co.uk. Open all year. 6 en suite rooms. Small hotel with a big reputation, especially for its wonderful cooking (4-course set dinner is £40 a head). Lovely location, good disabled facilities and also offers romantics accommodation in a cosy, self-contained barn. Self-catering available from £300 per week.

F Gatliff Trust Youth Hostel, Rhenigidale, www.gatliff.org.uk. Spectacular location at the head of remote Loch Seaforth. Here you'll find a converted croft house (no phone), which sleeps 13 and is open all year. If properly equipped you can walk the 5 miles from Tarbert using the path once trod by the schoolchildren.

Tarbert and around p356

Harris isn't lacking in places to stay, most notably there are luxurious self-catering accommodation and comfortable hotels or guesthouses. Some hotels may offer a room-only rate if you are catching the 0730 ferry back to Skye on Mon, Wed and Fri.

B Hotel Hebrides, beside the ferry pier, Tarbert, T01859-502364, www.hotel-hebrides.com. Extensively refurbished in 2008, this boutique-style 21-room hotel includes luxurious family and double rooms. From the revamped **Pierhouse Restaurant** you can enjoy views over the sea whilst tucking into breakfast or a dinner of fresh seafood (♥♥♥-♥♥).

A Harris Hotel, on the main road from Stornoway, on the left, before the turning for the ferry, Tarbert, T01859-502154. Built in 1865 and sporting the initials of the acclaimed 19th century novelist J M Barrie

in its window, this welcoming hotel has 22 comfortable bedrooms to retire to after enjoying a fine meal or malt in the bar.

B Ceol na Mara, at Direcleit, just mins drive from Tarbert, T01859-502464. Stands above a sea loch and offers 4 comfortable rooms and the option of a 3-course Hebridean dinner (♥♥♥). The Gaelic name translates as 'Music of the Sea.'

D Avalon Guesthouse, 12 West Side, Tarbert, just under a mile before Tarbert on left-hand side of road coming from Stornoway, T01859-502 334, www.avalonguesthouse.org. Open all year. 3 rooms. Comfortable B&B on family croft, wonderful views over Loch West Tarbert.

D Hirta House, Scalpay, T01859-540394, www.hirtahouse.com. Open all year. 3 lovely en suite rooms. Great sea views and a guest lounge and library. Good value.

D Mrs C MacKinnon, Highcroft, Ardnakillie, Scalpay, T01859-540305 www.harriscroft.com. Open year-round. 3 rooms in a modern crofthouse. 5 miles from Tarbert with views to East Loch Tarbert and the surrounding hills.

D Mrs Flora Morrison, Tigh na Mara, Tarbert, T01859-502270 www.tigh-na-mara.co.uk. A B&B within 5 mins' walk of the ferry pier, very friendly.

South Harris p357

L-A Scarista House, Scaristabeg, T01859-550238, www.scaristahouse.com. Open all year. 5 tastefully furnished rooms and 2 comfortable self-catering cottages at the rear of this 19th century former manse. The bedrooms are well equipped in a residence that truly oozes old world character. Antiques and books greet guests, who can then relax by the roaring open fire with a malt or bottle of fine wine (there's an extensive collection). Forget the TV. This is where to enjoy fantastic company, an evening meal (£42 for 3 courses and £50 for 4) and even impromptu live ceilidh music. Recommended.

B Rodel Hotel, Rodel, T01859-520210, www.rodelhotel.co.uk. Closed Jan to mid-Feb. 4 en suite rooms. Overlooking a tiny harbour at the southern tip of the island and close to St Clement's Church. Comfortable, with a reasonable restaurant (¶¶).

C Beul Na Mara, Seilebost, T01859-550205, www.buelnamara.co.uk. A 3-bedroom guesthouse on the west coast between Tarbert and Leverburgh, that enjoys the backdrop, golden beaches and of Taransay off-shore. Also offers dinner (¶¶¶ (£25 per person)).

B Grimisdale, Leverburgh, T01859-520460, www.grimisdale.co.uk. Run by Effie MacLeod is a friendly, 3-bedroom family guesthouse with wonderful views.

C Carminish House, 10 mins' walk from the Leverburgh ferry, T01859-520400, www.carminish.com. Offers views over the sea. Dinner is offered (£21) (**C**).

C Mrs Paula Williams, Sorrel Cottage, 2 Glen, Leverburgh, T01859-520319, www.sorrelcottage.co.uk. Open all year. 3 rooms. Relaxing place to stay, with meals available, including vegetarian (**C** with dinner, **F** for room only), and cycle hire.

E Am Bothan Bunkhouse, Leverburgh, T01859-520251, www.ambothan.com. Open all year. A fabulous, well equipped and friendly bunkhouse packed with character and situated close to the pier. Space for tents.

F Drinishader Bunkhouse, Drinishader, 3 miles south of Tarbert, Bays, T01859-511255. Open all year. 12 beds. Traditional crofters cottage by the sea, with a cosy coal fire. Easily accessed by bus from Tarbert, and there's a shop close by but the nearest pub is 4 miles away.

Self-catering

Blue Reef Cottages, overlooking Scarista beach, T01859-550370, www.stay-hebrides.com. Couples who seek the ultimate in luxurious self-catering need look no further than here. Fashioned from local stone and timbers, these identical 2 croft cottages built into the hillside enjoy breathtaking views over the machair (and golf course) to the Atlantic and offshore Isle of Taransay. There's champagne and home-baking on arrival, bikes and golf clubs to use, a fabulous kitchen, comfy sofas, a wood burning stove and after a day hillwalking or at sea, a jacuzzi and sauna to enjoy before retiring into the tastefully furnished bedroom with its hints of Harris tweed and Queen-sized bed. You'll never want to leave. From £950 per week. Recommended.

Croft Cottage, 5 mins walk from Tarbert T01859-502338, www.croftcottageharris.co.uk. A wonderfully luxurious self-catering option. Ingeniously converted from a former byre and with stunning views over East Loch Tarbert towards the Minch. 3-bedroom, family-friendly hideaway packed with stylish finishes, including solid oak floors and an irresistible sauna and jacuzzi. From £500 (3 days) or from £945 per week. Recommended.

Camping

In Luskentyre, you can **camp** on the machair, but ask for permission at the 1st house.

❶ Eating

Harris may be small and remote but the enterprising islanders can guarantee that even in the depths of winter you can enjoy a snack, lunch or full-blown candlelit dinner in style. However, it's advisable to book ahead just to ensure the restaurant/café is open. For more information on Harris in winter, see www.winterharris.com.

Tarbert and around *p356*

¶¶¶-¶¶ **Harris Hotel**, see Sleeping, above. Serves tasty food every day till around 2100. They do a 3-course fixed menu and reasonably priced bar meals.

¶ **First Fruits Tearoom**, Tarbert, T01859-502439. Easter-end Aug Mon-Sat 1030-1700. Cosy traditional Hebridean tea room serving delicious home-baking.

Self-catering
▦▦-▦▦ **Atlantic Edge**, T01859-520766, T077866-85156. It's the self-caterers dream with the home-delivery of delicious, gourmet, home-cooked starters (from £3.50), mains (from £12) and desserts (£5.50) right to your door. Feast on the likes of smoked fish pâté with oatcakes, or lemon and ginger soup followed by local lamb with apricots and chocolate roulade.

South Harris *p357*
▦▦-▦▦ **Scarista House**, Scaristabeg, T01859-550238, www.scaristahouse.com. For a mouth-watering 4-course dinner that may include local lamb, freshly caught shellfish and heavenly desserts, followed by a malt or glass of wine by the fire, you'll not beat the culinary experience at this homely former Georgian manse with views towards the sea. Book ahead. Fabulous and recommended.
▦▦-▦ **The Anchorage**, by the pier, Leverburgh, T01859-520225. Open Mar-Sep. Café/restaurant near the bunkhouse, offering reasonable lunches and dinners including seafood.
▦▦-▦ **Skoon Art Café**, Geocrab, T01859-530268, www.skoon.com. Open all year. Overlooking the rocky Bays area on the east coast, this cosy, bright traditional croft house is adorned with the artworks of the resident artist-cum-chef, Andy. His wife, Emma, serves up the delicious soups, sandwiches and home-baking. Recommended.

⊙ Activities and tours

Tarbert and aroun,d *p356*
Fishing
Obbe Fishings, Leverburgh T01859-520466, www.obbefishings.com. Will help you hook the freshest supper.

Tour operators
Angus Mackay, T01859-550260, www.visit-taransay.com. The man to call for a boat trip to the tiny Isle of Taransay. Leaves from Horgabost Beach and costs £20, children £10.

Bill Lawson, Leverburgh, T01859-520488, www.billlawson.com and **Mike Brigg**, T01859-502376, www.mikeandpeggybriggs.co.uk, offer informative walking trips to spot wildlife.
Hamish Taylor, T01859-530310, www.scenic-cruises.co.uk. Provides wonderful offshore wildlife cruises on the east coast.
Sea Harris, East Tarbert, T01859-502007, www.seaharris.co.uk. Skipper Seumas Morrison offers wildlife and sea trips to the Shiants and St Kilda.

Watersports
For watersports, contact **Adventure Hebrides**, www.adventurehebrides.com; and **Lewis Surf Trek**, T07939-194880, www.lewissurf trek.com. Both based on Lewis.

⊙ Transport

Harris *p354*
Bus There's a regular bus service between **Tarbert** and **Stornoway**, Mon-Sat, 1 hr 15 mins.
There's also a bus service from **Tarbert** to **Leverburgh** via the east coast (for the ferry to North Uist), 3-4 times daily, 1 hr 5 mins, along the so-called 'Golden Road' and 'Bays' route. This bus service (W13) includes stops at **Drinishader**, **Geocrab** and **Rodel**. To **Huisinis**, 2-4 daily on school days, 45 mins; to **Reinigeadal**, 2 daily on school days; to **Scalpaigh**, 2-5 daily, 10 mins. Bus timetables are available at the TIC or see www.cne-siar.gov.uk.
Cycle hire Harris Cycle Hire, Sorrel Cottage, 2 Glen Kyles, Leverburgh, T01859-520319, www.sorrelcottage.co.uk. Prices for bikes start from about £15 per day. Also rents children's bikes.
Ferry A ferry sails from **Leverburgh** to **Berneray**, 3-4 times daily. The trip takes 1 hr and a one-way ticket costs £6.50 per passenger, £29.50 per car (£11.10 and £51 for 5-day saver return). Note that though this is a short crossing, the service can easily be disrupted by high winds so try and be flexible with your travel plans.

The Uists, Benbecula and Barra

South from Harris lies the southern 'half' of the Outer Hebrides. The Uists, north and south, and Benbecula are all connected by a series of causeways; you can drive their length, past a never- ending series of fish-filled lochs, windswept beaches backing onto wildflower rich machair and tiny, straggling crofting communities. The quality of the seafood, livestock (and baking) on the Uists also sees these islands make a notable contribution to the acclaimed Outer Hebrides Speciality Food Trail, www.foodhebrides.com. At South Uist's southernmost tip, you cross a half-mile long causeway to the tiny and beautiful Isle of Eriskay where within sight of the beach where Bonnie Prince Charlie first stepped ashore on Scotland in his bid to seize the Scottish Crown for the Stuart's, the road runs out at the CalMac ferry slipway for Barra. Alternatively, you can fly from Glasgow to Barra and land on its famous famous cockle strand – at low tide, of course! ▸▸ *For listings, see pages 371-375.*

Ins and outs

Getting around

In recent years, the network of public transport on the islands has improved. Nonetheless, if relying on a bus to get around, don't expect one every five minutes – or hour. It is highly recommended to get hold of a free copy of Uist and *Barra, Bus and Ferry services* from TIC's or view the timetables online at www.cne-siar.gov.uk. There are six to seven buses per day (except Sunday) from Berneray to Lochmaddy. Some of these buses continue to Baile a Mhanaich (Balivanich) on Benbecula, where there is an airport, see page 365, and Lochboisdale and Ludag on South Uist, see page 366. There are six to seven buses per day from Lochmaddy to the island of Bearnaraigh (Berneray) just off the north coast in the sound of Harris. There are three buses per day from Lochmaddy to Clachan na Luib (Clachan-a-Luib) which run in an anti-clockwise direction around the north and west coasts. Two buses per day connect Clachan-a-Luib with Baile Sear (Baleshare) and also with Saighdinis (Sidinish).

A mile long causeway connects South Uist to Benbecula by road and regular buses (four per day Monday to Saturday) run between Lochboisdale and Lochmaddy on North Uist, stopping en route at Dalabrog (Daliburgh), Tobha Mòr (Howmore) and Lionacleit and Balinavich on Benbecula. There is also a regular bus service between Lochboisdale and Ludag (for ferries to Barra). A causeway links Eriskay to South Uist. CalMac operates a ferry to Eriskay from Barra, see page 375.

Uibhist a Tuath (North Uist)

→ *For listings, see pages 371-375.* *Colour map 1, C1. Phone code 01876. Population 1815.*
North Uist is the largest island in the southern chain of the Outer Hebrides, about 13 miles from north to south and 18 miles east to west at its widest point. At first sight it comes as something of a disappointment after the dramatic landscapes of Harris. In fact, it's barely a landscape at all, as over a third of the island's surface is covered by water. The east coast around Lochmaddy, the main settlement, is so peppered with lochs it resembles a giant sieve. But, heading west from Lochmaddy, the island's attractions become apparent, particularly the magnificent beaches on the north and west coasts. Also on the west coast, is the Balranald Nature Reserve, the ideal place for birdwatching. You're also likely to see

otters. There are numerous prehistoric sites scattered across the island and, with all that water around, there's obviously plenty of good fishing to be had.

Ins and outs

Getting there There are two car ferry services to North Uist. One is to the northern Isle of Berneray (joined to Uist by a causeway) from Leverburgh on South Harris, the other to Lochmaddy from Uig on Skye (one or two daily, the journey takes one hour and 40 minutes), a one-way ticket is £5.35 per person, £24.20 per car. Contact **CalMac** ① *T01876-500337*, in Lochmaddy, for further information. North Uist is joined to the islands of Benbecula and South Uist to the south by a causeway and bridge. There are several buses daily (Monday to Saturday) from Otternish to Lochmaddy and on to Lochboisdale on South Uist.

Loch nam Madadh (Lochmaddy)

Lochmaddy, the island's main village and ferry port, is a tiny place; so small you're almost through it before you realize. Though it's on the east coast and not close to the beaches, it's a good start point (and if devoid of camping equipment) base for exploring the island as it boasts most facilities. It has a bank (next to the tourist office), a hotel and pub, a tourist office, a few shops, post office, hospital, petrol station and the well run **Uist Outdoor Centre** ① *T01876-500480, www.uistoutdoorcentre.co.uk*, where you can enjoy a range of watersports, notably sea kayaking, and stay at its bunkhouse (see Activities and tours, page 374).

If you have time, the **Taigh Chearsabhagh Museum and Arts Centre** ① *T/F01876-500293, www.taigh-chearsabhagh.org, Mon-Sat 1000-1700, free*, is worth visiting and has a small café. You can also purchase home-made preserves, crafts and even Harris tweed handbags. The **TIC** ① *near the ferry pier, T01876-500321, Apr-Oct Mon-Sat 0900-1700, and for the arrival of the evening ferry*, will provide transport timetables and sells a number of useful walking maps if you plan to hike the beaches and hills.

Around the island

There are a number of interesting archaeological sites of different periods dotted around the island. The most notable is **Barpa Langass**, 7 miles southwest of Lochmaddy on the slope of Ben Langass, just off the A867, which cuts across the bleak peaty hinterland of North Uist. This is a huge chambered burial cairn dating from around 3000 BC. Unfortunately, it is now too dangerous to enter. About a mile away, on the southern side of Ben Langass, is the small stone circle known as **Pobull Fhinn**, standing on the edge of Loch Langass. Three miles northwest of Lochmaddy on the A865 are three Bronze Age standing stones called **Na Fir Bhreige** (The False Men), said to be the graves of three spies who were buried alive.

The real charms of North Uist, though, are the fabulous beaches on its north and west coasts. Heading anti-clockwise from Lochmaddy, the A865 runs northwest, passing the turning for Otternish and the wild and beautiful lands of Bearnaraigh (see below), which is now connected to North Uist by a causeway. It continues west through the township of **Sollas (Solas)**, where there are a couple of B&Bs, and then passes the beautiful sands of **Bhalaigh (Vallay) Strand**. Near the northwestern tip of the island, standing on an islet in Loch Scolpaig, is **Scolpaig Tower**, a 'folly' built to provide employment and income for local men in the 19th century.

Three miles south of here is the turning to **Balranald RSPB Reserve**, an area of rocky coast, sandy beaches and dunes, machair and lochs. The reserve is ideal for birdwatching, especially waders. A two-hour guided walk along the headland allows you to see Manx shearwaters, gannets, skuas and storm petrels, and, during the summer, you can listen out for the distinctive rasping call of the corncrake, one of the rarest birds in Britain. There's a basic visitor centre which is open from April to September.

As the road continues south, pop into the sparse but tasty **Claddach Kirkibost Centre and Café** ⓘ *Mon-Sat 1000-1600*, a community enterprise that sells peat smoked salmon, jams and an amazing selection of home-baking, including their famous tablet. A mile further south the A865 meets the A867, which heads east back to Lochmaddy. Staying on the A865, after another mile you can turn off for the tidal and sparsely inhabited island of **Baile Sear** (**Baleshare**), now connected by a causeway to North Uist and with a three-mile- long beach from where you can just see the low lying **Monach Isles** (also known by their old Norse name of *Heisker*) lying 5 miles off the west coast. They were once connected to North Uist at low tide until the 16th century, when a huge tidal wave swept away the sand bridge, thus isolating them. Even so, the islands were inhabited until as recently as the 1930s. Now they are populated by the largest breeding colony of grey seals in Europe.

South of Clachan, where a **viewing gallery** ⓘ *Mon-Sat*, provides an insight into the fish smoking process of the acclaimed **Hebridean Smokehouse** ⓘ *T01876-580209, www.hebrideansmokehouse.com*, the road runs past **Cairinis** (**Carinish**) and the **Carinish Inn** before heading across a series of causeways to the little-visited lobster-fishing island of **Griomasaigh** (**Grimsay**), before heading across another causeway to Benbecula. Near Cairinis is **Feith na Fala** (**Field of Blood**), site of the last battle fought in Scotland solely with swords and bows and arrows, in 1601, between the MacDonalds of Sleat and Macleods of Harris. The bloodshed was provoked by one of the MacDonalds divorcing his Macleod wife. When 60 Skye Macleods set off to North Uist to wreak revenge, they were met by 16 MacDonalds who literally chopped them to pieces, proving that divorce was a messy business even back then.

Bearnaraigh (Berneray) → *For listings, see pages 371-375. Colour map 1, B1. Phone code 01876.*

Ferries from Leverburgh on Harris arrive at the low-lying island of Bearnaraigh (believed to be Old Norse for Bear Island) now connected by a causeway to North Uist. The island, rich in birdlife, is famous as the place where Prince Charles spent a holiday helping out on a croft. It's also the birthplace of Angus 'Giant' MacAskill, see page 313. Its real attraction, though, apart from the splendid isolation and its cosy **Lobster Pot Café** (see Eating, page 373) at Ardmaree is the three-mile-long sandy beach along its western shoreline. On the east coast, there's more stunning white sands, behind which stands the fabulously earthy bunkhouse of the Gatliff Trust with views over the skerries and to the brooding rounded hills of Harris. A ½-mile east of the Lobster Pot is the **Berneray Historical Society and Visitor Centre** ⓘ *Mon-Fri 1100-1500, £1, internet access*, with photographs and exhibits highlighting the hardy life islanders once lived.

A booklet for Bearnaraigh, *Visit Berneray* is available from Lochmaddy TIC. It describes all of the key places of interest, including the 16th-century gunnery at **Baile**, the beaches and machair of the north and west coasts, and archaeological sites dating from the Viking period near **Borgh**. It also highlights a lovely 7½-mile-long circular walk. **Berneray Week** (late July) is a busy week with several ceilidhs held in the community hall and attracting visitors from far afield – including Gaelic speaking Germans!

Beinn na Faoghla (Benbecula)

→ *For listings, see pages 371-375. Colour map 1, C1. Phone code 01870. Population 1803.*

Tiny Benbecula may be suffering from delusions of stature. Its Gaelic name means 'mountain of the fords', but the highest point is a mere 407 ft, with the rest of the island as flat as a pancake. It lies between Protestant North Uist and Catholic South Uist, and most visitors use it solely as a means of getting from one to the other via the A865, which cuts straight through the middle.

Ins and outs

Getting there and around Benbecula's airport is at Balivanich and there are direct flights from Glasgow, Barra and Stornoway. **Flybe/Loganair** ① *T0871-700 2000, www.flybe.com,* flies from Glasgow to Benbecula, Monday to Saturday, twice a day and the flight takes one hour. The island is connected by causeways to North and South Uist, and buses travelling from Lochmaddy and Lochboisdale pass through the villages of Balivanich, Lionacleit (Liniclate) and Creag Ghoraidh (Creagorry). There are also regular island buses which run between these settlements. ►► *For further details, see Transport, page 375.*

Sights

Like North Uist, the east of the island is so pitted with lochs that most people live on the west coast. Until recently, a large percentage of the population were Royal Artillery personnel stationed at **Baile a Mhanaich (Balivanich)**, a sprawling, army base of utilitarian buildings in the northwest of the island. There's little to hold your interest in this village dominated by the (albeit diminishing presence) of the military and civilian airport. There is a Bank of Scotland (ATM), a post office and you can browse for high quality tweeds, hand-knitted jumpers, confectionery, prints and jewellery at **MacGillivrays** ① *T01870-602525,* or visit the notable **The Stepping Stone** restaurant.

South of Balivanich, the B892 runs around the west coast offering the opportunity to stroll down miles of white sands before joining the main A865 at the southern end of the island. It runs past **Culla Bay**, overlooked by **Baille nan Cailleach (Nunton)**. It was from here in 1746 that Bonnie Prince Charlie set off with Flora MacDonald over the sea to Skye, disguised as her maid, see box, page 311. To the south is **Poll-na-Crann**, better known as 'stinky bay' because of the piles of seaweed deposited there by fierce Atlantic storms. From the mid-18th century this kelp was used to provide soda ash for making glass, and provided a source of income for many communities. By 1820 the so-called kelp boom was over, but it is still gathered today and used for fertilizer.

The B892 ends at **Lionacleit (Liniclate)**, where the community school serves the Uists and Benbecula. It has extensive facilities, including internet, a swimming pool, library, theatre and even a small local history **museum** ① *Mon, Tue and Thu 0900-1600, Wed 0900-1230, 1330-1600, Fri 0900-2000, Sat 1100-1300, 1400-1600, free.* Close by, there's a very large Co-op supermarket, the only one for miles around.

Uibhist a Deas (South Uist)

→ *For listings, see pages 371-375. Colour map 3, A1. Phone code 01870. Population 2285.*

South Uist is the largest of the southern chain of Outer Hebridean islands and like North Uist and Berneray isn't lacking in wildlife, fishing and dramatic scenery. However, like its southern neighbour, Barra, South Uist is Roman Catholic and generally more relaxed about

Sunday openings. Its 20 miles of west coast is one long sandy beach, backed by dunes with a mile or two of beautiful, flowering machair behind. To the east of the main A865 which runs the length of the island, rises a central mountainous spine of rock and peat dotted with numerous lochs. Its two highest peaks, **Beinn Mhor** (2034 ft) and **Hecla** (1988 ft), tower over the rocky cliffs of an inaccessible eastern coastline indented by sea lochs.

Ins and outs

Getting there The island's main ferry port is Lochboisdale, which is reached from Oban four times a week (arriving at night) and twice a week from Castlebay on Barra. There's one direct sailing from Oban on Tuesday, Thursday and Saturday (five hours and 20 minutes), and one via Castlebay (Barra) on Sunday (six hours and 30 minutes). There are also early morning departures (0700) from Castlebay on Wednesday and Friday, and at 2010 on Sundays. A Oban to Lochboisdale one-way ticket is £11.80 per passenger, £53 per car. A private passenger-only ferry sails from Barra to Ludag, at the southern tip of South Uist, on Sunday. There are limited bus services on Sundays. ➤➤ *For further details, see Transport page 375.*

Background

The dominant family in South Uist was Clanranald, who also owned Benbecula. They were descendants of the first Lord of the Isles, who was a MacDonald. The island's connections with Clanranald came to a sorry end, however, in 1837, when it was sold, along with Benbecula, to pay off bad debts, and became the property of the infamous Lieutenant-Colonel John Gordon of Cluny. Though all the southern isles suffered during the brutal Clearances of the 19th century, the experiences of people on South Uist were particularly cruel and inhumane. Between 1849 and 1851 over 2000 were forcibly shipped to Quebec in Canada. Those who refused to board the transport ships were hunted down by dogs and bound, before being thrown on board and shipped to Canada, where they were left to starve. Today, owned by the community, the destiny of South Uist fortunately lies in the islanders' hands.

Loch Baghasdail (Lochboisdale) → *Colour map 3, A1. Phone code 01878.*

South Uists's largest settlement is set on a rocky promontory in a beautiful island-dotted sea loch. The imposing entrance is guarded by Calvay Island with its 13th-century castle ruin. Lochboisdale is a tiny place, with little in the way of tourist sights, though it does have a hotel, bank, post office and **TIC** ① *Pier Rd, T01878-700286, early Apr to mid-Oct.*

About 10 miles south of Lochboisdale, on the southern coast of the island, is **Ludag jetty**, the departure point for the small private passenger ferry to **Eòlaigearraidh (Eoligarry)** on (45 minutes) Barra T01851-701702. At **Cille Bhrìghde (West Kilbride)** nearby is **Hebridean Croft Originals** ① *open daily*, which has a wide range of local crafts on show, as well as a photographic display of local history and a tea room.

Around the island

At the north of the island a causeway leads across **Loch Bi** (pronounced 'Bee') to the distinctive modern statue of Our Lady of the Isles, standing by the main road on the lower slopes of **Rueval Hill**. Further up the hill is the Royal Artillery control centre, known by the locals as 'Space City', due to its forest of aerials and 'golf balls', which tracks the missiles fired from a range on the northwestern corner of the island out into the Atlantic. However, to home in on delicious food and a comfortable stay, it's worthwhile following the signs

Tight little island

Between Eriskay and South Uist is the wreck of the famous SS Politician, the island's other claim to fame. In 1941 the 12,000 ton ship went aground just off the island of Calvey and sank with its cargo, which included 20,000 cases of whisky. This not only provided many islanders with a supply of whisky for many years, but also provided the plot for Compton Mackenzie's book Whisky Galore!, which was later made into the famous Ealing comedy of the same name (called Tight Little Island in the US) and filmed on Barra. It's very difficult to spot the wreck, even at low tide, but if you pop into the friendly Am Politician pub in the village on Eriksay, Baile (Balla), you'll find more information and some memorabilia.

for the **Orasay Inn** ⓘ *T01870-610298, www.orasayinn.com*, by Lochcarnan and where just 1½ miles further down the road, you can further tickle your tastebuds by popping into the shop of the acclaimed **Salar Smokehouse** ⓘ *www.salar.co.uk*.

Just to the south of here is **Loch Druidibeag Nature Reserve**, on the site of the large freshwater loch, one of the largest breeding grounds in the British Isles for greylag geese and also a favourite haunt of mute swans (there's a warden nearby at Groigearraidh Lodge). From here the main road runs down the spine of the island; all along the way little tracks branch off to the west, leading down to lovely beaches.

Not far south of Loch Druidibeag is the turning to the tiny village of **Tobha Mòr** (**Howmore**), where you can see a collection of old traditional thatched blackhouses beside the seemingly endless stretch of golden sand. One of the houses has been converted into a **Gatliff Trust Youth Hostel**, see Sleeping, page 372. From the hostel, it's a five-minute walk across the machair to the sandy beach which stretches almost the entire length of South Uist.

Periodically, down the A865 you'll spot signs for accessing paths across the machair. In addition, from Tobha Mòr, there are superb walks through the lonely hills of **Beinn Mhor** (620 m), **Beinn Corodale** (527 m) and **Hecla** (606 m) to the picturesque and dramatic valleys of Glen Hellisdale, Glen Corodale and Glen Usinish on the east coast. In 1746 that ubiquitous troglodyte, Bonnie Prince Charlie is reputed to have taken refuge in a cave above **Corodale Bay** for three weeks after his defeat and escape from Culloden.

Near **Bornais** (**Bornish**) another minor road can be followed east of the A865 to **Loch Eynort**, which penetrates far inland from the Minch. An old stalkers' path can be followed along the north shore of the loch towards the sea, with views of numerous seals, the occasional otter and the steep upper slopes of Beinn Mhor towering above to the north.

A few miles south, at **Gearraidh Bhailteas** (**Milton**), a memorial cairn sits amidst the ruins of the cottage that was Flora (Flory) MacDonald's birthplace, that famous Hebridean lass who helped save the skin of Bonnie Prince Charlie, see box, page 311. Nearby is the **Kildonan Museum** ⓘ *Apr-Oct Mon-Sat 1000-1700, Sun 1400-1700*, with exhibits of the area's history, craft work and archaeology. There's also a tea room. A few miles further on, the A865 cuts east to the island's main ferry port of **Lochboisdale**. For those in search of great food and tremendous views towards Eriskay and Barra, leave the A865 for the B888 and enjoy the hospitality of the 17th century **Polochar Inn** (see Sleeping, page 372) on the southwestern tip of South Uist.

Eirisgeidh (Eriskay) → For listings, see pages 371-375. Colour map 3, A1. Phone code 01878.

The tiny island of Eriskay, with a population of less than 200, gives its name to the native breed of pony, said to have been ridden by King Robert the Bruce at the Battle of Bannockburn in 1314. In the late 1970s the ponies nearly became extinct, but one surviving stallion saved the breed and numbers are growing. A series of paths take you around the island in about three hours. For more details, see the *Cuairt Eirisgeidh* leaflet published by Visit Hebrides and available at the Lochboisdale TIC.

Most people come to Eriskay to pay a visit to **Coilleag a' Phrionnsa (Prince's beach)**, the sandy beach on the west coast and just 220 yds from the CalMac jetty that will take you to neighbouring Barra. The beach is where Bonnie Prince Charlie first stepped on to Scottish soil on 23 July 1745, at the start of the ill-fated Jacobite Rebellion. The rare pink convolvulus (field bindweed) which grows there today is said to have been planted by the Prince himself from seeds brought from France. A small memorial cairn in the dunes behind the beach was erected by the local school to commemorate the occasion.

It's now almost impossible to see the wreck of the *SS Politician* (see box, page 367) when crossing the causeway from South Uist (look left), but at the **Am Politician** pub you can (carefully) hold an original whisky bottle taken from its hold and look at other artefacts from the wreck. Another sight worth seeing is **St Michael's**, the Roman Catholic church built in 1903 and funded by the local fishing fleet.

Bharraigh (Barra)

→ For listings, see pages 371-375. Colour map 3, A1. Phone code 01871. Population 1316.

It may be tempting to overlook the little island of Barra, only about 8 miles long by 5 miles wide, but that would be a mistake, as it's one of the most beautiful of all the islands in the Outer Hebrides – 'Barradise' indeed. Here, despite an appalling lack of public toilets (there's only three: at the Ardmhor Ferry Terminal, Eoligarry and Castlebay Hall) and much needed facilities for campers (wild camping is tolerated) you'll find the best of the islands in miniature – beaches, machair, peat-covered hills, tiny crofting communities and Neolithic remains. A couple of days spent on Barra, including excursions to the wild and beautiful lands of Vatersay and the outlying (deserted) Isle of Mingulay, gives a real taste of Hebridean life. Gaelic and the traditional fishing culture is also strong here but, with its Catholicism, Barra is arguably more laid-back than its northern neighbours which strictly observe the Sabbath.

Ins and outs

Getting there The best way to arrive is by air at Tràigh Mhòr ('Cockle Strand'), the famous airstrip on the beach at the north end of the island. This is the only airport in the UK where flight schedules are shown as 'subject to tides' and wild campers are warned to keep off the beach on hearing the drone of an aircraft! **Flybe/Loganair** ① *T0871-700 2000, www. flybe.com*, flies from Glasgow to Barra, Monday to Saturday once a day. The journey takes one hour and five minutes.

Barra is most easily reached by car ferry from Oban on the mainland, by car ferry from Lochboisdale on South Uist (Monday at 0730, Tuesday at 1900 and Thursday at 2100, one hour 40 minutes, £7 one-way per passenger, £20.30 per car) and from Eriskay, or by a private passenger-only **ferry** ① *T01878-720238*, that sails from Ludag on South Uist to Eoligarry. There is one direct sailing a day from Oban, except Tuesday and Thursday.

The journey takes four hours and 50 minutes. The sailing from Oban to Castlebay via Lochboisdale is on Tuesday and Thursday (seven hours and 20 minutes) and one-way costs £11.80 per passenger and £53 per car.

Getting around There is a regular bus/postbus service (Monday to Saturday) that runs from Castlebay to the ferry port of Eòlaigearraidh, via the airport. There are also buses (Monday-Saturday) from Castlebay to Bhatarsaigh (Vatersay). You can hire a car or a bicycle to tour the island at your leisure. It's 14 miles round the main road. ▸▸ *For further details, see Transport page 375.*

Bàgh a' Chaisteil (Castlebay)

The main settlement is Castlebay, on the southern side of the island, situated in a wide sheltered bay and overlooked by **Sheabhal** (383 m), on top of which is a marble statue of the Blessed Virgin and Child. It's a short but steep walk up to the top from the town, and the views are well worth it. The once-thriving herring port is also overlooked by the large Roman Catholic church, **Our Lady, Star of the Sea**.

As the main ferry port, rather drab Castlebay provides the full range of services: hotels, B&Bs, shops, petrol, a bank (with ATM) and post office. The **TIC** ① *T01871-810336, Apr to mid-Oct Mon-Sat 0900-1700, Sun 1200-1600 and also open for the arrival of the evening ferry*, is on the main street near the ferry terminal. It sells handy leaflets on local walks (50p) including Vatersay, tickets for the castle (below) and will book accommodation.

Castlebay's most notable feature is the impressive 15th-century **Kisimul Castle** ① *T01871-810313, Apr-Sep daily 0930-1230, 1330-1730, £4.70, concessions £3.80, children £2.80, including boat trip*, reached by boat from Castlebay pier (five minutes), weather permitting, built on an island in the middle of the harbour. This was the ancient home of the Chief of the MacNeils, one of the oldest Scottish clans, who owned the island from 1427 until 1838. It was then sold to the notorious Colonel Gordon of Cluny, along with neighbouring South Uist and Benbecula (see page 366), and the poor people of Barra suffered the same cruel fate, 600 of them being shipped to Canada to starve. One hundred years later the castle and much of the island was bought back for the MacNeils by an American architect, Robert Lister MacNeil, who became the 45th Clan Chief and restored the castle to its present state before his death in 1970. His son, Ian Roderick MacNeil, used it as his residence when visiting the island, before handing it over to Historic Scotland in 2000 on a 1000-year lease, in exchange for a rent of £1 and a bottle of whisky.

If you're interested in finding out about the island's history, you should visit the Barra Heritage Cultural Centre, known as **Dualchas** ① *T01871-810413, May-end Aug Mon-Sat 1030-1630, Mar, Apr and Sep Mon, Wed and Fri, £2, concessions £1.50, children £1.*

Around the island

The A888 follows a circular route of 14 miles around the island, making an ideal day's bike tour from Castlebay. Heading west, it passes the turning for the causeway to **Vatersay** (see below), then runs north past stunning beaches including **Halaman Bay**, near the village of Tangasdal (**Tangasdale**) and overlooked by the **Isle of Barra Hotel** (see Sleeping, page 373), before climbing between two hills (Sheabhal to the east and Beinn Tangabhal to the west). Before reaching the north coast, at the turning for **Borgh** (**Borve**) there are standing stones followed by the small settlement of **Baile Na Creige** (**Craigston**), where you'll find the **An Dubharaidh Thatched Cottage Museum** ① *Easter-Oct Mon-Fri 1100-1700, £2*, an original whitehouse and the chambered burial cairn of **Dun Bharpa**. From Dun

Net profit

Rather than watch their island be destroyed by the elements, the redoubtable inhabitants of tiny Vatersay have taken matters into their own hands. The northern and southern ends of the island are linked by a narrow, 600-yd-long isthmus and, in recent years, raging Atlantic storms have washed away parts of it. Fearing that their island might be split in two, crofters have fixed some old salmon nets from fish farms onto the beach, secured with wires and old wooden pallets, to prevent the sand being scattered by the gales. Over time, the build up of sand

trapped in the netting can link up with the machair, thus allowing grass and flowers to grow. Hopefully, over time, successive layers of sand and earth will be built up to protect the coastline. About 100 yds of beach have so far been protected using this rudimentary method, and the island's local authority is donating £3000 so that the whole 600-yd stretch linking the two ends of Vatersay can be saved. News of the crofters' ingenuity and resourcefulness has spread and the plan is being adopted on nearby Barra, where erosion is also a serious problem.

Bharpa there are pleasant walks into the surrounding hills, with the summit of **Sheabhal** offering tremendous views from the highest point on the island.

Near **Allathsdal** (**Allasdale**), is another lovely beach, and just beyond are the remains of **Dun Cuier**, an Iron Age fort. Make a short detour at Greian, and follow the headland to the rugged cliffs at **Greian Head**.

The A888 then descends eastwards to **Bagh a Tuath** (**Northbay**), where a branch left leads to the village of **Eòlaigearraidh** (**Eoligarry**), near the northern tip, surrounded by sandy bays washed by Atlantic rollers. A private passenger ferry leaves from here to Ludag on South Uist.

The road to Eoligarry passes the island's airport at **Tràigh Mhòr**, the 'Cockle Strand', which once provided 100 to 200 cartloads of delicious cockles each day. Now the cockle-shells are gathered and used for harling, the roughcast wall covering used on many Scottish houses. By the beach is the house that was once the home of Compton MacKenzie, author of *Whisky Galore!*, see box, page 367. He lies buried at picturesque **Cille Bhara**, to the west of the village of Eòlaigearraidh, along with members of the MacNeil clan. This was one of the most important religious complexes in the Outer Hebrides, built in the 12th century, and consists of a tiny church and two chapels. One of these, St Mary's, has been re-roofed and houses several carved medieval tombstones and a copy of a runic stone. Much to the chagrin of locals, the original stone is in the Museum of Scotland in Edinburgh.

Bhatarsaigh (Vatersay) and Mingulay → For listings, see pages 371-375.

A worthwhile trip from Castlebay is to the island of Vatersay, linked since 1990 to Barra by a causeway built in an effort to stabilize the tiny community (around 70) on what is the most southerly inhabited Outer Hebridean island. Home to the acclaimed folk singing group The Vatersay Boys, it boasts several idyllic sands including two shell-sand beaches backed by machair, only a few hundred yards apart on either side of the narrow isthmus that leads to the main settlement of Vatersay. On the west beach, Bagh Siar, is the **Annie Jane Monument**, commemorating the terrible tragedy in 1853, when the emigrant ship *Annie Jane* was wrecked off the coast of Vatersay, with the loss of 333 lives, many of them islanders. There's a scenic 4-mile circular walk from the monument and the Barra TIC sells a map of the route. You can buy coffee and sandwiches at the **Vatersay village hall** ① *Apr-Oct 1000-1700,* (also, note, the only public toilets on the island), and wild camp or park your campervan nearby (£4 donation to the Vatersay Township).

On a clear day from Vatersay you can enjoy the view of the smaller islands to the south – Sandray, Pabbay and Mingulay. The latter was inhabited until 1912 and can still be visited from Barra. It was acquired by the National Trust for Scotland in 2000. ▸▸ *For details of tours, see Barra Fishing Charters, page 374.*

◉ The Uists, Benbecula and Barra listings

For Sleeping and Eating price codes and other relevant information, see Essentials pages 38-45.

● Sleeping

North Uist *p362*

B Langass Lodge, near Pobhull Fhinn, T01876-580285, www.langasslodge.co.uk. 12 en suite rooms. Stylish and comfortable accommodation in this secluded hotel over-looking a sea loch. Friendly, and welcomes children. The restaurant has a menu rich in local seafood and game (dinner ♥♥♥). Recommended.

L Tigh Dearg Hotel, Lochmaddy, T01876-500700, www.tigh-dearg-hotel.co.uk. Open all year. 8 en suite rooms. Stylish and contemporary, from the bright red exterior (the name means 'Red House') to the designer rooms, it offers DVD/CD players, a highly rated restaurant and a leisure club with fully equipped gym, sauna and steam room. By the way, it's pronounced 'tie-jerack'.

C Bagh Alluin, 21 Baleshare, T01876-580370, www.jacvolbeda.co.uk. Has 3 very spacious, modern bedrooms.

B-C Lochmaddy Hotel, right by the ferry terminal, Lochmaddy, T01876-500332, www.lochmaddy hotel.co.uk. Open all year. 15 en suite rooms (8 with sea view). Recently refurnished and fully Wi-Fi accessible. rooms. The restaurant and bar serve good-value food (♥♥-♥) in a pleasant setting. Also offers takeaway (♥) burgers, fish, etc, daily 1730-2030. This is the place to ask about fishing, as they rent out boats and sell permits for trout and salmon fishing. Proud of its walker- and cycle-friendly status, and this is reflected

in its drying rooms and lockable bike storage facilities for guests.

B Temple View Hotel, on the main road, Carinish, T01876-580676, www.templeview hotel.co.uk. This is a lovely, modest family-run guesthouse with views towards the 13th century ruin of Trinity Temple.

D Ardnastruban House, just off the A865, Grimsay, T01870-602452, www.ardnastruban house.co.uk. Open Jan-Dec. This friendly guesthouse is surrounded by wildlife and rugged scenery.

D Sgeir Ruadh , near Balranald, Houghgarry, T01876-510312, sgeirruadh@aol.com. Run by Mrs Simpson this good value B&B is open all year. It has 3 en suite rooms, overlooks a beautiful beach and is perfect for bird-watchers as it's within the Clanranald Reserve.

D Mrs Morag Nicholson, The Old Shop House, Bayhead, T01876-510395. Has 2 en suite rooms and offers friendly and comfortable B&B. **F**

Self-catering

Tigh na Boireach, Clachan Sands, T01876-560403. Sleep in a 4-poster bed in 1 of 2 modernized yet traditional thatched croft cottages surrounded by wildlife and rugged scenery. From £350 per week. Sleeps 2.

Uist Outdoor Centre, half a mile from the ferry pier, Lochmaddy, T01876-500234, 500480, www.uistoutdoorcentre.co.uk. Open all year. Independent hostel with room for up to 20 in 4-person bunk rooms (£15 per person per night). Offers a full range of facilities, outdoor activities and courses (see Activities and tours, page 374). Full board is also available. Prices on application.

Berneray p364

E Burnside Croft, near 3 mile west beach, T01876-540235, www.burnsidecroft.com. Here you can share Prince Charles' (not the Bonnie one) crofting experience with Don Alick (Splash) MacKillop and his Australian wife Gloria, who cooks up a storm in the kitchen. Guests can place a stone on the 'mosaic of friendship', a drystone dyke that attests to the welcoming atmosphere here. The hosts also offer fishing and boat trips to uninhabited islands and Don Alick is a storyteller in the great Hebridean tradition for evenings round the fire. Excellent walking, birdlife and beaches in the area. From £680 per week. Sleeps 2.

F Gatliff Trust Hostel, 1 mile up the east coast from the old ferry pier, www.gatliff. co.uk/berneray.php, T0870-1553255. Open all year, no advance bookings. Affiliated to the SYHA. Relax in 2 restored and truly rustic blackhouses overlooking a lovely sandy beach and old Viking pier. 12 beds, shower, no phone. It's far from luxurious but it's true old-world, earthy hostelling and the views are priceless. £10 for a hostel bed, £5 to camp. Recommended.

Benbecula p365

B Isle of Benbecula House Hotel, Creag Ghoraidh, T01870-602024, www.isleshotel group.co.uk. Open all year. 20 en suite rooms. Meals served in conservatory dining room (à la carte dinner £30 per person ⍦⍦-⍦⍦), with sea views.

C Creag Liath, 1½ miles off the road, Griminish, T01870-602992. Comfortable 2-bedroom option on a working croft.

Camping

Shellbay Caravan and Camping Park, Lionacleit, T01870-602447. Open Apr-Oct. £6 per pitch.

South Uist p365

B-C Borrodale Hotel, at the junction where the road splits south to Eriskay and east to Lochboisdale, Dalabrog, T01878-700444, www.isleshotelgroup.co.uk. 12 room hotel. Hearty lunch (⍦) from 1200 and dinner (⍦⍦) from 1800-2100.

B Lochboisdale Hotel, close to the ferry terminal, Lochboisdale, T01878-700332, www.lochboisdalehotel.com. Open all year. 16 en suite rooms. Family-owned hotel with music sessions every fortnight and frequent, spontaneous outbreaks of fiddling by the open fire.

C Orasay Inn, Lochcarnan, T01878-610298, www.orasayinn.com. Open all year. 9 en suite rooms. Small, friendly, family-run hotel. Reasonable rooms but the restaurant (1200-2100) is the star attraction, serving up delicious lunches (⍦) and dinners (⍦⍦): seafood such as scallops with bacon or freshly caught crab. Recommended.

B Polochar Inn, a few miles to the west of Ludag, Pollachar, T01878-700215, www.polocharinn.com. Open all year. 11 comfortable en suite rooms. Terrific food (see Eating, below), stunning views towards Barra. A small, refurbished hotel steeped in history, with its 1750 built walls and Neolithic standing stone by the shore. Recommended.

D Anglers Retreat, Ardmore, T01870-610325, www.anglersretreat.net. Mar-Dec. 4 en suite rooms. Comfortable, modern guesthouse that's perfect for the keen angler and birdwatcher.

D-E Caloraidh, Milton, T01878-710365. Open all year. 2 bedrooms including one suitable for disabled visitors. Friendly, comfortable and handy for the Askernish golf course, Kildonan Museum and Flora MacDonald's birthplace.

F Gatliff Trust Youth Hostel, Howmore, www.gatliff.co.uk/howmore.php, T0870-155 3255. Open all year. Converted black-house which overlooks the ruins of an ancient church and graveyard, beside the seemingly endless stretch of golden sand. 13 beds, no phone. The warden of the hostel also runs **Rothan Cycles**, see Transport, page 375.

Eriskay p368
Self-catering
Aird na Haun There is a 2-bedroom self-catering flat (T0141-3392143, www.visit eriskay.com), by the beach that can be rented from £300 per week.

Camping
You can wild camp but there are few amenities other than a shop, post office and the pub.

Barra p368
It's a good idea to book in advance if arriving on the evening ferry from Oban. There are neither independent hostels nor a Gatliff Trust Hostel on Barra. Complex crofting laws mean that provision for campers and motorhomes remains woefully inadequate, although one is planned for Borve in Spring 2011.

A-C Isle of Barra Hotel, 2 miles west of Castlebay, T01871-810383, www.isleofbarra hotel.co.uk 38 en suite rooms, and a good restaurant (ŦŦŦ-ŦŦ) and selection of bar food (Ŧ). Fabulous views of the white sands below, though the 1970s exterior isn't exactly in keeping with the landscape. It's only open Apr-Sep.

B-C Castlebay Hotel, overlooking the ferry terminal and Kisimul Castle, Castlebay, T01871-810223, www.castlebayhotel.com. Open all year. 10 en suite rooms. **B** including dinner (1800-2100). Arguably, the best place to stay on the island, combining comfort with tasty, good value food (ŦŦŦ-ŦŦ) and a lively, adjoining public bar.

B-C Craigard Hotel, Castlebay, T01871-810200, www.craigardhotel.co.uk. Open all year. 7 en suite rooms. Great views from the conservatory over the bay, reasonable food and walls adorned with photos from the filming of *Whisky Galore!*.

C Heathbank Hotel, T01871-890266, www.barrahotel.co.uk. 5 spotless en suite rooms of varying sizes with a pub downstairs.

D-E (£60) **Tigh-Na-Mara**, Castlebay, T01871-810304, www.tighnamara-barra.co.uk. Open all year. 5 rooms. Comfortable guesthouse only a few mins' walk from the ferry terminal.

E-F Dunard Hostel, just along from the Co-op and **Heritage Museum**, Castlebay, T01871-810443, www.dunardhostel.co.uk. This bright, well-equipped hostel offers family rooms (£52) and bunks (£15), and if you wild camp outside will charge only £3 for its toilet and shower facilities. This is also the place to come to arrange sea kayaking with **Clearwater Paddling**.

Self-catering
There are many options on Barra, as well as the Visit Hebrides website (see page 340), check out www.isleofbarra.com.

Camping
For some reason, the local powers that be seem to have ignored the needs of campers on Barra so you'll need to wild camp. The machair by the airport (not the runway) at Traigh Mhor and Borve Point (west Barra) are popular. To ensure you don't risk the wrath of the crofters ensure all waste and litter is removed when you leave the site. For provisions, there are 2 well-stocked mini-supermarkets in Castlebay.

Vatersay p370
Self-catering
Those who find Barra too busy can escape to the silence and golden sands of neighbouring Vatersay.
Vatersay School, Mrs Patricia Barron, T/F01871-810283, www.vatersayschool.co.uk. A converted schoolhouse overlooking a glorious south-facing beach. It sleeps 6 and costs £575-850 per week.

❶ Eating

A number of additional eating options can be found under Sleeping, above.

Berneray p364
ŦŦ-Ŧ Lobster Pot, Berneray, T01876-540288. Wed-Mon 0900-1700, Tue 0900-2000. Aside from a packed grocery shop (they'll deliver to the **Gatliff Trust Hostel**), there is a friendly

café (the only on the island) where you can tuck into toasties, crayfish salads, Salar salmon and home-baking.

Benbecula p365
ψψψ-ψψ The Stepping Stone Restaurant, Balivanich, T01870-603377. The best place to eat on Benbecula, with family links to the acclaimed MacLeans Bakery (of Hebridean Oatcake fame), half a mile up the road. Lunch-time specials may include cockles in oatmeal whilst in the Sinteas restaurant dinner (from 1800-2130) includes the likes of local lamb and dessert of traditional Crowdie and cream. 3 course set Sun lunch (£15).

South Uist p365
ψψψ-ψψ Orasay Inn, in the northeast, Lochcarnan. Isobel, the owner/chef, is a 'Natural Cooking of Scotland' trainer. Expect fresh and locally sourced game, lamb, beef, shellfish and vegetables, as well as freshly baked breads, scones and home-made desserts. The dining is relaxed, the service attentive and expect a warm welcome. Recommended.
ψψψ-ψψ Polochar Inn, see Sleeping, above. Good range of lunch and dinner options, with an emphasis on locally sourced produce. Try the hearty cullen skink (seafood) soup, the flakey smoked salmon with mussels or the leg of Uist lamb. Rustic interior with attentive service. Terrific food.

Eriskay p368
ψψ-ψ Am Politician, Baile, see page 368. This pub serves food (1200-2100), and occasionally hosts live bands. Its small conservatory offers lovely views over the sea.

Barra p368
ψψψ-ψψ Castlebay Hotel, Castlebay, T01871-810223, www.castlebayhotel.com. Overlooking Kisimul Castle and offering excellent fish and seafood.
ψψψ-ψψ Isle of Barra Hotel, Tangasdale Beach, T01871-810383, www.isleofbarrahotel.co.uk. Family-run hotel with an evening seafood restaurant and à la carte dining.

ψψ Café Kisimul, on the main street, Castlebay, T01871-810645, www.cafekisimul. co.uk. The place to feast on tasty Italian and Indian fare with a seafood twist.
ψψ-ψ The Deck and Hebridean Toffee Shop, on the main street, Castlebay T01871-810898. Open Mar, Apr and May Mon-Sat 1000-1700, Jun-Aug Mon-Sat 1000-1800, Sun 1200-1700. Produces 1st-class toffee and will serve you tea, sandwiches and great home-baking on its deck overlooking the castle.
ψ The Otter Café, clearly signposted, by the Ardmhar ferry terminal, T01871-890269. Open daily. A great tea room and you can catch the ferry to Eriskay nearby.

⊙ Activities and tours

North Uist p362
Uist Outdoor Centre, Cearn Dusgaidh, Lochmaddy, T01876-500480, www.uistoutdoor centre.co.uk. Runs week-long kayaking courses as well as weekend beginners' trips; scuba-diving; rock climbing and abseiling from sea cliffs; survival courses; and power-boat courses. For those wishing for even more solitude there are overnight expeditions to Pabbay and Boreray, where you can see dolphins, porpoises, minke whales, grey seals and basking sharks. You can also charter an RIB for a trip to St Kilda (38 nautical miles west), the Shiants, Monach and Flannan Islands. The centre provides accommodation (see Sleeping, page 371).

South Uist p365
Golf
Askernish Golf Club, Lochboisdale, South Uist, T01878-700083, www.askernishgolfclub. com. Recently 'rediscovered' amidst the machair, this may soon be promoted far and wide as one of the world's classic links courses, having been laid out in 1891 by the legendary Scottish golfer, 'Old Tom Morris.'

Barra p368
Boat trips
Barra Fishing Charters, Northbay, T01871-890384, www.barrafishingcharters.com. Run

by local fisherman Donald MacLeod, who offers a range of trips aboard his 10-m-long cruiser, *Boy James*. Fishing enthusiasts (free tackle and rods) pay £40 for a 4-hr offshore trip. Those who wish to take to the high seas without fishing kit can instead explore the remote but spectacular Hebridean isle of Mingulay from £50 per person (£25 per child). This 6-hr trip includes a 2-hr sail from Barra past the neighbouring islands of Sandray and Pabbay, a circumnavigation of Mingulay to view the spectacularly high western sea cliffs, and a landing on the east coast for a 3-hr exploration of the beautiful beach of Mingulay Bay, the deserted village and surrounding hills and coast. There are also fine views to the lighthouse on Barra Head, the most southerly outpost of the Outer Hebrides island chain where, weather permitting, the *Boy James* will also sail. It's also possible to charter the boat for private hire or wildlife excursions – call for prices.

Kayaking
Clearwater Paddling, just along from the Co-op and **Heritage Museum**, Dunard, Castlebay, T01871-810443, www.clearwater paddling.com. Experienced operator that offers a range of half-day (£30), full-day (£60) and week-long sea-kayaking trips from Barra. Also run the **Dunard Hostel** in Castlebay.

Taxi tours
Campbell Taxis, T01871-810216; and Lochmaddy, T01876-500215, for island tours.

⊖ Transport

For information on local bus journeys, see Getting around, page 362.

Berneray *p364*
Ferry From **Berneray** to **Harris**, 3-4 times daily, 1 hr. A one-way ticket costs £6.50 per passenger, £29.50 per car.

Benbecula *p365*
Air Flybe/Loganair flies to **Glasgow** from Benbecula, Mon-Sat, twice daily, 1 hr. There are also flights from **Benbecula** to **Barra**, Mon-Fri 1 daily, 20 mins.
Car hire Ask Car Hire, Linicleit, T01870-602818 www.askcarhire.com; **Maclennan Bros Ltd**, Balivanich, T01870-602191.

South Uist *p365*
Car hire Laing Motors, Lochboisdale, T01870-700267, www.laingmotors.co.uk.
Cycle hire Rothan Cycles, by the Gatliff Trust Hostel, 9 Howmore, T01870-620283, www.rothan.com. Hires basic bikes for £10 and tourers for £12. It's £18 and £20 respectively for 2 days. Will also repair your bike and deliver to/pick-up at Eriksay (£20), Lochboisdale (£15) and Berneray (£28).
Ferry No boats leave South Uist on Sun. **Lochboisdale** to **Oban**, 1 daily, Tue, Thu and Sat, 5 hrs 20 mins and via **Castlebay** (Barra) on Sun, 6 hrs 30 mins.

Barra *p368*
Air Flybe/Loganair flies to **Glasgow** from Barra, 1 daily, Mon-Sat, 1 hr 5 mins.
Car hire Barra Car Hire, Hugh MacNeil, Northbay, T01871-890313. **Barra Cycle Hire**, 29 St Brendans Rd, Castle- bay, T01871-810284. Hires bikes (starting from £10), booking recommended.
Ferry **Castlebay** to **Oban**, Mon, Wed, Fri, Sat, Sun, 4 hrs 50 mins. Also sailings via **Lochboisdale** on Tue and Thu, 7 hrs 20 mins. There is also a sailing via **Coll** and **Tiree**, Thu, 6 hrs 45 mins. To **Tiree**, £7.35 per passenger, £36.50 per car. Ferry from **Castlebay** to **Lochboisdale**, Tue and Thu, £6.70 per passenger, £19.55 per car.

There are also early morning departures to **Lochboisdale**, Wed and Fri, 0700, Sun 2050. Ferries sail from Barra to **Eriskay** at least 3 times daily. A one-way ticket costs £7 per passenger and £20.30 per car, a 5-day return is £11.85 per passenger and £35.50 per car. Bikes are free.

St Kilda

Forty one miles west of the Outer Hebrides lie the spectacular and isolated islands of St Kilda, Scotland's first UNESCO World Heritage Site and home to the largest colony of seabirds in northern Europe. St Kilda consists of several islands, remnants of an ancient volcano, and manages to capture the imagination of most visitors to the Outer Hebrides, whether they actually get there or just dream about romantic voyages to mysterious lands across perilous seas. Inhabited for almost 4000 years until evacuated by its remaining 36 islanders on 29 August 1930, the isles which are also a National Nature Reserve were bequeathed to the National Trust for Scotland in 1957. Each year, during the brief summer months teams of volunteers work on Hirta, maintaining what remains of the abandoned houses, studying the wildlife and glorying in the peace and isolation of a dramatic island group inhabited by a million seabirds and where the Soay sheep has bred for thousands of years.

Ins and outs

A 14-hour boat journey from Oban and eight hours from the Outer Hebrides, St Kilda is a long way out in the North Atlantic. The cost and the sea conditions are the two factors that will make or break your plans to reach St Kilda, but from expert sea kayakers on an expedition, to yachts and cruise boats, it is possible … at a price. **Island Cruising** ① *1 Erista, Uig, Lewis, T01851-672381, www.island-cruising.com*, arranges boat trips to St Kilda from April to October starting from £580 (four-day all-inclusive). The tour comprises the journey to and from St Kilda and a landing on Hirta with a visit to the museum, the old village and a wider exploration of the island, including a climb up to the highest sea cliffs in the British Isles at Conachair (430 m). They also run a six-day cruise (£795) allowing an extra day or two on St Kilda and will often try to visit the isolated, wildlife rich isles of the Monach's and North Rona en route. **Seatrek** ① *16 Uigean, Uig, Lewis, T01851-672469, www.seatrek. co.uk*, run day trips to St Kilda, departing at 0730 with three to four hours spent ashore (weather and tides permitting) before returning for 1900. The cost is £180 per person. **Uist Outdoor Centre** ① *North Uist, T01876-500480, www.uistoutdoorcentre.co.uk*, say their 1½-hour power- boat trip to St Kilda is the fastest way to get there. For trips to St Kilda, see www.outdoor hebrides.com, and the 'Visiting St Kilda' portal at www.nts.org.uk.

National Trust for Scotland ① *www.nts.org.uk, T0844-493 2237*, also organizes fortnight long voluntary work parties in the summer months every year to undertake restoration, maintenance and archaeology projects around the old village on Hirta. The groups are very popular and each volunteer must complete an application form, so apply early. The fortnight costs over £750 per person and this covers transport from Oban to St Kilda and all food and basic lodging costs while on the island. Note that the sea journey can be arduous.

Sights

In 1957 the islands become the property of the National Trust for Scotland, and in 1986 a UNESCO World Heritage Site. St Kilda is the most important seabird breeding station in northwest Europe. The islands are home to a quarter of the world's population of northern gannets, the largest colony of fulmars in Britain and one of the largest colonies of puffins in Scotland. These huge numbers of seabirds were vital to the islanders' survival. Their eggs provided food in the summer, and gannets and fulmers were caught each season to be plucked, dried and stored for the winter. Their feathers and oil were kept for export, whilst their bones were shaped into useful tools and their skins into shoes.

How St Kilda was killed off

Friday 29 August 1930 was the end of life as it had been for centuries on St Kilda. For at least 1000 years the inhabitants of this remote group of islands had been tenants of the Macleods of Dunvegan on Skye. In earlier days the trip from Skye, undertaken in longboats, would require 16 hours of rigorous rowing and sailing. Even now, the trip to St Kilda is no easy matter.

Until 1930 the islanders had been supported from the mainland by the provision of a nurse and a post office. But the Scottish Office decided that their subsidy of the islands was no longer economic. This meant that life for the residents without those facilities would be untenable.

In 1930, to the younger of the 36 residents, including a man with nine children, evacuation was an attractive prospect. There would be better schooling for the children, and better health care. Although many had never seen a tree, a new life in forestry appealed. The more elderly residents, most of whom had never left the island and who could not speak English, must have viewed the drastic change with alarm but the younger majority view prevailed and evacuation was planned.

There were 500 Soay sheep to be moved first. Their coats of fine wool were not sheared but plucked by the inhabitants using only a penknife. The resultant locally woven tweed, either shipped ashore or sold to rare visitors, had provided the inhabitants' only contact with actual money. No taxes on income or on anything else were paid. Their internal economy took the form of barter. The plentiful supply of gannets, when dried, provided winter food. No inhabitant had ever fought in any war. Their distance and isolation earned them no consideration by the rest of Scotland.

Despite protestations by the Canine Defence League, all dogs were destroyed. Just two were put down by injections of hydrocyanic acid. The rest, at the islanders' insistence, had stones tied around their necks and were hurled from the jetty. Small boats were used to ferry only a dozen or so sheep out to the SS Dunara Castle. Ten cows with four calves were also evacuated. Then HMS Harebell, of the Fishery Protection Service, came on the final day to take the islanders to the mainland. The Under Secretary of State for Scotland imposed a ban on photography, thus ensuring the people of St Kilda privacy during the evacuation. It was not possible to house all of the inhabitants in Argyll, as had been hoped, so the community was split, their communal lives coming to an end.

The history of the island has been documented in a number of scholarly works, including The Life and Death of St Kilda by Tom Steel, and Island on the Edge of the World by Charles Maclean.

The largest of the islands, **Hirta**, was the remotest community in Britain, if not Europe, until 1930, when the remaining 36 Gaelic-speaking inhabitants were evacuated at their own request, in one of the most poignant episodes of Scottish history (see box, page 377). Today, Hirta is partly occupied by the army as a radar-tracking station for the rocket range on South Uist and managed by Scottish Natural Heritage. Across a narrow channel lies **Dun**. Nearby **Boreray** is home to the world's largest colony of gannets, and **Soay** on which the rare Soay sheep breed, completes the group. There are several dramatic 'stacs' rising sheer from the Atlantic Ocean. At 430 m, the sea cliffs at Conachair are the highest in the British Isles.

Contents

Footprint features

At a glance

⊖ **Getting around** Excellent inter-
island ferry services, good bus links,
some flights and it's easy to travel
around by car. A great place to cycle,
but be prepared for strong winds.
✿ **Time required** Allow at least
1 week on Orkney or Shetland, or
a fortnight if planning to capture
the key sights around both.
☽ **Weather** From the end of
Oct to Mar, the weather conditions
are unsettled.
✖ **When not to go** In Jan there are
only a few hours of daylight.

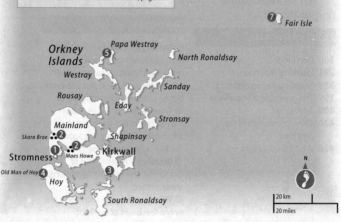

20 km
20 miles

N

To some, these two archipelagos will never be anything other than distant and overlooked specks of land peppering the wild North Atlantic, above an already distant north coast of mainland Scotland. They certainly are remote and they have maintained a social and political, as well as geographical, distance from the rest of Scotland, which goes a long way to explaining the relatively few visitors each year. Both were under Norse rule until the mid-15th century and, somehow, seeing them as a part of Scotland can be very misleading. Each must be seen within the context of its own unique cultural background and unusual geography.

Shetland's northern islands, on the same latitude as Alaska, are as strange and different as Britain gets, while beguiling Orkney just smiles serenely as the rest of world races headlong into the future at alarming speed. It is these qualities that make the islands worth visiting and the ones that the tourist boards are keen to plug. Both Orkney and Shetland are littered with outstanding archaeological evidence, not just of six centuries of Norse occupation, such as at Jarlshof at the very southern tip of Shetland, but also of life back in 3000 BC at Skara Brae and the Knap of Howar in the Orkneys. They are also among the best places in Britain to see wildlife as yet untamed by the 21st century. Here you can sail alongside porpoises and seals and potentially spot killer whales (orca) and watch a million migratory seabirds nest and raise their young during the summer months. And, thanks to fast and frequent transport links, it doesn't take an Arctic expedition to get here.

Orkney

Orkney may be separated from the north coast of Scotland by a mere 6 miles of the notoriously changeable waters of the Pentland Firth, but to the fiercely independent Orcadians, 'Mainland' means the largest of the Orkney islands and not the Scottish mainland. Mainland is also the site of the two main towns and ferry terminals: the capital Kirkwall and the beautiful old fishing port of Stromness. Orkney has the densest concentration of prehistoric monuments in Britain and Mainland is where you'll find many of these archaeological relics: the Stones of Stenness, Maes Howe, the Broch of Gurness and the remarkable Neolithic village of Skara Brae, all of which give Orkney a rare continuity of past and present. Aside from Mainland, there are a dozen smaller islands to explore, including Hoy, with its wild, spectacular coastal scenery. The even more remote northerly islands offer miles of deserted beaches and nothing but the calls of birds to shatter the peace and quiet. Quiet also describes the taciturn locals. They aren't unfriendly – quite the opposite, in fact – but it's said that Orcadians will rarely use one word where none will do. ▸▸ *For listings, see pages 403-411.*

Ins and outs

Getting there
There are direct flights to Kirkwall airport Monday to Saturday from Aberdeen, Edinburgh, Glasgow, Inverness and Shetland, with connections to London Heathrow, Birmingham, Manchester and Belfast. These are operated by Flybe/Loganair and can be booked through **Flybe** ① *T0871-700 2000, www.flybe.com*, or **Loganair** ① *T01856-886210, www.loganair.co.uk.*

There are several ferry routes to Orkney: Aberdeen to Kirkwall (six to seven hours); Scrabster, near Thurso, to Stromness (90 minutes, the boat sails close to the Old Man of Hoy); John o'Groats to Burwick, on South Ronaldsay (from May to September, 40 minutes) and Gill's Bay, near John o'Groats, to St Margaret's Hope. There's also an 'Orkney Bus', which leaves daily from Inverness, direct to Kirkwall. ▸▸ *For further details, see Transport, page 410.*

Getting around
There are flights from Kirkwall to many of the islands which are operated by Loganair (see above). They are very reasonable, costing £17 one way to North Ronaldsay and Papa Westray, and £35 one way to Eday, Sanday, Stronsay and Westray. There are also inter-island flights costing £20 return, and excursion flights (requiring a minimum of one night's stay at the destination), which cost £12 return. There are also sightseeing flights in July and August costing £39, which can only be booked 30 minutes prior to departure.

Orkney Ferries ① *T01856-872044, www.orkneyferries.co.uk*, operates daily car and passenger ferries to Rousay, Egilsay and Wyre from Tingwall with return fares costing £7.20, concessions and children £3.60 and per car £23. Ferries to Shapinsay from Kirkwall also cost £7.20 return (concessions £3.60, car £33.50). Ferries to Eday, Stronsay, Sanday, Westray and Papa Westray from Kirkwall cost £14.10, concessions and children £7.10 and per car £33.50. To Graemsay and Hoy from Stromness and to Hoy and Flotta from Houton it costs £7.20, concessions £3.60 and per car £23; An inter-island fare for the North Islands is £7.20, concessions and children £3.60 and £23 per car. If travelling by car, book ferry journeys in advance. All these prices are return with single fares 50% of the return price. A seven-day Island Explorer Ticket can be purchased for the North and South Isles, costing £42, concessions and children £21. Bikes can be carried for as little as £1.

Learning the lingo

Despite the disappearance of the Norse language, many of the Viking place names have survived. Here are some of the most common Old Norse elements which will help explain the meaning of many place names:

a(y)	island	holm	small island
a, o	stream	howe	mound
aith	isthmus	kirk	church
ayre	beach	lax	salmon
bard	headland	ler	mud, clay
bister	farm	lyng	heather
brae, brei	broad	minn	mouth
fell, field	hill	mool, noup	headland
fors	waterfall	setter	farm
garth	farm	thing	parliament
geo	creek	toft	house site
grind	gate	voe	sea inlet
ham(n)	anchorage	wick, vik	bay

Only the main population centres on Mainland are served by public transport, and having a car is highly recommended to visit many of the most interesting sights. Bringing a car to Orkney is expensive, but there are several car hire firms on the Mainland and on the other islands. An alternative could be taking to a bike. Orkney is relatively flat and most of its roads are quiet, which makes it ideal for touring on two wheels, though the wind can make it difficult if it's blowing in the wrong direction. Bicycles can be hired in Kirkwall, Stromness and on many of the other islands. Those with limited time may prefer to book a tour of the islands. ▶▶ *For further details, see Activities and tours, page 408, and Transport, page 410.*

Tourist information

Orkney Tourist Board ① *www.visitorkney.com*, has tourist offices in Kirkwall and Stromness. They will book accommodation for you, or provide a list of what's available, though many B&Bs are not included in the tourist board scheme. They can also provide information on various sights, walks and the islands' wildlife. Those wishing to leave Mainland and visit the smaller islands should pick up a free copy of the tourist board's excellent information and travel guide, *The Islands of Orkney*. Packed with information, their Orkney, irresistible islands brochure is also worth a browse.

Many of Orkney's monuments are managed by **Historic Scotland** ① *www.historic scotland.gov.uk*. They include the Bishop and Earl's Palaces, Broch of Gurness, Maes Howe, Skara Brae and Skaill House, Brough of Birsay and Hackness Martello Tower. If you plan to visit all or most of these sights, it may be cheaper to buy a **Historic Scotland Explorer Pas**s. There are various types: three days out of five costs £25 (concessions £20, family £50) and seven days out of 14 costs £34 (concessions £27, family £68).

Seal Skerry
Dennis Head
North Ronaldsay
North Ronaldsay Firth
Start Point
Lop Ness
Tofts Ness
Bay of Lopness
▶ To Lerwick
Sanday
Tres Ness
Otters Wick
B9069
Scar
Kettletoft
The Swarf
Sanday Sound
Vat of Kirbuster
Stronsay
Burgh Head
Ness of Brough
Quoyness
Hacks Ness
Whitehall
Papa Stronsay
Lamb Head
Auskerry Sound
B9070
Huip Ness
B9069
Auskerry
Tor Ness
Ingale Skerry
The North Sound
Calf of Eday
Loth
Holm of Huip
St Catherine's Bay
Linga Holm
Bay of Holland
Bee Taing
Firth
Mull Head
Papa Westray
Holm of Papa
Head of Moclett
Red Head
Mill Bay
Vinquoy
Tops
Eday
Holm of Ork
Stronsay
Rothieshom Head
Rothies-holm
Stanger Head
Sound of Faray
Backaland
B9063
Ness of Ork
Nettle Gee
Bay of Linton
Shapinsay
Papa Sound
Rapness
Faray
Ramsness Sound
Mae Ness
Egilsay
Muckle Green Holm
Ness
Veantrow Bay
B9058
Gairsay Sound
B9059
Shapinsay Sound
Bow Head
Knap of Howar
Head of Papa
Berst Ness
Point of Neven
Taracleff Head
Sweyn Holm
Gairsay
The String
Bay of Noup
Pierowall
Noltland
Fitty Hill
B9067
Westray
Inga Ness
Skea Skerries
Soviskaill Head
Soviskaill Bay
Rousay
Midhowe Broch & Cairn
Trumland Reserve
Eynhallow Sound
Broch of Gurness
Wyre
Wass Wick
Balfour
Wide Firth
Noup Head
Westray Firth
Sacquoy Head
Eynhallow
Evie
EVIE
Tingwall
RENDALL
Bay of Firth
Scabra Head
Costa Head
Whitaloo Point
Birsay
Brough of Birsay
Birsay Bay
Boardhouse Loch
Twatt
B9056
BIRSAY
Loch of Isbister
B9057
Dounby
HARRAY
A966
FIRTH
Finstown
A965
Loch of Harray
Maes Howe & Stones of Stenness
Markwick Head
Marwick
Oushore Point
A967
B9055
SANDWICK
Bay of Skaill
Skara Brae
Ring of Brodgar

Orkney's rugged, Nordic-feeling capital is built around a wide sheltered bay and is the main departure point for ferries to the northern islands. First impressions are a little misleading, as the harbour area has been blighted by modern development. More appealing, however, are the narrow winding streets and lanes of the old town, which has not changed much over the centuries. There are many houses dating from the 16th, 17th and 18th centuries, as well as Kirkwall's greatest attraction, its magnificent cathedral, the finest medieval building in northern Scotland.

Ins and outs

Getting there and around The **airport** ⓘ *T01856-886210 (information desk) or T0871-700 2000 (Flybe desk)*, is three miles southeast of Kirkwall on the A960. There are no buses to and from town. A taxi will cost around £6. **Northlink Ferries** ⓘ *T08456-000449, www.north linkferries.co.uk*, sail from Aberdeen to Kirkwall (six hours) on Tuesday, Thursday, Saturday and Sunday at 1700. Northlink Ferries also sail from Lerwick (Shetland) to Kirkwall on Monday, Wednesday and Friday at 1730, the journey takes seven hours and 45 minutes. Cars should be booked in advance and all passengers must check in at least 30 minutes before departure. **John o'Groats Ferries** ⓘ *T01955-611353, www.jogferry.co.uk*, run a ferry from John o'Groats to Burwick, with a bus connection to Kirkwall (45 minutes). The ferries leave twice a day and four times a day between June and August. The journey takes 40 minutes. John o'Groats Ferries also operate the Orkney Bus, a daily direct bus/ferry/bus service between Inverness and Kirkwall, via John o'Groats. It leaves Inverness at 0730 and 1420 from June to September (at 1420 only in May). and costs £49 return, advance booking is essential. The bus station is five minutes' walk west of the town centre.

The town is compact and it's easy to get around on foot. The main street changes its name from Bridge Street to Albert Street, then to Broad Street and Victoria Street as it twists its way south from the busy harbour. The cathedral is on Broad Street, and most of the shops and banks are on Broad Street and Albert Street. ▸▸ *For further details, see Transport, page 410.*

Tourist information On Broad Street, near the cathedral, is the very helpful **TIC** ⓘ *T01856-872856, www.visitorkney.com, Jun-Aug daily 0830-2000, Sep-Mar Mon-Fri 0900-1700 Sat 1000-1600, closed Sun*. Services they provide include booking accommodation and changing money; they also have various useful free leaflets including *The Islands of Orkney*, the *Kirkwall Heritage Guide*, and *The Peedie Guide* – a pocket-sized guide to eating, drinking, shopping and entertainment. They also stock a wide range of guidebooks and maps, and have details of forthcoming events. Another good source is the weekly newspaper *The Orcadian*.

Sights

The town's outstanding sight is the huge and impressive red sandstone **St Magnus Cathedral** ⓘ *T01856-874894, Apr-Sep Mon-Sat 0900-1800, Sun 1300-1800, Oct-Mar Mon-Sat 0900-1300, 1400-1700, free*, built by masons who had worked on Durham Cathedral in the north of England. It was founded in 1137 by Rognvald Kolson, Earl of Orkney, in memory of his uncle, Magnus Erlendson, who was slain by his cousin, Haakon Paulson, on Egilsay in 1115. Magnus was buried at Birsay and it is said that heavenly light was seen over his grave. It soon became a shrine, attracting pilgrims from as far afield as

Norway. Magnus was canonized in 1133, and four years later his nephew commissioned construction of the cathedral. The building wasn't completed until the 14th century. Major additions have been made over the centuries, the most recent of which was a new west window for the nave, to celebrate the cathedral's 850th anniversary in 1987. The bones of St Magnus now lie in the north choir pillar, while those of St Rognvald lie in the south one. There's also a memorial to John Rae, the 19th-century Arctic explorer who is buried in the

Kirkwall

Sleeping	Ayre **2**
Albert **1**	Foveran **3**
	Kirkwall **4**
	Kirkwall Youth Hostel **5**
	Lav'rockha **6**

Orkney **7**
Peedie Hostel **8**
Pickaquoy Caravan
& Camping Site **9**
West End **10**

Eating
Lynfield Hotel **1**

Scandanavian settlements

The history of Orkney and Shetland is bound up with the history of the Vikings, who first came to the islands in the latter half of the ninth century and stayed for about 650 years. This was part of a great Viking expansion westwards, and in less than a century emigrants from Norway and Denmark settled in Orkney, Shetland, Iceland, Greenland, Caithness, the Western Isles, Isle of Man and parts of Ireland and the northern half of England.

In 872 the King of Norway set up a Norse earldom in Orkney, from which the Vikings ruled Orkney, Shetland and the Western Isles and took part in raids around Britain and Europe, creating the popular image of Vikings as aggressive, bloodthirsty invaders. At home, however, they lived a peaceful life, adhering to the laws of their parliament, the 'thing', and many converted to Christianity.

In the late 14th century Norway, Denmark and Sweden were united under a Danish king. In 1469 the Royal estates and prerogatives in Orkney and Shetland were pledged to Scotland as part of the marriage dowry of Margaret, daughter of the King of Denmark, on her marriage to Prince James of Scotland, later to become King James III. Orkney and Shetland were to revert to rule by the kings of Norway when the debt was paid, but the pledge was never redeemed and the islands remained under Scottish control.

Soon after assuming control, the Scots began to change the old Norse laws, which they had agreed to maintain, and Scottish influence grew. In 1564 Mary, Queen of Scots granted the control and revenues from Orkney and Shetland to her half-brother, Robert Stewart. His prime motivation, however, was to extract as much money as possible through taxes. He was succeeded by his son, the infamous Patrick Stewart, who demanded even more rents, dues and fines. Earl Patrick eventually got his come-uppance when he was executed in Edinburgh for treason, but the changes he had made continued and Scots and English gradually began to usurp Old Norse as the native language of the islands.

graveyard, as well as a monument to the 833 men of the *HMS Royal Oak* who died when it was torpedoed in Scapa Flow in 1939.

Looming impressively nearby are the ruins of the **Bishop's Palace** ① *T01856-875461, entry by combined ticket with Earl's Palace*, built in the 12th century as the first Kirkwall residence of the Bishop of Orkney. Here King Haakon of Norway died in 1263 after his defeat at the Battle of Largs. The palace was repaired and extended in the mid-16th century by Bishop Reid, and most of what you see dates from that period. There's a good view of the town from the top of the 'Moosie Too'r'.

The adjacent **Earl's Palace** ① *T01856-875461, Apr-Sep daily 0930-1730, £4.50, concessions £3.60, children £2.70*, was built around 1600 by the notorious Patrick Stewart, Earl of Orkney, using forced labour. Still very much intact, it is one of Scotland's most elegant Renaissance buildings and was occupied by the tyrannical Stewart only for a very short time, until he was imprisoned and later executed. Wandering around both these impressive and solid palaces is a very good way to get a feel for this period of Orkney's history.

Opposite St Magnus Cathedral is **Tankerness House and Gardens**, a 16th-century former manse which has been restored and now houses the **Orkney Museum** ① *T01856-873535, Oct-Apr Mon-Sat 1030-1230, 1330-1700, May-Sep 1030-1700, free*, which highlights 5500 years of human presence on Orkney, including archaeological artefacts from

Neolithic times to the Vikings. If you are spending any time in Kirkwall at the beginning of your stay, then this is an exceedingly worthwhile exhibition. It is a great way to whet your appetite for the archaeological treats that are lying in wait for you all over the islands, and it also puts them into a useful chronological context.

Old radio buffs should not miss the **Orkney Wireless Museum** ① *Kiln Corner, at the harbour end of Junction Rd, T01856-871400, www.owm.org.uk, Apr-Sep Mon-Sat 1000-1630, Sun 1430-1630, small entry fee*, which houses a jumble of domestic and wartime communications equipment from the 1930s onwards.

A mile south of the town centre on the road to South Ronaldsay is the 200-year-old **Highland Park Distillery** ① *T01856-874619, www.highlandpark.co.uk, tours on the hour every hour with the last tour 1 hr before closing Apr and Sep Mon-Fri 1000-1700, May-Aug Mon-Sat 1000-1700, Sun 1200-1700, Oct-Mar Mon-Fri 1300-1600, £6*. This is one of the few distilleries that still has its own floor maltings – as well as its own mouser cat – and there's a dram of this particularly fine single malt at the end. Don't leave without buying a bottle, for this is one of the great all-round whiskies, with a distinctive smoky flavour. It rivals those from more fashionable Islay.

Stromness and West Mainland

→ *For listings, see pages 403-411. See map, page 384. Phone code 01856.*

Ferries from Scrabster arrive in Stromness, and newcomers are greeted by rows of stone-built houses hugging the shore, each with its own jetty. Stromness is a much more attractive town than Kirkwall, and its narrow, winding main street, its *wynds* and *closes*, its fascinating shops, and its unique atmosphere make it the ideal base for exploring the West Mainland, the name given to everything west of Kirkwall. It's an area of rich farmland, rolling hills and moorland, fringed by spectacular cliffs along the Atlantic coastline and with the greatest concentration of prehistoric monuments in Britain. Here you'll find, amongst many others, the well-preserved Neolithic village of **Skara Brae**, silent monuments to human endeavour in the form of the **Standing Stones of Stenness** and the **Ring of Brodgar**, and the chambered tomb of **Maes Howe**, with its many still-unresolved mysteries.

Ins and outs

Getting there and around Northlink Ferries sail from Scrabster to Stromness (1½ hours) three times a day Monday to Friday and twice a day on Saturday and Sunday. Between mid-June and mid-August, they sail three times a day Monday to Saturday. Passenger fare is £17 single and a car costs £51, in peak season. **Rapstons Coaches** ① *T0871-200 2233*, and **Citylink** ① *T08705-505050*, operate bus services between Thurso and Scrabster and there are regular bus and train services to Thurso from Inverness.

There are several buses between Kirkwall and Stromness, Monday to Friday, and two buses daily between Kirkwall and Birsay Palace. To get to Skara Brae you'll need your own transport, or you can visit as part of a guided tour (see the TIC), or walk north along the coast from Stromness, via Yesnaby. ►► *For further information, see Transport, page 410.*

Tourist information Stromness **TIC** ① *T01856-850716, Apr-Oct Mon-Sat 0900-1800, Sun 0900-1600*, is at the ferry terminal. Its exhibition, *This Place Called Orkney*, is a useful introduction to the islands, and its free *Stromness Heritage Guide* takes you round all the town's buildings.

Stromness

Stromness is a classic Scottish fishing town and a perfect introduction to Orkney. Though referred to in the Viking Saga as *Hamnavoe*, the town dates from the 17th century. Its importance as a trading port grew in the 18th century when wars and privateers made the English Channel too dangerous and ships used the northern route across the Atlantic, calling in at Stromness for food and water and to hire a crew. Until the late 19th century, ships of the Hudson Bay Company made Stromness their main base for supplies. Whaling ships bound for Greenland also hired local labour. By the late 19th century the herring boom had reached Stromness and there were 400 boats using its harbour, but within two decades the boom was over due to over-fishing. Today Stromness remains a fishing port, as well as Orkney's main ferry terminal and the headquarters of the Northern Lighthouse Board.

Stromness consists largely of one narrow, winding main street, paved with flagstones, which hugs the shoreline. Running off the street are numerous little lanes and alleyways, many with names such as **Khyber Pass**, and full of interesting buildings that reflect the town's proud maritime heritage. The houses on the seaward side of the street are gable end to the waterfront and each has its own jetty. The town is not designed for the car, so you'll have to park by the harbour and explore its delights on foot. The main street changes its name from Victoria Street to Graham Place, Dundas Street, Alfred Street and South End as it runs south from the harbour.

Stromness Museum ⓘ *52 Albert St, T01856-850025, www.orkneyheritage.com, Apr-Sep daily 1000-1700, Oct-Mar Mon-Sat 1100-1530, £3.50, concessions £2.50, children £1, family £7,* run by a community trust, it's packed to the gunnels with exhibitions on Stromness' social and maritime history, including the story of Arctic whaling and artefacts from Scapa Flow and the days of the Hudson Bay Company. Upstairs the beautiful Victorian glass cases house a complete collection of Orkney birds and butterflies. Recommended. Opposite the museum is the house where George Mackay Brown (1921-1996), Orkney's most famous poet and story writer, spent the last two decades of his life, see also page 454. On a jetty to the south of the new harbour is the excellent **Pier Arts Centre** ⓘ *T01856-850209, www.pierartscentre. com, Mon-Sat 1030-1730 Sun 1200-1600, free,* housing a permanent collection of works of the St Ives school, including Barbara Hepworth, Ben Nicholson and Patrick Heron, amongst others, in a lovely contemporary gallery.

Skara Brae and Skaill House

ⓘ *T01956-841815, www.historic-scotland.gov.uk. Apr-Sep (joint ticket) daily 0930-1730. £6.90, concessions £5.50, children £4.10. Oct-Mar (Skara Brae only) daily 0930-1630, £5.70, concessions £4.70, children £2.25.*

Eight miles north of Stromness, in the magnificent setting of the dazzling white sands of the Bay of Skaill, is Skara Brae, the best-preserved Stone Age village in northern Europe. Explore here and you may feel you have just joined the cartoon world of The Flintstones. First revealed in 1850 after a violent storm blew away the dunes, this amazing site dates from around 5000 years ago and was occupied for about 600 years.

The houses contain stone furniture, fireplaces, drains, beds, dressers and even have damp-proof coursing in the foundations. The whole complex presents a unique picture of the lifestyle of its inhabitants, and there's also a replica 'house' that you can wander around in the gloom, empathizing with that 3000 BC lifestyle.

The swish, modern visitor centre has a useful introductory video and exhibition which is definitely worth seeing before you look round the site (and it's also worth buying their guidebook). After leaving the visitor centre, you walk down a 'path of time', which takes you back through landmark achievements of the last seven millennia, gradually building up the suspense and putting the achievements of Skara Brae in perspective – they may only be rudimentary buildings that once had turf for their rooves, but they were built 2000 years before the pyramids of Egypt, and in one of the world's most northerly outposts.

During the summer a ticket to Skara Brae includes admission to nearby **Skaill House** ① *T01856-841501, www.skaillhouse.com*, an early 17th-century mansion which contains a few old artefacts, including Captain Cook's dinner service from the *Resolution* and the trappings and frippery of the Lairds of Brackness over 400 years. Seeing these Orcadian dwellings, hundreds of thousands of years apart, is remarkable. Sandwick and Yesnaby.

A short distance inland from here, at Sandwick, is Orkney's only brewery, housed in the old Quoyloo School. It brews the island's **Raven Ale** and various bottled beers, including **Skull-splitter**, named after the Viking earl, Thorfinn Skull-splitter.

South of the Bay of Skaill is Yesnaby, one of the most spectacular places on the islands, where the cliffs have been eroded into a series of stacks and geos by the fierce Atlantic seas. An exhilarating, and precarious, half-mile walk south from the car park and old Second World War lookout post brings you to **Yesnaby Castle**, a huge sea stack similar to the Old Man of Hoy. It's a dramatic sight, especially in a full force gale.

Standing Stones of Stenness and Ring of Brodgar
Northeast of Stromness on the road to Kirkwall is the tiny village of **Stenness**, near some of Orkney's most interesting prehistoric sites. The Standing Stones of Stenness comprise the four remaining stones from an original circle of 12 stones, dating from 3000 BC. The largest of the stones stands over 15 ft high. A path leads from the stones to the nearby **Barnhouse Settlement**, a recently excavated Neolithic village.

About a mile northwest of Stenness is another stone circle, the **Ring of Brodgar**. This is a particularly impressive henge monument. It is over 100 yds in diameter and 27 of the original 60 stones are still standing, some of them up to 15 ft high. Given the importance of these sites, it is particularly refreshing to realize when you get there that you can walk amongst the stones in the calm of a summer evening, with only a few oystercatchers for company, but both get busy with coach parties during the day.

Maes Howe
① *T01856-761606, www.historic-scotland.gov.uk. Apr-Sep daily 0930-1700, Oct-Mar daily 0930-1630, £5.20, concessions £4.20, children £3.10. Tickets can be bought from Tormiston Mill, on the other side of the road, where there's an exhibition, introductory video and café. Tours at 45-min intervals, call to book.*
Less than a mile northeast of the Stones of Stenness is Maes Howe, the finest Neolithic burial chamber in Europe. It was built around 2750 BC, making it contemporary with the Standing Stones and Skara Brae, and is amazingly well preserved. A huge mound covers a stone-built entrance passage which leads into a central chamber – over 12 ft square and the same in height – with three smaller cells built into the walls of the tomb.

When it was opened in 1861, no human remains or artefacts were found, giving no clues as to its usage. However, in the 12th century Vikings returning from the Crusades broke into the tomb searching for treasure. They found nothing, but left behind one of the largest collections of runic graffiti anywhere in the world, as well as carvings of a dragon, serpent and walrus. Many of the inscriptions are pretty basic, along the lines of 'Thorfinn wrote these runes', but some are more intriguing, such as "Many a woman has come stooping in here no matter how pompous a person she was".

A guide gives you an excellent overview of the chamber's mysterious architectural attributes, but the fact remains that the history of this extraordinary place is still largely unsolved – something that obviously adds to the site's attraction. Unfortunately, you do not get to spend much time in the chamber, so you are unlikely to uncover any great secrets.

Orphir

On the southern shores of West Mainland, overlooking Scapa Flow, is the scattered community of Orphir, which has a few sights worth visiting, especially if you're heading across to Hoy from the ferry terminal at **Houton**, a little further west. The main point of interest in Orphir is the **Orkneyinga Saga Centre** ① *T01856-811319, open all year daily 0900-1700, free*, where a small exhibition and video introduces the saga, written circa 1200, possibly by an Icelander, which tells the history of the Viking Earls of Orkney from around AD 900 to 1200, when the islands became a part of Scotland rather than Norway. As you would expect, there's plenty of gore and Machiavellian goings-on, including an assassination attempt that went disastrously wrong, when a poisoned shirt meant for Earl Harold was unwittingly and fatally worn by his brother Paul instead.

Behind the centre is **The Earl's Bu**, looking out across Orphir Bay south to Cava Island. These are the 12th-century foundations of the home of the Norse Earls of Orkney written about in the saga. Inside the cemetery gates is a section of the circular church built by Haakon and modelled on the rotunda of the Church of the Holy Sepulchre in Jerusalem.

Markwick Head

At the southern end of Birsay Bay are the wild and spectacular 300-ft-high cliffs of Marwick Head, topped by the distinctive **Kitchener Memorial**, erected after the First World War to commemorate Lord Kitchener and the crew of the *HMS Hampshire*, which was sunk by a German mine off the coast in 1916 with the loss of all but 12 of her crew. Marwick Head is also an **RSPB Reserve**, and during the nesting season in early summer is home to many thousands of guillemots, razorbills, kittiwakes and fulmars, as well as a few puffins.

A mile inland, by the Loch of Isibister, is another RSPB reserve, **The Loons**, an area of marshland where you can see breeding and migrating wildfowl and waders. Further east, between Boarhouse Loch and Hundland Loch, is the **Kirbuster Farm Museum** ① *T01856-873535, Mar-Oct Mon-Sat 1030-1300, 1400-1700, Sun 1400-1900, free*, the last surviving Orkney blackhouse which was inhabited till the 1960s and gives an insight into 19th-century rural life on the islands.

Birsay

At the far northwestern corner of the Mainland is the parish of Birsay, which was a favourite residence of the Earls of Orkney in Viking times as well as the first seat of the Bishop, before the building of St Magnus Cathedral in Kirkwall. Earl Thorfinn the Mighty lived here (1014-1064) and built Orkney's first cathedral, **Christchurch**, for the new Bishop.

In the centre of the village are the ruins of the **Earl's Palace** ① *T01856-721205, open at all times, free*, built by the infamous Earl Robert Stewart in the late 16th century, and once described as "a sumptuous and stately dwelling". Not much remains today, but enough to give some idea of the sheer scale of the place. Close by is **St Magnus church**, built in 1760 on the site of an earlier church, which in turn was built on the foundations of what is believed to be the original Christchurch. Also in Birsay, just south of the A966 and A967 junction, is **Barony Mills** ① *T01856-721439, www.birsay.org.uk, May-Sep daily 1000-1300, 1400-1700, free*, the last working water-powered mill in Orkney.

Lying half a mile off the coast near the village is the **Brough of Birsay** ① *phone the Earl's Palace (see above) or T01856-841815 for crossing times, open (when tides permit) mid-Jun to end Sep daily 0930-1730, £4, concessions £3.20, children £2.40.* The tidal island, managed by Historic Scotland, juts out into the north Atlantic and is visible from several other points all the way down the west coast of the Mainland. It is only accessible for a couple of hours at low tide (times available from Kirkwall and Stromness tourist offices) but, if possible, it is best seen at the end of the day, as the sun sets – you'll probably have the whole island to yourself. Pick your way over the causeway and wander at your leisure (but don't forget the tide) amongst the remnants of a Pictish, and then Viking, community. The island was an important Pictish settlement from around the sixth century, and many artefacts have been found here. Some of these can be seen at the small ticket office at the entrance to the island. The Brough was also the site of an important Viking settlement, and there are extensive remains, including the 12th-century **St Peter's church** where St Magnus was buried after his murder on Egilsay. You can also walk out to the island's lighthouse along the top of the cliffs and see puffins – amongst other migrating seabirds – and possibly minke whales, pilot whales and killer whales.

Evie and the Broch of Gurness

Nine miles northwest of Kirkwall is the tiny village of Evie. A track leads from the village towards the coast, past a sandy beach, to the **Broch of Gurness** ① *T01856-751414, Apr-Oct daily 0930-1730, £5, concessions £4, children £3.* Standing on a lonely, exposed headland on the north coast, with gentle views across towards the island of Rousay, this is the best-preserved broch on Orkney, thought to date from around 100 BC. It is surrounded by an Iron Age village whose houses are also remarkably well preserved, with the original hearths, beds, cupboards and even a toilet still in evidence. The broch and village were occupied by the Picts up until Viking times, around AD 900. Many Pictish artefacts have been found on the site, and the grave of a ninth-century Norse woman was also discovered.

To the southwest of Evie is the **Birsay Moors RSPB Reserve**, and at **Lowrie's Water** on Burgar Hill there's a bird-hide from where you can watch breeding red-throated divers. Also on Burgar Hill you'll see several huge aerogenerators built to take advantage of Orkney's fierce winds.

East Mainland and South Ronaldsay

→ *For listings, see pages 403-411. See map, page 384. Phone code 01856.*

The East Mainland is mainly agricultural land and though it contains little of the amazing archaeological wealth of its western counterpart, there are some attractive fishing villages, fine coastal walks and many poignant reminders of Orkney's important wartime role. Linked to East Mainland by a series of causeways, South Ronaldsay is the southernmost of the Orkney islands, only 6 miles from the Scottish mainland across the stormy Pentland Firth, the most dangerous stretch of water in the British Isles. A small passenger ferry crosses to Burwick on the southern tip of the island from John o'Groats: from May to September **John o'Groats Ferries** ① *T01955-611353, www.jogferry.co.uk,* leave twice a day for Burwick, or four times a day between June and August. The journey takes 40 minutes.

Ins and outs

Getting there **Pentland Ferries** ① *T01856-831226, T01856-611773 (Gill's Bay), www.pentlandferries.co.uk,* sail from Gill's Bay (between John o'Groats and Thurso) to St Margaret's Hope, three times a day (£13 single, children £6, car £30, including driver).

Deerness

There is not much to see inland on the road running southeast from Kirkwall past the airport, but head on towards the Deerness Peninsula and you will be richly rewarded by a truly serene, gentle beauty. There are sandy bays, which make for very pleasant short walks and picnics (if you can find a sheltered spot), jutting cliffs and a great variety of birdlife. The peninsula makes the West Mainland seem positively crowded by comparison, and is one of the best places on the Mainland to get away from it all.

When the weather's good, the view southwest from Sandside Bay to the Isle of **Copinsay** (an RSPB reserve) is glorious, and is a perfect example of the whale-like properties that have been attributed to the Orkneys by the islands' most famous poet George Mackay Brown. There is a footpath following the coast from Sandside Bay to Mull Head (a nature reserve) and round the tip of the peninsula to the **Covenanters Memorial** (1679), a 5-mile circular walk.

If you continue along the B9050, the road ends at The Gloup car park at Skaill Bay, from where it's a 200-yd walk to **The Gloup**, a dramatic collapsed sea cave, separated from the sea by a land bridge about 80 yds wide. The word comes from the Old Norse 'gluppa', meaning chasm, the local name for a blow-hole. A network of signposted footpaths covers the northeastern part of the peninsula and there are circular walks of between two to five miles which start from The Gloup car park. At the northeastern tip is **Mull Head**, a clifftop nature reserve which is home to guillemots, shags, fulmars, razorbills, terns and skuas.

On the south coast of East Mainland, near the northern end of the Churchill Barriers, is the old fishing village of **St Mary's**, once a busy little place but largely forgotten since the building of the causeways. To the east of the village is the **Norwood Museum** ① *T01856-781217, May-Sep Tue-Thu and Sun 1400-1700 or by appointment, £2.50, children £1.75*, which features the large and eclectic antique collection of local stonemason Norris Wood.

The Churchill Barriers

East Mainland is linked to a string of islands to the south by four causeways, known as the Churchill Barriers, built on the orders of Prime Minister Winston Churchill during the Second World War as anti-submarine barriers to protect the British Navy which was based in Scapa Flow at the time. Churchill's decision was prompted by the sinking of the battleship *HMS Royal Oak* in October 1939 by a German U-boat which had slipped between the old blockships, deliberately sunk during the First World War to protect Scapa Flow, and the shore. After the war, a road was built on top of the causeways, linking the islands of Lamb Holm, Glimps Holm, Burray and South Ronaldsay to Mainland.

On the island of **Lamb Holm** camps were built to accommodate the men working on the construction of the barriers, many of whom were Italian prisoners of war. The camps have long since gone, but the Italians left behind the remarkable **Italian Chapel** ① *T01856-872856 (for mass times), open all year during daylight hours, donations welcomed*, fittingly known as 'The Miracle of Camp 60'. It is difficult to believe that such a beautiful building could have been made using two Nissen huts, concrete and bits of scrap metal, and the chapel's enduring popularity with visitors is a tribute to the artistic skill of the men involved. One of them, Domenico Chiochetti, returned in 1960 to restore the interior paintwork.

Burray

On the island of Burray the road passes the **Orkney Fossil and Vintage Centre** ① *T01856-731255, Apr-Sep daily 1000-1800, Oct Wed-Sun 1030-1800, £3.50 to enter the display rooms*, which houses a bizarre collection of old furniture, various relics and 350 million-year-old

The graveyard of Scapa Flow

The huge natural harbour of Scapa Flow has been used since Viking times, and in the years leading up to the First World War the Royal Navy held exercises there, sometimes involving up to 100 ships. But Scapa was vulnerable to attack, and over the course of the war defences were improved with 21 blockships sunk at the eastern approaches. Scapa Flow continued to be used as the main naval base in the Second World War, but the blockships were not enough to prevent a German U-boat from torpedoing HMS Royal Oak, and the huge task of building the Churchill Barriers began, see page 394.

Scapa Flow's most famous incident happened at the end of the First World War,

when, under the terms of the Armistice, Germany agreed to surrender most of her navy. Seventy-four German ships were interred in Scapa Flow, awaiting the final decision, but as the deadline approached the German commander, Admiral Von Reuter, gave the order for all the ships to be scuttled, and every ship was beached or sunk.

The scuttled German fleet, however, proved a hazard for fishing and a massive salvage operation began. Today seven German ships remain at the bottom of Scapa Flow – three battleships and four light cruisers – along with four destroyers and a U-boat and the Royal Navy battle-ships HMS Royal Oak and HMS Vanguard, which blew up in 1917.

---

fish fossils found locally. There's also an archive room where you can browse old books and photographs. Not really something to go out of your way for, but worth a look if it's raining.

South Ronaldsay

The main settlement is the picturesque little village of **St Margaret's Hope** on the north coast. It is said to be named after Margaret, Maid of Norway, who died near here in 1290 at the age of seven while on her way to marry Prince Edward, later Edward II of England. She had already been proclaimed Queen of Scotland, and her premature death was a major factor in the long Wars of Independence with England. The word 'hope' comes from the Old Norse word *hjop* meaning bay.

The village smithy has been turned into the **Smiddy Museum** ① *T01856-831567, May and Sep daily 1400-1600, Jun-Aug daily 1200-1600, Oct Sun 1400-1600, free*, with lots of old blacksmith's tools to try out. The museum also features a small exhibition on the annual **Boys' Ploughing Match**, a hugely popular event first held circa 1860. Each year in August, boys from the village (and now girls as well) dress up as horses and parade in the village square (prizes are given for the best costume). Afterwards the boys and their fathers, or grandfathers, head for the **Sand of Wright**, a few miles west, and have a ploughing match with miniature ploughs, which are usually family heirlooms. The categories are: best ploughed ring, best feering or guiding furrow, neatest ends and best-kept plough. This sheltered beach is well worth a visit anyway, ploughing or no ploughing. The views stretch in a spectacular 180° panorama, south across the Pentland Firth to Caithness on mainland Scotland, west to South Walls and Cantick Head on Hoy, and northwest to Flotta and the west Mainland. It is yet another good place to spot snipe, lapwing, curlew and redshank. Arctic terns nest nearby and you can spot them diving dramatically as they fish in the bay.

To the north of the beach is the **Howe of Hoxa**, a ruined broch where Earl Thorfinn Skull-Splitter was buried in AD 963, according to the Orkneyinga saga. South Ronaldsay is a good place to buy local arts and crafts, and there are several workshops dotted around the island.

One of these is the **Hoxa Tapestry Gallery** ① *T01856-831395, www.hoxatapestrygallery. co.uk*, 3 miles west of the village on the way to Hoxa Head. Local artist Leila Thompson's huge tapestries are well worth a visit; you cannot help but marvel at the extraordinary amount of work and dedication involved in their creation; many of them take years to finish. Due to the success of the gallery, Leila Thompson now works mostly to commission with lengthy waiting times, but if you are interested, the gallery is worth a visit.

At the southeastern corner of South Ronaldsay is the **Tomb of the Eagles** ① *T01856-831339, www.tomboftheeagles.co.uk, Apr-Oct daily 0930-1730, Mar daily 1000-1200, Nov-Feb by arrangement, £6.50, concessions £5.50, children £2-3*, one of the most interesting archaeological sights on Orkney. The 5000-year-old chambered cairn was discovered by local farmer and amateur archaeologist, Ronald Simison, whose family now runs the privately owned site and museum. The contents of the tomb were practically intact and there were up to 340 people buried here, along with carcasses and talons of sea eagles, hence the name. Various objects were also found outside the tomb, including stone tools and axes.

Before visiting the tomb you can handle the skulls and other artefacts at the small 'museum' in the family home, which actually means their front porch. Then you walk for about five or 10 minutes through a field to visit a **burnt mound**, a kind of Bronze Age kitchen, where – if you're lucky - Ronald Simison will regail you with insider information about the excavation process, before walking out along the cliff edge to the spectacularly sited tomb which you must enter by lying on a trolley and pulling yourself in using an overhead rope. It is particularly eerie being here because there is generally no-one else around, and as you haul yourself into the tomb, with the sound of the North Sea crashing into the cliffs nearby, you wonder to yourself how those buried here met their fate. There is also a lovely, but generally wild and windy, walk back along the cliffs, via a different route, to the car park.

In South Ronaldsay too is the **Orkney Marine-Life Aquarium** ① *Pool Farmhouse, Grimness, T01856-831700, www.orkneymarinelife.co.uk, daily 1000-1800, £5.50, concessions £4*, that as the name suggests offers visitors of all ages an insight to the creatures of the deep around these shores. Year round, it's well worth a visit.

Hoxa → *For listings, see pages 403-411. See map, page 384. Phone code 01856.*

To the southwest of the Mainland is Hoy, the second largest of the Orkney islands. The name is derived from the Norse *Ha-ey*, meaning High Island, which is appropriate as much of the island is more reminiscent of the Scottish Highlands than Orkney, with only the southern end being typically low and fertile.

Ins and outs

Getting there and around There are two ferry services to Hoy, both run by **Orkney Ferries** ① *T01856-872044, www.orkneyferries.co.uk*. A passenger ferry sails between Stromness and Moaness Pier in the north (30 minutes) three times a day from Monday to Friday, twice on Friday evenings, and twice a day on Saturday and Sunday. There's a reduced winter service from mid-September to mid-May. There's also a car and passenger service (T01856-811397) between Houton and Lyness and Longhope (45 minutes) up to six times daily, Monday to Saturday. There's a limited Sunday service from mid-May to mid-September.

Transport on Hoy is very limited, **North Hoy Transport** ① *T01856-791315*, runs a minibus service between Moaness Pier and Rackwick, which meets the 1000 ferry from Stromness. Call the same telephone number for a taxi around the island. From May-Sep the Hoy Hopper T01856-872856 departs from Kirkwall at 0840 and stops at all the sites for just long enough to see them before returning you to Kirkwall for 1820 £16, concession £8. There are shops and petrol stations in Lyness and Longhope. >> *For further details, see Transport, page 410.*

Sights

Orkney's highest point, **Ward Hill** (1571 ft) is in the north of the island, and the north and west coasts are bounded by spectacular cliffs. At **St John's Head**, the sheer cliffs rise out of the sea to a height of 1150 ft, the highest vertical cliffs in Britain. The island is most famous for its **Old Man of Hoy**, a great rock stack rising to 450 ft. This northern part of Hoy forms the **North Hoy RSPB Reserve** which has a variety of habitats ranging from woodland to tundra-like hilltops and sea cliffs. The reserve is home to a huge variety of birds including great skuas and Arctic skuas, Manx shearwaters and puffins. On the hills there are red grouse, curlews, golden plovers and dunlins, peregrine falcons, merlins, kestrels and even golden eagles. Mountain hares are quite common and, if you are lucky, you can also see otters along the Scapa Flow coastline.

On the southeast coast of the island is **Lyness**, site of a large naval base during both world wars when the British fleet was based in Scapa Flow. Many of the old dilapidated buildings have gone, but the harbour area is still scarred with the scattered remains of concrete structures, and there's also the unattractive sight of the huge oil terminal on **Flotta**. Lyness has a large **Naval Cemetery**, last resting place of those who died at Jutland, of Germans killed during the scuttle of the German fleet and of the crew of *HMS Royal Oak*. The old pump house opposite the new ferry terminal is now the **Scapa Flow Visitor Centre** ① *T01856-791300, mid-May to Sep Mon-Fri 0900-1630, Sat-Sun 1000-1600, free*, a fascinating naval museum with old photographs, various wartime artefacts, a section devoted to the scuttling of the German fleet and an audio-visual feature on the history of Scapa Flow. It's well worth a visit and is reached by a short ferry trip across Scapa Flow. At South Walls, overlooking Longhope Bay, is **Hackness Martello Tower and Battery** ① *T01856-811397, Apr-Oct daily 0930-1730, Oct 0930-1730, £4.50, concessions £3.60, children £2.70*, which, along with another tower on the north side at Crockness, was built in 1815 to protect British ships in Longhope Bay against attack by American and French privateers while they waited for a Royal Navy escort on their journey to Baltic ports.

Walking on Hoy

Hoy's great attraction is its many excellent walking opportunities. A minibus runs between **Moaness Pier**, where the ferry from Stromness docks (see Transport, page 410), and **Rackwick**, on the opposite side of the island, but it's a lovely two-hour walk by road through beautiful **Rackwick Glen**, once populated by crofters and fishermen, but now quiet and isolated. On the way you'll pass the **Dwarfie Stone**, a huge, lonely block of sandstone which is the only rock-cut tomb in Britain, dating from around 3000 BC. Be careful, though, because, according to Sir Walter Scott, this is the residence of the Trolld, a dwarf from Norse legend. On your return you can take a different route through a narrow valley between the **Cuilags** (1421 ft) and **Ward Hill** and **Berriedale Wood**, the most northerly woodland in Britain. The most popular walk on Hoy is the spectacular three-hour hike from Rackwick to the cliffs facing the **Old Man of Hoy**. The path climbs steeply westwards from the old crofting township, then turns northwards before gradually descending to the cliff edge.

Rousay, Egilsay and Wyre → *For listings, see pages 403-411. See map, page 384.*

These three islands lie a short distance off the northeast coast of Mainland and, together with Shapinsay to the southeast, are the closest of Orkney's North Isles to Kirkwall.

Ins and outs

Getting there A small car ferry operated by Orkney Ferries sails from Tingwall to Rousay up to six times a day Monday to Saturday, and five times a day on Sunday. Most of the ferries call in at Egilsay and Wyre, but some are on demand only and should be booked in advance, T01856-872044. ▸▸ *For further information, see Transport, page 410.*

Rousay

Rousay is a hilly island about 5 miles in diameter and is known as the 'Egypt of the North' due to the large number of archaeological sites. It also has the important **Trumland RSPB Reserve**, home to merlins, hen harriers, peregrine falcons, short-eared owls and red-throated divers, and its three lochs offer good trout fishing.

A road runs right around the island, and makes a pleasant 13-mile bike run, but most of the sights are within walking distance of the ferry pier on the southeast side of the island, where most of the 200 inhabitants live. A short distance west of the pier by the road is **Tavershoe Tuick**, an unusual two-storey burial cairn, which was discovered in the late 19th century by Mrs Burroughs, wife of General Traill Burroughs who lived at nearby Trumland House. A mile further west, to the north of the road, is **Blackhammer**, a stalled Neolithic burial cairn. Further west still, and a steep climb up from the road, is **Knowe of Yarso**, another stalled cairn, which contained the remains of at least 21 people. The tomb dates from around 2900 BC.

Most of the island's archaeological sights are to be found along the **Westness Walk**, a mile-long walk which starts from Westness Farm, about four miles west of the ferry pier, and ends at the remarkable Midhowe Cairn. The walk is described in detail in a leaflet available from the tourist offices on Mainland. **Midhowe Cairn** is the largest and longest cairn – over 100 ft long and 40 ft wide – excavated on Orkney thus far and, like the others, dates from around 3000 BC. Housed in a large building to protect it, the 'Great Ship of Death', as it is known, contained the remains of 25 people in crouched position on or under the eastern shelves of the chamber, which is divided into 12 sections. Standing nearby, with fine views across to Eynehallow island, is **Midhowe Broch**, one of the best-preserved brochs on Orkney, occupied from around 200 BC to AD 200. The outer walls are about 60 ft in diameter and up to 14 ft high in places.

Another fine walk on the island is around the **RSPB Reserve**. A footpath leads from beside Trumland House and heads up towards the island's highest point, **Blotchnie Fiold** (821 ft). A leaflet describing the walk is available from the tourist offices on Mainland or the **Trumland Orientation Centre** by the pier.

Egilsay and Wyre

These two small islands lie to the east of Rousay and have a couple of interesting sights of their own. Egilsay's claim to fame is the murder here of St Magnus in 1115, and a **cenotaph** marks the spot where he was slain. The island is dominated by the 12th-century **St Magnus church**, built on the site of an earlier church, possibly as a shrine to St Magnus. It is the only surviving example on Orkney of a round-towered Viking church. Much of Egilsay has been bought by the RSPB as a reserve to preserve the habitat of the very rare **corncrake**, whose distinctive rasping call may be heard.

Tiny Wyre features strongly in the Viking saga as the domain of Kolbein Hruga, and the remains of his 12th-century stronghold, **Cubbie Roo's Castle**, and nearby **St Mary's chapel** can be still be seen. Kolbein's home was on the site of the nearby Bu Farm, where the poet Edwin Muir (1887-1959) spent part of his childhood. The far westerly point of the island, known as **the Taing**, is a favourite haunt of seals, and a great place to enjoy a sunset.

Less than 30 minutes by ferry from Kirkwall is the fertile, low-lying island of Shapinsay, home to **Balfour Castle** ① *T01856-711282, www.balfourcastle.com*, an imposing baronial pile which is in fact a Victorian extension to a much older house called 'Cliffdale'. The house, and the rest of the island, was bought by successive generations of the Balfour family who had made their fortune in India. Today the castle is the home of the Zawadski family and is rented to small house parties (see Sleeping, page 405). The castle can also be visited as part of an inclusive half-day tour, which leaves from Kirkwall on Wednesday and Sunday at 1415, from mid-May to mid-September. Arrange in advance at the tourist office in Kirkwall. The ticket includes a guided tour of the castle and gardens (at 1500) and complimentary tea and cakes in the servants' quarters. You can also take an earlier ferry if you wish to explore the island. The small car ferry makes up to six sailings daily (including Sunday in summer) to Shapinsay from Kirkwall (25 minutes).

In the village, built by the Balfours to house their estate workers, is the **Shapinsay Heritage Centre** ① *T01856-711258, open daily May-Sep, free*, in the old Smithy. It has displays on the island's history and a tea room upstairs. There's a **pub** in the village, in the old gatehouse, a couple of shops and a post office.

A mile north of the village is the **Mill Dam RSPB Reserve**, where there's a hide overlooking a loch from which you can see many species of wildfowl and waders. Four miles from the pier, at the far northeast corner of the island, is the well-preserved **Burroughston Broch**, with good views of seals sunning themselves on the nearby rocks. West of here, at **Quholme**, is the original birthplace of the father of Washington Irving, author of *Rip Van Winkle*.

The long, thin and sparsely populated island of Eday lies at the centre of the North Isles group. It is less fertile than the other islands, but its heather-covered hills in the centre have provided peat for the other peatless Orkney islands. Eday's sandstone has also been quarried, and was used in the building of St Magnus Cathedral in Kirkwall.

Ins and outs
There are flights from Kirkwall to Eday airport, called London Airport, on Wednesdays with **Loganair** ① *T01856-872494*. There are ferries also from Kirkwall twice daily via Sanday or Stronsay. Note that the pier is at Backaland, on the southeast of the island, a long way from the main sights. **Orkney Ferries** ① *T01856-872044*, also run the Eday Heritage Tour (see page 408). ▶▶ *For further details, see Transport, page 410.*

Sights
The island has numerous chambered cairns and these, along with the other attractions, are concentrated in the northern part. They are all covered in the signposted 5-mile **Eday Heritage Walk**, which starts from the Community Centre and leads up to the cliffs of Red Head at the northern tip. The walk takes about four hours to complete, and it's worth picking up the *Eday Heritage Walk* leaflet.

The walk heads past **Mill Loch**, where an RSPB hide allows you to watch rare red-throated divers breeding in spring and summer. Further north is the huge, 15-ft tall **Stone of Setter**, the largest standing stone in Orkney and visible from most of the chambered cairns. Close by are the **Fold of Setter**, a circular enclosure dating back to 2000 BC, and the **Braeside** and **Huntersquoy** chambered cairns. Further north along the path is **Vinquoy Chambered Cairn**, one of the finest in Orkney and similar to the better-known tomb at Maes Howe, dating from around the same time. An acrylic dome provides light to the main chamber, which can be entered by a narrow underground passage.

The path continues to the summit of **Vinquoy Hill**, which commands excellent views of the surrounding islands of Westray and Sanday. From here you can continue north to the spectacular red sandstone cliffs at **Red Head**, home to nesting guillemots, razorbills and puffins in summer, or head southeast along the coast to **Carrick House** ① *T01857-622260, guided tour mid-Jun to mid-Sep, Sun by appointment, free, donations to charity only.* Built for Lord Kinclaven, Earl of Carrick, in 1633, the house is best known for its associations with the pirate, John Gow, whose ship ran aground during a failed attack on the house. He was captured and taken to London for trial and hanged. Sir Walter Scott's novel, *The Pirate*, is based on this story.

Sanday → *For listings, see pages 403-411. See map, page 384. Phone code 01857.*

Sanday is the largest of the North Isles, 12 miles long and flat as a pancake except for the cliffs at Spurness. It is well-named, as its most notable feature is its sweeping bays of sparkling white sand backed by machair, and turquoise seas. There are Loganair flights to Sanday from Kirkwall twice daily from Monday to Friday and once a day on Saturday. Ferries run twice daily from Kirkwall (1½ hours) and arrive at Loth, at the southern tip of the island, where they're met by a minibus.

There are numerous burial mounds all over the island, the most impressive being **Quoyness Chambered Cairn**, a 5000 year-old tomb similar to Maes Howe. The 13 ft-high structure contains a large main chamber with six smaller cells opening through low entrances. Most of the burial tombs remain unexcavated, such as those at **Tofts Ness** at the far northeastern tip, where there are over 500 cairns, making it potentially one of the most important prehistoric sites in Britain. At **Scar**, in Burness, a spectacular Viking find was made, and at **Pool** a major excavation has uncovered the remains of at least 14 Stone-Age houses.

Sanday is known for its knitwear, though the factory unfortunately closed down. You can still visit the **Orkney Angora craft shop**, in Upper Breckan, near the northern tip of the island.

Stronsay → *For listings, see pages 403-411. See map, page 384.*

Ins and outs → *Phone code 01857.*
Getting there There are **Loganair** flights from Kirkwall twice daily from Monday to Friday. A ferry service runs from Kirkwall twice daily Monday to Saturday and once on Sunday (1½ hours), and the ferry from Eday runs once a day from Monday to Saturday (35 minutes).

Sights
The peaceful, low-lying island of Stronsay has some fine sandy beaches and cliffs, which attract large colonies of grey seals and nesting seabirds. There are few real sights on this largely agricultural island, but the coastline has some pleasant walks. One of the best is to the **Vat of Kirbister** in the southeast, a spectacular 'gloup' or blow-hole spanned by the finest natural arch in Orkney. To the south of here, at **Burgh Head**, you'll find nesting puffins and the remains of a ruined broch, and at the southeastern tip, at **Lamb Head**, is a large colony of grey seals, lots of seabirds and several archaeological sites.

The main settlement is the quiet village of **Whitehall**, on the northeast coast where the ferry arrives. It's hard to believe it now, but this was one of the largest herring ports in Europe. During the boom years of the early 20th century, 300 steam drifters were working out of Whitehall and nearly 4000 fishing crew and shore workers were employed. In the peak year of 1924 over 12,000 tons of herring were landed here, to be cured (salted) and exported to Russia and Eastern Europe. Whitehall developed considerably and the **Stronsay Hotel** was said to have the longest bar in Scotland. On Sundays during July and August there were so many boats tied up that it was possible to walk across them to the little island of Papa Stronsay. By the 1930s, however, herring stocks were severely depleted and the industry was in decline. The old Fish Mart by the pier houses a **Heritage Centre** ⓘ *T017856-616386, May-Sep daily 1100-1700, free,* with photos and artefacts from the herring boom days. It also has a café and hostel (see Sleeping, page 406).

Westray → *For listings, see pages 403-411. See map, page 384. Phone code 01857.*

Westray is the second largest of the North Isles, with a varied landscape of farmland, hilly moorland, sandy beaches and dramatic cliffs. It is also the most prosperous of the North Isles, producing beef, fish and seafood, and supports a population of 700. Flights to Westray with Loganair depart Kirkwall twice daily from Monday to Saturday and there's a car ferry service to Rapness, on the south coast of the island (1½ hours). It sails twice daily in summer (mid-May to mid-September) and once daily in winter.

The main settlement is **Pierowall**, in the north of the island, but, though it has one of the best harbours in Orkney, the main ferry terminal is at Rapness, on the south coast. Pierowall is a relatively large village for the North Isles and there are shops, a post office, a hotel and the **Westray Heritage Centre** ⓘ *T01857-677414, www.westrayheritage.co.uk, early May-late Sep Mon 1130-1700, Tue-Sat 1000-1200, 1400-1700, Sun 1330-1700, £2.50, concessions £2, children 50p,* with displays on local and natural history, and a tea room. Also in the village is the ruined 17th-century St Mary's church. About a mile west of the village is Westray's most notable ruin, **Noltland Castle**, a fine example of a 16th-century fortified Z-plan tower-house. To explore inside, pick up the key from the back door of the nearby farm.

Walks on Westray

There are some great coastal walks on the island, particularly to the spectacular sea cliffs at **Noup Head**, at the far northwestern tip, which are an **RSPB Reserve** and second only to St Kilda in terms of breeding seabirds, with huge colonies of guillemots, razorbills, kittiwakes and fulmars, as well as puffins. The cliffs on the west coast of Westray are five miles long and there's an excellent walk down the coast from Noup Head, past **Gentleman's Cave**, used as a hiding place by four Jacobite lairds in 1746. Near the southern end of the walk is **Fitty Hill** (554 ft), the highest point on the island, which you can climb for great views, and the walk ends at **Inga Ness**, where you can also see puffins. The best place to see them is at **Castle o'Burrian**, a sea stack on **Stanger Head**, on the southeastern coast near the Rapness ferry terminal.

Papa Westray → *For listings, see pages 403-411. See map, page 384. Phone code 01857.*

Tiny Papa Westray, known locally as 'Papay', is best known as being the destination for the world's shortest scheduled flight, from Westray; all of two minutes, or less with a good following wind, and there's no shortage of that. The famous two-minute flight leaves

Westray twice daily (Monday-Saturday). There is also a direct flight to Papay from Kirkwall, daily Monday to Saturday. There's a passenger ferry from Pierowall on Westray three to six times a day, and the car ferry from Kirkwall to Westray continues to Papa Westray on Tuesdays and Fridays (two hours and 15 minutes).

But there are other reasons to visit this little island, one of the most remote of the Orkney group. Papay is home to Europe's oldest house, the **Knap of Howar** ① *open at all times, free*, which was built around 5500 years ago and is still standing (they knew how to build 'em in those days). It's on the west coast, just south of the airport. Half a mile north is **St Boniface Kirk**, one of the oldest Christian sites in the north of Scotland, founded in the eighth century, though most of the recently restored building dates from the 12th century. Inland from the Knap of Howar is **Holland Farm**, former home of the lairds of the island, where you can rummage around the farm buildings and museum.

Papay is famous for its birds, and **North Hill**, on the north of the island, is an important RSPB Reserve. The cliffs are home to many thousands of breeding seabirds, and at **Fowl Craig** on the east coast you can see nesting puffins. The interior is home to the largest arctic tern colony in Europe, as well as many arctic skuas. If you wish to explore you have to contact the warden at **Rose Cottage** ① *T01857-644240*, who runs regular guided walks.

It's worth taking a boat trip to the even tinier, deserted **Holm of Papay**, off the east coast. This is the site of several Neolithic burial cairns, including one of the largest chambered cairns on Orkney. You enter the tomb down a ladder into the main chamber which is nearly 70 ft long, with a dozen side-cells. For boat trips between May and September T0776 4569790.

North Ronaldsay → For listings, see pages 403-411. See map, page 384.

Remote and storm-battered, North Ronaldsay is the most northerly of the Orkney islands and a place where old Orcadian traditions remain. It seems remarkable that anyone should live here at all in these extreme conditions, but 'North Ron' – as it is known locally – has been inhabited for many centuries and continues to be heavily farmed. The island's sheep are a hardy lot and live exclusively off the seaweed on a narrow strip of beach, outside a 13-mile stone dyke which surrounds the island. This gives their meat a unique, 'gamey' flavour.

This small, flat island, only three miles long, has few real attractions, except to keen ornithologists who flock here to catch a glimpse of its rare migrants. From late March to early June, and mid-August to early November there are huge numbers of migratory birds. The **Bird Observatory**, in the southwest corner of the island by the ferry pier, gives information on which species have been sighted, as well as providing accommodation. There are also colonies of grey seals and cormorants at **Seal Skerry**, on the northeast tip of the island. There are Loganair flights from Kirkwall, twice daily from Monday to Saturday and there's a car and passenger ferry which sails from Kirkwall twice a week (usually Tuesday and Friday). Contact Orkney Ferries for details.

Orkney listings

For Sleeping and Eating price codes and other relevant information, see Essentials pages 38-45.

Sleeping

Kirkwall *p386, map p387*

There are plenty of good value B&Bs, though don't always expect en suite.

B Ayre Hotel, Ayre Rd, T01856-873001, www.ayrehotel.co.uk. Open all year. 33 en suite rooms. Kirkwall's most upmarket hotel sits right on the harbour front. Very comfortable with a good restaurant and a bar.

B-C Orkney Hotel,40 Victoria St, T01856-873477. Whilst investing in an upgrade of its comfortable 30 bedrooms, some with jacuzzi baths and 4-poster beds, the hotel has retained the charm and period features of a dwelling that dates back to 1670. Its **Victoria Restaurant** is also pleasant and good value.

B Foveran Hotel, 2 miles from town on the A964 Orphir road at St Ola, T01856-872389, www.foveranhotel.co.uk. Open all year. 8 en suite rooms. Modern, chalet-style hotel overlooking Scapa Flow. Friendly and comfortable, it's renowned for its food (♥♥♥-♥♥), including scallops, beef and lamb. Food critics have praised the Foveran fudge and cheesecake. Definitely worth a bite.

B-C Kirkwall Hotel, Harbour St, T01856-872232, www.kirkwallhotel.com. Open all year. 37 en suite rooms. Large, imposing building overlooking the harbour. Rooms are reasonably comfortable, service is friendly and efficient, and the restaurant serves good food.

A-B Albert Hotel, Mounthoolie Lane, T01856-87600, www.alberthotel.co.uk. This old Kirkwall hotel has been revamped mixing modern (stylish rooms) with traditional (the cosy Bothy Bar).

B West End Hotel, Main St, T01856-872368, www.westendkirkwall.co.uk. The former house of an old sea captain, this is just along from the cathedral. Has a great restaurant and nicely done rooms.

D Lav'rockha, Inganess Rd, T01856-876103, www.lavrockha.co.uk. 5 rooms. Superior B&B in modern bungalow. Breakfasts are superb and they also provide a 3-course dinner (♥♥). Great value. Recommended.

F Kirkwall Youth Hostel, Old Scapa Rd, T01856-872243, www.syha.co.uk. Mar-Oct. Large SYHA youth hostel (60 beds) about 15 mins' walk from the town centre.

F Peedie Hostel, Ayre Rd, T01856-875477, kirkwallpeediehostel@talk21.com. A smaller and more intimate alternative to the SYHA hostel. 11 beds and on the waterfront.

Camping

Pickaquoy Caravan & Camping Site, on the western outskirts of Kirkwall, off the A965, T01856-879900. Open Apr-Sep. £10.50 for a pitch.

Stromness and West Mainland *p389*

B Merkister Hotel, on the shores of Loch Harray, Stenness, T01856-771366, www.merkister.com. 16 rooms, including 3 new terraced garden suites. A favourite with anglers, but also handy for archaeological sites, this place has a great location, an excellent restaurant (♥♥♥-♥♥) and a popular bar. Deals out of season. One of the best in Orkney. Recommended.

B Stromness Hotel, Pier Head, Stromness, T01856-850298, www.stromnesshotel.com. Open all year. 42 en suite rooms. The best hotel in town is this imposing old building overlooking the harbour. Good-value meals.

B-C Woodwick House, Evie, T01856-751330, www.woodwickhouse.co.uk. 8 rooms. Lovely, old country house in beautiful surroundings. Perfect peace, walks through woods and views across to the islands. Very good food (3-course dinner ♥♥♥). Recommended.

C Barony Hotel, Marwick Head, Birsay, T01856-721327, www.baronyhotel.com.

May-Sep. 10 rooms. On the north shore of Boardhouse Loch, this small hotel specializes in fishing holidays and is about the only place offering food around here. Central to main bird life sanctuaries and archaeological sites.

C-D Mill of Eyreland, Stenness, 3 miles from Stromness, T01856-850136, www.millofeyreland.co.uk. 3 rooms in a lovely converted mill with maintained workings.

D Orca Hotel, Victoria St, near the harbour, Stromness, T01856-850447, www.orcahotel.com. Open all year. 7 en suite rooms. Clean and tidy rooms in this small hotel. Good self-catering deals available Nov-Mar. **F** for room only. Also has a cellar bistro, Bistro 76, serving good food.

D-E Primrose Cottage, Marwick Head, Birsay, T01856-721384. 2 en suite rooms. Comfortable B&B overlooking Marwick Bay. Evening meal and vegetarian options available.

D Mrs Sinclair, 45 John St, T01856-850949. Close to the ferry, this 2-bedroom B&B serves fortifying breakfasts and will do packed lunches (with home baking).

F Brown's Hostel, 45 Victoria St, Stromness, T01856-850661, www.brownshostel.co.uk. 14 beds. This popular independent hostel has no curfew and is open all year round.

E Hamnavoe Hostel, 10a North End Rd, Stromness, T01856-851202, www.hamnavoehostel.co.uk. 12 beds. Private, family, twin and single rooms. Recommended.

C Netherstove, Sandwick, T01856-841625, www.netherstove.com. May-Oct. 2 rooms. Neat B&B near Skara Brae, overlooking the Bay of Skaill, run by the delightfully named Mrs Poke. Also has 2 self-catering chalets and a cottage (available all year).

Camping

Eviedale Centre, beside the junction of the road to Dounby, T01856-751254/751270, www.eviedale-orkney.co.uk. Apr-Oct. Has accommodation in a former workshop, barn and stable (**F**) from £275 per week)) and a campsite.

Ness Point, 1 mile south of the ferry terminal, T01856-873535. May to mid-Sep. A well-equipped campsite with incomparable views, but is very exposed.

East Mainland and South Ronaldsay *p393*

There's a good selection of accommodation in St Margaret's Hope.

C Creel Restaurant & Rooms, Front Rd, St Margaret's Hope, T01856-831311, www.thecreel.co.uk. 3 en suite rooms. Offers comfortable rooms and delicious food drawn primarily from the day's catch. (ŦŦŦ-ŦŦ, dinner only). Good choice.

B-C Eastward Guest House, St Margaret's Hope, T01856-831551, www.eastwardhouse.com. The accommodation in this converted kirk is smart but it's the food made by owner Keiko that's the draw. Her Japanese buffet makes the most of Orkney's seafood (from £18-40). Recommended.

D-E St Margaret's Cottage B&B, South Ronaldsay, T01856-831637, www.stmargaretscottage.com. 3 rooms. Comfortable B&B offering early breakfast option for guests using the Pentland Ferries.

D-E Commodore Chalets, St Mary's, Holm, T01856-781319, www.commodorechalets.co.uk. This place looks like an army barracks but offers good-value accommodation in nine self-catering chalets and 6 overnight lodges. Good location, with views of Churchill Barriers and within walking distance of Italian Chapel. Breakfast provided.

F Wheems Bothy, Wheems, Eastside, a few miles southeast of St Margaret's Hope, T01856-831556, www.wheemsorganic.co.uk. Apr-Oct. Organic farm offering cheap and basic hostel accommodation for 8 (from £250 per week). Camping available.

Hoy *p396*

There's not much accommodation in the north of the island, except for the 2 SYHA hostels. There are a few very good B&Bs in the south.

D Stromabank Hotel, Longhope, T01856-701494, www.stromabank.co.uk. 4 rooms. Great views across to Orkney and the Scottish mainland. Also serves evening meals to residents and the public during the summer months (phone to book). Meals served Sat-Sun only in winter.
E Quoydale, one mile from ferry, T01856-791315, www.orkneyaccommodation.co.uk. 2 rooms. B&B on working farm. Taxis, tours and evening meals available.
F Hoy Centre, about 1 mile from Moaness Pier, T01856-876327, 873535, www. hostels orkney.co.uk. May-Sep. Refurbished hostel sleeping 32 in 8 rooms. Family room also available and groups catered for. Book ahead.
F Rackwick Outdoor Centre, Rackwick Glen, north Hoy, T01856-873535 www. hostelsorkney.co.uk. Mid-Mar to mid-Sep. 8 beds, book ahead.

Rousay, Egilsay and Wyre *p397*
Accommodation is very limited on Rousay, and non-existent on Egilsay and Wyre.
D Taversoe Hotel, near Knowe of Yarso, about 2 miles west of the pier, T01857-821325, www.taversoehotel.co.uk. 3 rooms with lovely views over Eynhallow Sound. Offers excellent-value meals, the seafood is particularly recommended. Restaurant closed Mon to non-residents. Bar stocks local ales. Transport available to/from the pier.
F Rousay Hostel, half a mile from the ferry, Trumland Organic Farm, T01856-821252, trumland@btopenworld.com. Open all year. Accommodation for 13. Laundry facilities and camping available. Bikes for hire.

Shapinsay *p399*
A Balfour Castle, T01857-711282, www. balfourcastle.com. Live the life of a would-be aristo in this impressive baronial Victorian mansion, set in 70 acres of wooded grounds and still part-family home. The castle has a private chapel and a boat is available for birdwatching and fishing trips for residents. This exclusive retreat does not come cheap:

prices start at £2,700 per day all inclusive for 6 guests.
D Hilton Farm House, T01857-711239, www.hiltonorkneyfarmhouse.co.uk. 3 rooms. Very comfortable B&B, which offers evening meals as well as transport and fishing tours.

Eday *p399*
B-C Sui Generis, Redbanks, 2 mins' walk from ferry, T01857-622219, www. suigenerisfurniture.co.uk. Beautiful guesthouse/furniture maker. The 2 en suite rooms are truly imaginative and unlike anything else in this part of the world. 3-course dinner, £15. Recommended.
E Blett, Carrick Bay, opposite the Calf of Eday, T01857-622248. 2 rooms. Very friendly. Evening meal and packed lunch provided if you wish. Mrs Poppelwell also has a self-catering cottage for up to three nearby.
F Youth Hostel, London Bay, T01857-622206. Open all year. Run by Eday Community Enterprises, just north of the airport. Basic lodging but recently refurbished.

Sanday *p400*
C Kettletoft Hotel, Kettletoft, T/F01857-600217, www.kettletofthotel.com. Most rooms are en suite and are clean, though simply furnished. Serves meals using local produce and has a lively bar. Fish and chip takeaways available on Wed and Sat.
D-E Backaskaill B&B, Backaskaill, T01857-600298, www.backaskaill.co.uk. Open all year. B&B housed in a Victorian property with a cosy woodburning stove in the lounge. Self-catering evening meals on request.
C The Belsair, Kettletoft, T01857-600206 www.belsairsanday.co.uk . 3 rooms. Large house overlooking the old harbour. Meals served in the bar and dining room, packed lunches available on request.
F Ayre's Rock Hostel, Ayre, T01857-600410, www.ayres-rock-sanday-orkney.co.uk. Good facilities but only 7 beds. Also a campsite (£7 per pitch) and a chip shop takeaway service available on Tue and Sat evenings.

Stronsay *p400*

C-D Stronsay Hotel, near the ferry terminal, T01857-616213, www.stronsayhotelorkney. co.uk. Offers 3 doubles and 1 family room, all en suite. Cheap bar food available. Operates as the islands' hotel, restaurant and pub.
C Stronsay Bird Reserve, Mill Bay, south of Whitehall, T01857-616363. B&B and full-board options available or you can camp overlooking the wide sandy bay.
F Stronsay Fish Mart Hostel, next to ferry terminal, T01857-616386. Open all year. Well-equipped and comfortable and only mins walk from the ferry, see page 400. 3 bedrooms with bunk beds to sleep 10. Their café does cheap meals.

Camping

Torness Camping Barn, at the southern end of the island, on the shore of Holland Bay near Leashun Loch, T01857-616314. Very basic and very cheap camping facilities. They also organize nature walks to the nearby seal-hide. Phone for pick-up from the ferry.

Westray *p401*

B Cleaton House Hotel, 2 miles southeast of Pierowall, T01857-677442, www.cleaton house.co.uk. 7 rooms. This converted Victorian manse is the best place to stay. Also serves excellent evening meals (3 courses for £30 per person) (♥♥♥♥).
C Pierowall Hotel, Pierowall, T01857-677472, www.pierowallhotel.co.uk. 4 en suite rooms. Less stylish than Cleaton House Hotel, but comfortable and friendly. Also serves good-value bar meals, try their fish and chips.
D No 1 Broughton, Pierowall, T01857-677726, www.no1broughton.co.uk. Newly renovated house overlooking the bay, with 3 nicely furnished rooms. Packed lunch and light supper on request.
E The Barn, Chalmersquoy, T01857-677214, www.thebarnwestray.co.uk. Sleeps 13 in 5 rooms. High-quality hostel accommodation with great views.
F (now self catering) **Bis Geos**, T01857-677420, 677238, www.bisgeos.co.uk.

3 well-equipped self-catering cottages with great views. Minibus available from the pier. From £250 per week.

Papa Westray *p401*

E Beltane House Guest House, T01857-644321. A row of converted farm workers' cottages to the east of Holland House. It offers dinner (♥♥ (£14 per person)). Run by the island community co-operative.
D School Place, T01857-644268. Homely B&B with lunch and evening meals available.
F Papa Westray Hostel, T01857-644267, www.syha.org.uk. Open all year. In the same complex at **Beltane**. A 12-bed hostel run by the island community co-operative which also runs a shop and restaurant serving lunch and evening meals. They have a minibus which takes ferry passengers from the pier to anywhere on the island.

North Ronaldsay *p402*

C full board **Brigg & Garso House**, about 3 miles from the ferry pier, T01857-633244, muir886@btinternet.com Full-board B&B at Garso House. They also have a self-catering cottage – Brigg - (up to 5 people) and can arrange car hire, taxis or minibus tours.
D Observatory Guest House, T01857-633200, www.nrbo.co.uk. Offers wind- and solarpowered accommodation that's popular with birdwatchers and serves a great-value hearty dinner (£12). It also has a small hostel next door (£13 per bunk or £18 per person B&B)

♥ Eating

Eating options are very limited but most B&Bs and guesthouses will provide evening meals.

Kirkwall *p386, map p387*

♥♥♥-♥♥ **Lynnfield Hotel**, Holm Rd, T01856-872505, www.lynnfieldhotel.com. Next to the Highland Park distillery, this hotel is renowned for its food, including bere bunno' (Orcadian bannocks) and cooked-to-perfection lobster and scallops (6 courses for £48 per person).

¶ **Foveran Hotel**, see Sleeping, above. Just out of town but the food is worth the trip. Friendly service but not the quickest.

¶¶-¶ **Albert Hotel**, Mounthoolie Lane, T01856-876000, www.alberthotel.co.uk. Serves decent bar meals made with home-grown produce. Variety of dining options available, from fine dining to traditional 'bothy' bar which is a favourite with locals and visitors.

Stromness and West Mainland *p389*
¶¶¶-¶¶ **Hamnavoe Restaurant**, 35 Graham Pl, Stromness, T01856-850606. Apr-Oct Tue-Sun from 1900, Fri-Sat Nov-Mar 1200-1400, Sat-Sun from 1900. The best place to eat in town. It specializes in local seafood but also offers good vegetarian dishes.

¶¶ **Julia's Café and Bistro**, opposite the ferry terminal, Stromness, T01856-850904. Mon-Sat 0900-1700, Sun 1000-1700. Open some evenings in summer. Very good home-cooked food and huge cakes right on the harbour.

¶¶ **Stromness Hotel**, see Sleeping, above. Good bar meals and the hotel also has an à la carte restaurant. Children welcome.

¶ **Ferry Inn**, near the ferry terminal, John St, T01856-850280, www.ferryinn.com. Decent bar food and lively bar. Children welcome.

East Mainland and South Ronaldsay *p393*
¶¶¶ **Creel Restaurant & Rooms**, see Sleeping, above. Superb food using deliciously fresh, locally grown ingredients. Dinner only. Best on the islands by some way.

¶ **Murray Arms Hotel**, Back Rd, St Margaret's Hope, T01856-831205, www.murrayarms hotel.com. Not exactly haute cuisine but good-value bar meals served until 2100.

Hoy *p396*
¶¶-¶ **Stromabank Hotel**, Longhope, South Walls, T01856-701494, www.stromabank. co.uk. A bar and restaurant which serves local produce, including beef and lamb. Open to non-residents but book May-Sep.

¶ **Beneth'hill Café**, 5 mins' walk from the Moaness ferry. Evening meals and early breakfasts served.

Rousay, Egilsay and Wyre *p397*
¶¶-¶ **Pier Restaurant**, Rousay, beside the pier, T01856- 821359. Serves food at lunchtime (they stop serving at 1400) and evenings (last orders 1900) closed Wed and Sun. Standard or gourmet picnics can be ordered.

North Ronaldsay *p402*
¶-¶ **Burrian Inn and Restaurant**, T01857-633221. Orkney's most northerly pub, also serves food.

♪ Bars and clubs

Kirkwall *p386, map p387*
Nightlife revolves around its lively pubs. Check in *The Orcadian* for folk nights, etc.
Ayre Hotel, see Sleeping, above. Quiet and relaxed but also stages folk music nights.
Bothy Bar, Albert Hotel, Mounthoolie Lane, T01856-876000, www.alberthotel.co.uk. A good place for a drink, and sometimes has live folk music.

Stromness and West Mainland *p389*
The best places for a drink in Stromness are the **Stromness Hotel**, see Sleeping, above; the **Ferry Inn**, 10 John St, T01865-850280; and the bar of the **Royal Hotel**, Victoria St, T01856-850342.

● Entertainment

For details of what's going on, buy *The Orcadian*, www.orcadian.co.uk, which comes out on Thu, or pick up a free copy of the Tourist Board's guide.

Kirkwall *p386, map p387*
The town's **New Phoenix cinema** is in the Pickaquoy Leisure Centre, Pickaquoy Rd, T01856-879900, www.pickaquoy.com. Also has sports and fitness facilities, a café and bar.

✪ Festivals and events

Orkney *p382*
There are numerous events which take place throughout the year.

May Orkney Folk Festival, www.orkney folkfestival.com. An excellent event, which takes place for 3 days at the end of May at various locations throughout the islands. It is always well attended and can be rather boisterous.

Jun St Magnus Festival, www.stmagnus festival.com. This high-brow event is one of the UK's most prestigious and popular festivals. Held in Kirkwall, it consists of six days of music, drama, literature and the visual arts, with many internationally renowned performers.

Jul Regattas, during this month there are several regattas held on most of the islands. Visit the TIC or read The Orcadian for more information.

Aug Festival of the Horse and Boys' Ploughing Match, South Ronaldsay, www.orkneyjar.com. There are numerous agricultural shows in Aug which culminate in this festival, see page 395.

Sep Orkney International Science Festival, T01343-540844, www.oisf.or. 1st week in Sep. Offers visitors the chance to participate in a range of talks and exhibitions about astronomy, zoology and even renewable energy. The week also includes a ceilidh and concerts.

Dec The Ba' (ball), in Kirkwall, www.ba game.com. Amongst the best-known annual events. It takes place on Christmas Eve and New Year's Eve and is a bit like rugby, basketball and a full-scale riot all rolled into one, and is contested between 2 sides – the Uppies and the Doonies – representing different districts of the town. As many as 200 'players' may be involved, and a game can last up to 7 hrs as both sides attempt to jostle the ball along the streets until one reaches their 'goal' to win the prized ba'.

✪ Shopping

Kirkwall *p386, map p387*
The Odin Stone, 14 Junction Rd, T01856-877785. You can browse and buy the work of over 50 local crafts-folk at this delightful store that includes a replica of dresser of Skara Brae!

Orkney Handcrafted Furniture, Dellovo, New Scapa Rd, T01856-872998. Authentic and award winning range of traditional Orkney chairs.

Ortak, Hatston, T01856-872224, www.ortak. co.uk Popular jewellery with designs are influenced by Viking, runic carvings.

Stromness and West Mainland *p389*
Stromness Books and Prints, 1 Graham Pl, Stromness, T01856-850565. A wee gem. No '3 for 2' offers, no sofas, no internet, no skinny lattes with cinnamon, just books – ones that you might want to read – and an owner who knows what he's talking about. A real bookshop for real people.

✪ Activities and tours

Nor'West Tours/Go-Orkney, in Inverness, T01463-717181, www.go-orkney.com, run a series of tours of Orkney.

Kirkwall *p386, map p387*
Tour operators
Discover Orkney Tours, 44 Clay Loan, T/F01856-872865, www.discoverorkney. com. Offers tours of Mainland as well as trips to Westray and Papa Westray. Run day tours which can be tailored to suit requirements.
Orkney Ferries, Shore St, T01856-622260, T01865-622248, www.orkneyferries.co.uk. Run the Eday Heritage Tour, mid-Jun to mid-Sep every Sun. Leaves Kirkwall at 0920, returns at 1955 and costs around £32 per person, which includes ferries, guided walks or mini- bus tour, entry to Carrick House and lunch.

To dive for

Orkney offers some of the best scuba-diving in the world, thanks to the part played by Scapa Flow in both world wars, see box, page 395. The wreckage on the sea bed, combined with the wildlife that teems around it – sea anemones, seals, whales and porpoises – make for great diving. Visibility is sharp and the water is not as cold as you expect, thanks to the Gulf Stream. Several companies offer diving courses for beginners and wreck diving for more experienced divers. This can be as a dive package, including accommodation, meals and boat charter, or simply as a boat charter. Most companies are based in Stromness, see below. For a list of dive operators, check out www.subaqua.co.uk.

Stromness and West Mainland *p389*
Diving
The Diving Cellar, 4 Victoria St, Stromness, T01856-850055, www.divescapaflow.co.uk. Dive charter operating in Scapa Flow. Package including accommodation and minibus.
Scapa Flow Diving Holidays, Lerquoy, Outertown, Stromness, T01856-851110, www.scapa-flow.co.uk. Offers liveaboard packages or day trips on the *MV Invincible*.
Scapa Scuba, Lifeboat House, Stromness, T01856-851218, www.scapascuba.co.uk. Guided dives from £138. Range of PADI courses available.

Tour operators
Dawn Star Boat Trips, St Ola T01856-876743 www.orkneyboattrips.co.uk Departing at the pier at St Mary's, Holm, these tours take you all round Scapa Flow with an emphasis on both history and wildlife. The boat hold 6 passengers so prices depend on how many are in your party (for a 2-3 hr trip £110).
Wildabout Orkney, 5 Clouston Corner, Stenness, T01856-851011, www.wildabout orkney.com. Offers highly rated wildlife, historical, folklore and environmental tours of Mainland for £35-52 per person for a full day (child and concession reductions).

Rousay, Egilsay and Wyre *p397*
Tour operators
Rousay Traveller, T01856-821234. Run very informative minibus tours from Jun to early Sep Tue-Fri, meeting the 1040 ferry from Tingwall, they last 6 hrs and cost £17, children £6.

Shapinsay *p399*
Tour operators
Orkney Island Holidays, Furrowend, T01856-711373, www.ornkneyislandholidays.com. Paul and Louise Hollinrake have 20 years' experience running week-long all-inclusive tours of the island from their home base, with different holidays exploring the wildlife, archaeology, flora and fauna, history, crafts and local way of life on the islands.

Eday *p399*
Tour operators
Orkney Ferries, Kirkwall, T01856-622260, T01865-622248, www.orkneyferries.co.uk. Run the Eday Heritage Tour, book with Orkney Ferries or at the tourist office in Kirkwall.

Sanday *p400*
Tour operators
Roderick Thorne, Sanday Ranger, T01857-600341, ranger@sanday.co.uk. Guided walks and tours of the island.

Westray *p401*
Discover Orkney in Kirkwall. Runs day tours to Westray from Kirkwall.

Tour operators
M&J Harcus, Pierowall. T01857-677212. Bus tours and car hire.

☉ Transport

Kirkwall *p386, map p387*
Air Loganair, T01856-872494, www.
loganair.co.uk, flies an 8-seater aircraft
from Kirkwall Mon-Sat to **Stronsay,
Sanday, North Ronaldsay, Westray**
and **Papa Westray**, and on Wed to **Eday**.
To Papa Westray and North Ronaldsay
costs £17 one way, and to the other
islands listed £35 one way.
Bus There's a limited bus service around
the Mainland, the timetables of which can
be found at the TIC or on the transport
pages of www.orkney.gov.uk . Stagecoach,
T01856-870535, runs buses Mon-Sat from
Kirkwall bus station to **Stromness**,
30 mins. It also runs 3-5 buses a day,
Mon-Sat, to **Houton**, 35 mins, which
connect with ferries to **Hoy**; and a daily
bus, Mon-Sat, to **East Holm**, 25 mins, and
Stromness via **Dounby**, 45 mins. There are
buses daily to **St Margaret's Hope**, 30 mins
and there are also buses to **Tingwall** and
Evie. Note that there is a very restricted Sun
bus service on Orkney.
Car hire Orkney Car Hire, Junction Rd,
T01856-872666; WR Tullock, Castle St, T01856-
876262, and Kirkwall airport, T01856-875500.
Cycle hire Cycle Orkney, Tankerness Lane,
T/F01856-875777 www.cycleorkney.com.
Mountain bikes from £10 per day.
Ferry Northlink Ferries, T0845-6000449,
www.northlinkferries.co.uk, sails from
Kirkwall to **Aberdeen**, Mon, Wed and Fri,
2345, 6 hrs. A single passenger fare costs
£27.30 (peak season, Jul-Aug). A car costs
£97. They also sail from Kirkwall to **Lerwick**
(Shetland) on Tue, Thu, Sat and Sun, 2345,
7 hrs 45 mins. A passenger fare costs £21.60
single. A car costs £89.40 (in peak season).
Return fares are double the cost of single
fares and children under 16 travel for 50%
less. Cars should be booked in advance and
all passengers must check in at least
30 mins before departure. 2-berth cabins
are available on all journeys, up to £121.20
per cabin per journey in peak season.

John o'Groats Ferries, T01955-611353,
www.jogferry.co.uk, operates a passenger-
only (and bicycles) ferry service from
Burwick to **John o'Groats**. There are bus
connections between Kirkwall and **Burwick**,
45 mins, for all ferry sailings. It also operate
the Orkney Bus, a daily direct bus/ferry/bus
service between Kirkwall and **Inverness**, via
John o'Groats.

Stromness and West Mainland *p389*
Bus There are several buses Mon-Sat
between Stromness and **Kirkwall**, 30 mins.
Car hire Brass's Car Hire, Blue Star Garage,
North End Rd, Stromness, T01856-850850
www.stromnesscarhire.co.uk.
Cycle hire Orkney Cycle Hire,
54 Dundas St, Stromness, T01856-
850255, www.orkneycyclehire.co.uk.
Ferry Northlink Ferries from Stromness
to **Scrabster**, 1½ hrs. Passenger fare is £17
in peak season and a car costs £51. A bus
links Stromness with **Kirkwall**, via Hatston
Ferry Terminal.

East Mainland and South Ronaldsay
p393
Ferry John o'Groats Ferries, T01955-
611353, www.jogferry.co.uk, operates a
passenger-only (and bicycles) ferry service
from **Burwick** to **John o'Groats**.

Hoy *p396*
Ferry A passenger ferry sails between
Moaness Pier and **Stromness**, daily,
30 mins. There's a reduced winter service
(mid-Sep to mid-May).

Rousay, Egilsay and Wyre *p397*
Bus A bus connects **Tingwall** and **Kirkwall**.
Ferry A small car ferry operated by Orkney
Ferries sails from **Rousay** to **Tingwall**, daily,
20 mins.

Shapinsay *p399*
Ferry Small car ferry makes up to 6
sailings daily (including Sun in summer)
to Kirkwall (25 mins).

Eday p399

Air There are flights from **Eday** to **Kirkwall** with **Loganair**, T01856-872494, Wed only.

Cycle hire Mr Burkett, at Hamarr, near the post office south of Mill Loch.

Ferry Orkney Ferries sail to **Kirkwall** (1 hr 15 mins to 2 hrs) twice daily.

Taxi Mr A Stewart by the pier, T01857-622206.

Sanday p400

Air There are Loganair flights to **Kirkwall** twice daily Mon-Fri and once on Sat.

Ferry There's a ferry service twice daily to **Kirkwall**, 1½ hrs.

Stronsay p400

Air There are Loganair flights to **Kirkwall** from **Stronsay**, twice daily Mon-Fri.

Car hire and taxis DS Peace, Samson's Lane, T01857-616335.

Ferry A ferry service runs to **Kirkwall** daily, 1½ hrs, and once daily Mon-Sat to **Eday**, 35 mins.

Westray p401

Air Flights to Kirkwall depart twice daily Mon-Sat, **Loganair**.

Cycle hire Alena, the proprietor of Bis Geos hostel on Westray, see Sleeping above, will hire out bikes for £5 per day. **Barn Hostel**, see Sleeping, above, is another high quality hostel that can arrange bike hire.

Ferry There's a car ferry service to **Kirkwall** from **Rapness**, 1½ hrs. It sails twice daily in summer (mid-May to mid-Sep) and once daily in winter. There's also a passenger ferry from **Pierowall** to **Papa Westray**.

Taxi Kenneth Harcus, T01857-677758.

Papa Westray p401

Air The 2-min flight to **Westray** leaves twice daily Mon-Sat, £16, one way. There is also a direct flight to **Kirkwall**, daily Mon-Sat, £17, one way.

Ferry There's a passenger ferry to **Pierowall** on Westray, 3-6 times daily, 25 mins.

North Ronaldsay p402

Air There are Loganair flights to **Kirkwall** twice daily Mon-Sat.

Ferry There's a car and passenger ferry which sails to **Kirkwall** twice a week (usually Tue and Fri), 2 hrs 40 mins.

❶ Directory

Kirkwall p386, map p387

Banks Branches of the 3 main Scottish banks with ATMs are on Broad St and Albert St. Exchange also at the tourist office.

Laundry The Launderama, Albert St, T01856-872982. Mon-Fri 0830-1730, Sat 0900-1700. **Medical services** Balfour Hospital, Health Centre and Dental Clinic, New Scapa Rd, T01856-885400.

Post Junction Rd, Mon-Fri 0900-1700, Sat 0930-1230.

Stromness and West Mainland p389

Banks There are branches of Bank of Scotland and Royal Bank of Scotland, both with ATMs, on Victoria St, Stromness.

Laundry Next to the coffee shop, Stromness, T01856-850904, self-service or service washes.

Shetland

Shetland is so far removed from the rest of Scotland it can only be shown as an inset on maps. It is closer to the Arctic Circle than it is to London, and it's easier and quicker to get there from Norway than it is from the UK's capital. This seems entirely appropriate, for Shetland is historically and culturally closer to Scandinavia than Britain. Indeed, whilst the Scottish debate on independence waxes and wanes, so too do some Shetlanders argue that the Islands should go it alone. Many of its place names are of Norse origin, and people here still celebrate the vikings in the annual Up-Helly-Aa festivals. Modern-day visitors tend to come by plane rather than longboat, and usually bring binoculars, for Shetland is a birdwatcher's paradise. It is home to countless species, many of them seeking refuge from the madding crowds. And there's no better place than here to get away from it all. Moreover, due to its latitude, in high summer there's daylight for more than 20 hours of day so if you want to pack as much as possible into your visit this is the place where you can enjoy a coastal walk or round of golf at midnight. ➤ *For listings, see pages 425-432.*

Ins and outs

Getting there

Getting to Shetland by air can be expensive. Though there are seats available online from around £39, expect to pay from £100 one way from Aberdeen and over £200 return. Shetland has good air connections with the rest of the UK and there are regular flights from several mainland airports which are operated by Flybe/Loganair (see page 382). For details see **Flybe** ① *T0871-700 2000, www.flybe.com* or call **Loganair** ① *T01595-840246, www.loganair.co.uk*, in Lerwick. There are direct daily flights from Aberdeen, which has frequent services to all other major British airports and there are also direct flights from Glasgow (daily), Edinburgh (Monday to Saturday), Inverness (Monday to Friday), Orkney (Monday to Saturday) and Belfast (Sunday to Friday). There are also regular international flights from Bergen (Norway) to Sumburgh and Kirkwall. Shetland's main **airport** ① *T01950-460654*, is at Sumburgh, 25 miles south of Lerwick and there are regular daily buses (No 6) from **Sumburgh airport** to Lerwick, which connect with flights. These buses also stop at several main sights, including Jarlshof and Sandwick (for Mousa Broch).

Ferry links with the UK are provided mostly by **Northlink Ferries** ① *T0845-600 0449, www.northlinkferries.co.uk*. It operates daily car ferry sailings to Lerwick from Aberdeen (and to Kirkwall, Orkney), the journey takes 12 hours (14 hours if it goes via Kirkwall). There are also ferries from Norway, Iceland and the Faroe Isles, see page 33. ➤ *For further information, see Transport, page 431.*

Getting around

There is a regular scheduled inter-island service with **Directflight** ① *T01595-840246, www.directflight.co.uk*, from Tingwall airport near Lerwick to Foula, Fair Isle, Papa Stour and Out Skerries. Bus No 4 runs to Scalloway (Monday to Saturday) and there are also buses (Monday to Saturday) to Walls (No 9), Sandness, Aith (No 9 and 12), North Roe (No 21), Hillswick (No 21), Vidlin (No19), Toft (No 23) and Mossbank (No 23). Buses leave from the **Viking bus station** ① *Commercial Rd, T01595-694100, Mon-Sat 0900-1715*, in Lerwick to destinations all over the Mainland.

Frequent ferry services also link many of the islands with the Shetland mainland. These services are operated by **Shetland Islands Council** ① *T01595-693535, www.shetland.gov*.

Shetland

Muckle Flugga
Hermaness
Reserve
Saxa Vord
Burraforth
Haroldswick
Skaw
Norwick

Unst
Baltasound

Gloup
Cullivoe
Gutcher
Sellafirth
Westing
Uyeasound
Belmont
Muness
Haaf Gruney

*The
Herra*
Mid Yell
West
Sandwick
Otterswick
Aywick
Gossabrough
Ulsta
Hamnavoe
Burravoe

Yell

Hascosay

Fetlar
Oddsta
Tresta
Houbie
Funzie

Fethaland
Isbister
North Voe

Ronies Hill
(1477ft)
Northmavine

Hamnavoe
Heylor
Urafirth
Ollaberry

Esha Ness
Stenness
Hillswick
*The
Drongs*
Sullom Voe
Oil Terminal
Toft
Firth
Mossbank

Lunna
Lunning
Skaw
Brough

*Out
Skerries*
Housay

Mavis
Grind
Brae
Busta

Muckle Roe

Vidlin
Laxo

Isbister
Huxter
Symbister
Whalsay

Papa Stour
Hurdiback
Sandness
A971
West
Burrafirth
Clausta

East
Burrafirth
A970
North
Nesting
Laxfirth
Skellister

Brig o'Waas
Walls
Bixter
Aith
Weisdale
Tresta

South Nesting
Eswick
Gletness

*Wats
Ness*
Burrastow
Stanydale
Gruting
Garderhouse
Sand

Girlista
Whiteness
Tingwall
Gott
Dale
Heogan
Maryfield

Vaila
Culswick
Reawick
Skeld

Loch of
Tingwall
Scalloway
Lerwick
Noss

Bressay
*The
Ord*
Bard Head

Westerwick

Trondra
Gulberwick
Quarff

Hamnavoe
Burra
A970
Fladdabister
Ocraquoy

Cunningsburgh

Maywick
Channerwick
Bigton
St Ninian's Isle
Hoswick
Leebitton
Sandwick
Levenwick
Mousa
Broch

Scousburgh
Loch of Spiggie
Reserve
Fitful Head
Boddam
Southvoe
Quendale

Old Scatness
Sumburgh
Jarlshof
Sumburgh Head
Grutness

To Foula
To Norway
To Fair Isle
To Fair Isle, Kirkwall & Aberdeen

N

5 km
5 miles

uk. Fares vary according the route and booking in advance is essential. Times and fares can be found on the Shetland Council website or are available from the TIC in Lerwick. A *Shetland Transport Timetable*, published by the Shetland Council, contains details of all air, sea and bus services throughout the islands. It is available from the tourist office in Lerwick. Note that fares quoted in the transport section are for return trips. Shetland has around 500 miles of good roads, and an extensive public bus service links Lerwick with all towns, villages and tourist sights (there are several bus operators). The best way to explore the islands is with your own private car, but note that it is cheaper to hire a car in Lerwick rather than at the airport. Hitching is a feasible way to get around and is relatively safe, and cycling is a good way to experience the islands, though most places are very exposed and the winds can be relentless and punishing (Force 8 is considered pleasant is these parts).

➤➤ *For further details, see Transport page 431.*

Tourist information

The main tourist office is the Lerwick TIC ⓘ *Market Cross, Commercial St, T08701-999440, May-Sep Mon-Fri 0800-1800, Sat 0800-1600, Sun 1000-1300, Oct-Apr Mon-Fri 0900-1700*, which is an excellent source of information, books, maps and leaflets. They will also change foreign currency and book accommodation. It's also worth checking out the excellent www.visitshetland.com, with links to events, transport, accommodation and local operators.

Lerwick and around

→ *For listings, see pages 425-432. See map, page 413. Phone code 01595. Population 7600.*

Lerwick is the capital and administrative centre of Shetland and the only sizeable town, containing over 7000 of the islands' 22,000 strong population. Though the islands have been inhabited for many centuries, Lerwick only dates from the 17th century, when it began to grow as a trading port for Dutch herring fishermen, thanks to its superb natural sheltered harbour, the Bressay Sound. The town spread along the waterfront, where merchants built their lodberries, which were houses and warehouses with their own piers so that they could trade directly with visiting ships. By the late 19th century Lerwick had become the main herring port in northern Europe. Lerwick has continued to grow: the discovery of oil in the North Sea in the early 1970s led to the building of the Sullom Voe Oil Terminal, and the effect on the town has been dramatic. It is now the main transit point to the North Sea oil rigs and there have been major extensions to the harbour area, bringing increased shipping and prosperity to the town.

Ins and outs

Getting there and around Ferries from Aberdeen arrive at the main Holmsgarth terminal, about a mile north of the old harbour. There's a regular bus service between Lerwick and Sumburgh airport (50 minutes) run by **John Leask & Son** ⓘ *T01595-693162, www.leaskstravel.co.uk*. Taxis (around £25) and car hire are also available. All island bus services start and end at the Viking bus station, which is on Commercial Road, a short distance north of the town centre. The town, with about six pubs – including the Thule bar, frequented by hardy fishermen – is small and everything is within easy walking distance.

Lerwick

The town's heart is the attractive **Commercial Street**, which runs parallel to the Esplanade. At the southern end are many old houses and lodberries, and you can continue south along the cliffs to the **Knab** or to lovely **Bain's beach**. Lerwick Walks is a leaflet detailing many interesting walks in and around town.

Overlooking the north end of Commercial Street is **Fort Charlotte** ⓘ *Jun-Sep daily 0900-2200, Oct-May daily 0900-1600, free*, built in 1665 and later rebuilt in 1780 and named after Queen Charlotte, George III's consort. It has since been used as a prison and Royal Naval Reserve base and, though there's little to see in the fort, there are fine views of the harbour from the battlements. As an aside, if you're hungry, the Fort chip shop below the fort by the war memorial serves up cheap and tasty fish suppers. One of Lerwick's most impressive buildings is the Victorian **town hall** ⓘ *Mon-Fri 1000-1200, 1400-1530, free*, on Hillhead. The stained-glass windows of the main hall depict episodes from Shetland's history. Built on the historic site of Hay's Dock, is the fabulous and very recently reopened **Shetland Museum and Archives** ⓘ *T01595-695057, www.shetlandmuseumandarchives.org.uk, Mon-Sat 1000-1700, Sun 1200-1700, free*, which uses interactive technology to give an introduction to the islands' history. Amongst the artefacts on display are Viking runes, whale bones carved by

Lerwick

Sleeping		
Brentham House 1	Lerwick 5	Osla's Café Bar & Bistro 3
Clickimin Caravan &	Westhall B&B 6	Peerie Shop Café 4
Camp Site 2		
Glen Orchy House 3	**Eating** 🍴	**Bars & clubs** 🍸
Kveldsro House 4	Brasserie Restaurant 1	Lounge 5
	Monty's Bistro & Deli 2	

N

200 metres
200 yards

fishermen and all manner of things knitted in the Fair Isle style. Across the dock is Mareel, the new music and cinema venue that's due to open in early 2011.

Also in town, in the Galley Shed off St Sunniva Street, is the **Up-Helly-Aa Exhibition** ⓘ *www.uphellyaa.org, mid-May to mid-Sep Tue 1400-1600, 1700-1900, Fri 1700-1900, Sat 1400-1600, £3, concessions and children £1.* This gives a taste of the famous fire festivals, the biggest of which is held annually in Lerwick on the last Tuesday in January, when there's a torch-lit procession through the town with hundreds of people dressed in Viking costumes (*guizers*). The procession is followed by a replica Viking longship built especially for the event. At the end of the procession the ship is set ablaze when the guizers throw their flaming torches on to it.

A mile west of town are the substantial remains of **Clickimin Broch**, a fortified site occupied from 700 BC to around the fifth or sixth century AD. A path leads to the site from opposite the supermarket on the A970. About a mile north of the ferry terminal is the **Böd of Gremista Museum** ⓘ *T01595-695057, May to mid-Sep Tue-Sat 1000-1300, 1400-1700, free,* a restored 18th-century fishing *böd* (booth) which was the birthplace of Arthur Anderson (1791-1868), co-founder of the Peninsular and Oriental Steam Navigation Company, now P&O. One of the rooms features an exhibition on Anderson's life and involvement with P&O.

Bressay

Lying to the east of Lerwick across the Bressay Sound is the island of Bressay (pronounced 'bressah'), which creates a sheltered harbour for the capital and led to its establishment as a major trading port. Seven miles long by three miles wide, it makes an ideal day trip for cyclists. Another good way to get around is on foot, and there's a fine walk to the top of **Ward Hill** (742 ft), the highest point, from where you get great views of the island and as far afield as Foula and Out Skerries. There are also good coastal walks, particularly along the cliffs from Noss Sound south to **Bard Head**, **The Ord** and **Bressay Lighthouse**, where you can see large colonies of seabirds. For wildlife cruises to Bressay and Noss, see page 430.

Noss

Serious birdwatchers should head for Noss, a tiny, uninhabited island off the east coast of Bressay, which is a **National Nature Reserve** with over 100,000 pairs of breeding seabirds. A walk around the perimeter of the island takes at least three hours but is highly recommended. At the east side is the **Noup of Noss**, where the 600-ft cliffs are packed full of nesting gannets. The reserve is managed by Scottish Natural Heritage who have a small visitor centre at **Gungstie**.

Central Mainland → *For listings, see pages 403-411. See map, page 413. Phone code 01595.*

The Central Mainland is Shetland's slim waist, and only a few miles of land separates the east and west coast. There's not a huge amount of tourist interest here but the area's history is fascinating and the Scalloway Museum is certainly worth a visit.

Scalloway and around

Six miles from Lerwick on the west coast is Scalloway, once the capital of Shetland and now a fishing port and fish-processing centre. In 1942, during the Second World War, Scalloway became the headquarters of the **Shetland Bus** operations. This was the name given to the Norwegian fishing boats which sailed to Shetland during the night from German-occupied Norway, bringing refugees to safety and returning with ammunition and resistance fighters. An interesting and poignant exhibition on the Shetland Bus can be seen at **Scalloway Museum** ① *Main St, T01595-880608, May-Sep Mon-Sat 1000-1200, 1400-1630, free.*

The harbour is dominated by the ruins of **Scalloway Castle**(the key is available from the Shetland Woollen Company or on a Sunday, the Scalloway Hotel), built in 1600 by the notorious Earl Patrick Stewart using local slave labour (see box, page 388). After his execution the castle fell into disrepair, though the four-storey main block and one wing remain. Inside, an interpretative display explains its history.

South of Scalloway lie the islands of **Trondra** and **Burra**, now connected to the Mainland by bridges. At the south of the promontory at Houss, East Burra is the workshop of **Burra Bears** (call to arrange a visit T01595-859374, www.burrbears.co.uk), where you can buy teddy bears made from recycled Fair Isle jumpers. On the road back, over towards West Burra is the attractive little fishing village of **Hamnavoe**.

Tingwall
North of Scalloway, the B9074 runs through the fertile Tingwall Valley, past a nine-hole **golf course** at Asta, and the **Loch of Tingwall**, which is good for brown trout fishing and also home to swans and otters. At the northern end of the loch is a promontory called **Law Ting Holm**, which was the site of the Althing, or parliament, during the period of Norse rule. Overlooking the loch is **Tingwall Kirk**, built in the late 18th century on the site of the earlier church of St Magnus which dated back to the early period of Norse Christianity. In the graveyard is the old burial vault with several interesting old grave slabs. Nearby is **Tingwall Agricultural Museum** ① *T01595-840770, Jun-Aug Mon-Sat 1000-1300, 1400-1700, £2,* which houses a collection of old crofting implements.

Weisdale
The A971 continues northwest towards Weisdale, a district with some worthwhile attractions. At the head of **Weisdale Voe** the B9075 branches north to **Weisdale Mill** ① *T01595-830400, Tue-Sat 1030-1630, Sun 1200-1630, free (also café Tue-Sat 1100-1600, Sun 1200-1600),* which now houses the **Bonhoga Gallery**, a purpose-built art gallery featuring varied exhibitions of local, national and international works. There's also a nice café serving snacks. Weisdale Mill was part of the Kergord Estate, known until 1945 as Flemington, and was built from the stones of evacuated crofthouses. Over 300 crofters were forcibly evicted in the mid-19th century during the Clearances, when lairds expanded their more profitable sheep-farming activities. In 1940 the mill was requisitioned as the intelligence and administrative HQ for the **Shetland Bus** operations (see Scalloway, above). The Kergord estate today is the largest area of woodland in Shetland, and attracts migratory birds.

On the west shore of Weisdale Voe, south of the mill, are the ruins of the house where John Clunies Ross (1786-1854) was born. He settled in the Cocos Islands in the Indian Ocean in 1827 and the islands were owned by the Estate of the Clunies Ross family until purchased by the Australian government in 1978. In 1984 the islanders voted to become part of Australia.

The Westside

→ *For listings, see pages 403-411. See map, page 413. Phone code 01595. OS Landranger Nos 3 & 4.*
The western Mainland of Shetland, stretching west from Weisdale to Sandness, is known as The Westside. This part of Shetland is notable for its varied landscape of spectacular sea cliffs, rolling green hills, bleak moorland, peaty freshwater lochs and numerous long sea lochs, or voes. This is excellent walking country, with many fine coastal routes, especially

around **Culswick** and **Dale of Walls**. It is also great for birdwatching and trout fishing, and there are many opportunities for spotting whales, dolphins and otters.

Stanydale, Walls and Sandness

There are a few interesting archaeological sites here, too. At Stanydale, signposted from the road between the villages of **Bixter** and **Walls**, is the site of a Neolithic settlement with the remains of houses, field boundaries and clearance cairns. Near the **Brig o' Waas**, just north of Walls, is the **Scord of Brouster**, a prehistoric farm which has been excavated.

The pretty little village of **Walls** (pronounced *waas*) is set around a sheltered natural harbour and is a popular spot with visiting yachts. It also attracts many visitors during its Agricultural Show in August, the biggest such event on Shetland. Walls is the departure point for ferries to the remote island of Foula, see below.

Northwest of Walls, the A971 crosses bleak moorland before descending to the crofting township of **Sandness** (pronounced *saa-ness*), surrounded by fertile land and facing little Papa Stour, about a mile offshore. There's a good beach here and also a **woollen spinning mill** where you can watch how they spin the famously fine wool into yarn.

Foula

Lying 15 miles west of the Shetland Mainland, tiny Foula – whose name derives from the Norse *fugl ey*, meaning 'bird island' – is the second most remote inhabited island after Fair Isle. It supports a population of around 40 people, who are greatly outnumbered by the many thousands of seabirds, including a small colony of gannets and the rare Leach's petrel. There are also about 2500 pairs of great skuas, the largest colony in the UK. The island is dominated by its sheer cliffs, which reach their peak at **The Kame** (1220 ft), the second-highest sea cliffs in Britain after St Kilda.

An interesting feature of the island's people is that they still observe the old Julian calendar replaced in 1752 in Britain by the present Gregorian system which deleted 11 days from the year. Remote areas of the country kept to the old calendar, adding an extra day in 1800, which was a leap year, and some parts of Shetland continued to observe festivals 12 days after the dates in the new calendar. The most remote areas kept to the old calendar longest, and the people of Foula still celebrate Christmas on 6 January and New Year's Day on 13 January.

Papa Stour

A ferry sails from West Burrafirth on the Westside, near Sandness, to the little island of Papa Stour, only a mile offshore. The island, which has a population of around 30, is mostly made up of volcanic rock which has been eroded to form an amazing coastline of stacks, arches and caves, most spectacular of which is **Kirstan's Hole**. The island is home to large colonies of auks, terns and skuas, and also has an interesting history of its own. Pick up the island trails leaflet from the tourist office in Lerwick.

South Mainland → *For listings, see pages 403-411. See map, page 413. Phone code 01950.*

From Lerwick a long, narrow finger of land points south. The main road runs down the east coast for 25 miles till it ends at **Sumburgh Head**, near Shetland's main airport. This southern part of the Shetland Mainland holds the islands' two most important archaeological sights and main tourist attractions.

Isle of Mousa

ⓘ *Mousa Boat Trips, T01950-431367, www.mousaboattrips.co.uk, sail to the island from Leebitton harbour in Sandwick: Apr-Sep daily 1400 (Fri and Sun also at 1230), returning at 1700; Jun-Aug also daily at 1230, weather permitting. This allows two and a half hours to see the island and the trip takes 15 mins and costs £13, concessions £12, children £6.50. Entry to the broch is free.*

Fifteen miles south of Lerwick, the scattered crofting communities of Sandwick look across to the Isle of Mousa, site of the best-preserved broch in Scotland. This fortified tower was built around 2000 years ago and still stands close to its original height of 45 ft. It's a very impressive structure when you see it from the inside and has chambers, galleries, an internal staircase and a parapet. The broch features in a Viking saga of the 12th century when the mother of Harald, Earl of Orkney, took refuge there with her lover. The Earl, who did not approve of the liaison, laid siege to the broch, but it proved impregnable and he gave up.

Mousa island is also home to many seabirds and waders, most notably the storm petrel – or alamootie, as the locals call it – which is best seen at dusk as they return to their nests amongst the beach rocks. Mousa Boat Trips run late evening trips from late May to mid-July to see storm petrels swarm the broch: a sight, sound and indeed a vibration you will never forget. You can also see seals on the white sand beach at West Voe. If you have time, it's a good idea to walk right around the coast, starting from the landing stage at West Ham and first heading south to the broch. Watch out for dive-bombing bonxies (arctic terns).

South of Sandwick

Further south on the east coast, at Boddam, is the **Shetland Crofthouse Museum** ⓘ *T01595-695057, May-Sep daily 1000-1300, 1400-1700, donations welcome*, a restored thatched crofthouse built in the early 19th century. This was inhabited by a crofting family until the 60s, with the women working the land whilst the men went to the fishing or whaling. The two rooms – the but and the ben – hold all the original furnishings and utensils and there is a typical kale yard and upturned boat shed outside. During the evenings of the summer months, Elma Johnson of Island Trails (see Tours) tells old Shetland stories by the fireside. For more information check with the TIC in Lerwick. St Ninian's Isle to Quendale On the west coast, near Bigton village, a signposted track leads to the spectacular sandy causeway (known as an ayre or tombolo) which leads to St Ninian's Isle. The tombolo is the best example of its kind in Britain, and you can walk across to the island which is best known for the hoard of Pictish treasure which was discovered in 1958 in the ruins of the 12th-century church. The 28 silver objects included bowls, a spoon and brooches, probably dating from around AD 800, and are now on display in the Royal Scottish Museum in Edinburgh, though you can see replicas in the Shetland Museum in Lerwick.

The west coast south of Bigton is beautiful with long, sandy beaches interspersed with dramatic cliff scenery. On the other side of the road from the long, sheltered beach at **Scousburgh Sands** is the **Loch of Spiggie RSPB Reserve**. The loch is an important winter wildfowl refuge, particularly for Whooper Swans, and during the summer you can see various ducks, waders, gulls, terns and skuas. There's a hide on the northern shore with an information board. Nearby is the **Spiggie Hotel** which offers afternoon tea or dinner.

A few miles south of the loch is the village of **Quendale**, overlooking a wide, sandy bay. Here you'll find the beautifully restored and fully working 19th-century **Quendale Mill** ⓘ *T01950-460969, www.quendalemill.shetland.co.uk, Apr-Oct daily 1000-1700, £2, craft shop and tourist information point*, the last of Shetland's watermills. You might not see it but you will hear the groan of the wreck of the Braer oil tanker that lies, between Garth's Ness and

Close encounters of the bird kind

Shetland is famous for its birds. As well its huge seabird colonies, the islands attract Arctic species and are an important crossroads for migrating birds. Over 340 species have been recorded on Fair Isle, including rare and exotic birds from Asia and America. Twenty-one out of the 24 seabirds common to Britain breed in Shetland. These can be found around the coastline, but the largest colonies are at the Hermaness and Noss reserves.

Amongst the many species which can be seen are the puffin. About one fifth of Scotland's puffins breed in Shetland. Its cousins in the auk family, guillemots, and razorbills, are also here in abundance during the summer months, along with kittiwakes, shags and that most common of seabirds, the fulmar. Britain's largest seabird, the gannet, can be seen diving spectacularly for fish at Hermaness, Noss, Fair Isle and Foula, while its smallest seabird, the storm petrel, is best seen around dusk on the tiny island of Mousa.

Summer heralds the return of the Arctic tern which breeds along low coastlines, as do the eider, oystercatcher, ringed plover and black guillemot, or tystie, which stays here all year round. The best place to see waders and shelduck are the nutrient-rich tidal mudflats at the Pool of Virkie in the South Mainland.

Many birds breed on agricultural land, and these include the lapwing, skylark, meadow pipit and wheater. The hills and moorland provide breeding grounds for many summer visitors such as that pirate of the skies, the great skua, or bonxie, and the Arctic skua. Another Arctic species, the whimbrel, also nests here, mainly in Unst, Yell and Fetlar. Moorland habitats are also favoured by the curlew, golden plover and merlin, Shetland's only bird of prey, while the lochs are home to large numbers of red-throated divers. Fetlar is home to 90% of the population of one of Britain's rarest birds, the red-necked phalarope.

Many of Shetland's bird habitats are protected as RSPB Reserves and National Nature Reserves, and it is an offence to disturb the birds and their young at or near their nests. You also risk being dive-bombed by some of the more aggressively protective species. For a full list of all species recorded on the islands and more practical bird-watching information, get a copy of the *Shetland Bird Chart*, by Joyce Gammack, available from the tourist office in Lerwick.

Fitful Head. It ran on to the rocks in 1993. A disaster of epic proportions was averted by the hurricane-force gales which dispersed the huge oil spillage.

Sumburgh and Jarlshof

At the southern tip of Mainland is the village of Sumburgh, site of Shetland's main airport for external passenger flights and for helicopters and planes servicing the North Sea oil industry. South of the airport is Shetland's prime archaeological site, **Jarlshof** ① *T01950-460112, late Mar-Sep daily 0930-1730, £5.50, concessions £4.40, children £3.30*, a hugely impressive place which spans 4000 years of occupation from Neolithic times through Norse settlement to the 16th century. The original Stone Age dwellings are topped by a broch, Pictish wheelhouses, Viking longhouses and, towering over the whole complex, the ruins of a 16th-century mansion. This remarkable site was only discovered at the end of the 19th century when a violent storm ripped off the top layer of turf. Jarlshof is, in fact, not a genuine name, but the exotic invention of Sir Walter Scott in his novel *The Pirate*. A useful guidebook available from the visitor centre helps bring the place to life.

Another fascinating excavation has been going on nearby, at **Old Scatness**, and looks set to become just as impressive. Since 1995, a team from Bradford University have been working here and have revealed a mound over 5m high and 80m in diameter thought to have been inhabited for over 3000 years. In its centre is a an Iron Age tower, or broch. Visitors are welcome at the site May to October (winter group visits by arrangement). For more details visit www.shetland-heritage.co.uk/amenitytryst, or T01595-694688.

South of Jarlshof the Mainland ends abruptly at **Sumburgh Head**, an RSPB Reserve. The **lighthouse** on top of the cliff was built by Robert Stevenson in 1821, and the keepers' cottages are now rented out as self-catering accommodation. The lighthouse isn't open to the public, but from its grounds you can see many nesting seabirds such as puffins, kittiwakes, fulmars, guillemots and razorbills. Just to the east of the airport is **Pool of Virkie**, another good birdwatching area.

Fair Isle → *For listings, see pages 403-411. See map, page 413. Phone code 01595.*

Fair Isle, 24 miles southwest of Sumburgh and 27 miles northeast of North Ronaldsay in Orkney, is the most isolated of Britain's inhabited islands. Only three miles long by one and a half miles wide, the island has a population of around 70 and is best known for its intricately patterned knitwear, which is still produced by a co-operative, **Fair Isle Crafts**. Co-operative could be said to sum up the friendly islanders, whose lifestyle is based on mutual help and community effort.

Ins and outs
Getting to Fair Isle requires patience, persistence and a strong stomach to survive the white-knuckle 4½-hour ferry sailing. Costing just £3.40 each way, these can be booked through **Good Shepherd** ⓘ *T01595-760363*. There are also flights from Tingwall airport. A day-return flight allows about six hours on the island and costs £56 return. You can also fly from Kirkwall on Orkney, which allows 2½ hours on the island, T01856-872420. For more information on Fair Isle and on boat and flight times visit www.fairisle.org.uk, or call the **National Trust for Scotland** ⓘ *T0844-493-2100, www.nts.org.uk.* ▸▸ *For further details, see Transport page 431.*

Sights
Fair Isle is a paradise for birdwatchers, and keen ornithologists form the majority of the island's visitors. Celebrity birdwatcher and former Goodie, Bill Oddie, has dubbed it the 'the Hilton of the bird world'. It stands in the flight path of many thousands of migrating birds, and over 340 species have been recorded here at the **Fair Isle Bird Observatory** ⓘ *T01595-760258, www.fairislebirdobs.co.uk, Apr-Oct*, which also offers accommodation and where visitors are welcome to take part. As well as the almost obscenely rich birdlife there are around 240 species of flowering plants, making the island an especially beautiful haven for naturalists. Fair Isle's coastline, especially in the north and west, also boasts some outstanding cliff scenery.

The bird observatory was the brainchild of George Waterston, an ornithologist who first visited in 1935 and then bought the island in 1948 to begin his task of building the observatory. The island was given to the National Trust for Scotland in 1954 and declared a National Scenic Area. It was recently designated a place of outstanding natural beauty and cultural heritage by the Council of Europe. The **George Waterston Memorial Centre** ⓘ *T01595-760244, May to mid-Sep Mon and Fri 1400-1600, Wed 1000-1200, donations welcome*, has exhibits and photographs detailing the island's natural history, as well as the history of crofting, fishing, archaeology and knitwear. **The Textile Workshop** ① *T01595-760248*, offers demonstrations in textile techniques and is open year round (by prior arrangement). Individuals and small groups can be accommodated for short courses.

North Mainland → *For listings, see pages 403-411. See map, page 413. Phone code 01806.*

The main road north from Lerwick branches at **Voe**, a peaceful and colourful little village nestling in a bay at the head of the Olna Firth. One branch leads to the Yell car and passenger ferry terminal at **Toft**, past the turn-off to the massive **Sullom Voe Oil Terminal**, the largest oil and liquefied gas terminal in Europe. The other road heads northwest to Brae (see below).

Brae
Brae is not a very pretty place and was built to accommodate workers at the nearby Sullom Voe oil terminal. It does boast a good selection of accommodation and decent facilities – such as Frankie's, Britain's most northerly fish and chip shop – and makes a good base from which to explore the wild and wonderful coastal scenery around the Northmavine peninsula to the north. There's also good walking and spectacularly good westerly views around the island of **Muckle Roe** to the southwest, and up the island's small hill, **South Ward** (554 ft). But be careful of the overly protective bonxies which will attack if you get too close to their nests in the grass. The island is attached to the mainland by a bridge.

Northmavine
The charmingly named **Mavis Grind**, the narrow isthmus where it's claimed you can throw a stone from the Atlantic to the North Sea, leads into Northmavine, the northwest peninsula of North Mainland. It is one of Shetland's most dramatic and beautiful areas, with rugged scenery, spectacular coastline and wide empty spaces. This is wonderful walking country, and it's a good idea to abandon the car and explore it on foot. **Hillswick Ness**, to the south of **Hillswick** village, is a nice walk, but further west, around the coastline of **Eshaness**, is the most spectacular cliff scenery and amazing natural features, all with unusual and evocative names.

North of the lighthouse are the **Holes of Scraada**, **Grind o' da Navir** and the **Villians of Hamnavoe**, which are not the local gangs but eroded lava cliffs with blowholes, arches and caves. East of Eshaness are the **Heads of Grocken** and **The Drongs**, a series of exposed sea stacks, which offer superb diving. Further north, overlooking the deep sea inlet of **Ronies Voe**, is the dramatic red-granite bulk of **Ronies Hill** (1477 ft), with a well-preserved burial cairn at the summit. The coastal scenery to the north and west of here is even more breathtaking, but very remote and exposed. You should be well equipped before setting out.

Between Eshaness and Hillswick, a side road leads south to the **Tangwick Haa Museum** ① *T01806-503347, Apr-Sep daily 1100-1700, free*, which features displays and photographs on the history of fishing and whaling and the hardships of life in these parts.

Whalsay and Out Skerries

→ *For listings, see pages 403-411. See map, page 413. Phone code 01806.*
South of Voe, the B9071 branches east to Laxo, the ferry terminal for the island of **Whalsay**, one of Shetland's most prosperous small islands owing to its thriving paelagic fishing industry, which helps support a population of around 1000. There are regular daily car ferries from here to Whalsay for £3.60 per passenger and £8.50 per car including driver. The

journey takes 30 minutes. There are rumoured to be more millionaires here per head of population that anywhere else in Scotland. Certainly its golf course above the cliffs is rich with sea views. In the seas around Whalsay you can see porpoises, dolphins, minke whales and orcas, hence its viking name which means 'island of whales'. The fishing fleet is based at **Symbister**, the island's main settlement. Beside the harbour at Symbister is the **Pier House**, a restored **böd** which was used by the Hanseatic League, a commercial association of German merchants who traded in Shetland from the Middle Ages to the early 18th century. Inside is an exhibition explaining the history of the Hanseatic trade, and general information on the island. One of Scotland's great poets, Hugh McDiarmid (Christopher Grieve), spent most of the 1930s in Whalsay, where he wrote much of his finest poetry, until he was called for war work in 1942, never to return. His former home, at Sodom near Symbister, is now a **camping böd**, see Sleeping, page 426.

The Out Skerries is a small group of rocky islands about 5 miles from Whalsay and 10 miles east of Shetland Mainland. It's made up of three main islands: the larger islands of **Housay** and **Bruray**, which are connected by a road bridge; and the uninhabited island of **Grunay**. The Skerries boast some spectacular and rugged sea cliffs which are home to many rare migrant seabirds in spring and autumn.

Yell, Fetlar and Unst → *For listings, see pages 403-411. See map, page 413.*

Yell → *Phone code 01957.*

Yell, the second largest of the Shetland Islands, was described rather damningly by the Orkney-favouring writer Eric Linklater, as 'dull and dark'. And it's true that the interior is consistently desolate peat moorland. But the coastline is greener and more pleasant and provides an ideal habitat for the island's large otter population. Yell is also home to a rich variety of birds, and offers some good coastal and hill walks, especially around the rugged coastline of **The Herra**, a peninsula about halfway up the west coast.

At **Burravoe**, about 5 miles east of the ferry terminal at **Ulsta**, is the **Old Haa Museum** ⓘ *T01957-722339, late Apr-Sep Tue-Thu and Sat 1000-1600, Sun 1400-1700, free, donations appreciated, garden open every day,* housed in Yell's oldest building which dates from 1672. It contains an interesting display on local flora and fauna and history.

The island's largest village, **Mid Yell**, has a couple of shops, a pub and a leisure centre with a good swimming pool. About a mile northwest, on the hillside above the main road, are the reputedly haunted ruins of **Windhouse**, dating from 1707. To the north is the **RSPB Lumbister Reserve**, where red-throated divers, merlins, great and Arctic skuas and many other bird species come to breed. The reserve is also home to a large population of otters. A pleasant walk leads along the nearby steep and narrow gorge, known as the **Daal of Lumbister**, filled with many colourful flowers. The area to the north of the reserve provides good walking over remote moorland and coastline.

The road continues north past the reserve and around **Basta Voe**, where you can see otters. North of **Gutcher**, the ferry port for Unst, is the village of **Cullivoe**, with some good walks along the attractive coastline. There's a bus service which runs between Ulsta and Cullivoe and stops at villages in between, T01975-744214.

Fetlar → *Phone code 01957.*

Fetlar is the smallest of the North Isles but the most fertile, and is known as 'the garden of Shetland'. Indeed, the name derives from Norse meaning 'fat land', as there is good grazing and croftland and a wide variety of plant and bird life. The whole island is good for birdwatching, but the prime place is the 1700 acres of **North Fetlar RSPB Reserve** around Vord Hill (522 ft) in the north of the island. This area has restricted access during the summer months, and visitors should contact the warden at Bealance (T01957-733246). The warden will also let you know if and when you can see the one or two female snowy owls which sometime visit.

The north cliffs of the reserve are home to large colonies of breeding seabirds, including auks, gulls and shags, and you can also see common and grey seals on the beaches in late autumn. Fetlar is home to one of Britain's rarest birds, the **red-necked phalarope**, which breeds in the loch near **Funzie** (pronounced 'finnie') in the east of the island. You can watch them from the RSPB hide in the nearby marshes. Red-throated divers and whimbrel also breed here. The island is also good for walking, and a leaflet describing some of the walks is available from the tourist office in Lerwick.

The main settlement on the island is **Houbie**; on the south coast. Here you'll see a house called Leagarth, which was built by the island's most famous son, Sir William Watson Cheyne, who, with Lord Lister, pioneered antiseptic surgery. Nearby is the excellent **Fetlar Interpretive Centre** ① *T01957-733206, www.fetlar.com, May-Sep Mon-Fri 1100-1500, Sat-Sun 1300-1600, £2, concessions £1, under 16s free*, which presents the island's history and gives information on its bounteous birdlife.

Unst → *Phone code 01957.*

Unst is the most northerly inhabited island in Britain and some believe where the Vikings first landed on Shetland, but there is more to the island than its many 'most northerly' credentials. Aside from being where the local bakery makes 'oceanic' oatcakes from sea water, it is scenically one of the most varied of the Shetland Islands, with spectacular cliffs, sea stacks, sheltered inlets, sandy beaches, heather-clad hills, fertile farmland, freshwater lochs and even a sub-arctic desert. Such a variety of habitats supports over 400 plant species and a rich variety of wildlife. Unst is a major breeding site for gannets, puffins, guillemots, razorbills, kittiwakes, shags, Arctic and great skuas and whimbrels, amongst others, and in the surrounding waters you can see seals, porpoises, otters and even killer whales.

In the east of the island, north of **Baltasound**, is the **Keen of Hamar National Nature Reserve**, 74 acres of serpentine rock which breaks into tiny fragments known as 'debris', giving the landscape a strange, lunar-like appearance. This bleak 'desert' is actually home to some of the rarest plants in Britain. Baltasound is the island's main settlement, with an airport, hotel, pub, post office, leisure centre with pool and Britain's most northerly brewery, the **Valhalla Brewery** ① *T01975-711658, www.valhallabrewery.co.uk, visited by appointment Mon-Fri 0900-1700, £3.50.*

To the north of here is the village of **Haroldswick**, home of Britain's most northerly post office, where your postcards are sent with a special stamp to inform everyone of this fact. Here you'll also find **Unst Boat Haven** ① *T01957-711528, May-Sep daily 1100-1700, £2, children free*, where you can see a beautifully presented collection of traditional boats and fishing artefacts. A little way further north is the **Unst Heritage Centre** ① *May-Sep daily 1100-1700*, which has a museum of local history and island life. Nearby is an RAF radar-tracking station at Saxa Vord. The road ends at Skaw, where there's a lovely beach and Britain's most northerly house. The road northwest from Haroldswick leads to the head of **Burra Firth**, a sea inlet flanked by high cliffs, and site of Britain's most northerly golf course.

To the west of Burra Firth is the remote **Hermaness National Nature Reserve**, 2422 acres of dramatic coastal scenery and wild moorland which is home to over 100,000 nesting seabirds including gannets, and the largest number of puffins and great skuas (or 'bonxies') in Shetland. There's an excellent **visitor centre** ① *T01975-711278, mid-Apr to mid-Sep daily 0800-1700*, in the former lighthouse keeper's shore station, where you can pick up a leaflet which shows the marked route into the reserve, and see the artistic efforts of many of Unst's children. Whilst in the reserve, make sure you keep to the marked paths to avoid being attacked by bonxies; they are highly protective and they will attack if they think that their territory is being threatened.

The views from Hermaness are wonderful, out to the offshore stacks and skerries including **Muckle Flugga**, and then to the wide open North Atlantic Ocean. Muckle Flugga is the site of the most northerly lighthouse in Britain, built in 1857-1858 by Thomas Stevenson, father of Robert Louis Stevenson. The writer visited the island in 1869, and the illustrated map in his novel *Treasure Island* bears a striking similarity to the outline of Unst. Beyond the lighthouse is **Out Stack**, which marks the most northerly point on the British Isles. With nothing between you and the North Pole but water, this is the place to sit and contemplate what it feels like to be at the end of the world.

◉ Shetland listings

For Sleeping and Eating price codes and other relevant information, see Essentials pages 38-45.

● Sleeping

Lerwick and around *p414, map p415*
B Westhall B&B, Lower Sound, T01595-690364, www.bedandbreakfastlerwick.co.uk. A big old house, just 20 mins' walk from the centre along the bay. 3 rooms en suite. They also offer a cottage from £560 per week (sleeps 5). Recommended.

Most of Shetland's best accommodation is outside Lerwick, where hotels are mostly geared towards the oil industry. During the peak months of Jul-Aug and the Folk Festival in Apr, it's a good idea to book in advance. There are several decent guesthouses and B&Bs in town, which are all much of a muchness. The tourist office can supply details.
C Scalloway Hotel, Main St, Scalloway, a few miles west of Lerwick, T01595-880444, www.scallowayhotel.com. A comfortable, modest hotel with a growing reputation for serving up the best seafood and hearty steak pie dinners (♥♥-♥) for miles around.
C Brentham House, 7 Harbour St, T01950-460201, www.brenthamhouse.com. 3 en suite rooms and 1 suite. Luxurious rooms featuring Victorian bathtubs and with a continental breakfast waiting in the fridge.

B Kveldsro House Hotel, Greenfield Pl, T01595-692195, www.shetlandhotels. com. The most luxurious hotel in town. Pronounced 'kel-ro', it overlooks the harbour and has an upmarket restaurant (♥♥♥) as well as cheaper bar food.
C Glen Orchy House, 20 Knab Rd, T01595-692031, www.guesthouselerwick.com. Excellent guest house with 23 en suite rooms and its own Thai restaurant.
E SYHA hostel, Islesburgh House, King Harald St, T01595-692114, www.islesburgh. org.uk. Open Apr-Sep. Clean and well-run with 64 beds, with an excellent café.

Camping
Clickimin Caravan & Camp Site, near Clickimin Leisure Centre and loch on the western edge of the town, T01595-741000, www.srt.org.uk. Open May-Sep. £5.80-£12 for a pitch.

Central Mainland *p416*
B Herrislea House Hotel, Tingwall, near the airport, by the crossroads, T01595-840208, www.herrisleahouse.co.uk. 13 en suite rooms. Country house in lovely setting with well-furnished rooms. Their Phoenix restaurant (♥♥♥) specializes in local meat (Mon-Sat 1830-2045), The **Starboard Tack** bar has live music.

C The Westings Inn, Wormadale, near Tingwall, T01595-840242, www.originart. com/westings. 6 rooms. Whilst it wins no prizes for décor, you'll be well looked after at this B&B with views over Whiteness Voe. Decent bar food and real ales, also has a campsite.

D Hildasay Guest House, Scalloway, in the upper part of the village, T01595-880822. Has disabled facilities and arranges fishing trips.

The Westside *p417*

B Burrastow House, 2 miles southwest of Walls, T01595-809307 www.burrastow house.co.uk. Open Apr-Nov. 6 rooms. A restored 18th-century house overlooking Vaila Sound, it's full of character. The owner cooks magnificent seafood, see Eating, below. Recommended.

D Pomona, Gruting, east of Brig o' Waas, T01595-810438. Friendly and comfortable, modern bungalow. An excellent base for seal, otter and birdwatching. 4 miles from Walls, where there's a shop and petrol station.

D Skeoverick, a mile or so north of Walls, T01595-809349. A welcoming B&B with 4 rooms. The owners allow guests to use the kitchen to prepare meals.

Camping

Voe House www.camping-bods.com. Walls, is a camping *böd* – a restored 18th-century house overlooking the village. Open Apr-Sep. Book through Lerwick tourist office.

Foula *p418*

C Leraback, Foula, T01595-753226, www. originart.com/leraback/leraback. Modern crofthouse bungalow with three bedrooms. 3-course dinner included in the price (served at 1815) and self-catering also available. Free collection from, and drop off at, the pier.

Self-catering

There is self-catering accommodation available on Foula in a cottage sleeping 4-6 people. Contact Mr R Holbourn, T01595-753232.

Papa Stour *p418*

F Hurdiback Hostel, T01595-873227. 2 rooms of 4 bunks means this is a small whilst it location means it's often quiet. You can order off, bread and eggs before you arrive. www.hurdibackhostel.co.uk.

South Mainland *p418*

There's accommodation in Bigton and Scousburgh, around Sumburgh, but it is limited.

C-D The Spiggie Hotel, Scousburgh, Dunrossness, T01950-460409, www.the spiggiehotel.co.uk. Less than 30 mins' drive from Lerwick and close to Sumburgh airport. A small, family-run hotel with 6 rooms, overlooking Spiggie Loch, with a cosy bar (think postage stamp size) serving good real ales and tasty seafood. Also sells permits for fishing.

D Setterbrae, Scousburgh, T1950-460468, www.setterbrae.co.uk. 3 rooms overlooking the Loch of Spiggie.

C Sumburgh Hotel, next to Jarlshof, Sumburgh, T01950-460201, www. sumburghhotel.com. 32 en suite rooms. 19th-century former home of Laird of Sumburgh, with great views across to Fair Isle and 2 bars and a good restaurant (♟).

D Hayhoull, Bigton T01950-422206, www. bedandbreakfastshetland.com. This spick and span B&B has 3 rooms with beautiful views of St Ninian's Isle and towards Foula, Evening meals are available. Recommended.

Camping

Betty Mouat's Cottage, next to the excavations at Old Scatness and the airport, is this camping *böd*. It sleeps up to 8 and is open Apr-Sep. Book through Lerwick tourist office.

Fair Isle *p421*

There are a few places to stay on the island, but accommodation must be booked in advance and includes meals. There are no hotels, pubs or restaurants.

C South Lighthouse, T01595-760355, www. southlightfairisle.co.uk. Stunning location, the price includes dinner and a packed lunch.

C **Upper Leogh** www.kathycoull.com, T01595-760248. Situated beside a working crofthouse, with sea views. Offers full board and is run by Kathy Coull.

B-C **Fair Isle Lodge and Bird Observatory**, T01595-760258, www.fairislebirdobs.co.uk. The price is for full-board accommodation in private rooms. (**E**).

Self-catering
Self-catering cottage, T01595-760225. Available at Springfield Croft House.

North Mainland *p422*
A-B **Busta House Hotel**, Brae, T01806-522506, www.bustahouse.com. Open all year. 20 rooms. The best place to stay around Brae, and probably the next best on Shetland, is this luxurious and wonderfully atmospheric 16th-century country house overlooking Busta Voe about 1½ miles from Brae village. The superb restaurant (♛♛♛) is one of the finest on Shetland, with a selection of malts to match, and there are also meals in the bar. Recommended.
C **Almara**, Upper Urafirth, T01806-503261, www.almara.shetland.co.uk. This friendly and comfortable B&B is the pick of the bunch.
C **Westayre**, Westayre, Muckle Roe, Brae, T01806-522368, www.westayre.shetland. co.uk. A working croft.

Camping
Johnny Notion's Camping Böd, in **Hamnavoe**, Northmavine, www.camping-bods.com, reached by a side road which branches north from the road between Hillswick and Eshaness. This is the birth-place of John Williamson, an 18th-century craftsman who developed an effective inoculation against smallpox. Apr-Sep, has no electricity. Book through Lerwick tourist office.
Sail Loft, in Voe by the pier. This former fishing store is now Shetland's largest camping *böd*. Open Apr-Sep.

Whalsay and Out Skerries *p422*
Hugh Mc Diarmid's Camping Böd (The Grieve House), near Symbister, www.camping-bods.com. Open Apr-Sep. The former home of this great poet, see page 423. No electricity.

Yell *p423*
D **Norwind B&B**, Mid Yell, T01957-702312. Offers 2 double and twin rooms (all en suite) in a comfortable, modern bungalow where if requested in advance she'll provide an evening meal and a packed lunch. 15 mins from the ferry.
D **Pinewood Guest House**, South Aywick, between Burravoe and Mid Yell, T01975-702427.
D **Post Office**, Gutcher, T01957-744201. Friendly and welcoming.

Camping
Windhouse Lodge www.camping-bods.com. Open Apr-Sep. A well-equipped camping *böd* below the ruins of haunted Windhouse.

Fetlar *p423*
C-D **The Gord**, Houbie, T01975-733227. B&B attached to the shop in Houbie. 3 en suite rooms, offers dinner and is easy to find.

Camping
F **The Garths Campsite**, Fetlar, T01975-733227. Open May-Sep. Overlooks the beach at Tresta and has good facilities. Pitch up for £7.

Unst *p424*
There's a decent selection of accommodation on Unst.
B **Buness House**, T01975-711315. Top choice has to be the faded grandeur of this 17th-century Haa in Baltasound which has fine views. Staying here is a bizarre and rather surreal experience, given that you are on the most northerly island in Britain. The house is crammed full of Indian Raj relics, and the stuffed eagle, tiger and leopard skins hanging in the hallway are a wildlife

A böd for the night

There is only one youth hostel in Shetland, but budget travellers shouldn't panic. **Shetland Camping Böd** project has developed a network of camping *böds* (pronounced 'burd') which provide basic and cheap digs throughout the islands.

A *böd* was a building used to house fishermen and their gear during the fishing season and the name has been used to describe these types of accommodation which are similar to English 'camping barns'. They are all located in scenic places and each has its own fascinating history. They are very basic and the more remote ones have no electricity. You'll need to bring a stove, cooking and eating utensils, a sleeping bag and a torch (flashlight). All *böds* must be booked in advance through the TIC in Lerwick and cost £6 per person per night without electricity, or £8 per person per night with electricity. They are open from April till the end of September. There are at present nine camping *böds* on Shetland (listed in the relevant places). See also www.camping-bods.com.

close up almost as impressive, though considerably more unsettling and un-'PC', as the Hermaness Nature Reserve in the north of the island that the family own. The food is excellent (♥♥♥) and accommodation comfortable.

E Prestegaard, T01975-755234. A Victorian house at Uyeasound on the south coast near the ferry. Terrific sea views.

C Baltasound Hotel, T01957-711334, www.baltasound-hotel.shetland.co.uk. Wooden chalets and a small but well-stocked bar serving decent food.

D Gerratoun, Haroldswick, T01975-711323. Claims to be Britain's most northerly B&B. Located within walking distance of Hermaness and with excellent views, this restored crofthouse offers 1 twin bedroom. Caters for special diets.

F Gardiesfauld Hostel, Baltasound, T01975-755259, www.gardiesfauld.shetland.co.uk. Open Apr-Sep. An independent hostel, which also hires bikes.

⊕ Eating

Lerwick and around *p414, map p415*
Despite a ready supply of fresh local produce, with a few notable exceptions (and of course during its excellent 'Flavour of Shetland' food festival in Jun), the archipelago can feel like a gastronomic desert. The hotels and guest-houses listed above under Sleeping are far and away the best options, especially **Burrastow House** and **Busta House Hotel**.

♥♥♥ **Monty's Bistro & Deli**, 5 Mounthooly St, T01595-696655. Open Tue-Sat. Directly across from the **Lounge** (see bars below), this is the best place to eat in Lerwick. It offers good modern Scottish cooking, including huge thick-cut halibut steaks and a selection of fine wines in a cosy, informal setting.

♥♥♥-♥♥ **Hay's Dock**, Shetland Museum, www.haysdock.co.uk, see Sights, page 415. This café/restaurant is worth a try – as is their salt beef Shetland bannock,- but just like **Monty's** their main dishes are a little pricey.

♥♥ **Brasserie Restaurant**, Lerwick Hotel, see Sleeping, above. For dinner or bar lunch. Its carvery is a roast dinner lover's dream, with seaweed-fed Shetland lamb served with Shetland Black potatoes. Recommended.

♥♥ **Gallery Restaurant**, Kveldsro Hotel, see Sleeping, above. Offers the chance to watch the boats sail by as you eat. Pan-fried scallops, crab and Shetland lamb pâté, and a traditional roast menu on Sun.

♥ **Osla's Café Bar & Bistro**, 88 Commercial St, T01595-696005. Open Mon-Sat until 2000, Sun 1200-1700. Bustling café serving a wide range of coffees, pancakes and other snacks, and boasting the islands' only beer garden.

☙ **Peerie Shop Café**, Esplanade, T01595-692816. Mon-Sat 0900-1800. The best cappuccino in Shetland and muffins the size of Bressay. Also does cheering soups.

Central Mainland *p416*
☙ **Castle Café**, New Rd, Scalloway, near the castle, T01595-880270. Damn fine chippy serving takeway or sit-in fish and chips.
☙ **Da Haaf Restaurant**, NAFC Marine Centre, Porth Arthur, Scalloway, T01595-772480, www.nafc.ac.uk. Open Mon-Fri 0830-1600. A canteen-style restaurant in the North Atlantic Fisheries college specializing in seafood. Does a good fish supper, as well as a more upmarket menu for the evenings.

The Westside *p417*
☙☙-☙ **Burrastow House**, see Sleeping, above. Open to non-residents Sat-Sun. The new Belgian owner of this restored 18th-century house cooks magnificent seafood. This is the best place to eat on the islands, so you'll need to book ahead. Recommended.

North Mainland *p422*
☙☙ **Busta House Hotel**, Brae, see Sleeping, above. The best option hereabouts, serving Shetland hill lamb, free range pork from Unst and Yell Sound scallops. Has a good malt whisky selection.
☙☙ **Frankies Fish and Chips**, Brae T01806-522700. Serves all sort of fried seafood (squid, skate wings, prawns) as well as the old classics. They also steam the fattest juiciest local mussels for those watching their waistlines.
☙☙-☙ **Pierhead Restaurant and Bar**, Voe, T01806-588332. Serves decent meals: locally caught fish and shellfish are the mainstays of the menu. And in the evenings, Shetland's young fiddle players play for pints.
☙ **Da Bod Café**, Hillswick, T01806-503348. Open Thu-Sun 1200-1800. Shetland's oldest pub, now converted into a vegetarian café serving light bites and snacks. Café also hosts live music and storytelling events.

Yell *p423*
☙ **Old Haa Museum Café**, Burravoe, south-east Yell. Open 1000-1600. A small café on the ground floor of the museum. Serves teas, coffees, great home-baking and sandwiches.
☙ **Wind Dog Café**, opposite the Post Office, Gutcher, T01957-744321, www.winddog cafe.co.uk. Open Mon-Fri 0900-1700, Sat-Sun 1000-1700. Evening meals are served from 1830. Internet access in cosy surroundings, where you can enjoy home-baking, coffee, soup of the day or a burger. Recommended.

Unst *p424*
☙☙☙-☙☙ **Baltasound Hotel**, T01975-711334. Serves meals and drinks to non-residents.

⊙ Bars and clubs

Lerwick and around *p414, map p415*
Lounge, Mounthooly St, near the TIC. The locals mingle downstairs, whilst upstairs the bar is quite touristy but definitely one of the best places for a drink. Moreover, this remains a magnet for enjoying planned and impromptu sessions of Shetland's wonderful fiddle and folk music. Whenever you arrive, there's usually someone playing.

⊕ Festivals and events

Lerwick and around *p414, map p415*
The *Shetland Times*, www.shetlandtimes. co.uk, has details what is going on. Also check the tourist board's website, www. visit shetland.com, or ring T08701-999440.
Jan Up-Helly-Aa, www.uphellyaa.org. Lerwick's annual fire festival is celebrated on the last Tue in Jan with torch-lit processions, Viking costumes and the burning of a Viking longboat. If you miss this one, there are a number across the islands over the next 2 months. See also page 416.
May Shetland Folk Festival, www.shetlandfolk festival.com. Folk music has a strong following in Shetland and this is one of Scotland's top folk events. Over 3 days in early May musicians from around the globe come to play.

Jun Shetland Food Festival, www.visit
shetland.com. The 4-day 'Flavour of
Shetland' food festival is a gastronomes
dream with the best of Shetland lamb and
shellfish among the treats to be found by
the harbour in Lerwick. It's a major festival
with dozens of boats sailing across from
Norway to enjoy the festivities, so if you
fancy a mid-summer party you know
where to come.
Mid-Oct Shetland Accordion and
Fiddle Festival, for details of both events
contact the Folk Festival office, 5 Burns
Lane, Lerwick, T01595-693162 or www.
shetandaccordionandfiddle.com.

○ Shopping

Lerwick and around *p414, map p415*
Ninian, 110 Commercial St, T01595-696655
For new takes on traditional Fair Isle knitting.
Peerie Shop, Esplanade T01595-692816
Colourful homeware, postcards and knits.
Shetland Times, Commerical St, T01595-
695531. For books about Shetland.
The Spiders Web, 51 Commercial St,
T01595-695246. Open Mon-Sat 0900-1700.
The place to buy authentic Shetland knit-
wear sourced directly from the local knitters.
Hand-spun yarn and hand-knitted Fair
Isle jumpers, waistcoats, cardigans,
scarves and shawls.

Central Mainland *p416*
Shetland Woollen Company, next to
Scalloway Castle. Where you can buy the
famous Shetland wool and Fair Isle jumpers.

The Westside *p417*
Shetland Jewellery, Soundside, Weisdale,
T01595-830275, www.shetlandjewellery.
com. Open Mon-Fri 0900-1700, Jun-Aug
also Sat 1000-1700 and Sun 1400-1700.
This small workshop and studio is set
right beside a sea loch. Great place to buy
authentic gold and silver Shetland rings
and brooches, etc. Guided tours available
over a cup of tea.

○ Activities and tours

Lerwick and around *p414, map p415*
Boat trips
A boat trip to the seabird colonies on Noss
and Bressay is unmissable, so don't even
think about coming here and not doing it.
Seabirds-and-seals, Bressay, T07831-
217042 or T07876-550224, www.seabirds-
and-seals.com. Award-winning wildlife
cruises run by Jonathan Wills. If you go
at the right time of year, you are almost
guaranteed to see seals, porpoises and the
astounding gannetry on the spectacular
cliffs of Noss' east coast. Trips leave at 1000
and 1400 mid-Apr to mid-Sep, weather
permitting, £40, concessions £35, student
£30, under 16s £25, under 5s free.
   If you want to learn about the Island's
stunning geology and how man and nature
has made these Islands their own Allen
Fraser of **Geo-Tours**, Burra Isle, T01595-
859218, www.shetlandgeology.com, has
a fine grasp of the last 500 million years.
Mousa Boat Trips, Sandwick, T01950-
431367, www.mousa.co.uk. Runs daily
trips from Apr-Sep to Mousa aboard *M/V
Solan IV*. The 15-min crossing provides the
chance to spot seals and seabirds before
exploring well preserved Pictish brochs on
Mousa. £13, children £6.50. Trip also suitable
for wheelchairs.

Photography
Island Trails, Bigton, T01950-422408, www.
island-trails.co.uk. Guides tours by Shetland's
acclaimed storyteller, Elma Johnson. She also
does evening suppers and stories in her own
home. From £25pp.

Sea kayaking
Tom Smith, 56 Whitecraigs, Kinnesswood,
Kinross, T01592-841160, T07787-535659,
www.seakayakshetland.co.uk. Half-day trips
£40, full days £70, including packed lunch.

Tour operators
John Leask & Son, the Esplanade, T01595-693162. Travel agent and tour operator. Can arrange fly-drive packages to Shetland with car hire and accommodation. Also offer a variety of bus tours costing from around £12 up to £25 depending on the destination.

⊖ Transport

Lerwick and around *p414, map p415*
For more information, see Getting there, page 412.

Bus Bus No 4 runs to **Scalloway** (Mon-Sat) and there are also buses to **Walls** (No 9); **Sandness**, **Aith** (No 9 and 12); **North Roe** (No 21); **Hillswick** (No 21); **Vidlin** (No19); **Toft** (No 23), 1 hr; **Mossbank** (No 23). All buses leave from Lerwick's Viking bus station. There are several buses daily between **Lerwick**, **Sandwick** and **Sumburgh Airport**. 2 buses daily Mon-Sat to **Quendale**, with a change at **Channerwick junction**. Regular daily buses from **Lerwick**, which stop at the Sumburgh Hotel, **Scatness** and **Grutness Pier** (for Fair Isle) en route to the airport.

Regular buses Mon-Sat to **Brae** and **Hillswick** to the northwest, and **Toft** and **Mossbank** to the north, pass through **Voe**. To **Hillswick** and **Toft/Mossbank** stop in **Brae**. There is a daily bus service from here to **Hillswick**, Mon-Sat, 1710. From there, a feeder service (No 21) continues to **Eshaness**, 20 mins. Contact **Johnson Transport**, T01806-522331. There are daily buses to **Laxo** and **Vidlin**, run by Whites Coaches, T01595-809443.

For detailed information on all bus services, T01595-744868, or see www.zettrans.org.uk.
Car hire Bolts Car Hire, Toll Clock Shopping Centre, 26 North Rd, T01595-693636; www.boltscarhire.co.uk. **John Leask & Son**, the Esplanade, T01595-693162, www.leaskstravel.co.uk; **Star Rent-a-Car**, 22 Commercial Rd, T01595-692075,

www.starrentacar.co.uk, which also has an office at Sumburgh Airport.
Cycle hire Grantfield Garage, North Rd, T692709, www.grantfieldgarage.co.uk. Mon-Sat 0800-2300, Sun 1100-2300. Hires bikes for £5 per day or £30 per week.
Ferry Ferry links with the UK are provided mostly by **Northlink Ferries**, T0845-600 0449, www.northlinkferries.co.uk. They operate car ferries from Lerwick to **Aberdeen**. A single fare for a passenger seat costs £35.80 in peak season (return fare is double). A car costs £127.90 up to £123.70 single. A 2-berth cabin costs up to £121.20 for a 'Premium' berth in high season. Children aged 4-16 half price and under 4s free.

There are regular daily car ferries between Lerwick and **Bressay**, £3.60 per passenger, £8.40 per car, 5 mins. To **Skerries**, Tue and Thu, 2½ hrs, £3.40 per passenger, £4.20 per car, call G W Henderson, T01806-515226; to **Lerwick** and **Fair Isle**, alternate Thu, 4½ hrs, £3.40 per passenger, £15.80 per car.

Bressay *p416*
Ferry Noss can only be visited from late May-late Aug Tue, Wed and Fri-Sun, 1000-1700. From the 'Wait here' sign overlooking Noss sound on the east side of Bressay an inflatable dinghy shuttles back and forth to Noss during the island's opening hours. In bad weather, call the tourist office, T01595-693434, to check if it's sailing. A **postcar** service runs once a day Mon-Sat from Maryfield ferry terminal to Noss Sound, T01595-820200.
Taxi There are several taxi companies in Lerwick: **6050 Cabs**, T01595-696050; **Abbys Taxis**, T01595-696666; **Allied Taxis**, T01595-690069; **Sinclairs Taxis**, T01595-694617.

Central Mainland *p416*
Air Tingwall airport, T01595-840246, has flights to most of the smaller islands, including the **Skerries**, and getting to the airport is straightforward, as the regular buses between Lerwick and Westside stop in Tingwall.

Bus There are buses Mon-Sat between **Scalloway** and **Lerwick**, John Leask & Son, see Activities and tours, page 431.

The Westside p417
Bus A minibus (No 10 and No 11) runs to **Sandness** from **Walls** once a day Mon-Sat. Contact A&K Transport, T01595-809337.
Ferry There's a passenger/cargo ferry service between **West Mainland** and **Papa Stour**, £3.40 per passenger, £4.20 per car, Mon, Wed, Fri, Sat and Sun, 40 mins; to **Foula**, Tue, Sat and alternate Thu, 2 hrs, £3.40 per passenger, £15.80 per car. Ferries should be booked through W Clark, T01595-810460.

South Mainland p418
Air Flybe, www.flybe.com, flies directly (using **Loganair**, T01595-840246) from Sumburgh to **Aberdeen**, **Kirkwall**, **Inverness**, **Glasgow** and **Edinburgh**. The airline also connects with **Bergen** in Norway in the summer. **Loganair** also operates a regular service from Sumburgh to **Fair Isle**. **Ferry** Regular daily car ferries from **Scalloway** to **Foula**, alternate Thu, 3 hrs, £3.40 per passenger, £15.80 per car; and **South Mainland** to **Fair Isle**, Tue, Sat and alternate Thu, 2½ hrs, £3.40 per passenger, £15.80 per car.

North Mainland p422
Ferry There are frequent car and passenger ferries from **Toft** on North Mainland to **Ulsta** on the south coast of **Yell**. It's not essential, but it's a good idea to book in advance, T01975-722 259, £3.40 per passenger, £8.40 per car, 20 mins.

Whalsay and Out Skerries p422
Ferry There's a less frequent car ferry service between **East Mainland** and **Skerries**, Mon, Fri, Sat and Sun, 1½ hrs, £3.40 per passenger, £4.20 per car. There are regular daily car and passenger ferries between **Laxo** and **Symbister**. To book, call

T01806-566259. There are ferries to the Skerries from **Vidlin**, about 3 miles northeast of Laxo. For bookings, call G W Henderson, T01806-515226.

Yell p423
Ferry There are regular daily car ferries to **Belmont** on **Unst**, free, 10 mins; and **Fetlar**, 25 mins, free, from **Gutcher**. Booking is advised, T01975-722259.

Fetlar p423
Bus There's a post car service which runs around Fetlar from the ferry once a day on Mon, Wed and Fri, T01975-733227.
Ferry There are regular car and passenger ferries between **Oddsta** in the northwest of Fetlar, **Gutcher** (Yell) and **Belmont** (Unst).

Unst p424
Bus There's an island bus service, which runs a few times a day, Mon-Sat between **Baltasound**, **Belmont** and **Haroldswick**, P&T Coaches, T01975-711666.

Directory

Lerwick and around p414, map p415
Banks Bank of Scotland, Clydesdale and **Royal** are on Commercial St. Lloyds TSB is on the Esplanade. **Embassies and consulates** Denmark, Iceland and Netherlands, Hay & Company, 66 Commercial Rd, T01595-692533; Finland, France, Germany and Norway, Shearer Shipping Services, Garthspool, T01595-692556; Sweden, Iain Tulloch, Linnabretta, 13 Stout's Court, Lerwick T01595-692991. **Laundry** Lerwick Laundry, 36 Market St, T01595-693043, Mon-Sat, service washes only. **Medical services** Gilbert Bain Hospital, South Rd, T01595-743000; Lerwick Health Centre, opposite Gilbert Bain Hospital, T01595-693201. **Post** 46 Commercial St, Mon-Fri 0900-1700, Sat 0900-1230; Toll Clock Shopping Centre, 26 North Rd, T01595-695362.

Contents

Background

History

Prehistory

Scotland's earliest known inhabitants are the hunter-gatherers of around 6000-5000 BC. By 2000-1500 BC these Mesolithic people had been joined by Beaker folk, so named from their distinctive pottery, and grain-cultivating Megalithic people, arriving by sea via Spain and Portugal, who were tempted to settle by a then prevailing near-Mediterranean climate. Several climate changes for the worse triggered much population movement and also, along with extensive deforestation, caused the formation of peaty soil, now characteristic of much of Scotland, by around 1000 BC.

The pottery and other artefacts of the Beaker people have been found in burial mounds or cairns, such as Maes Howe on the Orkney Mainland (see page 391). They suggest a complex social structure and perhaps, more importantly, a belief in the afterlife, as do the prehistoric settlements and monuments in Caithness, Orkney, Shetland and the Outer Hebrides, notably at Skara Brae (see page 390), Stenness, and the Ring of Brodgar on Orkney Mainland, and Callanish on Lewis (see page 348). But throughout Scotland there are hundreds of standing stones and circles, a legacy of the megalithic peoples. In Aberdeenshire surveys reveal precise orientations indicating their use as observatories charting lunar cycles and eclipses. The layout of Clava Cairns, near Inverness (see page 199), bears similarities to the great temple at Newgrange in Ireland. And at Kilmartin in Argyll (see page 80), cup and ring marks, stone alignments and burial cairns, formed in a complete 'landscape temple', suggest a geomantic sophistication that has now been forgotten.

At the beginning of the first millennium BC, Bronze Age traders from far afield were busy around the coasts. Celts arrived from Germany, bringing with them new agricultural technology and weaponry such as swords and shields, which in turn necessitated impressive earthwork defences in the form of hillforts and crannogs (see page 138) as competition for land increased. In about 200-100 BC more Celts arrived with superior iron-working skills, and consequently, more fortifications were also built. The brochs, or towers, the remains of many of which can still be seen dotted along the west coast and in the islands, date from this time (see also page 393).

The Picts and the Romans

Indigenous Iron Age tribes inhabited most of the country and were identified by the Romans as 'Picts' – possibly meaning 'painted, or tattooed, people'. They thwarted Roman imperial ambition in Alba, the land north of the Forth and Clyde, in around AD 80, and a string of Roman military outposts along the Highland line remain from this abandoned campaign. At Fortingall near Aberfeldy, the ancient yew tree is said to mark the birthplace of Pontius Pilate, possibly the son of a Roman soldier who later found preferment in Rome. To add credence to this theory, a gravestone marked 'PP' was found.

Defensive walls built by Emperors Hadrian (circa AD 123 from the Solway Firth to the Tyne) and Antoninus (from the Clyde to the Forth circa AD 143) against the Picts inadvertently set a precedent for the eventual polarization of Scotland and England, beginning around the ninth century, out of the mass of tribal kingdoms. An endlessly disputed border led to centuries of retaliatory raids and devastation on either side.

Picts south of the Antonine wall became semi-Romanized and were known as Britons, kin to the Welsh. Their kingdom of Strathclyde, with a stronghold on Dumbarton Rock near Glasgow, once extended into Lancashire and retained a separate identity into the 11th century. The Lothians, territory of the British Gododdin, was overrun by Anglians from Northumbria. In the seventh century the Anglians challenged the Picts in Alba and were finally defeated at Dunnichen.

Meanwhile an Irish tribe, the Scots, who claimed descent from an Egyptian Pharaoh's daughter, had been settling in Pictish territory in Argyll from around the fourth century. Once in Argyll, the sons of the Scots' leader, Erc, established a kingdom called Dalriada, sharing it between themselves under a high king at Dunadd (see page 81). When their fellow countryman, Columba, arrived in the sixth century on Iona, they were aided in their cause by his diplomatic skills at the hostile Pictish court of King Brude, in Inverness. In the ninth century the Scots under Kenneth MacAlpin took over the Picts. Although their written records were destroyed, or falsified by the conquering Scots, they left a rich legacy of unique sculptured stones denoting a civilized and artistic culture. When Kenneth set up at Scone, and Alba became Scotland, the seven kingdoms of Pictland in the north and east survived as great earldoms.

The early church

Some claim Joseph of Arimathea brought Christianity to Whithorn in Galloway, which had been a religious centre since the first century. Around AD 397 Ninian founded a Christian Mission in Whithorn, along eastern Mediterranean monastic lines vastly different from the Roman model. From here he and countless missionaries such as Kentigern, Moluag and Comgan went north to convert the Picts, as far as St Ninian's Isle in Shetland. Their communities, oak churches and cells are remembered in innumerable place names, wells and simple cross-marked stones, often established on pre-Christian sacred sites.

In AD 563 Columba arrived on Iona (see box, page 108), where he went on to found the Celtic Church, or the Church of the Culdees, with centres throughout Scotland, which differed in many ways from the Church of Rome. Iona became known as the 'Cradle of Christianity in Scotland', but the arrival of the Vikings inhibited sea travel and the monks were driven from Iona. About this time, the Scots took over the Pictish nation and the Columban church moved to Dunkeld, with Columba's relics transported in the breacbannoch, or Monymusk reliquary. This was carried at Bannockburn and is now in the Museum of Scotland in Edinburgh.

St Andrews later became the principal seat of the church, although Iona retained special status. Communities of Culdees (one of which was at St Andrews) survived into the 13th century, outwith the Columban and later Roman church. These were thought to be adherents of Ninian's church, preserving elements of pre-Christian druid religion.

A common origin for the cross symbol found on both the Pictish cross slabs and the free standing crosses of Iona and Islay is the *chi-ro*, or wheeled cross, as found at Whithorn. However, the enigmatic symbols, vivid hunting scenes and mythical beasts of the Pictish stones found throughout Pictland are unique, and their function remains a mystery. Another mystery is the brief flourishing in the early 13th century of an accomplished school of sculptors around Loch Awe, in Argyll. In ancient burial grounds throughout Knapdale are found grave slabs depicting swords, warriors and foreign ships, thought to mark the graves of the Knights Templar who fled here from France.

The Vikings

Pagan Norsemen in dragonships are first heard of in Argyll in AD 795, the first of many such coastal raids of unimaginable savagery, which included ritual killings. Colonies of monks were not spared; 68 suffered the 'red martyrdom' on Iona in 807, and its library, 'a shop window crammed with the loot of centuries' was a magnet for raiders. By the late ninth century Norsemen had colonized Orkney (see box, page 388), and from Birsay Palace Earl Sigurd wielded power as far south as Moray. A renegade bunch of mixed Norse and Gaelic ancestry, the Gall-Gaels, appeared in the Hebrides and Galloway. Some of these, like chieftain Ketil Flatnose's family, became early settlers of Iceland.

Once surrounded by aggressive Norse colonies, now also in Dublin and York, the newly formed 'Scotland' survived through a combination of fighting spirit and a network of shifting alliances with the various Norse powers. Some of these alliances were enduring. In the ninth century 'Torf' Einar, credited with introducing peat cutting, founded a dynasty from which sprang the Earls of Angus.

After the Dublin colony collapsed in 1014, a Viking kingdom of 'Man and the Sudreys' (Hebrides) filled the vacuum, and the isles continued to be ravaged by warring Norsemen. By around 1100 Norwegian king Magnus Barelegs' empire included the entire northern and western seaboard. Against this backdrop, pursuing his own interests, appears Somerled, Hebridean hero of Norse-Gaelic blood, progenitor of Clan Donald and the powerful Lordship of the Isles. In 1153 he supported a rebellion against the Scottish crown. Later, in the early 13th century, he built a series of castles around the coast, such as Sween, Tioram, Mingary and Dunstaffnage, which foiled the intermittent attempts made by the Scottish crown to assert control.

The last of the great Norse kings, Hakon, was defeated by the Scots in 1263 at Largs, with the aid of bad winter weather. Orkney and Shetland were only returned to Scotland in the 15th century. A Norse dialect was spoken there into the 18th century, and vestiges of Norwegian law still survive, as does the Viking St Magnus Cathedral in Kirkwall.

Macbeth and the battle for kingship

Macbeth, the earl-king of the vast land of Moray, rose to high kingship with popular support, reigning for a relatively long (1040-1057) and peaceful time with his queen Gruoch, grand-daughter of Kenneth III of Scots. The popular image of Macbeth as portrayed by Shakespeare is, in fact, a false one. The great bard vilified Macbeth in order to please his James VI, who claimed descent from Duncan, Macbeth's rival. But it was Duncan who was the nasty piece of work, and he was slain not at Glamis, as in the play, but on the battlefield, while invading Macbeth's territory. Duncan features in the *Orkneyinga saga*, a Viking history, as Karl Hundason, 'low-born son of the hound'.

Competition for the throne was a part of Pictish custom. A suitable 'tanist' or candidate was elected from anyone whose great-grandfather had been king, and the candidates would then fight it out: in practice, survival of the fittest. This competition for the right to be king was complicated by the ancient dynastic rivalry among the Dalriadic Scots and perpetuated when they merged with the Picts under Kenneth MacAlpin. This later precipitated the Wars of Independence.

One part of Shakespeare's Macbeth which is historical fact is the Birnam Wood incident, when Malcolm, Duncan's son, and his Northumbrian allies used tree branches as camouflage to advance on Macbeth in his Dunsinnan stronghold near Perth. He was later hunted down and slain at Lumphanan by Malcolm's ally, MacDuff, Earl of Fife, and is buried on Iona.

Macbeth, the last truly Celtic king, was also one of the most able early kings. He was the first to establish and implement a fair legal system and, a firm supporter of the Celtic church, he went on pilgrimage to Rome where an Irish monk observed him liberally scattering money to the poor; further evidence of the great disservice done to his memory by Shakespeare.

The Canmores and the Norman conquest

Macbeth's usurper, the uncouth Malcolm III, Canmore (meaning 'big head'), was an illegitimate son of Duncan and a miller's daughter. In 1067 Malcolm married Margaret, a Saxon princess born in Hungary and sister of Edgar Atheling, the English heir to the throne, who had fled north with his family to escape William the Conqueror and the Norman conquest. Margaret was a devout Catholic and was largely responsible for introducing the religious ideas of the Roman Catholic Church into Scotland, for which she was canonized in 1251. In 1072 she founded Dunfermline Abbey and introduced southern manners to the Scottish court.

Malcolm's belligerent instincts were not curbed by the influence of the saintly Margaret, however, and one of his many raids into Northumberland provoked a visit from William the Conqueror. The result was that Malcolm was forced to swear allegiance to William, an oath he didn't take too seriously, as he continued to raid England at whim, but one which would lead to a greater degree of southern interference in Scottish constitutional matters.

The Normans began to exert their influence over Scotland in many other ways. They were granted land as far as the Highland fringes, establishing a feudal system based on loyalty to the crown. The traditional patriarchal tribal culture was eroded, causing constant rebellions in the North and Galloway. The Norman successor to the Scottish throne, David I, like many of his Norman friends, had English estates, acquired through his wife. This wealth built the great Border abbeys and established the Roman church more fully. New parishes and dioceses revolutionized administration, and burghs were founded to develop international trade, attracting Flemish settlers. Society in medieval Scotland became more typically European than England or even France.

One of the depressingly familiar themes running through Scottish history has been the unwillingness of the Scots nobility to resist English ambitions towards Scotland. This has always been their Achilles heel and, in 1290, it provoked a crisis of succession, when the new child queen, Margaret, Maid of Norway, died en route from Norway. Margaret had been recognized as heiress of Scotland, the Hebrides and the Isle of Man, and the planned child marriage to the prince who would become Edward II, son of Edward I, was not to be. Following her death, no fewer than 13 rival contestants materialized. Two main factions emerged: the Balliols and Comyns against the Bruces. But instead of reverting to the traditional method of tanistry, or 'natural selection', the pusillanimous Scots nobles appealed to Edward I of England to adjudicate.

Wallace and Bruce: the Wars of Succession

Edward eventually chose John Balliol, and he was crowned king at Scone in June 1292. Balliol was anxious to prove to his fellow Scots that he was not as weak as they claimed him to be. He negotiated a defensive agreement with the French, the beginning of the Auld Alliance. He then invaded Cumberland in 1296, but in retaliation Edward attacked Berwick and slaughtered its inhabitants. The Scottish army was then defeated at Dunbar, and thereafter the castles of Edinburgh, Roxburgh, Perth and Stirling were captured.

In the same year, Balliol abdicated at Stracathro and went into exile. Edward then destroyed the great Seal of Scotland and, worse still, moved the Stone of Destiny, the traditional crowning throne for all Scottish kings, to Westminster Abbey, where it lay under the Coronation Chair for 700 years. Scotland, as a result, was left in disarray.

However, resistance found a leader in William Wallace, son of a Renfrew laird. He began a revolt against the English in 1297 and built up a substantial army. By September of that year he he had secured a small but strategic victory against English forces at Stirling Bridge.

This galvanized support, and he was quickly declared 'Guardian of the Realm'. Following his defeat at Falkirk he was betrayed to Edward by one of the Scots noblemen, captured and taken south to be executed (disembowelled, then hung, drawn and quartered) in Smithfield, London, in 1305.

This stirred Robert the Bruce to take up the cause of independence. Encountering his treacherous rival, 'Red' Comyn, in a Dumfries church, he seized the initiative, stabbing him at the altar. With Comyn dead, and the support of patriotic church leaders, as well as Sir James, 'The Black Douglas', Bruce was able to consolidate his gains, and he was crowned king with full ceremony at Scone before the inevitable blow of Papal excommunication fell. But it was not only that Rome refused to recognize Bruce as king. Edward I, the self-proclaimed 'Hammer of the Scots', was not best pleased, and for the next seven years Bruce was a virtual outlaw fighting a guerrilla campaign against Edward from hiding in the west.

During this time the indomitable Edward died, and Bruce felt bold and confident enough to raid the northern counties of England as far south as Appleby and Richmond. Of his castles captured by the English, only Stirling remained to be wrested from Edward's successor, Edward II. So the scene was set for the most significant battle in Scottish history: in 1314 at Bannockburn, near Stirling, Bruce confronted Edward II's vastly superior army. His incredible victory, aided by Angus Og of the Isles, and a number of Knights Templar recently arrived seeking sanctuary from persecution in France, has ensured him a place in the heart of every patriotic Scot.

Bannockburn brought the Scots a rare victory over their southern enemy, and led to the 'signing' of the Declaration of Arbroath, manifesto of Scotland's independence, in 1320. There followed a temporary peace with England, and Bruce was finally recognized as king by the Pope, before he died in 1329. His friend Douglas, as requested, took Bruce's heart on pilgrimage to the Holy Land, but when Douglas died en route it was returned to Melrose Abbey.

The Stewart dynasty

From Robert the Bruce's title of 'High Steward' sprang the dynasty of Stewart kings. The early Jameses (of whom there were seven in all) all followed a tragic pattern: succeeding as infant kings, imprisoned throughout childhood, and suffering untimely deaths. James I and III were both murdered, and James II blew himself up accidentally with a cannon. Unscrupulous regents frequently took charge, and hugely powerful nobles like the house of Douglas competed both amongst themselves and against the king. James II hot-bloodedly murdered the Earl of Douglas over dinner at Stirling Castle by throwing him out of the window. The Lords of the Isles were put down by the Earl of Mar and his followers in one of the bloodiest battles of all, 'Red Harlaw' near Inverurie. Like the Douglases, they too were finally forfeited, in 1543.

However, the early Stewarts made progress towards rescuing the country from anarchy by laying the foundations for a modern state through a series of constitutional reforms. Mostly cultured and progressive, they found time to write poetry (James I wrote the *King's Quair*), to build Renaissance palaces, and to father sufficient illegitimate 'James Stewarts' to fill numerous ecclesiastical sinecures (James IV and V). James IV was a true Renaissance prince with a glittering court, but a self-destructive streak led to his early death – along with most of the nobility – at Flodden, in 1513, sacrificed for the long-standing 'Auld Alliance' with France.

Mary, Queen of Scots

There is no more tragic and romantic figure in Scottish history than Mary, Queen of Scots. Raised in France for safekeeping as a Catholic, her brief reign was dogged by bad luck, bad judgement and bad timing. She arrived back in Scotland in 1561, a young widow, at the height of Reformation turmoil in which both France and Catholicism were inimical. Something of a loose cannon, she was embroiled in a power struggle not helped by her disastrous choice of husbands. Implicated in the celebrated murder of the first husband, her cousin, Henry Lord Darnley, she then swiftly married one of the chief suspects, the Earl of Bothwell, incurring the fury of everyone else. Imprisoned after the Battle of Carberry on the island fortress of Loch Leven, she escaped only to throw herself on the mercy of her cousin Queen Elizabeth I, who, mindful that in Catholic eyes Mary had the better claim to the English throne, locked her up at Fotheringhay for 19 years before deciding to do away with her altogether.

Reformation and the roots of Scottish education

The Reformation, converting the Catholic church to Protestant, came relatively late to Scotland and the motives were as much political as religious, though, of course, in 16th-century terms the two were inextricably linked. A pro-English Protestant faction had grown over decades, opposing the French Catholic Regent, Mary of Guise, and in 1560 a rebel parliament banned Catholic Mass, thus shattering for good the Auld Alliance with France, first formalized in 1295.

The casualties of the Reformation were countless, and included religious buildings, works of art and even whole libraries. It amounted to a complete obliteration of the past over which even today amnesia prevails, though, unlike in England, there were very few martyrs. So began 100 years of bitter struggle to establish the reformed church. Cue the Protestant exile, John Knox, a Calvinist rabble-rouser of dubious character and little diplomacy who was prone to blasting his trumpet off against the 'monstrous regiment of women,' namely Mary, Queen of Scots. Knox's skills as a colourful orator, and his self-appointed role as official historian of the Reformation, have allowed him to eclipse the real hero, Andrew Melville, who sacrificed his career of reforming university education to devote himself to the nuts and bolts of church reform.

Schooling for all as a passport to intellectual freedom and moral probity was a dream of the reformers. While grammar and song schools already existed, by the end of the 17th century most parishes had schools using the bible as textbook. The 'Dominie' (schoolmaster) was, until recently, a hugely influential community figure. Prior to the Reformation the Universities of St Andrews (1412), Glasgow (1451) and Aberdeen (1495) had been established, and Edinburgh University was added to the list in the 1580s.

James VI and the Union of Crowns

After Elizabeth's death, Mary's son became James VI of Scotland. Jacobean Scotland was vibrant and vigorously European. Religious extremists were checked by James VI, the 'Wisest fool in Christendom,' and unprecedented peace allowed Renaissance culture to blossom. But trouble was brewing. In 1603 James VI ascended to the English throne as James I, with the Union of Crowns. At this time the Scottish Parliament had so little power that James VI/I was able to write from his palace in London: "Here I sit and govern Scotland with my pen. I write and it is done." In contrast, the English parliament had begun to assume some genuine power.

What's in a name?

Before Culloden and the Clearances, Highland tradition decreed that a person's loyalty lay first and foremost with their own particular clan, or family group. There were two classes of clan: clansmen of the clan who were related by blood and shared the same family name, and individuals and groups who sought and obtained the protection of the clan. This resulted in a clan having septs, or sub-groups, of different surnames. The first Scots to be organized into clans or kindreds were known in early Scots Gaelic as cenela, and there is documentation of three such clans in the seventh- century kingdom of Dalriada, present-day Argyll. Certain features persisted from those early days until the demise of the clan system in the 18th century, in that chiefs could be elected or deposed, but there was no need for kilts or tartans. What held the clan together was a shared knowledge of history and genealogy, reinforced through the oral tradition of the bards and story-tellers. The great majority of 'clan' tartans are, in fact, a 19th-century invention, inspired by the creative genious of Sir Walter Scott.

Charles I and the Covenanters

James believed in the Divine Right of Kings – the God-given right of monarchs to rule their subjects. It was a belief that he passed on to his son Charles I, who succeeded in 1625 and quickly proved that he had little desire to consult parliament in either Scotland or England. Although he was born in Dunfermline, he showed little interest in Scotland and was essentially an absentee monarch. He did not even bother to come to Scotland to be crowned until 1633, calling a parliament at the same time – and then overseeing proceedings, making sure that the voting went his way.

Charles also showed little tact and diplomacy in matters ecclesiastical, and by reasserting the powers of the bishops he rode roughshod over the authority of the General Assembly of the Church of Scotland. Not surprisingly, the rumblings of revolution could soon be heard.

The struggle of the kirk (church) against the king erupted into full-scale civil war, with hostility towards bishops the recurrent theme. A riot in St Giles in Edinburgh expressed public feeling and resulted in The National Covenant, signed in Edinburgh in 1638, pledging faith to 'the true religion' and affirming the authority of the powerful General Assembly of the Church of Scotland in all matters spiritual. Covenanters and king came to blows, followed by an extremist group of Presbyterians allying with the English parliament against the king, in the Solemn League and Covenant. Battle-hardened Scots flooded back from European campaigns to take up arms.

A supporter of the original Covenant, Montrose, led a spirited but doomed campaign for the king against the extremists. At Ardvreck in Assynt he was betrayed to his arch-enemy 'King Campbell', Duke of Argyll, who gave him a traitor's death in Edinburgh. After the Restoration Argyll found himself on the wrong side and met the same end on the same spot.

Civil War

Throughout the 17th century the dark side of religious idealism – fanaticism and paranoia – were epitomized by the 'kirk sessions': courts in which the church conducted an orgy of scapegoating and witch-hunts. Fundamental differences of ideology, constitution and culture between two countries only recently 'twinned', opened cracks in the alliance with the Parliamentarians. The following year Civil War broke out in England, with parliamentarians led by Oliver Cromwell fighting to wrest power from the king. In 1649 Charles was executed and England became a republic. The Scots, however, wanted to keep the monarchy and proclaimed his son, Charles II as their king, despite falling under Cromwell's military 'Protectorate'. Cromwell acted swiftly to bring the country under his control. In 1651 he forbade the Scots from holding their own parliament – forcing them to send representatives to Westminster instead.

Charles II and Restoration

The Commonwealth under Cromwell lasted until 1660, when Charles II was restored to the English throne. The Scottish Parliament was revived and met again in 1661. This time the Presbyterian Covenanters, who had gained such control of Parliament prior to the Commonwealth, were tamed. The Scottish Parliament was again largely run by nobles loyal to the king.

Although Charles II was greeted with wild rejoicing, the reinstatement of the bishops once again proved problematic. Some unconsenting ministers of the church were outlawed and, finding a loyal following, especially in the southwest, they held illegal services, 'Conventicles', in the open air. Crippling fines and brutal persecution from officers of the crown, including Graham of Claverhouse, merely increased their resistance, and many died in the 'Killing Times' as martyrs to high principle.

Religion and the monarchy

Scotland and England continued to disagree, both about the succession and about religion. Charles II's brother and successor, James VII/II, was a Roman Catholic, and in 1687 he tried to introduce more tolerant policies towards Catholics. His actions were seen as a threat to the privileged position held by the Church of England, which since the time of Henry VIII had been the official church in England, and also displeased Presbyterians in Scotland. At first the feeling was that this state of affairs wouldn't last: James was ageing, and as both his daughters were Protestants, the Protestant succession seemed safe. However, when his heir James Francis Edward was born and brought up as a Catholic, a crisis was precipitated, James was ousted from the throne, and fled ignominiously in 1689. His Protestant daughter, Mary, and her husband William of Orange, were invited to take the throne of England, and were later reluctantly accepted by the Scots under the terms of the Revolution Settlement.

The Darién Scheme

Although both countries shared a monarch, England was growing significantly wealthier than Scotland. Like other European countries, it was thriving economically through trade generated by its colonies. Scotland, however, had no colonies of its own. To remedy this, a monopoly company was founded with the approval of the king, modelled on the English East India Company. Wealthy Scots helped to fund it, but much of the capital was raised in England. However, the English East India Company exercised its considerable power to protect its monopoly. Strings were pulled and the House of Commons soon threatened to prosecute the Scottish company's English directors. The king, who had agreed to its establishment, now came under pressure to oppose it. Not surprisingly, most of the English backers withdrew and Scotland saw it as a matter of national pride to raise the starting capital itself – a sum of £400,000, roughly half the nation's capital.

The intention of the scheme was to establish a permanent colony at Darién, on the Panama Isthmus in Central America. Darién was a strategically important site, and the plan was that goods sent to and from Europe would sail to Panama, be carried overland across the isthmus, then reshipped – the new Scottish company carrying out this lucrative work.

However, the project had not been thoroughly researched. For one thing, the land was owned by Spain, a major world power who King William could not afford to offend. Consequently, he ordered English colonists in the area not to help the Scottish settlers defend their new home against the Spanish. In addition the terrain was hostile (which was why the Spanish had not set up a similar scheme already), and diseases like malaria and yellow fever were rife. Within months large numbers of colonists had died. Another attempt was made and was also unsuccessful, and by 1700 the colony had been abandoned.

The consequences were far reaching. Scotland lost a vast proportion of her wealth; national pride and confidence were dented; and the country lost faith in the dual monarchy. The king had sided with his wealthiest subjects – and Scotland felt betrayed.

Union of Parliaments

While Darién produced much anti-English feeling, a number of Scots began to feel that greater co-operation with England could be economically advantageous. At around the same time a further constitutional crisis was brewing. William of Orange had no children and was to be succeeded by James VII/II's daughter, Anne, who was Protestant. However, Anne had no surviving children and English politicians began to search for an heir – who had to be both Protestant and have Stuart blood. They decided on the Hanoverians, who were descended from the daughter of James VI/I. In 1701 the English parliament passed the Act of Settlement, ruling that on Anne's death the throne should pass to the House of Hanover. In 1702 William died and the throne passed to Anne.

The assumption was that the Scots would follow England's lead and accept the Hanoverian succession. But the nation was still smarting over Darién and, as Anne turned out to have little interest in Scotland, relations were strained. The difficulties over having two separate governments under one monarch would not go away. In 1703 the Scottish parliament passed the Act of Security which declared that on Anne's death Scotland would take a different successor to England, unless some settlement could be agreed upon that restored "the honour and sovereignty of this Crown and Kingdom". They wanted to guarantee the power of the Scottish parliament; the freedom of Scottish religion; and freedom of trade. In addition Parliament ordered people to arm themselves and prepare to fight. It was sabre rattling that the English could hardly ignore.

Although Anne signed the Act of Security, Scotland's triumph was shortlived. England passed the Alien Act, which declared that all Scots except those resident in England should be treated as aliens, and Scottish trade with England was to be blocked. The act was to remain in force until Scotland agreed to make moves towards parliamentary union, or accepted Hanoverian succession.

There were obvious economic advantages to closer ties with England, and Scotland was in a vulnerable position. Not only had the Darién venture weakened the economy, the country was also suffering from several years of harvest failure which had led to famine. Although public opinion was against Union with England, it counted for little. It certainly appealed to many in parliament. Financial inducements were offered – and accepted – causing Robert Burns to comment later that Scotland had been "bought and sold for English gold". The Church of Scotland, initially suspicious of Union, withdrew its objections when it was assured that Presbyterianism would be safeguarded. A propaganda campaign was carried out on both sides of the border, many of the pamphlets being written by the author Daniel Defoe. The English were assured that Union would end the threat of invasion from Scotland; the Scots assured of great economic benefits.

The people were not swayed. There were violent demonstrations in the streets, and riots in Glasgow, Dumfries and Edinburgh. Opponents even went as far as claiming that Union would be sinful. The riots in Edinburgh were particularly violent, causing Defoe, who was acting as a spy for the English government, to say: "A Scots rabble is the worst of its kind." The Scots – he said – were a "hardened and terrible people". Pro-Union MPs were attacked, and plans were made in Lanarkshire to raise an army to march on Edinburgh. But public opinion was not of consequence. The Duke of Argyll, for instance, stated that anti-Union petitions were only fit to make paper kites out of. Although some members, notably Andrew Fletcher of Saltoun, were opposed to Union, the treaty was comfortably passed by the Scottish Parliament on 16 January 1707. It had to be signed in secret in Edinburgh to protect politicians from the mob.

In April the act was passed in the English Parliament, and on 1 May 1707 the Union came into effect. The Kingdoms of Scotland and England were united into Great Britain, though Scotland preserved its separate legal system, educational system and church. Despite the vigorous opposition, threats and bribery assured that a bankrupt and exhausted Scotland was, in popular mythology, sold to England for £398,085 – part compensation for Darién, part wages for the Commissioners who closed the deal.

Jacobite rebellion

Rebellion against the imposition of William of Orange began in 1689, when William's government redcoats clashed with supporters of James II (the Jacobites) at Killiecrankie (see page 135). They were led by Graham of Claverhouse, 'Bonnie Dundee', who was killed in the battle. In 1692 an expedition to weed out the Jacobites in the Highlands resulted in the Glencoe massacre, which provoked unprecedented public outcry (see box, page 231).

The Act of Settlement was not forgotten, and dwindling trade and increased taxation fuelled dissatisfaction with the Union. A lively underground resistance, aided by long-standing French connections, revolved around the Jacobite court in exile at St Germain. Sympathy also came from English quarters.

Four attempts ensued to reinstate a Stewart monarchy, supported erratically by France, and culminating at Culloden in 1746 (see box, page 199). Much support came from north of the Tay, which was Catholic and Episcopalian country. The term 'Jacobite' popularly denoted anti-establishment and Episcopalian. There was also a linguistic, social and cultural divide between Lowlander and Highlander which had grown since the 15th century.

Highland culture and independence was not diminished after the demise of the Lords of the Isles, hence the rise of the Campbells to enormous power as government agents, dealing for instance with the troublesome MacGregors. Claiming descent from Kenneth MacAlpin, the MacGregors were almost annihilated in 1603, and outlawed until 1774. They played a significant part in the Jacobite rebellions.

Although traditionally indifferent to the monarchy, many clans came out in support of Prince Charles (of 'Bonnie Prince Charlie' fame) in 1745. After defeat at Culloden, savage reprisals were led by the 'Butcher' Cumberland. Rebels were beheaded or hanged, estates confiscated, and the pipes and Highland dress proscribed until 1782. Clansmen were enlisted into Highland regiments and 1150 were exiled, swelling the ranks of emigrants to the colonies. Gaelic culture was effectively expunged and Scotland as a whole suffered disgrace. See also box, page 444.

Death of the clans

Though events such as Culloden played a part in the demise of traditional clan society as central government sought to 'civilize' the lawless fringes of society, the repression of clanship had already been effected largely by the changing role of the clan elites.

By the time of Bonnie Prince Charlie's defeat at Culloden in 1746, the clan chief had virtually become a commercial landlord, no longer trustee of his people's territory but sole owner of the land, thanks to the new, legalistic definition of clanship agreed between the clan chiefs and central government.

Tensions between the state and the leading clans over authority and control of the Highlands and Islands of Scotland had grown in the wake of the Union of Crowns in 1603 and the government introduced a series of measures, known as the Statutes of Iona, in 1609 (revised 1615-1516) to curb the most disruptive aspects of clanship and to educate the clan chiefs about their responsibilites as members of the Scottish landed classes.

These new laws defined the clan elite's superior position at the expense of their clansmen. Traditionally, all clansfolk considered themselves noble, due to their relationship with previous chiefs, but the Statutes limited the wearing and use of arms, lowered expectations of hospitality, restricted the deployment of military retinues and made the clan elite accountable to the Scottish legal establishment. This had particular impact in the Hebrides where further measures such as the promotion of English schooling and establishment of a Protestant Church ministry were designed to force the pace of change and assimilation.

During the course of the 17th century central government control was further extended. The notion of heritable trusteeship exercised by the clan chiefs over their clan territories gave way to the more legalistic alternative of heritable title, ending the notion of collective land rights and replacing it with sole ownership of the land by the clan elite.

The spread of agrarian capitalism further changed the nature of the clan system, as the clan elites took a more propietorial role in their dealings with their kinsfolk. Civil War, occupation by Oliver Cromwell's forces and the massive ideological and financial pressures generated by the Covenanting movement all had a devastating effect on the Scottish Gaeldom, leading to social dislocation and a polarization of the clans.

The policies of the restored regime of Charles II only made things worse. The increased burden of high taxation and accountability for his clansmen consolidated the tendency of the clan chiefs to act in their own interests rather than as patrons and protectors. So clansmen became alienated from their elite and the role of the chief changed as head of the kindred was sub-ordinated to his role as head of the elite.

The Jacobite Rebellions of 1715 and 1745 not only gave the British government the excuse to wipe out all traces of the clan system, and, in the process, the Gaelic language, in favour of commerce and 'civility', but also provided clan leaders with an excuse to end their traditional responsibilities.

Rise and fall of Bonnie Prince Charlie

Charles Edward Stuart, the 'Young Pretender', grandson of James II, was born in Italy. First setting foot on Scottish soil aged 23 with seven companions (the Seven Men of Moidart), his forceful personality persuaded reluctant clan chiefs to join him in raising the Standard for his father at Glenfinnan in 1745. Inadequately prepared government troops under 'Johnny Cope' enabled his swift progress to Edinburgh, where he held court at Holyrood, dazzling the populace with a grand ball. Edinburgh was charmed but embarrassed.

With sights set on the English throne, he reached Derby. Encouraging reports about panic in London were offset by news of advancing government troops which prompted retreat. The pursuing redcoats were outwitted as far as Inverness, and the ensuing bloodbath at Culloden, though Charles' only defeat, was decisive. Fleeing to the Hebrides, he was given shelter by Flora MacDonald (see box, page 311) and then spent a summer as a lone fugitive. Despite a £30,000 reward for his capture, he managed to escape on a French frigate in 1746. Too late by just a fortnight, 40,000 Louis d'ors then arrived from France, enough to have revived the whole campaign.

This failure has been ascribed to a fatal weakness of character and a collapse of resolve at Derby. He ended his days a degenerate and broken man, ensuring the complete collapse of the Jacobite cause. But Bonnie Prince Charlie is remembered in numerous nostalgic songs, a toast to 'the King over the Water', and a host of memorabilia.

The Enlightenment

Intellectual life flourished in late 18th-century Scotland. Embracing all the arts, its roots lay in the philosophical nature, shaped by European thought, underlying Scots law, education and the church. The sceptic David Hume (1711-1776) was the foremost of a school of philosophers, best known for his *Treatise on Human Nature and Essays, Moral and Political*. Kirkcaldy-born Adam Smith pioneered political economy in his *Wealth of Nations* (1776), a powerful impetus to later political reform.

An emphasis on research and practicality in the sciences fostered inventiveness in applied science, contributing much to industry and agriculture. James Watt developed the steam engine which powered the machinery of the Industrial Revolution, medicine flourished at Edinburgh University, and further generations spawned engineers and inventors like Alexander Graham Bell and John Logie Baird, inventors of the telephone and television.

Classicism was espoused in architecture and by painters like Allan Ramsay, Raeburn and Naysmth, and gave way in literature to the Romanticism of Robert Burns whose work profoundly influenced popular culture and notions of democracy.

Sir Walter Scott's best selling historical novels worked miracles for Scotland's public image. It was he who stage-managed the visit of George IV, who sportingly donned a kilt and, for modesty's sake, pink tights for the occasion. Later on, Queen Victoria was inspired to adopt a Highland home and, with the craze for 'Balmorality', the Highlands assumed a romantic glamour, becoming a fashionable resort for southern sportsmen.

Industrial revolution and the Clearances

Until around 1750 a large percentage of Scotland's population lived north of the Clyde and Tay. Emigration to the Lowlands or North America was already a problem, as a money economy threatened traditional ways of life. The decision of landlords to resettle their tenants on the coasts, replacing black cattle with sheep, was a disastrous economic and social experiment, with brutal evictions in some areas – although popular myth forgets that famine, disease and overpopulation were rife and many went willingly. Eventually, in 1886, crofters' rights were to some extent recognized (see also box, page 345).

The gap between Highland and Lowland life continued to widen as overgrazing, deforestation for industry, and deer 'forests', led to desolation in the Highlands, while improvements and drainage transformed Lowland agriculture.

At the same time industrialization was soon to bring a massive population shift. Wool, cloth and linen, long established as cottage industries, were undergoing mechanization. By 1820 mills were established in the coalfields of Lanark, Renfrew and Ayr. Linen declined in favour of cotton, spun and woven in Paisley and New Lanark, while tweed was first woven in Galashiels in 1830. Dundee substituted jute for linen and Kirkcaldy developed linoleum. Thriving on trade with America, Glasgow's population mushroomed, absorbing many from the Highlands, as well as thousands of Irish refugees from the potato famine of the 1840s. Poor housing, overcrowding and disease became chronic.

20th-century Scotland

By 1900 iron and later steel, mainly in the west, had become manufacturing mainstays, serviced by new canals, railways and roads. As well as emigrants, Scotland supplied goods to North America: locomotives, girders, bridges, textile machinery and tools. Shipyards flourished on the Clyde. The first iron steam ships were launched around 1800, although fast wooden clippers like the *Cutty Sark* were still competitive in the mid-19th century, when major shipping companies such as Cunard came to the fore. From 1880 skilled labour built steel ships for world markets as well as for the Royal Navy. Business boomed during the First World War, when political activity among skilled workers, inspired by the Bolshevik revolution and led by Marxist and Scottish Nationalist John Maclean, gave rise to the myth of 'Red Clydeside'.

Post-war slump hit all industries in the 1920s, from which they never really recovered. A dangerous dependency on mining, metalworking and heavy engineering was a crucial factor in industrial decline, and the innovative spirit of the 19th century is only now re-emerging among pioneering computer software development companies in the central belt.

In a long Liberal tradition dedicated to political reform, the issue of Home Rule reared its head repeatedly after the 1880s. The first stirrings of nationalism were heard after the First World War and voiced by writers in the 1920s, such as Lewis Spence, Hugh MacDiarmid and Neil Gunn. These sentiments took political shape as the Scottish National Party (SNP) in 1934. Support grew through the 1950s and 1960s, and in 1967 the SNP was revealed as a potent political force when Winifred Ewing won the Hamilton by-election.

Nationalist fervour reached its height in the 1970s, roused by expectations that revenue from the oil and gas recently discovered in the North Sea would reverse economic decline. These hopes were dashed by oil revenues disappearing into the British Treasury at Westminster. In 1974, 11 SNP MPs were elected to Westminster – and, although many felt that this was a protest vote, Labour was concerned. In 1979 it held a referendum on the establishment of a Scottish Assembly. Turnout was low and support was luke warm, so no assembly was established.

Labour were soon ousted from office and the Thatcher government swept to power in 1979, bringing with it a disdain for Scotland that was to have far-reaching consequences. The new Conservative government also introduced policies that did not sit easily with most Scots. When the unpopular Poll Tax, which notoriously taxed 'dukes the same as dustmen', was introduced in Scotland a year earlier than in the rest of Britain, the country felt that it was increasingly being governed by politicians who cared little for its people.

Sunny side up for Eigg

The 12 June 1997 was not just a momentous day in the history of the Isle of Eigg, but a cornerstone in the long, hard struggle by successive generations of Highlanders to end 250 years of oppression and feudal law. This was the day that the Eigg Heritage Trust successfully bought their own island (for £1.6 million), thus bringing it back into community ownership.

It brought to an end a decade-long battle with their rather idiosyncratic landowner, Keith Schellenberg, who had a penchant for flying in his rich buddies for a spot of good-natured war gaming (shooting the local peasants having already been declared illegal), and would tour the island in his Rolls Royce, issuing proclamations (until said Rolls mysteriously 'caught fire' one day in 1994,

provoking a humorous headline in *The Sun* – "Burnt Eigg Rolls").

With the 60 or so residents behaving like "ungrateful children", "IRA terrorists" and even "Islamic fundamentalists", the "misunderstood" Schellenberg finally got the message and, in 1995, sold to a singularly bizarre German artist by the name of Professor Maruma. Even by the standards of Highland landlordism, Maruma cut an eccentric figure, and was discovered by the German press to be neither an academic nor an artist.

It couldn't last, and so the people of Eigg won a famous victory that would cause a seismic shift in Scottish landownership, paving the way for the landmark ruling of 2003, ending centuries of colonial abuse and injustice, and ensuring a viable future for the islanders.

Years of Tory rule served only to widen the gap between Scotland and Westminster, and it was almost inevitable that some form of devolution would follow.

The new parliament

Twenty years on, the Scots voted emphatically in favour of devolution, and the Scottish Parliament reconvened after 292 years on 12 May, 1999. The new Parliament has 129 MSPs (Members of the Scottish Parliament) who were elected by proportional representation. It has the power to pass legislation and to alter the rate of taxation. However, defence and foreign affairs are still handled by Westminster. The early years of the parliament have not been without controversy, and its relationship with Westminster has at times proved frosty. The most pressing issue is the so-called 'West Lothian Question', the anomaly that allows Scottish MPs at Westminster to vote on issues solely affecting England, while English MPs cannot vote on solely Scottish issues. MSPs, for example, recently voted to fund personal care for the elderly in Scotland. Yet this went against the policy of the Labour government, leading to the possible scenario of Scottish Labour MPs at Westminster voting against such funding for the elderly in England. As one commentator said: "The English have been the silent and uninvited guests at the devolutionary feast". In addition, Scotland still benefits from higher spending per head than any other part of Britain – a situation which is almost certain to change in the near future.

The bold, stunning new parliamentary building, which finally opened in October 2004, has more than its fair share of critics and was even subject to a public inquiry into why its costs increased tenfold (from an estimated £40 million to over £400 million), and why it opened three years later than planned. Blame was eventually apportioned to beaurocrats and politicians (so what's new?). But now, at least, it's there, fittingly overshadowing the

The winds of change

Unsurprisingly, renewable energy companies are keenly following developments on the Isle of Lewis, the most northerly of the 140-mile-long Outer Hebridean archipelago. This is a landscape where powerful waves roll off the Atlantic pushed by gale force winds, and there are potentially rich financial rewards for those who can perfect the technology and gain the necessary council permissions to harness this raw natural wave and wind power. However, in April 2008 a proposal by Lewis Wind Power to build over 100 giant wind turbines, each over 140 m tall and potentially generating over 1000 megawatts of electricity, was finally rejected on environmental grounds after the bitterly contested application went to the Scottish Executive for a decision.

Although Lewis is a potentially lucrative location for renewable energy developments, and consequently job creation, the Scottish Government's decision to reject the Lewis Wind Power scheme also recognized the island as a haven for wildlife.

Lewis is home to one of the largest remaining peatland habitats in Europe. This blanket bog, which is only found in a few widely scattered areas such as Tierra del Fuego, Kamchatka in Russia and New Zealand, supports dozens of rare birds and insect species and is acknowledged as equivalent to the Amazonian rainforest in South America. Some residents on Lewis argue that construction of wind turbines would destroy this precious environment, and the Royal Society for the Protection of Birds (RSPB) also has serious concerns for the rare bird populations living on the moor. They estimate that 50 golden eagles and up to 250 red-throated divers could be killed by collisions with rotor blades if dozens of wind turbines are erected.

Consequently, as politicians, environmental groups and developers argue and debate there are currently just three wind turbines in operation across the whole of the Isle of Lewis. The Scottish Government is currently deliberating whether or not to grant an application for the building of 57 wind turbines at Pairc in the Lochs (west coast) area of Lewis, whilst another proposed development for 53 turbines at Eishkean is also currently the subject of a government enquiry.

Whilst the issue of wind power continues to generate a storm on the island, there are whisperings that in the very near future the west coast site of Siadr will be granted permission to develop a wave energy facility. As a result, there are those who believe it's no pipe dream that Lewis will soon be a major player in producing renewable energy to meet Scotland's needs.

queen's residence. Whether devolution is a step on the road to full independence remains to be seen, as does the Scottish Parliament's ability to continue to go its own way in the face of economic recession. In early 2011, Alex Salmond's minority SNP government continues to buck the trend of the coalition's cost-cutting policies south of the border.

Culture

Architecture

Early structures: from brochs to towers

A thousand years before Stonehenge, a Neolithic architect was supervising the construction of Maes Howe (see page 391) in Orkney. Dramatically accompanied by two stone circles, its massive precision-cut stonework houses a tomb. Religious architecture evolved into the Bronze Age, and over 22 centuries of chambered tombs survive, notably at Camster and Kilmartin. Henges and stone circles, as at Cairnpapple, also abound. At Skara Brae (see page 390) is a 5000-year-old village, a Neolithic Pompeii where stone furniture and utensils survive in rooms straight out of the *Flintstones*.

Brochs, fortresses not dissimilar to diminutive industrial cooling towers such as at Mousa on Shetland (see page 419), appeared around 75 BC. A staircase ascended within double walls and a well often provided water for the besieged within. On duns and hilltops, timber-laced forts, built from 700 BC into the Middle Ages, are sometimes found to have been fired to such an extent that stonework fused solid or vitrified. Whether this was intentional, or the result of attack, remains a mystery.

Ninth-century wheelhouses, with stone piers radiating from a central hearth, are visible at Jarlshof on Shetland, and appeared later in the Hebrides. Timber began to be used for Pictish hall houses, crannogs (lake dwellings on wooden rafts) and early churches.

In the 11th century round towers, such as those at Brechin and Abernethy, were used for defence and as belfries by Culdee communities. Around this time the first cathedrals were built. The one at Birsay on Orkney, founded in 1050 by Earl Thorfinn, was soon replaced by another in Kirkwall commemorating the Norse St Magnus (see page 386). This was built by masons from Durham Cathedral after working at Dunfermline Abbey, also Romanesque, built for St Margaret. She also commissioned St Rule's in St Andrews, whose tall square tower suggests Northumbrian influence, echoed in those at Muthill, Dunning (in Strathearn) and Dunblane.

Abbeys and cathedrals

David I (1124-1153) granted land to Roman monastic orders and two centuries of abbey and cathedral building ensued, though mostly in the Lowlands. Years of neglect and depredations by English troops and iconoclastic reformers left many as picturesque ruins, stripped of magnificent wood and stone carving, stained glass and wallpainting. The wallpaintings at Fowlis Easter, 15th-century collegiate churches, are a rare survivor. The ruins of Oronsay Priory and the Valerian-clad cloisters of Iona's nunnery (see page 106) are the legacy of the Augustinians.

Medieval castles

Symbols of feudalism built by Norman settlers appear in the form of timber motte and bailey fortresses – timber towers with defensive earthworks – though they are found mostly south of the Forth and Clyde.

Square or oblong tower houses, with a defensive entry at first floor level, barrel vaulting and great hall, were to be an enduring form of dwelling, evolving from the 14th century into the 17th. More elaborate are L-plan and Z-plan versions, with one or two towers added at the corners to defend the entry.

Renaissance palaces

While ordinary folk lived in thatched turf and stone hovels (some into the 20th century), the cosmopolitan and cultured Stewart kings set about building new palaces and improving existing residences. The old castle at Linlithgow had emerged by 1540, a wholly residential Renaissance palace ranged around a quadrangle, which even impressed the French Mary of Guise. While the Great Hall at Stirling is a triumph of late Gothic, the later Palace block (1540–1542) reveals many Renaissance features, such as the recessed bays along the exterior with sculpted figures, and the famous carved wooden ceiling medallions, the 'Stirling Heads'.

The tower house

A minor building boom in the late 16th century was a result of church land being transferred over a long period into private hands. The old tower house formula found favour, preferred over earlier royal examples of Renaissance innovation. Everyone from nobility to minor gentry was afforded both defence against troublesome neighbours as well as gracious living. Claypotts in Dundee is a good example of 'the castle with a country house built on top', while at Craigievar (see page 165), finished as late as 1626, idiosyncratic inventiveness reaches its apogee where the roofline explodes in a flurry of fairytale turrets. Families of masons developed individual styles detectable in Aberdeenshire where many tower houses, great and small, are still inhabited or have been recently revived. Defensive features like gun loops (apertures for guns) survived less out of necessity than as status symbols, and interiors, especially timber ceilings, were vividly painted, with exuberant imagery, as at Crathes (see page 157).

16th- to 18th-century townhouses

'New towns' to promote trade were established by David I and settled with English and Flemish merchants, with a strict hierarchy of trading rights and privileges. Stone houses first replaced wood in the east coast burghs in the 16th century, setting a precedent for future urban design. Every burgh had its symbols of commerce and government at its centre: the Mercat (market) cross and the Tolbooth (town hall).

Two centuries later, the spirit of vernacular architecture had not changed dramatically. Nor had urban layout, many houses still being built gable end on to the street. The multi-storey tenement became a distinctive feature of urban living, pioneered in Edinburgh's Canongate, where buildings such as Gladstone's Land are still intact. Culross Palace and Argyll's Ludgings in Stirling are outstanding examples of grand town houses.

William Bruce and the 17th-century mansion

The country mansion was a concept pioneered by Alexander Seton, paragon of a new kind of architectural patron, at Pinkie House in Musselburgh, a daring essay in elegance and erudition. Post Restoration, William Bruce exemplifies a new concept: the architect. Introducing classical symmetry to existing buildings such as Holyrood and Thirlestane, he also designed Hopetoun in 1699–1703. The innovative oblong shape and hipped roof of Kinross are characteristic of his many other country house designs with their Anglo-Dutch interiors and plasterwork. He also revolutionized garden and landscape design. Bruce's protégé, James Smith, was a pioneer of British Palladianism. Rising from master mason to King's Master of Works and private architect, his own house, Newhailes (circa 1690), was the inspiration for countless lairds' houses, both grand and humble, built throughout Scotland in the 18th century.

Victorian Baronial

Not content with Classicism, architects raided the Gothic, Tudor, Jacobean and Scottish past, even Asia and Europe, for ideas. Late 18th-century country houses by Gillespie Graham were asymmetrical and castellated. Inspired by the picturesque movement, they are the harbingers of the High Victorian revival of Scottish baronial which reached its peak in the 1860s. New and unprecedented wealth found industrial tycoons and landowners beating a path to the doors of fashionable architects like Burn and Bryce, to build colossal and fantastic country seats with room for entertaining on a huge scale, and the latest in comforts – like plumbing. Some followed Queen Victoria's example at Balmoral, building extravagant Highland shooting lodges. Most eclectic of all is Mount Stuart on Bute (1870s) a neo-Gothic/Renaissance palace whose sumptuous interior even includes details from Charlemagne's tomb (see page 88). Flamboyant design extended to monumental industrial buildings like textile mills and foundries, also railway stations, viaducts and bridges.

Literature

Any overview, no matter how brief, of Scotland's literary tradition must begin with a poet who has become inextricably linked with the image of Scotland and all things Scottish across the globe. **Robert Burns** was born on 25 January 1759 in Alloway, Ayrshire, in very humble surroundings, later referring to himself as "a very poor man's son". Burns wrote in the dialect of plain country people and about the lives they led, but the emotions he described were so genuine that they appealed to all classes.

His poetry mainly concerned itself with life as he was living it. He was also keen to point out what he saw as a kinship between all living things, such as in his famous *To A Mouse*. The most frequently quoted lines of this poem; "The best laid schemes o' mice an' men – Gang aft a-gley," has entered the language, as have many sayings originated by Burns, and is a perfect summing up of his point of view. His most celebrated work, *Auld Lang Syne* expresses the joys of human companionship and is practically an anthem when friends gather to celebrate New Year around the world. His love of the companionship of friends is also a focus of *Tam O'Shanter*, which also serves as a cautionary warning against overindulgence and is a ghost story in the tradition of the mythic, while his irritation against the assumed superiority of some was put into words in *A Man's A Man For A' That*, which also returns to his theme of kinship.

The 'heav'n-taught' Ayrshire ploughman died on 21 July 1796, and was buried in St Michael's Churchyard, Dumfries. Such is his standing that his memory is celebrated every year on 25 January, his date of birth, now referred to as Burns Night.

Another writer forever associated with the Borders is **Sir Walter Scott**, who not only ruled the roost of his native Scotland but the world of literature in general. Born in 1771, the son of a wealthy Edinburgh lawyer, Scott spent much of his childhood in the Borders during which time he immersed himself in tales and ballads of Jacobites and Border heroes, giving him a passion for history which would infuse his later work. It was this material which would eventually become poems in his three volumes of *Minstrelsy of the Scottish Border* which established his name as a literary figure. Other romantic poetic works followed, such as *The Lady of the Lake*.

In 1811 Scott purchased Abbotsford, a farmhouse near Melrose, and during the following years developed the style which would remain his best-remembered contribution to literature, the historical novel. Collectively known as the Waverley novels, these included *Old Mortality*, *Rob Roy* and *The Heart Of Midlothian*. The original Waverley was a romantic tale of the Jacobite Rebellion of 1745 and the Highland society of the time. By 1819 Scott had moved beyond purely Scottish history and wrote *Ivanhoe*, set in 12th-century England. It remains his most enduring work, and he followed it with *Kenilworth*, *Redgauntlet* and *The Talisman*.

Scott died on 21 September 1832. His huge popularity was believed to have kept the spirit of Scotland alive and he is commemorated by the Scott Monument in Princes Street, Edinburgh.

A contemporary of Scott's, though far less well known, was **James Hogg**, the Ettrick Shepherd, born at Ettrickhall Farm in Selkirkshire in 1770. Like Burns before him, Hogg was of humble origins and did not receive a proper education he but inherited a vast store of balladry from his mother, Margaret, some of which Scott published in his *Minstrelsy Of The Scottish Border*. Like Burns, Hogg was lionized by the Edinburgh elite as another heaven-taught rustic with a flair for poetry, but that is to severely undermine his importance to the world of philosophy and psychology as well as literature. His writings dealt with the notion of a divided nature within a single individual, reflecting Hogg's own double life as rough Border shepherd and sophisticated urban intellectual. Hogg's thinking and writing reached their apotheosis is his extraordinary *The Private Memoirs and Confessions of a Justified Sinner*, published in 1824 and one of the true masterpieces of Scottish literature. There is nothing else like it and, prior to the Freudian era, nothing to match its insight into fractures of human nature.

This exploration of the dual nature of man received its quintessential expression in **Robert Louis Stevenson**'s *The Strange Case of Doctor Jekyll and Mister Hyde*, published some 50 years after Hogg's death and one of the classics of horror literature. The tale was inspired by Edinburgh's notorious Deacon Brodie, a seemingly respectable pillar of the community by day and a criminal, gambler and womanizer by night.

Stevenson's fondness of the macabre is also apparent in stories like *The Bottle Imp* and *The Bodysnatcher*, but it is for his romantic historical adventures that he is best known. Born at 8 Howard Place, Edinburgh, on 13 November 1850, Stevenson was fond of travel which led to his employment as a writer of travel articles and essays. While staying in Braemar in 1881, Stevenson drew pirate maps of an island, and these became the basis of his tale, *Treasure Island*, published two years later. For Stevenson it was just the first of the many adventure tales, including *Kidnapped*, its sequel, *Catriona* and *The Master of Ballantrae*, he wrote before his death in Samoa on 3 December 1894. The tradition of the adventure story has continued throughout the 20th century in the works of Perth-born **John Buchan**, author of *The Thirty-Nine Steps*.

One of Stevenson's contemporaries at Edinburgh University was **Sir Arthur Conan Doyle**. Born at Picardy Place, Edinburgh, on 22 May 1859, Conan Doyle was schooled in Lancashire before returning to study medicine at Edinburgh University in 1876. It was while serving as an out-patient clerk at Edinburgh Royal Infirmary that Doyle met Doctor Joseph Bell, the man who was to influence most the creation of his famous character. "His strong point", Doyle later noted, "was diagnosis, not only of disease, but of occupation and character".

Doyle was living in London and had published several short stories and essays when memories of his former mentor, combined with a love of the detective fiction of Edgar Allan Poe, inspired him to write *A Study In Scarlet*, which first appeared in the 1887 edition of *Beeton's Christmas Annual*. Doctor Watson recounted Sherlock Holmes' unique detective skills in this, followed by a further three novels and 56 short stories, with all but *The Sign Of Four* making their initial appearance in *The Strand Magazine*.

Holmes became a phenomenon that not even Doyle could control. In fact, by 1893 he was so annoyed that his more serious literary endeavours were being neglected that he

Gaelic writers

Not surprisingly, given the relatively low numbers of people who can speak the language (around 80,000), Gaelic writers have never enjoyed anything like the same success of their English-language counterparts. Two writers who have managed to transcend the linguistic barrier are Sorley Maclean (1911-1996) and Iain Crichton Smith (1928-1998).

Sorley Maclean in particular is something of a cult figure, and it has been argued that he did for the Gaelic language what Hugh MacDiarmid did for Scots. The fact that Maclean translated much of his work into English made him accessible to a much wider audience and this sparked a Renaissance in Gaelic literature. He was also influencial in the preservation and promotion of the teaching of Gaelic in schools.

It was the publication of Gordon Wright's *Four Points of a Saltire* – poems from Goerge Campbell Hay, Stuart MacGregor, William Neill and Sorley Maclean – that brought his work to the outside world in the 1970s, and the bilingual *Selected Poems* of 1977 brought him a whole new generation of readers. He won the Queen's Gold Medal for Poetry in 1990 and died in 1996, at the age of 85.

Another important Gaelic writer of the 20th century was Lewis – raised Iain Crichton Smith. Like Sorley Maclean, Crichton Smith was bilingual, allowing him to reach a wider audience, as well as translate other Gaelic works – including the 'Gaelic Homer', Duncan Ban McIntyre. Smith was awarded an OBE in 1980 and won numerous literary prizes, travelling frequently to read his work around the world. His heart, though, remained in the Highlands of Scotland, and he lived in the village of Taynuilt, near Oban, until his death in 1998.

achieved what many criminals had failed to do. He killed Holmes. Following publication of *The Final Problem*, in which Holmes and his mortal foe, Professor Moriarty plunged over the Reichenbach Falls, there were public displays of grief and mourning. It was clear that the public were not going to let Holmes rest in peace, and eventually Doyle was forced to find an ingenious way of reviving the character. He penned his last Holmes story in 1927, a mere three years before his own death. Doyle's other famous character was Professor Challenger, who famously discovered the Lost World, which later inspired Steven Spielberg's *Jurassic Park*.

Another classic of literature was written by Doyle's older literary friend, **JM Barrie**. Born in Kirriemuir in 1860, James Matthew Barrie was the son of a weaver. Educated at Glasgow Academy and Edinburgh University, Barrie spent some years in Nottingham as a journalist before returning to Kirriemuir to write. He moved to London in 1885, and it was there that he wrote his first novel, *Better Dead*. More novels and plays followed, best known of which is *Peter Pan* and *The Lost Boys*. First published in 1904, it was written for the children of a friend, Llewelyn Davis. Before his death in 1937, he bequeathed the copyright for Peter Pan to Great Ormond Street Hospital in London.

'th century

common criticism of 19th- and early 20th-century Scottish literature was the relative sence of novels dealing with the whole issue of industrialization, growing social division and immigration. Rather than explore the vexed issues of poverty, class division and the growing Celtic influence, most writers belonged to the 'Kailyard School', which presented a romantic, sentimental and completely unrealistic image of Scotland, perhaps reflecting the overwhelmingly middle-class background of novelists at that time.

The Kailyard came to be detested by a growing band of writers in the 20th century, and a new phase of realistic literature – known as the Scottish Renaissance – began in the 1920s, inspired by one of the greatest novels to emerge from Scotland, **George Douglas Brown**'s ground-breaking *House of the Green Shutters*. Published in 1901, the novel brings Greek tragedy to 19th-century rural Ayrshire and, more than any other, destroyed the bucolic escapism of the Kailyard School.

In the same year **James Leslie Mitchell** was born in rural Aberdeenshire. Better known by his pseudonym **Lewis Grassic Gibbon**, his novel, *Sunset song*, published in 1932 (only three years before his untimely death), has become one of the mainstays of modern Scottish literature, and taught as part of the national curriculum. It was written as the first book in the trilogy, *A Scots Quair*, which charts the life of Chris Guthrie, from late 19th century through to the 1920s. Written from the girl's perspective, it is remarkable not only for its strong evocation of this part of Scotland, but also for its uncanny emotional resonance.

Another renowned northeast writer is **Neil Gunn**, born in Dunbeath, Caithness, in 1891. His writings, which deal with the disintegration of the old Highland way of life in the wake of the Clearances and the struggle to adapt to new conditions, also convey a strong sense of place and are as important to Scottish literature and identity as Faulkner and Dostoevsky are to the USA and Russia. Amongst his best-known works is *Silver Darlings* (1939), the title of which refers to the booming herring industry. Gunn died in 1973.

For its size, Orkney has produced a disproportionate number of well-loved and much-read authors. The poet, novelist and playwright, **George Mackay Brown**, gained even more popularity after the posthumous publication of his autobiography, following his death in 1996. Like Gunn and Grassic Gibbon before him, Brown is inextricably linked to his homeland and evokes the spirit and landscapes of his beloved Orkney with a deft sensitivity, bringing a strong poetic impulse to bear on the social realism of his novels. Amongst his best is *Greenvoe*, published in 1972. **Eric Linklater** (1899-1974) is another Orcadian whose copious output of books and poems gained him international recognition. *The Dark of Summer* best represents his compelling style.

One of the most important 20th-century Scottish writers, perhaps *the* most important, is **Hugh MacDiarmid** (1892-1978). Born Christopher Murray Grieve, in the Scottish border town of Langholm, MacDiarmid, as with many Scottish writers of the 20th century, was fiercely political, becoming a founding member of the Scottish National Party (SNP) in 1928. During the 1930s, MacDiarmid moved to the remote Shetland island of Whalsay. He continued writing ground-breaking poetry, becoming increasingly convinced that the essential Scottish human condition could not be fully expressed through the English language alone but rather through a plurality of voices, including Lowland Scots dialect and the Gaelic language. Though recognized as the major force behind the Sottish Literary Renaissance, MacDiarmid's life was a frugal one and he died a man of modest means, near Biggar, in 1978. His best-known work, *A Drunk Man Looks at the Thistle*, was published in 1926.

Another 20th-century giant is **Robin Jenkins**, referred to as 'the Scottish Thomas Hardy'. It was Jenkins who put his native city of Glasgow firmly on the literary map. His most Glaswegian of novels, *A Very Scotch Affair* (Gollancz, 1968), is still regarded as a high point in pre-1970s Glasgow fiction. Jenkins is also recognized as the founder of new Scottish fiction and a precursor to Kelman and Welsh as portraying an unsentimental view of Scottish life. Among his other novels are *The Cone Gatherers* (MacDonald 1955), *Fergus Lamont* (Edinburgh Canongate 1979) and *Childish Things* (Canongate 2001).

Another Glasgow literary talent of this time is **William McIlvanney**. Though he had already published two Glasgow novels in the 1960s, it was the following decade which saw him emerge as one of the city's greats. In *Laidlaw* (Hodder and Stoughton, 1977), McIlvanney explored Glasgow's seedy, criminal underbelly through the eyes of the eponymous police Detective-Inspector, who became as much a part of the city as Ian Rankin's *Rebus* has become a part of Edinburgh. Two subsequent crime thrillers featuring Laidlaw, *The Papers of Tony Veitch* (Hodder and Stoughton, 1983) and *Strange Loyalties* (Hodder and Stoughton, 1991) helped McIlvanney transcend the crime novel genre, in the same way that Ian Rankin has done today.

Writers, of course, are interested in people and as Ian Rankin says: "Edinburgh's dualism makes it perfect for tales of people who are not what they seem. It's a very secretive place, its residents reticent". It was this characteristic that **Muriel Spark** captured in her classic novel *The Prime of Miss Jean Brodie* (1965). In 1981 **Alasdair Gray**'s totally original debut novel, *Lanark: A Life in Four Books* (Canongate, 1981), changed everything. It single-handedly raised the profile of Scottish fiction. Suddenly, the outside world stood up and took notice. Since then, Scottish writers have gone from strength to strength, most notably with **James Kelman**, a giant on the literary scene, whose brilliant fourth novel, *How Late It Was, How Late* (Secker and Warburg, 1994), won the Booker Prize. A one-time bus conductor, Kelman is a committed and uncompromising writer whose use of dialect has attracted as much criticism from the literary establishment as it has praise from fellow writers at home. When some reviewers accused him of insulting literature, he retorted that "a fine line can exist between elitism and racism. On matters concerning language and culture the distinction can sometimes cease altogether."

Kelman has revolutionized Scottish fiction by writing not just dialogue but his entire novels in his own accent, and the debt owed to him by young contemporaries is immense. Writers such as **Duncan Mclean**, **Alan Warner** and **Irvine Welsh** all cite Kelman as a major influence on their writing. Cairns Craig, who has written widely on the modern Scottish novel, states that Kelman's real importance lies in his original use of the English language. "He can be seen as a post-colonial writer who has displaced and reformed English in a regional mode". Among Kelman's finest is his first novel, *The Busconductor Hines* (Polygon Books, 1984) and *A Disaffection* (Secker and Warburg, 1989). Kelman's *Translated Accounts* (Secker and Warburg, 2001) is believed to be his most 'difficult' to date. One literary critic claimed that, while it took Kelman three years to write, it might take the reader three years to understand it.

There are many other notable Glasgow novelists who began to make their name from the 1980s onwards. **Jeff Torrington**, the Linwood car-plant shop steward who was discovered by Kelman, won the Whitbread Prize for his debut novel *Swing Hammer Swing* (Secker and Warburg, 1992), which is set in the Gorbals of the late 1960s. **Janice Galloway** received much praise for her first novel, *The Trick is to Keep Breathing* (Vintage, 1990), which was on the short-list for Whitbread First Novel, and followed it up with an excellent collection of short stories, *Blood* (Secker and Warburg, 1991). Another brilliant collection of mostly Glasgow short stories is **AL Kennedy**'s *Night Geometry and the Garscadden Trains* (Edinburgh: Polygon, 1991), while *So I am Glad* (Jonathan Cape, 1995) is a Glaswegian take on Magic Realism.

Scottish literature has long been known for its dark hue. Crime, poverty and social dysfunction have provided rich copy for writers in a world where detectives are never less than hardened and profanity is as prevalent as punctuation. **Irvine Welsh** whose 1994 cult novel, *Trainspotting*, shone a spotlight on the city's drug-ridden underbelly, spawned an entire generation of gritty, realist writing. After a succession of hit and miss follow-ups,

Welsh is back to rude health with his latest, *Porno* (2002), a sequel to *Trainspotting*, which sees the return of Renton, Sick Boy, Spud and Begbie.

From the same stable is **Alan Warner**, whose bleakly humorous *Morvern Callar* not only put Oban on the literary map but also signalled the arrival of a major and serious new talent, and **Laura Hird**, whose debut novel, *Born Free* (Rebel Inc 1999), tells the tale of a dysfunctional family trying to cope with life in one of West Edinburgh's most notorious housing schemes.

One of the most successful and best-known Scottish authors is **Iain Banks**, whose shocking debut, *The Wasp Factory* (1984), heralded a new Scottish writer of considerable imagination and wit. Banks has gone on to become one of the most prolific writers around, penning his best-seller, *The Crow Road*, and many others, as well as science fiction novels written under the name **Iain M Banks**.

Perhaps the most successful current Scottish writer is Fife-born **Ian Rankin**, currently the finest exponent of so-called 'Tartan Noir'. Rankin's Inspector Rebus novels give a striking depiction of contemporary Edinburgh. Rankin lives in Edinburgh and walks around the city a lot while researching new titles. He uses real locations and gruesome historical events in his books. Rebus drinks in a real city pub, the Oxford Bar, and in one book *Set in Darkness*, Rankin uses the story of an act of cannibalism which took place in the 18th century Scottish Parliament. Like the rest of Rankin's Inspector Rebus novels, this paints a stark, honest picture of contemporary Edinburgh through the eyes of a cynical detective straight out of the Philip Marlowe school of hard cops. His other Rebus novels include *The Falls* (2001), *Black and Blue* (1998), *A Question of Blood* (2003), and *The Naming of the Dead* (2006), his most recent. Rumour has it that, like Conan Doyle with Sherlock Holmes, Rankin is planning to get rid of Rebus.

Music

It could easily be argued that, in its music, Scotland produces the finest and clearest expression of its culture. All tastes are currently catered for within its music scene, reflecting the cosmopolitan nature of a country standing at the threshold of a new era with its own parliament and a deep sense of love of its history and traditions, while keeping a weather eye on the future. Although the words 'Scottish music' often conjure up images of a tartan-clad piper on a mist-covered moor, that same piper is just as likely to be found supplying stirring melodies to the decidedly 1990s edge of 'drums and bass' styles heard in clubs around the country. And that's not all – the sheer number of options available to those seeking any style of music, ranging from folk to funk, from 'Tattoo' to 'T In The Park', is truly remarkable.

Yet, despite the fact a new millennium has come and gone, bringing with it so many changes in music and technology, Scotland as a nation still responds, virtually as one, to the skirl of a full set of **Highland bagpipes**. Little wonder the pipes have been a dominant instrument for centuries – in celebration, in battle, in mourning – and are never far from the traveller's notion of all things Scottish. The pipes' unique sound is enjoyed the world over, not just in Scotland – witness the large numbers of pipe bands in the USA, Canada, across Europe, Australia and New Zealand. However, perhaps the best way to enjoy the pipes is to visit the country in summer when, accompanied by a full complement of drummers, many pipe bands can be seen taking part in competitions or playing at Highland Games in the open air. It would also be totally remiss not to mention the **Edinburgh Military Tattoo**, which takes place annually during August at the world-renowned Edinburgh Festival on the esplanade of Edinburgh Castle.

Great Scots

For such a small country, Scotland has produced a remarkable number of intellectual geniuses who have been peculiarly influential. Many of them were great scientists, like James Clerk Maxwell, described by Einstein as the most important physicist after Newton, and who paved the way for Einstein's theory of relativity. There was also John Napier, the inventor of logarithms, Lord Kelvin, who devised the second law of thermodynamics, and James Hutton, Roderick Murchison and Charles Lyell, who together created modern geology.

In medicine, Scotland led the world. Robert Liston and James Young Simpson discovered the benefits of chloroform, and Alexander Fleming discovered penicillin, the most effective antibiotic ever devised.

The number of techno-logists is incredible, and includes James Watt, who developed the steam engine, R W Thomson, who invented the fountain pen and pneumatic tyre, John Macadam, who gave us the metalled road, Charles Mackintosh, who invented waterproof fabric, Alexander Graham Bell, who invented the telephone, and not forgetting John Logie Baird, the father of television.

Scotland has also given the world the Bank of England, the decimal point, colour photographs, the fax machine, the photocopier, the bicycle, the bus, the thermos flask, the thermometer, the gas mask, the gravitating compass, the fridge, the grand piano, finger- printing, Bovril, interferon, insulin, the gel-filled bra and Dolly, the cloned sheep.

Traditional Scottish music can be passionate or jocular, mournful or joyous. In the hands of a good player, few instruments compare to the violin, or '**fiddle**'. For confirmation, simply seek out the work of **Ally Bain**. With The Boys Of The Lough, Phil Cunningham or solo, his handling of all traditional Scottish styles is superb. The folk circuit is alive and well and, crucially, features many contemporary songwriters as well as tradionalists. Apart from those already listed above, the players worth checking out include Dougie Maclean, Eric Bogle, Hamish Imlach, the Battlefield Band, Dick Gaughan and the Tannahill Weavers, all of whom have a worldwide following.

Delving a little deeper into traditional Scotland's music, you may come across Strathspey and Reel societies. These are groups of fiddlers, large or small, which are well attended across the length and breadth of Scotland. Most welcome visitors to their meetings to enjoy the music and, as most of these take place in pubs and hotels, to enjoy the local brew. On a more informal level, there are ceilidhs which often employ the help of a 'caller' to call out the moves to beginners and experienced dancers alike. The emphasis here is on enjoyment rather than precision and it is well worth seeking out some of the finest ceilidh dance bands, such as Tayside's Benachally Ceilidh Band, featuring former members of Silly Wizard and Capercaillie, The Craigenroan Ceilidh Band, The Occasionals and Alisdair MacCuish and the Black Rose Ceilidh Band. Two rapidly emerging contemporary Scottish folk bands are the **Vatersay Boys** from Vatersay and Barra on the Outer Hebrides and **Skipinnish** from the Isle of Tiree.

There are also numerous Scottish music festivals, which range from the massive **Celtic Connections** and the well-respected **Shetland Folk Festival**, to smaller events which feature ceilidhs and more informal jam sessions.

Folk fusion

Scottish folk music struggled hard to shake off its couthy image, no doubt fuelled by too many dreadful hogmanay TV shows and shameless shysters in kilts. Things then took a turn for the better in the 1970s with the emergence of bands such as North Uist's **Runrig**, who married Gaelic lyrics to rock stylings and even reached the UK Top 10, and **Capercaillie**, whose reworkings of traditional West Highland songs with Karen Mattheson's haunting vocals have brought them significant commercial success. These two in particular have managed to promote Gaelic language and culture as well as promoting the image of traditional music as an exciting, innovative and relevant medium. Another innovative folk fusion band is **Afrocelts**, formerly the Afro Celt Sound System, which has been at the cutting edge of Celtic/World Music for several years and strongly identified with the new age/rave scene. Others worth checking out include **Silly Wizard** (featuring Phil Cunnigham), **Salsa Celtica**, **The Easy Club**, **Mouth Music**, **Deaf Shepherd** and **Shooglenifty**, whose radical mixing of folk music with trance – 'acid croft' as they call it – has made a huge impact internationally. Also worth listening to are **The Peatbog Faeries**, from Skye, with their high-octane fusion of Celtic folk with reggae, dub and soca, and newcomers **Pipedown**, from Edinburgh, who successfully marry the pipes with guitar, mandolin and percussion. Their debut album, *The First Measure*, has won many plaudits.

Scottish rock, pop and dance

The Scots may be stereotyped as a bunch of kilt-wearing, haggis-munching bagpipe players, but there's so much more to the country's musical heritage. This is the country that gave the world **Lonnie Donegan**, **Lulu**, **Donovan** and **The Incredible String Band**. Ex-Faces lead singer and sun-tanned bad-hair boy, **Rod Stewart**, though born in England, still remembers his roots and wraps himself in tartan every time Scotland (used to) qualify for a World Cup. And speaking of tartan, there's the **Bay City Rollers**, who blazed a trail in the 1970s as the forefathers of the teeny-bop market. The 1970s were also notable for the peerless white funk of **Average White Band**, whose singles *Pick up the Pieces* and *Let's Go round Again*, dented the charts. Glasgow-born **Sheena Easton** made it big stateside in the 1980s, while that decade was dominated by the **Eurythmics**, led by Aberdeen-born singer, **Annie Lennox** and **Dave Stewart**. Also big in the 1980s were **Simple Minds**, whose early post-punk sound and look gave no hint of their later stadium rock credentials.

One of the most influential bands of the 1980s were the **Jesus and Mary Chain**, whose distinctive feedback-drenched sound and notoriously shambolic live gigs brought them a huge cult following. Their drummer, **Bobby Gillespie** went on to form the equally influential **Primal Scream**, whose prodigious alcohol and drug consumption was only matched by the size of their egos.

The 1980s also saw the emergence of the innovative Postcard label, which launched the careers of **Orange Juice**, whose frontman **Edwyn Collins** went on to huge international solo success with A Girl Like You, Josef K, the Bluebells (featuring Lonnie Donegan's son) and the 16-year old **Roddy Frame** and his band, **Aztec Camera**. Also big in the 1980s was the Celtic-influenced guitar sound of **Big Country**, fronted by former Skids man, **Stuart Adamson**, **Wet Wet Wet**, who still hold the record for the number of weeks at number one (15) with *Love is all around*, and who could forget **The Proclaimers** who released the unashamedly sentimental *Letter from America*. Other notable Scots names from that decade include **The Cocteau Twins**, **Love & Money**, **Altered Images**, **Texas**, **Del Amitri**, **Blue Nile**, **Billy Mackenzie** and **The Associates**, **Waterboys**, **Danny Wilson**, **Goodbye Mr Mackenzie** (who featured Shirley Manson on vocals, later of Garbage). As dance began to take hold in the latter half of the decade, another Scottish band provided one of the key albums of the period, namely **Primal Scream**'s epic *Screamadelica*.

The 1990s were no less productive with **Bronski Beat**, **The Shamen**, **Soup Dragons**, the hugely important **Teenage Fanclub**, and the bizarre and enigmatic **KLF**, who produced one of the soundtracks of the time with their 1990 ambient classic, 'Chill Out'. The 1990s also saw the arrival of **Travis**, whose 1999, *The Man Who*, brought them massive commercial success.

Behind the scenes, too, Scots have been influential, and none more so than **Alan McGee**, whose Creation label signed up the cream of talent north of the border in The Jesus and Mary Chain, Primal Scream and Teenage Fanclub (as well as a bunch of Mancunian upstarts by the name of Oasis). And Glasgow's fecund indie scene continues to produce a stream of contenders. There are established favourites like **Belle and Sebastian**, **Idlewild**, **Mogwai**, **Arab Strap**, **The Delgados**, **The Cosmic Roughrider** and **Uresei Yatsura**, and the fabulous avant garde funk of **Franz Ferdinand**. Not to be outdone, Edinburgh, too, has produced some fine pop bands, including the very melodic **Aberfeldy**, named after the Perthshire town. One of the most interesting performers of recent years is **Kenny Anderson**, whose Anstruther-based Fence Collective spawned the massively successful **KT Tunstall**. His own band, **King Creosote**, feature regularly in Highland music festivals with their own folk-inspired music.

Language

Though the vast majority of Scots speak English, one ancient Scottish language which survives is Scottish Gaelic (*Gaidhlig*, pronounced 'Gallic'). Preceded by the speech of the Celts, it is now Scotland's oldest surviving language. Often referred to as the national language, it has been spoken the longest. Introduced to the country by Irish immigrants in the third and fourth centuries, its use soon spread and became well established. The language is spoken by about 60,000 people in Scotland (just over 1% of the population). This is in the **Gaidhealtachd**, the Gaelic-speaking areas of the Outer Hebrides, parts of Skye and a few of the smaller Hebridean islands. Gaelic is one of the Celtic languages, which has included Irish Gaelic, Manx, Welsh, Cornish and Breton. Today only Scottish and Irish Gaelic, Welsh and Breton survive.

Argyll (which means 'coastland of the Gael') was the prime Gaelic-speaking area from the time Columba landed there in 563. Scottish Gaelic expanded greatly from the fifth century to around the 12th century and became the national language, spoken throughout most of the country with the exception of the Norse-speaking Orkney and Shetland isles. Galloway had a Gaelic community which was separated from the Highlands, but the language died out there about the 17th century.

From that point, Gaelic began a steady decline over the following centuries and, even before Union with England, was being usurped by English as more and more wealth and power passed into non-Gaelic hands. This transfer of power was given a major boost by the Reformation in the mid-16th century, as strong anti-Gaelic feeling was to the fore in the Church of Scotland.

Gaelic culture still flourished in the Highlands, but the failure of two successive Jacobite rebellions in the 18th century helped to seal its fate. In the wake of Culloden, all features of traditional Gaelic culture were proscribed and the clean sweep by government and landlords culminated in the Highland Clearances of the 19th century. The final nail in the coffin came in 1872, with the Education Act that gave no official recognition to Gaelic.

After two centuries of decline, Gaelic is now staging a comeback, thanks to financial help from government agencies and the EU which has enabled the introduction of bilingual primary and nursery schools and a massive increase in broadcasting time given to 'Alba' – Gaelic-language digital broadcast programmes. This renaissance can also be seen, and heard, in the fields of music and literature, and the recent return of the Scottish Parliament and with the Scottish National Party (SNP) in power can surely only help to strengthen the position of Gaelic in Scottish society.

Arts and crafts

Many of the handicrafts you'll see during your visit to the Highlands and Islands, such as pottery and jewellery, though undeniably beautiful, are produced by non-indigenous residents. Two traditional craft skills which have survived are weaving and knitting. Two areas where these skills reach their apotheosis are Harris and Orkney and Shetland and Fair Isle.

Knitting

Scottish sheep, particularly Orkney and Shetland, are characterized by their fine wool. The sheep of the original breed of Orkney and Shetlands, small bodied with low carcass weights, were probably a cross with Scandinavian animals. These Moorit sheep still thrive on North Ronaldsay, protected by the Rare Breeds Survival Trust. For most of the year they feed on seaweed but are moved on to grass in the lambing season. All the males and 20% of the females are horned.

Gossamer fine shawls made from Shetland wool are soft but hardwearing. Shetland wool is very loosely spun, which adds to the lightness of the finished garment. Knitted on fine needles the famed characteristic of the shawls is that they can be pulled effortlessly through a wedding ring.

Intricate patterns in bright colours characterize Fair Isle knitting. When not being worked into the design, the wool in the spare colour is taken across the back of the work, caught at regular intervals in the stitches so that there are no long loops. It is important for the tension to be correct as too tight carrying of the spare wool would distort the finished garment. This double use of wool also means that Fair Isle garments as well as being extremely colourful, are very warm, consisting as they do of two or more layers of wool.

Before the advent of mass-produced fleece clothing and other warm store-bought wear, a Scottish fisherman wore a sea jersey, sometimes known as a Guernsey or a Gansey. Tradition says that each village had its own peculiar design. Thus, if a man were lost at sea, his jersey pattern might be the only means of identification if he were not found very quickly. But in reality, every family and knitter in that family would have their own pattern. Cable stitch represented rope; hearts, anchors and waves could also be part of a design. The jerseys were made from five-ply Yorkshire 'wheeling', still available from Richard Poppleton of Wakefield, Yorkshire. This is a pure wool worsted yarn, tightly spun which makes it warm and hardwearing. When unwashed, the wool would contain lanoline, the natural oil, which would make garments practically waterproof too. Wool with the natural oils would be widely used for the knitting of seaboot stockings.

The jerseys are knitted in the round on four or five needles. There is no sewing together of the garment, all is done by knitting. Some jerseys have three little pearl buttons to close the neck. The sleeves are knitted from the armholes downwards and are never too long as they get wet as the seamen work with the nets. Also, when the wrist edges eventually become frayed, the knitter unravels the cuff and knits it up afresh.

The needles are long as more than 500 stitches are cast on. In order to make the work easier to handle, the right-hand needle would be anchored at the waist by a 'shield', a pouch of straw or a bunch of feathers. Quite an intricate design might be woven into the shields and they fetch a good price in auctions today. Alternatively, a knitting stick or knitting goose would anchor a needle under the right arm.

It is said that Kaffe Fasset, who is now one the world's leading knitwear designers, began his career thanks to Scottish wools. He was in the north and saw for sale wools of every delicious colour. Knowing little about knitting at that point, he nevertheless bought wool of every shade and also two needles. Boarding the train from Inverness back to London, he was in a carriage with several women. Soon after they began the journey he said 'I'm sure that some of you ladies can knit?' Indeed they could. By the time that they reached London, they had shown Kaffe Fasset how to cast on and off and how to increase and decrease. This was all that was needed to start his amazingly successful career. To this day, his designs use no complicated stitches, their unique beauty derived from inspired use of vibrant or subtle colours.

Religion

The Highlands and Islands of Scotland are largely Protestant, and religion, as in the rest of the country, plays a relatively small part in the lives of most people. This does not apply, however, in the Outer Hebrides, where religion plays a vitally important role in the islanders' lives, and priests and ministers still wield considerable power in the community. This particularly applies in the Calvinist Protestant islands of North Uist, Harris and Lewis, which still strictly adhere to the creed of Sabbatariansim. Here, Sunday is the Lord's Day and the whole community stops work. But despite the fact that the Outer Hebrides are sharply divided between the Protestant northern islands and the Roman Catholic southern islands of Benbecula, Barra and South Uist, there has been little confrontation.

The only conflict has arisen within the Presbyterian Church of Scotland (or Kirk) itself, which has split into various factions over the years. The main split had its roots in the 1712 Patronage Act, which allowed a landlord the right to choose the parish minister, thus breaking the fundamental rule of the church ministers and elders. In 1843, in protest at the state's refusal to change the Patronage act, a third of Scottish ministers walked out of the established Church of Scotland to form the Free Church of Scotland – the so-called 1843 Disruption. In 1893 a second disruption occurred, this time within the Free Church of Scotland itself when a minority seceded and formed the Free Presbyterian Church. Now it becomes really confusing. In 1900 most congregations in the Free Church of Scotland and the United Presbyterian Church joined together to form the United Free Church of Scotland. However, a large proportion of people in Lewis were opposed to this union and the largest congregations decided to continue as the Free Church of Scotland, or 'Wee Frees' as they are popularly known. Later, in 1929, the United Free Church joined with the Established Church of Scotland. And it doesn't end there. As recently as 1988, the Wee Frees split over the threatened expulsion of a minister who attended a requiem mass during the Catholic funeral of a friend. He and his supporters have since formed the breakaway Associated Presbyterian Churches.

Now all this may seem pedantic to many outsiders, but to the people of Lewis, Harris and North Uist (and also much of Skye and Raasay), the Free Church is of enormous social and cultural, as well as spiritual, importance. Not only did it organize resistance to the Highland Clearances but it has also done the most to preserve the Gaelic language.

Land and environment

Geographically, Scotland can be divided into three areas: Southern Uplands, Central Lowlands and Highlands. The Southern Uplands is the area south from Edinburgh and Glasgow to the English border, and consists of a series of hill ranges sandwiched between fertile coastal plains. The Central Lowlands, the triangle formed by Edinburgh, Glasgow and Dundee to the north, contains most of the population, and is the country's industrial heartland. The Highland Boundary Fault is the geographical division running northeast from Helensburgh (west of Glasgow) to Stonehaven (south of Aberdeen). To the north of this line lie the Highlands and Islands, which comprise roughly two-thirds of the country. This is an area of high mountain ranges punctuated by steep-sided valleys, or glens, and deep lochs. The northwest coastline is indented by numerous steep, fjord-like sea lochs, and offshore are some 790 islands, around 130 of which are inhabited. These are grouped into the Outer Hebrides, or Western Isles, the Inner Hebrides, and, to the north, the Orkney and Shetland Islands.

Much of Scotland was long ago covered by the Caledonian forest, which consisted mainly of the Scots pine, along with oak, birch and other hardwoods. Over the centuries, the trees were felled for timber and to accommodate livestock, and now only around 1% of this ancient forest still remains. Small pockets of native Scots pine can be found scattered around the Highlands, at Rothiemurchus, near Aviemore, at Glen Tanar, near Ballater in Deeside, around Braemar, at Strathytre near Callander and Achray Forest near Aberfoyle, at Rowardennan on Loch Lomond, in Glen Affric and on the shores of Loch Maree.

Several decades ago the Forestry Commission, a government body, set about fencing off large areas of moorland for reforestation. Now much of the landscape is dominated by regimented rows of fast-growing sitka spruce, which are not particularly attractive. There are also serious concerns over the damage coniferization causes to the unique habitats in many areas, in particular to large areas of bogland in the 'Flow Country' of Caithness and Sutherland, a unique natural environment as precious as any tropical rainforest. This and other endangered habitats are registered as an SSSI – a Site of Special Scientific Interest – but this has proved less than adequate. The only real guarantee of protection is for such areas to be owned or managed by environmental organizations such as Scottish Natural Heritage, the Scottish Wildlife Trust, the Royal Society for the Protection of Birds, the Woodland Trust and John Muir Trust.

In recognition of this, the new Scottish Parliament produced a draft bill to establish a series of national parks, based on advice from Scottish National Heritage. This is aimed to reduce the conflict between social and economic development and long-term protection of the natural and cultural environment. In April 2002 Loch Lomond and Trossachs National Park opened, and in early 2003 Cairngorms National Park.

Wildlife

The Scottish countryside plays host to some of Europe's rarest and most celebrated wildlife, though much of it has disappeared over the centuries. The ancient Caledonian forests were once home to wildlife that we now identify with other far-flung countries: including the brown bear, lynx, wolf, reindeer and beaver to name but a few. Small numbers of beaver and reindeer have been reintroduced in recent years and there is the ongoing controversial debate regarding the reintroduction of the wolf in the far northeast

Munros, Corbetts and Grahams

There are 284 mountains over 3000 ft (914 m) in Scotland, known as 'Munros', after Sir Hugh Munro, first president of the Scottish Mountaineering Club (SMC), who published the first comprehensive list of these mountains in 1891. In the 1920s a further list was published, of the 221 summits between 2500 and 3000 ft, by J Rooke Corbett, and these became known as 'Corbetts'. A third list, of summits between 2000 and 2500 ft was compiled by Fiona Graham and published in 1992. This list was subsequently revised and corrected and now all peaks that are between 2000-2500 ft are called 'Grahams'.

This is where the term 'Munro-bagging' comes from – one of Scotland's favourite pastimes – climbing as many peaks over 3000 ft as possible.

of Scotland. Meanwhile, wildlife enthusiasts and nature conservation body's continue to press for tighter legislation and resources to tackle illegal hunting and baiting of Scotland's birds of prey.

Coastal wildlife

Scotland boasts over 13,000 km of the British coastline. As a result seabirds and some sea mammals abound and both the resident and visitor list is impressive. Some of the more notable avian 'stars' include the eider duck, most famous for its feather down which the birds use to keep their eggs warm and we use in quilts to keep us cosy. Both sexes are about the size of a small goose yet are quite different in appearance. The male, for courting purposes, looks very regal, being predominantly black and white with lime green cheeks and a pastel pink breast, while the female, for the purposes of camouflage, is a dull brown colour. During the breeding season on the coast fringes and off-shore islands it is not unusual to encounter the females at very close quarters while sitting on the nest. They are very confident about their camouflage and will stay perfectly still even when you are within a few feet.

During the winter the firths (large coastal inlets) and estuaries play host to large numbers of predominantly arctic seaduck including the beautiful jet black common and velvet scoter, the scaup (very similar to the common tufted duck) and the spectacular and rare king eider. Waders too are present in large numbers around the coast and again, especially in winter. Knot, dunlin and turnstones are also common along the beaches and mudflats. During the summer perhaps the most commonly seen coastal wader is the oystercatcher which is black and white with a conspicuous orange beak. While around estuaries keep your ears open for the high-pitched call of the curlew.

These estuaries, along with many of the offshore islands also play host to Scotland's two resident seal species, the common seal and the grey seal. Although the two are at long range quite hard to distinguish, the common is generally lighter in colour and smaller with more delicate dog-like facial features. The common seal breeds in summer and generally tend to be independent of one another, while the grey breeds in mid-winter in rookeries predominantly on offshore islands. Both species can be seen throughout the year with the most common on the west coast and the grey on the east.

Dolphins, porpoises, basking sharks and some species of whale can also been seen regularly around the Scottish coastline. The resident pod of bottlenose dolphins in the Moray Firth is best viewed between May and September, while minke whales, basking sharks and even orca (killer whales) are spotted off the west coast and Western Isles far more frequently than you may imagine.

Island wildlife

The many offshore islands scattered around the Scottish coast provide sanctuary to a wide variety of seabirds, often in huge numbers. These islands are important both nationally and internationally for many breeding species and as such are designated National Nature Reserves (NNRs) and Sites of Special Scientific Interest (SSSIs). The most noted are the islands around Orkney and Shetland and on the west coast Handa Island near Cape Wrath.

To visit these islands and the massive seabird colonies that inhabit their towering cliffs in the breeding season (April to September) is an unforgettable experience. Classic residents include members of the auk family, including the guillemot, razorbill and the puffin, without doubt the most colourful and charming seabird in Britain. Unlike the hardy guillemots and razorbills that nest precariously on the cliff ledges, the puffin nests in burrows, which they excavate with razor-sharp claws. After the eggs are incubated and the eggs hatch the chicks are raised in the burrow and this is the best time to view the birds.

The best places to see puffin and the seabird colonies are in Orkney and Shetland, or Handa Island in the far north west of the country, near Cape Wrath. Several other species inhabit other neighbourhoods within these seabird cities including the Manx shearwater and fulmar, which are both specialist pelagic petrels. The fulmar is worth special mention because it has the admirable habit of vomiting all over you should you stray too close. One of the most famous seabirds around Scotland is the large and very stern looking gannet which is black and white in colour with a 6-ft wing span and an ochre-coloured head. Its most famous international breeding site is the Bass Rock in the Firth of Forth (see *Footprint Scotland* for more details) where over 50,000 pairs breed annually. So famous is the Bass that it lends its name to the Northern or Atlantic gannet's official scientific name, Morus bassanus.

Other more unusual rare and resident species you might be very lucky to see on the coast are the white-tailed sea eagle around the Western Isles or the beautiful snowy owl on Fetlar in Shetland. The sea eagle used to be fairly common but was wiped out in Scotland by early last century. Now, after a successful reintroduction on the Isle of Rùm on the west coast, several pairs breed. The specific nesting locations are understandably kept secret but you may still see one on a fishing foray over its huge territorial range. Like the golden eagle its sheer size is an instant give away while the tail distinguishes it from its more common relative. The snowy owl is rarely seen outside Shetland and is instantly recognizable.

Some islands around the coast of Scotland are also well known internationally as migratory stopovers for vagrant species. Fair Isle between Shetland and Orkney is particularly important and well known often providing life-saving shelter in spring and autumn storms for such exotically named species as the jack snipe or black redstart.

Rivers, lochs and wetlands

Otter are more commonly found along riverbanks in Europe but in Scotland are best observed on the tidal fringes searching for seafood. The Isle of Skye and Shetland are the best venues. The otter was for decades almost hunted to extinction in Britain but is now fully protected. It is often confused with the feral mink or ferret, which is far more commonly seen in the countryside throughout Britain.

Loch Garten in Speyside near Aviemore is the home to the osprey and the venue of one of Scotland's most successful avian conservation stories. After being absent for many years the Loch Garten breeding site became a catalyst for what is now the successful national comeback of the species. You can view the birds nesting in summer at Loch Garten but if you are really lucky you will see one catching fish in a spectacular display of aerial acrobatics on the lochs and rivers of the region. The rivers Tay and Spey are world famous for their salmon. Some of the hydroelectric dams in Scotland have fish ladders where you can observe this archetype of inherent motivation as the fish struggle relentlessly upstream to breed. Pitlochry is one such venue.

Although not endemic to Scotland one of the most beautiful bird species you may encounter on the more remote lochs are divers (or loons as they are called in North America) – most commonly the red-throated diver, the rarer black-throated diver and occasionally the largest, the great northern diver. All three can be seen on the coast in winter. The best time to see these birds is in their superb summer breeding attire but it is perhaps their call that is most memorable. The haunting cry of the great northern or black throat that carries for miles across the moors and wide-open spaces is quite simply unforgettable. Red-throated divers breed on lochs throughout the Highlands while black-throated divers can be found in the far north, especially round Lochinver and in Caithness. Also both rare and beautiful is the delicate black-neck grebe which supports a headpiece in the breeding season to beat any human fashion label at the annual Royal Ascot horse races. Loch Ruthven near Inverness is an excellent place to observe this particular avian fashion parade.

For any Scot who is in tune with the countryside the first calls of greylag and pink-footed geese are a sure sign that summer has ended. Huge numbers winter in Scotland especially in the central lowlands and parts of the west coast. Similarly, barnacle geese invade the Solway Firth in the south in their thousands. The V-shaped flying formations and constant honking of course make the type of bird if not the actual species instantly identifiable. Of course no mention of Scotland's waterways and wildlife would be complete without mention of Scotland's most famous aquatic creature – the Loch Ness Monster. Nessie does of course exist but like the wild haggis is very very shy and elusive.

Forests and lowlands

As opposed to its introduced North American cousin the native red squirrel is a delicate and shy creature. Their beautiful rustic colours can often herald their occasional public appearance in the forests of the Central Highlands, especially Speyside. If it were not for the grey squirrel pushing them out of former habitats and man destroying the habitat itself they could once again be classed as common. Even rarer is the elusive and rarely seen wildcat and pine marten. The wildcat is larger than the domestic 'moggy' and has a much courser, thicker fur coat, piercing, wild eyes and untamed attitude. Over the years the feral cat and wild variety have interbred and now it is very unusual to see the species in its rawest form. The pine marten is about the size of a mink and is occasionally seen in forested areas of more remote and unpopulated areas of the country.

The forests and lowlands are also home to some familiar bird species. The quite bizarre and wonderfully named capercaille (pronounced 'capper-kay-lee') is a member of the grouse family and the largest of the three species found in Scotland. It is the handsome black male that is most often seen deep in the forests, most commonly crossing forest paths and fire breaks while guarding his extensive territory. This is necessary not so much as protection from predators, but invasion by other highly sexed males intent on one thing and one thing only. An encounter and subsequent dispute results in audible threats and much puffing up of the plumage. Even more spectacular are the fights between the capercaillie's smaller relative the black grouse. Their version of a 'boxing ring' is called a 'lek' and can be the sight of spectacular displays of male hormonal overload.

Other unusual birds of the forest includes the crossbill, which is about the size of a overweight canary and has a beak that intersects, which it uses to expertly extract pine seeds from the cone. Crossbills can regularly be seen in the Central Highlands with National Nature Reserves like Loch Garten being a good bet. While in the Loch Garten area you may also see the delicate little crested tit, which although not endemic, only breeds in this part of Scotland. In much of western Scotland the hooded crow, or 'hoodie' replaces the common crow found throughout Britain. The hooded crow can be distinguished by the diagnostic grey patches on its plumage.

Britain's only venomous snake, the adder, is relatively common throughout Scotland and is mainly found on open ground covered in bracken or heather. It is rarely seen and generally keeps well out of your way, though you may be lucky enough to encounter one sunning itself on rocks early in the day. In 2007, a man required emergency medical help after he picked up an adder on the Isle of Arran. The lesson – don't touch!

Highlands

The red deer are as much an environmental problem as a feature of the Scottish landscape. They now number over 300,000 and in the absence of natural predators are essentially out of control in the Central Highlands. However, steps are increasingly being taken to sustainably manage wild deer numbers, including through targeted culling. Indeed, in November 2008, an new 'Approach' to deer management was launched by the Minister for the Environment. In summer, deer remain in herds on high ground and, despite their size, they are actually very hard to spot. In winter however you can often see them in large numbers on lower ground in the glens and beside the main roads. During the 'rut' in autumn the males (stags) become highly aggressive and use their impressive antlers in fierce combat to win the females (hinds). This fighting is often accompanied by a loud roar that carries for miles. Other deer species seen commonly in Scotland in the Highlands, Central Lowlands and Borders are the roe, sitka and fallow deer.

Another famous Highlands inhabitant is the golden eagle. After periods of decline they are now present in relatively healthy numbers especially in the Central and Western Highlands but are not exactly widespread or commonly seen. To the uninitiated the eagle is very often confused with the common buzzard, though the latter is actually much smaller. The golden eagle also dwarfs the large and menacing raven that is also a regular sight in central and western Scotland – usually accompanied by a raucous, 'throaty' call. Another regal and masterful lord of the highland skies is the peregrine falcon. In both flight and appearance they are the epitome of power. To watch a peregrine hunting other birds in flight is to witness one of the most spectacular acts in nature.

Two quite common masters of camouflage on the mountain slopes are the mountain hare and the ptarmigan, a bird similar in size and appearance to a red grouse. Both go through an incredible phase of moult from dark browns in summer to pure white in winter. They do this of course in order to blend in with their surroundings and avoid predators like the peregrine. Any time spent around the ski-fields in summer or winter should reveal one or both species.

Other rarer birds found breeding on the inhospitable high tops, especially in the Cairngorms, are the dotterel, a small attractive wading bird and the sparrow sized snow bunting. The snow bunting, like the mountain hare and ptarmigan, assumes a predominantly white plumage in summer. Few breed in Scotland as it is mainly a winter visitor to the coast. On the lower slopes the red grouse is a common sight. Vast tracks of land are maintained to provide the ideal breeding habitat for this 'game bird' which are then hunted for sport.

Books → See also page 451.

History, politics and culture

Herman A *The Scottish Enlightenment* (Fourth Estate, 2001). A brilliant account of Scotland's contribution to the world.
Kennedy, L *In Bed with an Elephant* (Corgi, 1996). An entertaining account of Scotland's often turbulent relationship with England.
Lawson, B *Harris in History and Legend* (Birlinn, 2006). Essential read for all interested in the land of the Hearrachs.
Lynch, M *Scotland A New History* (Pimlico 1999). A worthy contender.
Macdonald, M *Scottish Art* (Thames & Hudson, 2000). Good overview.
Magnusson, M *Scotland the Story of a Nation* (Harper Collins, 2000). A mighty tome.
McIntosh, A *Soil and Soul: People Versus Coporate Power* (Aurum Press, 2004). Ecology, spirituality and politics woven into a spell- binding tale of the power of the community.
Nairn, T *The Break-up of Britain* (Common Groundb, 2003). Radical perspective of independence. *Scotland's Story* (Fontana).
Prebble, J *1000 years of Scotland's History*, *The Lion in the North, Glen Coe, Culloden* and *The Highland Clearances* (Penguin). Emotive and subjective view of highland history.
Smout, T C *A History of the Scottish People (1560-1830)* (Fontana, 1998); *A Century of the Scottish People (1830-1950)* (Fontana, 1997).

Biographies and travelogues

Banks, I *Raw Spirit: In Search of the Perfect Dram* (Arrow, 2004). Slightly uneven but enjoyable romp around Scotland's distilleries.
Bathurst, B *The Lighthouse Stevensons* (Harper Collins, 1999). Well-documented account of Robert Louis Stevenson's family.
Boswell and Johnson, S *A Journey to the Western Islands of Scotland* (UK Penguin). If you only read one travelogue, make it this.

Crumley, J *A High and Lonely Place and Gulfs of Blue Air – A Highland Journey* (Mainstream).
Duff, D (ed) *Queen Victoria's Highland Journal* (UK Hamlyn). Another interesting read.
Fraser, A *Mary, Queen of Scots* (UK Mandarin).
Grant of Rothiemurchus, Elizabeth *Memoirs of a Highland Lady* (Canongate).
Maclean, F *Bonnie Prince Charlie* (Canongate).
Maxwell, G *The Ring of Bright Water* (Penguin). One of the best known Highland memoirs, a tale of otters and other wildlife set in Glenelg.
Miller, K *Electric Shepherd: A Likeness of James Hogg* (Faber & Faber, 2003). A study of the life and works of one of Scotland's most enigmatic literary figures.
Morton, H V *In Search of Scotland* (Methuen).
Nicolson, A *Sea Room* (Harper Collins, 2002). Beautiful and lyrical 'love letter' to the Shiant Islands, written by the man who owns them.
Skinner Sawyers, J (ed) *The Road North – 300 years of Classic Scottish Travel Writing*, (The Inn Pinn, 2000). A selection of the best, including **Daniel Defoe, Edwin Muir** and **Jan Morris**.
Tomkies, M *A Last Wild Place*, An account of life in a remote West Highland croft.

Outdoor activities

Walking
There are numerous walking guides available, 2 of the best are *Great Walks Scotland* by **Hamish Brown**, and *100 Best Routes on Scottish Mountains* by **Ralph Storer**.
Helpful hillwalking guides published by the **Scottish Mountaineering Trust** are

The Munros by **Donald Bennett** and The Corbetts by **Scott Johnstone et al**. The SMT also publishes a range of district guides listing mainly high level walks. Also useful are The Munro Almanac and The Corbett Almanac by **Cameron McNeish**.

Those wishing to attempt one of the long-distance walks should read The West Highland Way or The Southern Upland Way, both highly informative guides by **Roger Smith** (HM Stationery Office).

An excellent guide for both walkers and mountain bikers is **Ralph Storer**'s Exploring Scottish Hill Tracks.

Ian Mitchell's Scotland's Mountains before the Mountaineers (Luath press, 1999), offers insights about those who may have beaten you to the summit.

Cycling
With 40 illustrated routes **Fergal MacErlean**'s Bike Scotland pocket guide is a must read for anyone planning on putting pedal to the metal (Pocket Mountains). Other recommended cycling guides include: The Scottish Cycling Guide by **Brendan Walsh**; 101 Bike Routes in Scotland by **Henry Henniker** (Mainstream); Cycling in Scotland by **John Hancox** (Collins Pocket Reference, Harper Collins); and Cycling in Great Britain: Bicycle Touring Adventures in England, Scotland and Wales by **Tim Hughes & Jo Cleary** (Bicycle Books, US).

Birdwatching
A good birdwatching guide is Where to Watch Birds in Scotland by **Michael Madders and Julia Welstead** (UK Christopher Helm).

Miscellaneous

Black, G The Surnames of Scotland: their origin, meaning and history (New York, 1940). Available in most public libraries.
HM Stationery Office Exploring Scotland's Heritage. A beautifully illustrated series of books on historic buildings and archaeological sites in different regions of Scotland.

Jackson, M The Malt Whisky Companion (UK Dorling Kindersley). Those wishing to bone up on their malt whiskies should refer to this.
MacDonald, Lady C The Claire MacDonald Cookbook (UK Bantam). An excellent Scottish recipe book, Lady Claire, runs a hotel on Skye.
Prior, C Scotland The Wild Places (Constable). Colin Prior's stunning photographs of the nation's landscape and wildlife.
Sinclair, C Tracing your Ancestors (HM Stationery Office). For more detailed genealogical study.
Smith Haswell, H The Scottish Islands (2004, Canongate).A wonderful reference book to the history, wildlife and ownership of Scotland's myriad of islands.
Stuart, M and Balfour Paul, J Scottish Family History (Edinburgh, 1930). For a comprehensive history of Scottish clans and families. In most public libraries.

Poetry

Crawford, R and Imlah, M (eds) The New Penguin Book of Scottish Verse, (2000). An excellent overview.
Crichton-Smith, I Collected Poems. Bilingual (English and Gaelic) poet writing passionately about life in the Outer Hebrides.
McCaig, N Selected Poems. Challenging poet whose work is deeply rooted in the landscapes of the Highlands.
McDiarmid, H Selected Poems. A huge figure on the Scottish literary landscape. His nationalist views and use of Scots have been as influential as they have been provocative.
Morgan, E New Selected Poems. Scotland's new poet laureate is one of the country's foremost living writers and both entertaining and experimental.
Muir, E Collected Poems. One of the most distinguished poets of the last century.
Paterson, D Landing Light. The latest work of an innovative voice in Scottish poetry.

Contents

Footnotes

Glossary

Scottish terms

ben	hill or mountain
bothy	farm cottage/mountain hut
brae	hill or slope
brig	bridge
burn	brook
clan	tribe bearing same surname
crannog	Celtic lake or bog dwelling
croft	small plot of farmland and house
dram	small measure of whisky
factor	manager of estate/landlord
firth	estuary
ghillie	personal hunting or fishing guide
howff	traditional pub/haunt
kirk	church
lade	mill stream
laird	landowner/squire
Mac/Mc	prefix in Scottish surnames denoting 'son of'
machair	sandy, grassy coastal land used for grazing
manse	vicarage
merse	saltmarsh
Munro	mountain over 3000 ft
provost	mayor
Sassenach	literally 'Saxon', ie English
sept	branch of clan
Wee Frees	Followers of the Free Church of Scotland
wynd	lane
yett	gate or door

bealach	mountain pass
beg, beag	small
cairn	heap of stones marking a spot
camas	bay or harbour
ceilidh	social gathering involving singing, dancing and drinking
cnoc, knock	hill
coll or coille	wood or forest
corran	point jutting into the sea
corrie, coire	hollow in mountainside or whirlpool
craig, from creag	rock, crag
drum	ridge
dubh	black
dun	fort
eas	waterfall
eilean	island
fin or fionn	white
gare, gear	short
garv, garbh	rough
geodha	cove
glen, glean	valley
inch, innis	meadow or island
inver, inbhir	river mouth
kyle, caolas	narrow strait
liath	grey
loch	lake
more, mór	great, large
rannoch	bracken
ross, rubha	promontory
sgeir	sea rock
sgurr	sharp point
sheiling	shepherd's hut
strath	wide valley
tarbet, tairbeart	isthmus
tigh	house
tir, tyre	land
torr	hill, castle
tràigh	shore
uig	shelter
uige	water

Useful Gaelic

abhainn	river
aonach	ridge
aros	dwelling
ault, allt	stream
bagh	bay
bal, baile	town or village
ban, beinn	mountain

Acknowledgements

A huge number of people need to be thanked for helping with this new edition. Firstly, a big thank you to the dedicated staff of the tourist offices throughout the highlands and islands of Scotland who answered my many, many questions with patience, politeness and a smile (always). Thanks also to Ian Gardner at the National Trust for Scotland and Emma and Laura at Historic Scotland, and to the good folk at Caledonian MacBrayne (who didn't even bat an eyelid when I had to reverse my car off the Armadale to Mallaig ferry as it was about to leave because I'd left my laptop in the hotel).

A massive shout to all the people who tirelessly strive to improve Scotland's reputation as a first-class tourist destination by continually raising the bar for standards of food and accommodation. I hope you're all mentioned in this guidebook. If I've missed you then please email or write and tell me about it.

Finally, and most importantly, to my wife, Philippa, for her selfless and unstinting help, support and love, and for putting up with many rain-soaked family holidays in the Scottish Highlands. Without her this book would not exist.

Credits

Footprint credits

Project editor: Alan Murphy
Layout and production: Emma Bryers
Cover and colour section: Pepi Bluck
Maps: Kevin Feeney

Managing Director: Andy Riddle
Commercial Director: Patrick Dawson
Publisher: Alan Murphy
Publishing Managers: Felicity Laughton, Nicola Gibbs
Digital Editors: Jo Williams, Jen Haddington
Marketing and PR: Liz Harper
Sales: Diane McEntee
Advertising: Renu Sibal, Elizabeth Taylor
Finance and administration: Elizabeth Taylor

Photography credits

Front cover: Urquhart Castle, Loch Ness/ Mauritius
Back cover: Monarch of the Glen/ Photolibrary

Printed in India by Nutech Print Services

Every effort has been made to ensure that the facts in this guidebook are accurate. However, travellers should still obtain advice from consulates, airlines, etc about travel and visa requirements before travelling. The authors and publishers cannot accept responsibility for any loss, injury or inconvenience however caused.

Publishing information

Footprint Scotland Highlands & Islands
5th edition
© Footprint Handbooks Ltd
March 2011

ISBN: 978 1 907263 32 3
CIP DATA: A catalogue record for this book is available from the British Library

® Footprint Handbooks and the Footprint mark are a registered trademark of Footprint Handbooks Ltd

Published by Footprint
6 Riverside Court
Lower Bristol Road
Bath BA2 3DZ, UK
T +44 (0)1225 469141
F +44 (0)1225 469461
footprinttravelguides.com

Distributed in the USA by Globe Pequot Press, Guilford, Connecticut

Colour section photography credits

P1: Photolibrary/Olivier Seydoux. P2-3: Photolibrary/Simon Butterworth. P6 top: Alamy/ Les Gibbon. P6 middle: Shutterstock/Ttphoto. P6 bottom: Alamy/Design Pics Inc. P7 top: Robert Harding/Patrick Dieudonne. P7 bottom: Alamy/Alan Majchrowicz. P8-9: Hemis/ Christophe Boisvieux. P10 top: Alamy/Chris Knapton. P10 bottom: FLPA/Michael Krabs. P11 top left: Alamy/Colin Palmer Photography. P11 top right: Paul Miller. P11 bottom: Photolibrary/Colin Weston. P12: Robert Harding/Charles Bowman.